zip it up!

THE BEST OF
TROUSER PRESS MAGAZINE
1974 - 1984

EDITED AND ANNOTATED
BY IRA A. ROBBINS

TROUSER PRESS BOOKS

Cover and interior pages designed by Kristina Juzaitis / February First Design

ISBN 979-8-9898283-0-2

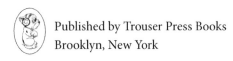 Published by Trouser Press Books
Brooklyn, New York

First printing March 2024

A3

www.trouserpressbooks.com
facebook.com/trouserpressbooks
E-mail: books@trouserpress.com
www.trouserpress.com

CONTENTS

START THE PRESSES

PREFACE

Writing about rock music before the advent of Wikipedia, the Internet, YouTube, e-mail — not to mention libraries full of biographies and reference books, college courses and, err…, computers — meant scouring what magazines existed at the time, Lillian Roxon's wonderful *Rock Encyclopedia*, liner notes and record company press releases for scraps of information and then convincing yourself you knew enough to pontificate with confidence and authority. Of course, it helped if you could interview the artist, but that was not always an option.

We did the best we could, sometime relying on received wisdom (and dates and names) that was not fully factual; mistakes made early in the game sometimes lasted for decades, repeated ad infinitum by what appeared to be primary sources but were not reliable. Skepticism about the stories artists told was not really an option; there was little to no way to check the credibility of assertions made in interviews. These days, all it takes is a few keyboard clicks.

When *Trouser Press* began publishing in early 1974, we were reliant for information and inspiration on two British weekly papers, *Melody Maker* and *New Musical Express* (via sea mail), American magazines like *Phonograph Record* and *Crawdaddy!*, collectors' fanzines like *The Rock Marketplace* and *Bomp!*, cutout record racks around New York and not much else. We spoke to artists whenever we could and asked them about releases, lineups, history and whatever else we could get to fill in the gaps in our knowledge. We were all about their history and their catalogues in the beginning, an obsession that tapered off as we embraced more contemporary concerns.

Reading this selection of articles from the magazine's ten-year run four-plus decades later, I'm struck by the depth of what we, and our freelance contributors, were able to come up with, both in terms of creative ideas and solid reporting. Sure, a lot of this stuff now seems elementary or even uninformed; many of the artists we devoted a few words to have since been the subjects of full-scale biographies, documentaries and extensively researched magazine profiles. It's important to keep the perspective of when these were written and the tools we had to work with. Getting artists on the record about subjects that interested us at a time when the rock press was respected (a bit), allowed us a lot of leeway; we were granted far more access than is generally on offer by major artists. In many cases, the courage of *Trouser Press* interviewers to ask tough or uncomfortable questions is surprising, given how unlikely even polite confrontation would be the order of business today.

In turn, the openness of artists who spoke to us then now is shocking; perhaps because the impact a quote in a music magazine 45 years ago, unamplified by social media and clickbait, would not have been too great (except, of course, for John Lennon's one unfortunate turn of phrase), they could feel free to express themselves more freely. We often sought out artists who were not being barraged with the same questions often enough to formulate stock answers; we were winging it, maybe some of them were as well.

Another point that always needs to be stressed when reading vintage criticism is that, when we wrote about a record, it was new, often by a band or artist who had yet to make a mark. Upon release, every LP has an equal opportunity to succeed or fail. We responded to what we heard, with no foresight or really any concern about how they might be heard or thought of decades later. If a record that got a lukewarm (or even negative) review in *Trouser Press* went on to sell ten million copies and land the group in the Rock and Roll Hall of Fame, such acclamation may make what we wrote at the time seem clueless, wrong or short-sighted. And, sure, it may have been all of the above. But it was new to our reviewer at the time; future airplay, sales and endurance all have an effect on the perspective of a contemporary reader. So, while you may enjoy the hindsight that a half-century affords, don't blame our writers for not knowing what was to become of the music they were writing about.

You may also find information in feature articles that is so commonplace it's hard to see why it was mentioned; bear in mind that it wasn't commonplace when these were written. (I did, however, remove one reference to U2 as being from Ireland.) If observations made herein now seem quaint, obvious or even wrong, credit the incredible onslaught of information about past cultural figures that has emerged in the years since.

Our world was not what Cameron Crowe depicted in *Almost Famous*; we didn't tour with bands, share their drugs or shag their groupies. We rarely got offered the free trips that brought our British writer pals to town a couple of times a year. Most of the time, we sat in our small Times Square office (eventually decamping to a larger space on Fifth Avenue (hoo-boy!) facing Madison Square Park — a building that was later made into a residence and now contains a New York penthouse owned by Jeff Bezos), answered the phone, wrote and opened snail mail and typed on IBM Selectrics. We interviewed bands in record company conference rooms and hotel rooms. We went to concerts and press parties, but debauchery was not on the agenda, work was. Putting out a monthly magazine with a small staff took a lot of time and effort; keeping it afloat always took precedence over the perks others in our profession may have enjoyed.

Trouser Press existed for ten years, from 1974 to 1984, and the focus of our coverage followed, to a degree, the evolution of rock music over that span. Other than glam, there wasn't much we loved in the early '70s, so we focused on musicians who first made their mark in the '60s. We covered the early stages of progressive rock because it was out of the mainstream and mostly foreign-based; that appealed to our sense of mission to write about music otherwise being overlooked. We were excited about the grit and spirit of pub rock and absolutely thrilled by the concurrent explosion of punk and American indie music in 1976–77. In the early '80s, while embracing post-punk and its myriad offshoots, we dabbled in other genres — hardcore, reggae, arena rock, classic rock — while tentatively appreciating the colorful young chart bands popularized by MTV.

Over the course of its existence, *Trouser Press* published a total of 5,508 pages, which included 859 feature articles. We reviewed a total of 3,320 albums.

The story of *Trouser Press* resembles the story of a band. We met in high school, got things going in college, had fun for a while, involved a lot of great people, made no money, broke up and then got famous. We never had a clear sense of what the magazine meant to anyone — until we stopped. Since 1984, I have been amazed by how durable a concept, a memory, an ideal *Trouser Press* turned out to be. People on our message board still refer to "Trouser Press bands," meaning an ethos more than a sound. Whatever that ethos is, *Trouser Press* represents it even more strongly now than it did 40 years ago, when *Rolling Stone* ran our obituary: "Voice of pop-rock underground folds after 10 fan-filled years."

The writing presented here runs from straightforward historical documentation — a resource generally in short supply in the '70s, which made it seem important for us to carefully gather and present — to rampantly creative freestyle criticism. That led us down rabbit holes of discographical detail and genealogical spelunking. (In our early issues, a box containing a careful listing of releases, with U.S. and UK label information, dates and catalogue numbers, accompanied many articles. As those would now be hopelessly outdated and incomplete, they do not appear here.)

Our approach to the artists we interviewed was sometimes, in retrospect, surprisingly confrontational, or at least challenging in ways rarely seen in music journalism nowadays. We took many of our cues from the British weeklies, which led us to believe that being sarcastic and cynical was the requisite alternative to being giddily fannish (which we could certainly be as well). Our commitment to snark extended to the liberal distribution of editor's remarks in the middle of articles, taking our own writers and subjects to task in a dialectic not every writer appreciated.

We were determined to never patronize our readers, who we assumed to be intelligent, curious and willing to make a little effort — just as we were in our reading. We used big words, tossed around arcane references, even the occasional sophisticated concept to put across what we wanted to convey. None of us were academics or scholars, but there were some ample vocabularies in our company, and we never (well, almost never) discouraged their deployment. So, yes, the German word *gemütlichkeit* (geniality, friendliness) and the phrase *Blut und Eisen* (blood and iron) did appear in our pages. And "hejira," "abjured," "etiolated," "pataphysics" and "fustian." "Defenestrate" was randomly trotted out for the headline of an article about the Buzzcocks; "agonistes" was hung on Bryan Ferry. "Penultimate" got misused, maybe more than once. A reference to the Tasadays, a tiny indigenous population of the Philippines, found its way into a profile of Iggy Pop, as did lacuna (an unfilled space or interval). James Joyce got a namecheck.

For this collection, I've made some minor cuts so things would fit. I've added a few emendations [usually in brackets but sometimes not] where needed to provide context or clarification, especially of references that may have been common knowledge all those years ago but now have very little chance of being correctly apprehended. As the magazine staff's editing, proofreading and typesetting skills improved significantly over the years, some of the early stuff needed cleaning up. I've second-guessed the occasional clumsy phrase, cut small bits of throat-clearing chaff and corrected formatting, misspellings, typos, wordos, punctuation and factual errors that appeared in print, not in the interest of hiding imperfections (we made plenty of boo-boos) but for the sake of clarity, stylistic consistency and contemporary readability. Oxford comma, begone! No one has ever been able to agree on the correct rendering of "rock'n'roll," but Trouser Press Books house style is "rock and roll," so that's been adjusted throughout.

Album titles, which the magazine always intentionally rendered in boldface (we just *had* to be different), are now italicized. Thanks to online resources like www.Discogs.com, song and LP titles have been corrected where necessary. But artist names that have undergone revision in spelling over the years (looking at you, Steve Naive / Nieve / Neive…) have been left as they originally appeared in articles. Like everyone else at the time, we mistakenly assumed that the singer of U2 was Mr. Vox.

The racial-cultural designation "black" has been, in line with current usage, capitalized. Apologies to anyone offended by once-tolerated slurs and outmoded viewpoints preserved in quotations from artists. In the interests of respecting copyrights and avoiding legal matters, lyrics that were quoted in the original articles (fair use in journalism, not generally allowed without license in books) have been excised. You can look 'em up.

Guarantee: no opinions, perceptions or arguments have been harmed in the editorial process.

OUR READERS WERE as opinionated, engaged and outspoken as we were: the letters page, which we named *Hello It's Me* after the Todd Rundgren song, routinely ran finicky corrections, withering attacks, fulsome praise and everything in between. Whatever it was people praised the magazine for, an equal and opposite number took us to task for being too mainstream, too critical, too smart, too dumb, full of shit … and we printed a lot of it.

Starting in TP 26, we ran a monthly column called *Raving Faves* in which we posited a question and tallied the replies — crowd-sourced listicles, long before either term existed. That lasted as long as the magazine did: 70 in all, with topics ranging from Best Song Titles and Best/Worst Drum Solo to Favorite Record Company and Worst Rock Rip-Offs.

What was the editorial selection process?
The goals here were:
To document the best, most consequential or most timely writing that appeared in the magazine.
To honor and showcase some of the many fine writers who contributed over the years.
To follow the magazine's changing editorial focus through a variety of musical eras.
To offer a minor corrective to the historical record about the dearth of women in '70s/'80s music journalism. (I will, however, not suggest that we covered female musicians adequately. Only ten of our 95 covers pictured women, and only four of those did not also include men.)
To share what was written at the time, without benefit of foresight, as a snapshot of history.
It was hard to cut out sizable features on important bands, but space put constraints on what it was possible to include. Some worthy candidates were omitted because we didn't locate the writers to seek permission. In any case, the entire run of issues are indexed and can be read for free at www.TrouserPress.com.

FOR STRICTLY practical reasons, none of the "Autodiscographies" published in *Trouser Press* are included in this volume. We did 18 of these extensive interrogations of artists about their work, album by album. The subjects: Blondie, Buzzcocks (Pete Shelley), John Cale, Damned, Dave Edmunds, Genesis, Roy Harper, Ian Hunter, Jefferson Airplane/Starship, Jethro Tull (Ian Anderson), Steve Marriott, Bill Nelson, Iggy Pop, Ramones, Sparks, Stranglers and Steve Winwood. They're all highlights of the magazine's archive, but there was no way to include them all, so I've held them out with the thought of devoting a

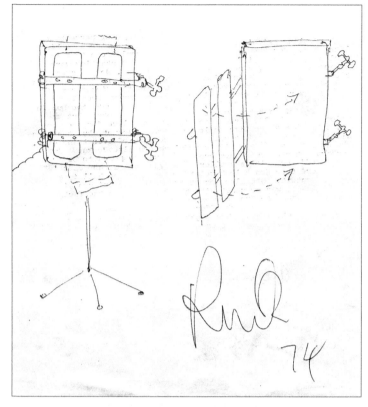

Sketch of a trouser press by Roger Ruskin Spear of the Bonzo Dog Band.

down prints and scans — not to mention the impossibility of selecting photographs for all these articles— put that prospect of illustrating this book well beyond the resources available for this endeavor. Apologies to all the photographers whose work appeared in our pages and who are not represented here.

What about record reviews?

Nope. It would have been an impossible — and deadline-busting — task to read and weed through the thousands of albums and singles that got reviewed in our pages. Iron man Jon Young alone, in his *Hit & Run* column, covered a couple of dozen a month for six years.

What's a trouser press, anyway?

Introduced in the 1930s, it's a wooden device used to flatten out the wrinkles and put the crease in pants. In the 1960s, the British firm John Corby Ltd. (whose family later included Mike Corby of the Babys) electrified its models, and they became common in hotels and such. Roger Ruskin Spear (who provided us with an explanatory drawing of the device) made it the title of a 1968 song by the Bonzo Dog Band. For us, it provided a handy (if unintended) journalistic pun and conveyed the dada whimsy we envisioned for our little magazine.

I've been asked many times in the past why there's never been a book anthologizing the work of *Trouser Press*. Many other music publications — *Crawdaddy!, Punk, Jamming!, Bomp!, Creem, Rolling Stone, Spin, No Depression, Touch & Go* — have already done them (many of those are on my bookshelf) but it wasn't until Trouser Press Books became an ongoing concern that I came to see the feasibility of doing it as a way of marking the magazine's 50th birthday. Hope you enjoy our back pages.

—Ira Robbins
February 2024

separate volume to them down the road.

The same space considerations meant there's nothing here from *Trouser Press Collectors' Magazine*, the bi-monthly newspaper we spun off and published between 1978 and 1983 (30 issues in all) to provide a vehicle for the auction and set sale record advertising we inherited from Alan Betrock when he shuttered *The Rock Marketplace* in preparation for launching *New York Rocker*. Under the editorship of Jim Green and then Mark Fleischmann, with great contributions from John Leland, Steven Grant, Thomas Anderson, Jamie Kitman, Dean Johnson, Robert DuPree and many others, *TPCM* ran rock histories, discographical and scholarly articles of the sort that no longer fit in the new wave era of *Trouser Press*. A few of them are posted on www.trouserpress.com.

Why are there no photographs from the magazine in this book?

The space, time, cost, logistics of tracking

ACKNOWLEDGMENTS

Regardless of how responsibility or credit for the magazine may now be perceived, *Trouser Press* was very much the collective result of the hard work, enthusiasm and talent of many, many people: staffers, writers, photographers, cartoonists and interns. We also benefited from the encouragement, logistical assistance and, at one crucial point, the generosity of our families, some of whom loaned us money and were not fully repaid.

What ultimately made *Trouser Press* worth its ink and paper was the incredible wealth of talent we were granted. Somehow, what we set out to do attracted many creative characters who got what the magazine was about and wanted to be part of it. They made it great; we just gathered their work, put it on paper and got it out to readers.

And they (and we) did it for peanuts. It was pathetic how little we were able to pay such valuable people and how generous they were to accept a pittance in exchange for whatever appearing in our pages meant to them. (We were all young in those days; life wasn't as complicated or as expensive as it has become.) We didn't have much money, but our staff and contributors worked their tails off all the same. We operated as a collective of sorts, and everyone's contribution was part of a group effort to accomplish something worthwhile. It's both a vindication and a relief that so many of them went on to far more lucrative and recognized success.

For those reasons, this book is humbly dedicated to everyone who contributed directly, as well as those whose support allowed it to survive for a decade: subscribers, readers, advertisers, bands, publicists, labels and distributors.

Trouser Press was created by Ira Robbins, Karen Rose and Dave Schulps. Jim Green, Scott Isler and Susan Weiner joined early on as core staff; those six were the corporate owners and directors of the business. We all took on various roles over the course of the decade.

Barbara Wolf was the magazine's initial art director, producing the first eight issues. One-time Fillmore East usher Scott Isler wielded the T-square and wax machine, starting with TOTP 10, until the arrival (TP 42) of Judy Steccone-Sitz, who gave the magazine its characteristic visual identity. Dan Zedek took over when she left (after TP 91) and saw things through to the end.

Our additional full and part-time staff over the years included Steve Korté, Joel Webber, Linda Danna Robbins, David Sheridan, Louise Greif, Kathy Frank, Tim Sommer, John Gallagher, Rod Granger, David Fenichell, Craig Campbell, Linda Francischelli, Frank Horowitz, Kenn Lowy, Wayne King, Mark Fleischmann and Frederick Wasser.

Interns, many of whom subsequently built illustrious careers in and out of the music world: Linda Walker, Pearl Lieberman, Fran DeFeo, Miriam Kuznets, Eric Hoffert, Adam Auslander, Claus Castenskiold, Joanne Long, Eric Blumberg, Jay Paquette and Marcelo Romero.

Columnists: Jon Young (*Hit and Run*), Paul Rambali and Brian Hogg ([*English*] *Ramblings*), Jim Green, Robert Payes, Tim Sommer, John Leland and countless local correspondents (*America Underground*), Jim Green (*Green Circles*), Mick Farren (*Surface Noise*), Allen Gunnison, Michael Bloom and Barry Taylor (*Across the Channel*), Dr. Joe Sasfy (*Rock Therapy*), John Paige and John Diliberto (*Outer Limits*), Jon Tiven and many others (*Media Eye*).

Photographers: Ebet Roberts, Mitch Kearney, Linda Danna Robbins, Laura Levine, BC Kagan, Ron Gott, David Arnoff, Janet Macoska, Neal Preston, Anastasia Pantsios, Lisa Haun, Chuck Pulin, Sheila Rock, Godlis, Charles Charas, Richard E. Aaron, Roberta Bayley, Stephanie Chernikowski, Bob Leafe, Paul Natkin, Lou Kish, Brian Aris, Ann Summa, Lisa Tanner, Teri Bloom, Lynn Goldsmith, F-Stop Fitzgerald, Theresa Kereakes, Craig Dietz, Robert Matheu, Mike Putland, Bob Gruen, Harrison Funk, Marie Scuderi, Waring Abbot, Steve White, Tom Bessoir, James Lee Soffer, Ron Akiyama and many others.

Writers: Lauren Agnelli, Trip Aldredge, Daniel Alexander, Barry Alfonso, Carter Allen, Greg Allen, Lynne Allen, Tom Anderson, Rick Atkinson, Raj Bahadur, Cary Baker, Glenn A. Baker, Brad Balfour, Lester Bangs, Joseph Barnett, Allen Barra, Philip Bashe, Bruce Bauman, Tom Beach, Alan Betrock, Michael Bloom, Ray Bonici, Lou Bonilla, Galen Brandt, Myron

Bretholz, Mark Brown, Roy Carr, Stuart Cohn, Danny Cornyetz, Suzan Crane, Giovanni Dadomo, Cary Darling, Mike Davies, Kris DiLorenzo, Scott Duhamel, Todd Everett, Jim Farber, Ann Ferrar, Hugh Fielder, Bill Flanagan, Mark Fleischmann, Gordon Fletcher, Al Flipside, Bill Foreman, Pete Frame, David Fricke, Dale Funtash, Barry Geiger, Harry George (Robinson), Craig Gholson, Holly Gleason, Michael Goldberg, Toby Goldstein, Richard Grabel, Steven Grant, W. Vann Hall, Ed Hanel, Danny Heaps, Richard Hogan, Brian Hogg, Don Howland, Barry Jacobs, Blair Jackson, Ira Kaplan, Scott Kempner, Nick Kent, Wayne King, John Koenig, David Koepp, Frank Kornelussen, Rick Krieger, MT Laverty, Kurt Loder, Steve Lorber, Jane Lupo, Janet Macoska, Sal Manna, Phillipe Manoeuvre, Dave Marsh, Dan Matovina, Charles McCardell, Moira McCormick, Joseph McGrath, Marianne Meyer, Dominic Milano, Jerry Milbauer, Kathy Miller, Barry Millman, Uday Mohan, Anthony Morra, Jonathan Morrish, Steve Morse, Burt Muirhead, Charles Shaar Murray, Peter Olafson, Jeffrey Peisch, Sukey Pett, j. poet, Ruth Polsky, Parke Puterbaugh, Mario Quinones (where *is* that Epiphone Melody Maker?), Steven X. Rea, Ben Richardson, Eddie Rivera, Bruce Rosenstein, Alec Ross, Leo Sacks, Chris Salewicz, Janis Schact, Elizabeth Schaffner, Nick Schaffner, Karen Schlosberg, Davin Seay, Karl Seebacher, Pete Silverton, Tom Silvestri, Ihor Slabicky, Gary Sperazza!, Cole Springer, Gloria Stavers, Duncan Strauss, Jim Sullivan, Adam Sweeting, Nick Taquinto, Jon Tiven, Lori Twersky, John S.P. Walker, Ted White, Peggy Wolfe.

Cartoonists and artists: Roman Szolkowski, Savage Pencil, Nick DeBenedetto, Amy Hill, Pete Frame, Carl Bianucci, Roger Ruskin Spear, Marc Nadel, Rob Burger, Brad Hamann, Alba Acevedo, John Ebersberger. The panels of *Savage Square* (Savage Pencil) and *Don't Believe a Word!* (Roman Szolkowski) are reproduced here with permission of the artists.

Invaluable assistance and/or inspiration: Frank Reda, Pete Townshend, the Bonzo Dog Band, Alan Betrock, Marty Scott, Greg Shaw, Suzy Shaw, Paul Black, Dennis Diken, Donna Diken, Lisa Fancher, Joseph Fleury, Susan Ollinick, John Visnaskas, Nipo Antonucci, Neil Kempfer-Stocker, Barry Kramer, Bob Merlis, Susan Blond, Bruce Harris, Gregg Geller, Lois Marino, Art Collins, Janine Safer, Doreen D'Agostino, Carol Kaye, Hilly Kristal, Jim Charne, Barb Pepe, Jerry Jaffe, Michael Searles, Ed Chapero, Ted Gottfried, Roger Armstrong, Glen Colson, Ken Weinstein, Jem Aswad, Ida Langsam, Seymour Stein, Jeff Stein, Ellie Smith, Kris Needs, Andy Ferguson, Andy Childs, Barry Margolis, Arthur Levy, Lenny Kaye, Michael Pietsch, Rich Kuba, Tom French, Ted Carroll, Neil Spencer, Marie Scuderi, the Residents, Twin/Tone Records, Jol Dantzig, Jake Riviera, Harold Bronson, Gary Stewart, R. Stevie Moore, Harry Palmer, Nick Nicholis, Jol Dantzig.

And a special note of appreciation for the enormous creativity and dedication that Kristina Juzaitis of February First Design brought to designing and producing this book.

Apologies to anyone who deserves a mention and did not get one.

HOW IT ALL BEGAN...

On Friday, August 3, 1973, the Mercer Arts Center collapsed into a pile of rubble in Greenwich Village, ending, with its existence, New York Rock Phase I. That night, however, the foremost proponents of the genre, the New York Dolls, were not at the Mercer, but uptown a few miles, second-billed to (also defunct) Mott the Hoople at the Felt Forum (still standing but since renamed).

Before that gig, Karen Rose — Jeff Beck freak and staunch Anglophile since the Beatles' days — had her first encounter with a Fanatical Record Collector who claimed to be able to spot a Yardbirds/Kinks/Zombies fan a block away and therefore approached her. After same gig, Ira Robbins and Dave Schulps, high school friends who had been saluting the Union Jack of rock since Pete Townshend decided to wear one as a jacket, had their second meeting with the self-same Fanatical Record Collector, whom they had met in the elevator of a record company office building.

A week later, on Sunday, August 12, the FRC convened a gathering of the tribe — record nerds and Anglophiles — at his parents' home in Yonkers. The invited guests included his new friends Karen, Ira and Dave. While others listened to tapes of old *Shindigs* and *Hullabaloos*, Karen approached Ira and Dave, seated at the dining room table amid piles of *Melody Makers* and *NME*. They were deep in research, they explained, for their still incomplete masterpiece, an encyclopedia of the history and bands of every British rock musician who had ever lived. The afternoon ended with an exchange of telephone numbers and promises to keep in touch.

A week later, on Monday, August 20, our heroes and heroine found each other at a Central Park concert featuring Foghat, Mark-Almond and Robin Trower, the former Procol Harum guitarist making his American debut as a bandleader. In the brisk evening air, words to the following effect were spoken:

Ira: "Wanna start a magazine?"

Karen: "Sure!"

Ira: "Everyone always says, 'Sure.'"

Karen, a Brooklyn College grad who had been editor of her school's paper, was working at her first real world job, which had nothing to do with newspapers, rock or England. Ira, an engineering student at the Polytechnic Institute of Brooklyn, was writing about music for his college paper and dreaming of placing reviews in a national magazine: rejection slips from *Creem* and other magazines were tacked up on the one wall of his bedroom uncovered by posters and photos of the Who. Dave was attending George Washington University in D.C., where he soon was to become a journalism major. He, too, was taking the college paper and radio routes for the love of British rock (and Todd Rundgren).

A few months later, Karen and Ira attended a Foghat/Strawbs/Back Door concert at the Academy of Music (later the Palladium, now an NYU dorm). The notion of starting a magazine bubbled up again. In December '73, they drew up an outline for the Anglo-angled fanzine and, during a long-distance phone call to Dave, *Trouser Press* went from a whim to a plan.

The three decided to take their humble venture, literally, to the streets. They guessed a rough date for the likely completion of the first issue and

edited the contents to comport with a New York concert date. So, *Trans-Oceanic Trouser Press* issue one would make its debut on the 14th Street sidewalk outside the Academy of Music on March 9, 1974, 7:30 pm, to catch the attention of attendees at the Rory Gallagher/Brian Auger/10cc concert therein. Barbara Wolf, an art student, agreed to serve as art director, and the project was finally, seriously, under way.

With a scheduled homage to the Who for the cover story, articles were prepared on Rory Gallagher, the Pink Fairies, the Beatles and King Crimson. A unique (albeit completely impractical) ten-point guide to record rating was conceived and a handful of reviews written using it. Although *Trouser Press* would later become "America's Only British Rock Magazine," at its inception it was cover-sloganed "For the Rock Consumer."

Articles were written by late February, and it was Karen's job to type the whole deal onto stencils with Ira handling messenger chores until he was felled one week before release date with a 104-degree fever. (Karen waited until a week after the issue to collapse.) Once recovered, Ira got to cranking his father's mimeograph machine and, on Friday, March 8, 1974, 8:00 p.m., the first copy of *TOTP*'s first issue was collated, stapled and autographed by Karen and Ira. "This will be worth a lot of money someday," they joked. "If it sells out, we'll do a number-two."

The following evening, Ira, Karen, Barbara, Dave (in town for the occasion), two other friends and shopping bags containing 400 copies of their humble 24-page fanzine met on the corner of 14th Street and 4th Avenue. *Trans-Oceanic Trouser Press* cover price: 25 cents) was about to make its debut. And the rain fell in torrents.

We started with lots of ideas, many of them bad (or at least unworkable) and abandoned them quickly, letting the magazine evolve organically rather than stuck to a bunch of ill-conceived sections. One thing that took a bit longer to get over was the article that we appended to the name: perhaps *The Trouser Press* seemed right at the outset, but it sounds clumsy and weird now.

The biggest course correction that we made was abandoning the idea — emblazoned on our

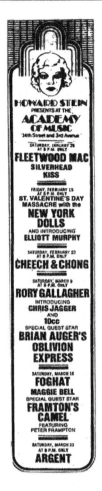

The advertisement that led to the creation of the Rory Gallagher article in the first issue, which we signed to commemorate the occasion.

front cover and retained for three additional issues — that the magazine's purpose was to help readers choose which records to buy and which to avoid. That was simplistic and in defiance of the real object of criticism, which didn't quite dawn on us at first.

Obviously, any media that practices criticism is going to be perceived as a consumer guide of some sort, but we stopped thinking of that as our purpose. Sure, some of what we did was to spread the word about bands and records we liked, but we came to see our role as more about judging quality for its own sake. We rejected the idea of giving records grades or stars.

The inescapable and foundational commercialism of rock was something we acknowledged without quite accepting; we made it a mission to put those concerns aside and write about music that mattered, whether it was likely to attract ten

fans or ten million. It may be an overly fine distinction to parse and certainly out of our control as to how people would respond, but — at least to our minds — our reviews were meant to document and appraise rock music that we considered significant, not tell people what to buy. And that was an important idea, one that allowed us to cover whatever we wanted to without much concern for what was happening in the proverbial rock marketplace. We evolved an aesthetic that guided (not perfectly, but generally) our editorial decisions and attracted a core readership that got it.

In the beginning, we intuitively followed all the universal characteristics of the fanzine genre: more enthusiasm than writing skill, a blinkered view of the world at large, wobbly self-importance, absolute critical certainty, proselytic fervor bordering on zealotry and an electric typewriter. But, like the man says, you gotta start somewhere.

```
Contents
Intro by Karen & Ira -------2
Outro by Karen & Ira -------3
24 Neat Things I Bet Somebody
Doesn't Know About The Who by
Ira Robbins ---------------4
Rory Gallagher by Ira Robbins
                         ----6
King Crimson by Ihor Slabicky
                         ----8
A Defense of the Pink Fairies
by Richard Kuba -----------11
The Complete Discography of
Beatle Bootlegs by Mario
Quinones -------------------13
RECORD REVIEWS ---
Fiendish Ten-Point Rating
System --------------------17
Scraping the Bottom - Bargain
Bin Classics --------------18
Neophytic Notables --------20
Vintage Vinyl -------------22
Classified Ads ------------23
Subscription Blank --------24
```

Contents of TOTP 1

This is how we explained our mission in the first mimeographed issue, which we stapled together on a card table in a Manhattan apartment:

The *Trans-Oceanic Trouser Press* will hopefully be the first consumer-oriented, (inter-)national rock fanzine, concentrating on cheapie bin finds throughout the U.S., analysis of concerts here and abroad and reviews of records which the major rock press has or will ignore. All of this will be approached from an "is it worth it?" viewpoint, because when you get down to basics, what has the Carpenters' craver got in common with the Slademaniac? Yup, he/she is spending money — on records, concerts, T-shirts, whatever. It's money. We'd like to help you decide if your pennies are better off in the piggy bank, or, if, indeed, a given double-album English import is worth goin' without food for a month. Taste aside, as rock consumers, we're all in the same boat.

"Trouser Press" is the name of a song by the Bonzo Dog Band. It became our name because one of our editors has an odd attraction to the word "press." "Trans-Oceanic" joined "Trouser" (and our hero, "Press") in order to define our scope of interest, information and, we hope someday, readership. Yeah. "Trans-Oceanic" also comes in handy in forming our initials, TOTP, which cleverly stand for *Top of the Pops*, the British TV show, and "Top of the Pops," the Kinks song it provoked. So, we're the *Trans-Oceanic Trouser Press*, the *Trouser Press* or just plain *TOTP*. Call us what you will.

WARNING: Expect a lot of English! Although *TOTP*'ll be concerned with Anyband from Anyplace, with the exception of our love for Todd Rundgren, the editors are severe Anglophiliacs.

In addition to each issue's major articles — which this issue include a scholarly history of King Crimson and a quite definitive discography of Beatle bootlegs — the *Trouser Press* will contain some regular columns.

In each issue, *Scraping the Bottom — Bargain Bin Classics* will contain standardized reviews of records found in cheapie bins all around the country. Since we have not yet gotten together our "foreign" correspondents, our first column will deal exclusively with the NY bins. In the future, the records mentioned will be cross-referenced. That is, if we find and review a record in New York, but it's available in Cleveland, we'll let you know.

Neophytic Notables will deal with new and already obscure discs — the records which, for reasons of "What the hell is this?" do not stand too strong a chance of being reviewed in the rock press but may be worth either keeping or avoiding if they should accidentally fall into your hands. These are the cheapie bin residents of the future, unless they're fated to become *Vintage Vinyl*. Here we'll find our old and obscure discs. These records are not rare. They are not cheap. They were merely ignored at the time of their release. They, too, may be worthy of your attention (or lack of)

In the future, the *Trans-Oceanic Trouser Press* hopes to also have standardized national concert reviews. We think it would be interesting to follow Anyband's tour — watching them have the Spectrum on its collective feet in Philly, for example, and bombing in Seattle and trying to figure out (other than "it was just a bad night") why. This, like our cheapie bin feature, will once again depend on our finding national correspondents.

Odds 'n' Sods will be a wrap-up, by Ira, of

British musical news, meant especially for those readers who live in places where *Melody Maker* and *New Musical Express* aren't as readily available as they are in New York.

WE MAILED A COPY of the first issue to Pete Townshend (every self-respecting Who freak knew his address) and got this reply to the article cautiously titled "24 Neat Things I Bet Somebody Doesn't Know About the Who":

Dear Ira,

Nearly 24 neat things you should know about the oo.

1) "Waltz for a pig" was dedicated to Shel Talmy for screwing us down to 1%. He put out "Legal Matter" ha ha (at the same time)

2) Ronnie Lane played bass on "Warm Heart Pastry"

3) The Who were called "The Detours", then "the Who", then the "High Numbers", then "the Who" again. We were first the Who in early 64.

4) Roger was never scheduled to appear on any of John's songs in the early days neither was I. (We really did hate one another)

5) On Roger Spear's next album he uses my whole drum kit.

6) I smoke 4 beedies a day. Just 4. (occasionally 5) (sometimes 6) (rarely more?)

7) Since Stevie Wonder didn't get excited because I told him I was a Taurus too my favorite musician is Link Wray again.

8) I use regular strings not light nor heavy — in fact it is the very top strings that are heavier than normal — E 0.14 B 0.16 etc.

9) Keith Richards is not staid.

10) (including 11-24) Link Wray's next album has my liner notes on — as did his first (intentionally), had the printers printed them on the cover. I said "Link was an early influence blah blah"

Much love & respect to your fine paper
Pete T.

P.S. Tell Karen my two favourite names are Karen and Rose. Great eh? Isn't that just great? Huh? Great? Fab eh? Good good. ∎

That was great encouragement for us to carry on.

Contents

Contents

Contents of TOTP 2 (top) and 3

Trans-Oceanic Trouser Press

February 1974

Dear Whoever:

Ever see the TV commercial where the agency guy says to Abe Lincoln, "I kno' you're smart, and you know you're smart, but you ain't goin' nowhere without that sheepskin?" Well, rock writing works the same way. You sit down and write a really good review of an album by a band you know a lot about, send it out to one of the national rags, and what do you get? Rejected, that's what! Without that imaginary membership card, the only person who gets to read your article is an editor and a postman. The reason, simply, that we all get wiped out is because all the major releases are reviewed by assigned super-pens almost before they're recorded, and the obscure stuff never gets reviewed, by anybody, just because it's obscure. The college-type writer or genuine record freak hasn't got a chance at journalistic stardom.

As a result of their advancing age and secure positions, most of the big guns are burnt out -- they're dull as donuts. The main function being served today by the major magazines is as a hip, musical version of Mad. That's okay, but for music news (of the U.S. and U.K.) you have to read Melody Maker, and for reviews, well, let's drop that debatable question.

So here we are -- a new fanzine. Why? Well, usually a zine is put out as a grad-A ego-trip for whoever puts it out. Nobody who wasn't in it from the start ever really gets involved, and the establishment cycle begins again. Now there's us -- an alternative to the alternate alternatives -- a chance to be different. We need lots of writers (as well as money) from all over so that we can print the city-by-city comparative bargain bin surveys and nationwide concert reviews (entire tours reviewed) that we intend to do with your help. We have nothing to alienate anybody -- no famous writers, no big names, no money, or anything that might make us elitist (or successful). The TRANS-OCEANIC TROUSER PRESS needs you to help wirte, sell, push, and build a great zine that'll blow away the stiffs. THINK!!!

Now the hitch. This whole affair was our idea, so we get to be the editors. (Also, we stand to lose all the money unless people kick in some bread.) We reserve exclusive rights to review everything by a couple of bands that are special favorites (they'll be enumerated at a later date), but otherwise we want each writer to take responsibility for all the features and reviews of his/her favorite band(s). Hopefully, this will work itself out without too much friction, so be authoritative, but, most of all, BE ESOTERIC.

There is, of course, no money to be made here by anybody (unless we should strike oil or sell out), only a chance to write about music if you love it, and the satisfaction which comes from having a zine to call your own.

> Write for details and further instructions
> if we've grabbed ya (and send some stamps
> if you can),
>
> The TRANS-OCEANIC TROUSER PRESS,
>
> Ira, Karen, Dave

THE SIXTIES

> 66
>
> *The first time that I saw them they were playing sitting down. Mind you, if you had to play those sweaty clubs you'd be sitting down, too.*
>
> 99
>
> **—ANDREW LOOG OLDHAM,**
> original manager and producer of the Rolling Stones

One of our impulses for creating *Trouser Press* was to publish detailed historical appreciations of '60s bands we loved, and our early issues regularly presented lengthy accounts (some of them running across multiple issues), complete with discographies, of the Yardbirds, Animals, Pretty Things, Free, Left Banke, Tommy James and others. We never let that become the magazine's sole purpose, but it was one expression of our enthusiasm; while we stopped including discographies after a while, we never lost our taste for digging up the past. Once we began publishing *Trouser Press Collectors' Magazine* as a spinoff, we generally consigned the dustbin of historical work to its newsprint pages.

As noted in the Preface, our sources for these sorts of articles were limited and, in some cases, less than reliable. It took writers who were devoted fans and had been following their idols for a good while to have, or know where to look for, the information it took to assemble them.

In 1975, a large envelope from England appeared in our mailbox at the Grand Central Station Post Office. Inside, typed on translucent onionskin, were a pair of articles, one about Ducks Deluxe, a rocking pub band we were aware of, not just from our assiduous perusing of the British weeklies but because RCA had seen fit to release their first album in the States. The handwritten letter of introduction read, in part, "Here are two unsolicited manuscripts for you to throw in the dustbin. Like the magazine." (We took that second sentence to be part of a compliment, not a suggestion.)

The writing was smart and strong, and we were delighted to publish it in our next issue (TOTP 11). But, as a result of misreading the handwritten name scrawled at the top of the piece, we credited the work to "Pete Silvester."

We apologized for that and stayed in touch. The following year, we got another piece from Pete, filling both sides of ten sheets of foolscap, about a band we didn't know: the 101'ers. It was a tremendous piece of writing, but ended with the band broken up, leaving one posthumous single as its legacy. We were cool with covering the obscure and the defunct, but 6,000 words on a defunct group we'd never heard — and likely never would hear — made the idea of publishing it a non-starter for us. (It's now available at https://trouserpress.com/letsagetabitarockin/)

Silverton soon became one of our prized London correspondents (Paul Rambali being the other, later joined by Harry George [Robinson]), writing about the Clash, Elvis Costello and Van Morrison. (Pete used to say that he and Paul had agreed to share the spoils: he would handle Joe Strummer, and Paul would write about the Pistols.)

A diehard Elvis Presley fan, Pete was versant in many eras of music, and this fine piece of rock history ran in an issue that had Johnny Rotten on the cover and articles about Phil Manzanera's prog rock ensemble Quiet Sun, saxophonist Lol Coxhill and the Stranglers. We may not have been entirely open-minded, but we were eclectic.

Pete went on to long and illustrious career in British journalism. He co-wrote the first memoir by ex-Pistol Glen Matlock and a brilliant book about cursing called Filthy English. An incredible wit with wide-ranging knowledge, curiosity and cooking skills, remained a treasured friend until his death in 2023.

ALL OR NOTHING: THE SMALL FACES STORY

TP 22, OCTOBER 1977

By Pete Silverton

It's 1968, alright. Me and a mate are lounging around in his garden. His parents are out for the day. School's out for the summer. Free from the two biggest bugaboos of adolescence, we're getting a little crazy with the freedom. Talking about anything that comes into our heads. Mostly about sex (what did you talk about at that age?) but also about such fashionable topics of the day as how to smoke banana skins and more mundane matters such as the idiocy of our English teacher. Then, fueled by the contents of a quart bottle of light ale, we have a go at coming on like real rebels. Wire up the lead on the record player so it reaches into the garden. Shuffle through a pile of singles. Crank up the volume till the four-inch speaker's screeching its guts out all 'round the garden and over the neighbor's fence. Slap on the Small Faces' "Lazy Sunday." Go little Stevie, go.

Ah, the bliss of trying to be outrageous. But there's more to it than that. Y'see, of all the socio-psycho-anthropological academic theories that have been chucked up in the last hundred years, there ain't but a damn few of them that help you understand rock and roll. Except Tinbergen's theory of imprinting, that is. [Nobel prize-winning Dutch biologist Nikolaas] Tinbergen would take a baby chicken, let it run around a little and then drag a ball along in front of it. The dumb chicken would figure the ball was its mother and follow it around. The ball was big; therefore, it was the mother. Imprinting.

That's exactly how tastes in rock and roll are formed. They're pretty well set in concrete by the first thing you really hear, the one that hits you so hard you sit up and go, "What was *that*?" It's happened to everyone I've ever asked about it. There's always that one record that sets you on the fast road to terminal vinyl junkiedom.

The first record I can remember liking was "Nut Rocker" by B. Bumble and the Stingers, but the one that turned me into a rock and roll nut was "Lazy Sunday" by the Small Faces. Pace, humor, raunch, production tricks, a singalong chorus, innocence — it's got 'em all. I loved it then. I love it now. It's that one record, the keystone of my listening since. It's probably the reason why I hate monsters like the Floyd and Zeppelin. If you start out smiling — life is just a bowl of All-Bran — you carry on that way.

Forget the Beatles, forget the Stones. Back then my heroes were the Small Faces. My parents liked the Beatles, so they were out. The Stones were just a little too weird for me then. But the Small Faces — they were cool and hip like I could only dream about. There were all tiny. An important point at the time. How could I, at five-six, ever identify with Long John Baldry? (That's why he never really made it; there just weren't enough tall people around to fantasize about being him.) And their clothes! You wondered how they had time to choose all the different outfits, let alone have the front to wear some of the more outlandish ones. In short, they were mods.

A lot of bilge has been written about mods. Sometimes it seems like anyone who was under 45 and over three-and-a-half and lived in England between 1960 and 1966 reckons they were a mod. The nearest most of them ever got was a short stroll down Carnaby Street long after the real scene had moved on. Pete Townshend wasn't

a mod. He might have expressed their feelings with uncanny insight, but he was no mod, just a sensitive voyeur. Marc Bolan was a mod, even a face (a super mod); he got his picture in *London* magazine when he was only twelve or so and lived for clothes. The Small Faces (see how they got their name? It was a girlfriend's idea.) were mods.

Mods were no rabble. In point of fact, they were so elitist they made hippies look positively democratic. The elitism focused on clothes, records and more clothes. New jacket every time you went out. Change your socks after every dance. Two-tone tonic suit with patch pockets this week, three-button cuffs next week, but always cut just so. This obsession with street couture and neatness fooled outsiders, made parents still ranting about bearded beatniks look upon these sweet and tidy boys (and girls) with something approaching benevolence (until they started trading punches and broken bottles with their enemies, the contemporary bike-boy Rockers, down at the seaside). They all had day jobs; they had to if they wanted to afford the clothes. Most of them worked in banks or as solicitor's clerks; with a "nice" job like that, you could still wear your gear to work.

But the smiling parents were being conned. The mods were the ultimate double agents of teenage society. Presenting that *almost* staid image all week, they'd only come into their own at the weekend. Speedball straight through from Friday night to early Sunday morning, gather at that week's fashionable club, parade in the latest threads, get hip to some new sounds (mostly black American imports; "Hey, have you heard that Dobie Gray?") and generally "make the scene." It's amazing what a few little pills can help you do, innit?

If all mods were double agents, the Small Faces were the smartest double agents of all. They came on so sweet and innocent that your mother would say, "Aren't they nice boys?" And they're on *Top of the Pops* bopping along straight-faced, singing stuff like "Here Comes the Nice."

You're giggling up your sleeve and your mother's still going on about what nice boys they look.

They had their cover down perfect. I mean, my god, you have to be good to get away with singing a hymn of praise to amphetamine dealers on a ten-million audience teeny-bopper (though they weren't called that then) show and have all those kids skipping around and singing the chorus for the next month. Now that I think about it, it was so insidious that they ought to have been locked up for corrupting the morals of the young. What kind of pervert would advocate speed as a cure-all? Still, the last laugh was on Stevie. Someone spiked his water supply with methedrine, and he didn't realize till he'd been up for a week and had more spots than David Cassidy. Serves him right.

But they were double agents in more ways than one. I don't care about you precocious bastards who were into the San Francisco sound when you were thirteen — when I was that age, the only psychedelia I got to hear was on hit singles. The Beatles aside, that meant the Move (maybe) and the Small Faces. Any new idea that came along, they'd think it out, slim it down and slot it into a three-minute slice of Top 10 fodder. Pop plus.

But that was later. They started out like a million other '60s beat groups. First, decide you want to be a star. Get hold of an instrument. Find a song in a key you can play and sing. Play every hole of a club that'll let you past the door. Sign a management contract with the first shyster that offers you a few quid. Have one hit single. Put out an atrocious follow-up. Go back to the car factory where you worked after leaving school, taking with you a few memories of fleeting fame and a big debt for the 85 pairs of trousers you charged to account on Carnaby Street. It's such a common story that I'm surprised anybody stayed at the top for more than the Warholian 15 minutes. Sure, those that did make it generally had talent (whatever that is). But so did a lot of those that didn't make it. And the Small Faces very nearly didn't make it.

LET ME INTRODUCE the villains of the piece one by one:

Cheeky Stevie Marriott is sitting around, bored, in the J-60 Music Bar, an instrument shop in London's East Ham. He's had a taste of fame already, playing the Artful Dodger in the London production of *Oliver*. Now, too old to be a child actor, he's certain he doesn't want to work in this shop for a few bob on Saturdays for the rest of his life. He's a soul fanatic. He's been the leader of the Frantics and the Moments, but they didn't really get anywhere, despite a few recordings.

Then this other little geezer walks through the door. Ronnie Lane, guitarist with the Pioneers and instrument checker for Fender, has decided to switch to bass, and he's come in to buy one. He's seen Steve with his band before, but it's not until he asks for a Harmony bass and Steve remarks on the wisdom of his choice that they really get to talking for the first time. Seems they're both really into Booker T. So, come closing time, they nip 'round to Steve's house and play some of his records, real unusual stuff for those days: Bobby Bland, James Brown and all the new Stax sounds.

Ronnie's playing a local boozer that night with his band (the drummer's Kenney Jones) and he gets Steve to come along and have a blow. They get along great. So great that they get pissed out of their tiny fifteen-year-old brains and are barred from playing there again. All in the same boat, they decide to pool their misfortunes, roping in a mate of Stevie's on piano, Jimmy Langwith, who changes his name to Winston. They call themselves the Small Faces and start out hustling gigs. Up and down the M1 on egg, beans and sweet lukewarm tea. That's the life.

They get a bit of a name for themselves in Sheffield and London, even if they do play the same set three times a night and have only got about six numbers. Natch, along comes their very own shyster.

"Hello, Mrs. Marriott. Is your Stevie there? No? Well, look, my name is Don Arden, and I'm interested in working with your boy. I think he can go places. Tell him to give me a ring at the office and we can set up an appointment. That's right: A-R-D-E-N.

"...Come in boys. Let me come straight to the point. I want to sign you. I'll either give you all thirty quid a week flat or I'll put you all on a percentage with twenty a week guaranteed. Do I look like I'd twist you? You'll take the percentage? Wise decision. Don't worry about clothes and instruments and so on. I'll arrange for you to have charge accounts the length of Carnaby Street. Now, here's the pen. No, don't worry about a song either. I'll get one for you. I know just the man! Ian Samwell. Alright?"

Yeah, alright! Our man Samwell does an outrageous steal on Solomon Burke's "Everybody Needs Somebody to Love" (which is fine by the band, they'd rather be black anyway) and calls it "Whatcha Gonna Do About It" — talk about more front than Selfridges. Quick, sharp drum patter; bouncing organ; Stevie takes a deep breath, fills himself with mod aggression, opens his mouth and, for the first time, the record-buying public gets a chance to knock their lobes to the greatest male English white soul singer ever. Ronnie and Jimmy shout along behind him like East End Ikettes who've undergone a sex-change operation. And it gets better. Steve's voice gets looser, more relaxed and confident. Then, in the middle eight, he steps out with a harsh, tense (dare I say minimalist?) guitar solo that must have ruined his AC30.

So, it's hello charts, but it's goodbye Jimmy. Winston was too tall, couldn't play very well and wanted to be the star. Ex-Twickenham Art College student Ian McLagan, then with the Muleskinners and the Boz People (yeah, it was Boz Burrell's band) was short, could play a mean organ and also wanted to be a star. But they forgave him that. The band had seen a complimentary review of him in *Beat Instrumental*, so they got Arden to phone him up and come into the office for an interview. He'd just walked out on the Boz People when their van broke down on Chiswick flyover, so when he got the call, he went straight in.

It was love at first sight. And Don Arden made Mac an offer he couldn't refuse.

"How much you earning now, my boy?"

"Twenty pounds a week," replies Mac, lying through his back teeth. ("I was smarter than I realized, 'cos I was only really taking home about a fiver," Mac says now.)

"I'll make it thirty. You're on a month's probation; but first we'll have to get you some new

clothes and your barnet, well..."

Mac gets taken down Carnaby Street. Socks, socks, socks. Shoes, shoes, shoes. Trousers. More trousers.

Mac: "I was on the road with them for a week before I had a chance to phone my parents. They didn't know what I was doing. 'Look mum, I've got a good job. but it's top secret so I can't tell you anything at the moment. I'll phone you later.' After six weeks, I finally plucked up the courage to ask Ronnie if I was still in the band. He said, 'What you talking about?' They didn't know anything about this one-month probation business. So, I joined and me wages went down to twenty pounds. I'd thought they were earning fortunes, not less than me."

When Mac joined, the second single, "I Got Mine," had just been released. It failed to make the charts, but they were still tearing round the country fitting more gigs into a week than there were days. They used the song again as the instrumental "Ogdens' Nut Gone Flake."

As much by default as anything else — they just wanted to play R&B — the Small Faces were now full-fledged teen idols, a state of affairs reinforced by their next single. "Sha La La La Lee" was released early in 1966 and reached number-three in the charts. As it was written by showbiz hacks Kenny Lynch and Mort Shuman, it's not surprising that it's very much a standard boy-plus-girl-equals-marriage pop song. Luckily, the raw power of Marriott's vocals and occasional bit of phasing do more than save it.

It wasn't a classic; nor was the next single, the rather ordinary "Hey Girl" (although it was a Marriott/Lane composition). After that, though, came their first killer and chart-topper, the sublime "All or Nothing." From the opening tom-tom roll (a Kenney Jones specialty) to the first subtly savage chord, right through to the ride chorus when everybody on the dance floor would join in pretending they were Stevie Marriott, it's a perfect vehicle for Marriott's voice, then maturing as fast as his personality was retarding under the isolation of fame. The build to the crescendo is magnificent; the chaotic cymbal-crashing finish is cathartic. It was the first great English soul record. It also marked, by dint of its excellence, the entry of the Small Faces into the main rock and roll action of the mid-'60s: the competition among major groups to make the one perfect single of all time. They were all in the game: the Beatles, Stones, Yardbirds, Kinks. They all knew you were only as good as your last single, and if you wanted to show how good you were, you had to top not only your own last release but also the last Who single or whatever. It was probably — no, certainly — the most competitive period ever in rock history. It also produced some of the best music. Singles really were the best things around then.

Between the burgeoning producer cult (e.g., Andrew Oldham wanted to think he was Phil Spector), the new technology (multi-tracking, unusual instruments like the accursed sitar, feedback tricks) and the discovery of hallucinogenic drugs, the good old pop single was jet-lifted into a whole new universe. Whereas before you had a verse, a chorus, a middle eight, another verse and goodnight, suddenly not only did you have to have all that (or at least some of it), you had to make weird, wonderful and profound statements on top of a backing track that had to be strange, adventurous and instantly accessible. If the imposition of an outside discipline encourages tightly focused, finely honed work, never was that discipline more draconian.

It worked best in the period of tension before drippy psychedelia took over wholesale: before that wretched excrescence *Sgt. Pepper*, when all the groups still believed in the importance of singles. They aimed their best work at the least sophisticated audience and attempted to stretch that audience's notions of what pop music is about without being either pompous or condescending.

Where the Small Faces differed from the other bands was that they weren't quite as earnest. A po-faced Stevie, Mac or Ronnie would be like a laughing assassin — uncanny and slightly disturbing. Their first album — the only original one on Decca — was apparently recorded out of their trees on acid, standing on chairs upside down, making strange noises and generally treating it

with less respect than normal. (It's still in catalogue, but when I told Mac that, he just shrugged: "We never got any money from it. It was a tape deal with Contemporary Records. Decca paid the money to Contemporary [an Arden firm] but it never reached us.")

Such levity would be just what you would expect from a band in the Small Faces' position then. They were teen idols to the point where live gigs were the sort of screaming farce you can hear on the live Beatles album. Neither the band nor the audience could hear what was being played; both rapidly ceased to care. The band were stuck in a chauffeured limo, hotfooting it from hall to hall, never seeing anything past the fortieth joint of the day and their own very in-group sense of humor; the audience were stuck in their belief in the Small Faces as objects to scream at.

Steve: "It reduced our mentality by ten years. We were going 'round shooting water pistols and pop guns at each other. We all got a bit crazy. I remember Ronnie on Carnaby Street one day, for no reason just jumping up in the air and turning 'round three times or so. We just didn't know what was happening to us. We couldn't handle it."

Kenney: "We were totally cut off. One day I went into Lord John (a Carnaby Street clothes shop) and bought a checked jacket, a checked shirt, checked trousers and a checked tie. All real loud bright-colored checks. Then I went into Toppers and bought some checked shoes. And when I walked down the road, I couldn't understand why everyone was looking at me."

Their press agent at the time (he's working for them again now) had them walk baby alligators around Berkeley Square. Mac: "It was either that or run for parliament. That was always a good one."

They had another hit with the whimsical "My Mind's Eye," but by now relations between them and Arden were becoming a little strained. This didn't improve when their parents decided to ask Arden where all the money was going. He told them all their sons were junkies and that the money was going straight into their veins. They still haven't got the money they're owed.

The Small Faces left Arden ("He was so tight

he wouldn't even pay for session musicians on our records") and, after a short spell with Harold Davidson, teamed up with that archetypal '60s wunderkind, Andrew Loog Oldham. Oldham, hedging his bets on the Stones and believing himself to be the ultimate rock and roll Svengali, had set up his own management and record company, Immediate, with its own yukky motto: "Happy to be part of the industry of human happiness."

It was the first major British independent and, although it later collapsed in rather messy circumstances, it was an early, brave attempt at creating a viable musical force separate from the dictates of the mindless pap-oriented majors. Oldham might have been a pain in the arse as a person and utterly and childishly egocentric, but at least he had good taste and the guts to put his money where his mouth was. He was certainly the savior of the Small Faces. Whereas before they'd been treated as a moronic bunch of star-struck kids who could be ripped off for a few bob, Oldham gave them back their self-respect and helped launch them into the peak of their career.

Mac: "Immediate was great. We got paid for the first time. When I say we got paid, I mean our wages went up from twenty pounds to sixty pounds a week."

Steve: "And we got into the studio. Given our heads for the first time. But we put all our eggs in one basket, didn't we? They managed us. They were our recording company, and they were our publishing company. Talk about juggle bread. We used to receive a sheet saying where all the money had gone to. That's all. It could have been done by any typist. Nine times out of ten we found out it hadn't gone there at all. So, we still owed people all these vast amounts of money that had supposedly been paid out. Which is why we didn't receive any royalties [to this day].

"Andrew managed us for about three years [it can't have been much more than two and a half, actually]. He was terrific really. A loon. We had a good laugh. We didn't get any money, but we had a good laugh."

So did everyone who bought the Small Faces' Immediate singles. First up was the aforementioned dissolute "Here Comes the Nice." It was in a whole different league to their Decca singles. Beyond the superficial quirky poppiness of the tune and the double-entendre hip of the words, the band had their tongues deep in their cheeks. For the first time they'd tapped into their own cultural background rather than that of destitute Blacks across the Atlantic. If there's been a lot of guff spouted about the mods, there's been almost as much spewed out about the influence of the English music hall. Nobody seems to be able to mention Ray Davies without going on about how he's part of an ongoing link with the rich traditional British working-class music-hall culture. Quite simply, Davies has no connection with it at all. Ultimately his songs are reserved, diffident, elitist and literate. Music-hall culture was earthy, simplistic, sentimental and robust. Often unbearably crass, all emotions were laid on with a mechanical digger. Nothing (except Queen and Country) was taken seriously. Which is just how the Small Faces approached "Here Comes the Nice." Anyone could sing along to it. No one could believe a word of it. In 50 years' time, if there are still any boozers left, "Here Comes the Nice" will be sung at chucking-out time, as if it had always been a revered pub singalong classic.

Their production techniques had improved beyond the wildest expectations of their audience. While adhering more or less to the basic four-piece unit, they'd added all sorts of neat little twists and the occasional novelty. Marriott's gut-wrenching voice, Mac's insistent piano and warm-toned organ, Ronnie's reliable bass and idiosyncratic voice and Kenney's muscular drumming had always been there, but now they had their very own instantly recognizable sound.

The next three singles were, and I don't use this word too often, brilliant. They all sound like the masterstrokes that quite a few bands manage once and never again. The Small Faces did it not once but three times: "Itchycoo Park," "Tin Soldier" and "Lazy Sunday."

When "Itchycoo Park" appeared, hippiedom was just starting to raise its stoned head. Trust the Small Faces to take the piss out of it. One step on from the ultra-cool speed dealer we meet the East End street kid acid freak. The Marriott/ Lane writing team apparently started the song as a joke. They ended up with demonstrative proof of their songwriting excellence. And while it is a big piss-take, Stevie's voice invests it with enough soul to make it sound as if he really felt for the kid who never got closer to the idylls of the country-side than Itchycoo Park.

"Tin Soldier" was a partial return to their earlier R&B days, if only because of the delicious and talented P.P. Arnold (who came over with the Ikettes and stayed) on prominent backup vocals. I remember seeing 'em do it on *Top of the Pops*. Slow drift into the number. Stevie leans back, finds his spot and slams into a Telecaster (or is it an Esquire?) chord. He turns sideways, checking out the band around him, urges "Come on!," revitalizes the song, then immediately drops the volume for the first lines and sings almost delicately over Kenney's crisp hi-hat touches. Have these boys no limits? Now they're rewriting fairy stories (Hans Andersen, if I remember correctly). Into the first chorus. and Pat Arnold's hollering along, adding harmonies to Steve's raucous rabble-rousing but moving rasp. From there, it's all power, marred only slightly by the lack of control and overstatement.

Perhaps the most remarkable thing about the Small Faces' period with Immediate is that, as well as the classic singles, they managed to fit in another album while still carrying on touring at the same spirit-crushing rate. More and more they felt distant from an audience that only wanted to hear them do the hits and see them wiggle their arses around a little. Gradually they withdrew into the studio and began work on their magnum opus, *Ogdens' Nut Gone Flake*.

Everything they'd learned from "All or Nothing," from their old soul favorites, from "Itchycoo Park" and from Andrew Oldham was squeezed into *Ogdens*. They'd gone into the studio intent on proving to the scoffing (and self-evidently stupid) cynics that they could produce an album which worked as an album; one which, if not quite a concept LP, had an underlying unity that took it beyond their previous "two hits and 12 unrelated tracks" approach. But they were still the same old

cocky, humorous Small Faces.

The second side is a six-track linked narrative, but they went one different by getting screwball English humorist Stanley Unwin to write his own word-warping script. How seriously can you take a story about someone thinking the moon's disappeared just because it's on the wane? First time I heard it I thought it was great, but I must admit that, while over the years the actual songs have continued to grow in stature, the spoken story line has started to grate and seems both dated and ingenuous. It was a brave experiment, but like a lot of its kind it fails because the words just don't stand up to repeated listenings. Trite words in songs don't matter because they're not the only component; with words alone, there's no tune to carry your attention over the boring bits. And anyway, you can't dance to them.

The first side of *Ogdens* is a mixture of styles, loosely based around the same techniques they'd used on "Lazy Sunday" (the last track on the side). After the opening title track, a pleasant but not astounding instrumental, comes Marriott's raw soul-belter showcase, "Afterglow." It's probably the best Small Faces record that never became a big hit. Then a short, wry McLagan song, "Long Agos and Worlds Apart" — I've been listening to it for nine years and still haven't managed to make out more than a fraction of the lyrics. "Rene" is the East End belly laugh. Crude and full of local references, even now it sounds totally outrageous. It's about a dockside whore and her manifold delights. I suppose you could get sanctimonious about it and claim it was some kind of deep comment on waterfront low-life. It ain't nothing of the kind. It's just the Small Faces having a laugh and giving you one at the same time. Unfortunately, after that arresting start, they slip into another instrumental which, good and funky though it is, slows things down too much. The next to last track, "Song of a Baker," is strange. Every time I play it, I think it's a real neat little song. And then when it's finished, I forget it totally. Enjoyable but not memorable.

Last but hardly least is the utterly wonderful "Lazy Sunday," with its innumerable different sound effects (birds, church bells, flushing toilets and more). Stevie Marriott registers what may well be a first: a true rock song sung not in an American or transatlantic accent, but in broad (and heavily hammed) Cockney. "Rene" is sung in the same voice but isn't really what you would call a rock song. Playing it at the end of the side makes you realize what a cleverly crafted and crazily inspired piece of work "Lazy Sunday" is.

Going through the album track by track as I have hardly makes it seem particularly great. But it is when you listen to it. I'm not sure why, but let me just say that the whole is decidedly greater than the sum of its parts. The album has a very original (if impractical) sleeve: it's meant to look like an old-fashioned tobacco tin from the outside. Inside, you get all sorts of hippy-dippy cracked lens pictures of the band. The round cover looks pretty, but the record keeps falling out. In the U.S., this problem was solved by placing the cover in a snap-sealed clear plastic "tobacco pouch."

Ogdens reaped a large amount of critical acclaim and went to the top of the charts [in England] but, far from launching the Small Faces on a new, dynamic stage of their career, it confused them. Their stage show was still in the old "wham bam and off" style. Although they experimented with using Georgie Fame's horn section (the results of which can be heard on the live tracks of *Autumn Stone*), people hoping to hear them perform *Ogdens* were disappointed. They only played two songs from it live: "Rollin' Over" and "Song of a Baker." (They did eventually perform "Lazy Sunday," but only much later.)

Even their last proper Immediate single was a strangely dispiriting affair. "The Universal" was partly recorded on a cassette player at Stevie's house. It had some of the same warm, slightly silly humor that was the Small Faces' trademark, but it also seemed to have a hollow center — or perhaps one of despair. Not even the jaunty brass section could hide the pathos of Steve singing, "I mind my own and my own minds me." He sounded lost.

Mac: "It was on the Australian tour, after *Ogdens,* that we realized we weren't cutting it. We should have kept both things going. We should

have juggled gigs and the studio."

They still needed a follow-up single to "The Universal" (which only reached number-16, a very low position for them). Steve: "We took 'Autumn Stone' into Immediate and played it for them. They turned it down. They didn't like it, but that's what they called the album."

Autumn Stone was the double compilation album Immediate put out after the band broke up. Besides nearly all their hits and the live stuff already mentioned, Immediate included whatever new songs they could find, whether they were properly finished or not. Despite that, it's almost certainly the best Small Faces album. The title track is a dynamite ballad and almost worth the cost of the album by itself. There are superb oddities like Tim Hardin's "Red Balloon" and the unfinished "Collibosher" ("I had the words for 'Collibosher,'" said Steve, "but I didn't have time to put 'em on"). There's an ace all-out rocker, too, in "Wham Bam Thank You Mam."

On New Year's Eve 1968 the Small Faces were to play as one of the bands at a big gig at Alexandra Palace. Before they went on, they arranged that at the end of "Lazy Sunday" Alexis Korner and maybe some others would join them onstage for a jam. At the end of the song, Steve just upped and walked offstage.

Mac: "I didn't understand why. He just walked off. We're going, 'What the fuck's happening? Oh no. What are we supposed to do now?' I just didn't know what had gone on. We still didn't know what was happening when we got to the dressing room."

Stevie was just sitting there looking blank, uncomprehending. "It was my fault really. If anything, Ronnie and I were very close, and we just drifted apart in lots of ways. I got really insecure as a person, as a musician and with the people I was working with. I had to leave before my nut went. I dunno. It was just growing up, I suppose."

So, it was finito, kaput, end of the Small Faces. You know all about after then, about Rod and Pete, the riches and the bitches. Which would have been a nice and tidy ending but then the Small Faces had to go and mess it up by reforming, didn't they?

Kenney: "I phoned 'em up. We were just trying to get a couple of gigs."

Mac: "We had a play. It was great with the four of us. So, we thought we'd get in the studio so we could get to know each other again and put down some songs. But after one night, Ronnie was talking about going back to Wales. We'd ditched our projects, but he wanted to keep on Slim Chance. We agreed to go with his management company. We'd bend with the wind."

"But," adds Steve, "there was an insult given out, and I still take it as one today. At which point I whacked him, and Ronnie said goodbye. It was a minor fracas, but it was heavy. It'll obviously turn round to be all my fault."

If they were to carry on, they needed a new bass player. Enter Rick Wills, late of Frampton and Roxy Music. "I'd had him up me sleeve all along, but I didn't know if he was free," says Steve. Rick, in fact, was filling in time on a building site and only too pleased to join the Small Faces.

There were still problems. The major one was obviously the negotiations over management and record contracts. These took a year to sort out. Meanwhile, the newly reformed Small Faces had to rehearse in secret. They finished an album nearly a year ago but it wasn't until this spring they were able to go out and play.

I saw the first and last nights of the tour. The first night in Sheffield was chaos, everything went wrong. Steve dropped his guitar. Mac's electric pianos (all three of 'em) went out of tune. It was a night I'd rather forget. But the last night at the Rainbow was great. The whole band, including Pat Arnold, who they were taking along with them again, had fun and communicated it to the audience. Marriott did his whole Jack the Lad bit, getting the crowd to shout out "Alright, guv'nor" instead of "yeah" (a bit hammy, but a laugh). And it was a total gas hearing "All or Nothing" done how it should be done. The new songs I wasn't quite so sure about. By the time you read this the album will be out anyway; it's going to be called *Playmates*. Whether they'll ever be as good as … well, I don't know, nor do I much care. They've given me enough great memories already. To expect more would seem greedy. ∎

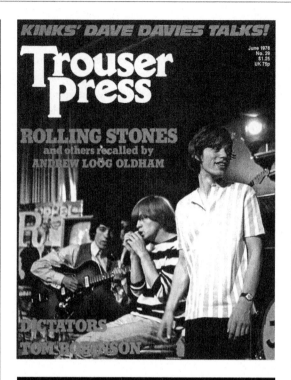

ANDREW LOOG OLDHAM

TP 29, JUNE 1978

By Dave Schulps

One of the most interesting personalities of the first decade of British rock was the Rolling Stones' sharp-tongued, red-headed manager, Andrew Loog Oldham. Along with Brian Epstein, Oldham represented a new breed of music biz entrepreneur, the manager who was himself a celebrity of sorts. Unlike Epstein, whose role was confined to management and who was, in show-biz tradition, quite a bit older than the bands he managed, Oldham was actually younger than the members of the Stones. Also, he took an active part in their music, becoming their record producer.

Many writers through the years have credited Oldham with totally creating the Rolling Stones' image, but if, as Oldham insists, that's not the case, the role he played in establishing that persona was nonetheless tremendous, although he ended his association with the band in 1967 during the recording of *Their Satanic Majesties Request*.

In 1965, having "hustled," as he would put it, the Stones to international prominence, Oldham formed Immediate Records in partnership with Tony Calder. Immediate was one of the first independent labels in Britain, "the infant bastard of the music industry," as they liked to call it. While Immediate was not especially successful in the area of album sales during its brief existence [1965-1969] and was eventually forced to dissolve, both artistically and in terms of what the label's acts would go on to become in the '70s, the label was just a bit too farsighted for its own good. A list of musicians who contributed to Immediate in one capacity or another reads like a who's who in British rock: the Stones, of course, Jimmy Page, John Paul Jones, John Mayall, Eric Clapton, Keith Emerson with the Nice, Steve Marriott (first with the Small Faces and later coupled with Peter Frampton in Humble Pie), Fleetwood Mac and a good stock of slightly less illustrious talents like Chris Farlowe, Nico, the McCoys, P.P. Arnold and Billy Nichols.

Following the dissolution of Immediate in 1969, Oldham moved to America — along with the Stones, who were also dodging the taxman — and greatly reduced his public profile. For a while, he was a staff producer at Motown's Rare Earth label, but that association proved unprofitable. After a short sabbatical from "the biz," Oldham returned to activity last year both as a producer and in a managerial capacity with the Werewolves, a Texas rock and roll band with Stonesish overtones and a guitarist who could be mistaken for Keith Richards's brother. Their debut album is expected momentarily on RCA. As a producer, he has also recently worked with Reddy Teddy and Benny Mardones.

With the advent of the new wave in England and the rise of such hustler-manager "personalities" as Malcolm McLaren, Jake Riviera and Bernard Rhodes, we decided last December that it was a good time to pay Mr. Oldham a visit. The parallels between Oldham's role in the first wave of British rock and McLaren's in this one are astonishing.

Here, then, is Andrew Loog Oldham at his best — talking about himself.

What got you into the music business? You started out working with Brian Epstein, didn't you?

Before that, I worked for [*fashion designer*] Mary Quant, doing things like pouring drinks and helping them dress windows. That was a very good education, if for nothing else than how to dress windows — which you could use for album covers later — or how to throw parties.

Then I gave that up and went to France and was involved in nice little things like kidnappings and got deported from there. Then I was working for an industrial public relations firm, but when their doors shut at six, I would open up my own agency. I was handling people like Johnny Tillotson, Brian Hyland, Chris Montes, Little Eva, Phil Spector, Gene Pitney and those bulk-rate cinema tours — the equivalent of Dick Clark things. I was moonlighting out of this place — I think they call it "conflict of interest" now —[laughs] until eventually I had to go out on those tours. I remember one tour Don Arden promoted with Sam Cooke and Little Richard which I got thrown off of because the cinema chain said, "Either the publicist goes or the tour goes."

So, I left that and took an office with this agent named Eric Easton [laughs]. My mainstay was Mark Wynter, who at the time was having hits covering Steve Lawrence. I was making about £7 per week. Solid money. I could afford to be flippant. Mark Wynter was doing a weekly show from Birmingham which came out every week called *Thank Your Lucky Stars*. I went up once and there was Brian Epstein and the Beatles doing their first television appearance with "Love Me Do."

Epstein already had a publicist called Tony Barrow, who was also working for Decca Records at the time. He was moonlighting, but only doing

Epstein's written stuff, so I hustled him into letting me do the on-the-street stuff. I think I started off at £10 per week. After the first results — when I had gotten them into places where rock and roll had not gotten into before, the equivalent of *Cue* magazine or *New York*, whatever — they took me out to Liverpool so I could see where the talent was being grown. There was this poor shop assistant sitting there, and Epstein tells me this is his next act. It was Gerry Marsden of Gerry and the Pacemakers. Then he upped me to £25 a week, so who was I to disagree?

Did you "hustle" Epstein, as you put it, for a job because you felt there was a good chance that the Beatles would be huge? Did you feel they had something special that first time you saw them?

I liked them, but in terms of the first time I actually sat there with a Lana Turner lump in my throat and really got choked up about it, that didn't come until the Bedford Odeon, when these kids started breaking all the windows backstage. Although they'd already been getting that kind of response in certain places, the first tour with Tommy Roe and Helen Shapiro was still sort of spotty — it would depend on where you were. Further north and south they did well, but not in the areas around London and the Midlands. That Bedford gig, though, the noise level just hit you emotionally. I felt all those things that Sid Bernstein would later find a cute way to say.

Did Epstein have grand designs on America from the start?

Yeah. America was already becoming a possibility, but it was still also an unreality, because no one knew what to expect. There's an equation between that and what's happening now with new wave.

Epstein's vision was terrific. I've spoken before about Epstein and about George Martin. George Martin would have been a terrific producer, as far as I'm concerned, if he'd only known the right time to go to the toilet. I'm not saying it was the case, but if he knew when to get out during certain uptempo situations and leave the Beatles to it…

Anyway, the great thing about Epstein's vision was that you couldn't knock a dent in it, you could only agree with the guy — and that I love. Consider the facts. There it was, out of the box, the records were number-one.

I stayed with him through the first two records of the Beatles, the first record of Gerry and the Pacemakers, up to a few weeks before the first Billy J. Kramer record. By then, I was already involved with the Rolling Stones. It came down to a case of either pooling the Stones with Epstein or splitting — it might have been a totally different story, folks — so I left. But he was terrific.

Why did you decide not to pool the Stones with him?

I didn't think either of our egos could take it. It was as simple as that.

When you got the Stones, did you totally transform them, as some people have suggested?

No.

Their image was pretty much set before you came in, then?

Yeah. Well, the first time that I saw them they were playing sitting down. Mind you, if you had to play those sweaty clubs you'd be sitting down, too. Actually, I'm being a bit facetious, it was probably more conducive to the whole blues structure they were playing in. You take something more seriously when you're sitting than when you're standing up. There were six of them, since Ian Stewart was still with them, but they looked the same as they would later on.

Then there was no calculation of their image?

Well, there's calculation just by saying, "Stay the way you are."

But there were certain tendencies that were exaggerated. Was that your input or theirs?

Everything was pretty much a two-way street. We had our own little fantasies that we would run in-between each other — this or that schtick or the *Clockwork Orange* thing — but if you're asking me if I created the whole image, the answer is "no." Those things were us rehearsing between each other and hyping each other up. The only time I changed them was when I got them to wear a particular costume for a particular television show like *Thank Your Lucky Stars*. The guy who did *Thank Your Lucky Stars* was some 50-year-old guy who was, as we say in England, educated in the RAF. There was no way he was going to have them on, in terms of his ego, if it didn't look like they had made some effort to show their appreciation for being on this majestic show. We all liked buying clothes just as much as anybody else, so we went and got the costumes. Gradually, over the course of a few shows, the costumes disappeared anyway, but faced with the prospect of either wearing the costume or not getting on, they went and did it. You can't force somebody, though.

You mentioned that the Stones wanted to do a film of A Clockwork Orange. *Were they always into doing films?*

Clockwork Orange started it. What happened was that Kubrick, without having finished *2001*, already had the rights to the movie. He bought it for almost nothing off Anthony Burgess — something like one grand. The story is amazing.

Burgess had been told he was dying of cancer, so he began selling off everything he had cheap to make some money to support his family. He started drinking more and taking Benzedrine, because he didn't want to sleep away the last two years of his life, and he wrote four great books. Two years passed, though, and he was still there — the doctors had been wrong — but his writing has never been as good as when he thought he was dying.

Didn't you at one point have the rights to A Clockwork Orange, *though?*

We never had the rights. I believe if you lie enough, it becomes a reality. In that instance, it didn't, but we had a great four or five months with it. I wouldn't have done all those great sleeve notes without Anthony Burgess.

Weren't you going around saying the Stones were going to do Clockwork Orange *for quite a while?*

The whole thing then was to get in the *New Musical Express* and papers like that, because you could just measure your success by how many inches you'd get a week.

That was all during the *Clockwork Orange* period. Eventually, though, we had to face the fact that we didn't have the rights to do it. It reached a point where I was reading the newspapers and believing the stories I'd planted in the first place,

forgetting that it was me who told it to them.

Eventually, we settled on a book called *Only Lovers Left Alive* to replace *Clockwork Orange*. It fitted the bill. It was no way as well-written. It was written by a teacher from Yorkshire called Dave Wallis, but if you forgot that it wasn't as interestingly written, and you just reduced the plot to two pages, it ran fantastically. The mind just boggled. By that time, Allen Klein was in the picture.

How did Klein initially enter the picture?

It's a very incestual world. He represented Sam Cooke, though I never met him in the days that I worked for Sam Cooke. He handled the catalogue for Kags Music, which had "It's All Over Now."

Our habits then were that, if we had recorded an outside tune, I would go around knocking on the doors of the various publishers going, "Could be a single, but we want a piece" — 'cause we were making money, but not that much. I arranged a meeting with this guy called J. W. Alexander, who was the administrator of Kags Music, but Klein really owned it. I rolled up for breakfast at the Hilton to ask him for my percentage for the Stones for doing the song. Klein was sitting there asking all the right questions like, "Do I want to be a millionaire?" and "Do the Stones want to be famous?" Yes. About a day later, I brought Mick and Keith around to see him, and they were as enchanted as I was. It was all go. It was really as simple as that.

Getting back to the movie, our Decca deal had one of these great clauses in it — if they wanted a soundtrack album, they would have to put up the money. So, for a while it looked like the movie could actually happen. Then it got bogged down in detail. I bought the idea that we must be packaged with what are now called "bankable people." I remember taking Mick to meet Nicholas Ray — he was sitting in a corner with a drink going on and on about James Dean. Even to us it was apparent that the guy hadn't worked since he was called in to resurrect some Biblical film. I don't think Mick actually said it, but it was pretty apparent that he was thinking, "Don't ever put me through that again," because it was light years away from what we wanted. A few encounters like that with the "establishment" end of film just got everybody a little sour on the whole thing. The fantasy was becoming too real. There was also too many other things to do. It was now getting a little harder to keep up with how many records you had to have out.

The fun had already been had, and if you can't keep the momentum going there are other things that you have to do. I don't think anybody ever completely forgot the importance of doing a film, but it was like, "If we can't do it the way we want it, fuck it."

What year was that?

'65.

What about the band in the studio? Did Spector play any role in production or was that all you? You never produced a record before the first Stones album — was it sink or swim?

We did the first record at the old Olympic Studios, which was four-track. I think we had the wonderful sum of about £40. So, at £6 an hour, it was log in and get out. I was really watching the clock. I just said to the Stones, "Okay guys, I'll see you next week. Out of everything you know, just play me everything that you think's the most commercial." That's how we arrived at the first record ("Come On").

At the end of that first recording session, I went, "Hmmm, right, let's go." And the engineer said to me "What about mixing it?" I said, "What's that?" and he looked at me like, "What the fuck is this?" I think he tried to be as nice about it as possible. The thing was that everybody in the group was just as interested to hear what mixing was. So, he said, "Well, you know, we have four tracks, and in order for it to become a record we have to get it down to one." I said, "Oh, you do that, I'll come back in the morning," figuring that if I stay it will probably take longer.

After that experience we decided that was too complicated, and we went to recording in mono, which was how we ended up doing the first album and a few other things we did at Regent Sound, because recording in mono did have the element — which we all needed — of what you see is what you get.

After the first single, was it decided that their

material wasn't commercial enough?

It wasn't their material that we were recording for the first single. It was all other people's stuff.

I mean, the material they were doing — the R&B stuff.

Yeah. It was one of those unspoken things.

Was there a problem with the Stones in the beginning because they were five guys who thought they were an R&B band, unlike the Beatles, who were into pop? They were very serious about the blues at that time, weren't they?

Not that serious. In terms of me saying to them, "Well, we're going to make a single, play me the five things you think are most commercial" — they knew we were dealing with reality.

How willing to compromise were they?

The first record went to number-18, but I don't think they were actually compromising. I think they thought the record sucked, which it did. And the second record, "I Wanna Be Your Man," they just wouldn't have recorded if they didn't want to. They never recorded anything to please me or my taste.

So, they were actually fairly committed to their music...

It depends, looking back. If you look at some of the earliest songs that Mick and Keith wrote, in no way would they appeal to their more staunch blues fans. But that was them working as songwriters — writing to order. I was already starting to run that fantasy alongside the reality of wanting them to write. Also, they didn't mind writing for other people.

Did you urge them to write?

Oh yeah, from the word go. Not only because you could see how self-contained in one way or another the Beatles were, but because a lot of the things that I'd been following that were coming from America were written by established songwriters like Goffin-King, Sedaka, Pomus and Shuman and Leiber and Stoller. That was reality. The record companies were saying things like, "This one's terrific for Cliff Richard." That was "Blue Turns to Grey," which was an English single and a hit for him before the Stones did it.

"Heart of Stone" was the first song Mick and Keith wrote that we figured was too good to give to someone else. "Tell Me" was just done in Regent Sound, but the first version of "Heart of Stone" had Jimmy Page and John McLaughlin on it and was cut in Decca Studios just as a demo.

Did that version ever come out?

No, it was just a case of the more the merrier. Anyway, they wanted to write. It didn't take much urging. I've always considered that the first song they wrote was "Not Fade Away," anyway. At that time, Mick, Keith and I were living together. They were into the last half bottle of wine and going through it — it was one of those magical moments: "We gotta record it." But there's no way if someone had just said coldly, "Right, let's do 'Not Fade Away,'" that we would have wanted to do it without hearing the way that Keith was playing it on the guitar. To me, they wrote that song. It's a pity we couldn't have gotten the money.

How important do you think you were to the Stones' success?

Very important.

Do you think they would have made it without you?

I can't be overly modest. I'm talking to myself, too. I can look at it two ways: First, "Would I have made it without them?" And the answer is undoubtedly that I would have hustled myself in some way. There was never any doubt in my mind that I'd make money at something. I mean, I'd gotten kicked out of school for bringing hard-to-get records back from France where I was on holiday. Records were then [five shillings and seven pence] and [I was] selling them for 10 shillings. That was called extortion.

It's capitalism.

Right, and I was in a capitalist school — the straw hats and everything.

I don't know. Who knows what would have been? There's no doubt that they would have been the Rolling Stones, but whether they would've been what they are...

They're still a point of reference for everything I do, and I would hope that some of the things that I did are still points of reference for them, that is, when they're faced with a situation, they have a reference point from the time when I was involved.

Whether they would have been even more extreme in arriving at where they are today or whether it would have gone the other way and turned into a Chicago blues type of more esoteric music had I not been there...well, who knows?

When you say the Stones are a reference for everything you do, how will you use, say, with the Werewolves, what you did with the Stones? People are going to be looking at you with the Werewolves and saying, "Can he do another Stones?"

Oh, I'm not even thinking about that. I mean I do, but when I talked about points of reference, I wasn't thinking of that particular aspect of it. What I meant was just your life experience with these people. It's mainly a matter of taste, in terms of what I got out of it and what I put into it. It's just a barometer that always stays in your head. It can pertain to anything to do with the music, or it can be if I'm buying luggage, and I'm going, "I wonder if Charlie would like that luggage?" because that is a point of reference of something we used to do, and it just doesn't leave your head.

Do you still have any contact with the Stones?

Yeah. We don't go out of our way to join each other for weekends, but it's fine. The only one that my relationship was ever a little rusty with is now departed, so with the ones that remain it's fine.

When the songwriting thing started, everyone was encouraged to write. If some people can't write, they might get a little frustrated. We really tried. I even had Gene Pitney sit down and try to write with Brian [Jones] once.

How much did you have to manipulate the Stones image-wise?

You've gotta be stupid if you're standing there among a bunch of journalists and you realize something is wrong, and that is that they think that, looking at the Rolling Stones, they are really looking at a pretty scuzzy bunch. Now, there's no way you can change that, so you might as well play it up. They would. In terms of what is manipulated and what's not, if you think of them as an act and someone is putting out the kind of vibe to you that the press was to us, you normally react that way back.

The Rolling Stones would react like that. If a journalist walks into the room and gives you that,

"Hey, you're the greatest thing since God" shit, then the chances are you'll feel like it, if you're performing. I mean, none of them ever looked at Jethro Tull like that, regardless of what they wrote about [Ian] Anderson.

How did you come to leave the Stones? Was it basically to start Immediate?

No. I started Immediate in '65. It made a lot more noise in Europe because the first record we had out there was a hit — "Hang on Sloopy" — which was a hit on Bang [in the U.S.]. We bought the European rights for $2,000 and got a number-one record. The Immediate thing didn't really relate to me leaving the Rolling Stones except that it kept me busy. It was getting pretty crazy, playing executive in the daytime and then — *da-da* — quick change into the studio. The only time I'd ever stop was to watch *The Prisoner*. Anyone who knew you and dared call you between 7:25 and 8:25 on a Sunday was a friend no more. And most of Monday was blown out — everybody was so stoned during that time — trying to work out who number-one was. That would be the whole of Monday morning. People would call and my secretary would tell them I was in a meeting. Meanwhile I'd be talking to somebody going, "Who is number-one?"

But really, splitting with the Stones had nothing to do with Immediate. It was really like when a relationship is more than just on paper and you have to go through the accumulation, then the results of success and wealth — and not be able to have the time where each of you develops your own private lives. If you start to drift apart, you might as well recognize it for that.

You just realized it was over?

Yeah. If you just look at the situation as it was then, where I'm saying to myself, "Right, he got busted and I didn't," then that's another thing that comes into your life and creates a certain tension.

The tension materialized. It became a reality during the first time we were in the studio during the making of *Satanic Majesties*, which I left in the middle of. Because of the lifestyles going apart, it was the first time I'd been in the studio when I didn't understand what they were doing.

I don't think they did either.

No. It was ironic. The only one with a complete tune was Bill Wyman. It was as simple as that. I looked at it and said, "Well, what the fuck am I doing here?"

Fortunately, our split was before the days when everybody had lawyers, so it was really very clean. It was done just like that. [Snaps fingers.]

I asked you before about production in the studio, with Spector...

Right. Spector came in during the sessions of "Not Fade Away." His contribution was production, but it was also not production, in a sense. I'm not detracting from his influence on me — or on anybody — but his influence in that particular instance was more in spirit, because the reality of watching him work, apart from liking his records, had nothing to do with the way we worked just by virtue of the fact that the Rolling Stones were a band. When you walk into a studio and hear Bill Medley's part and then you hear this rather squeaking voice which was him, because the two of them [the Righteous Brothers] wouldn't go into a studio at the same time, you know that his trip's got nothing to do with what you're doing. But his spirit was definitely a great asset to that session. Gene Pitney was in on it, too. Have you seen that bootleg that's out on a single that's got "Cocksucker Blues," with "Andrew's Blues" on the other side? On "Andrew's Blues" the vocal is by Mick and Phil Spector with bits of the Hollies and Gene Pitney in the background. It was cut during the same session as "Not Fade Away."

Do you consider yourself more as a producer than as a manager? How do you see your own image?

I think in America it's more as a producer. I never get asked to manage people. I think it is just because my production credit is on all the labels. For management, well, Allen Klein, by being based here, was more out front than any of us.

You were involved in the release of the Stones' Metamorphosis *album on Abkco. Where was that material from?*

A lot of it was stuff they'd done with Jimmy Miller and not completed. And then most of Side One — well, "Out of Time" was the Farlowe track with Jagger's voice over it. A lot of the other stuff on Side One was out of the sessions cut for Screen Gems Publishing with Jimmy Page, John Mc-Laughlin and all those people that were just demos, with Jagger's voice on them. What people got quite clearly is not the Rolling Stones. That was all done when Decca thought they were paying for the Andrew Oldham Orchestra, and I was running my publishing company out of it by cutting the tracks and selling them elsewhere.

What was the actual thing with the Andrew Oldham Orchestra? Was it basically Stones tracks?

No. I used to deliver an album, but Decca used to pay for recording all the tracks. So, I had the chance of a lifetime. For instance, the John Paul Jones single, I'm quite certain that Decca paid for it and then I sold it to Pye. Decca would get an album by the Andrew Oldham Orchestra, but they didn't know what else I'd cut.

In other words, you were cutting extra tracks they didn't know they were paying for, then selling those to other companies as finished masters.

Yeah. I mean, we weren't rich, we had to....

Decca was richer than you, let's put it that way.

They still are. Things on *Metamorphosis* like "Blue Turns to Grey," "Somethings Just Stick in Your Mind," "Try a Little Harder," "Each and Everyday of the Year" — if Joe Smith of Warner Bros. wanted to delve into the whole early Warner Bros. vaults, he'd probably be able to find records of Dick and Dee Dee singing over the same tracks. When *Metamorphosis* came out, he found me out. He suddenly realized that he had paid for the tracks, too. Now, he doesn't mind because he has a sense of humor, and he can tell the story at the different dinners he goes to. Though he did tell me that if I ever came to a deal with him, he would hold it against me at the first auditing.

Why did you decide to put out "I'd Much Rather Be With the Boys" after it had been held back for so long? That, to me, is part of the Stones' myth. Is "Cocksucker Blues" ever coming out? Are there other songs we've never heard?

You mean on *Metamorphosis*? I wanted that one to stay — with "Andrew's Blues" in it — but no one would listen to me because I didn't manage the act anymore and couldn't go, "This is what the act wants." I wanted to shove it in just as a single,

but nobody else would have it. I mean, you got to have a sense of humor. That album was really quite old, because a lot of the work had been done about three years before that, when it was called *Necrophilia*. There are covers around that were printed up — the same stuff. But they thought it reflected on the state of the late guitarist and was in bad taste.

Those early Stones covers were great.

We were very lucky. Two of the main photographers, David Bailey and Gered Mankowitz, really had a line on the group, too, so inasmuch as the Stones trusted me, I trusted these people, 'cause they really knew what to do.

The liner notes — when you wrote those, did you go in with a specific idea of how you wanted to sell them? The one that's written in the Clockwork Orange *style [on the original UK edition of* No. 2, *which more or less became* 12x5 *in the U.S.] is probably the best liner I've read.*

No, but I was just obviously influenced at that time by all the film shtick that was going on because that took place over quite a length of time. It was probably written — well, you just had to get it to them the next morning. Those notes were probably down to *Clockwork Orange* and amphetamines.

Were there any other film plans after Only Lovers Left Alive? *We heard about one called* Gather No Moss.

I don't remember what that was. There used to be a lot of wrong information that would get thrown about in the press, just based on the fact that somebody was offering something. We were very hot on the idea, though. So much so that we were actually rehearsing making movies. There's a film around that I did with them in Ireland — *Charlie Is My Darling* — that I think we almost spent more money on the credits than we did on the film. I think it was actually two grand on the credits, four grand on the film. Looking back, it seems like it was just an exercise in bullshitting ourselves. We just wanted to be able to see the credits. Then we said, "Well, go on with this," but we never did.

How much recording was done in that period of 1964 and 1965, around the time of those Page–

McLaughlin demos, that hasn't been released?

Nothing, really. I think you've pretty much seen all of it. There's possibly a lot of stuff afterwards, from the period when Jimmy Miller produced them. By then, the method of recording had changed. Also, things had started to slow down, demo-wise, as the time in England got less. In terms of writing for other people, they had begun to concentrate on writing for themselves. The benefit of writing for other people had been gotten.

Were you interested in the production side of things when you started with the Stones?

Not really. I became a producer by default. Decca tried to bring another producer in. The guy who was producing Brian Poole was probably on something like £20 a week. George Martin may have been on £40 — a guy didn't really have that much incentive to become a producer. They actually did go through meetings with Decca where they were told they had to have their sound this way or that, but by that time I'd had a bite of it and wanted to keep going. They didn't really want to work with all these staff producers, and I didn't want them to, either.

What influence did Spector have on your productions?

I went through a period when I was over the top with my infatuation with his records. At the same time, I loved the Four Seasons' records. What prompted me and Keith to write "I'd Much Rather Be With the Boys" was some sort of a private joke to do with Bob Crewe, as to what you might call his "persuasion." [Crewe] used to send me some of their tracks without the vocals and write that if we wanted to use them, we should just have Mick and Keith write another song around them. He didn't send me "Sherry" or "Rag Doll," but there were a lot of good tunes. It was nice to receive them. He had a follow-up to "Rag Doll" by a girls group doing an answer record. That was a valuable input to my own career with Immediate. I learned if you have one hit, then whatever you can put out that people will connect with it will sell something. It was those outside deals that allowed Bob Crewe to live in splendor, because the record deal he had with the Four Seasons wasn't paying them very much.

What do you think of the Stones now?

Well, they're still a constant source of entertainment. Forgetting about whether I see them a lot or anything like that, the basic necessity is still to be a fan and have a parallel between that and when I was working for them. In that way, they're still entertaining me. I like some albums more than others, but it's hard to talk about them right now, coming off a live record with no tour to plug into. Their spaces have been pretty constant over the past six years as to when they'll come up with another anthem. They're due for one very, very soon.

What do you consider was their last anthem?
"It's Only Rock 'n' Roll."
Even though it was stolen from Marc Bolan...
They were just paying him back.
Is there anything about the climate of the music business now that interests you more than it would have, say, a few years ago?

No. The only climate I go by is my own. It's just a particular time when I feel like working. There probably wasn't anything wrong with the music business, it wasn't any worse or better, but as for my attitude, well, I probably just went through a couple of years of sleep. You look at it and there's a time to work and a time not to work. My sleep period came after I was working for the sake of it. I'd gone through a horrendous deal with Motown when they had that Rare Earth label. Financially, it was incredible, but what they were doing hiring a British producer to get them British rock and roll acts when that producer couldn't even go back into England, I don't know.

Why couldn't you go back to England?

In 1970, the same time the Rolling Stones left England, I left, and the first year you weren't even allowed back. The guy who was supposed to be running Rare Earth's business at that time called me up and told me it was about time I found a group and went in to record for this deal. I said, "Oh, really?" 'cause I was sleeping up in Connecticut at the time. So, I went down to Westport and pranced around the village green for a while and the first group that vaguely sounded like Crosby, Stills, and Nash — well, that was it. That was a group called Repairs. [*Repairs released* Already a

Household Word, *produced by Oldham, on Rare Earth in 1971.*]

Luckily, none of the acts I did for them were either super-talented or I didn't care for them at all — one way or another — because the setup was horrendous. There was no way they could get away with it. As far as getting radio play on [the group] Rare Earth records, okay, they could get away with that. They were doing Black songs produced by a Black producer and they had the pipes to get away with it. When they went out on the road, they died. The rest of the record industry would not accept white rock and roll bands from Motown. Not that I gave them anything that would've helped them move it ...

It was an incredible experience, though. You would roll up in Detroit to do string overdubs — which I did for the Repairs album and one other that never even came out — you'd arrive and everybody you'd meet was a potential Temptation. The driver who picked you up at the airport, the guy who carried your bags... Anyway, they used to block time for the orchestra at the studios, from 10:00 a.m. to 1:00 p.m., say, they'd tell you, "Okay, we're doing four tracks: Norman Whitfield's doing one and three, you're doing two and four," and regardless of your requirements, they'd have this whole orchestra booked in. I only wanted string quartets because we were going for this dipsy Joni Mitchell shit, and they had 36 strings there. It didn't matter what you wanted; it was like music coming off a conveyor belt. It worked for them, though.

I cut one Detroit act for them, a sort of sleaze would-be Mitch Ryder thing. Sunday Funnies, and we used that original old Motown studio. It was incredible, the monitor system was just one bass amp. The Motown thing was a two-way street, though. They didn't exactly get the best years of my life, either.

The reason I asked if anything about the music business today excited you was because a lot of people seem to be drawing parallels between what's happening in England now and the first wave of English rock and roll which you played a big part in.

I was in England from Christmas 1976 to April 1977. The thing then was that the media coverage didn't equal the sales. Bands were getting all this press, but the only people who had a shot at selling anything at all were the Sex Pistols, and they were passing from one record company to another at the time. It was already getting to the point where every record company was signing one band "just in case."

It's great if it instills a little fear into the record business in general. I like the economics, because you just do your small deal and get on with it. New wave's great, but there are certain things that are out of perspective about it. The media will kill a lot of the bands off here before they even get started, because they're being asked to live up to such a big build-up. Few of them will be able to do it.

Do you know Malcolm McLaren?

No, but I've been told I really should meet him.

The parallels in the way he's gone about publicizing them seem to be pretty striking.

Yes, but a lot of those things rollercoast for you. Okay, you give somebody credit for opening the door, but a lot of times all you've got to do is to know when not to talk. I would like to see him and the group together before I judge. Mind you, he's done pretty well so far.

What do you think of their records?

Actually, I haven't heard one.

You're pretty much divorced from the new wave in England then?

Yeah. It actually meant going out and seeing these bands, and I was too busy getting married. It doesn't matter, it doesn't really make any difference.

But that was similar in the Beat Boom. Dozens of groups had one hit and were never heard from again.

It's different sitting here and looking at it coming from England, because you see the incredible resistance that is coming from record companies and agencies over here.

Was there the same type of resistance when you first started working with the Stones? We've all heard stories about Decca.

Yeah. It was pretty similar, but a lot of what's

happening now is this political thing. Kids are gonna produce music whatever happens; the political label's got nothing to do with it.

In England, it's always been the same for any kid who's ever left school and had to decide what he was gonna do. That doesn't make it any less valid, but there's really no difference from Cliff Richard to the Rolling Stones to the Sex Pistols.

The only thing that makes it difficult to compare is that one of the divergent points would be where all these '60s acts were working. I haven't been able to see any of these new bands work, because they couldn't work, with all these Greater London Council bannings and such. We used to watch the Rolling Stones go out and play ballrooms in virgin territory and just die.

How did the Stones react to that?

The numbers would get faster. Everyone just wanted to get the hell out of there. The whole thing was very uncomfortable; those ballroom dates where the equipment and the group were all shoved in the back of one van. How they ever got up on stage and moved I still don't know. You would get out after four hours driving on the motorway and ... well, god knows how we made it as far as we did. ∎

HELLO IT'S ME

TP 36, FEBRUARY 1979

Peter Meaden, the Who's first manager — and author of their first two sides, "I'm the Face" and "Zoot Suit," — and later manager of Jimmy James and the Vagabonds and, most recently, the Steve Gibbons Band, died last August 7th of a barbiturate OD at age 35. Although we ran a short news item on his death (TP 33), an old friend and associate of Meaden's felt that some more words were in order.

Peter Meaden and I grew up, hung up and out in Hampstead NW3, a sort of London upper west side middle-class Tarrytown, around speed and Gene Vincent time. I worked for Mary Quant. He kept a job at McCann-Erickson and made the big move from Edmonton to NW3.

The first company we formed, in 1960 when we were an odd 16 and 17 years old, was called Image; we were a public relations company which my mother incorporated. (That was a heavy meeting, my mum and Peter's aunt.) We did catalogues and brochures for a Ted Lapidus-alike shop called John Michaels. We then formed the Hampstead Literary Society (Town Halls in England did not charge rental to non-profit intending organizations) and held an R&B night, which for 1961 was ahead enough for prospective failure. Gordon and Peter (before they became Peter and Gordon) double-headed the bill. Gordon topped the bill under the name Marc Conquest. Peter's girlfriend's father (who owned a Greek restaurant) handled the catering, and Peter and I decided it was better to leave early to keep the door money safe.

The same funds were later blown trying to take the project to downtown Chelsea. Beautiful dreamers that we were, we went our own ways: I to my Stones, Peter to his Who.

The last time I saw Peter for a long while he took me to see a group called the High Numbers who did a great Temptations tune or two. I asked Peter who the two quiet gentlemen sitting near us in the same Islington Hall were. Peter replied that one of them was the brother of the actor Terry Stamp and the other was the wayward son of the legendary classical figure Constance Lambert. They both had the secure look of managers. I can only remember Peter as up, I didn't listen to his friends. Be it the Who, Jimmy James and the Vagabonds, or whatever cause, Peter was always selling, hustling and performing — which is where we all came in, isn't it? The last time I saw him was February of '77 in timeless Wardour Street. Peter gave me all his eyes and went into a 180 mph rap on the wonders of life with Steve Gibbons, Bill Curbishley and the family of Who. The last time was like the first time and who could ask for anything more ...

Andrew Loog Oldham
New York, NY

SYD BARRETT: CAREENING THROUGH LIFE... FROM THE FLOYD TO THE VOID

TP 26, FEBRUARY 1978

By Kris DiLorenzo

he color black is not a solitary real color. Nor is it the total absence of color. A black hole in space, in fact, is a concentrated area so densely packed that nothing, not even light, can penetrate it. Black-ness is actually all colors at once, so many colors merging at such intensity that the riot of their profusion produces, to the superficially perceptive eye, only nothingness: black. Try it with your crayons or magic markers: everything at once, too much simultaneous input layered repeatedly, gives you blackness.

You all know who Syd Barrett is even if you think you don't. Without him there would have been no Pink Floyd. Barrett dominated the band during their first years, writing most of their material, singing lead vocals and playing lead guitar. He left the band (or the band left him) for reasons of mental health and, in 1970, with the aid of his replacement in the Floyd, Dave Gilmour, recorded two solo albums: *The Madcap Laughs* and *Barrett*. Syd then performed briefly with Stars, an ensemble in the Cambridge area, but left them after three gigs and virtually vanished from the public eye.

For the past five years, Barrett has generally been written off as an acid casualty — but more often lamented as a musical visionary whose interior landscape became too disorienting for him to handle. Some of the stories one hears about Barrett are disconcertingly true, others only sound like Syd, but most of his acquaintances express the same conclusion: intuitive and fragile, Barrett was a unique talent and an erratic mind on the edge of a different type of existence — as well as a man who indelibly affected those who came into contact with him.

Several people close to Syd at various times in his life offer their perspectives in this article, and the resulting portrait is Picasso-like: a profile viewed simultaneously in different dimensions of seeing. Many thanks go to the following for their help: **Glen Buxton** (formerly guitarist with Alice Cooper), **Duggie Fields** (designer, artist and Barrett's flatmate for several years), **Lindsey Korner** (Barrett's girlfriend during the Pink Floyd days), **Bryan Morrison** (former Pink Floyd manager and publisher, still Barrett's publisher), **Mick Rock** (photographer for Hipgnosis in London during the '60s), **Jerry Shirley** (formerly with Humble Pie and Natural Gas, drummer on Barrett's albums and currently with A&M's Midnight), **Twink** (drummer for Pretty Things, Pink Fairies, Tomorrow, Stars and Rings, who still believes in Syd), **Dave Gilmour**, for devotion above and beyond the call of rock and roll.

There is no question that Syd Barrett was one of the "umma" (the brotherhood of prophets — see Frank Herbert's *Dune*) and "just mad enough to be holy." Barrett's madness was not quite a sudden explosion, however, but rather a gradual implosion, the clues to which he articulated in his music long before his behavior signaled distress. Syd's songs contained warnings from the beginning: he dealt with instability and the primal need for comfort via authority's fairytales ("Matilda Mother"), the desire for control of a situation and the outsider/observer role ("Flaming"). The lyrics of "Jugband Blues" (on Floyd's *Saucerful of Secrets*) also spell out some of his conflicts. By the time of *The Madcap Laughs* and *Barrett*, Syd's songs clearly revealed raw spots in his psyche amid the poetically jumbled voodoo of his writing.

Ten years since the release of Pink Floyd's first album, *The Piper at the Gates of Dawn*, it's difficult for those unfamiliar with Pink Floyd's music or the burgeoning British music scene of the '60s to attribute great importance to Syd Barrett. All it takes to be convinced of Barrett's significance, however, is a careful listen to *Piper*, *A Saucerful of Secrets* (the second LP) and the singles he wrote for the group (on the Dutch *Relics and Masters of Rock* collection). What Syd created in sound and imagery was brand new: at the time, America hadn't heard of Hendrixian feedback and distortion as part of a guitar's capabilities, and the Beatles were just recording *Sgt. Pepper* (at the same time and in the same studios) as Pink Floyd were cutting *Piper*. Barrett's music was as experimental as you could get without crossing over entirely into freeform jazz; there simply were no other bands extending the boundaries of rock beyond the basic 4/4 sex-and-love themes.

Syd certainly listened to American jazz, blues, jug band music and rock (as did most young British rock and rollers of the time). He cited Bo Diddley as his major influence, yet these inputs are no more than alluded to in his music, which contains every style of guitar playing imaginable: funky rhythm churns up speeding riffs that distort into jazzy improvisation. At times, an Eastern influence surfaces, blending vocal chants, jangling guitar and devotional hum in tunes like "Matilda Mother" and the lovely "Chapter 24," based on the I Ching.

Barrett's guitar work maintained a psychedelic, dramatic ambience of incongruous contrasts, violent changes and inspired psychosis. No technician à la Eric Clapton, Barrett simply knew his own particular instrument well and pushed it to its limits. Compared by critics to Jeff Beck, Lou Reed (in the early Velvet Underground days) and Jimi Hendrix, Barrett lacked only the consistency to match their achievements. His trademark (and Achilles heel) was sudden surprise: trance-like riffs would slide abruptly into intense, slightly offbeat strumming ("Astronomy Domine"), choppy urgency gives way to powerful, frightening peaks ("Interstellar Overdrive"), harmless lyrics skitter over a fierce undertow of evil-sounding feedback and menacing wah-wah ("Lucifer Sam"). Stylized extremes made Barrett's guitar the focus of Floyd's early music; his instrumental mannerisms dominated each song even when Syd merely played chords. Barrett's rhythms were usually unpredictable; one never knew what process in Syd's brain dictated when to speed up or slow down the pace, when to sweeten or sour the sound and when to wrench the tempo totally out of joint, shifting gears to turn rhythms inside-out. As a result, Barrett's playing was variously described by critics as "clumsy and anarchic," "adventurous and distinctive," "idiosyncratic," "revolutionary" or "brilliant and painful."

Barrett was indisputably an innovator. Whether he was entirely conscious, or in control, of his art is impossible to determine; perhaps it's enough to say that he was indeed effective. His work with Pink Floyd still ranks as some of the most expressive, sensational playing recorded by a rock guitarist. Even ten years later, Barrett's solos stand as fixed entities in the overall scope of Pink Floyd's music; it's a rare long-term Floyd fan who doesn't know every note, each frenzy of feedback and electronic eccentricity. Yet Syd borrowed no familiar blues licks as the young Eric Clapton, Jeff Beck and Jimmy Page were wont to do.

Barrett's songwriting genius was original and

extremist as well. His singing was highly stylized: obscure chanting vocals, high-tension verses and explosive choruses alternating with deadpan storytelling and hypnotic drawls. He utilized fairytale technique, surrealistic juxtaposition of psychedelic detail and plain fact, childhood experience and adult confusion. Like the Beatles, Barrett combined dream imagery and irony with simple, direct tunes, strong, catchy melodic hooks with nonsense rhymes and wandering verses that sound like nothing so much as what goes on inside people's heads when their minds are running aimlessly.

Although some of Barrett's songs seem to be straightforward stories, one always discovers a twist: multiple meanings to a line that belie the childlike wonder of the words ("Gnome"), innocuous lyrics devastatingly undermined with a questing guitar or unlikely special effects ("Scarecrow," "Jugband Blues"). Certainly, psychedelia asserted its influence on Barrett's writing; there are descriptions and perceptions one can attribute only to drugs or hallucinatory schizophrenia, but others are strictly the products of his unaffected imagination.

As a songwriter, Barrett has been compared with Pete Townshend and Ray Davies. Dave Gilmour echoes that evaluation: "Syd was one of the great rock and roll tragedies. He was one of the most talented people and could have given a fantastic amount. He really could write songs and, if he had stayed right, could have beaten Ray Davies at his own game."

Syd's influence on Pink Floyd continued to manifest itself long after he left the band. Carrying on without him was difficult at first, since the public and music business obviously thought Syd was all the band had. Initially, Gilmour's style conformed to the Barrett prototype established on the first album, and the music retained Syd's spirit, but the songwriting gradually changed. In the years following Syd's departure, he remarked that the band wasn't progressing, and in a real sense this was true. Even Pink Floyd's three most recent albums, to a large extent, expand and develop themes and riffs Syd laid down with them in 1967. The point of view Barrett used in

his songs, an alternation (and occasional fusion) of second and third persons, still predominated in Pink Floyd compositions; pieces of his solos find their way into Gilmour's; tracks from *Saucerful* rearrange themselves on *Dark Side of the Moon* and *Wish You Were Here*. Even 1977's *Animals* displays Barrett's dark humor and takes off on his "Rats" premises. The dramatic mixes Syd applied to the Floyd's early recordings are now magnified by 16-track studios but employ the same technique: whole walls of sound rocket from one side of the room to the other, the guitar careens in and out of different speakers, submerged speech and incidental sounds chatter beneath instrumentals; their use of sound as an emotional tool is absolutely Barrettonian.

The most obvious impact of Syd Barrett in absentia has been on the concerns of much of Pink Floyd's music since 1969. They began dealing with the politics of reality in the outside world and became obsessed with the internal world of madness. The lyrics to "Shine on You Crazy Diamond" are in perfect context on an album that clearly expresses the band's outrage at the whoring business of rock and roll and its toll on a human being like Barrett.

Syd did indeed wear out his welcome with Pink Floyd. It became nearly impossible to follow him musically as he reached for more abstract constructs, constantly rephrasing, shifting and rewriting as he performed, expressing a compulsive need for uniqueness without considering logic. He worried about being considered "redundant," was anxious about growing older without accomplishing everything he wanted and at one point said in exasperation to his roommate, "Duggie, you're 23 and you're not famous!"

By 23, Syd was already internationally famous and began the rollercoaster ride to oblivion. Onstage, he often found it inconceivable to play, standing among the amps with his back to the audience, staring at his guitar as if he'd never seen one before. He occasionally exhibited flashes of virtuosity that dazzled audiences and made them hope for more, but Barrett was incapable of performing for its own sake. He wanted to achieve something indefinable each time he set out to play, and this Olympian vision could prevent Syd, worried it not be perfect, brilliant and innovative, from producing anything at all. Paralysis generated fear, and many Pink Floyd concerts saw Barrett treating his guitar as if it were a treacherous grenade; at other times he would simply disappear for the duration and a substitute guitarist would have to be called in. Barrett's musical ideas were metamorphosing, too; as he became more withdrawn personally, his songs tended to deal only with internal reality and became more obscure. He was becoming more of a conceptual artist than a musician, and eventually broke the barrier between form and content (and genius and insanity) by becoming what he had sung about.

Why didn't anyone see Barrett metaphysically [or metaphorically] waving his arms in the air? Perhaps because during London's turbulent '60s scene it was difficult, especially in a love-and-drug stupor, to distinguish incipient dementia from contrived brinksmanship. Barrett, as a genuine innovator and avant-gardist, probably had more leeway to act peculiar than most of the artiste/ intellectual crowd he hung out with. Certainly no one around Syd was in a stable enough state to estimate the strength or weakness of his grasp on ordinary reality. Most of Barrett's craziness was accepted as "just Syd" until it became impossible for the Floyd to perform with his spells of onstage paralysis and offstage freakouts. The incredible struggle Gilmour and Waters of Pink Floyd endured during the recording of Barrett's solo albums, the sheer energy and patience it took to motivate Syd and keep him on the track, was the final straw. When Barrett dissolved Stars, it was apparent that he could not continue musically until he recovered from his shellshock.

BY ALL ACCOUNTS, Syd Barrett's career began like thousands of others. among the crowd of young people during the first psychedelic rush of the '60s. He attended art school, became involved with other art and architecture students (among them the nucleus of the embryonic Pink Floyd) and finally left school for music. Syd's home in Cambridge, where his mother ran a boarding house, was the local social hangout for the Cambridge students and dropouts who later moved to London to form their own artistic enclave; until just a few years ago Barrett was still oscillating between his flat in London and his mother's in Cambridge. Like all local "freak" scenes, the Pink Floyd crowd had a nexus: flats in London's Cromwell Road and Earl's Court became mecca for Cambridge hippies and budding mods. Photographer Mick Rock remembers one of Syd's flats as "a burnt-out place, the biggest hovel, the biggest shit-heap; a total acid shell, the craziest flat in the world. There were so many people, it was like a railway station. Two cats Syd had, one called Pink and one called Floyd, were still living in the flat after he left. He just left them there. Those were the cats they used to give acid to. You know what heavy dope scenes were like."

When Pink Floyd "made it," Syd Barrett was about 21 years old. "They used to rehearse in the flat," Duggie Fields says, "and I used to go downstairs and put on Smokey Robinson as loud as possible. I don't know where they all arrived from, but I went to architecture school and so did Rick [Wright, the Floyd's keyboard player] and Roger [Waters, bassist). I don't quite remember how I met them all. I just remember suddenly being surrounded by the Pink Floyd and hundreds of groupies instantly."

Barrett felt the ensuing changes keenly. Within a few months after his "Arnold Layne" and "See Emily Play" (the first Floyd singles) made Pink Floyd stars, Lindsey Korner says "chronic schizophrenia" set in. It wasn't drugs particularly that set Syd off, she insists; from the time she first met him, Korner considered Syd one of the sweetest, most together people, even though Syd's previous girlfriend says he was off the wall a little even then. According to Lindsey "it got a bit crazed" during the fall of '67; by Christmas, Syd had started to "act a little bonkers."

"Oh, he went more than slightly bonkers," Fields affirms. "It must have been very difficult for him. I think the pressures on Syd before that time must have upset him very much, the kind of pressure where it takes off very fast, which Pink Floyd did — and certainly in terms of the way people behaved towards them. I used to be speechless at the number of people who would invade our flat, and how they would behave towards anyone who was in the group, especially girls. I'd never seen anything like it. Some of the girls were stunning, and they would literally throw themselves at Syd. He was the most attractive one; Syd was a very physically attractive person — I think he had problems with that.

"I saw it even when he was out of the group (by the beginning of 1969). People kept coming around and he would actually lock himself in his room. Like, if he made the mistake of answering the front door before he'd locked himself in his room, he found it very difficult to say no. He'd have these girls pounding on his bedroom door all night, literally, and he'd be locked inside, trapped. He did rather encourage that behavior to a certain extent, but then he didn't know what to do with it; he would resent it."

In 1967, Pink Floyd toured America for the first and last time with Syd Barrett. During their L.A. stay, the band was invited to visit the Alice Cooper entourage, quartered in a house in Venice during their stint as the Cheetah club's house band. Cooper and his band had heard the Floyd's *Piper at the Gates* and their reaction, guitarist Glen Buxton recalls, was, "Wow! These guys should be reckoned with!" So, Pink Floyd came to dinner.

"Syd Barrett, I remember," Buxton says emphatically. "I don't remember him ever saying two words. It wasn't because he was a snob; he was a very strange person. He never talked, but we'd be sitting at dinner and, all of a sudden, I'd pick up the sugar and pass it to him, and he'd shake his head like 'Yeah, thanks.' It was like I heard him say 'Pass the sugar' — it's like telepathy; it really was. It was very weird. You would find yourself right in the middle of doing something, as you were passing the sugar or whatever, and you'd think, 'Well, damn! I didn't hear anybody say anything!' That was the first time in my life I'd ever met anybody that could actually do that freely. And this guy did it all the time."

If leaving Pink Floyd was hard for Barrett, so were his last months in the band.

Jerry Shirley explains: "When he plays a song, it's very rare that he plays it the same way each time — any song. And some songs are more off-the-wall than others. When he was with the Floyd, towards the very end, Syd came in once and started playing this tune, and played it completely different. Every chord change just kept going somewhere else, and he'd keep yelling (the title), 'Have you got it yet?' I guess then it was Roger (who kept yelling back, 'No!') who kind of suddenly realized, 'Oh, dear.'"

Similar episodes became more frequent until the Floyd reached the breaking point. "It was getting absolutely impossible for the band," Shirley recalls. "They couldn't record because he'd come in and do one of those 'Have you got it yet' numbers, and then onstage he would either not play, or he'd hit his guitar and just turn it out of tune or do nothing. They were pulling their hair out, they decided to bring in another guitarist so Syd wouldn't have to play guitar and maybe he'd just do the singing. Dave came in and they were a five-piece for about four or five weeks. It got better because Dave was together in what he did. Then the ultimate decision came down that if they were going to survive as a band, Syd would have to go. Now I don't know whether Syd felt it and left or whether he was asked to. But he left. Dave went through some real heavy stuff for the first few months. Syd would turn up at London gigs and stand in front of the stage looking up at Dave; 'That's my band.'"

Syd had probably met Dave in the early '60s when Gilmour played in a Cambridge band. "They used to play things like 'In the Midnight Hour,'" Rock recalls, "and Syd would go watch Dave play 'cause I think Dave had got his chords down a bit better than Syd in the early days. Syd was always a bit weird about Dave. That was his band, the Floyd."

Even before Pink Floyd returned home from their American tour, Barrett was proving more than merely eccentric. As Buxton recalls, "The crew used to say he was impossible on the road. They'd fly a thousand miles, get to the gig, he'd get up onstage and wouldn't have a guitar. He would do things like leave all his money in his clothes in the hotel room or on the plane. Sometimes, they'd have to fly back and pick up his guitar. I didn't pick up that he was a drug casualty, although there were lots at the time who would do those exact things because they were drugged out. But Syd was definitely from Mars or something."

Fields and Gayla Pinion, Syd's girlfriend during the difficult years after Pink Floyd, were most continuously exposed to Barrett-crazies, and Duggie recalls many trying periods of life with Syd. "When he gave up the group, he took up painting again for a bit, but he never enjoyed it. He didn't really have a sense of direction.

"He used to lie in bed every morning, and I would get this feeling like the wall between our rooms didn't quite exist, because I'd know that Syd was lying in bed thinking, 'What do I do today? Shall I get out of bed? If I get out of bed, I can do this, and I can do that — or I can do that, or I could do that.' He had the world at his feet, all the possibilities, and he just couldn't choose. He had great problems committing himself to any action. As for committing himself to doing anything for any length of time, he was the kind of person who'd change in the middle. He'd set off, lose his motivation and start questioning what he was doing — which might just be walking down the street."

Fields attempted to alter Barrett's pattern, but nothing quite worked. "Sometimes he'd be completely jolly and then just snap — you could never tell what he was like. He could be fabulous. He was the sort of person who had amazing charm; if he wanted your attention, he'd get it. He was very bright. After he left the group, he was very much aware of being a failure. I think that was quite difficult, coming to terms with that."

At one point, when Gayla moved out of the flat, Syd rented her room (the smallest) to first three, then five people. Fields despaired; eventually, Syd couldn't deal with them either because they were always underfoot, wanting his attention, as did many slightly younger people who idolized him. Fields recalls visitors constantly bringing pills to Barrett: "Just give Syd mandrakes [Mandrax] and he'll be friendly." More visitors came "with their hounds as well" and Syd, unable to tolerate the situation any longer, went back to Cambridge. "He just left them," Duggie recalls, "and then rang me up and said that I had to get rid of them. I said he had to get rid of them, but I actually did in the end. I said, 'Look, Syd wants you out; he's coming back!' They were a bit frightened of him because he did have a violent side."

Barrett's first solo album, Jerry Shirley says, was a result of the Floyd finally convincing Syd "that he should get off his ass and make an album." Gilmour and Waters co-produced the LP, but after the experience Waters gave up ("That's it! I can't cope with that again!") and Rick Wright joined Dave as co-producer for the second one.

The two albums, released later in America as a double package, are curios even seven years after their appearance. Syd wrote all the material (some of it years before) except the lyrics to "Golden Hair" (a James Joyce poem), and every symptom of his personal problems is in evidence. The tone is somber and unsettling, with only three frivolous songs. Many tunes end abruptly or with contrived instrumental fades when Syd runs out of lyrics. Barrett's singing is a deep-pitched melancholy monotone. There are painful moments when his voice cracks or careens out of control reaching for notes he once could sing; he shouts the higher notes, not believing he can reach them. His acoustic guitar playing is mainly arrhythmic strumming full of arbitrary and often clever tempo shifts and reversals, punctuated with extreme dramatic bursts and tenuous pianissimo. There are no brilliant solo flashes, but several tunes display his instrumental ability: "Wined and Dined" and "Effervescing Elephant," with which Barrett was familiar enough not to have trouble with the chords; "Wolfpack," Syd's temporary favorite and a demonically energized number; "Gigolo Aunt," recorded in one take on a good day; and "Dominoes," the track on which Syd's spacey, chaotic playing most resembles his Pink Floyd style.

Syd's changes were foreshadowed musically on "Apples and Oranges," a late '67 Floyd single. That tune resembles the work on the solo albums: background drone, rushed verse and slow chorus, and intense vocal line ascending and descending uneasily became stock characteristics of Madcap and Barrett. The transformation in Barrett's self-image and confidence is evident if one compares the brashness and electricity of the early Floyd albums with the dead-sounding Syd of 1970, chanting rather than singing, vocal sometimes estranged from his rhythms, unnerved by his mistakes; literally falling apart several times, incapable of performing properly at that particular moment, but unwilling to give up entirely. His music is stark, eerie and often depressing despite some genuinely funny lyrics and the efforts of Syd's musicians to add lively touches to the bleakness.

Some Barrett traits, however, didn't change. His simple stories trade off with surrealistic half-sense and nonsense; nursery rhyme structures are bent with restless time signatures and startling chord progressions. Choruses switch tempos and lyrics (often unintelligible) function more as sound. Words become less communicative elements than instruments of sensation as Barrett meanders through inexplicable mental territory, sometimes resolving into straight songs and sometimes dissolving into multi-rhyming babble.

Despite some incredible songwriting, complicated structures and stunning sonic/verbal images, there's no way to avoid feeling that the two albums are the portrait of a breakdown. Scattered throughout the nightmare/fantasy lyrics are whispers and screams from a confused Syd, trying to carry on in the midst of utter disorientation and emotional turmoil. In "Long Gone" he sings about "wonder" for those he loves as he "cried in [his] mind."

"Waving My Arms in the Air" recalls Syd's early Floyd days when, attired in a long cape, he would stand onstage with his image projected onto a screen behind him and do exactly that. He sounds quite human on that track, but when he shifts into the love song "I Never Lied to You," the voice goes flat and lifeless. In "Late Night," however, Barrett articulates clearly: "Inside me I feel alone and unreal."

Was Barrett as out of control in reality as he sounds on the albums? "Well, yes and no," Fields says. "He really didn't have to have that much control before, but when you have to provide your own motivation all the time, it is difficult, certainly in terms of writing a song. When it came down to recording, there were always problems. He was not at his most together recording the album. He

had to be taken there sometimes, and he had to be got. It didn't seem to make any difference whether it was making him happy or unhappy; he'd been through that, the excitement of it, the first time around."

Jerry Shirley agrees that Barrett was bizarre during the sessions. On the day the backing tracks to "Dominoes" (a beautiful song with a haunting arrangement) were recorded with great success, enthusiasm was running high. Dave was with Syd trying to get a lead guitar track, but Barrett couldn't play anything that made sense. In a brainstorm, Gilmour turned the tape around and had Syd play guitar to the tracks coming at him backwards. "It played back," Shirley says, "and the backwards guitar sounded great; the best lead he ever played. The first time out and he didn't put a note wrong."

Shirley refers to "If It's in You," the track on which Syd can't find the melody and flounders, breaking stride throughout the song. "That is a classic example of Syd in the studio. Between that and talking in very obscure abstracts. It's all going on in his head, but only little bits of it manage to get out of his mouth. And then the way he sings he goes into that scream — sometimes he can sing a melody absolutely fine, and the next time 'round he'll sing a totally different melody, or just go off key. 'Rats,' in particular, was really odd. That was just a very crazed jam, and Syd had this lyric that he just shouted over the top. It's quite nuts. But some of his songs are very beautiful."

To ease the process for Syd, before they went into the studio to cut, Gilmour would sit with him and either make up demo tapes of the songs or, if possible, learn the song with him. Then he'd explain it to the other musicians and play along with Syd, although he made Syd do the leads instead of taking them himself. If Dave got a fair rough guitar track out of Syd he'd use it and overdub the other instruments. If it weren't for Gilmour, Shirley feels, there would have been little semblance of togetherness; working with Syd was mainly playing it by ear. "You never knew from one day to the next exactly how it would go."

Could Barrett have been pulling some numbers on purpose? Shirley answers with a baffled squeak. "I honestly couldn't say. Sometimes he does it just to put everybody on, sometimes he does it because he's genuinely paranoid about what's happening around him. He's like the weather, he changes. For every ten things he says that are off-the-wall and odd, he'll say one thing that's completely coherent and right on the ball. He'll seem out of touch with what's gone on just before, then he'll suddenly turn around and say, 'Jerry, remember the day we went to get a burger down at the Earl's Court Road?' — complete recall of something that happened a long time ago. Just coming and going, all the time."

Barrett's one public appearance during the LP sessions was a brief set during a three-day festival at the Olympia in London. Syd eventually even managed to play his guitar instead of holding it as if it were about to explode. Barrett's initial decision to play, however, kept unmaking itself. "He was going to do it, he wasn't going to do it, it was on and off, so finally we said, 'Look, Syd, come on, man. You can do it!' We got up, I played drums, Dave played bass and he managed to get through a few songs. It got good, and then after about the fourth song Syd said, 'Oh great, thanks very much' and walked off! We tried, you know."

For Barrett, the solo albums didn't change things much. He left London for Cambridge when he decided to become a doctor. "Yes, a doctor," Duggie affirms. "He and Gayla were going to get married and live in Oxford. He had a bit of the suburban dream. That was a very bizarre sort of thing underlying him. He had lots of concepts that he found very attractive like that; he didn't really like all the one-night stands; he wanted the marriage and that bit, in the back of his head." Syd and Gayla became engaged and left the flat to Fields, who never saw Barrett after that.

Drummer Twink, then with the psychedelic band Tomorrow, met Barrett in '67 when Pink Floyd played a European festival. The band brought gifts with them; Twink's, from Syd, was a hash pipe. Though they remained friendly afterwards, it wasn't until 1972 that they got together musically. "I didn't know him closely for that long, but I was in the same space, and I could understand exactly where he was at. I thought he was very together, you know. As a friend, it was

a very warm relationship; no bad vibes at all. We didn't have any crazy scenes."

Stars was originally brought together by bass player Jack Monk's wife Ginny, who took Barrett down to a Cambridge pub to jam with Twink and some others. A few days later, a more permanent arrangement coalesced, and Stars began rehearsing for their first gig, an open-air May Day celebration in Market Square. Their material, mostly Syd's, included some from the Pink Floyd days; Barrett recorded practice sessions and [did] one coffee bar gig and seemed genuinely interested in working again when a promoter friend of Twink's booked Stars into the Corn Exchange. At that gig, everything that could possibly go wrong did: the PA sabotaged Syd's vocals, Monk's amp acted up and somehow Barrett cut his finger open. Added to Syd's memory blanks and hesitant playing, the result was bad press and immediate depression for Syd.

"We just weren't ready for it," Twink concedes. "It was a disastrous gig, the reviews were really bad, and Syd was really hung up about it, so the band folded. He came 'round to my house and said he didn't want to play anymore. He didn't explain; he just left. I was really amazed working with him, at his actual ability as a guitar player."

Barrett made no further public appearances after Stars. Anecdotes from the years following are rife; one acquaintance reported Syd carrying his dirty clothes into the London boutique Granny Takes a Trip because he thought it was a dry cleaners. Duggie Fields ran into Barrett in London's Speakeasy club. "I wasn't sure he recognized me. I was with some people he'd known for years; we talked for about five minutes, but did he really know who we were? That was when he was starting to get heavy, and he didn't look like the same kind of person at all."

In 1975, a strange reunion took place at EMI Studios, attributable, Jerry Shirley feels, to Syd's uncanny sixth sense of timing. "The last time I saw him was possibly the last time the guys in the Floyd saw him, too. They were putting the finishing touches on *Wish You Were Here*. Earlier that day Dave Gilmour had gotten married, and they had to work that night, so EMI had this round-table dinner in the canteen for them. Across the table from me was this overweight Hare Krishna-looking chap. I thought maybe it was just someone who somebody knows. I looked at Dave and he smiled; then I realized it was Syd. The guy had to weigh close to 200 pounds and had no hair on his head. It was a bit of a shock, but after a minute I plucked up enough courage to say hello. I introduced my wife and, I dunno, I think he just laughed. I asked him what he was doing lately. 'Oh, you know, not much: eating, sleeping. I get up, eat, go for a walk, sleep.'"

That night the band finished the album and were playing back the final mix of "Shine on You Crazy Diamond." "When the song ended, Roger Waters turned to Syd and said, 'Well, Syd what do you think of that?' He said, 'Sounds a bit old.' I believe Syd just got up and split not too long after that. After two years of nobody seeing him, of all the days for him to appear out of nowhere!"

[2023 addendum: In the documentary *Squaring the Circle*, a principal of the design firm Hipgnosis recalls that Syd turned up in their London office that day, asking if Floyd was there. Told they were recording at Abbey Road, he left, evidently headed for the studio.]

Jerry Shirley is less then optimistic about the possibility of Barrett recording again. "The last person to make that sort of effort was Dave, and they barely got him to do it; it was like pulling teeth. Since then, I don't think there's anybody close enough to him to get him to do it. He would have to return to the planet long enough for someone to believe that he's got it in him to actually get through the sessions. And that would just be the first step. The guys really did persevere through those sessions, god! Especially Dave, particularly in light of the way Syd was to him before. But … if he showed that he really wanted to try for it, then maybe one of them would make the effort."

Have any of Barrett's friends made a serious effort to sit down and talk with him about his future? "Oh yeah," Shirley says. "No chance. You'd get some sort of sense out of him, and then he'd just laugh at you. Lots of people tried lots of different things."

Bryan Morrison cleared up a few of the mys-teries surrounding Barrett. He explained Syd's departure from Pink Floyd: "He didn't leave of his own free will, really. I mean, he kept threatening to leave. I think in the end it was by mutual agreement, because he was having some personal problems. He wasn't able to get it together anymore, and by agreement he left the band."

Did a similar thing happen with Stars, or did Barrett have a reason for leaving that band? Morrison hesitates a bit before answering. "Have you ever met Syd? Well, one of the main things — he had psychiatric problems and was actually in a sanitorium."

There are no other Barrett recordings outside the solo LPs and some "incoherent" tapes, Morrison says. Right now, Syd is living on his royalties in a London hotel. "He doesn't have any involvement with anything or anybody. He is a recluse with about 25 guitars around him. I see him very rarely. I mean, I know where he is, but he doesn't want to be bothered; he just sits there on his own, watching television all day and getting fat. That's what he does." Can nobody talk Syd into becoming musically active again? "No. It's impossible." To Morrison's knowledge, Syd hasn't been out of England since the Pink Floyd tour in 1967, and he gave his last interview in 1971. Barrett is firmly anchored in his shell.

Then is Barrett's extended schizophrenic episode (see *The Politics of Experience*, R.D. Laing) permanent insanity of just prolonged post-Floyd depression? Chemical ingestion coupled with chronic existential anxiety? Morbidly sensitized insecurity and a crumbling value structure? Or diabolically effective defense and legend material?

Let's put it this way. Anyone who's ever been in chronic pain and confusion can sympathize with Barrett. Anyone ever caught in the equally real dread of the principal's office or never returning from a drug experience has experienced Barrett's primal tears. Anyone who's ever teetered on the edge of chaos and felt the black panic of falling into the void can comprehend the Madcap. Someone who's almost grokked the universe and then lost the definition on the tip of their tongue knows what it's like to be a crazy diamond. Twink says Barrett's no acid freak. Shine on, Syd. ■

CLASSIC ROCK

Dave Schulps' skill, nerve and preparation made his lengthy interviews some of the most powerful and enduring pieces we ever published. While our focus was firmly (but not exclusively) on British rock icons of the '60s, he engaged Jimmy Page, Pete Townshend, Ray Davies, Andrew Loog Oldham, Kevin Ayers, Ron Wood and many others in thoughtful and detailed discussions of their careers and views, proving time and again that the more you put in, the more you get out. We didn't think of the music these folks made as "classic rock" then, but time and the quality of their work has made it so.

Trouser Press *co-founder Karen Rose, a short woman with a huge mane of red hair, a Brooklyn native who lived in a studio apartment in the heart of Greenwich Village, was a larger-than-life character: smart, organized, funny, enthusiastic, talented and charming. She was also, at the outset, the only one of us with any actual professional experience in journalism (or in any other field, for that matter).*

She was instrumental in bringing the magazine into existence and providing early momentum (as well as a floor on which to prepare subscription mailings) but ceased to take an active role in it after a few years and went on to found Rock Read, a mail-order music book business that now seems prescient in many ways. A lifelong non-smoker, Karen — who chose to keep her illness private — died of lung cancer in 1989. We were once close friends; the belated news of her death came as a complete shock.

Fandom was our collective motivation for starting the magazine: Dave and Ira were united in Who freakdom; Karen was, first and foremost, devoted to Jeff Beck (although Peter Frampton was not far behind in her estimation). This article in an early issue was her detailed paean to him.

(Despite the careful inclusion of discographical minutiae, none of us ever truly embraced the pursuit of rare vinyl. Even as the magazine ran page after page of minuscule record auctions and sales, we stood apart from the world of serious record collecting, so much so that we once teased that segment of our readership with the sardonic declaration, "The more you spend, the better it sounds.")

Jeff Beck was on our cover again six issues later, interviewed at length about Blow by Blow *and much more by* Rolling Stone *contributor Gordon Fletcher. Sample quote from the enigmatic guitarist: "Life is a joke... There are only a handful of things in my life that I can say I'm really glad I did."*

BECK BASIC

TOTP 4, JULY/AUGUST 1974

By Karen Rose and Nick Taquinto

For a skinny London kid, Jeff Beck is one of rock's foremost heavyweights, a title well-deserved for what he's done, what he's capable of doing and what we pray he'll do again.

After (a) quitting (b) being fired from (choose your favorite rumor) the Yardbirds in late 1966, Jeff Beck embarked on a "solo" career under the guidance of manager/producer Mickie Most. His first release, in April 1967, was the single "Hi Ho Silver Lining"/"Beck's Bolero" (Epic 5-10157), the A-side of which features one of those rare Beck vocals and is a pop effort certainly not indicative of the progressive band he just left behind. (It seems that no one knows who was playing on the "Hi Ho" session unless whoever it was is unwilling to admit to the fact.) The flip side, "Beck's Bolero" (same version as on the *Truth* album), showcases Jeff in a gorgeous instrumental written by one J. Page, accompanied by Pagey, Keith Moon, Nicky Hopkins and John Paul Jones and recorded while Beck and Page were still Yardbirds.

A bit prior to the time of this release, an official Jeff Beck Group was forming. This band made its first public appearance on March 3, 1967, in Finsbury Park, London, second bill to the Small Faces. The lineup was: Jeff Beck, guitar; Rod Stewart, vocals; Ron Wood, bass; Roger Cook, drums. (Up until a few weeks ago, we believed that anoth-

Trans-Oceanic Trouser Press

July-August 1974   For the Rock Consumer   #4   50¢

Yardbirds Part II: Jeff Beck

23 on the **Move**

Reviews A-plenty

JBG's '67-'75

(David) Bowie

Beck

er Beck Group — with Beck, Stewart, Viv Prince (Pretty Things) on drums and Jet Harris on bass — had previously rehearsed once, but that was it.

We have since learned that a Beck Group appeared on the BBC's *Saturday Club* with the following lineup: Jeff, Stewart, Wood on rhythm, Jet Harris on bass and Aynsley Dunbar on drums. This, of course, does not jibe with the fact that Jet Harris rehearsed with the band only once and did not perform with them at any time. Also, Jet's time of service in the Beck Group is difficult to ascertain. Let's say he played a minimum of twice. His first and second appearances cross the time of four drummers, because in the spring of '67 Rod Coombes (now with Strawbs) took Roger Cook's (now of Blue Mink) place, though he (Coombes) was replaced by Dunbar before the next Beck single was recorded.

Like Jeff says, "The continuity of my past is just about as messed up as it could be." We doubt if anyone other than Jeff would know what's going on here and we doubt if even he would care. Just us.)

Anyway, Beck's next single, released in October 1967, was Graham Gouldman's "Tallyman" backed with "Rock My Plimsoul" (Epic 5-10218). "Tallyman" is yet another rare and weak Beck vocal (for all his other talents, Jeff Beck can't sing!),

though the mike is handed to Stewart on "Rock My Plimsoul." "Plimsoul" was re-recorded for the *Truth* album months later, and it's that second version that appears on *The Best of Jeff Beck* (Columbia EMI 5C054-92207), a Dutch import. The original 45 is noteworthy, though, because toward the end of one guitar break, Stewart compliments Beck's playing with "Nice," to which Jeff, not usually the humble sort, answers "Thank you" ... ON HIS GUITAR! While not missing a note of the solo he happened to otherwise be in the middle of, mind you.

Jeff's following single (England only), released in April 1968, was "Love Is Blue"/"I've Been Drinking" (UK Columbia DB 8359), both sides of which were to surface much later on the above-mentioned *Best of Jeff Beck* album ("Tallyman" and "Hi Ho Silver Lining" are on this record, too). "Drinking," another superb Stewart vocal, also features Nicky Hopkins, who was to join the group on piano in fall '68.

At this point, Beck's career was still being controlled by Mickie Most, and the emphasis was on Beck as a "solo" artist. All three singles were credited to "Jeff Beck" and not "The Jeff Beck Group"; this solo push is what accounts for the B-sides of all three singles being better than the A-sides, where the soon-to-be-official Jeff Beck Group was hidden.

(From this point on, singles will not be discussed. Anything that Beck recorded with *his* bands — this eliminates work for Donovan, the GTO's, Stevie Wonder, and, most recently, Badger — can be heard on the five albums bearing his name.)

Dunbar was replaced, sometime along the line, by Micky Waller, leaving the lineup that was to record the priceless *Truth* album (Epic BN 26413). Released in August 1968 — two months after the Jeff Beck Group, in their American debut performance at the Fillmore East, June 14, 1968, was called back for so many encores at the early show that the top-billed "play all night" Grateful Dead had time for only a 30-minute set — is undoubtedly one of the three greatest rock albums of all time, a true desert island classic. And, for once, due to *Truth*, the commercial-minded Most takes on the hero role. Without him there would have been no album. To quote Mickie: "I personally financed their [Beck's] first tour to America and supported them. Epic Records didn't want to release *Truth*. It wasn't until Peter Grant (who worked for Most) took a *New York Times* review of Beck's first U.S. performance at the Fillmore East and telegraphed it to the president of Epic that he agreed to release the LP."

Serving mainly as a showcase for Beck's versatility, *Truth* contains not only the expected rockers and blues numbers, but a reworking of The Yardbirds' "Shapes of Things," interpretations of the traditional "Greensleeves" and Oscar Hammerstein's "Ol' Man River" and "Beck's Bolero," which stands alone as well. This album is the fulfillment of the promise Beck had shown with the Yardbirds. While he may have brought the guitar (and hence the guitarist) into the spotlight while with that band, it was with *Truth* that Jeff showed just how worthy of that up-front honor his talents were. His sharp chops and lightning leads simply dazzle the listening audience.

Jeff Beck's *Truth* — six years later and still no one can play guitar like that. Period. Simply stated, on *Truth*, Beck transcends the physical limitations usually placed upon those possessing only five fingers on one hand. At the time, Jeff had a more thorough knowledge of his instrument and equipment than any other guitarist around and, what's more important, he used it tastefully, not letting electrical devices dominate him, unlike other guitarists whose footwork (as in fuzz tone and wah-wah) demanded equal, if not more, attention, than their fingerwork. (Beck's tasteful use of electronics is apparent in "I Ain't Superstitious" and "You Shook Me," to name but two.) This was the time of the "Big, Better, BECK" campaign; probably some advertising man somewhere was very proud of his cute little alliteration. Fact was, BECK and BEST had indeed come to be synonymous. And, by fully utilizing stereo recording facilities and Rod Stewart's unique vocal abilities, Beck, in *Truth*, created the nearly perfect album.

With this masterpiece and his new band, Beck stormed the States twice to the delight of thousands. Problem was, in the beginning at least, people didn't know he was coming. The two American singles had received almost no airplay, if any at all, and *Truth*, as stated earlier, was not released until two months after that Fillmore debut in June '68. It's interesting to note that that first Fillmore concert was initially advertised as a Jeff Beck concert. But the new band from England must not have sold too well at the box office, because the Grateful Dead were added later to top the bill. However, it was no wonder that this band "tossed the Grateful Dead for a solid eight count," as Lenny Kaye once wrote. They had absolutely everything going for them.

Forgetting the guitar and vocals (if one could), this band even looked perfect. At this point it should be stated that we would both trade all the glitter, eye make-up, and hair dye in the world for a Rory Gallagher guitar solo. But crushed velvet pants, silk shirts and satin vests with fringes, especially coming a mere six months after "the year of the hippie," are a whole 'nother story. Beck had (has) class! He was what all the males in the audience wanted to be, and what all the females wanted. Considering the latter half of that statement, it's puzzling to note that the "Jeff Beck audience," which would later gain infamy for booing everyone but Beck off any given stage, was always 99 per cent male.

DURING BECK'S second tour, which began in October 1968, Nicky Hopkins, tired of being a session man, officially joined the band. Nicky, as everyone knows, had previously (and since) done session work for EVERYBODY. But the first band he was ever officially in was the Jeff Beck Group. Obviously, Nicky Hopkins knew where to find as talented a guitarist as he was a pianist. For once, things ran smoothly. But, immediately before a third tour was to begin in February 1969, Beck's temperament unfortunately got the better of him, and Wood and Waller, one of the finest rhythm sections of all time, were fired. Drummer Tony Newman (now a Bowie Diamond Dog) and bassist Doug Blake were hired. Blake, however, can claim only one date, a concert in Virginia, as a member of the Jeff Beck Group. Jeff just wasn't satisfied with Doug, and Wood was rehired and flown over to join the band. Cutting the tour short, it was this band that went back to Britain to hurriedly record and release a new album. It was felt that the group had been touring for too long on the strength of *Truth*.

The results of these sessions was *Beck-Ola* (Epic BN 26478), released in spring '69, and generally considered a disappointment because it wasn't nearly up to par with *Truth* and contained too much filler material: "a waste of time," as Beck himself described the album. While true that the only obvious purpose of most of "Rice Pudding" and all of Hopkins' "Girl From Mill Valley" was to help make the album the minimum required length, it cannot be said that *Beck-Ola* is without redeeming musical value.

Jeff once again executes some beautiful guitarwork here, draping it on a powerful repeating framework in "Plynth," churning and hammering out incredible sounds in "Jailhouse Rock" and gracefully spitting out neat little licks between Stewart's vocal lines in "Spanish Boots." Rod, by the way, again laid claim to the title of "World's Greatest Vocalist" with this recording (although he seems less emotionally charged than on *Truth*), and anyone who says that he sounds like Joe Cocker, well.... Anyway, to get back to the point, the last 30 seconds of "All Shook Up" alone are worth the price of the album.

With the release of *Beck-Ola*, another tour of the States was planned for July and August of 1969. Venues included the Fillmore East, Central Park, the *Newport Jazz Festival* and, of course, *Woodstock*. Beck once again made a public display of his moodiness when, at the end of one of the Fillmore concerts, the audience called for an encore (naturally). Returning to the stage, Jeff grabbed a mike and asked if the audience wanted to hear more. The response was overwhelming. "Well, then, come up to Newport," he said, and walked off and out. So, some of us went to Newport and witnessed a tantrum thrown by Jeff because of a blown amplifier, which included our boy throwing his guitar to the floor.

The band never made it to *Woodstock*, and it was soon announced that they had split up. The nasty stories are still flying on this one, as regards no one being paid for his work, etc. The press had Beck and Stewart at each other's throats. But, still, Stewart was scheduled to be in Beck's next proposed band.

IN SEPTEMBER, rumors circulated stating that Beck was planning a new band which would include himself, Stewart, and the two former Vanilla Fudgies, bassist Tim Bogert and drummer Carmine Appice. There had been a longstanding mutual admiration society on the part of Jeff and Tim/Carmine, quite understandable on the part of T and C. The story has it that Jeff was sitting around one day listening to some old albums with some old friends. One of the albums was Vanilla Fudge's *Near the Beginning*, and one of the friends was John Bonham. Supposedly, then and there, Jeff decided that Bogert and Appice were the rhythm section for him.

Vanilla Fudge was slowly melting, so when later doing a Canadian tour with Led Zeppelin and being told by Bonham of Jeff's feelings about them, B and A rushed to the nearest phone booth. It was decided that everyone's respective managers would get together as soon as possible to see what could be done about contracts and other assorted problems. Stewart was slated to be the new band's singer, of course, and Tim and Carmine had even thought up a name: Cactus.

Ron Wood, meanwhile, had lined up a job playing guitar with the three Small Faces left after Steve Marriott's departure from that group. By the end of October 1969, Stewart had become restless and also joined the Faces, taking with him a part of the public's attraction to the Beck group. Not waiting around for Jeff was a lucky move for Rod, because in November, one day before the scheduled meeting of the managers, Beck — who has always had a penchant for American hot rods — was involved in a crash in Maidstone, Kent, England, which left him with a fractured skull and removed him from the public eye for almost two years.

Following the accident, absolutely nothing was heard of Beck until July of 1970. Meantime, the Fudgies found substitute Cacti, and Rod Stewart found fame and fortune. But, by summer of 1970,

Jeff had picked up a drummer named Cozy Powell, who bears a striking resemblance to Jeff, and had also, it seems, been auditioning bass players in London — nearly one hundred bass players, in fact, according to Jeff. But none possessed quite the necessary qualifications. So, Jeff, along with Powell and Mickie Most, flew to Detroit to do some recording with Motown session musicians and, if possible, steal away a "funky" bass man.

Although some recording was done in Detroit, including versions of the Four Tops' "Reach Out" and the Temptations' "Losing You" (the latter of which was soon recorded by Rod Stewart backed by the Faces and included on one of his solo albums), it is highly doubtful that we'll ever hear any of that Jeff material. Beck supposedly didn't like any of the final results, but legend has it that the studio men didn't appreciate Jeff's Superstar attitude and walked out — a case where Limey Flash and Motor City Funk simply weren't compatible.

So, Jeff went back to England and back into hiding until the following May, when he was found rehearsing a new band. Besides Jeff and Powell, this group consisted of Max Middleton on piano, Clive Chaman on bass and Alex Ligertwood (now with Brian Auger) on vocals. In August, Ligertwood was replaced by Bob Tench, formerly of Gass, and the band began to record.

The results — Jeff's comeback, an event which had fans everywhere trembling with anticipation, and *Rough and Ready* (Epic KE 30973), the first new Beck album in over two years. General opinion on *Rough and Ready* seems to vary a great deal (it's supposedly selling up a storm in Germany at this very moment), but we feel it's easy to see why the disc disillusioned so many of Jeff's longtime followers. For one, its title, tailored for the old Beck image, and its contents have nearly nothing in common. In writing all of the songs, with the exception of "Jody," which he co-wrote, Beck shows where his musical weaknesses lie. No individual song stands out, and within a few listenings, all seem to fall into a nothingness blend from which it's easy to be distracted. The album has a certain jazz feel to it, which was almost totally alien to and unexpected by Beck fans and can be attributed to the precise drumming of

Cozy Powell, as well as to the jazz-oriented piano of Max Middleton. Occasionally, in moments of "Situation," *the* cut from the album, and "Train Train," glimpses of Beck's former glory can be caught. But these aren't enough. Jeff seems to be holding a lot back here, and while he may at times smolder, he fails to ignite.

Apparently, Jeff was aware of *Rough and Ready*'s shortcomings, because the next album, simply entitled *Jeff Beck Group* (Epic KE 31331) was an obvious step in the right direction — not far, mind you, but well-aimed, nonetheless. Still searching for that elusive "soulful" quality he so desired, Beck recorded the album in Memphis, complete with a black female back-up chorus and production credit to Steve Cropper of Booker T and the MGs fame. Variety is given to the album through five songs written or co-written by Jeff and four non-originals.

Among the latter is an interesting version of Dylan's "Tonight I'll Be Staying Here With You," for which Bob Tench attempts an impression of Rod Stewart. Beck shows that he's still capable of making his old "rude sounds" with "Ice Cream Cakes," but the album's real stand-out is Jeff's rendition of Don Nix's "Going Down," where, after a few introductory bars of piano from Max Middleton, Beck rips into a solid six minutes of his old well-known and loved tricks. Unfortunately, the album is weighed down by several throwaway cuts such as "Sugar Cane," where Beck mainly stays in the background fiddling with his wah-wah, and an uninspired cover of Stevie Wonder's "Got to Have a Song."

A U.S. tour followed the release of *Jeff Beck Group* in May of 1972; by the time the band returned to England, it seemed to be a rather secure, if not exciting, unit. In August, however, Beck suddenly fired Powell, Tench and Chaman. As Jeff stated later that year, "I just felt we'd reached as high as we were ever going to go. Somehow, the energy wasn't there. People said Max couldn't play and Bob couldn't sing, but that's so much bullshit. It wasn't that at all, the trouble was Bob isn't a hard rock singer; he's got a great, but very soulful voice. And Max, as everyone knows, is more jazz influenced, so there were too many different elements pulling against each other. Unfortunately, it took us a long time to see we weren't compatible." This, of course, is contradictory (so what else is new — this is a Jeff Beck article, isn't it?) to the facts that Beck *wanted* a "soulful" singer and that Max was not fired, but announced as a member of Jeff's new band, which was to include vocalist Kim Milford, a former *Jesus Christ Superstar* star, and finally, after at least four years of wishing it were so, Tim Bogert and Carmine Appice.

Jeff's decision-making pattern as regards musical styles and their subsequent performers in his various bands was summed up by Cozy Powell in a recent interview: "That's Jeff. A real Jekyll and Hyde. He never knows what he wants to do from one day to the next." But as Jeff once stated, "I can split from 20,000 groups if I want to. If a person is not happy with a job he leaves."

Anyway, a whirlwind tour of the States was immediately begun by this band. Among the dates scheduled was an early August night in the Bronx, now commonly referred to as "the Gaelic Park Disaster." Jeff, on this occasion, arrived nearly two hours late and went on to play a half-hearted half-hour set. (It must be said, however, in all fairness to the prime bad boy of Britain, that Beck was forced to cut the show short due to a park curfew.) Thrown bottles and a near-riot were the reaction that Wednesday night, and reports from L.A. didn't have the fourth coming of Beck doing much better there, either. Shortly after this, Middleton and Milford was discharged, the latter for allegedly hogging the stage and trying to steal the spotlight from Mr. B. And that left Beck, Bogert and Appice.

What can you say? It was the American dream come true for these two guys from the Island or Jersey or wherever. To be in a band with Jeff Beck! And as for that touch of class that was always Beck's trademark (getting back to fashion for a bit — forget the velvet pants and silk shirts by this time, no one can even look like Jeff in dungarees), the other B and A didn't move upward by association. Instead, they just brought Jeff down. The two kids make good and the main man is destroyed. Jeff Beck symbolized all that was flash, all that was London, all that was cool ... all right, an egomaniac, but if anyone ever deserved to be one, it's Jeff Beck. In reference to the Yardbirds, Jeff recently said, "...the way I played was different from anybody else then, and now everybody seems to play that way." Quite the understatement! It's heartbreaking: Jeff accompanied by a bassist who introduces a song with the dedication: "Dis one's for Brooklyn."

Beck, Bogert & Appice (Epic KE 32140) was released in March 1973, and is an album whose entire merit, what little there is to be found, is obscured by the absolutely awful vocals [*uncredited, by all three*] that dominate the disc. "Superstition" is far inferior to Stevie Wonder's original, on which Jeff played guitar, by the way. The vocals are so horrible here that Beck's guitar cannot compensate for them. "Livin' Alone" and "Why Should I Care" both show Jeff in fine shape, though, once again, the vocals kill both songs. "Black Cat Moan" features a Jeff vocal, which is valuable for its rarity, though certainly nothing else, which leaves "Lady," a well-structured composition, as the album's highlight.

We originally had suggestions for additions/ improvements to BBA as it stands now. Rather than murder the latter B and A, we felt that they should be relegated to their rightful places as Beck back-up men. That's to say, un-power the trio. Then let Beck get a good singer, someone he'd have to live up to, perhaps out of fear, guitar-wise. We first thought of Paul Rodgers, but he, unfortunately for our plans for Jeff, has fallen in with Bad Company (and there's the group we're counting on to cut through the glitter, like the Jeff Beck Group '68 made it through Flower Power!). Or, if Beck, as of this writing (like Cozy says, "from day to day") is still searching for the "soulful" sound he wanted a while back, some Black Philadelphia singer along the lines of Harold Melvin, for instance, could fill the bill. In the latter case, all the physical attention would be focused on Jeff, even more so than if he had someone like Rodgers who looked like Beck's "rough and ready" image. And, of course, instead of adding the fourth name to Beck, Bogert and Appice, the band would be a Jeff Beck Group once more, which is how this whole problem came to be.

Music fans can debate forever as to who was the innovator in guitar feedback, fuzz tone, wah-wah and flash in general. Okay. But there's no denying that Jeff invented the rock ego and developed it to such a degree that it was necessary to his art. When bands were falling apart because the lead singer decided he was holier than them — Eric Burdon and the Animals, for example — Jeff Beck was, and sometimes in *name* only (it *was* the Jeff Beck Group) hiding Rod Stewart, Nicky Hopkins and the like in the background. When egomania caught on, and now everyone is someone, Jeff went the opposite route. Instead of denying himself, though, he decided to give equal billing to two musical fools no less. You know who they are from the start, so there's no possibility of their stepping up from behind and stealing the spotlight from Jeffrey (as if they could), so there's no cause for Jeff to fight back. Why kill himself? Instead, he plays some ho-hum guitar, people go berserk 'cause Beck's a legend and the endeavor comes to naught. Beck, Bogert and Appice — now that's a laugh. What BBA amounts to is a psychological dilemma musically. Since teaming up with his "dream" band, Jeff has been on vacation.

And now rumor has it that Jeff is going into retirement. BBA has split up. *Melody Maker* has said it. Cozy Powell mentioned it in a *Sounds* interview. Reliable sources in Washington, D.C. report it. Tim Bogert, who has taken to hanging around outside New York concerts, won't talk to anybody. And, realistically, there's been no recorded effort released by the trio in 15 months.

So where to now, Jeff Beck? In 1965, Yardbirds rhythm guitarist Chris Dreja noted of Jeff, "He is 1975." Jeff's got six months on the backwards road to former glory. Whereas we'd anxiously await whatever combo Jeff has brewing up his guitar-playing sleeve, how many other people will be how loyal and for how long? As for retirement, the potential loss is frightening. We're honestly scared.

"If Jeff doesn't come back to us," we recently vowed, "we'll just go to him!" See ya in England, Jeff, and hope you remember the guitar break to "Blues De Luxe." ∎

BEST CONCEPT ALBUM

TP 61, MAY 1981

Although the conceptual rock album — in which the various tracks are more than an unrelated grab bag — first bloomed in the psychedelic '60s, it has proven a hardier breed than most whims of style. Curiously, *Sgt. Pepper*, which made the form prestigious overnight, has incurred a definite backlash. One respondent asked that if the Beatles album won, "I hope you will explain exactly what the concept is."

If nothing else, this survey established that there are more rock concept albums than anyone probably wants to hear. Most are united by a common song topic, but a few vary the formula. The Buzzcocks' *Singles Going Steady* is a structurally conceptual LP; M. Puyman mentioned the Residents' *Nibbles*, "which, by following a concept of being a non-concept album became a concept album." And Jim Nesbit wondered if *Sid* [Vicious] *Sings* isn't a concept album.

- *Quadrophenia*, the Who
- *The Lamb Lies Down on Broadway*, Genesis
- *Arthur*, Kinks
- *The Book of Invasions*, Horslips
- *The Dark Side of the Moon*, Pink Floyd
- *Tommy*, the Who
- *The Wall*, Pink Floyd
- *The Rise and Fall of Ziggy Stardust and the Spiders from Mars*, David Bowie
- *Berlin*, Lou Reed
- *Lola Versus the Powerman and the Moneygoround*, Kinks
- *Sgt. Pepper's Lonely Hearts Club Band*, Beatles
- *666*, Aphrodite's Child

As amazing as this piece was and is, the uncertain logistics threatening an implacable printing deadline made this an absolute nail-biter for those of us waiting anxiously in the New York office for the planned cover story to be completed and delivered from California. In the days before technology sped up a lot of the process of publishing, everything about this had to be done the old-fashioned way. Regardless, it was absolutely worth the agita to have this enormous feather in the magazine's cap. At the same time, it established Dave's reputation as a first-rate interviewer, a talent he has continued to apply professionally ever since.

JIMMY PAGE:
THE INTERVIEW

TP 21–23,
SEPTEMBER–NOVEMBER 1977

By Dave Schulps

What now seems like ages ago, when we first decided to gamble on a long shot and try to get a super in-depth interview with Jimmy Page, we were a bit skeptical about the whole thing. First off, we hadn't seen an interview with Page of the type we wanted to do (that is, a thorough run down of his entire career) since he spoke to the English fanzine *ZigZag* four years ago. Obviously, he must not be too interested in talking about his past, we figured, or someone else would have done a similar piece since then.

Next, we wondered whether he'd want to take the time to talk to a magazine whose circulation was not exactly in the league with, say, *People*, or even *Rolling Stone*.

Both of those fears were allayed by Janine Safer of Swan Song's New York office, who told us that not only would Jimmy grant us an interview but was even anxious to do the kind of interview we required.

Just prior to the appointed time on [a] Sunday afternoon, we received an ominous phone call from Swan Song saying that Jimmy was still sleeping and would we do it later that evening? Later that evening, another call: "Still sleeping, how about Tuesday afternoon?" OK, but we were beginning to get skeptical once again.

Sure enough, though, we arrived at the Plaza Hotel at the prescribed time on Tuesday and were taken up to a room on the same floor as Page's suite, where we were asked to wait while Jimmy readied himself to see us. To everybody's chagrin, however, repeated knocks on Page's door brought no answer. You guessed it; "still sleeping."

With Led Zeppelin set to leave for Los Angeles directly following that evening's Madison Square Garden show, hopes for our prized Page interview slowly began to fade. Oh well, it was too good to be true anyway, guess we'll just stick Donna Summer on the cover and forget the whole thing.

"Not so fast," said Janine. "Jimmy still wants to do the interview. One of you will just have to come out to Los Angeles with us and we'll do it there tomorrow. You can fly back in the evening."

Five hours later, I was sitting in Led Zeppelin's private Starship with Lisa Robinson on one side of me and Robert Plant on the other. "What the hell am I doing here?" I wondered. But, as they say, never look a gift horse in the mouth.

I didn't get to meet Page on the plane, though he was twice ushered by where I was sitting: once on his way into the plane, once on the way out. I was struck by how extremely frail he appeared, escorted by a bodyguard, who seemed almost to be propping him up.

Safely landed, we checked into the Beverly Hilton, where I was deposited in a poolside room of my own. I would be informed when Page was ready to see me. Until then, well, enjoy. I began to sense that I would probably not be on that night's flight back to New York.

The next day, I was told that Page would indeed see me that evening. When the time came, I made my way upstairs to Janine's room, tape recorder in hand, to wait for confirmation (shades of the Plaza!). This time, however, Jimmy was awake and ready to talk.

After a brief introduction he offered up a Heineken and asked if, since the interview was to be quite lengthy, I would mind doing it in two or three installments. Since I had nothing important to do back home until next week, I indicated I'd be quite happy to stay as long as necessary to get the whole story (goodness knows, I hadn't had a suntan in years).

We then proceeded with the first interview, covering Page's activities up through the time he joined the Yardbirds in late summer of 1966.

Remarkably thin and pale, his sideburns showing a slight touch of grey and his skin exhibiting a wraith-like pallor, I found it hard to believe this was the same person I had seen bouncing around the stage at Madison Square Garden earlier that week.

Speaking slowly and softly in a sort of half-mumble half-whisper which matched his frail physical appearance, Page showed an excellent memory for detail, considering the time that had elapsed since the period we discussed.

After about an hour of strolling down memory lane, we called it quits when Page, who seemed tired by this time, was visited by Michaels Des Barres and Monarch of Swan Song's Detective.

The next night we reconvened the discussion, Page going into great detail on the entire story of the Yardbirds and the formation of Led Zeppelin. Unfortunately, before we started talking Jimmy had asked me to shut off my microphone for a second, and when we resumed, I had started the tape recorder without turning the mike back on. This was discovered after forty-five minutes of great chat, and while I was about to have an ulcer right then and there, Jimmy just said, "Don't worry about it. Remember the questions and we'll go over it again next time."

Which we did, nearly word for word. Yer all right by me, Pagey.

Interview number-three took place the final night of my stay, Sunday, and was preceded by the fear that Page would again turn comatose and I would leave L.A. with a mere hour of tape (and a tan). "Don't worry," said Janine, and she was right.

Zep had just played a gig in San Diego that evening and Page entered bouncier and more awake than at either of the other two sessions. By the time we actually started talking it was probably around one o'clock Monday morning. The interview covered the remainder of Zeppelin's career (a sizable load, I might add) and the aforementioned Yardbirds-era rehash. It ran approximately three hours.

During the course of the interview, Page made reference to his original demos and "instrumental versions" of certain Zep songs. At one point he went and pulled out a box of cassettes which he revealed as those tapes. After the interview ended Page began illustrating certain points by playing for me a bunch of these tapes, including his original demo of "Kashmir," featuring just himself and Bonzo, a few rough but interesting instrumental workouts and a song featuring Page on guitar, Keith Richards on rhythm and vocal, Ronnie Wood on bass and Charlie Watts (I think) on drums, recorded at Wood's home.

After listening to all that, Page, still wide awake and peppier than I'd seen him the entire time, put on his favorite current record, [*Damned Damned Damned*], and danced around for a few moments while Vanian, Sensible, Rat and Brian blasted "New Rose" through the speakers.

Then Jimmy slapped on a rehearsal tape of Metropolis, the band made up of all the ex-Pretty Things sans Phil May, which we both felt sounded impressive. After a few minutes, I happened to look over my shoulder and realized that it was now getting light outside. I also realized I was quite tired and was scheduled to catch a noon flight back to New York, so in the interest of not arriving home a total wreck I left the still wide-awake Jimmy Page, crawled back to my room and collapsed.

A week after the originally scheduled interview was supposed to have taken place, it was finished.

It was well worth the wait. (DS)

PART ONE: SESSIONS

What were your ambitions as a young guitarist? You kept out of the limelight for quite a while, not playing with any groups except Neil Christian until you joined the Yardbirds.

Very early, once I started getting a few chords and licks together, I did start searching feverishly for other musicians to play with, but I couldn't find any. It wasn't as though there was an abundance. I used to play in many groups ... anyone who could get a gig together, really.

This is before you joined Neil Christian?

Just before Neil Christian. It was Neil Christian who saw me playing in a local hall and suggested that I play in his band. It was a big thing because they worked in London, whereas I was from the suburbs. So, there I was, the 15-year-old guitarist marching into London with his guitar case. I played with him for a couple of years.

Did he have a big local reputation at the time?

In an underground sort of way. We used to do Chuck Berry and Bo Diddley numbers — bluesy things — before the blues really broke. In fact, half the reason I stopped playing with Neil Christian was because I used to get very ill on the road —

glandular fever — from living in the back of a van. We were doing lots of traveling; the sort of thing I'm used to doing now. I was very undernourished then. It wasn't working right, either; people weren't appreciative of what we were doing. At that time, they wanted to hear Top 20 numbers. I guess you could put it pretty much akin to the pre-Beatles period in America, except that this was a couple of years before that. I was at art college for 18 months after I left Neil Christian, which was still before the Stones formed, so that dates it back a way. The numbers we were doing were really out of character for the audiences that were coming to hear us play, but there was always five- or ten-percent, mostly guys, who used to get off on what we were doing because they were into those things themselves — guitarists, record collectors. You'll find that nearly all the guitarists that came out of the '60s were record collectors and/ or had friends that were collectors of either rock or blues. I used to collect rock and my friend collected blues.

Did you swap?

He wouldn't have any white records in his collection. He was a purist. I remember going up to a blues festival in the back of a van the first time a big blues package tour came to England. That was the first time I met Jagger and Richard ... pre-Stones.

Were you into the blues as much as the Stones or was it more rock and roll for you?

I was an all-'rounder, thank God.

Do you think that's helped your career?

Immensely. I think if I was just labeled a blues guitarist, I'd have never been able to lose the tag. When all the guitarists started to come through in America — like Clapton, Beck and meself — Eric, being the blues guitarist, had the label. People just wanted to hear him play blues. I saw the guitar as a multi-faceted instrument, and this has stayed with me throughout. When you listen to the various classical guitarists like Segovia and Julian Bream — brilliant classical players — and Manitas de Plata doing flamenco, it's two totally different approaches to acoustic. Then there's Django Reinhardt, and that's another approach entirely.

Are you influenced by stringed instruments other than guitar?

Yeah...in a folk music context.

Things you've picked up from traveling?

Yeah.

Has it helped you expand your playing?

In those early days, I was very interested in Indian music, as were a lot of other people, too. Most of the "textbook" of what I was forced to learn was while I was doing sessions, though. At that point you never knew what you were going to be doing when you got to the session. In America, you were a specialist. For example, you would never think of Steve Cropper to do a jazz session or film session or TV jingles, but in Britain you had to do everything. I had to do a hell of a lot of work in a short time. I still don't really read music, to be honest with you. I read it like a six-year-old reads a book, which was adequate for sessions, and I can write it down, which is important.

What was your first guitar?

It was called a Grazioso; it was a Fender copy. Then I got a Fender, an orange Gretsch — Chet Atkins hollow body — and a Gibson stereo which I chucked after two days for a Les Paul Custom which I stuck with until I had it stolen ... or lost by [the airline] TWA.

What got you into guitar playing? Was it just hearing it on record?

Exactly. I've read about many records which are supposed to have turned me on to want to play, but it was "Baby, Let's Play House" by Presley. You've got to understand that, in those days, "rock and roll" was a dirty word. It wasn't even being played by the media. Maybe you'd hear one record a day during the period of Elvis, Little Richard and Jerry Lee Lewis. That's why you were forced to be a record collector if you wanted to be part of it. I heard that record and I wanted to be part of it; I knew something was going on. I heard the acoustic guitar, slap bass and electric guitar — three instruments and a voice — and they generated so much energy I had to be part of it. That's when I started.

Mind you, it took a long time before I got anywhere — I mean any sort of dexterity. I used to lis-ten to Ricky Nelson records and pinch the James Burton licks, learn them note for note perfect. I only did that for a while, though. I guess that after one writes one's first song you tend to depart from that. It's inevitable.

How old were you when you left Neil Christian and started going heavily into sessions?

I left Neil Christian when I was about 17 and went to art college. During that period, I was jamming at night in a blues club. By that time, the blues had started to happen, so I used to go out and jam with Cyril Davies's Interval Band. Then somebody asked me if I'd like to play on a record, and before I knew where I was, I was doing all these studio dates at night — still going to art college in the daytime. There was a crossroads, and you know which one I took.

Would you say your development at that time as a guitarist was your fastest ever?

During the studio period, yeah. When I left Neil Christian, I had some sort of reputation, but I just couldn't handle the road anymore.

Do you remember your first studio session?

I think it was called "Your Momma's Out of Town," by Carter-Lewis and the Southerners [1963]. Wait a minute; I'd played on one before that, "Diamonds" by Jet Harris and Tony Meehan, but that didn't mean anything to me. They were both hits and that gave me the impetus to keep on doing it. If "Your Momma's Out of Town" hadn't been a hit, though, I might have abandoned it then and there.

Were you influenced at all by the Shadows?

No, not at all. That was the kind of music they wanted to hear — I wasn't doing that. I think Hank Marvin's great and lots of guitarists were influenced by him, but I wasn't. I preferred James Burton and people like that. I think the only English guitarist at that time who was any good was Tony Sheridan, and there's only one record that would give any indication of how good he was, "I Like Love" and "Right Behind You Baby" by Vince Taylor. I like "conviction rock": something that sounds like it's got conviction behind the playing. Some of the Shadows things sounded like they were eating fish and chips while they were playing.

How long did you play with Cyril Davies?

That's an interesting story. He had the Interval band, and he asked me, as I was leaving Neil Christian, to join him. I rehearsed with them — Cyril, Nicky Hopkins — and I said, "I just can't join, I've been too weakened. I've got to build up some strength — have a musical retirement." He didn't seem to understand, but I knew if I joined him I'd be right back into where I was: out of the frying pan and into the fire.

In retrospect, do you think you made the right move by doing sessions?

I think so. It kept me off the road until such time as it became stagnant and it was time for a change. I was doing pretty well with Neil Christian, as far as money went, and to come out of that and go to art college on a $10 a week grant would seem like insanity to a lot of people, but I'd do it anytime if it were necessary — make a drastic change if it had to be.

What did you study in art college?

Fine art. Painting.

Did they discourage rock and roll there?

No, no, no. In the art colleges, they were always a couple of steps ahead of what was generally going on. The scenes that would be about to break about a year later would be happening in the art colleges, and there'd be interest in it. That's how I first heard about Bert Jansch.

Were you very influenced by him?

God, yeah. I thought he was the innovator of the time. He tied up the acoustic guitar in the same way that Hendrix did the electric. His first two LPs that came out in England had some instrumental work that was totally unbelievable. I watched him play once at a folk club and it was like seeing a classical guitarist playing. All the inversions he was playing were unrecognizable. I don't know whether this is true, but I'd heard it on good authority that he'd contracted arthritis, which is a total tragedy. His playing was amazing, but he doesn't play so much anymore. There are a couple of his early LPs still available here on Vanguard — *Lucky Thirteen* and *Jack Orion*.

Were there any other influential English acoustic guitarists?

Davy Graham was good. He used to go to Morocco and live there and play with the Arabs.

There's a guy over here, Solomon [Feldthouse], who used to be with Kaleidoscope, who played flamenco guitar and bouzouki at renaissance fairs.

When did you first travel?

During art school vacations I used to travel across the continent. Then, when I was in the Yardbirds, I remember we were playing Australia and it was time to come back; all the others wanted to come back through San Francisco, but I wanted to return through the East — India. Nobody else wanted to go. I arrived at three in the morning in Bombay with just my bag, on my own.

This period we've been talking about I was practicing a hell of a lot —all the time. Anytime I could get on the guitar. I can't put it down to hours, but I was practicing consistently until I started working sessions regularly.

I'D BE INTERESTED IN your reminiscences of some of the groups you did or were supposed to have done sessions with. If you wouldn't mind commenting, I'll just run down a few of them.

Go ahead.

You worked with Them...

A most embarrassing session. Before we even start, I should say that I was mainly called in to sessions as insurance. It was usually myself and a drummer, though they never mention the drummer these days, just me.

Who was the drummer?

Bobbie Graham. On the Them session, it was very embarrassing, because you noticed that as each number passed, another member of the band would be substituted for by a session musician. It was really horrifying. Talk about daggers! God, it was awful. There'd be times you'd be sitting there — you didn't want to be there, only you'd been booked — and wishing that you weren't there.

That seems to have happened to you often, from what I've heard.

What, the daggers? That only happened twice that I can remember. The Them sessions were the classics. "Here Comes the Night," "Baby, Please Don't Go," all that stuff. The group went in thinking they were going to record and, all of a sudden, they find these other people playing on their records. Okay, trouble with the guitarist ... fair enough ...

but with Them, the organist was replaced, then the bass player's position was in jeopardy. It's a miracle they didn't replace Van Morrison!

But they were still getting the royalties for playing on the records?

Yeah, I'm sure they did. I just got the session fee.

How did you feel about that?

I didn't care. I used to enjoy it, that was the absurd thing. I enjoyed playing. I didn't even think about royalties.

I heard Shel Talmy used to keep you around Who sessions and Kinks sessions, just in case you were needed, without really planning to use you in advance.

Well, I was on "Can't Explain," and on the B-side ["Bald Headed Woman"] you can hear some fuzzy guitar coming through, which is me.

And you played rhythm on "Can't Explain"?

Yeah, pretty much. Little bits here and there.

You co-wrote "Revenge" with Ray Davies.

No.

Well, you were credited with writing "Revenge" with Ray Davies.

Was I? That's good [laughs]. There is some justice in this world after all. Ray Davies said things like, "He wasn't anywhere near our sessions, he played tambourine." I never played tambourine on the damned records; I played guitar. But I didn't play on "You Really Got Me" and [people believing I did is] what pisses him off, so he uses that as his main contention.

But you've said many times you didn't play on "You Really Got Me."

I didn't. I played on the subsequent records.

Why, after Dave had created an amazing sound like on "You Really Got Me," did they need to call you in to play guitar?

On the album it's more apparent. There are a few little bits and pieces that come in where I'm just there. That's where I was at.

But you played on subsequent singles like "All Day and All of the Night"?

Right. There's more than that, though. I don't know their discography, but there were bits of feedback on "I Need You" that I can remember.

Was Dave playing on these?

Dave was playing as well, but Ray wasn't playing. Don't forget, they had a session pianist and a session drummer. If you really want to be silly about it, you should do an article about their session drummer rather than their session guitarist, because they carried on with a session drummer far longer than they did with a session guitarist.

But Mick [Avory]'s a great drummer.

[nods in agreement] But the whole point is that they were the ones who started getting nasty about things. I wasn't a public voice.

There was one group in England who really got smashed to pieces in the press because they'd used session musicians on their records.

Love Affair?

That's right, Steve Ellis. That vibe was going around at the time. Consequently, Ray wanted to squash all rumor that there had been session musicians on the records, and so who was going to come under the hammer but me? It doesn't matter, it just shows where he was at. I always thought the Kinks were alright, anyway, as far as what they did.

Did Pete Quaife play all the bass on their records?

Yeah. I don't know why there's such a fascination with the Kinks, though. Every time I'm interviewed, people still want to know about the Kinks more than anything else. It's just weird.

I guess a lot of people love them and are still interested. What about Herman's Hermits?

I didn't play on any of their records. John Paul Jones did.

Donovan?

I didn't do "Hurdy Gurdy Man." He wanted me to, but I was in the States at the time.

Who did it, then?

Beck had a whole day, but couldn't do it, so they got a session guy in at 10 o'clock in the morning and he did it. A guy called Alan Parker.

Did you work concurrently with Big Jim Sullivan when you were doing these guitar sessions?

At one point Big Jim was the only guitarist on the whole session scene. That's the reason they really picked up on me, because they just didn't know anyone else but Jim. Obviously, there were many people about, but I was just lucky. Anyone needing a guitarist either went to Big Jim or myself.

Weren't there any others who came in a little bit after you?

Only Alan Parker, that I can remember, and I didn't really rate him very much. There's probably a lot of good ones there now. It's a boring life. You're like a machine.

But you kept at it a pretty long while...

I kept at it as long as the guitar was in vogue, but once it became something that was like a tambourine or claves and they started using strings or an orchestra instead, I decided to give it up.

They stopped putting on guitar breaks?

Exactly. It just wasn't the thing anymore.

What about Fifth Avenue's "Just Like Anyone Would Do?" [Immediate IM 002, released in 1965]

That's a Shel Talmy thing, isn't it? Wait a minute! I produced that! What am I talking about? That's got a really good sound. It's really good, actually. I wrote that. It's not good because I wrote it, but it's got a fantastic sound on it. I used a double up-pick on the acoustic guitars. It had nice Beach Boys type harmonies. The other side was "Bells of Rhymney."

Did you play guitar on it?

No, I just produced it.

Who were the band?

Just session musicians that were around. I think Jonesy was on bass.

Was that your first production?

No, but don't ask me what the other ones were. That was during the period I was producing for Immediate Records — Andrew Oldham.

How did you get involved with Oldham?

I just knew him... I love Andrew, he's one of the few producers I really respect. That's true, I really do respect him.

What about an earlier band called the Mickey Finn Group, which had you on some publicity stills around 1965? Were you actually a member? What did you do?

Harmonica. I played on a few singles and they had me take the stills with the band, though I was never actually a member.

Do you still play harmonica?

Not really. I did a lot of studio work on it at one time, though.

You've never played it with Zeppelin, have you? That's all Robert.

Yeah.

THERE WAS A PERIOD *you were working with a lot of American acts, like the Everly Brothers. Were you doing those sessions in America or England?*

There were quite a few, all done in England. I actually did two Everly Brothers sessions: one that had a Hollies involvement (*Two Yanks in England*) and another one with Tony Hatch (who'd written "Downtown" for Pet Clark) producing them. They had a three-hour session and spent two and a half hours on this damn thing of his and then they pretty much said, "Alright, that's it, let's do the B-side" and Don Everly picked up his guitar and just started roaring away with fantastic rhythm, and I thought, "Wow, this is great." It could have never come out because of the politics involved with the A-side, but I remember really playing like mad on it.

Were the Everlys an early influence on your guitar playing?

Sure. I used to listen to them, of course. Anything that had a good guitar break on it, I listened to. Lots of odd and obscure artists.

Were they both good guitarists?

No, I think Don was the real guitarist. He didn't play lead, though, he just had this special rhythm thing — "Wake Up Little Susie" and all those. I asked them who did the guitar solos on "Lucille" and "I'm Not Angry," and it was their pedal steel guitarist, Johnny Day. I thought it was a bit too good for an ordinary guitarist.

Who were some of the other American artists you worked with in England?

Brenda Lee and Jackie DeShannon.

How did you come to work with Jackie De-Shannon?

Just happened to be on a session. She was playing guitar, and she said, "I've never found a guitarist who could adapt so quickly to the sort of things I'm doing." She had these odd licks, and she said, "It's usually a big struggle to get these things across." I didn't know what she was talking about because I'd been quite used to adapting.

We wrote a few songs together, and they ended

up getting done by Marianne Faithfull, P.J. Proby and Esther Phillips or [some other Black artist] did a few. I started receiving royalty statements, which was very unusual for me at the time, seeing the names of the different people who'd covered your songs.

Did you play behind Cliff Richard at all?

I played harmonica on a Cliff Richard cut.

After the Shadows had split with him?

No, he was with them, but it was a state of flux at the time.

What about First Gear's "A Certain Girl"?

Don't remember. Sounds like a Liverpool band that came down to London to record. [*Yorkshire, actually. Shel Talmy produced the single, released in 1964.*] You've got to understand, I did hundreds and hundreds of sessions. Really, a phenomenal amount. Film things, Bacharach sessions, jazz sessions, folk sessions ... the Dubliners. Anything and everything.

Did you work in the States at all?

No, all in England.

Burt Bacharach was recording in England?

Yeah. I played on his greatest hits album [probably *Hit Maker!*, 1965]. That was reading music.

What about Dave Berry? You were credited on the album as Little Jimmy Page.

That was to distinguish me from Big Jim Sullivan. I did do the solos on those things. Did you ever hear "My Baby Left Me" by him? That was a solo a lot of the groups got into. That was before "The Crying Game."

What about "Beck's Bolero"?

[I] wrote it, played on it, produced it ... and I don't give a damn what he says. That's the truth.

What about Keith Relf's solo singles?

Didn't have anything to do with them.

There's an album [on Atlantic] *by a Scottish group called Cartoone, from 1969, that credits you as "guest artist." Who were they?*

I really don't recall. I must've played some acoustic guitar on it. During the period of *Zeppelin I*, though, I did a few guest sessions that were tie-overs from a few sessions I'd been asked to do.

Which were those?

With a Little Help From My Friends by Joe Cocker and *Love Chronicles* by Al Stewart.

What about all those Immediate blues albums you did songs for with Eric Clapton? What were those tracks?

Jeff and I went to see Eric play one night with the Bluesbreakers, and Eric came and stayed at my house that night. In the morning we got up and were messing around, just plugged straight into the tape recorder. A little while after that I came to produce John Mayall and the Bluesbreakers, and it just so happened it was for Immediate: "I'm Your Witchdoctor," "Telephone Blues," "Sitting on Top of the World" and "Double Crossing Time." I'm absolutely positive the take I did of "Double Crossing Time" came out on the LP on Decca [London in the US].

I told Immediate that I had these tapes I'd done with Eric and they said, "They belong to us" because I was contracted to them at that time. They told me they were going to put them out and I said, "Oh, no." But they said I had to give them the tapes, so I told them if they were going to put them out, I'd at least try to do something with them, because all the tapes were, actually, just one long blues jam with Eric and I repeating the same blues over and over and over. Obviously, since it was Immediate, I was able to enlist a little help from the Stones in the overdubbing. Jagger played harmonica, and Stu [Ian Stewart], who's the all-time guv'nor of blues and boogie-woogie piano, came in and did a bit. I tried to separate the overdubs as much as possible, so that they would seem at least a little different from each other.

So, all those cuts were really just one continuous jam spliced into different pieces?

Yeah. It was a 45-minute tape of the same blues ... different attempts that sounded very similar. I had to do my best to camouflage that fact if they were going to release them. I know there were royalties paid to Eric and everything, but it was a bit of a drag that those should ever have come out. I just had no power at all to stop them.

Did you do sessions on all the early Immediate singles?

Not all. They had staff producers. I was on "Out of Time," though, the hit for Chris Farlowe. My linkup with Immediate did occur during the era I was doing sessions, though.

What about your solo single, "She Just Satisfies"?

I just did it 'cause I thought it would be fun. I played all the instruments except drums, which was Bobbie Graham. The other side was the same story.

Whatever happened to Bobbie Graham?

He just freaked out one day. Took his wife, his daughter and his dog and split for Ireland. He wanted to be a producer and get out of drumming. It's a shame because he was a good drummer. Bonzo likes him. You can hear him on those early sessions, the Kinks ... he was on "You Really Got Me."

Why didn't you ever do a follow up to "She Just Satisfies"?

Because I wanted to do "Every Little Thing" with an orchestra, and they wouldn't let me do it.

So, you refused to do anything else.

No, it was just left like that, and my contract ran out before I could do anything else. Simple as that.

Was "She Just Satisfies" purposely similar to the Kinks' "Revenge"?

It was tongue-in-cheek, let's put it that way. It wasn't the same as "Revenge." By that time, Ray Davies had already been hullaballooing, so I thought "Alright, I'll have a go..."

It was more a harmonica showpiece than guitar.

Yeah, well, I was doing a lot of harmonica sessions around then.

What about Mickie Most? You worked on his single and then later he produced the Yardbirds.

"Money Honey" I did with him, but the B-side, "Sea Cruise," wasn't me, it was Don Peek, who toured England with the Everly Brothers. He was bloody good. He was the first guitarist to come to England who was doing finger tremolo, and all the musicians were totally knocked out. Eric picked up on it straight away, and others followed soon after. Eric was the first one to evolve the sound with the Gibson and Marshall amps; he should have total credit for that. I remember when we did "I'm Your Witchdoctor," he had all that sound down, and the engineer, who was cooperating up to that point — I was producing, don't forget — but was used to doing orchestras and big bands, suddenly turned off the machine and said, "This

guitarist is unrecordable!" I told him to just record it and I'd take full responsibility; the guy just couldn't believe that someone was getting that kind of sound from a guitar on purpose. Feedback, tremolo— he'd never heard anything like it.

Was Eric the first guitarist to use feedback?

No, there were a few guitarists doing it. I don't know who was the first, though, I really don't. [Pete] Townshend, of course, made it a big feature of his scene, because he didn't play single notes. Beck used it. I used it as much as I could.

Did you like Townshend's style?

Oh, yeah. Lots of attack. Really good. He had his limitations, though. He was no Beck, but he was alright.

Were you getting off much on the other English guitarists at that time?

Sure. I really was, yeah. More so, then, than I do now.

Was it mostly Clapton, Townshend and Beck?

Well, yeah. It was just like a little clan, really. Beck, meself and Clapton were sort of "arch-buddies," and Townshend was sort of on the periphery. He came from another area of London.

Where were you living in London?

We were all in commuting distance from Richmond, which is where it was all going on. Townshend came from Ealing. Albert Lee was the only other guitarist really worth noting. He was like a white elephant. He was so good ... very much in the Nashville tradition. One thing I've noticed, though, is that all the good musicians who've stuck to it from those days have come through.

PART TWO: THE YARDBIRDS

You were originally offered the job as Eric Clapton's replacement in the Yardbirds but you turned it down, suggesting Jeff Beck instead. How did that come about?

Giorgio Gomelsky approached me and said that Eric wasn't willing to expand and go along with the whole thing. I guess it was probably pretty apparent to them after they did "For Your Love." He didn't like that at all. By that time, they had already started using different instruments, like harpsichords, and he was just fed up. The rest of the band, especially Gomelsky, wanted to move further in that direction.

The very first time I was asked to join the Yardbirds, though, was not at that time, but some time before then. Gomelsky said that Eric was going to have a "holiday," and I could step in and replace him. The way he put it to me, it just seemed really distasteful, and I refused. Eric had been a friend of mine, and I couldn't possibly be party to that. Plus, Eric didn't want to leave the band at that stage.

What did you think of Eric's guitar playing?

He put some really good stuff down. The blues on *Five Live* were really super, "I Ain't Got You" is great, and there's a few gems on the LP.

Do you think, in the long run, Eric was saddled with the toughest job out of the three Yardbirds guitarists, because he had the reputation as a blues "purist" while you and Beck could play pretty much anything?

It was a self-imposed identity, really. I wouldn't say he had the toughest job, though.

But he always had to play to a public who, regardless of what he wanted to do, saw him as a blues guitarist. You and Beck never had that kind of constraint.

He was obsessed with the blues, with wanting to sound really authentic, which is what he did. His expansion came through in a different way with Cream. There you had Jack Bruce, who was willing to go even further. I don't think it was really until Derek and the Dominos that he really found himself. As far as his musical character was concerned, I think he found himself then. The public, though, really enjoyed him most in the early Cream days, post-John Mayall, when he was really blasting out.

As far as your own expansion goes, you mentioned Jack Bruce, who had been greatly influenced by the English jazz scene; yet in your own playing I've never really detected a strong jazz influence, if any at all, though you pride yourself on being eclectic. Is there a particular reason you've steered clear of jazz?

In the formative years when, say, Johnny McLaughlin, far and away the best jazz guitarist in England at the time, had to work in a guitar shop because he couldn't get enough money out of it to be self-sufficient playing jazz there was a terrible snobbishness. Not from him, but from the jazz guitarist clique. They couldn't accept the fact of bending strings; they were totally into technique — no rude notes. Later, when Miles Davis started playing with a rock rhythm section, it suddenly became acceptable to use rock devices. They finally started bending notes then, and most of their intonation went down the chute. It was really curious that a lot of these chaps could play these chordal Johnny Smith-type things, but when they started bending strings their intonation got totally lost. A lot of them got it together, of course, but I personally wouldn't follow that type of music after knowing what their attitude was toward string bending and then hearing them sound like a bunch of cats wailing. I dabbled in the Johnny Smith stuff, but I was a rock and roller and string bender, so I wasn't about to put heavy gauge strings on and start playing what is basically just scales.

What about the kind of fusion music Beck has ended up doing?

It seems to be the most comfortable thing for Jeff. He certainly wasn't comfortable with BBA [Beck, Bogert & Appice], and he wasn't even comfortable with the Jeff Beck Group after Stewart. Having worked with him, even in the days of "Bolero," and knowing what kind of melodic sense he has, it makes a lot of sense for him to have lots of chords working underneath him and that kind of rhythm section. It's obviously much more fulfilling for him, personally. *Blow by Blow* was a fabulous LP, a pleasure. With any of the bands from the five albums before, he had a sort of inconsistency where you'd have a flow of pure genius one night, but if you hadn't known any of his previous phases, you'd wonder where it was all coming from. Another night you'd go along, and he'd just be standing there looking really disinterested. *Blow by Blow* seemed to capture all the hidden aspects you'd catch if you were following a tour. Beck's always been a really great player, and I was really pleased to hear *Blow by Blow* after all the transitions he'd gone through.

When Beck joined the Yardbirds he was supposedly asked to play in Clapton's style, at least in the beginning.

A lot of the things the Yardbirds were doing

with Eric other people were doing at the same time, so it wasn't really hard for Beck to fit in. When you say "playing in his style," there were obviously certain passages and riffs that had to be precise. It was only a matter of time until the next recording, at which time Beck could assert his own identity.

You mentioned you were good friends with Beck before the Yardbirds. How did your friendship come about? Did you see the Yardbirds often when Beck was with them?

When I was doing studio work, I used to go see them often, whenever I wasn't working. I met Beck through a friend of mine who told me he knew this guitarist I had to meet who'd made his own guitar. Beck showed up with his homemade guitar one day and he was really quite good. He started playing this James Burton and Scotty Moore stuff; I joined in, and we really hit it off well. We didn't become good friends until later on, when we played in different groups together at separate times. I think it happened twice. This was before Jeff was with the Tridents. I can't remember the names of the bands, there were a couple of them. One was a guy called Brian Gibb, I think, that was his real name, but he performed under the name of Johnny Howard. This was around the time I first started doing sessions and Johnny Howard asked me to come in and do a solo on "One of a Kind," a Tommy Sands song, and it turned out that Jeff was the guitarist in his band. We had a laugh about that.

We used to hang out a hell of a lot when he was in the Yardbirds and I was doing studio work. We both got very turned on to Rodrigo's Guitar Concerto by Segovia and all these sorts of things. He had the same sort of taste in music as I did. That's why you'll find on the early LPs we both did a song like "You Shook Me." It was the type of thing we'd both played in bands. Someone told me he'd already recorded it after we'd already put it down on the first Zeppelin album. I thought, "Oh dear, it's going to be identical," but it was nothing like it, fortunately.

Didn't he record his version long before yours?

Yes, I just had no idea that he'd done it. It was on *Truth*, but I first heard it when I was in Miami

after we'd recorded our version.

It's an interesting point of comparison.

It's a classic example of coming from the same area musically, of having similar taste. It really pissed me off when people compared our first album to *Jeff Beck Group* and said it was very close conceptually. It was nonsense. Utter nonsense! The only similarity was that we'd both come out of the Yardbirds, and we both had acquired certain riffs individually from the Yardbirds.

Why didn't you join the Yardbirds the second time Gomelsky asked, after Eric decided he wanted to quit the band?

I still wasn't certain about my health and whether I wanted to go out on the road. Besides which I was making good money playing sessions and still enjoying them at that time.

Under what circumstances did you finally join the Yardbirds when [bassist] Paul Samwell-Smith quite in late summer 1966?

It was at a gig at the Marquee Club which I'd gone along to. They were playing in front of all these penguin-suited undergraduates, and I think Samwell-Smith, whose family was a bit well-to-do, was embarrassed by the band's behavior. Apparently, Keith Relf had gotten really drunk and he was falling into the drum kit, making farting noises into the mike — being generally anarchistic, very much like Johnny Rotten tries to be now. I thought he'd done really well, actually, and the band had played really well that night. He just added all this extra feeling to it. When he came offstage, though, Paul Samwell-Smith said, "I'm leaving the band." Things used to be so final back then. There was no rethinking on decisions like that. Then he said to [rhythm guitarist] Chris Dreja, "If I were you, I'd leave, too." Which he didn't. They were sort of stuck.

Jeff had brought me to the gig in his car and on the way back I told him I'd sit in for a few months until they got things sorted out. Beck had often said to me, "It would be really great if you could join the band," but I just didn't think it was a possibility in any way. In addition, since I'd turned the offer down a couple of times already, I didn't know how the rest of them would feel about me joining. It was decided that we'd definitely have a go at it; I'd take on the bass though I'd never played it before, but only until Dreja could learn it — he'd never played it before either. We figured it would be easier for me to pick it up quickly, then switch over to a dual guitar thing when Chris had time to become familiar enough with the bass.

What was your first American tour (a Dick Clark "Caravan of Stars" production) with the Yardbirds like?

Painful. I don't know exactly how many dates it was. It was about 33 dates, and they were all "doubles," two shows [a day] in two different cities. It was a package tour, and we were the closing act in the first half. When we were done with the first show, we jumped into a bus and drove straight to the next town. Eighty percent of the tour was like that, and we played almost every day. There were probably only two or three days off out of more than 30 dates. It was a really grueling experience.

You weren't being paid very well either, were you? Which led to some mistrust of [manager Simon Napier-Bell]?

It wasn't really that, it was more a case at the end of this period of doing that tour and other tours of the States; a tour of England and maybe somewhere else as well, I think France; doing "Stroll On" for *Blow-Up* and a Great Shakes commercial. Simon Napier-Bell got out a piece of paper and started writing down some really weird mathematics. We ended up with about 200 pounds each for that entire three-month period. Not on.

HOW DID BECK leave the group?

It was on that Dick Clark tour — there were a few incidents. One time in the dressing room I walked in and Beck had his guitar up over his head, about to bring it down on Keith Relf's head, but instead smashed it on the floor. Relf looked at him with total astonishment and Beck said, "Why did you make me do that?" Fucking hell. Everyone said, "My goodness gracious, what a funny chap." We went back to the hotel and Beck showed me his tonsils, said he wasn't feeling well and was going to see a doctor. He left for L.A., where we were headed in two days' time anyway, When we got there, though, we realized that whatever doctor he was claiming to see must've had his office in the Whisky. He was actually seeing his girlfriend, Mary Hughes, and had just used the doctor bit as an excuse to cut out on us.

Prior to my joining the Yardbirds, apparently, he had pissed around on stage quite a lot — knocking over his amps, just walking off, whatever. At the time I came in, he was in a rut — I think he felt a bit alien in a way. I'm not sure, but I think so. When I joined, he pulled himself together and was far more disciplined, especially when I went on guitar; he didn't want to go walking off then. Instead, he went the other extreme and started messing about offstage, generally being late, not turning up until the end of a session, etcetera. These sorts of things went on and it must have revived all the previous antagonism between him and the rest of the band. I think that that, and a couple of other things — especially the horrible wages we were being paid — helped to bring about his behavior, which had obviously stewed behind everybody's back. I didn't even know about it, but by the time we got to L.A. they had already decided they didn't want to work with him anymore. They were just totally adamant, and there was nothing at this particular point that either Beck or I could say to make the rest of the group change their minds. Beck wasn't saying anything anyway, because he didn't have very much of an excuse. We had a meeting and when it was over Beck got up to leave and asked me if I was coming, too. I said, "No, I'm going to stay behind," because I wanted to try to work it out. Actually, it probably would have been better if I had left, but at that time I just really thought they could be talked back into it if I told them the more positive aspects of what had happened and what could be if we kept Jeff in the group.

That quote you mentioned, that Keith Relf had said, "The magic of the band left when Eric left," I think really has to be taken into account. They were prepared to go on as a foursome, but it seemed that a lot of the enthusiasm had been lost. Then Napier-Bell called up with the news that he was selling his stake in the band to Mickie Most. I think they must have cooked it up, actually, the three of them: Napier-Bell, Mickie Most and Beck. This way Jeff could have a solo career, which he'd

> 66 I never desired stardom,
> I just wanted to be respected as a musician.

already begun in a way with the recording [*"Bole-ro" was recorded while he was still in the Yardbirds*].

You said that when you joined the Yardbirds you knew a bit about the business aspect of music and were a bit suspicious of the Yardbirds' management.

I had worked with Andrew Oldham and Tony Calder at Immediate and had to be involved a little in that side of it. A lot of things just didn't seem right to me.

Did you swing the band away from Gomelsky when you joined?

No, I wasn't involved with the group at that time. It was Paul Samwell-Smith's girlfriend who knew Simon Napier-Bell. At the time they were getting a bit dissatisfied with Gomelsky; when Na-pier-Bell phoned up and said he could get them a record advance, something they'd never had 'til that time, that was it. It never occurred to them personally before that they should have a record advance, so when Napier-Bell called, they decided to go with this new, forceful manager. Of course, Napier-Bell then came in and paid their percentage to his agency, hee hee.

Gomelsky, for all his shortcomings — and there were a few — was a very good ideas man. He was the Rolling Stones' first manager. He was the one who got the Yardbirds involved in a lot of the good things that happened to them. He was the one who got them recording at Sun studios with Sam Phillips. Sam Phillips hadn't recorded an art-ist, even though a lot of records had come out on Sun subsequently, since Charlie Rich did "Lonely Weekends." Gomelsky got him out of bed at two or three in the morning because he had booked time at the studio and thought the engineer was a wanker. Sam Phillips actually came down and recorded with them.

What songs were done there?

"Train Kept A-Rollin'" and one other, I'm not sure which.

Getting back to the period when Beck left the Yardbirds, you mentioned that Napier-Bell had sold the rights to both the Yardbirds and Beck to Mickie Most.

That's right. Actually, when I think of it, Mickie Most as an A&R man/producer was probably more interested in Beck's career than ours. They knew Jeff had the potential, but it was necessary to get him the right material and produce him. Napier-Bell had already gotten the members of the group into doing solo material; Keith Relf had done some singles; Jeff had already record-ed "Bolero" and Jim McCarty was about to do a comedy record. It had started to go that way al-ready, so Napier-Bell probably had that in mind when he decided to sell our contract to Most.

What about the Little Games *album? What cir-cumstances was it recorded under? I've always felt it was not as good as it should have been.*

It was just so bloody rushed. Everything was done in one take because Mickie Most was basi-cally interested in singles and didn't believe it was worth the time to do the tracks right on the album. Stu [Ian Stewart] from the Rolling Stones played piano on those tracks, and when we finished the first take of the first track we were recording he said, "That'll sound much better the second take." Mickie Most was sitting in the control booth, and all of a sudden, he said, "Next!" Stu couldn't be-lieve it. I mean, it was all right, the take we had just done, but had we done it again it probably would have been a lot better.

The album was made as an album, then, not just taken from a lot of singles sessions?

"No Excess Baggage" was something Most suggested as a single, but we did it as an album session. There could've been a lot better stuff on the album. I remember him saying to me once, about guitar solos, "They're something you stick in the middle of the single where there isn't any vocal." He didn't share my view that a guitar solo, like the ones on the Ricky Nelson records, for instance, could be an uplifting experience.

He eventually began using guitar with Donovan.

I did a couple of Donovan sessions with him: *Sunshine Superman.* It was probably Donovan who got it all together and made that an album. It was only after that album started selling that Mickie Most realized that there was a potential in albums. But he was really a singles-oriented man ... mysterious.

Why was Little Games *never released in England?*

I don't know. I don't remember.

Who owns the rights to that now?

Mickie Most.

How did Peter Grant come to manage the Yardbirds?

Peter was working with Mickie Most and was offered the management when Most was offered the recording, of which the first session on our behalf was "Little Games" and the first on Beck's behalf was "Love Is Blue." I'd known Peter from way back in the days of Immediate because our offices were next door to Mickie Most's, and Peter was working for him. The first thing we did with him was a tour of Australia and we found that suddenly there was some money being made after all this time.

I was only on a wage, anyway, with the Yardbirds. I'd like to say that because I was earning about three times as much when I was doing sessions and I've seen it written that "Page only joined the Yardbirds for the bread." I was on wages with Napier-Bell, except it came to the point where — like at the end of that tour when he did his scribbling — the wages were more than what the rest of the band were making and it was cheaper for Napier-Bell to give me what everybody else was getting.

How lucrative was it to be a session musician?

It was very lucrative. I'd saved up a lot of money, which is why it didn't bother me that I was working for a lot less in the Yardbirds. I just wanted to get out of only playing rhythm guitar and have a chance to get into something more creative.

As they were a really creative band, there were obviously possibilities — especially the idea of dual lead — that really excited me. Nobody except maybe the Stones had done anything approaching what we wanted to do, and even the Stones didn't really use dual leads, at least not the way we had in mind. I mean we immediately settled into things like stereo riffs on "Over, Under, Sideways, Down" and all kinds of guitar harmonies on stage — everything fell into place very easily.

Had you jammed a lot with Beck while you were still doing sessions?

Yeah, plus I had him in on some session work as well. Not that much, just a few things.

But you were well acquainted with playing with him and knew his style?

Yeah.

What about the idea of the bowed guitar, which I believe you first started using when you were with the Yardbirds? It's on "Glimpses," from Little Games.

I had used it before I joined the Yardbirds. It was suggested to me by a session violinist. I didn't think it could be done at first — bowing a flat-necked instrument — but I took his advice and got a bow and started having a go and I could see the possibilities in it. I started trying to fit it in on sessions where I could. I was using it as soon as I joined the Yardbirds; I used it on the bass when I was playing that. On record I used it on "Glimpses" and "Tinker Tailor" — that's with the Yardbirds. As far as the session days go, I can't remember any of the specific tracks I used it on.

What's the story behind the Live *album recorded at the Anderson Theater?*

That was a total embarrassment. It was recorded on jet lag and by a guy who had never recorded a rock and roll band in his life, just orchestras. He had one mike on the drums, which was unthinkable, and he miked the wrong cabinet for the guitar so that the fuzztone which gave it all the sustain wasn't picked up. It wasn't a very good night in any way, least of all on the recording.

We had the option to refuse release should it not be right. However, he went into the studio and worked on it because we'd told him we wouldn't go along with it as it was. He said, "What's wrong with it?" and we told him: "For a start, you can't hear the bass drum," and so forth. So, he went into the studio and worked on it. He added bullfight cheers and people muttering in a cocktail lounge and clicking glasses during "Dazed and Confused" [*called "I'm "Confused" on the album*], but that was about the extent of it. Then he called us up and asked us if we wanted to come down and hear it, "because wonders can be done in the studio." He hoped we'd let it come out, but we all agreed that it shouldn't be released. So, they waited three years and then released it, but we had it pulled back. It just wasn't right. It wasn't a good night, it wasn't representative of how we were, and it certainly wasn't representative of Keith Relf, who is now not with us. It would have been much easier just to accept an advance and put it out, but there was more pride and vanity, if you like, among everybody concerned.

What are your favorite tracks you recorded with the Yardbirds?

In the studio I don't think we ever really had enough time to get together a good account of ourselves. We never rehearsed material for an album, it was like leaving Mickie Most to come up with the material. It's easy to be wise after the event, but when Donovan albums sounded so good, we figured we could probably trust Most to do as well for us. Maybe Donovan was just more headstrong in doing what he wanted. A lot of those things like "Ha Ha Said the Clown" and "Ten Little Indians" were done as experiments. He suggested that we try them and see what happens, but we just knew they wouldn't be any good. We had hopes for a couple of things we never got to do and for things like "Puzzles," but to him that was a B-side.

Why did the group finally split?

It just got to a point where [singer Keith] Relf and [drummer Jim] McCarty couldn't take it anymore. They wanted to go and do something totally different.

You wanted the band to continue. didn't you?

Yeah. When it came to the final split it was a question of begging them to keep it together, but they didn't. They just wanted to try something new. I told them we'd be able to change within

the group format; coming from a sessions background I was prepared to adjust to anything. I hated to break it up without even doing a proper first album.

What about your own desire for stardom, did that have any role in your quitting sessions to join the Yardbirds in the first place?

No. I never desired stardom, I just wanted to be respected as a musician.

Do you feel the extent of your stardom has become a burden for you?

Only in relation to a lot of misunderstandings that have been laid on us. A lot of negative and derogatory things have been said about us. I must say I enjoyed the anonymity that was part of being one-fourth of a group. I liked being a name but not necessarily a face to go with it. [*The Song Remains the Same*] film, I think, has done a lot to put faces to names.

AFTER RELF and McCarty said they were quitting the Yardbirds, you planned to keep the group going with Chris Dreja and bring in a new drummer and singer, is that right?

Well, we still had these dates we were supposed to fulfill. Around the time of the split, John Paul Jones called me up and said he was interested in getting something together. Also, Chris was getting very into photography; he decided he wanted to open his own studio and by that time was no longer enamored with the thought of going on the road. Obviously, a lot of Keith and Jim's attitude of wanting to jack it in had rubbed off on him, so Jonesy was in.

I'd originally thought of getting Terry Reid in as lead singer/second guitarist, but he had just signed with Mickie Most as a solo artist — quirk of fate. He suggested I get in touch with Robert Plant, who was then in a band called Obs-Tweedle. When I auditioned him and heard him sing, I immediately thought there must be something wrong with him personality-wise or that he had to be impossible to work with, because I just could not understand why, after he told me he'd been singing for a few years already, he hadn't become a big name yet. So, I had him down to my place for a little while, just to sort of check him

> **We were going to form a group called Led Zeppelin at the time of the "Beck's Bolero" sessions with me and Beck on guitars, Moon on drums, maybe Nicky Hopkins on piano.**

out, and we got along great. No problems. At this time, a number of drummers had approached me and wanted to work with us. Robert suggested I go hear John Bonham, whom I'd heard of because he had a reputation but had never seen. I asked Robert if he knew him, and he told me they'd worked together in this group called Band of Joy.

So, the four of you rehearsed for a short time and went on that Scandinavian tour as the New Yardbirds.

As I said, we had these dates that the Yardbirds were supposed to fulfill, so we went as the Yardbirds. They were already being advertised as the New Yardbirds featuring Jimmy Page, so there wasn't much we could do about it right then. We had every intention of changing the name of the group from the very beginning, though. The tour went fantastically for us, we left them stomping on the floors after every show.

Who actually named Led Zeppelin? I've heard that both John Entwistle and Keith Moon claim to have thought up the name.

It was Moon, I'm sure, despite anything Entwistle may have said. In fact, I'm quite certain Richard Cole asked Moon for his permission when we decided to use the name. Entwistle must've just been upset that the original Led Zeppelin never took off.

What original Led Zeppelin?

We were going to form a group called Led Zeppelin at the time of "Beck's Bolero" sessions

with the lineup from that session. It was going to be me and Beck on guitars, Moon on drums, maybe Nicky Hopkins on piano. The only one from the session who wasn't going to be in it was Jonesy, who had played bass. Instead, Moon suggested we bring in Entwistle as bassist and lead singer as well, but after some discussion we decided to use another singer. The first choice was Stevie Winwood, but it was decided that he was too heavily committed to Traffic at the time and probably wouldn't be too interested. Next, we thought of Stevie Marriott. He was approached and seemed to be full of glee about it. A message came from the business side of Marriott, though, which said, "How would you like to play guitar with broken fingers? You will be if you don't stay away from Stevie." After that, the idea sort of fell apart. We just said, "Let's forget about the whole thing, quick." Instead of being more positive about it and looking for another singer, we just let it slip by. Then the Who began a tour, the Yardbirds began a tour and that was it.

Remembering that session when we did "Bolero," the band seemed to be almost tied up; it was really close to happening.

When was that "Bolero" session? Had you joined the Yardbirds yet?

Yeah. It was around the time we recorded "Happenings Ten Years Time Ago" and "Psycho Daisies." I played an electric 12-string on "Bolero."

And you composed it?

I did the main construction on it — the opening and the riff. Then it sort of stops and hits these two chords and that was the essence of where the song came to be from. Keith Relf had a melody on tape, and we used that as a main part of the song. I don't think Beck actually came in on the backing tracks, he just did the overdubs.

What cuts did you and Beck both play guitar on while you were both with the Yardbirds?

"Happenings Ten Years Time Ago" (John Paul Jones played bass on that, by the way); "Psycho Daisies" — I think I played a bit of guitar on that and all the bass; and "Stroll On" from the *Blow-Up* soundtrack.

Did John Paul Jones do any other tracks with the Yardbirds?

He may have played on "Little Games." Yes, I'm pretty sure he did.

PART THREE: LED ZEPPELIN

What were the original ideas behind Zeppelin? Was it immediately decided to be a high-energy thing?

Obviously, it was geared that way from the start. When Robert came down to my place the first time, when I was trying to get an idea of what he was all about, we talked about the possibilities of various types of things — "Dazed and Confused," for example — and then I played him a version of "Babe I'm Gonna Leave You." It was the version by Joan Baez — the song is traditional — and I said, "Fancy doing this?" He sort of looked at me with wonder, and I said, "Well, I've got an idea for an arrangement," and started playing it on acoustic guitar. That's indicative of the way I was thinking with regards to direction. It was very easygoing.

How was the material chosen for Led Zeppelin I?

The stuff was all originally put forward by me as the material to include in the program we played in concert. It had all been well rehearsed as we'd toured Scandinavia as the New Yardbirds before recording the album. We also had a few other things we were doing at the time which never got recorded: "Flames," written by Elmer Gantry, was a really good number; "As Long as I Have You" was a Garnett Mimms number we had done with the Yardbirds which Janis Joplin had recorded. There were a lot of improvisations on the first album, but generally we were keeping everything cut and dried. Consequently, by the time we'd finished the first tour, the riffs which were coming out of these spaces we were able to use for the immediate recording of the second album.

Zeppelin I *is said to have been recorded in 30 hours.*

That's right, about 30 hours of recording time. We had already played the numbers live before we started recording, and I already had a good idea of what was going to go on as far as the overdubs went.

There weren't many overdubs done on Zeppelin I *at any rate, were there?*

Not many. On "Babe I'm Gonna Leave You" there's an acoustic guitar dubbed over, and there's some pedal steel on "Your Time Is Gonna Come."

When did you learn to play pedal steel guitar?

For that session. We also had worked out a version of [the Band's] "Chest Fever" in rehearsals, though we never played it on stage. That had organ and pedal steel on it.

What was the recording of Zeppelin II *like? How long did it take you as opposed to the first album?*

It was done wherever we could get into a studio, in bits and pieces, so I couldn't even tell you how long it actually took. I remember we did a vocal overdub in an eight-track studio in Vancouver where they didn't even have proper [headphones]. Can you imagine that? It was just recorded while we were on the road.

Was it recorded entirely on the road?

No. "Thank You," "The Lemon Song" and "Moby Dick" were overdubbed on tour, and the mixing of "Whole Lotta Love" and "Heartbreaker" was done on tour. In other words, some of the material came out of rehearsing for the next tour and getting new material together. The most important thing about *Zeppelin II* is that up to that point I'd contributed lyrics. Robert wrote "Thank You" on his own. That was the first one, and it's important because it's when he began to come through as a lyricist. I'd always hoped that he would.

There was a bit of a fuss made at one point because on the first couple of albums you were using a lot of traditional and blues lyrics and tunes and calling them your own.

The thing is they were traditional lyrics, and they went back far before a lot of the people that one related them to. The riffs we did were totally different, also, from the ones that had come before, apart from something like "You Shook Me" and "Can't Quit You Baby," which we attributed to Willie Dixon. The thing with "Bring It on Home," Christ, there's only a tiny bit of that taken from Sonny Boy Williamson's version, and we threw that in as a tribute to him. People say, "Oh, 'Bring It on Home' is stolen." Well, there's only a little bit in the song that even relates to anything that had gone before it — just the end.

ZEPPELIN III *presented a very different image of Led Zeppelin from the first two albums. Most importantly, it was predominantly acoustic. How and why did the changes that brought about* Zeppelin III *take place?*

After the intense touring that had been taking place through the first two albums — working almost 24 hours a day, basically — we managed to stop and have a proper break, a couple of months as opposed to a couple of weeks. We decided to go off and rent a cottage to provide a contrast to motel rooms. Obviously, it had quite an effect on the material that was written.

Was the whole group living together in the cottage?

No, it was just Robert and myself.

Did you write the whole album there?

Just certain sections of it. "That's the Way," "Bron-Y-Aur Stomp," quite a few things. It was the tranquility of the place that set the tone of the album. Obviously, we weren't crashing away at 100-watt Marshall stacks. Having played acoustic and being interested in classical guitar, anyway, being in a cottage without electricity, it was acoustic guitar time. It didn't occur to us not to include it on the album, because it was relative to the changes within the band. We didn't expect we'd get thrashed in the media for doing it.

Was there a rethink about the stage act, since you were faced with having to perform material from a predominantly acoustic LP?

It just meant that we were going to have to employ some of those numbers onstage without being frightened about it. They were received amazingly well.

Had you wanted to bring in more of the English folk roots to Zeppelin, or was it just the influence of living in the cottage that gives the album a pastoral feeling?

It has that because that's how it was. After all the heavy, intense vibe of touring which is reflected in the raw energy on the second album, it was just a totally different feeling. I've always tried to capture an emotional quality in my songs. Transmitting that is what music seems to be about, really, as far as the instrumental side of it goes, anyway. It was in us, everything that came out on

Zeppelin III can still be related to the essence of the first album when you think about it. It's just that the band had kept maturing.

Were you surprised when the critical reaction came out?

I just thought they hadn't understood it, hadn't listened to it. For instance, *Melody Maker* said we'd decided to don our acoustic guitars because Crosby, Stills and Nash had just been over here. It wasn't until the fourth LP that people began to understand that we weren't just messing around.

You did put a lot of stock in the criticism of Zeppelin III. *Personally, you seemed to be hit very hard by it at the time.*

To pave the way for 18 months without doing any interviews, I must've. Silly, wasn't I? That was a lot of the reason for putting out the next LP with no information on it at all. After a year's absence from both records and touring, I remember one agent telling us it was professional suicide. We just happened to have a lot of faith in what we were doing.

Was the cover of Zeppelin IV *meant to bring out that whole city/country dichotomy that had surfaced with* Zeppelin III?

Exactly. It represented the change in the balance which was going on. There was the old countryman and the blocks of flats being knocked down. It was just a way of saying that we should look after the Earth, not rape and pillage it.

Do you think Zeppelin III *was good for the band, regardless of the critical reaction, because it showed people that the band was not just a heavy metal group, that you were more versatile than that?*

It showed people that we weren't going to be a stagnant group. There were some people who knew that already and were interested to see what we'd come up with; there were others who thought we were just an outright hype and were still living back in the '60s. They just didn't take anything we did seriously. A lot of them have since come around. You should read that *Melody Maker* review, though, it's absolutely classic.

I felt a lot better once we started performing it, because it was proving to be working for the people who came around to see us. There was always a big smile there in front of us. That was always more important than any poxy review. That's really how the following of the band has spread, by word of mouth. I mean, all this talk about a hype, spending thousands on publicity campaigns, we didn't do that at all. We didn't do TV — well, we did a pilot TV show and a pilot radio show, but that's all — it wasn't as though we were thrashing about all over the media. It didn't matter, though, the word got out on the street.

What about "Hats Off to Harper," was that written as a tribute to [English singer-songwriter] Roy Harper?

In a way, because he'd stuck to his guns at that point. He wouldn't let anything dissuade him, and he was really coming up with some brilliant stuff. *Stormcock* was a fabulous album which didn't sell anything, which was really not just at all. Also, they wouldn't release his albums in America for quite a long time. For that I just thought, "Well, hats off to you."

Did you hope to draw some attention to him through the song?

In a way, sure. As far as I'm concerned, though, hats off to anybody who does what they think is right and refuses to sell out.

IT SEEMS THAT of the big groups, only you and the Who have managed to stay together for such a long time without personnel changes, and the Who don't really seem to get on with each other very well.

Yeah, we've always had a strong bond. It became very apparent when Robert was injured before we made *Presence.*

Zeppelin IV was to my mind the first fully realized Zeppelin LP. It just sounded like everything had come together on that album.

Yeah, we were really playing properly as a group, and the different writing departures that we'd taken, like the cottage and the spontaneity aspects, had been worked out and came across in the most disciplined form.

"Rock and Roll" was a spontaneous combustion. We were doing something else at the time, but Bonzo played the beginning of Little Richard's "Good Golly Miss Molly" with the tape still running and I just started doing that part of the riff. It actually ground to a halt after about 12 bars, but it was enough to know that there was enough there as a number to keep working on it. Robert even came in singing on it straightaway.

I do have the original tape that was running at the time we ran down "Stairway to Heaven" completely with the band. I'd worked it all out already the night before with John Paul Jones, written down the changes and things. All this time we were all living in a house and keeping pretty regular hours together, so the next day we started running it down. There was only one place where there was a slight rerun. For some unknown reason, Bonzo couldn't get the timing right on the 12-string part before the solo, other than that it flowed very quickly. While we were doing it Robert was penciling down lyrics; he must have written three-quarters of the lyrics on the spot. He didn't have to go away and think about them. Amazing, really.

"Black Dog" was a riff that John Paul Jones had brought with him. "Battle of Evermore" was made up on the spot by Robert and myself. I just picked up John Paul Jones's mandolin, never having played a mandolin before, and just wrote up the chords and the whole thing at one sitting. The same thing happened with the banjo on "Gallows Pole"; I'd never played one before either, it was also John Paul Jones's instrument. I just picked it up and started moving my fingers around until the chords sounded right, which is the same way I work on compositions when the guitar's in different tunings.

Why did Sandy Denny come in to sing on "Gallows Pole"?

Well, first off, it sounded like an old English instrumental. Then it became a vocal, and Robert did his bit. Finally, we figured we'd bring Sandy by and do a question-and-answer type thing.

"Misty Mountain Hop" we came up with on the spot. "Going to California" was a thing I'd written before on acoustic guitar. "When the Levee Breaks" was a riff that I'd been working on, but Bonzo's drum sound really makes the difference on that point.

You've said that when you heard Robert's lyrics to "Stairway to Heaven" you knew that he'd be the

> ❝
>
> I knew "Stairway to Heaven" was good. I didn't know it was going to become like an anthem, but I did know it was the gem of the album.

band's lyricist from then on.

I always knew he would be, but I knew at that point that he'd proved it to himself and could get into something a bit more profound than just subjective things. Not that they can't be profound as well, but there's a lot of ambiguity implied in that number that wasn't present before. I was really relieved because it gave me the opportunity to just get on with the music.

Did you know you'd recorded a classic when you'd finished it?

I knew it was good. I didn't know it was going to become like an anthem, but I did know it was the gem of the album, sure.

You recorded Zeppelin IV _at a few different studios, right?_

It was recorded on location at Headley Grange in Hampshire. "Stairway" was done at Island, as were the overdubs. "Four Sticks" was done at Island because it had a lot of chiming guitars and things. "When the Levee Breaks" is probably the most subtle thing on there as far as production goes because each twelve bars has something new about it, though at first it might not be apparent. There's a lot of different effects on there that at the time had never been used before. Phased vocals, a backwards echoed harmonica solo. Andy Johns was doing the engineering, but as far as those sort of ideas go, they usually come from me. Once a thing is past the stage of being a track, I've usually got a good idea of how I'd like it to shape up. I don't want to sound too dictatorial, though, be-

cause it's not that sort of thing at all. When we went into Headley Grange it was more like, "OK, what's anybody got?"

And it turned out that you had more than anyone else?

It usually does.

Was the idea of the symbols on the cover of Zeppelin IV _yours?_

Yeah. After all this crap that we'd had with the critics, I put it to everybody else that it'd be a good idea to put out something totally anonymous. At first, I wanted just one symbol on it, but then it was decided that since it was our fourth album and there were four of us, we could each choose our own symbol. I designed mine and everyone else had their own reasons for using the symbols that they used.

A lot of time was spent on the cover of Houses of the Holy.

We had a lot of trouble on that, processing the dye. The colors they applied didn't work. They kept getting the sky too red, making the sky the focal point and upsetting the balance.

Do you envision a relationship between Zeppelin cover art and the music on the albums?

There is a relationship in a way, though not necessarily in a "concept album" fashion.

HOW DID Houses of the Holy _come about?_

A lot of it was written in rehearsals. It didn't take long. "The Rain Song" I'd totally written at home and worked out the chords; "Over the Hills" as well. "The Crunge" just happened spontaneously. Bonzo started playing, Jonesy came in next, then I joined in. It happened as quickly as that. At the time it seemed to be undanceable, because it keeps crossing from the on- to the off-beat, as opposed to most James Brown things which are totally danceable. That's why we called it "The Crunge." We thought of putting steps on the cover to help you do the dance.

Does Robert usually come into sessions with the lyrics already written?

He has a lyric book and we try to fuse song to lyric where it can be done. Where it can't he just writes new ones.

Is there a lot of lyric changing during a session?

Sometimes. Sometimes it's more cut and dried, like on "The Rain Song."

There are a few jokey tracks on Houses: *it seems to exhibit more of a sense of humor than Zeppelin had been known for. "The Crunge" is funny, and "D'yer Maker" has a joke title which took some people a while to get.*

I didn't expect people not to get it. I thought it was pretty obvious. The song itself was a cross between reggae and a '50s number: "Poor Little Fool," Ben E. King things, stuff like that. I'll tell you one thing, "Song Remains the Same" was going to be an instrumental at first. We used to call it "The Overture."

You never performed it that way.

We couldn't, there were too many guitar parts to perform it.

But once you record anything with overdubs, you end up having to adapt it for the stage.

Sure. Then it becomes a challenge, a tough challenge in some cases. "Achilles" is the classic one. When Ronnie Wood and Keith Richard came to hear us play, Keith said, "You ought to get another guitarist; you're rapidly becoming known as the most overworked guitarist in the business." Quite amusing. There are times when I'd just love to get another guitarist on, but it just wouldn't look right to the audience.

Houses of the Holy was the last album that came out on Atlantic before you formed Swan Song. How did the label get started?

We'd been thinking about it for a while, and we knew if we formed a label there wouldn't be the kind of fuss and bother we'd been going through over album covers and things like that. Having gone through, ourselves, what appeared to be an interference or at least an aggravation on the artistic side by record companies, we wanted to form a label where the artists would be able to fulfill themselves without all of that hassle. Consequently, the people we were looking for for the label would be people who knew where they were going themselves. We didn't really want to get bogged down in having to develop artists, we wanted people who were together enough to handle that type of thing themselves, like the Pretty Things. Even though they didn't happen, the rec-

ords they made were very, very good. They've reformed as Metropolis without Phil May and they're really fantastic right now.

Physical Graffiti was not all new material. Why was this?

Well, as usual, we had more material than the required 40-odd minutes for one album. We had enough material for one and a half LPs, so we figured let's put out a double and use some of the material we had done previously but never released. It seemed like a good time to do that sort of thing, release tracks like "Boogie With Stu" which we normally wouldn't be able to do. [Stu is] Ian Stewart from the Stones. He played on "Rock and Roll" with us.

Which other tracks on Graffiti had been recorded previously?

"Black Country Woman" and "Rover" were both done at the same time we did "D'yer Maker," "Bron-Y-Aur" was done for *Zeppelin III,* "Down by the Seaside" and "Night Flight" and "Boogie With Stu" were from the sessions for the fourth album. We had an album and a half of new material, and this time we figured it was better to stretch out than to leave off. I really fancied putting out a song called "Houses of the Holy" on the album.

Where did you get the title Physical Graffiti from?

It came out in the usual panic of trying to find a title for an album. I came up with that title because of the whole thing of graffiti on the album cover and it being a physical statement rather than a written one, because I feel that an awful lot of physical energy is used in producing an album.

[*We begin discussing "Kashmir" and Jimmy plays me the cassette of his original demo of the song with just him and John Bonham.*]

Do you consider "Kashmir" one of your better compositions?

Yeah. There have been several milestones along the way: that's definitely one of them.

If you were to put together a best-of-Zeppelin album, what tracks would you choose for it?

That's very difficult to say. I haven't thought about it.

If you were to put those "milestones" together you mentioned?

"Communication Breakdown" ... It's difficult, only because I don't know the running times and if you mean a single LP or a double. It'd probably be about three songs from each LP. I'd be very conscious of a balance of the sides. There are some tracks which are obvious.

Are there any plans to put out an album like that?

Not at this moment.

Do you think you'll do one eventually?

I'm going to work on a quad[rophonic] thing. I had one idea for a chronological live LP which would be two or three albums going back through "Communication Breakdown," "Thank You" and all those sorts of numbers. We've got recordings starting with the Albert Hall in 1969 and '70, with two a year from then on. It'd go all the way through.

PRESENCE *WAS RECORDED AFTER Robert's accident, and you've said it was the album you were most intensely involved with since the first.*

As far as living it uninterrupted from beginning to end, yeah, definitely. I did 18-hour sessions ... 20-hour sessions to complete it. We overran our time allotment at the studio and Mick Jagger was coming in afterwards with the Stones, and I asked him if we could just have a couple of extra days to finish up. He said, "Sure." Anyway, the day we finished it, the Stones came in and asked how we'd gotten on. I said, "Alright, I've finished, thanks to the two extra days you gave us." They said, "The tracks?" And I said, "No, the whole thing," and they couldn't believe it. They knew how much we had left to do before those two days and couldn't imagine how we'd completed the whole thing.

Is there a reason Presence *is a totally electric guitar-oriented album?*

I think it was just a reflection of the total anxiety and emotion at the period of time during which it was recorded. It's true that there are no acoustic songs, no mellowness or contrasts or changes to other instruments. Yet the blues we did ["Tea for One"] was the only time I think we've ever gotten close to repeating the mood of another of our numbers, "Since I've Been Loving You"; the chordal structure is similar: A minor blues. We just wanted to get a really laid-back blues feeling without blowing out on it at all. We did two takes in the end, one with a guitar solo and one without.

I ended up sitting there thinking, "I've got this guitar solo to do" because there have been blues guitar solos since Eric on *Five Live Yardbirds* and everyone's done a good one. I was really a bit frightened of it, I thought "What's to be done?" I didn't want to blast out on the solo like a locomotive or something, because it wasn't conducive to the vibe of the rest of the track. I was extremely aware that you had to do something different than just some B.B. King licks.

You've always seemed to be conscious of not repeating blues clichés.

I probably do it more on stage than [on] record. It's evident on the live album when we do "Whole Lotta Love."

I'll tell you about doing all the guitar overdubs to "Achilles Last Stand." There were basically two sections to the song when we rehearsed it. John Paul Jones didn't think I could succeed in what I was attempting to do. He said I couldn't do a scale over a certain section, it just wouldn't work, but it did. What I planned, to try and get that epic quality into it so it wouldn't just sound like two sections repeated, was to give the piece a totally new identity by orchestrating the guitars, which is something I'd been into for quite some time. I knew it had to be jolly good, because the number was so long it just couldn't afford to be half-baked. It was all down to me how to do this. I had a lot of it mapped out in my mind, anyway, but to make a long story short, I did all the overdubs in one night.

Do you know how many tracks you did?

No, I lost count eventually.

Not many people picked up on that number, but I thought as far as I can value tying up that kind of emotion as a package and trying to convey it through two speakers, it was fairly successful. Maybe it's because it was a narrative, I don't know.

What was the object on Presence *supposed to represent?*

Ambiguity, in a way. The way the cover came about was that after we'd returned from the recording, we realized that the only feasible thing to do was to take a picture of the studio and its chaos, but we needed something better than that, so we contacted Hipgnosis and explained to the chap there, Po [Aubrey Powell], what had been going on. He returned and said that the thing that had always struck him about Led Zeppelin was a power, a force, an alchemical quality which was indefinable, which I guess he was relating to the magnitude of the band. He came up with this idea of interpreting this through an object which could be related to any object in a community that everyone was perfectly at home with.

I came up with the idea of "Presence," because there was the presence of this object, yet the word has other connotations, as well.

Were you upset that the first live LP was a film soundtrack [for The Song Remains the Same*]?*

Dead right. It was a shame. For a time, the movie was shelved, and we were going to come over here with what we'd learned, and do some more footage, but after Robert's accident we were forced to tie it all up — we'd done work with it already, and it had to come out. It was recorded over three nights, but in fact the music for the footage mainly came from the first night. It was the best vocal performance and wasn't like they had drop-ins and that sort of thing, but they just didn't have complete footage, so we had to come up with the fantasy sequences to fill it up. Had we been a band that's the same every night, it would have been very easy for them to link one night's performance with another. As far as live albums go, most groups will record over half a dozen nights and make the best of that, but as it was a visual, we couldn't do that.

Do you like the movie?

Oh, it was an incredible uphill struggle. We'd done a bit of work on it and stopped, did more, then stopped again ... three times in all. At that point, we'd decided to redo the thing, making sure the filmmakers did have everything covered properly.

As far as it goes, I'm really pleased that it is there. Purely because it's an honest statement, a

documentary ... it's certainly not one of the magic nights. It was not one of the amazing nights you get now and again, but you'd have to have the entire film crew travelling with you all the time to catch one. That'd be just too costly to do. We'd gotten to the point where we were so far into it, we couldn't pull out, we'd put so much money into it. By that point, we knew it was going to be alright, but the director was very stubborn, and it would've been a lot easier had he just done what he'd been asked to do.

Getting back to your original question, though, it was frustrating because I did have this concept of this chronologized live LP which really would've been a knockout.

It still sounds like a viable thing for you to do in the future.

I'll get to it. I'll do it eventually.

Try to get only things from magic nights on one collection?

The really ace nights you never get down, but there are some really good performances. "Dazed and Confused," when I was doing it, would change night after night, and over a period of a few months it would change quite dramatically. I really like listening to bootlegs of us sometimes — even though the recording quality is so bloody horrible — just to hear the different approaches we'd take to numbers. It's very interesting.

DO YOU ENVISION A TIME where you may be uncomfortable doing what you want to do with Led Zeppelin, that you may want to do some orchestration or something on your own?

I don't see why that couldn't be done within the vehicle of the band — unless it was totally instrumental, of course — but I've got a couple of things I'm working on which could pave the way to orchestrated pieces. As far as the band goes, the bond between us really showed at the time of Robert's accident. Our loyalty to each other and to what we're doing really showed at that point, we just really love playing together. And though things could've easily collapsed then, we all realized we just couldn't do it any other way.

Would you consider making a solo album?

As far as the kind of stuff I'm working towards,

as far as composition goes, it might require it, but it would just be a one-off and wouldn't interfere with the band in any way whatsoever.

It wouldn't be a solo career type of thing...

No way, I'm no Django Reinhardt.

What do you think of the term "heavy metal" being applied to Led Zeppelin?

It's a bastard term, really. It's just a marriage of two words, "heavy music" and "metal" ... the metallic feeling. I can't relate that to us because the thing that comes to mind when people said "heavy metal" was riff-bashing, and I don't think that we ever just did riff-bashing at any point, it was always inner dynamics, light and shade, drama and versatility that we were going in for — right from the start. I don't know what category we fit into, but it's not "heavy metal." It's just music, that's all. I've said a million times that it's music of the streets — street music, folk music — because that's where it's come from, it's come from the streets, self-taught. A lot of rock and roll is like a folk music when you think of the social statements made by somebody like Chuck Berry: "No Money Down," "School Days" ... things like that were incredibly powerful statements.

Is it your desire for your music to achieve an immortality?

I think we'd all like to, but I don't know whether there's a possibility. In relationship to whom did you mean that?

Beethoven...

Wagner, Stravinsky... I don't think there's anybody who can even be linked in the same breath on the rock and roll battlefield strewn with souls, I just don't think there is. Those people are just so far ahead in terms of construction.

Do you think any of today's rock and roll will be listened to 100 years from now?

Yeah, I do. But I've just got the feeling that at this particular point, if it wasn't for punk, which is taking it right back to the roots of shit-kicking rock and roll — back to "fuck you" music, the sheer adrenaline — rock would be in a sad state of affairs. Thank God for them, it's finally back to neighborhood rock. Maybe we're about to begin a new cycle.

What do you see in the future for the new wave?

I know it's going to be really big. I knew the minute I saw it [that] it was going to go over big in England, because you get all the kids coming out to London over summer vacations from the suburbs, sporting whatever is the current vogue at the time. One year it was Bolan, one year Bowie, another year it was the Osmonds. It's obvious with all the shops opening up selling punk fashions that it's to be for this summer.

I haven't seen any really strong philosophy emerge from any of it, though. As a political issue, I don't take it very seriously. All that rebellion and anarchy is a bunch of bullshit unless you've got a really headstrong philosophy toward change. What's to be there instead? I haven't really seen anybody eulogizing on any profound philosophical utopia which should be arrived at. I mean, we've all considered anarchy in our time, I'm sure, but sometimes it's more important to get to the grass roots and use the system for change. You've got to be realistic; you can't just wipe out everything that exists and expect a utopian existence to replace it. It just doesn't happen.

And I don't see how they can knock any of the forerunning bands, really. It's just the vogue. All of them seem to have traces of the Velvet Underground, Lou Reed, Who, bits of us, bits of this, bits of that... unless they all want to stop playing electric guitars entirely, they must realize it's all been done before them by somebody or another and they just ought to get on with the job at hand. I see its importance as bringing back neighborhood bands, and I think that's really good.

Everybody should have an attempt at doing something musically because it's such a joy to do, even if it's just banging a box along with some other people. You can get back to the old Victorian concept of "musical evenings," just people getting into music. That's the important thing. As far as the grace and the glamour of rock and roll goes, it changed after the demise of the Beatles, and took on a different shape. People are getting into lyrical content and instrumental virtuosity. I think the punks should just remember where they are and what they're doing, which is damn good, and try to realize that there's more to music and musical tastes than just one thing. ■

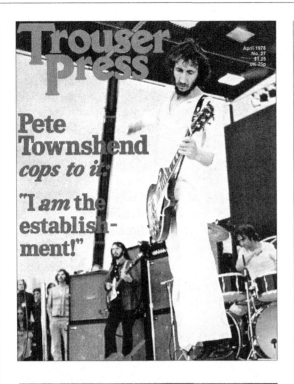

PETE TOWNSHEND

TP 27-28, APRIL-MAY 1978

By Dave Schulps

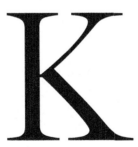

Karen Townshend answers the door wearing a puzzled look.

"Hello. I'm here to see Pete. We've got an interview scheduled for ten o'clock."

The puzzled look remains. "Pete was supposed to see you at his office."

"Well, you see..."

It's hardly an auspicious way to start a long

sought-after interview with Pete Townshend — an interview which became possible only when, after efforts through the normal channels had seemingly failed, a letter from Mr. T. himself arrived at *TP*'s doorstep, in which he agreed to an interview should we find our way to Britain in the near future. Now, I'm standing at the front door of his home in the London suburb of Twickenham trying to explain to his wife how a slight direction mix-up has landed me there instead of at his office in the nearby Meher Baba Oceanic Centre, where we're actually scheduled to meet. It's a slightly embarrassing introduction, but, after a couple of seconds' pause, she decides it's all right to let me in and asks me to have a seat while she goes upstairs to get Pete.

The house is located on the bank of the Thames directly across from Richmond, the Surrey town which was the center of the entire British R&B scene in the mid-'60s. It is quite modest, certainly not the opulent quarters one might expect from a rock star of Townshend's stature, although I'm told his weekend home at the seaside town of Goring is a bit more lavish. The downstairs area here consists of a rather normal-sized living room area — filled up, not with the usual furniture, but with synthesizers and other keyboards — and a kitchen. A pedal steel guitar greets you as the door swings open and, as I recall, is the only visible guitar, save for one hanging on the wall above the keyboards. In all, it is a decidedly unassuming abode, yet owns the kind of warmth and aging charm one would expect from a three-centuries-old English home.

Within a couple of minutes Pete Townshend stumbles downstairs. He obviously has not been awake for very long, but after a quick introduction he explains the real cause of his disheveled appearance: a night out drinking with Keith Moon at the Vortex, the London club which sets aside Monday and Tuesday nights for a continuous stream of punk bands. While Pete fixes a much-needed pot of coffee, we chat about the bands he had seen the night before — and he admits to having enjoyed nearly all of them. He also mentions having been asked by members of Generation X to produce their debut album, but obviously hasn't made a decision about it yet. All in all, he agrees, the scene over here is very healthy indeed, reminiscent perhaps of the bygone era which spawned the Who.

Ever since I started taking rock seriously, the Who have been my favorite band; or rather, when the Who became my favorite band, I started taking rock seriously — started thinking about it as more than just another form of entertainment, more than a couple of hours a day spent in the company of a radio or record player (I didn't have a "stereo" then). Pete Townshend was responsible for that. He approached rock not only as a musician but as a critic with a finely honed sense of what rock was, is and could be. Mainly, for me, he made it seem so very important. So, in a way, Townshend's vision of rock has very much helped put me where I am today and, yeah, shaped my life.

I'd go on more about what it's been like being a Who freak for the past decade, but I've neither the time nor the space. Suffice to say that I had only one hero as an adolescent and that this interview probably means more to me than you'd want to know.

When Townshend recently broke his public silence of over two years it seemed a good indication that something was once again astir in the Who camp. Townshend's last interview (the one that inspired a less than cordial rebuttal by Daltrey in another paper a few weeks later, thus leading to a long-term snub of the press) had taken place months before the release of *Who by Numbers*, a record which, more than any other Who album, could have stood an explanation from Townshend. From that time up until Townshend's *Rolling Stone* piece and his two recent interviews in connection with the *Rough Mix* album, there has been no communication at all between the Who and their public.

At long last, though, word started coming out as to the group's activities: the album they are currently recording, the *Kids Are Alright* film now in its cutting stages and some possible plans for future film projects. The *Rolling Stone* piece, if a bit vague and oddly oblique at times, at least let us know that Townshend had made it through his period of desperation and was ready to get down to business once again. In fact, after the interview today, he tells me, he'll be heading into the studio to do some more work on the album.

As we sit down and prepare to begin the interview, we are both wondering exactly what tack we're going to take in our discussion. In the letter in which he agreed to the interview, Townshend mentioned his interest in having us do something on his demos, perhaps sitting down and listening to all of them while he commented on each. This seemed like a great idea, and we were anxious to pursue it. Unfortunately, Pete says, the tapes are in his other house, and unless I'll be in London for a while longer, he won't be able to do it. As I'm leaving in a couple of days, it'll have to wait for a while. "I just thought it would be a drag if the first thing that *Trouser Press* actually did with me was just a hard-nosed interview. It would be nicer if it was more something special, something one wouldn't normally do with any other paper," Townshend offers as he sits down with me at a small wooden table by a window, coffee in hand.

As I look at my notebook, in which over the past week I've been scrawling out hundreds of questions and topics, I realize there's no way we'll be able to cover it all anyway, so I decide to abandon it entirely and instead ask one straightforward question, letting the discussion proceed from there. I figure the present is the best place to start.

What are the Who up to right now?

Townshend, rubbing his still half-asleep blue eyes, and trying to act as awake as one possibly can the morning after a night of boozing, replies: "We're recording; that's going very well. We've got the Jeff Stein film (*The Kids Are Alright*) on the board. We're also planning a revival of the *Lifehouse* film, which we're hoping will get moving in the middle of next year."

Lifehouse, for those unfamiliar with it, was a film project the Who were involved in back in 1970. It included a series of concerts before a small invited audience at the Young Vic theater in London. The idea was to create an interaction — through the intimacy of the theater and the familiarity of a returning audience — that would surpass anything that had come before it, creat-

66 I just find it so easy to make the clichéd noises.

ing a situation where not only would the audience feed off the band, but the band would feed off the audience.

Unfortunately, the project never shaped up quite right. Especially depressing to the Who were the results of the Young Vic shows, in which the audience refused to accept the all-new songs the Who were playing and called out mercilessly for old favorites. Those new songs, by the way, later went on to constitute most of *Who's Next* and Townshend's *Who Came First*.

Will this *Lifehouse* stick to the same concept as the original film?

"Roughly. What fell apart with it before was that I actually tried to make this fiction that I'd written happen in reality. That's where I went wrong, actually trying to make a perfect concept, whereas this time it'll be done like a film script."

Then he drops the bomb.

I ask about the persistent rumors that the Who don't want to play in America anymore.

"We don't want to play anywhere anymore."

I ask why.

"With the live gig thing I'd just reached a point where I don't really think — as things stand at the moment — that things are that promising for people who want to see the band, because basically we've been doing the same live act for such a long time now. We've had two albums worth of material which..." His sentence trails off. He begins again.

"I've always tried to make sure there was material which would work live, and [a lot of] it's never been used. *Quadrophenia* and *Who by Numbers* had a lot of raunchy material that never got on the stage. All that seemed to work was a couple of the old singles, the stuff from *Tommy*, a few rock and roll numbers and finish. That was the act we went out and did again and again and again. That was the act that we were acclaimed for. That was the list. And really it wasn't a list, it wasn't an act, it

wasn't a group, it wasn't anything. It was a fuckin' celebration of our history. I'm fed up of doing it.

"I'm as much a Who freak as any other Who freak, and I like what the band has done. I don't think there's anything as exciting as going into "My Generation" and seeing people go crazy, but after a while it's automatic. It's like being the Queen. People wave and shout just because you're there, they don't really care what you're doing. I've ceased trying to analyze that. I think that in itself it's a wonderful thing, but in the end, for somebody like myself, when you realize the price you have to pay emotionally — with your family and with everything else — to actually go and hawk your body on the road for six weeks at a stretch twice a year in the U.S.A., I don't think it really gets the right results anymore. I know it's going to make a lot of people angry. I've already had a lot of letters from kids that maybe haven't seen the band yet who are really pissed that we're not touring."

"That's probably why you've had to do the same act for so long," I suggest. "You get a new audience each tour in addition to the regulars."

Townshend looks up. His face seems older, more lined and careworn than I'd imagined it. He continues: "I don't think by any means that it's the audience's fault. I think what I've described is something weird that has happened to quite a lot of people. Maybe I've appeared to blame the audience, but I don't think that's really what it's all about. I think it's much more something that we've created. We've created a straitjacket of our own making."

Did he think that if the Who had gone on three or four years ago and refused to do the old material it would have gotten them out of it?

"I think it possibly could have, yeah. I think it would've stood for what we actually were at the time, as the records did. I mean, the weird thing is that *Who by Numbers* was an extremely effective record in putting across what was in my head at the time, and I think to some extent really what was happening to the band at the time. But, despite the fact that the record went out, people listened to it, people enjoyed it musically and people — some — were disturbed by the lyric content, nonetheless, when it came to going out and doing a gig, the Who went out and went" — he raises his arms and imitates a child making loud machine-gun-like noises — "nah-nah-nah-nah-nah. Same old stuff. Despite the fact that they'd already sort of done it all before. And in *Quadrophenia* as well, which we worked on for two years, we then went out and played *Tommy*."

I remind him that when the Who first performed *Quadrophenia* on stage they didn't do any of *Tommy* except "Pinball Wizard" and "See Me, Feel Me." Could it have just been a question of touring the States too soon after the album had come out, before the audience had a chance to get acquainted with it?

"With *Quadrophenia* we did tour too soon. *Quadrophenia* was an extremely slow album. In fact, it still hasn't sold very well in America to this day. It's a very good seller in this country because I think people are able to identify with it more, but it did very badly in America for a Who album. I think the answer is that we weren't prepared to work to gain our audiences' reactions. We wanted it instant and pat, and the way to do that is to go on and play something that they recognize, which whips people up immediately."

I mention how strange it seemed during that first *Quadrophenia* tour when he and Roger tried introducing the songs; nobody in the crowd seemed willing to pay attention.

Townshend was never very happy with the introductions. "I could never work out quite what was going on there. Roger thought that *Quadrophenia* wouldn't stand up unless you explained the story — and he's not the most verbose character. It was done sincerely, but I found it embarrassing, and I think it showed, so I was glad when we dropped it. I couldn't really work out what must be going on in the audience's mind when they were being told, 'There's this kid and he's just like you and me...' and then the music began; and

then, 'Then this kid he...' The whole thing was a disaster. Roger ended up hating *Quadrophenia* — probably 'cause it had bitten back."

"You must have been very disappointed," I speculate. "Here was this double album you'd worked on for two years that you couldn't even do on stage."

"Well, I suppose with that album, and with *Who's Next* as well, I was disappointed by the lack of good stage material to come out of it. When we went to rehearse *Tommy*, we went to some little rehearsal hall in Southall and ran through the whole album, everything on it; it all felt great, we couldn't believe it. *Quadrophenia* didn't work that way. Neither did *Who's Next*; just a couple of tracks came out of it. They were recording studio efforts, whereas the amazing thing about *Tommy* was that it was very organic, very simple, very pure, and it did work very well on stage."

HE PAUSES. Having finished his coffee, he picks an orange from a bowl of fruit sitting on the table and begins to roll it around in his hands. His mind seems to wander for a few seconds, but he returns to explaining his lack of desire to continue touring.

"It may seem, in a sense, that I'm groping for a reason, but there are a lot of other reasons. As I sit here now my ears are screaming." He puts his hands on his ears and notes sadly, "I've really fucked my hearing completely.

"The other thing is that, to some extent, I've fucked a lot of other things for the Who tours and I'm just not going to do it anymore. It's as simple as that. I can't really give rational reasons. It's not because I don't enjoy it, not because I don't think it's fantastic, not because I'm bitter, it's got nothing to do with that. You've got to draw a line somehow, and I think that what would be awful would be if the Who did just crash on and on and on until they became seedy and plastic. I think the trouble is that we're in a rut which is just so bloody deep that you couldn't step out of it easily. I don't think it's a nasty rut, a rut like a nine-to-five office job or anything, but I mean as far as stage material goes Keith has actually had his list of numbers printed on one of his drums. That's the list that we use. It hasn't been altered for the last two years.

"I think I'll miss it terribly. I think I'll miss playing with the band on the road, I'll miss live appearances, I'll miss the contact; but for me it was starting to become very much a non-event anyway. I'd almost prefer to stand with a guitar in the pub up the street."

Has he ever done anything like that?

"No, I haven't, 'cause I wouldn't."

Why's that?

"I dunno," he smirks. "Perhaps I'm not that desperate yet."

"What about the group?" I wonder. "Let's say you've given up live performances, what's in store for the future of the Who?"

"Up to a couple of months ago we didn't even know we had a future," he admits. "I thought the only way I was going to get off the road was to leave the band. I thought what would happen is: We'll do an album, we'll go in, [Who manager] Bill Curbishley will book a tour and I, like a puppy with a Pavlov bell ringing in my head, will get on the airplane and go. So, I said to Bill, 'The only way I'm going to get around it is to quit. I'll get me demos together, put out an album of my own and leave it at that.'

"Then I spoke to Roger. And it was amazing because he felt the same way I did. I couldn't really believe it. I was expecting him to be in accord with me to some degree, but I didn't expect him to be quite so sympathetic. Not only to me as a human being, but also on his account. He felt very similarly to the way I did."

I wondered if this was the incident Townshend described in the *Rolling Stone* piece.

"No, this happened quite recently; two months ago. We sat down and I said, 'Listen, I'm not up to doing any more tours, etc., etc.' Roger said, 'I feel the same way.' John's face fell because John loves touring. And Keith, believe it or not, also was quite pleased. He'd been getting incredibly nervous and that had partially been the cause of his emotional problems that had led him on to drinks and drugs — he was getting so hyped up over concerts.

"Keith's a funny guy," Townshend says, his voice revealing a great deal of warmth toward the subject. "On the outside he's all brash and confi-dent, but when he goes onstage to a Who concert he's often sick as he climbs up the stairs. Sick with fright."

"How is he doing these days?" I ask, having heard rumors of the aforementioned drinks and drugs.

"I was with him last night and he was still here. He was dressed in a dinner jacket down at the Vortex." He laughs loudly, then returns to explaining how the Who stuck together.

"We ended up with, I suppose, a choice as to whether to let everything slide or to carry on. I felt very, very strongly that I wanted the band to continue if possible as a working unit and to confront head-on what it was really supposed to be doing at this point. We were more now than just a rock and roll band, we were — are — probably the only group in the world capable of being both a rock and roll band and raising seven million dollars to make a film by snapping our fingers. And so, I felt that we should be making a film. I thought, too, that the Who are really the only band that's lasted with any kind of integrity whatsoever."

How does he define integrity?

"Well, having a track record, to use a hackneyed phrase, which is pretty clean. We haven't made too many of the obvious mistakes. Nobody has killed themselves off with dope, nobody has done anything wildly dishonest, nobody has killed anybody [he laughs]. We never put out what I feel was a dishonest record, we've never deliberately gone out to exploit large numbers of people, we've toured and worked hard whenever we could. Perhaps the only thing we've done wrong is focusing too much on America and not enough here. Really, that's because America to me is the workplace. I tend to think of Britain as the control room and America as the studio.

"Anyway, I rate the band and its past pretty highly. I feel maybe we should try to prove to people and to new bands — particularly since the new wave bands are so assertive in their attitudes — that it is possible to grow within the rock business; to grow old gracefully and to evolve in a way that doesn't lose the spirit of things. One constant criticism of successfully established bands by younger up-and-coming groups — especially new

Boardrooms and business meetings are a big part of our life now.

wave groups — is that they have not been putting money back into the industry that gave them their enormous takings, that they've been content to take the money and run, to become tax exiles."

The Who have certainly escaped this kind of criticism, but I wondered about Pete's feelings on putting money back into the business.

"I think it's weird, really, because ... well, I don't want to end up talking about tax, but ... the only way you can avoid giving your money away to tax people is to pour it back. If you pour it back, it's acknowledged as an investment back into the business. Just as if you were making doorknobs and you went to the tax people at the end of the year and you said, 'I've got $50,000 profit but I don't want to pay tax, what I'd like to do is put it into an investment program.' It's allowed. This is really what prompts us to put the enormous amounts of money that were earned on the *Tommy* film into Shepperton, into new bands, into record labels and things like that. To some extent, it's not necessarily what we really want to do."

What do they really want to do?

"I think we really want to work. Record and continue to communicate. There's part of me that really still wants to go crashing around on the road, but I just don't think it's on. Boardrooms and business meetings are a big part of our life now, like it or not, because that is what the responsibility is all about: not doing what we want, but doing what is necessary. I think when people say that money should be poured back — when a young guy says, 'When I get rich and famous, I'm gonna pour my money back into the industry' — what they don't realize is that it's no good just getting the money and throwing it somewhere; you've got to be responsible for it, you've got to do something with it. Money on its own doesn't do anything; you've got to make it work."

I suggest that certain things can obviously be done, such as rehearsal halls for young bands who can't afford them.

"Yeah, I've got one. The only trouble is that one rehearsal hall is packed solid all the time. I'm building another one down at Shepperton. Myself, not the group. That'll probably be snapped up just as fast. We don't charge the bands that come and work. I don't know, I don't think the rehearsal hall is the most important thing. The most important thing is that when a band is ready there should be someone to guide them."

He uses, as an example, John Otway and Wild Willy Barrett. Four years ago, Townshend produced some tracks for Otway, then totally unknown except in his home of Aylesbury. Townshend was even able to talk Track Records into putting two of the tracks out as a single, but it was not pushed at all and died an immediate death. Last year, Otway (with Barrett) reemerged via an album that he had pressed himself and was selling mail order from his home. The album got such good reviews and sold so well that Polydor became interested and picked up the rights to distribute it. They released a single from it, "Cor Baby That's Really Free!," which made the Top 30 in the UK charts. Otway was heralded as a genius by many members of the press here as well.

"Look at the scrubbing and scrapping that they've been through," Pete says. "It's partly the public who didn't have the sense to see that Otway was a genius and has been a genius for the last few years. He hasn't changed in my mind since I first met him. I can see. I can look at a man like that and know that he's good." His voice rises querulously. "Why can't anybody else?" he chuckles.

"It's rock and roll. Either somebody has got it, or they haven't. It's not something you debate; if somebody is it, they are it. It's not whether they're good or bad, they're either rock and roll or they're not, and he is. So, eventually he's going to do something marvelous. That's the way I felt years ago," he smiles. "And I'm still crowing about it to some extent.

"What I'm getting at is that when that moment comes — this is the important part of any band's career — then what they need is guidance, the kind of guidance we had from Kit Lambert, the kind the Stones had from Andrew Oldham. Behind every band is some sort of mentor figure, some Svengali. This is the thing. That can't be provided without love, care and full-time attention. At the moment, John Otway manages himself. He sends out newsletters to all his fans and stuff. He's got a Polydor deal, but how his career goes from now is in the hands of the gods."

WHAT DOES HE THINK of the veritable explosion of new bands on the scene right now?

"I think it's incredibly exciting, I must admit. I feel in perspective again. It's great. We get letters constantly from kids who say, "I'm in a band and blah, blah, blah." I must have a thousand letters from kids in groups sending me tapes and things like that. And a lot of them are really amazing. Their attitudes are amazing, you know: "We're gonna make it..." Of course, they never do. But what's nice now is to see that people are realizing that you don't have to "make it." You don't have to make anything. You either are it or you're not. You make your own scene. This is what's happened in this country. A whole scene has developed from in and around. In a sense, there's enough new bands to not only entertain one another, but also to be one another's audience. Down at the Vortex last night everybody was in a band."

I mention that musically the young bands I've seen here in England seem to be developing at an incredible rate. Townshend shrugs, not in disagreement but in a gesture that says he's not concerned.

"I must admit that I like the basic starting point. It's where we started exactly. They make exactly the same noise we used to make, and so, for my money, practically every record I put on I love. I love the noise of it. I like the use of the English accent a lot because it's comical but it's also ferocious."

"And more honest," I add.

"Yeah, it's more honest, really. It's a bit difficult to sing in an English accent, though; sometimes it's more contrived than you'd think. I suppose it's because for so many years we've lapsed into the American accent to sing that it just feels natural that way."

The discussion moves to the area of Townshend's own musical evolution, particularly the noticeable movement on *Rough Mix* away from straight-ahead rock and roll into more subtle but equally powerful stuff like "Street in the City" (on which Townshend is, for the first time on record, accompanied by a full orchestra). Pete continues playing with his orange as he expounds on the subject.

"I just find it so easy to make the clichéd noises. I can do it in my sleep. I just know the Who can play the Who's type of rock and roll better than anybody else. We can do it very easily, and as a result it tends to fall off the end of the guitar without any strain; also, without any real care somehow, because we're not really testing ourselves, stretching ourselves. I've stopped being afraid of parodying myself, becoming a caricature — these rich clichés I invented five years ago. Actually, Tommy Smothers invented that. He said to me, 'It's very weird what being on TV every week does to you.' When I asked him what he meant he said, 'Week after week I sit and watch myself. I study my face, I study my actions, I study what I say, and then I edit it mentally, remove everything I don't like and keep everything I like. In the end I'm an increasingly evolving, edited version of what I think is best about me. I've ended up being a copy of myself.'"

But, Pete, isn't that how any artist evolves?

"I suppose so, but I'm fairly keen to keep away from that. That's why I like working with Glyn Johns in the studio. He's got an incredibly open mind, and he's always on the alert to do something new. He knows that the easy way to pep up a particular passage of a song is for Keith to go blam-blam-blam-blam-boom-boom-boom and for me to go takka-takka-ta and for Roger to scream his primal scream. If we did that on every track it would be a bit pat."

Suddenly and very humorously, Pete blurts

out an admission. "Christ! My breath is on fire! I must've drunk about four pints of vodka last night." He excuses himself and gets up to brush his teeth, while I use the opportunity to turn my tape over.

I REMEMBER A QUESTION I'd been meaning to ask him. "You've spoken more about the meaning of rock and roll than almost anyone else around," I start. "What does rock and roll mean to you now?"

"The theory of rock and roll? What it is and whatever? I still think I'm one of the few people who really knows what it is, but I think there's a lot of people now who are learning. It's been around long enough in its current form for people to know what it is. When I talk about rock and roll, I'm only talking from my vantage point. I don't speak as a journalist, I don't write as a journalist, I don't write as a composer. When it actually comes to the moment where you sit down and somebody asks you a question like this, you try to answer from feeling like you've got some authority on the subject. Rock is not definable, really. Without becoming maudlin, rock is really very much a reflection on life like anything else.

"Look at everything. If you look at the ocean you can draw a parallel with everything else, with God; if you look at a leaf you can see the whole cosmos in it. I think, funnily enough, rock has now become society. It started off being an alternative, an expression of a new society, and now it is society, it is you and me. I'm in my thirties, I'm not only part of the establishment, I *am* the establishment. I *am* this country. People come to me to get money for their charities, people come to me to do this or that. It's a strange feeling, but that's what rock is.

"I've always known that rock would do it. I'm not talking from a money point of view; I'm talking about the fact that it would eventually take over. What we do with it now I don't know. We've demanded the responsibility, we've screamed out for it, we've accused, we've attacked, we've criticized, we've said, 'You've never done it right, you're all fuckin' wrong, we could do it better.' Now we have the chance.

"I'm not saying we're politicians, although Roger has said that we will all inevitably become so someday. I think there's a lot of potential truth to that, actually, but I think we're definitely part of the establishment and can't wiggle out of it now."

I mention that Britain seems extremely politicized right now. Everyone over here seems to be talking politics in one way or another, especially the young bands. In many ways, to an American it feels like slipping back ten years in time.

"I think a lot of the punk bands are a lot more political than I am; because I think politics is trite. I don't think politics has anything to do with anything. I think it's a game. It's like religion, which has nothing to do with God; it's very, very necessary, unfortunately, to large amounts of the population. How South America would manage without candles, I don't know. That's a nasty thing to say; I don't really mean it in that sense. I mean that Roman Catholicism holds South America together by giving simple people a connection with something grand, rich and beautiful. But does it really deal with spirituality? Does it really help them? Does it improve them or does it just make their week a bit more bearable? In the same breath, do politicians — though they organize to get the roads swept, which somebody has to do — actually improve the country and the way we live?"

Doesn't he think, then, in that sense, that rock and roll has failed?

"No, because now it's got its chance. The Who are one of the first — we're probably in the mainstream, aren't we? — to last enough time to make a lot of money, to have the ability to become part of the establishment. Plus, the fact that we've still — up to quite recently — been doing road work; we're in close connection with our fans, have a tremendous amount of direct feedback; we know what's going on in the streets; and suddenly we're there. We're a rock and roll band that's in the midst of society with the ability to change things. What do we do? Do we do it within the capitalist framework? Do we try to initiate a revolution? Do we have ourselves crucified? What do we do? That's really what we're saying now: 'What do we do?' We've asked for it, we've gotten it and we've got to do something about it.

"This is what I was saying about a lot of the punk bands. They really do care about what the Who do. They don't necessarily love our music or feel they'd die without it, that they couldn't carry on without it. They've created something which exists within itself, that takes our music and other bands like us as its basic roots. But there the similarity ends because this is '78, not '63."

In 1971, though, you said, "Meet the new boss, same as the old boss." Was that meant to be about yourselves?

"I don't like to try to explain 'Won't Get Fooled Again.' That song grows old quite gracefully — like 'My Generation.' I don't know. I think that if we can manage another couple of years and still maintain our integrity and honesty, we'll be over the hump. Then we can all look back and see whether or not rock and roll has been properly manifested and, rather than just being words, has become real life.

"It's easy to sit and write songs. You can write anything, you can say anything, you can do anything. The Who are on stage singing 'See Me, Feel Me,' then 15 minutes later they're smashing a hotel room to bits. Not that I care about inanimate objects. I suppose I care about the effect it has on the cleaning lady when she comes in the next day — the deep shock, the abhorrence, the horror, the fear it creates. I certainly don't attach any importance to a lump of wood known as a guitar, or a piece of plaster known as a lamp; on the other hand, I know the effects go much deeper than that.

"When I was talking about the Who's integrity, I think we've come through on a razor's edge, because we could have made terrible, terrible mistakes. There have been a lot of occasions where any one of us could've killed somebody, there were a lot of occasions when we could have easily been killed or easily have been part of a nasty drug scene. But we haven't, and we've been very lucky. Very, very lucky. And we're lucky to be together today, to be the same four blokes we always were. Because when you've known and worked with four people for 15 years, in the end you've got a power no one else can get unless they wait 15 years."

THE DOG BARKS.

"Shaddup," yells Pete. Then he slaps his leg, and Towser the dog comes running over. "Do you want to go out?" Pete asks, getting up to open the door which leads from the kitchen to the yard.

We're about halfway through what has turned from being a straight "question-answer" interview into a fairly freewheeling discussion on various and sundry Who- and Townshend-related topics.

"When I was doing the *Rough Mix* album with Ronnie Lane," he begins after sitting down once again, "Eric [Clapton] was sitting there one day and he said, 'You know, Pete, you're a lucky bastard having a band ... just having a band. All I've got is me.' I was startled. 'You've got a great band at the moment,' I said. But, he said, 'They're a band, they feel like a band; but it's like me *and* a band, I'm not part of a band.'" From Townshend's face, I could tell he understood.

I say that it amazes me that, while the idea of "groups" provides so much of the dynamic of rock and roll, so few have been able to survive intact for more than a few years. Townshend shakes his head. "I don't think it's amazing so few have survived, I think it's amazing that *we* have. I think it's the most natural thing in the world these days to separate, for people to do what they want rather than knuckle down, to compromise, to fit in with someone else."

Does he, then, consider himself old-fashioned?

"Yes," he replies without hesitation, "very old-fashioned. Yet to me it's more what rock is about than smacking cocaine up your nose, playing with whoever happens to be there at the time and fuck everybody else. In a sense, that's why I place such great weight on the Who. It's because I don't have much faith in the rest of the fucking music business. I wonder, what are they actually up to? Do they live on this planet? Sometimes I wonder if they do...

"For instance," he continues, "I think the Stones' *Love You Live* is magnificent, but I've got absolutely no faith in the Stones to do anything other than to just produce the occasional magnificent album. I'm really glad they did that album, though I don't think they'll get any thanks for

> **"I don't want to spend the rest of my life in fucking mud, smoking fucking marijuana. If that's the American dream, let us have our fucking money and piss off back to Shepherd's Bush, where people are people.'**

it. I don't think anybody realizes how long they struggled to get that live album together. There was a time in London where every studio you went in was full to the ceiling with live Rolling Stones concert tapes ... then Jagger would walk in bleary-eyed and start listening to them. Hundreds of hours of tapes.

"But apart from that — great album, great to hear them doing it — there's fuckin' Keith Richards in jail. That's what's happened to so many of them, they've either gone and been killed off, or its soppy brother..." His voice trails off.

Has being in a group been important to his own survival, then?

"Oh yeah," he answers with certainty, "I think what a lot of people probably don't realize about working in a group is that you've got a basis for learning all of life's hardest lessons very rapidly. In other words, you say, 'I think we should do such and such a thing,' and everybody says, 'Nonsense, we're going to do such and such a thing.' The first thing you realize is that if you want to do what you want to do you've got a choice: either you're going to fight like hell to get it done — convince the people you're working with that it's right or demonstrate that it's right — which is why I always do demos, or, alternatively, you can run away and do it on your own. In a group you

learn the art of compromise, you learn the art of diplomacy; I think most of all you learn the art of caring about other people's opinions. Whether you like it or not, you have to care about other people's opinions, otherwise you're not going to get anywhere. In a way, working in a group is like" — he searches for words — "well, it's the way God planned it, isn't it? You put people together and you get chemistry, you get experience.

"I feel we've had a very special and unique experience having been a group of people that hasn't been a football team or working in an office or making doorknobs — I always say doorknobs because our first manager made doorknobs — but we've been a successful rock and roll band as a group, so our experiences have been unique. I can't imagine what kind of person I'd be had I not done all the things I've done with the Who. When I look back on the last ten years, the important experiences seem mainly to be Who experiences — the important lessons — despite the fact that I have an amazing and powerful conviction toward Meher Baba. It seems that, despite that, all my philosophical decisions have been made from experiences with the Who. All I've really ever felt for Meher Baba is this overpowering feeling of love, but I've never actually gotten experience. Experience I've gotten on the street with the Who.

"What I'm driving at is a bit gratuitous in a way. I think it's common knowledge that living with somebody, getting married, if you like, is not just a convenient way to live, it's also a very natural human thing to pledge yourself to another person. Suddenly, when you realize the beauty of marriage — and I'm old-fashioned enough to say this and mean it — I hate the way marriage is played down today. I don't think marriage is anything where anybody gains anything, I think both people lose equally. Then you get a marriage that works, if both individuals feel they're doing all the work. In the Who, every one of us feels we're doing all the work. Every one of us feels we've got the weight of the band on our shoulders. So, every one of us is putting in 100 percent, or maybe a little bit more than that. That's how you get an effective unit. This is what's great about working with a group of people. As you share devastating experiences and exhilarating experiences, like standing on a stage in front of 60,000 kids all cheering you, you can look at the other person and know there's someone else there who knows what it feels like.

"On the other hand, there's the other thing ... like being marooned at Saskatoon Airport in the snow for three days. You know that all you need to do is turn around to one of the guys in the band, say 'Saskatoon' and they'll crack up. You start to develop a quality of intimacy which you can't get anywhere else outside a family."

Does he feel that the feeling of family and community that seemed to permeate rock in the '60s has been all but lost in the '70s? Has rock failed in this way?

"All those feelings are transitory anyway," he posits. "I remember at *Woodstock,* people were so appalled when the Who asked for their money — having just traveled 7,000 miles to get there. I said to some guy, 'Listen, this is the fucking American dream, it's not my dream. I don't want to spend the rest of my life in fucking mud, smoking fucking marijuana. If that's the American dream, let us have our fucking money and piss off back to Shepherd's Bush, where people are people.'

"I think that was the big mistake. Rock started celebrating itself too soon. I think this gets back to what I was saying before, that there are very few people in a position to prove that we're not just a bunch of big-mouthed gits who criticize everything in sight, that we're now in a position to actually do something about it — that we're adults. Our generation is now doctors and lawyers, schoolteachers and psychologists, even politicians. Now is the time people can actually do something to make their words good. When you ask has rock failed, the answer is that its aspirations haven't yet been reached. But its aspirations have been very fuzzy around the edges to me because they've been so negative some of the time. Rock's been so destructive and continues to be. The punk movement seems to be destructive by nature. It seems to be important that it destroys first in order to build — it's using that old standard — so that one doesn't get a compound thing. You don't get the value of experience, the value

of a build-up of social intercourse. There are no textbooks about rock and roll, we haven't got libraries, but they're starting in a way.

"Music has unified a whole group of people. I still think it's one of the greatest single things to ever have happened in the world. Really, I do. I think it's something that's shared; people that are interested in it, that love it, that listen to it, that play it, that write it are a different breed. They just are. There's just something I immediately have in common with them and I can count on it not just being a common interest musically but socially. It doesn't matter whether they come from Czechoslovakia, Japan, Australia, France, Germany or America; if they're into rock and roll their social conscience is going to be similar. That's all right by me, because if, at the moment, all the rock social conscience has created is a lot of people that said, 'We failed,' at least we're bloody admitting that we failed to do something we set out to do. At least we're aware of that rather than just sitting there and festering, rather than creating wars and blowing one another's heads off.

"I've always felt that one of the most tragic things about rock is that it isn't bigger. If you take the world population, then take all the people who buy rock records, I think you come to a modest little clique.

"I don't think it's down to the whole clique, though. I don't think it's fair to expect kids on the street to be able to change society. They can change themselves, but not society. What I'm driving at is that bands like the Who are now rapidly coming into a position where they're actually physically able to change society. The responsibility has finally arrived."

Does he feel a greater responsibility now than ever before?

"I've always felt a great deal of responsibility. I feel now it's just more practical to feel it. If somebody knocked on the door in 1967 and said, 'We run a boy's club that's doing great things in our neighborhood where there have been 14 murders. Since we have been running it, the kids have been coming and playing snooker and billiards but ... we need a disco,' we would have said [in a teasing, snotty and blasé tone], 'Oh really, how sad.' Today we can give them one. We decide what we do. That's just one example.

"I think if we can go on organizing ourselves so we can stand really close scrutiny; if somebody came in to pick us to pieces and said, 'OK, you wrote "My Generation," now what are you doing?' we could take them in and show them every aspect of what we've done and hopefully wouldn't find any flaws. Then we've achieved something, if only by example.

"I don't want to change the world," he says adamantly. "If Britain was a communist country, I wouldn't want to make it capitalist, and as it's a capitalist country, I don't particularly want to make it communist."

What if it were a dictatorship?

"I don't know. It depends what kind," he replies.

"Let's say fascist," I counter. "People are beginning to think it could happen here."

Townshend dismisses the notion. "Bah. Roger's always screaming about how the fascists will take over the country. They won't take over. They'll try. Let's face it, come on, the whole of Britain rose up against fascism. And the weird thing then was that fascism had been quite an acceptable thing in this country under Oswald Mosley. My father was saying that, as a 16-year-old kid at school, they used to play fascists; they used to goose-step down the street. Then the war broke out and everybody knew it was a thing to fight."

That's what's so scary, I remark. Wouldn't you think that people now know it? The war wasn't that long ago.

He pauses. "I think people do know it's a thing to fight. I don't think there are any wars coming; I don't think there are any nuclear holocausts coming. I don't think we're going to be that lucky. I think it might draw people together. I think if you could have a war without the senseless death, it might be good. It would bring people together. The last war gave the country a sense of community, of togetherness; we knew who our friends were. In the last analysis, America came and helped us. We also were able to demonstrate our care and love for our neighbor countries. But I don't think there will ever be a nuclear war. There will be little brushfire wars as in Vietnam and Israel, but — and maybe not in our lifetimes — I think things will end up peacefully."

FINALLY, HE RETURNS to the more mundane subject of rock and roll and its place in the grand scheme of things.

"Anyway, I think rock and roll is extremely small, and I think the Who are a very small part of rock and roll. As such we can only do our little bit. But I think it's important and it's important to be optimistic."

Has he always been this optimistic?

Townshend thinks for a second before replying. "I've always been optimistic about life. I've not always been optimistic about my role in it."

He adopts a jokingly didactic tone, as if imitating some age-old sage handing down advice. "You see, I've learnt a few very simple lessons in the past couple of years. One is that I would not be able to carry on working in the band or even — I suppose it sounds a bit melodramatic — living without my wife. I've always known that I loved her, but what I really didn't realize was that I needed her so implicitly. Of course, I didn't realize this until she walked out on me one day. Then I thought 'Well, this is it. The crunch has come. Victim of a show-business romance. Divorce number 4,589.' He imitates a newscaster: 'Pete Townshend's second wife said...' flashed through my mind; I thought, 'Well, fuck that,' and I just crumbled in a heap. It was a bloody shock, because I thought I'd be able to carry on, thought I was a complete person. I thought my wife needed me, not the other way around.

"That was one simple lesson. That's a form of ignorance, which leads to evil, which leads to lack of respect for the institution of marriage such as it is, which has existed four thousand years longer than I have, yet I chose to fuck around with it.

"I suppose the other simple lesson is that when I thought the only way to change life in the Who was to walk away from it, I actually realized that the guys in the band were very sympathetic to my problems, weren't over-anxious to force a compromise, loved me and were prepared to do whatever was necessary to keep me happy. And that was a fucking shock, because I've always regarded the Who as a bit of an enemy — I mean in a business sense, like when it comes to a tour — the way you regard your work as an enemy. Then suddenly it turns around on you and becomes the exact opposite. That's why the early part of this year I stopped talking about the Who as 'the Who' and started to talk about 'my band,' stopped talking about Daltrey, Moon and Entwistle and started talking about three people who I really do feel are friends. Quite how they feel about it I don't know; I think each person in the band oscillates, but I must admit I feel a damn sight closer to them now as people than I ever have."

Did this revelation about the Who come after *Who by Numbers*?

"Oh yeah."

Were certain songs on that album meant to cry out to the band in any way?

"To some extent. I think it was just me whining about certain things. I've never felt it's wrong for a man to cry, anymore than — I was going to say something chauvinistic, but I won't. You have to double think, don't you, make sure you're not sexist: 'My Baby Gives It Away.'"

That song, along with "Squeeze Box," seems so incredibly chauvinist. Did he intend them as jokes?

"No. That's what I was about to say. I'm not conscious, I don't sit and work out stances, I just write. This is the thing. Half the time I don't know what I'm doing until I've done it — that's why it's honest."

Does he ever regret writing that way afterwards?

Again, he answers negatively. "How can you regret anything when you've got no choice in the matter?"

I suggest he has the option not to use material he's written.

"Often that's not even my choice either, as regards material with the group, or when one publishes an article like the one I did in *Rolling Stone*, or things like that. I mean, I regretted that article to a great extent, but I still put it out because the process had been initiated and I thought I might as well do it. In a sense, it was sort of a journalistic

Who by Numbers — two years after the event."

But a little more optimistic, I add.

"Yeah, a little more. In the case of 'Squeeze Box,' that was supposed to be a funny song. It came from hearing somebody referring to a woman's tits as a 'squeeze box.' A squeeze box to me had always been an accordion, and I just wrote that little rhyme about it.

"I'm sexist to the extent that I" — he pauses and then bursts out with the end of his sentence — "love tits, and love women practically to the extent of being unstable on the issue, like a lot of men are. I just can't repress it; I just can't hold it back. It's not because I want to put them into a corner, they can do whatever they like. They can mother me or dominate me, or I can mother them and dominate them. I don't care, just as long as I can get it out of them.

"I dunno. Take 'My Baby Gives It Away.' That's actually a song about my old lady, and she didn't think it was sexist; she was the first person I played it to. I suppose it was a song about me. About my realizing what idiots men really are for chasing after what they have in their own backyard; chasing after trouble; chasing after wounding relationships; hurting people. Of course, women are half to blame for that as well."

He laughs. "I think maybe you don't realize until you're getting to the point where you begin to think you might be past it. You start to think about what is wound up in a casual affair, a quick one-night job with some bird in some hotel room. What is it? What does it mean? The spiritual ramifications are one thing, your own moral values are another. It's a declaration of mistrust but, most of all, most important, is that, for the sake of a physical thing, you're going into another human being, becoming enmeshed with them and then tearing yourself away." He demonstrates by clasping his hands together and slowly, painfully, tearing them apart. "It's just the craziest thing to go around doing — crashing into things, literally. It doesn't detract from the beauty of the experience or from the joy of sex as God bloody handed it down. It's just that, well, teenage promiscuity is one thing — experimentation — but when you get to be 22, 23, 24, by that time if you haven't got your shit together, forget it.

"'My Baby Gives It Away' is really about that. I suppose it is openly sexist, but it's not a self-conscious statement. It's sexist in that it says, 'I am a married man, and my old lady loves me enough to let me have it when I want it.' Which is a bloody lie." He laughs heartily.

I comment that he had written a few songs about women early in the Who's career, before there even was a well-organized women's movement. "Glow Girl" was the original setting of the *Tommy* theme: "It's a girl, Mrs. Walker, it's a girl..." "Join My Gang" was about a guy asking a girl into his clique, a move he reckons will "shake the world"; this 1966 song was recorded only by a guy called Oscar [*Paul Nicholas*].

Townshend shrugs, dismissing any hint that he was ahead of his time. "'Join My Gang' was a self-conscious thing. The reason the Who never did it was because it was very much an exercise. You know who used to rave about that song? David Bowie. He actually heard it in the publishing office before he was a big star — he used to work in an office that had a lot of my stuff then.

"I've had great difficulty writing about relationships, period. I still find it difficult to even mention the word 'love' in a song. I think it's a symptom of maturity — I like to talk about maturity as if it were a disease; a symptom of maturity — when you start writing love songs. Rock and roll to me has never been about love, it's been about care. I think the two things are different. I don't like to see the word 'love' bandied about; I think it's a very misused word."

He digresses. "Love. Adi Irani, who was Meher Baba's secretary and has been to England a few times and stayed at Oceanic [Townshend's Meher Baba Centre in Twickenham] — he's a great guy — was asked the difference between the various forms of love. One person thinks love is screwing in the back seat of a car, another thinks it's divine drops of water from heaven. He said that if you think of love as being like an ocean, a limitless ocean of, let's say, water; then lust is like water in a gutter, love between man and woman is beer, if you like; love from man to God is like milk; and love from God to man is like wine. There are

degrees in everything.

"This is something that I find very hard to express in rock songs. I find that the easiest thing to do is just to get mad. You know what I mean? Because there's always something to get mad about. I find that the hardest thing for me to do as a writer is to express optimism, general warmth and a feeling of good will to all men in a song. It feels trite, and I hate it. That song, 'I love every minute of the day' ["Blue Red and Grey"] on *Who by Numbers*, is a prime example. Glyn Johns wanted it on the album; I cringed when he picked it. He heard it on a cassette and said, 'What's that?' I said 'nothing.' He said, 'No. Play it.' I said, 'Really, it's nothing. Just me playing a ukulele.' But he insisted on doing it. I said 'What? That fucking thing? Here's me, wanting to commit suicide, and you're going to put that thing on the record.'"

Most people's initial impression of "Blue Red and Grey," I tell him, given its context, was that he was just being ironic, tongue-in-cheek.

He shrugs. "It's a bit weird, actually. It definitely doesn't fit into the *Who by Numbers* concept as described by Dave Marsh. He said it was the Who's first concept album. I like Dave Marsh, actually, he's a good bloke, but he takes rock *so* seriously." Isn't that a symptom of rock journalism?

"I think it's a problem of a lot of people who buy records, too. Because if it is life — our little chunk of life — well, you should treat life with respect, but you shouldn't be pompously serious about it."

In defense of us scribes, I suggest that we're probably just a bunch of people who take life too seriously — which is what sparks us to write in the first place.

"On the other hand," Townshend asks, "why the chemistry of putting on a record and going bananas?"

Probably to get out of it, I suggest.

"It's weird, isn't it," he says, and then gives the best definition of a rock record I've ever heard. "It's a black plastic thing you buy, and you can put it on and it clicks your social conscience — makes you think about the world, makes you think about life — and then makes you dance to forget about it."

DALTREY'S SIDE: "NOT SO FAST, PETE"

Pete Townshend's pronouncement that he does not want to tour anymore may come as a bit of a shock to Who fans hoping to see the band (again) in the future. You can put stock, though, in the fact that things are subject to change — especially with the Who.

Townshend himself prefaced his remarks with "as things stand at the moment," an indication of the possibility of a change in heart. Then there is this conversation with Roger Daltrey which took place stage-side at London's Gaumont State Theatre, where the Who were filming live footage for the upcoming *Kids Are Alright* film the day after I interviewed Townshend.

Daltrey, friendly and effusive, approached me during a break in the activity and began talking about the Who's laser show, which was being filmed that day for the movie. After a short chat about lasers and holograms (for which Daltrey expressed a particular fascination), he asked me what I thought of the tracks from the new album I'd heard in the studio the day before.

I mentioned that I thought it sounded a lot more cheerful than their last one (as if anything could sound less cheerful than *Who by Numbers*). "Yeah," he exclaimed, "but I love that album. I listen to it all the time. Maybe you've got to reach a certain age to appreciate it. I didn't like it when it was written. I argued a lot with Pete over it, but I've been through what he describes now, and I understand what he was writing about." The new album, he said, is "incredible. Pete's still the best writer there is. I mean, the new wave's given everybody a kick in the ass" — it was incredible to see Townshend, Daltrey and Entwistle sitting around the studio discussing what Paul Weller of the Jam was doing — "but this is amazing; it's got so much."

His next statement took me by surprise.

"I can't wait to get back on stage again," he said, almost bouncing on the floorboards of this stage.

"You're planning to go back on tour?" I asked.

"Every time I get out on a stage I want to go back. That's what rock's about, especially the 'Oo. Pete has bad problems with his ears, it's true, but we all want to go back. We'll work on him."

I mentioned I was glad to hear that the Who were finally going to get to do the *Lifehouse* film (after our interview, Pete told me they had already secured seven million dollars to make the film, and that either Nicholas Roeg or Alan Parker would probably direct it). Daltrey, however, didn't think it was going to happen:

"I don't think we're actually going to do it," he said. "The story's not really strong enough for a major film. *Tommy* was a bit naïve, but we want to follow it up with something a bit stronger. Maybe we'll buy the rights to a classic." ∎

WHO IN ACTION! GIG! FILM! RECORD!

TP 26, FEBRUARY 1978

By Dave Schulps in London

DECEMBER 13: From the outside it's not very impressive: an unassuming brick building in Battersea, a tough working-class neighborhood which stretches along the south bank of the Thames. There are no signs offering the identity of the building or its occupants; no indication at all of what is going on inside.

The building is, in fact, the recording facility owned and operated by the Who, and inside the Who are in the midst of working on their new and, as usual, long overdue LP.

Inside the control room, producer Glyn Johns is setting the levels for playbacks of some of the tracks the Who have already cut. In short order, he is joined by Pete Townshend, John Entwistle and Roger Daltrey, who have been upstairs discussing the week's activity, which will include two days set aside for filming a live performance for use in *The Kids Are Alright*, the upcoming screen documentary on the Who. Keith Moon is conspicuously absent.

He and Townshend were out drinking the night before at the Vortex, London's two-night-per-week punk club (live music Monday and Tuesday nights, disco the rest of the week); today is reserved for a hangover. The atmosphere among the other three, however, is surprisingly warm and easygoing. There is certainly none of the tension one might expect from a group recording their first album in over two years — two years that have seen them come very close to finally calling it quits a number of times.

In fact, the Who seem to be stronger now than at any point during those past couple of years, and maybe even farther back than that. Townshend [told me earlier] that the group seems to have ironed out most of the problems that have been plaguing them and are finally headed in a somewhat more specific direction than the seeming limbo of the recent past.

The tape op starts the machine and a wash of sound blares from the huge studio speakers. There can be no mistaking the sound of the Who. The song is called "Had Enough," and although written by John Entwistle, the vocals are handled by Daltrey. There is, however, another unusual feature: an orchestra. Not one of Townshend's synthesizer jobs, but the real thing. Pete tells me it's conducted by his father-in-law, who was also responsible for his first orchestral fling: "Street in the City" on *Rough Mix*.

If "Had Enough" isn't exactly typical Who, it's not a far cry from it, either. As on "Street in the City," the orchestra heightens the power and tension of the music without getting soupy, soppy or syrupy. The sound is extremely full, somewhat akin to parts of *Quadrophenia*, and a striking contrast to the barrenness and simplicity that characterized *Who by Numbers*, yet the chords are still archetypal Who — no surprises there.

Satisfied with what they have heard, the next number is readied for auditioning. First the drum levels are set, then the bass and finally the syn-

thesizer and guitar tracks are mixed into place. The backing vocals have already been recorded as well, and they are added next. A constant refrain of "Who are you, oo oo, oo oo" now repeats itself above the backing track. The lead vocal will be recorded today. Townshend, Entwistle and Daltrey all leave the control room.

About five minutes later, Daltrey returns with a lyric sheet in one hand and a cup of coffee in the other. He walks into the studio and begins singing the opening verse to "Who Are You." It's obviously a difficult bit; Daltrey has to sing the word "hiccoughed" so that it comes across as a hiccough, but he manages to get it nearly perfect each time — and makes it look easy.

After a few takes, all of them scrapped for one reason or another, he runs through the verse perfectly. Everyone in the studio knows this is the one ... except the engineer, who has forgotten to switch on the record button. Glyn Johns throws his hands up and flies out of the room muttering, "This just isn't my day." Soon after, though, Daltrey manages a comparable rendition and everyone is happy ... especially the engineer.

"Who Are You" is a typical Townshend rocker, which again recalls the style of *Quad* in its complex yet still direct approach. Lyrically, it recalls "5:15," with our hero once again finding himself on a train, this time making his besotted way back home from Soho. Could it be about Townshend's now-legendary "evening out" with the Sex Pistols?

Johns figures they're about halfway through recording, though no one seems certain which tracks will be used. Another Townshend song called "Sister Disco" is among those completed, and Entwistle says he should have one or two more songs on the LP. The album will be a single record and should be out soon.

December 14: *The Kids Are Alright* is the brainchild of American Who freak/film director Jeff Stein, and I can safely say it will be unlike any rock movie ever made. Stein has tracked down all available footage of the Who dating back to the High Numbers days. The film is scheduled for release sometime around mid-year.

Today and tomorrow have been set aside as

filming days for the Who. Today will be a test run of sorts, with the entire afternoon to be spent on "Won't Get Fooled Again," replete with laser display. Tomorrow, the Who will run through an entire set in front of an audience, though news of the show has not yet been announced.

The filming is taking place at the Gaumont State Theatre, an old cinema in Kilburn. Today, it's nearly empty save for the film crew, the Who's laser and sound teams, and the band themselves.

The atmosphere is, as at the recording studio, friendly and cheerful. Stein, after running through the laser sequence without the band, is heard muttering something about "blowing away *Star Wars*." Wondrously, a well-rested Keith Moon has arrived, looking fit as a fiddle.

The band takes the stage. After what seems like endless runs through "Won't Get Fooled Again," most of which are screwed up by either one of the light men or Townshend, the cameras finally get what they're after, and the Who adjourn for the day. Though the band was obviously a bit rusty, watching Townshend run through the song over and over without ever once repeating himself only serves to heighten my appreciation of his incredible talents.

December 15: A single radio spot announcing a free concert by the Who brings a thousand people to the Gaumont within a half hour. After an hour, more than two thousand [have shown up], and the doors are shut. Another radio spot advises listeners that there are no more seats available.

The show starts late, but no one seems to mind the wait. The Who take the stage and blast off into "I Can't Explain," followed by what has become pretty much the standard Who stage act over the past five years: "Substitute," "Baba O'Riley," "My Wife," "My Generation," "Behind Blue Eyes," "Pinball Wizard," "Uncle Ernie," "Tattoo," "Shakin' All Over" and "Summertime Blues." The only post-*Who's Next* material was "Dreaming From the Waist" and a snippet of "Who Are You" during the "My Generation" break. While there were isolated great moments to the show, it wasn't quite the transcendent experience most Who concerts turn out to be. The effects of not having played together

for quite a while were obvious, and Townshend repeatedly voiced his disapproval of the way things were going. Still, most groups would give anything to sound as good as the Who on a mediocre day.

After an hour and a quarter, it was over. Townshend flung his guitar over his head and let it fall noisily to the stage. It was that kind of day. He didn't smash it, but he didn't quite catch it either. ■

BASS DANCES: JOHN ENTWISTLE LOOKS OUT, UP AND AHEAD

TP 65, SEPTEMBER 1981

By Wayne King

Meeting a longtime hero can be a nerve-wracking experience. Not only are all your expectations supposed to be fulfilled, but you do not wish to impress as a dolt. The tension just about ruins any chance of coming across cool, calm and collected.

Recently an opportunity arose, by way of an interview, to trip over my feet and tie my tongue in front of John Entwistle, bearlike bassist for the fabled Who. Only a funny thing happened or, rather, didn't happen: the anticipated mumbling and stumbling never occurred. On the elevator up to his New York hotel room, my stomach was flashing a few nervous signals up to my brain. But when Entwistle opened the door and politely ushered me in, it became obvious I was there for a business transaction. Besides, not having felt too fannish toward the Who lately (and having more than a few reservations about *Face Dances*), there were some questions that needed asking. And so, after a comment on how thin he looked, we got on with matters.

The first thing we discussed was his upcoming solo album, *Too Late the Hero*, on which Joe Walsh figures prominently. Entwistle met the guitarist around 1970, when the James Gang toured England. The third member of Entwistle's power trio, drummer Joe Vitale, now plays with Walsh in the Eagles, but in 1975 he led a band of his own (Joe Vitale's Madmen) that opened for Entwistle's short-lived Ox during an English tour.

"It took me over two years to do the album because of the two Joes' commitments to the Eagles and my own commitments; there only seemed to be two months that coincided that we had off. I like to use the same musicians all the way through, so I had to wait until they were free. I'm a little bit worried that if we decided to go out on the road the same problems would occur: rehearse for one month in 1981, tour in 1982 and do another rehearsal in '83. It might get a bit spread out."

The last time Entwistle toured solo was with Ox six years ago. Despite favorable reviews prior to playing the U.S., the result was a musical and financial debacle. The latter aspect may have been an important reason for the lengthy gap in solo projects; Entwistle's reputation for penuriousness once led him sarcastically to dub himself "Silas Stingy."

"I broke the band up afterwards because I didn't want to support it financially anymore," he concedes. "It would have taken two or three more tours to get anywhere. I wasn't getting on with the guitarist [Robert Johnson] too well, and the Who commitments coming up [*Tommy* film premiere, *Who by Numbers* recording and tours] were going to keep me pretty well involved for a couple of years non-stop, so I figured it was time to put it on the shelf. Also, I was getting into a style of writing I didn't like, so I put my whole solo career on the shelf and decided to wait until my head turned 'round a bit and write something different."

Entwistle's traditional onstage spot with the Who, of course, is back in the shadows. Playing with Ox meant standing up front, but he adapted well.

"It was great, once I'd gotten used to the fact that I couldn't wander to the back of the stage and have a quiet drink while the announcements were going on. I realized that I had to stay up front all the time and sing and make all the announcements. It got me used to standing out front, and when I went back to work with the Who I didn't stand back in the shadows anymore. It did me a lot of good. It was worth losing the money."

Since Ox, the only hint of solo work from Entwistle was a since-abandoned science-fiction concept. "It turned into '905' and 'Had Enough' on the *Who Are You* album. Those were the two strongest songs I had for it. My science fiction idea was so close to Pete's, *Lifehouse*, that we decided to combine the two. If *Lifehouse* ever did come out, the songs would include 'Had Enough,' '905,' 'Won't Get Fooled Again' and 'Baba O'Riley.'"

NO GREATER EXAMPLE of the muddled state of mid-'70s Who affairs can be found than the attempt to revive *Lifehouse*. Pete Townshend's plans for a mind-boggling audience-participation cinematic project collapsed in early 1971, leaving *Who's Next* as its remains. The original project's focus was on the interplay between audience and band — an intention likely to be altered, to say the least, by Townshend's vow (before Moon's death) not to play live again. That tempestuous period saw changes in previously well-defined roles, and Entwistle finally got to contribute more than before. *Who Are You* has three of his numbers, *Face Dances* two.

"I wouldn't have offered the Who anything that went on the *Mad Dog* album or *Rigor Mortis*, because it just wouldn't have suited them. It was old-style rock and roll. After that, any songs I wrote were more or less with the Who in mind. I had put away my solo career, so everything was written for the band. Out of maybe five or six songs I presented we'd do two or three; this time I offered the Who two."

Entwistle's "Trick of the Light" and "The Quiet One" are the most straightforward, guitar-heavy songs on the last two Who LPs. *Face Dances* particularly finds Townshend downplaying his guitar, leaving the rockers to his bandmate. What's caused this change?

"Keyboards had a lot to do with that. Pete didn't write the guitar solos into his songs, and keyboards took a much stronger part than guitar. The way we usually recorded was without keyboards, adding them later if the song needed it. This album, we tended to use keyboards [played by Rabbit Bundrick] whether or not the song needed it. It may have been a mistake; the guitar was the instrument that suffered. One of my two songs was written on eight-string bass [as was *Who Are You*'s "Trick of the Light"], so guitar played a much more dominant role in my stuff. When we looked back at the end, the only two strong guitar songs were my two. It wasn't deliberate, it was just the way the album was recorded."

THE WHO HAS toured England twice this year, once before *Face Dances*' release. For the occasion, the band added "You Better, You Bet," "Another Tricky Day," "Don't Let Go the Coat" and "The Quiet One" to its live repertoire.

"They started out a bit sticky because we weren't used to them, and the audiences hadn't heard them before and hadn't time to get into it. But by the end they started taking shape. We have to perform a song 15 to 20 times onstage before it actually starts fitting together. I wrote 'Quiet One' especially to replace 'My Wife' onstage; I had gotten tired of singing that and 'Boris the Spider.'"

Entwistle continues. "In 1979, we were playing with two different lists, and we'd change it every night. At the beginning of the latest English tour, things weren't quite right, so we jumbled a few songs around, and by the end of the tour it was sorted out. I think there's still a possibility of playing more tracks from the new album; I'd like to try 'How Can You Do It Alone' and 'Daily Records.'"

"How Can You Do It Alone" did make it onstage two years ago, as "one of those things that turned up at the end of jams — that, and 'Dance It Away,' which didn't get on the album."

Surprising, since it went over well live.

"I was disappointed as well. Two of my favorite tracks didn't get on the album. It was a matter of having enough time to finish everything; we'd got too much material, so we had to decide which ones were going to go on the album and we were gonna finish. The backing tracks for the two I liked needed to be redone; that would have involved more time, so that's probably the reason they didn't get included. if we'd had a couple of more songs, we could have turned this into a double album, but I don't really know who wants a double album." (Outside of the Clash, probably no one.) The glut of new material is welcome news, compared to conditions surrounding the two Who albums preceding *Face Dances*. Throw in Townshend and Entwistle's offshoot careers, and you get too much of a good thing — for live shows, anyway.

"We made it a golden rule that we never play solo material onstage; we felt there was too much Who material that would suffer." [Parts of Townshend's *Empty Glass* LP *were* previewed on the 1979 tour.] "Now I think things might change. We've realized it's stupid to have a vehicle like the Who and not be able to play solo material as long as it's distributed fairly. It could give us something new to play; the stage show doesn't change fast enough." Which of the older songs are on their way out?

"'My Generation' goes back and forth like a yo-yo. 'See Me, Feel Me' was dropped."

Who-ray!

"It's very difficult to cut material out because you're so used to playing it that it feels like a gap — unless you've got something really exciting to replace it with. We don't want to extend the stage show to two-and-a-half, two-and-three-quarter hours again. If you've got three in a row, the last two shows suffer because you're tired."

If the Who didn't include his numbers, would frustration cause Entwistle to hit the boards on his own again?

"Probably not with this album so much. My solo career has now started again, though, and I've got another two albums planned after this; then I might start getting a little bit frustrated. I've always considered going out on the road with Joe Walsh and Joe Vitale. I've never felt like that about a set of musicians other than the Who."

THE 12 MONTHS between Keith Moon's death and the film premieres of *The Kids Are Alright* and *Quadrophenia* seem finally to have put the old Who out to pasture.

"It was the year of Who nostalgia," Entwistle agrees. "We did start to feel we were looking back and not forward. But it's nice to be able to get out your old photographs occasionally, and the films helped the new audience catch up."

By playing a heavy schedule around the respective movies, the Who paradoxically moved its image firmly into the '80s. As musical director for both films, Entwistle was especially relieved to hit the road again. "I had no intention of getting back into the studio in connection with the films," he states decisively. "It was enough to last me the next five years."

Townshend and Entwistle have openly expressed displeasure with the *Kids* venture. Entwistle and Who manager Bill Curbishley even trimmed the movie's one true find — "A Quick One," from *The Rolling Stones' Rock 'n' Roll Circus* TV show — from the European print. How come?

"We finished dubbing the film. In between my going home and the film actually being cut together properly, an extra ten minutes of dialogue was added in such a way that I couldn't cut it out without half of the 'Quick One' segment; it fit together that way. So, I had to cut 'A Quick One' short. The English distributor wanted the film cut down to 100 minutes; they were cutting out parts I wanted left in and leaving in parts I wanted cut out, so I went into the cutting room and cut 10 minutes. It made for a faster-paced film.

"Also, I felt after Keith's death that [director Jeff] Stein was cashing in by sticking lots more Keith in than he had done before. I didn't think that was right; it completely unbalanced the film. There was also far too much dialogue and not enough music, so I tried to cut out enough dialogue to balance the music."

So much for attic-cleaning. Back in the present, Entwistle foresees more touring towards the end of this year, including a probable Stateside visit. It's been nearly two years since the last U.S. shows, but things could be worse: Australia has gone Wholess since 1969, and Japan has never seen the band in the flesh.

"I think we've always been known as a famous touring band and not as a famous recording band. Our records don't sell that amazingly, but as far as live concerts are concerned the band has done very well."

The Who is among the elite rock acts (also including the Stones, Led Zeppelin and maybe Bruce Springsteen) for whom ticket demand increases logarithmically regardless of artistic progression. Entwistle has noticed his group's younger, more diverse audience.

"We just played England, where we hadn't toured for a long time, and about 30 per cent of the people had never actually seen us before. It's a bit off-putting playing for people with their mouths open, 'cause they really didn't know what to expect. They didn't really expect us to be that good, I suppose.

"In the States, I think as the audience gets older, they go to far less concerts, so your audience gets younger. It's more challenging and a lot more satisfying to win over a member of the audience that hasn't seen you before or hasn't grown up with the band. It's more fun to play for that younger audience."

Talking about audience regeneration makes the Who sound like a lifetime project, but Entwistle denies the band members think of their group in those terms. "It's just happened to carry on and on and on and on. When we first started, I never thought we'd still be going at this time; we figured we had about 18 months. But then music started to change and musicianship became more respected. We just seem to carry on as long as the record contract carries on."

Having just signed with Warner Bros., that means quite a while.

"At the rate we turn out records, yeah."

SPEAKING OF RECORDS prompts a remark on *Face Dances'* squeaky-clean sound, even more of a letdown coming after the physical punch of much of Townshend's *Empty Glass*.

"It is very tidy," Entwistle acknowledges. "Looking back on it, there are several reasons why the album is like it is, but we never realize what's going to happen until the album is actually out. It sounded a lot heavier while we were doing it. *Who's Next* also came out a lot softer than we intended. I don't think the Who have actually made their greatest album. I have a feeling the next album has to be a heavy rock album. I felt this about the last one; it just didn't turn out that way. That's why I wrote two extremely up numbers."

Will Entwistle's songs pick up the slack if Townshend can't supply the bite?

"No, I'll probably write a broader spectrum of songs with the Who in mind. My style of writing is along the same lines as 'The Quiet One' and 'Trick of the Light'; that's the sort of material I'm writing now. I do write slower, more melodic tunes, but I'm starting to write songs in the same way I play onstage. I just hope the next Who album is going to turn into the one we're after. We'll probably attempt it in our own studio, which is a lot more suited to the Who. I really believe the Who should produce the next album themselves."

How involved was the Who with [the sound of] *Face Dances*?

"It's not [producer] Bill Szymczyk's fault, and it's not our fault. He wanted one of us (me) there for the mixing, and everything got put back two weeks. I was rehearsing for the English tour at the same time the album was being mixed. I really regret not being there for the mix because I could have made it..." Heavier?

"The bass sound was there but it just didn't get mixed properly. I think it's very important to get the right balance, but it's almost impossible to get a live Who sound on record. The last one to do it was *Live at Leeds*. That sounds more like the Who than any other record."

John Entwistle is not the Who member to ask about the band's mental health or current ideology; he has a deserved reputation for being reclusive and softspoken. Ironically, however, he is anything but that when it comes to playing his own music, as the heavy metal blast of *Too Late the Hero* shows. If the Who's interminable problems should ever prove fatal, Entwistle will undoubtedly carry on with his rock and roll — very loudly. ∎

This was the first article about an American artist to become a cover story in Trouser Press. We'd stopped running the Creem-aping cover slogan "America's Only British Rock Magazine" with issue 20 in the summer of 1977, but it appeared inside, on the contents page, for another ten issues. (After that, we just made up silly shit every month.)

We'd covered Rundgren before, and an interview with his former colleague Mark "Moogy" Klingman was the first interview ever conducted for the magazine, so putting Todd on the cover was not a difficult decision. Neither was having a dude from Philadelphia write about a hometown hero and give a master class in the backstory of the city's musical scene.

NOTHING/EVERYTHING: THE BALLAD OF TODD RUNDGREN, FROM HERE TO UTOPIA

TP 30, JULY 1978

By David Fricke

Todd Rundgren lies comfortably against a pillow on the living room floor of his Bearsville, New York retreat, located just off a winding, ill-paved driver's challenge called Mink Hollow Road. Against one knee-high landing is a row of records encroaching its way across the room. The first one, front and center, is a copy of Rundgren's first solo album, *Runt*, no doubt the result of a quiet stroll down memory lane.

Trouser Press

July 1978 • $1.25
No. 30 UK 75p

TODD RUNDGREN
Everything You
Wanted to Know
but Didn't Think
He'd Remember

RITCHIE BLACKMORE
Escapes the
Purple Haze

IAN DURY
DAVID BOWIE
BUDDY HOLLY
FLAMIN' GROOVIES

CAN YOU TRUST A ROCK MAGAZINE OVER 50?

"Actually, I just produced a punk album by Jean-Yves Labat — M. Frog — the original synthesizer player in Utopia. One of the tunes is a reworking of a song from that album called 'I'm in the Clique.' His new album is called *Froggy Goes a Punkin'*." *

Right there, in barely over 25 words, is the gist of Todd Rundgren's stormy ten-year career as one of American rock's most prodigious and, at times, petulant geniuses. Alternately a defiantly individualistic solo artist, a much-sought-after producer of hits for other occasionally less talented folk and the democratically inclined lead guitarist for a band and ideology called Utopia, Todd Rundgren is all things to only a few understanding people. His records with and without Utopia since 1973's *A Wizard, a True Star* have sold at a modest but discouragingly fixed rate of approximately 200,000 a pop — enough to keep his commercial momentum at a respectable pace, but not enough to keep him from languishing in the shadowed obscurity that is the scourge of all cult figures.

But Rundgren would seem totally unaffected by his inability to make a large-scale artistic impact on an audience he feels is brainwashed by the false promises of '70s pop and the insensitive record industry prophets that make them. Much like the Number 6 character portrayed by Patrick McGoohan in *The Prisoner*, Rundgren writes for himself the role of a man who consistently defies the powers-that-be who, in this case, would emasculate the creative potential of any single musical project he might care to name. He will cite such scurrilous activity as going back as far as his celebrated late '60s stint with Nazz and then detail the problems he claims he faces in pursuing a musical career, either on his lonesome or in the company of fellow Utopians. Take, for example, his solo recording contract with Bearsville Records.

"I deliver albums on approval. I'm not obligated to deliver any albums to them, but I can't take an album to another label, either. I just sort of do what I feel like doing, and they have the option of putting them out or not putting them out. The way they behave when I deliver them, I don't understand why they bother. You'll have to ask them."

I did just that, calling Bearsville's California office to ask company head and long-time Rundgren confidante Paul Fishkin about Rundgren's business circumstances and the company's attitudes toward the music Rundgren says they have no commercial faith in.

"There is a certain level," Fishkin replies, "on which Todd likes to think of himself as independent. He's also a very — what's the word? — mercurial personality, and much to his credit he's never wanted to be categorized. That's what makes him so unique. But that also makes it very frustrating for us because we would like to sell more records."

So would Todd, but for him, that's not the bottom line. "That's another argument I have with the record company. They feel that selling 150,000 albums in this day and age makes you irrelevant, that it has to be a million and a half albums to be worth anything. Their whole attitude is ... like world conquest or manifest destiny, where you're just supposed to expand and expand and expand in the same way the economy does until you hit your recession and your economy collapses.

* That M. Frog project was shelved, but its contents — titled *Froggy Goes a Pumpkin* — surfaced in 2001 on a Japanese Rundgren Archive release called *Demos and Lost Albums*.

"I don't particularly feel that way. I feel that it seeks its own level. I can't force it any greater. I'm not attempting to be anyplace, underground or overground. I'm just attempting to do what I feel I should do in terms of making records."

A week later and 3,000 miles away, Fishkin makes Todd's point for him.

"He makes the music in his head at a given moment. And that music is the story of his life at that moment."

RAZ-A-MA-NAZZ

The fourth largest music market in the country, Philadelphia nevertheless endures a perennially bad rock and roll reputation. The East Coast industry focus makes an occasional stop there, paying due respect to the bastard children of Dick Clark's *American Bandstand* — that South Philly brigade of acne-free faces like Frankie Avalon and the imminently forgettable Fabian — with more recent tribute paid the R&B factory run by Philadelphia International's Gamble and Huff.

As a result, the city's young white rockers still fight an uphill battle trying to make even their own local audience aware of the talent developing there, only to find their fortune in a two-hour drive to the north. The psychedelic joyride we now know as the late '60s found many of Philly's aspiring rock bands coming about as close as they ever would. Mandrake Memorial, Edison Electric Band, Elizabeth, Sweet Stavin Chain, High Treason — they all snagged fleeting moments of recognition with albums of fair to excellent quality. But, by 1968, there was no question about who reigned supreme, even if they didn't gig with the same regularity and took a casual pass on hippie ethics. Nazz — generally through the services of the still-18-year-old Todd Rundgren — were unanimously, if begrudgingly, voted most likely to succeed. That, in the end, Nazz dissolved in a flurry of infighting and managerial mishaps, Rundgren attributes more to the times than the place.

"Nazz was certainly out of context in the sense that it wasn't typical of what was happening at the time."

Rundgren has been talking about his own musical tendencies at any given time *vis a vis* those considered in vogue at that given time. It is a theme he sounds throughout the conversation, and Nazz is just another case in point.

"It wasn't exactly out of context," he submits, "because we were the premiere local band at the time. We did have a large following. But the Nazz was considered out of context because the music that was happening was not at all like ours.

"First of all, everybody was taking a lot of drugs. The whole thing was that late-'60s music evolved out of this street-level thing, like San Francisco and so on. Like, 'Hey, blues.' Except I'd already gone through the blues trip with Woody's Truck Stop."

Actually, Rundgren had been through that and more by 1967, when Nazz first reared its Anglo-foppish head. He could count to his credit the usual Beatle-copy and Britrock cover bands like Money (the same heard at the start of Side Four of *Something/Anything*). As an impressionable lad growing up in the depressingly nondescript Philadelphia suburb of Upper Darby, he ignored Elvis Presley ("A lot of people who emulated him were machismo-greaser-killer types who were always out to kill me"), opting for what he describes as the "art school personality" personified by the Beatles, "wanting to be a little different and strange and still have people like you."

Come 1966, Rundgren fancied himself a budding white bluesman, heading for center city Philadelphia and joining forces with an early hippie configuration, Woody's Truck Stop, which held forth at the bohemian Walnut Street hangout called the Artist's Hut. Paul Fishkin, who managed the Truck Stop for a time, describes the group as "sort of the Grateful Dead of Philadelphia." However, their few claims to fame were Todd, a marginally excitable album on Smash (post-Todd) and a guitar player by the name of Alan Miller, who raised a court ruckus when his high school suspended him for not cutting his hair to a regimental length. Such were the times, and the times were not with Todd who was (depending on whom you believe) either tossed out of the Truck Stop for not taking drugs (Fishkin's story) or because he didn't like the band's drug scene (Todd, natch).

His next stop was what he calls "high concept," a very Beatle-y trip to include singer-organist Stewkey (né Robert Antoni, from the group Elizabeth), bass guitarist, occasional songwriter and old friend Carson Van Osten and ex-Munchkins drummer Thom Mooney. Stewkey remembers that it was Todd and Carson who formulated the idea for Nazz, then recruited him and Mooney to complete the band. As Nazz, they eventually released the first so-called progressive rock record out of Philadelphia ("Open My Eyes" b/w "Hello It's Me") and, with the debut album *Nazz*, defined an entirely new 1967 sound that could be described in today's terminology as "power pop."

"Nazz was a high concept band," reiterates Rundgren. "We emulated a lot of English bands like the Who and Small Faces and really wanted to be as big as the Beatles, so we conceptualized everything on that level. The music was designed to have more of a common denominator, play more of an eclectic thing — a lot more vocals than what was happening at the time. At the time, everything was endless guitar solos. We had long conceptual songs, but even those were a high level of composition, as opposed to dropping acid and jamming."

But was it just guitar solos and acid? Few of the bands, local or otherwise, who played Philly's psychedelic showplaces like the Trauma, the Electric Factory and the Second Fret coffeehouse even dented the charts with their extended paeans to the new consciousness. A glance at any one of the Top 100 lists of the late '60s would reveal the Beatles at the height of their power, the Who slipping in every once in a while and American groups like the Grass Roots, the Union Gap and Paul Revere and the Raiders taking their turns with alarming regularity. If anything, Nazz's neo-Whoish energy wedded with Rundgren's gift for writing inescapable melodic hooks should have made them prime contenders.

"Well, Nazz wasn't really counter to things that were happening," he'll say, implying that maybe it was more the creative atmosphere which was at fault.

"As I recall, a lot of my influences at the time were popular, but in other aspects. Like Jimmy Webb and the type of things he was doing influenced me to write 'A Beautiful Song' (the extended orchestral opus on *Nazz Nazz*). It's just that we were joining a lot of disparate influences in the Nazz, and it was a combination that wasn't necessarily accessible.

"It's also conceivable that the Nazz could have been more successful if our management had been a little more realistic. If we had played around more consistently and had a chance to develop our performance to the extent that we were developing our recording, then things might have happened differently. But our manager had this theory that if we had played around too much, we would establish ourselves as having a low price tag. He was very money-oriented, mostly because he spent money at an incredible rate."

So, even with the first album, Nazz were left to their own devices. Despite production credits for Chicago producer Bill Traut (Shadows of Knight, etc.) and, on "Open My Eyes" and "Hello It's Me," Michael Friedman, Rundgren says that Nazz went the whole thing alone. "He [Traut] just sat there and read the trades while we were working. Then he mixed the album and a couple of hours later flew back to Chicago. We wound up remixing the whole album anyway. Michael Friedman was the partner of our manager at the time, and he just wanted to have his name on the record somewhere. But all he did was sit around..."

...and read the trades, no doubt. But the end result soon obscured any of the shit flying around in the managerial arena. *Nazz* was — and still is — a refreshing, uplifting experience, totally lacking in artistic pretension. The rock ("Open My Eyes," "Lemming Song," "When I Get My Plane") is raw at the core, with a distinctive and imaginative polish to complement the gentility of ballads like "If That's the Way You Feel" and "Hello It's Me" (still an undeniable classic, reflecting the urban soul colorings of Rundgren's musical upbringing). Only "Crowded" bears compositional credits other than Todd's ("Wildwood Song" is a group effort), in this case Stewkey and Mooney. So, while *Nazz* was not totally a Rundgren showcase, it set an auspicious example for the future.

Somebody then had the ingenious notion of

sending Nazz to London in the fall of '68 for recording purposes, sheer brilliance when you consider the wealth of English influences displayed on *Nazz* (the opening chords of "Open My Eyes" are straight out of the Who's "I Can't Explain"). Work permits being what they are, Nazz finished only one track in their two weeks there — a Carson Van Osten song called "Christopher Columbus" that later showed up in re-recorded form on *Nazz III*. (The original version of "Christopher Columbus" along with a different studio take of "Open My Eyes" can be heard on *The Todd Rundgren Radio Show*, a 1972 Bearsville promotional issue.) Nazz then headed for California's sunny climes to do the second album, and there the problems began in earnest.

"The Nazz always had internal problems, personality conflicts. For instance, the lead singer, Stewkey, was not inspired to do a lot except sing. Originally, he was supposed to be an organ player, but he never practiced organ. I had been playing piano in the meantime and subsequently, by the time we got to the second record, I ended up doing most of the keyboard work.

"The drummer, Thom, and I had constant conflicts of an ego nature that had nothing to do with the professional direction of the band. We would get in the studio and if I were to say, 'Play it this way,' he would purposely play it another way, just to keep things going. By the time we got to the second album, we were just stomping in and out of the studio, fights all the time and shit like that. It was not the best set-up internally."

Stewkey takes some exception to Todd's criticisms, concurring that, yes, there were internal problems, but Todd was just as much a part of the proceedings. As for his own role as organ player, "Todd knew that I didn't play well. I never took piano lessons or anything. I just started to play as a music fill-in at the time. And I proceeded to get into the singing aspect of it. I never thought I was meant to be a virtuoso." He does, however, play all of the ivories heard on *Nazz*.

Queried about Todd's domineering role as composer, arranger and de facto producer, Stewkey claims, "Todd always felt like he was the only one, anyway. It got to a point where we weren't even important anymore. On the second album, for instance, there are some tunes that I'd never heard before I even got into the studio. He would be off by himself, and we didn't even know what he was doing. A lot of hassles went down with the band and he just separated himself from them."

For Rundgren, though, the breaking point came with a controversy involving the group's second album, released in 1969 as *Nazz Nazz*. As he explains it, all of the material found on both *Nazz Nazz* and *Nazz III* came from the same 1968 Hollywood sessions, done after Nazz returned from London. Together they would comprise a double album — at least, he thought so — entitled *Fungo Bat*. ("We were really getting out there...") But the real bone of contention for Todd was the fact that on most of the *Nazz III* tracks he, not Stewkey, had originally sung lead vocals.

"I wanted that record to be a double album, including all the material. In fact, we had a whole double album mix. Somewhere around here" — Rundgren gestures casually across his living room — "I have the lacquers or the master tapes of it.

"But they [meaning a combination of band members and record company higher-ups] decided to make it a single album and, on the songs I sang, [they] removed my voice from the master tapes and put Stewkey on instead. That became *Nazz III*."

Stewkey was just as surprised to see *Nazz III* in a record store in Madison, Wisconsin almost two years later. Regarding the erasure of Todd's voice from the tapes he comments, "They just didn't sound good as far as I was concerned.

"I didn't want a double album. I thought it was bad timing — we had a hard enough time selling a single one. And a lot of that material on *Nazz III* shouldn't have come out."

If that was the case, why bother to overdub the new vocals? "They — the record company and the people involved in it — wanted me to."

While Rundgren claims that was only one of the points of dispute within Nazz, the *Nazz Nazz* controversy was his last. He and Carson Van Osten took their leave almost simultaneously. "Carson was a pretty mellow, easygoing guy and just didn't like the situation," says Todd. "I split shortly after that."

Stewkey and Thom Mooney kept a version of Nazz alive until mid-1970, when Mooney split for California (only to resurface briefly on albums by the Curtis Brothers and Tattoo with ex-Raspberry Wally Bryson). Carson retired to a promising career as an animation artist, Stewkey eventually hooked up with Cheap Trick's Rick Nielsen for a couple of short-lived projects, and Todd set his sights on production work. With hardly more than two years and three mildly successful records to show for them, Nazz dissolved without a whimper. Easily years ahead of their time, they swam upstream in a river of sonic psychodaisical jive that, with their Marshall stacks and tie-dyed shirts, had no time for classic pop melodies. Today, the rock and roll pundits would call it power pop and "Open My Eyes" would be a Top 10 charter all over again. Or would it?

Stewkey: "We went too fast. I think if we had played around and functioned like any band that takes two or three years to get up the ladder, we would have hit really big."

Todd: "If Nazz were together now, it would be really sick!"

PROMISE 'EM SOMETHING, PROMISE 'EM ANYTHING, BUT GIVE 'EM THE HITS

Ironic, isn't it? Todd Rundgren's latest solo opus, *Hermit of Mink Hollow*, currently garners more airplay and public attention within a month of release than most of his recorded output since the puzzling *Wizard*. Both the solo and Utopian Rundgrens have been making undeniably curious if not totally accessible music for nigh on those ensuing five years, and while even Todd admits to certain flaws in the flow, he won't even recognize criticisms of his refusal to follow the pop path laid out by the gold record success of 1972's *Something/Anything*? Add to that a prestigious track record of hits produced for other folks and you wonder where one — Todd, Runt, Utopia, etc. — ends and the other begins. They all, in fact, begin in 1969.

More interested in "developing a musical style without having to deal with someone's reaction to it," Rundgren passed on both forming a band and going solo in order to acquaint himself with the wonders of the studio. It would be fair enough, then, to say that Rundgren's decision to head straight off for the console instead of the microphone has colored his solo and group activity since. Although his voice has become almost immediately recognizable, all Rundgren records possess a studio gleam, a definitive "sound" that can only be his, and the same goes for, among others, the Hall and Oates, Grand Funk and Meat Loaf records he has produced with variable success. Whatever the content, however recorded, they all literally scream "Rundgren."

About his "sound," Todd says, "It's very hard for me to describe it in words, but I know the difference between the way I produce and the way other producers work. For instance, my main area is in terms of the sound, and the arrangements can vary very broadly. For example, I probably do the widest variety of types of production of almost any producer — country, blues, jazz-rock, straight-ahead rock and roll, nearly MOR, and then my own albums. That's opposed to, say, Richard Perry who only does a certain MOR-type of album. He uses the same musicians, the exact same drum sound — it sounds like a Richard Perry record with a different lead singer on it."

Todd describes his first production assignment, a Philly band called the American Dream, as a "chance to learn certain basics," which proved beneficial in more ways than one. With the 1969 job came the opportunity to christen the just-opened Record Plant in New York. A brand-new console and similarly shiny new equipment presented considerable deterrents for the three or four engineers who tried their hands at the Dream album. Finally, Todd took the matter into his own eager hands, working the board and subsequently learning the most advantageous thing you could possibly know as a budding young producer — how to engineer.

That ability allows him maximum control when recording himself or Utopia. Still, he insists that recording all by your lonesome — instruments, vocals, the works — is no big deal if you know your way around the limitations. Most of the instrumental and vocal work on his first two solo works, *Runt* (1970) and *The Ballad of Todd Rundgren* (1971), were his own with only rhythmic help from the Sales brothers (Hunt and Tony), some guys from the Band and, on one *Runt* track, from the American Dream.

In fact, *Runt* was recorded on speculation by Todd after Bearsville Records, where he was staff producer, gave him a budget ("as a concession") and told him, literally, to go make an album. Prior to that, Todd had done some writing, little outside playing and a lot of session engineering, including the Band's *Stage Fright*. Apparently Bearsville expected nothing much above the ordinary because, as Todd tells it, "when I brought back *Runt*, they were more or less shocked that I had actually done it and that it displayed a certain amount of originality. So, they signed me up after the album was finished."

Nine months later, Bearsville figured they had some hot property. Through the good promotional offices of the aforementioned Paul Fishkin, "We Gotta Get You a Woman" (written for and about Fishkin) went Top 10 and everybody waited with bated breath for the follow-up. But *The Ballad Of...* spawned no hits, even if the stuff of which they are made was there in spades. "That was my least successful album in terms of sales, although people say it is the most coherent in terms of songwriting and nowadays could be one of your across-the-board MOR-type records. But at the time it wasn't fashionable. Nothing I do is fashionable at the time I do it."

But if *The Ballad of Todd Rundgren* is an album Billy Joel would kill to call his own, then *Something/Anything?* is the best album Paul McCartney never made and, in retrospect, it is easy to see how *S/A?* can be singled out by (generally former) fans as the quintessential Todd, the absolute height of his melodic and lyrical powers. Here was a four-sided, 24-song declaration of independent genius, further set apart from the mainstream by two common denominator hits, the extraordinary "I Saw the Light" and a re-recording of "Hello It's Me," and, as Todd calls it in the liner notes for Side One, "a bouquet of ear-catching melodies."

Besides, recording it was a cinch.

"I originally planned to do *Something/Anything?* all myself because on the previous albums I did everything except the bass and drums — the bass just being sort of a big guitar and the drums I had sort of fooled around with to some extent.

"The only challenge in doing that was playing the drums. Since everything was so highly arranged, it didn't amount to a lot of complexity. It was essentially just arrangements, which was no problem for me. Y'know, sit down, take a half hour, and work out the part. After that, it was easy.

"You usually start with the drums and it's hard to play the drums to nothing, the reason being that halfway between the song you forget where you are. It's hard going through the song, trying to sing it all to yourself, the whole arrangement, and keep it in your head without getting lost. A lot of times, I would have to use an edit or two to get through the song. I'd forget and stop, but the first part would be so good that I couldn't do it over again. I'd start in the middle, edit it together and overdub everything from there.

"Since then, I've been influenced by a lot of R&B drum players, so the style's a little different, a little more syncopated, more complicated turn-arounds and things like that. On *Something/Anything?*, for the most part, I was playing rhythm, whereas on my new album, I'm playing, to some degree, what they call "melodic rhythm."

"The operetta ('Baby Needs a New Pair of Snakeskin Boots') only took a day or so to do three songs in one session and the rest in another. The other three sides only took like three weeks to do. I would essentially do a track a day, working on some stuff at home on the 8-track. I did 'Breathless' and 'One More Day' at home.

"I can't remember, but I think *Something/Anything?* was conceived as a single album and just turned into a double. I was writing material so fast that it became a double album. That was one reason why I changed my style so radically on the next album, because it just became too simple to write songs like that, almost mechanical. I would sit down at the piano and there would just be standard changes and combinations and lyrically it was the same subject matter. I had to break out of that rut. I didn't feel I was doing myself creative justice."

OOOPS! WRONG RUNDGREN!

"In terms of cycles, I guess my apogee is their perigee and vice versa. I'm just cyclically 180 degrees off from whatever else is happening. But it's a big world and there's a lot of people in the same boat as me and somebody's gotta appeal to them."

If only by default, that somebody is Rundgren, a rationalization that accounts for the continued release of records bearing his name, even if the general public and press corps eye each waxen item with the suspicion that there is something on that record they want little or no part of. To some, it's the frantic instrumental deluge marking "A Treatise on Cosmic Fire," a 30-minute epic from *Initiation* which Todd admits will appeal "to very few people that aren't musicians. It appeals to musicians who want to hear something different as well as on a technical level, particularly people who are more or less removed from the mainstream of pop music."

To others, the idealistic sociology coloring his Utopian lyrics should have nothing to do with the business of making popular music, a criticism that Todd vehemently denies. In again referring to the roundly panned *Initiation*, he insists that, like with any record or song, "I was determined to write lyrics entirely about something I believed in, rather than something I simply speculated about or had idle thoughts about." The success and subsequent constant critical referrals to *Something/Anything?* drained him, at least temporarily, of the urge to write love songs of the moon-June-spoon variety. *A Wizard, a True Star* and *Utopia* were the almost disastrous result.

"After doing *Something/Anything?*, I had become deeply involved with production and sound. From that, I conceptualized this whole recording studio and built it from scratch. That was Secret Sound in New York, and *Wizard* was the first album done there. The studio was designed to be able to produce all these sonic illusions, and the whole *Wizard* album was an attempt to do that."

A collection of songlets ranging from the fluid electronic backdrop of "International Feel" to the hard pull of those Philly-soul roots in the "Cool Jerk"/Smokey Robinson/Curtis Mayfield medley, *Wizard* was certainly, as Rundgren indulges in characteristic understatement, "the most radical departure that I'd made up to that point." His follow-up to *Something/Anything?*, it could not help but alienate his substantial singles-buying audience. And the album scarfers had a time of it, too, something for which the aborted first Utopia tour can be properly blamed.

Undertaken in the spring of '73 and lasting no more than three gigs, the first Utopia tour was an unmitigated bomb. Even in his hometown, Rundgren found few believers. While he admits that not a lot of folks had yet made the transition from *S/A?* to *Wizard*, he feels it might have worked if his manager at the time, Albert Grossman (Dylan, Band, etc.) had shown a little more faith in financing the stage extravaganza. Still, survivors of the Philadelphia show — opened appropriately enough by King Crimson — can only babble about lengthy Mahavishnu-like jams, a large dome under which M. Frog conducted extensive business on synthesizer and the black outfits offset by shocks of white fur on top of each head. It was hard enough telling Rundgren from Moogy Klingman, much less sitting back and trying to catch a few bona fide songs.

Since then, Utopia — now a streamlined four-piece with Todd the only original left, in the company of Roger Powell, Kasim Sulton and John Wilcox — has developed a stage show so high on P.T. Barnum showmanship that it's no small wonder that Utopia's tours are underwritten by record advances and royalties. Despite that, Rundgren says that all the Utopia records have been performance-inspired. "In all cases, the material was either performed live first or was designed to highlight the stage show, as with the *Ra* album and the sphinx and pyramid staging that went with it."

But for every Utopia album, there is a solo Rundgren issue, a pattern for which he has no explanation. "Actually, *Faithful* preceded *Ra* by a considerable stretch of time and then, after *Ra*, there was *Ooops! Wrong Planet!* which was another Utopia album. I'd been pretty much totally involved with the Utopia road concept and, as a result, didn't record a Todd Rundgren record in something like two years. We've been touring extensively, so our records have reflected our touring experience, whereas my solo albums are more or less closed environment things."

The latest in the lengthening line of Rundgren solo projects, *Hermit of Mink Hollow* takes that assessment to its logical conclusion. Where *Todd*, *Initiation* and *Faithful* were all recorded with a variety of Utopians and sympathetic outsiders, *Hermit* takes *Something/Anything?* that final step further — it was produced, arranged, written, played and sung by Todd R. with the unsolicited help of absolutely no one. What that has to do with the fact that it is his most immediately accessible album since *S/A?* is anybody's guess. Even Todd's. "In my solo albums, except for a few instances, I have always dealt in song styles. *Initiation* had at least one side of songs. *Todd* was very song-related, too, although it incorporated the instrumental stuff that came to a head on *Initiation*. *Wizard* was more like songlets, an attempt to break certain restrictions in songwriting. *Faithful* was all songs as well. In fact, *Faithful* was the penultimate song album in a way because I took archetypal songs of the '60s like 'Good Vibrations' and 'Strawberry Fields Forever' and reviewed those with a '70s approach. Then, on the 'original' side, I did my interpretation of those '60s influences. So, for me, that was the ultimate song album, totally self-conscious song stylizations.

"As for the recent album, I wrote songs as an opportunity for me to sing as opposed to playing, which is what I mostly do with Utopia. It is a chance to do a number of different styles of singing and essentially highlight my voice."

Case in point is the opening track, "All the Children Sing," a light, harmonic exercise of vocal expertise overlaying a rhythm track of guitars, basic bottom and harpsichord. The choral break in the middle, though, is a classic example of Rundgren's studio methodology. You think you hear about a dozen little Rundgren's ooh-aahing in the background when, in fact, Todd has overdubbed himself maybe three times to achieve the effect. And the same goes for the lead vocal harmonies.

"When I do vocals, I essentially have a lead voice and three background voices. The way that they are arranged is what gives you the impression that there are more or less. Essentially, it's studio dressing. I used to double each voice in the background vocals. Now I just do them all with one voice. So, there are actually less voices than there have been on previous albums. But the point is that I have different vocal control now and there is different technology for creating sound..." Here, he pauses, as if to think of a way to summarize the recorded effect. "...sound-picture sound."

Technology notwithstanding, *Hermit of Mink Hollow* literally glows with melodic light, a vivid aurora borealis of lyrical changes, high harmonies and instrumental gloss. "Hurting for You," "Bag Lady," "Bread" and "Fade Away" are all living testament not only to Todd's wizardly control of the mixer but also [his ability] to write songs that, despite possessing the obvious hooks upon which commercial success is hung, are head and shoulders above the AM and FM wallpaper against which Rundgren incessantly rails.

"Any record company executive now will tell you that people don't listen to music, and that's what music now is designed to be — not listened to. It's essentially wallpaper and people don't want to hear music that puts them through an emotional trip, some kind of spectrum of feelings."

On that account, notice the legend appearing on each side of your copy of *Hermit*. Side One is tagged "The Easy Side"; Side Two is "The Difficult Side." Be not dismayed —Todd assures you that this is merely a clever in-joke. When he first delivered the album to Bearsville for release, the twelve songs were in an entirely different order. However, the company felt that demographic theories on such matters made a difference in his case. ("These different theories about listener response are supposed to override whatever it is you intended, the mood you want to create.") Bearsville prexy Paul Fishkin feels that Rundgren "could make those changes and not affect the album as a whole, but he considers it meddling."

In any case, Bearsville presented Todd with a list of songs they felt would program better together on one side ("Those tunes acceptable on the MOR crossover theorem...") with the ones they figured were too challenging — in other words, "annoying and grating" — on the other. Hence, "Easy" and "Difficult."

"The funny thing is that it makes no difference to me whatever. I don't know what the fuck they were talking about. So, I did it, figuring it was their particular wank, and they can think what they want.

"You see, record companies just sell the record, so they say it can be done. But it's not their obligation to play it and then live with it once they do. That's what is so hypocritical about the business. The artist has to live with what he creates. In that way, most things that record company people say to me goes in one ear and out the other."

Todd's relationship with Bearsville and the industry at large cannot be all that bad, since he still makes records and at least gets them on the street, which is more than a lot of other diehard idealists can say. And Fishkin admits to an undying respect for Todd's independent stance. Still, respect doesn't count in the $7.98 retail race.

"I guess," he says, "I'll always be a revolutionary because I don't want to be part of the establishment. I don't care who the establishment is, either. I just want the option to be exactly who I am and, as a result, I will always be on the outside."

MEANWHILE, BACK IN PHILLY...

What, I'm sure you're all asking, happened to that post-Rundgren Nazz that went to Dallas and eventually went the way of all has-beens? And what does Cheap Trick have to do with it?

Yes, these are questions to which you no doubt want the answers. Ex-Nazz lead singer Stewkey was more than happy to oblige.

"After Todd and Carson quit the band, Thom Mooney and I went to Dallas bringing two people with us from Philly, a bass player named Greg Simpler and a guitar player named Craig Bolan, who used to play with Thom a long time ago in the Munchkins. As the Nazz, we played around the Southwest. We tried to hook up with some management people out there, but that didn't work out. So, we finally disbanded the group after about six or seven months. That was in mid-1970.

"Thom went to California, while I stayed in Texas. Maybe a year or so later, I got a phone call from Rick Nielsen. He wanted to know if I wanted to come to Illinois to sing with his band. So, I went up there and sang with his band — it was called Fuse at the time."

This version of Fuse came together after their lone Epic album (of which Nielsen has little good to say), was recorded. According to Stewkey, Thom Mooney played with Fuse for a time in Illinois, but left again, and eventually Fuse headed to Philadelphia and were rechristened Sick Man of Europe. The personnel changed with some regularity, with the band including at times Nielsen, Stewkey, Tom Petersson (also of Cheap Trick), and Philadelphians Hank Ransome (a longtime local drummer) and Cotton Kent (jazz-rocker and Sigma Sound session regular). As Sick Man of Europe, they recorded a number of demos which have since turned up on a bootleg album, *Retrospective Foresight*, as a collection of Nazz outtakes, although most of the tracks actually aren't. It actually features *Nazz III* tracks, a live take of "Open My Eyes" that Stewkey thinks might be the Texan Nazz, and rough takes of "Lemming Song" and "Train Kept A Rollin'." The Sick Man of Europe tunes on the record are "I Ain't Got You" (a Stewkey original), "He Was" (another Stewkey comp) and Nielsen's "So Good to See You" (billed there as "Ready I Am").

In any case, Sick Man eventually brought in a drummer from Illinois (not Bun E. Carlos) whose name Stewkey can't remember. And then... "I don't know. I left again. Actually, I got fired. I just had bad luck with two bands."

Stewkey is now living in Philadelphia, doing sporadic writing and, for a while, was gigging acoustically in a duo. When asked about his personal relationship with Todd during the Nazz period, he refers back to Todd's aversion to drugs.

"When I was playing with Todd when Nazz was first together, I'd like to go out and get high. And he didn't like that. I thought Todd really got impossible after a while. If we weren't working and I wanted to go out and see a chick or get high with a couple of friends, he'd really get upset about that. Which I didn't understand. Y'know, people like to have fun, Todd." ∎

Trouser Press

RAY DAVIES
Ol' Gap-Tooth Is Back

PETER GABRIEL
ROBERT FRIPP
BRIAN ENO

DEAD BOYS
BLONDIE

Caught up in the reflexively disrespectful ageist thrill of new wave rebellion, and keen to be as irreverent as the British weeklies we devoured, we, for a time, out-snarked ourselves by slapping a gratuitous "B.O.F." (Boring Old Fart) label on articles about rock's elder statesmen (who, of course, were only in their forties at the time, and while perhaps not storming barricades alongside the punks, were still capable of real artistic achievement). Belated apologies to Ray, who was tagged number seven, and the other venerable icons (Paul McCartney, Pete Townshend, Keith Emerson, Greg Lake, Carl Palmer and Ritchie Blackmore) who we undercut our admiration for in that regrettable series.

RAY DAVIES, MISFIT AND CONCERNED CITIZEN, TALKS

TP 32, OCTOBER 1978

By Dave Schulps

"If I were offered a door that said 'Immortality, Riches and Fame,' I'd think about it, but the fact that the door was there would probably be enough to satisfy me. You don't have to go through it. I think we had the door there at one point, but we chose to find it again rather than go through it."

Ray Davies sits casually on the sofa of his midtown New York hotel room and reflects on the Kinks' position in the rock pantheon. The band has a large and extraordinarily devoted cult following, larger than most groups one might reasonably call "cult bands," but has yet to make that last step up to stadia, triple-platinum and, ultimately, what they refer to as "superstardom." Yet if it hurts Davies deep down inside to watch a stream of performers far less gifted than himself attain those goals, on the surface he seems genuinely content to remain just outside that door, playing to an audience that cares about him and what he has to say, not about who he's dating, what he eats for breakfast and what position the Kinks occupy in the charts.

"We've never really reached what they call 'the big time,'" he continues. "That did us a lot of good, because it's allowed us to keep our feet on the ground. We started out playing huge gigs — Hollywood Bowls and the like — but by flukes, incidents, things going wrong or maybe going right, I don't know, we didn't continue like that. We decided to settle where we are, and I just kept writing. Some people are in rock and roll because they want to play music or write songs, some want to use it as a vehicle to do something else. I think I'm one of the unfortunate ones who wants to write songs. Maybe because I really enjoy what I do I don't want to walk through that door that says: 'You've done it.'

"Maybe I want to keep in a hungry situation because it's the only way I can keep writing. I don't

> " If fitting in with the world is following the river and knowing where it's going, I'd rather go my own way and not know where I'm going.

want to live in a capsule. It's odd, usually I'm dissatisfied with things. I guess in a way I'm happy being dissatisfied because it enables me to keep functioning. Once you reach the top and play the Garden, where else are you going to play? Me, I think the Palladium's too big."

Less than a week before, the Kinks had indeed played New York's 3,500-seat Palladium, putting on what most people agreed was one of their finest New York performances ever, introducing in the process the two new Kinks: bassist Jim Rodford (ex-Argent) and keyboard player Gordon Edwards (ex-Pretty Things). The personnel changes seem to have had a tremendous revitalizing effect on the other Kinks. The band has never sounded tighter or more energetic. Rodford and Edwards both sing beautifully, which has enabled the Kinks to drop the female backing vocalists they used in the past and still pull off the most exquisite performance of "Waterloo Sunset" I've ever seen.

"I think the changes were due to happen for a long time," Davies reveals. "I think the most important change, without putting the other guy down, was John Gosling, since Andy Pyle was only with us about 11 months. John was unhappy touring with us right from *Preservation*, I don't think he totally agreed with doing the shows. He didn't really make this clear until a few years afterwards, though. I think it was brewing within him. That, and personal things. I sat down with him and said, 'John, I've always wanted the band to be 100 percent from everyone, and there's a hint that you can't give 100 percent.' He said he didn't think he could." Gosling and Pyle have since formed a band of their own called United.

"But anyway," Davies adds, "the positive thing was that it gave us the chance to get players who

could sing, because neither John nor Andy could. Jim's good, and Gordon's got very good range. Vocally, it's working out real well. I think it's sounding nearer the records, and we've only been working together for about five weeks. The good thing about Jim is that he's an aggressive bass player, one of the most aggressive we've had, certainly more so than Andy or John Dalton. He's got a subtlety with it, as well, and he brings out Dave [Davies]. That's the amazing thing. And Gordon's got a really good right hand. He was a bit rusty to start with, he's been off the road for a while and hadn't played the piano very much, but now he's really getting into it. It's brought [drummer] Mick [Avory] out, too, because Mick's the kind of guy who, if the atmosphere is good, plays much better. And I'm enjoying it, too. I feel like I'm playing in a group. And it's a great feeling." He smiles a satisfied smile, as I ask whether that feeling was not present in the past.

"Not last year," he answers. "During the tour I was really feeling lonely. Do you know that one of the guys who left actually got so drunk at one show that he fell asleep during a number. I mean, I like getting drunk after the show and..." he smiles coyly, "having a few on stage, but ... Dave got so pissed off that he kicked Mick's drums, because Mick was the closest to him, which caused Mick to throw his drums on the floor and say, 'That's it...' Fortunately, we were able to straighten things out after the show.

"At the moment, though, everything is great. I'm getting excited about doing the next album. I think it could be amazing." And, given the contribution made by the new members to the live show, it should be. Especially coming, as it will, on the heels of *Misfits*, which for me anyway, is one of the most puzzling and least satisfying

Kinks albums; a record which took too long to make and which was, as we now know, the product of a band in a state of flux during the time of its recording. Still, despite an overall feeling of sluggishness, like any Kinks album it has its moments of brilliance, and, of course, serves as yet another message from the Kinks to kroniklers everywhere. I wondered if "A Rock 'n' Roll Fantasy," a song in which Ray speaks about the need for keeping the band going, was written about the departures of Messrs. Gosling and Pyle.

"No. I wrote that last August when everything was still alright. Strange, that. It was more directed at Dave than the band as a whole. Obviously, being very close, it was a statement about us. Also, it was a statement about rock and roll. Presley died the week I was writing it, so obviously that was an influence. I was never a great Presley fan, just a real admirer of the bravado, the style, some of his musicians — James Burton and people like that. Everybody in rock and roll was affected by it in some way." I wondered, then, if Dave was thinking of leaving the Kinks at that point.

Again, the answer is negative. "It's just that I had wanted him — I've always wanted him — to do other things. Maybe it was a mixture of that and me wanting to write more and do more things. The weird thing is that when the other two decided to leave, Dave came up to me and said, 'This could be the best thing that's happened to us. Now we have the chance to be the band we want to be.' So, the song is really about losing touch with reality by being kind of protected from it by what you do. I don't want to get out of rock and roll, but I don't want to live in a bubble, either. I want to be creative, but I can only be creative if I'm in touch with what being creative's about. The lampshade isn't going to read my book or listen to my music, people will."

AFTER SEEING *MISFITS* described by reviewers as a concept album, I asked Ray whether he had intended it to be one. "It wasn't meant to be a concept album, because the idea was to make it a lot of tracks that didn't fit in with a concept. But as it wore on and I actually got down to writing the lyrics to "Misfits," things changed. The lyrics

and the music to the first verse came out at exactly the same time, and it wasn't until I got into writing the lyrics for the rest of the song that I realized that it was the key track that could tie the whole thing up: it could say a lot about the band, a lot about me and a lot about the album... So, really, though it wasn't intended to be a concept thing, it ended up one, purely and simply because it was tied together by one track. If we'd taken that one track off, the rest of the album wouldn't have fitted together. It wasn't intended to be a story album."

I was surprised to find out that much of the album had been written quite a long time ago: "Get Up" was a year-and-a-half old; "Black Messiah" dates back two years; "Hay Fever" is three years old; and "In a Foreign Land" was actually written in 1974. Yet despite the age of the material, lyrically, *Misfits* is extremely contemporary, with songs like "Live Life," "Get Up" and, oddly enough, "In a Foreign Land" relating directly to what's been going down in England this past year. In fact, it's the Kinks' most political album since *Preservation Act II*, though Davies' politics seem moderate compared to some of the more radical songwriters of the new wave. A review of *Misfits* in *Sounds*, in fact, attacked Davies for his conservatism, singling out "Foreign Land" in particular for supporting the tax exiledom of "rich" old rock stars like himself. Davies, however, is no tax exile: he still lives in England.

"The song is about a character who's not just pissed off with the tax, he's pissed off more with the culture itself. If I ever left England, it wouldn't be because of tax, it would be because I didn't want to live there anymore. If you talk about escaping from tax, people naturally assume that you have a lot of money. The problem in England is that everybody working class has to escape from tax, really, but the song is more about escaping from a lifestyle, or what you see happening to a place. The character is a guy who wants to be nothing, he doesn't want to be recognized, he doesn't want to be anybody."

SINCE HE'D WRITTEN *Arthur (or the Decline and Fall of the British Empire)* nearly 10 years ago, I asked Ray his feelings on England in 1978. "I think it's on the verge of being truly screwed up. As soon as you get off the plane in England they're hitting you with the past, whereas in America people seem more willing to accept reality. In England, you've got to be one thing or another, there's no tolerance there, it's become a very intolerant country. What I've found is that if you don't go and vote socialist, you're branded as an ultra-conservative. I was brought up socialist, but I've noticed that the extreme way is not my way. You've got to be able to have an argument, and the way I see it going is that we're going to end up in a society where it's not possible to have one. As much as you dislike the guy on the street and say, 'I think you stink' or 'I think you're wrong,' the fact that you've got the right to say that is enough. But I think there's a difference between saying you're unhappy and saying you want to bring down the government. I don't want to get too involved in it, but, well, unions in England are being manipulated a bit by the extremes, I think. England seems to me to be ripe for totalitarianism."

Does the National Front scare him? "It's always scared me. I was brought up to be afraid of Adolf Hitler. All through my life I was taught, 'This is what a bad person is.' But then the two extremes seem the same to me. There was a track that I left off *Misfits* called 'East/West': 'East, west, what's the difference? You might be going east or west until somebody tells you...' That sort of lyric; I guess I didn't put it on because I didn't like the tune. Anyway, I feel that both extremes are equally corrupt. It's not money that corrupts people, it's power. It's when people think they have ultimate power over people that they get together and torture people, because they have them at their mercy. I might be totally wrong, but that's what I see, that's what I feel. Maybe I'm mixing up my songwriting and my politics — composing the future — but I can see it ending up like the ending of *Preservation*.

"That's why my interest in *Preservation* has been rekindled. I want to make it a movie. I've got to. I've been looking at Cleveland as a place to film it. The movie needs a stadium by a river, which they've got. It's a very industrial town with a lot of alleyways. I'd like to make it partly there and partly in London. Make it everywhere. I've been working on an outline of it with a friend of mine."

HIS DISCUSSION of the film brings us back to what he had said in connection with "A Rock 'n' Roll Fantasy," about getting out and doing things not directly connected with rock and roll, rather than living the ivory-towered existence that goes along with rock stardom. I asked Ray what his feelings are on superstardom.

"The idea of attaining total stardom is that you do cut yourself off from the world. That's what it's all about. That is freedom, perhaps. I'm saying that I don't want that kind of freedom, maybe I feel that I should stay where I am. At the same time, I think about the lyric to '20th Century Man' and I feel really close to that lyric now, too. I just don't want to be here sometimes, because one person who's a songwriter can't do that much. Maybe it's good to have the choice of not being here, but maybe it's good to stick it out, too. That's what I'm going to do. That's what "Brother" [on *Sleepwalker*] is about. It's not just about someone leaving on a boat. It's people ratting on you and leaving you behind to face the consequences. The song says a bit about me, that I'll work with the first person I see on the street. I think everyone's got something they can give. 'I'm your brother, don't even know your name,' sounds great, very poetic. But really, I think on a work basis, people have got to be a bit more like that."

But, I interject, the whole thrust of technological society is to... "...eliminate people." He finishes my sentence. "Yes, that's what Mr. Black will do. A lot of people are becoming automaton without knowing it. When we fly from gig to gig, especially in America, I see a guy with a briefcase and I know in a minute he's going to pull out a sheet with figures on it. I know what the problems are going to be, what he's going to have to drink, what's going to happen when he gets home. People are becoming like the red ant who adapts to what's going on around him very quickly."

Does he think it's particularly noticeable in the music business?

"I think I'd notice it in whatever business I was in, because I'm me," he says with a tinge of sadness. "Maybe I notice it more because I do think about people a lot when I'm writing. I think, 'How can I communicate this to people?' I don't know why I think about political things so much. I guess I'm concerned. The thing I hate most is people doing what they don't want to do. When I see it happening — people ignoring what's going on, even though they don't like it — the most horrible things have resulted. I think about Nazi Germany and Hitler. Sometimes it's maybe the will of the people that does it. Was it Adolf Hitler or was it the will of the people being manifested in one person? Once again, it's having power and nobody to question it.

"There's always got to be a question and someone to answer to. Someone bigger up there to confront. It stands to reason. You've always got to have an objective and someone to be objective with you. It's like in an Alan Bennett play called *40 Years On,* where this rich, old lady is being wheeled around in a wheelchair throughout the whole play. She's left on stage alone for a minute and she gets up and starts walking around and addresses the audience, 'You may be wondering why I'm walking around,' she says. 'It's because I'm so rich I don't have to walk.' She pretends that she's a cripple. That's the one red light, watch for it. Power corrupts, fame corrupts."

I ASK IF HE'S HAPPY being a misfit. "If fitting in with the world is following the river, going along with the current, and knowing where it's going, I'd rather go my own way and not know where I'm going." Doesn't he feel that it's a very elitist stance to take?

"If it is elitist to be an individual and to want that right to be an individual, then I'll be an elitist, but I think it's elitist to want everyone else to be like you. I just reject the crowd. The fact that the Kinks get maybe two or three thousand people at a gig is a kind of, not so much acknowledgment of my belief, but an acknowledgment that those people believe in themselves.

"It's almost uncool to see the Kinks play, yet they come see us anyway." ∎

HELLO IT'S ME

TP 28, MAY 1978

I enjoyed Jonathan Morrish's Traffic retrospective (TP 25) very much; however, there are a few misconceptions I'd like to clear up.

The way the article reads it looks as if Chris Blackwell didn't enter the picture until Steve Winwood had split from me. Actually, Chris was in on the beginning of the Spencer Davis Group.

The right-hand photo of the two captioned "Chris Wood then and now" on page 12 was actually Ric Grech.

The initial single by the Spencer Davis Group ("Keep on Running") didn't involve any of Traffic except Steve. However, we were all on subsequent singles like "Somebody Help Me" and "I'm a Man." Peter York was probably one of the best drummers in the UK at the time and is currently playing with Chris Barber's Jazz Band. Muff Winwood was a more than adequate bass player. When we added people on those records it was because we wanted them in to add to the sound of the record, not because we couldn't play the songs ourselves. I also played guitar on most of those things as well.

The line-up on "I'm a Man" was myself on guitar, Pete York on drums and finger cymbals, Muff on bass, Steve on keyboards. Chris Wood played maracas. Jimmy Miller was in on it as well. It was an exciting session which, incidentally, was actually recorded as a soundtrack to a film about mods called *Swingin' London.* We liked the track so much we decided it would be our next single. We were right; it was a major hit, although Chicago's version was an even bigger hit.

"Gimme Some Lovin'" had everyone on it as well. Also, after Steve had left the SDG and I'd split from Island, I had a number of singles out. One was called "After Tea" and had Dave Mason on sitar. Chris Wood and Jim Capaldi were on it as well, though Steve didn't appear at all.

Spencer Davis
Los Angeles, CA

PRODUCT REPORT: KISS, INC.

TP 34, DECEMBER 1978

By Dave Schulps

WINTER 1974: When I saw the cover of the first Kiss album, I laughed. I mean, here were these four geeks looking like rejects from last year's Halloween party. Did somebody forget to tell them that glitter-rock was dead? I had to hear it.

I chuckled as I opened the shrink wrap. "Smart guy," I thought after the needle had made its way across the platter for a couple of minutes, "Had 'em pegged from the start. They'll never make it." It was minimally competent loud glitter stuff. So what. Who needs this stuff when I got T. Rex?

When I first saw Kiss play, I shuddered. It was purely by accident, anyway. I was working for my college radio station then, and the opening act was a new Anglo group I wanted to interview after their set — the Heavy Metal Kids. Kiss was headlining, and after my interview was over, we went back downstairs (the radio station was conveniently located right above the concert hall — the stairway led right backstage) to see this band that looked so ridiculous, actually had a second album out and were reportedly into such stunts as rising drum platforms, fire breathing and blood spitting onstage. Sure enough, things were as bad as expected. "Terrible," I thought, "they'll never last."

Still, the crowd had packed the place, and they were getting off. Just what they were getting off on was hard to say. Drugs? Sure. Beating each other up? Yeah, a few of them were doing that. The music? Well, obviously they were. When the band left the stage, these kids went crazy. Since I was standing backstage (a first for me) I got to see and hear these schleps as they walked off stage. The tall one with the armadillo boots was dripping dirtied makeup and pulling singed hairs out of his head. His fire-breathing trick had not worked quite right that evening. As the applause rang fiercely from in front of the stage, their conversation went something like this:

"God, did you see those guys up front, they were beating the shit out of each other."

"I'm not going back out there, those people are insane."

"My back is killing me. I don't know whether I can drum anymore. Somebody rub my back."

"C'mon, let's do an encore, I wanna see what's happening with that fight."

They did the encore. And another. And another.

I was still backstage when they changed out of their make-up and costumes. Don't ask me why I stayed, but I wanted to ask one of them a question. I was introduced to Gene Simmons, who sat down and looked at the copy of *Trouser Press #2* I handed him. "British rock, huh? It's a nice magazine. I used to put out a science-fiction fanzine myself. You should write about your own groups right here in America, though." (Soon after, he subscribed, anyway.) "Hah!" I thought, "That'll be the day when I write about these guys." I was less than tactful when I finally got down to asking my question.

"Why?" I asked. "Why do you go out there and act like that?" I was very serious (and more than a little obnoxious). He wasn't hurt. "Why?"

He replied in an almost pedantic tone. "Did you see those kids out there? They loved us. They ate it up. We're giving them exactly what they want." ("But is that what they need?" I thought.) After about 15 minutes of discussion of the merits of Kiss and the question of British vs. American rock, Kiss left for their hotel. Gene gave me his number and said to call him the next day. I didn't.

WINTER 1975: "Rock and Roll All Night" was blaring out of portable radios and jukeboxes all over the Apple. It was almost like you couldn't walk outta the house without hearing it somewhere. The barriers were being broken down. Not just mine — though I have to admit that the refrain began to carve a niche for itself somewhere in my cerebrum — but radio's, too, and that meant something. Wherever these guys had gotten to before they'd done it by word of mouth and satisfied concert-goers, radio (at least New York radio) had resisted them like the plague. Now, *Kiss Alive* was selling like hotcakes, and the kids who hung out at the local pizza joints were dropping their dancing dimes into the slot, pushing the buttons marked "Kiss," and talking 'bout Gene and Paul and Ace and Peter like they'd known them all their 15-year-old lives. Face it, guy, you blew it, these guys had made it.

Whether I like it or not — and, in principle, I didn't — Kiss had placed their finger on the pulses of these kids, or at least their fantasies, with a simple eleven-word reprise: "I wanna rock and roll all night, and party every day." This was an anthem, a teenage anthem, nothing more and nothing less; and while I could argue 'til doomsday that my faves the Dictators were writing better teenage anthems — funnier, crazier, less simplistic, more biting — you didn't have to be a genius to see why one was getting through while the other wasn't. Simply, Kiss were, on one hand, larger than life, totally unapproachable and unreal, and, on the other hand, spoke the audience's language in terms anyone could understand. You didn't have to be cool to dig Kiss; they were merely four distinct images up there acting out your fantasies of stardom and superherodom — there was nothing to understand, no secret meanings to grasp. They didn't even exist as people, not really, and if whatever was under that makeup and costume was any smarter or any better in any way than you were, they sure weren't letting on to it.

What's more, they were beginning to write some better-than-average rock songs — churning out teenage anthems ain't easy, you know — and their performances were no longer sloppy but had evolved into a strikingly professional extravaganza which was both excessive and tight at the same time. And, after all, they did play hard rock: no troubled troubadour music, no jazz-rock fusion shit, no dippy laid-back L.A. country-rock, no disco. Sure, they were simplistic and a bit crass, but hasn't rock always been simplistic and crass? — were the Beatles mass-marketed any more tastefully once it was found that there was an audience that would buy anything they put their name to? So, while I wasn't about to go out and enlist in the Kiss Army, I had to admit that I liked some of their stuff and, most of all, I admired them for so shrewdly being able to calculate who their audience was and what they wanted, and then going out and giving it to them.

WINTER 1976: Since the breakthrough achieved by the platinum *Alive*, there has been no stopping Kiss. They've released two more LPs. *Destroyer* proved they could duplicate the success of *Alive* with a studio album. Perhaps their best album in terms of material, containing three bona-fide anthems in "Detroit Rock City," "Flaming Youth" and "Shout It Out Loud" (though, oddly enough, the hit single was "Beth," a Peter Criss-sung ballad that was initially supposed to be a B-side), its main drawback was Bob Ezrin's overproduction, which sapped much of the power it should've had. *Rock and Roll Over* was back to basics, with Eddie Kramer handling the production in a straight-ahead, no-punches-pulled manner.

In the year since *Alive*, Kiss has become almost an American institution. *Creem* and *Circus* seem to have them on the cover every other issue, and there are rumors that Marvel Comics is working on a comic book based on Kiss. They have literally become the superheroes of a generation. Strangest of all, though, is the audience at their Madison Square Garden concerts. Where two years ago the crowd seemed to range in age from 15 to 20, this crowd ranges from eight to 80. For me, the show in the audience comes close to upstaging the show onstage. There are at least a hundred fully made-up Kiss lookalike kids parading around the hall — some of the smaller ones holding onto mommy's hand. One fan breathes fire from the balcony seats and is arrested by the Garden cops as thousands of boos go up. The whole thing is an amazing spectacle. Regardless of what you think of Kiss, you have to be just a little bit amazed by it all. The band's performance is almost anticlimactic next to the event. itself, but the crowd, of course, goes wild.

WINTER 1978: Two years on, three more group LPs — *Love Gun*, *Alive II* (another double live album) and *Double Platinum* (a double greatest hits package) — ensure that Kiss stock hasn't dropped a point. They've also now got the world's only "gold" (500,000 sales) comic book ever published, with a sequel due out shortly. Just out is another first, four simultaneously released, similarly packaged, solo LPs — each one shipped "gold" — which stress each group member's individual persona while maintaining the Kiss identity through the packaging concept. And if you think the barrage of Kiss product up to now has occasionally seemed overwhelming, well, we've only just glimpsed the tip of the iceberg. Love 'em or hate 'em, it's going to be pretty hard to ignore Kiss in the coming months, for it seems they're going to be just about everywhere you can turn.

The questions are, of course, why and how all of this has happened and, ultimately, where is it all leading to? How much farther can this group that couldn't last go? In search of some answers, I spoke to Paul Stanley (face to face) and to Gene Simmons (over the phone from Los Angeles, where he was finishing up work on his LP), the two members who founded and conceptualized Kiss. The interviews were not only revealing, but (especially in Simmons' case) fairly mind-boggling. Each was eager to discuss his solo album and, more surprising to me, both seemed extremely proud of what they had done. I asked why they had all decided to do solo albums.

Paul: "Everyone in the band had wanted to do one. Solo albums usually have connotations of bands breaking up, or one guy showing he's the force behind the band because his LP sounds like the band. We did some stuff that the band couldn't get away with because it wasn't the 'Kiss-sound,' y'know, two guitars, bass, drums, vocal, background vocal — straight ahead. Mine

is one-quarter of that sound. I wanted to take my quarter further and make it the whole of the sound.

"I didn't want to get into using session people, though, guys who at 7:00 are going to do your album and at 8:00 a McDonald's commercial. I just used some people I enjoy playing with. The nucleus was myself and Bob Kulick, who's played with Meat Loaf, Lou Reed and Alice Cooper. We never actually rehearsed the material, we just went in and did it cold. You may get technically better performances after rehearsing a few days, but you don't get the heart. The songs for the album were all written within the last six months especially for the album. I wanted to steer clear of doing Kiss rejects. I didn't want to put out an album of songs indicative of where I was five years ago."

Which is exactly what Gene Simmons did: "You see, the secret about Kiss is that we were not born with high heels, and I was not born with a long tongue... I just kind of grew into it. Before Kiss, Paul and I were in a different kind of band that was doing exactly the kind of material that's on my album. In fact, some of the material, some of the more obvious Beatle-esque stuff, is the stuff I did back then, eight years ago. I still have about a hundred tunes left over from that period — that kind of stuff, I mean, you don't always feel like sawing your brains in half. I guess more than anything else the album is a kind of open book on the influences of that period of my career."

I asked what that band was called, knowing full well he wasn't going to tell me. "That's not really important, because Paul and I had cut an album which we sold to another record label — under different names and all that — and that record company still has that album with all this different kind of material on it so — well, I'd rather not have that stuff come out.

"Anyway, the kind of material we were doing back then was a mishmash of all different kinds of styles, and nobody really gave two shits whether or not we were coming or going, and we realized our own failings, failings of that last band, and that last band — it was kind of nondescript. There were all kinds of guys, all different sizes, all different shapes. You know, one guy with an afro, another guy with long hair, another guy with a beard, another guy with a moustache and two guys without moustaches. I mean there was just kind of no unity. One guy was fat, one guy thin. It looked like the UN, you know."

And we all know how popular they are. "So, that band was short-lived, but it was a good learning experience for me, because I realized that to make any kind of statement from music or anything else, you really have to simplify it, really bring it down to the LCD — the Lowest Common Denominator, so that people out there that don't play instruments can, you know, appreciate what you are doing, that they don't have to sit there and go to school to realize that what we've done is good. Anyway, Kiss is really a band that Paul and I always pretty much wanted to see on stage, the culmination of all the bands I've ever seen, from the Who to Alice, through early Genesis, to the Dolls — lots of different kinds of bands that I liked, but were not complete bands in the sense that if the lead singer had an off-night, you really wouldn't give two shits about the rest of the band. So, if the lead singer, the front man, or whoever it was that has the visual thing happening, was not on, then it was the end.

"My album initially was going to be called *Man of a Thousand Faces*, until we decided as a band not to mislead people, because we were simply putting out four Kiss albums, and that the fact that I was putting out my own album didn't infer anything more than the fact that it was going to be my album, but also an extension of Kiss, and that there were, in fact, four Kiss albums instead of four solo albums, because we're not breaking up and we're not arguing and we're not doing any of the stuff that solo albums necessarily infer.

"So, the album is really a collection of songs that I always liked. That was the prerequisite for the songs being on the album, but what happened without my initially knowing it is that there developed a kind of lyrical theme running through the whole thing and then, all of a sudden, it hit me that the end, the last song, ('When You Wish Upon a Star') was really, you know, Gene Simmons realizing his dream.

"Until now, I've never really thought about doing any of this stuff, because it's very personal. It's very vulnerable kind of stuff. You can't be stomping on the stage and killing chickens to the beat of the music, which is what we're usually doing, while singing 'Mr. Make Believe' or 'Man of a Thousand Faces' or any of that stuff. You've got to come out and sing about strutters and about cops and about the kinds of things that everybody thinks about anyway. Because it's fun, and especially because it's easier to put a big, strong backbeat to that stuff. But since this is a solo album, I really wanted to do something special, something different. 'When You Wish Upon a Star' is the last cut. I planned to do it for about a year, but it wouldn't have fit with Kiss — not then, but now that I've heard it through, I see that lyrically, at least, it really is what we're about. We're just four guys who are walking the streets of New York, you know, paying with everybody else, going to see Led Zeppelin at Madison Square Garden, and wishing we were up there doing it. There's nothing very original about what we wanted to do and what we wanted. I'm sure there are millions of people walking the streets nowadays that have the same thing going."

Why have Kiss been able to step off the street and become superstars when nearly everyone else who's tried has failed?

Paul: "We decided that we were gonna be a kick-ass rock band that's theatrical, rather than a theatrical band that plays rock and roll. When we put together Kiss, we looked for people with a vibe about them who played English-style hard rock. Gene's an English freak, Ace is an English freak, I'm an English freak. We wanted a drummer who was solid, originally, we wanted two bass drums. We didn't want someone with a moustache, didn't want someone who was 5'1" and fat. We were looking for a group image — the right chemistry. Ace came in and was doing all those Jimmy Page licks, that was what we wanted, a classic English hard rock guitarist with the trills and the triplets and that whole trip.

"We were determined to cut across to a wide audience on a lot of levels. There's ten reasons you could think of that people could like us. Maybe we're a little more intelligent than a lot of other people... I'm sure that doesn't hurt."

Gene: "We are not stupid, which probably has something to do with it. We don't believe our own press. Also, most rock and roll people are so fucked up with things going through their veins that by the time success or any kind of exposure starts to happen, they're already in the ground, or have done themselves in. Just look at the Dolls. Everybody in this band knows exactly what we're doing. We created the thing by ourselves, and it was not an accident. It was us trying to figure out who we'd like to see on stage, what kind of a band would we like to see on stage, how many people should be in it. It was a very thought-out thing, and especially the songs. The songs were the kind of songs that we sat down and figured out what appealed to most people, the kind of music that I liked to listen to live. We knew that the concept of selling music on radio is self-defeating in the long run, because you get typecast very quickly — somebody like Carol Douglas can come out and sell two million copies of "Doctor's Orders" and then the album sells a thousand. And in the back of all this, we really wanted to be big and famous and rich and all the rest of the stuff that comes with being famous, and probably at the end of all of this, it could be luck."

Did he feel he needed those "name" guest stars to help sell the album or did he just want them there because they were friends?

"They were friends, number one. Number two, I reject very strongly the unwritten law in rock and roll, that certain musicians in certain rock and roll genres can't associate with other people. For instance, 'Death to Disco' by the rock and roll segment of the populace, and the guys who like the old British style of music thinking that punk is nonsense, and the punksters thinking the rest of the stuff is nonsense. There is a lot of division in rock and roll that I could never really understand. I think a record is good if it's good. If it moves me on whatever grounds, then it's simply good and it works on that level. I may have my own favorite kinds of bands, I may prefer to play in a special kind of band, but certainly the kind of music that I play is not all that I am — I don't listen to Kiss records all day. Sometimes I turn to Lawrence Welk

on television, because it's sick. You know, Lawrence Welk is a much sicker person than I am."

Why?

"Oh, the man lives in a time capsule. The man is in the '20s someplace. I mean, you can't be normal and have bubbles floating around the stage."

I'm sure he'd say something similar about Kiss.

"Well, of course, but that's why it's wonderful, because everybody's sanity is based on their own conception of it. The guy who walks the streets who is crazy, probably has people who are saying the same thing about him that he's saying about them. That's the kind of stuff that I don't understand in rock and roll when it's all based on a concept of a strong backbeat. Everything else is just a variation of that. What is so different from the Dolls to the Pistols to even Zeppelin, except for the fact that it's different styles?"

It's just a matter of taste and the level on which a certain listener may be able to understand the material.

"There's no accounting for that, certainly, but with my album I also wanted to get some people pissed off, because I'm not so much interested having people saying that I'm great, I just don't want them to say: 'Ho hum, that's interesting.' You just tell me that it's the worst piece of trash that you ever heard and you are so adamant about it that you have to go tell your friends about it, or it's the best thing you've ever heard and you have to go tell your friends about it. Either way, what I want is that you go tell your friends about it, discuss it or just talk about it, but just don't say 'So what,' because apathy is nothing."

How would he feel, then, if he received an apathetic reaction to his album?

"I wouldn't feel badly about it at all, it wouldn't matter to me at all because it's exactly what I wanted to do, because you would have to be crazy to be affected by it now when it's never affected you before. We were never really a critics' band."

I didn't mean critics, I meant, if the Kiss audience listened to it and said, "Ho hum, that's nice."

"Oh, my fans. I would feel hurt by that. Of course, I would. It's the people that have embraced me and said, 'Look, we accept what you do, we like what you do.' If they put their thumbs down on that, I would feel hurt by it. I think the only criteria for that is sales. You and I could argue from now until doomsday about how good or bad something is, but the one thing we can't argue about is, if something is really a piece of trash, then fewer and fewer people will tend to buy it. There is such a thing as peer group pressure and all the rest of that, but when you're talking about millions of records, there's got to be something there that people like. It's the old Elvis Presley adage: 50 million Elvis fans can't be wrong."

True, but the fact that Kiss has more money to put into advertising and promotion than another band might have is a big factor.

"Yes. I'll never negate that fact. However, there are classic examples like the millions of dollars that was spent to promote the *Tonight Show* album and you know that flopped like no other album I ever heard of. You and I know that no matter how big a group is they can slip. Jethro Tull can go from two million units to five hundred thousand units within one album, which he [sic] did. I don't care who you are, if the public decides you are no longer doing the kinds of stuff they are interested in, then you're on your way out."

So, with your album, let's say, you're taking a chance.

"I don't think I am. I think I'm expanding the audience. There's enough Kiss stuff in there that makes it me as people are used to me, and what it is, is it's also some stuff for little sister and mom and dad, and I think it's also from the point of view of being sick, you know, Gene Simmons on stage. It's also pretty sick to hear me singing 'When You Wish Upon a Star.'"

Oh, I think so. (Laugh.)

"It's Bellevue material."

I thought it was pretty funny.

"Yeah."

Did you think it was funny while you were doing it?

"I was very serious about it."

Really?

"Yeah. You know, Kiss has never really been anything more than Disney, 100-megaton bomb-size. You know, there is no difference. Disney never had a message. The only thing he ever offered was

escapism. That's it. Visual escapism, and that's all we ever hope to do. The only thing we hope to do as a band and individually is when you come into the concert hall, wherever the thing is, that while you are in there you are completely into what we are doing."

How far can they see taking the Kiss concept in the future?

Gene: "I'll tell you. We are taking a year off. In that time, in September, the four Kiss solo albums are coming out, I think five million copies are shipping, the largest in recorded history. Two days before that, the second Marvel comic book is coming out, and we're making up our own awards called Gold Comics. The first Kiss comic book was gold, and now it's almost platinum. The second Kiss comic is shipping gold."

Is that the largest selling comic book ever? "Yes. Especially in that size. What happens is most comic books sell about 200,000 to 300,000 units as 35-cent comic books. Our comic book sells for $1.50. So, that's coming out in September along with the Kiss transistor radio, the Kiss back-to-school books, Kiss jeans, Kiss garbage pails, believe it or not, and Kiss dolls put out by Meco, the same people who put out the Cher doll. Then there's the Kiss Bally pinball machine and Kiss bubblegum cards."

What are the Kiss jeans going to look like? "They're gonna have a tongue as an overlap, and you pick the tongue up to put your hand in your pocket. And there are Kiss jackets, very fancy kind of baseball jacket things that are going on sale. But anyway, that's happening in September. Then in October — Halloween — the Kiss Halloween outfits are going on sale, and the two-hour movie that we did for NBC is going to be broadcast October 28. The movie was a co-production between ourselves and Hanna-Barbera Productions, costing over two million dollars to make, and it's going to be released as a movie outside of the United States. And then we're starting our first feature movie in January/February, all of which is going to lead to the soundtrack album coming out in late spring, which is going to be a double album of new material."

Whew! When I'd asked the question, I hadn't

been prepared for the kind of incredible list Gene rattled off. I was amazed at his knowledge of the current Kiss marketing strategy, but I'd actually wanted to know what he thought would happen to Kiss over a longer span of time. After all, they've done nearly everything that I could think of already.

"Are you kidding? It's just beginning. What are you talking about?"

What more could Kiss do, short of entering politics?

"Eventually, what we'd like to do, is open up Kiss World."

Uh-huh. A kind of Disneyland, I guessed. "Oh, Disney's got nothing on us. I think we can make it a little bit more exciting, and certainly we never — you know, we never said we were anything original, or anything new under the sun. It's very pompous to even think in those terms. But so what, who cares if something is new or old? The important thing is that it works, and that it gets people off and that people like it. So, eventually, we are going to be thinking of obvious central points and build something called Kiss World."

Any plans for where it might be? You could drop it right in the middle of New York City.

"That sure would be nice, wouldn't it?"

How did Gene feel Kiss differs from the Bay City Rollers, conceptually, aside from the obvious differences in costume and music?

"Probably conceptually we are similar, in the fact that our fans idolize us. I don't want to be a punk band, you understand, and have the audience think they're the same as me. I don't. I want to be up on that stage, and I want you to grovel at my feet, and just be amazed by how big and amazing, truly wonderful, I am. I don't want you to come up and pat me on the back and say: 'Say, you and I are the same, look, I have the same haircut, and we can walk down the street together — we're just two punks.' No way.

"If I wasn't doing this, I would have to do something else that would make somebody come over and pat me on the back and say: 'Gee, you're really wonderful,' which is really what it's all about for me. I don't really give two shits about money or any of that stuff. The only reason the toys and

records and anything else really knocks me out, and the reason I collect everything to do with myself, is because I get a kick out of it. It soothes my ego. It's recognition. You don't have to jump off the highest building just to get your picture in the paper. That's what it's all about."

So, it's not money or anything like that. I found that hard to believe.

"If you ask anybody that's ever known me for any amount of time, you will find out that I still don't drive and I still don't have a car, but I do just call up whatever company is around and they pick me up. I don't want possessions, I don't want things, but I do want to have all the money that I could ever conceive of so that I can do whatever I want to do."

Would he ever consider taking off the makeup?

"No. Well, sure, I do every once in a while. I do have to go to sleep, take showers and other things."

I've seen you in public without it.

"As long as Kiss is around, I don't think I'd ever appear without it. It's too important. You don't want to find out that your father is really Santa Claus coming down the chimney. It would ruin the magic. No. While there is Kiss, I don't want to take it off. If I do ever decide to do anything else besides Kiss, and right now, you know, all my needs and wants are satisfied with the band, sure I'll take it off sometime in the future, but it won't be the same. And I certainly wouldn't try to do the same thing. It would be blasphemic [sic], blasphemic for me to do that."

"You know what I just saw in front of me?" Gene asked rhetorically. "The Kiss Phono by Tiger Electric Toys. It's amazing what they've done. It's like this record player and a suitcase."

He seemed to be auditioning new Kiss products even while we were talking on the phone. I asked how a Kiss phono is different from a regular one. He began to read off the label:

"Here's what it says: 'Deluxe Kiss Phono with exciting Kiss scene' — that's a good picture. 'Rich, clear sound from dynamic three-and-a-half-inch speaker. Sapphire needle, star protective tone arm guard,' whatever the fuck that means. 'Solid state amplifier, two-speed turntable,' blah blah."

It doesn't spit blood, or anything? I asked. This was getting ridiculous.

"It does have a period once a month."

Oh well, that's nice.

"That's about all. It looks neat. Boy, I'd buy that instead of Mickey Mouse any day. Mickey Mouse doesn't have a dick."

This does?

"Sure. Anything with Kiss on it's got a dick."

How big?

"A mile long. Ask anyone."

Fan or non-fan?

"What?"

Fan or nonfan?

"Even a non-fan's got to say, 'God, I hate those guys, but they sure have big dicks!'" ∎

HELLO IT'S ME

TOTP 11, NOVEMBER/DECEMBER 1975

Recently picked up your tenth number and must say it really is one of the better written rock journals...

Yes, I did pay for it off the newsstand!

Gordon's Beck interview was superb. Nice digging ... but I do take exception with some of the things Beck said...

"The Faces and Zeppelin are catering to the public..." Well, without mentioning any names, Jeff!!! Alright then, what if, in fact, both are doing the self-same thing (catering)? Is it any less important? And since when has rock become so elitist (self-indulging?). I mean, can you picture Chuck Berry saying what Beck said about Bill Black's Combo??? If you can take a figurative step backward and consider for a moment. Rock 'n' Roll (Rock, or whatever else you want to call it...) is mass-culture oriented ... it's here and now music, played by people for people of the same comparative age group (goodness, I got a lump in my throat). No need to say that about yer mates, Jeff. People that buy their records/see their concerts are happy, as are the people that see you. I'm sure!

OBVIOUSLY!! Otherwise they wouldn't spend the $4. for the stuff...

Then again, I'm one of those who liked the *Truth/Beckola* period, anyway...

Kindly pay attention to New York bands. This is important ... and very healthy for you, as well as, obviously, the bands.

Recently saw some of the newer bands and I'm knocked out to see that feyness (at least "forced feyness") has disappeared from the scene ... I liked the Planets much, and Movies are a very un-New York-ey kind of group — I mean they can actually play well...

Looking forward to future issues.

Best regards
Gene Simmons

TOTP 13, APRIL/MAY 1976

Another nice one...

Layout & pics are all very pleasing...

I like [Alex] Harvey. The man seems most sensible, and not at all uncomfortable with his age or position in popular music (Rock!)... Why you guys could get this kind of depth out of Alex, when the newsstand 'zines can't is beyond me...

Wish I could've been around to live through the first real British invasion (i.e. actually sweating along with everyone else on a weekday night at Ronny Scott's or at the Marquee, for an off-night of the Beatles...) Alex obviously has fond memories of the whole thing..

Lately, Mott's been doing a row of dates with us and we've grown close ... but that has little to do with my disagreements over Scott Isler's Mott review... For my money, Mott (in many ways) is a stronger outfit this time. Agreed, Hunter had strong presence and wrote some fine tunes, but Mott is playing in tune and with balls...

Then again, Scott may have caught one of the formative gigs of the new ensemble... I say Mott is hot!

Sweet--Yes!

Cheers
Gene Simmons

CHEAP TRICK: GREETINGS FROM ROCKFORD

TP 57, DECEMBER 1980

By Ira Robbins

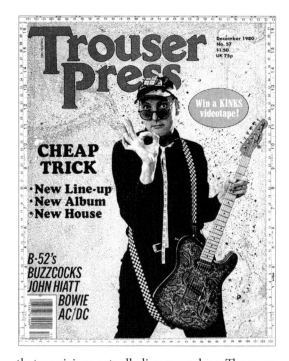

Rockford, Illinois (population 140,000) has made two notable contributions to the entertainment world: [1980 presidential candidate] John Anderson and Cheap Trick. While there is little similarity between the two — no one in Cheap Trick has white hair — their roots, outlook and ethics (industriousness, seriousness, sense of commitment) are the same.

Rockford hardly seems the kind of place to inspire wild rock and rolling. It's neither bustling nor sleepy; whatever extreme impulses might lurk behind the middle-American *Gemütlichkeit* can be funneled into constructive community activity. Amid fair Swedish and Teutonic descendants, however, a rock band lives and works, brewing platinum potions for the youth of America. Cheap Trick, well into their fourth year as a top draw, continue to reside there and have no intentions of leaving. You'd expect successful rock musicians to move to one of the US rock biz power centers after grabbing the gold ring, but the ties that bind the Cheap Trick organization to their spawning ground are so strong that bassist Tom Peterson's relocation to Beverly Hills two years ago culminated in his departure from the band this past August.

It's easy for rock writers (and fans) to forget that musicians actually live someplace. The press and public sees them only in hotel rooms, concert halls, bars, dressing rooms, recording studios or record company offices, none of which serve as anything more than transient roosts from which to conduct business. The most successful ones stay on the move, never stopping anywhere for long. If they have normal off-the-road families and lives, we neither see nor consider it, and that's probably the way everyone involved would like it to remain. But where do rock professionals go when their obligations are over and done? Into hibernation? Long vacations in exotic resorts? Foreign hospitals for blood transfusions?

A few days after Rick Nielsen and company tendered the offer to come out and observe Cheap Trick's native habitat, I found myself seated on a TWA flight with the festively adorned guitarist. As usual, Nielsen sported a baseball cap, a custom sweater and a batch of gold-colored Sportsacs from which he produced a tiny cassette recorder [*it was a first-generation Walkman, not yet available in the U.S. but given to him by Sony on a recent trip to Japan*], earphones and a tape of the group's then-forthcoming LP, *All Shook Up*. While the stewardesses tried to ignore his pleas for free refreshments that are a privilege of first-class air travel, I parked myself in the economy section with a musical menu the inflight program just couldn't challenge.

Nielsen's jeep is parked across the street from the Rockford airport (a 12-minute hop from Chicago). The guided tour provided by our host/chauffeur reveals Rockford to be the sort of place in which no adventurous type would ever remain. Nothing wrong with a handsome burgh, but this place's major industry is the manufacture of screws.

Everyone in Maria's Italian restaurant — kids, parents — knows who Nielsen is, but only a few take any notice. Enough of them have known the band since the beginning not to be especially surprised by their success. Nielsen obliges the autograph requests and is full of repartee for everyone who comes over and sits in an extra chair that, for all I know, might have been left on purpose by the waitress. He has opted to live in the town where he was raised and doesn't seem to find the burden of fame troublesome. He could move to some metropolis where the night spots' clientele would never dream of asking for an autograph, but who knows if they'd tolerate a guy in a baseball cap? Welcome to Rockford!

With the exception of new bassist Pete Comita, who's moved back to Chicago after a few years in Los Angeles, all the members of Cheap Trick live within a 10-minute drive of each other. Until recently, drummer Bun E. Carlos and singer Robin Zander lived in the same apartment building. Most of the band's road crew and administrative personnel also live in Rockford. Those who don't — like manager Ken Adamany — reside in Madison, Wisconsin, 100 miles due north. Rockford, Madison, Chicago and Milwaukee form a geographic rectangle, and Cheap Trick's early days were spent playing clubs in those four spots. Many fledgling bands in the region continue to do the same, although venues have changed over the years. One, in Madison, was owned and operated by Adamany in the '60s (and was the site of Otis Redding's last gig before the singer's plane nosedived into a nearby lake); it has been converted into a small commercial building housing his offices.

There's a sense of loyalty and solidarity among people in the Cheap Trick organization. Most go back a long ways, and they've all watched (and helped) the band get to where it is now. There don't seem to be any glory hounds or ladder-climbers, just a bunch of hard workers who really believe in the band. Cheap Trick is almost a cottage industry around here, and their forays into the world take on a pioneering quality against this setting.

Nielsen's new home is a beautiful large house that could belong to any prosperous Rockford citizen. There are no neon signs or gates with musical notes, yet as we pull up the driveway, a kid in a station wagon pulls around and drives away, apparently caught in the act of night-time sightseeing.

The tour of the house takes a while — Nielsen is as proud as a new father — but almost nothing about it suggests its owner's livelihood. The furnishings' taste and sophistication don't jibe with the cartoon character familiar to Cheap Trick fans.

When you're a kid you think each concert is unique, an event witnessed by a houseful and never repeated. I remember the first time I saw a major band two nights in a row (I think it was the Stones, about a dozen years ago) and the awful realization that the show was prearranged; what had seemed spontaneous was actually rehearsed. It's a lot easier to understand touring's shortcuts and unavoidable pressures after seeing how little time bands spend together on the road. Apart from soundchecks, they're never near equipment, which, by necessity, travels ahead of the band, and the opportunity to rehearse new material or even alter standards just isn't there. In the '60s, bands could always get up onstage and jam, but how many people would enjoy seeing that again? So, there's nothing wrong (only lamentable) with bands sticking close to format night after night.

Somewhere along the line, though, Cheap Trick hit a rut. Their shows — even from tour to tour — varied so little that it became hard to work up enthusiasm each time they came around. On the last tour, which brought them to New York's Madison Square Garden, they played only four songs from their then-current *Dream Police*, and one of those had been in their set for a year already. Although the band dredged up some early retirees and did a few things differently, the show's routine nature signaled the end of a phase in their development.

The next time Cheap Trick ventures out — which in America will be in December (after a 10-day November tour of England, France and Portugal) — they'll have to do things a bit differently due to the group's new bassist, Pete Comita. The obvious question is why Peterson (now officially spelled with one "s") — longtime friend and musical associate of Nielsen and Carlos's — is no longer in the band.

"It's really no one's business," Nielsen replies, with a tinge of annoyance. "I don't think Cheap Trick was his main concern. He wants to do some things that would take him away too much from the band. It was his decision as much as our decision. He's got things he wants to do; I think he'll do well."

Nielsen sounds genuine in his good wishes; the split doesn't seem to have been based on or to have fostered any hostility. Peterson, reached by phone in his Jacuzzi [ha-ha] in California, seconded the emotion: "There's no hard feelings. I feel good, they feel good. If I had no direction, it'd be horrible, but I'm not worried about anything. I've never been happier." What Peterson has been doing is recording a solo album that was begun back in the winter, right after the *All Shook Up* sessions were completed.

"We had some time off, and the people I wanted to work with were available, so it just fell into place." The group he has assembled for recording (and future performances, once the record is released in early 1981) consists of ex-Nazz drummer Thom Mooney, with whom Peterson and Nielsen worked years ago; keyboard player Joachim Kuhn; and Peterson's wife Dagmar sharing vocals with hubby (who has taken up guitar in addition to bass). "It's a strange group," Peterson admits. "The record is pretty unconventional." No one in Cheap Trick has heard it yet.

According to Nielsen, Cheap Trick first met Pete Comita "about seven years ago when we were playing clubs. He was in other groups, and he'd come see us play in the Chicago area. We never played together, although we may have, as they say, "jammed' [a grimace of embarrassment crosses his face] or something unplanned like that."

During a stay in Los Angeles, Comita cut demos with various players; Nielsen insists on playing a tape for me of good FM pop-rock originals that resemble Cheap Trick tunes. Comita had circled around the big leagues before. On Nielsen's recommendation, Foghat signed him to replace guitarist Rod Price; unfortunately for Comita but fortunately for Cheap Trick, Price changed his mind about leaving.

Nor is the newest Trickster a dark horse. Peterson developed a viral infection during a Canadian tour this past August. With a Japanese tour looming immediately afterward, the band called Comita and suggested (strenuously, one would imagine) that he learn the bass repertoire in a hurry. On the same day that Peterson (who had flown to California on business) was advised by his doctor not to travel for at least a week, the band held a long afternoon soundcheck with their deputy bassist before that evening's gig.

"I was as nervous as Pete was when he first got out there," Carlos remembers. "I didn't know if he was gonna look out there and see 20,000 people and freeze up. We were all kind of nervous, but by the seventh job he fit right in. The guy's on the ball; he knows what he's doing."

In Japan, the altered Cheap Trick played three open-air festival dates on a package tour (*Japan Jam Two*) with the Atlanta Rhythm Section and some local talent. "The weather was terrible," Nielsen says. "The shows weren't as good as they should have been. I want to go back and make amends. It wasn't our fault; being in a monsoon dampens your perspective." Little notice was reportedly taken of the new face, although the size of the gigs [*and Comita's resemblance to Peterson*] may have contributed to fans' acceptance. Upon returning to the U.S., Nielsen says, "The decision was made for Tom to leave the group." He adds that Peterson's illness was not the reason.

Bun E. Carlos doesn't think the shift will appreciably affect the group's live sound. (Studio fallout will have to await next year's LP: *All Shook Up* was completed before the change.) He notes only that Comita has a higher voice than Peterson, "so it'll sound better on the high vocal parts." But, he adds, enthusiastically, "He's already taking stuff Tom was doing on the bass a step further. After a few gigs, Pete was already coming out musically as opposed to a guy playing all of Tom's riffs. Musically, he fits in better at this point than Tom did."

There seems to be an overwhelming sense of relief about the new face in the band — not just that he fits in, but that the situation is significantly better than it was. For his part, Peterson is also quite pleased with his solo status. No one, though, has much to say on the subject, taking a "you'll see" approach. Meanwhile, Carlos is using some of the group's off-road time prior to the European dates to break in the rookie."I've just got to sit down with him and go over stuff. It's a pain, but it's interesting."

As regards the upcoming tour, Carlos suggests that "We'll probably do the whole new album. We were getting stale on songs like "Big Eyes," which are limited for changing around live." Stroking his chin philosophically, however, Cheap Trick's timekeeper observes, "In a concert situation, there's always something to keep you interested. You can always watch to see if someone's gonna fire a beer bottle or something. That didn't happen too much this summer; because of the economy, nobody's throwing anything with a deposit on it."

All of Cheap Trick's past albums were recorded at near-breakneck pace, crammed into a few weeks between touring commitments and other activities. After the first, recorded in New York's Record Plant with Jack Douglas, there were two constants in their studio work: all of it was done in California, and all of it was produced by Tom Werman. Douglas was called in again to mix *Live at Budokan* but no one received producer credit; fair enough for a live LP. The *Found All the Parts* EP, assembled in New York early this year, listed the band as producer and noted that the four songs were "recorded by Jack Douglas."

The group made several strategic changes for *All Shook Up*. They enlisted George Martin to produce and booked time in AIR Studios, Mont-

serrat, the newly built dream studio Martin owns and operates in the West Indies. To cap off the new approach, they scheduled sessions in February and the delivery of finished tapes to Epic in August allowing for a six-month incubation period in which to perfect the album. (Although the preceding *Dream Police* was held up for about eight months due to *Budokan*'s unexpected popularity, that situation was so moment-to-moment that the finished album could hardly be tampered with.)

Whatever Cheap Trick would do with its six-month holiday, it wouldn't be spending it all in the studio. Basic work was completed in several weeks in Montserrat, followed by a spell in AIR London, where strings and Vocoder were introduced, and some vocals and overdubs added. The group then went home, leaving the record with Martin, who mixed and sent tapes back to the U.S., a few tunes at a time. The band considered each track, informed Martin of any changes they desired, and waited for the next version to arrive. Nothing much was done to change the record, although some titles were resequenced. The six months may have been unnecessary, but the band seem satisfied, and their praise for Martin and engineer Geoff Emerick is unanimous. Nielsen enthuses, "We'd tell 'em what sound we want, and one minute later we'd have it. George Martin would say, "Don't do that, Geoff: you make it look too simple.' It's up in his head, it's not messing around with dials, or moving the amps around for 20 minutes or two hours, or never getting it. He knows how to get it."

The album's *déjà entendu* title represents (for Nielsen at least) the style of the record. "I believe that this, in a way, is an interpretation of the '50s without being a rockabilly album: 1950s with 1980 tendencies. That's what we tried to do on the album cover; I don't know if it came across."

Martin has not overpowered Cheap Trick, as some feared. He has made an LP that sounds vastly better than any of their Werman efforts. Yet *All Shook Up* has a few flaws. Clocking in at a mere 34 minutes, it's about two songs shorter than *Dream Police* or *Heaven Tonight*. (Maybe Martin charges by the minute of finished music...) There was more in the can. Carlos: "Originally there were 11 songs. "Machines Make Money," one of Tom's songs, was on there, but he said he could do it better on his solo album." The track was removed by mutual consent, necessitating some song-shuffling to maintain the desired balance between loud and soft tunes. Another Martin production, "Everything Works If You Let It," was on the *Roadie* soundtrack and released earlier this year as a 45. Whether legal or musical obstacles kept in from being included isn't known.

All Shook Up's material sticks to the usual Cheap Trick blend of wild ravers, slow ballads, throwaways and a few surprises, with Nielsen's lyrical wit featured throughout. You'll have to rely on your ears to catch the words this time, as there's no lyric sheet. As Nielsen points out, "The Rolling Stones never print lyrics for their LPs": too bad the two Cheap Trick albums that didn't have as good lyrics as this one. Another element missing on this record is the garbage-can guitar sound so prominent on previous records. Here it's been replaced by a wide variety of guitar styles and sounds.

"Stop This Game" kicks off the LP on a totally unexpected note: a sustained piano drone that sounds like a Fripp / Eno tape loop. "It's layered piano without the attack," Nielsen explains. "George knew how to do it. We hit a piano chord, counted off 12 measures and hit it again. The next time you wait one measure before hitting the chord, then two, and so on. It makes for a floating piano chord that just sits there throughout the song." Originally dubbed "Can't Stop the Music," the song was renamed after the Village People's movie appeared. It's an impressive tour de force, demonstrating the band's theatrical flair; rock instruments are used symphonically in much the same manner as "Dream Police"'s bridge. Saxophone accents and Peterson's swooping bass will remind many of *Quadrophenia*, and Zander's Daltreyesque vocals further the resemblance; yet the track retains a Cheap Trick ambience. It is the album's first 45.

"Just Got Back" begins with Zander accompanied only by Carlos's jungle rhythms (which he says are "hell for one drummer to do" live). "This is more of a slam bang rocker," Nielsen observes,

and it certainly is in the style of the group's other ravers. The song just starts to rev up when it fades out before two minutes are up.

"Baby Loves to Rock" is a catalogue of styles and personalities. With Clashlike guitars and a bunch of identifiable clichés from Marc Bolan, Eddie Cochran, Alice Cooper and the Who, there's so much going on that it takes a few listens to untangle. Nielsen describes it as "big drums, big guitars — probably a half-dozen tracks of guitar. It's straight-ahead '50s rock, then real heavy guitar stuff, plus a bridge where you have the stereo going back and forth, and then back to the '50s stuff" — and that doesn't fully explain all the song's neat tricks and turns. "I used a string bender (the Telecaster modification invented by Gram Parsons and Clarence White of the Byrds) for the guitar solos, so I get these notes no one can play." Nielsen remarks cheerfully. "I showed John Lennon that guitar and he said, "Oh man, I'm gonna write some songs with this,' so I loaned it to him."

The nasty, throbbing sound of *Heaven Tonight*'s "High Roller" (which sounds like *Exile*-period Rolling Stones) has been recaptured on "Can't Stop It but I'm Gonna Try." Acoustic guitar on the bridge is a weird Cheap Trick touch. Nielsen's rhyming of "stops" and "talked" and "fucked" (implied but not enunciated) qualifies him for a Dylan poetry award. "To really put this song across the vocals should be a full octave higher than the verses," he says. "We've talked about doing it that way live."

Carlos calls "World's Greatest Lover," the first side's closer, "kind of old. It used to be faster and about 10 minutes long." Nielsen, who wrote it (as well as seven other tracks here, co-writing the remaining two), elaborates: "I wrote that about eight years ago, around the same time as "I Want You to Want Me.' It was very difficult coming up with the arrangement. Sometimes you get 90 per cent of a song in ten minutes, but then you can't get the other 10 per cent for 10 years." It's a slow ballad with an expansive vocal, and impressive, dramatic production encompassing strings and horns. Nielsen's guitar solo proves that besides all the goofing around he can play scintillating runs that add to a sensitive song. There's a certain amount of ELO on this track, but it remains one of the group's best recordings. Nielsen: "We're working on it as a stage number, but we may do a video of it and show that in concert."

Side Two starts with another of Nielsen's good-versus-evil psychodramas: "High Priest of Rhythmic Noise" pits an innocent Zander ("I'm just a singer in the mind choir") against the demonic High Priest, played by Nielsen via gravelly Vocoder. ("Herbie Hancock and ELO make the Vocoder sound nice and romantic; I think it has nasty tendencies.") While the lyrics battle it out, the music consists of awesome, unpleasant-sounding chords built on a bass anchor. "This song needs noise. It doesn't sound like a rock and roll riff or a blues riff; it needed an obtuse lick. It sounds like an orchestra, but it's just guitars." Can action film soundtracks be far off?

The lyrics of "Love Comes A-Tumblin' Down" are largely a tribute to AC/DC's Bon Scott. The drum work is impressive, but the rest is quite pedestrian. "It has these completely off-the-wall tom-tom licks in the chorus," Carlos says. "When we got to the end of a take, George announced that he wanted the drums doubled and then tripled for stereo. I said, 'You're kidding! Why didn't you tell me before we did it so I could have done something I'd remember?' I had to spend that night in my room listening to the track 20 times and writing it down in Bun E. drum language. I can't read drum music."

The tune was originally titled "*Life* Comes A-Tumblin' Down," but was changed, Nielsen says, because it looked too stupid. "A spoken part — a little prophecy about the supreme healing force of music" — is in the tradition of "Dream Police" and others. Recorded in the studio by persons unnamed, it has been handed over to Carlos for stage purposes.

The album continues to flounder with the following song, a sloppy Faces soundalike called "I Love You Honey but I Hate Your Friends." Nielsen's right about the title being great (it's borrowed from another song of his, "It Must Be Love," performed by Rick Derringer on a recent LP), but the song has little to recommend it beyond a

tremendous out-of-place (hence thoroughly fitting) mambo bridge. "It's just a silly rock tune," he admits, "real slopped out. It sounds like Rod Stewart; no doubt about it."

With a roaring bass explosion, the record regains momentum on "Go for the Throat (Use Your Own Imagination)," which demonstrates the musical intricacies Cheap Trick can handle. It also delivers Rick Nielsen's Message to the Rock Fan, which he iterates a few times during the interview. "We could make songs that would show exactly the thought we had, but that's silly. People write to me and ask what a particular song means: to me when I wrote it? To me today? To me after I've heard some other person's interpretation of it?"

The song itself is a Spectorian construction which Nielsen describes as "all melody and counter-melody. It's a crazy riff, and everything's going on: something's descending, another thing is ascending. The vocals are up and down. I think it's a lesson in melody. It's gonna be hard to do live." Vocals are great, but Peterson's phenomenal bass playing really shines through.

All Shook Up closes on an incongruous note: after all the subtlety and complexity. "Who D'King" is an overdubbed percussion orchestra and chorus chanting "Who d'king o' d'whole wide world?" over and over. It was, according to co-writer Carlos, "originally gonna be a non-LP B-side around 30 seconds long" until he got carried away and ended up with five drum tracks. He then decided the track also needed brushes, cowbells, tambourines and who knows what else.

The vocals weren't as simple. "Me, Robin, Rick and Tom went in and did the basic melody. Then we got a group we called the Four Nites — these guys who worked in the kitchen down there. Then we put a couple of the engineers and a bunch of locals on, and then we took it to London. George had this idea of what to do: We got a case of wine and a case of champagne and gathered up about 45 of the younger people who work for Chrysalis [the label has an interest in AIR Studios]. We held up cue cards for them to sing along." What emerged — besides being funny as hell — could be "a great Third World hit" in Carlos's mind. "I think you could go to Zimbabwe and hear it on a jukebox. It's very international; anybody can get into the lyrics."

Four years of touring, an enormous amount of press and public contact and the extra pressure of maintaining control and sanity in a difficult period for the rock industry can hardly have left Cheap Trick unaffected. "I haven't changed," Nielsen insists, "everyone else has. I've always just kept on going. With success, maybe things are more buffered, but you still have as many heartaches and headaches as when you're struggling along. Sure, we have some things to show for it, but I still think we're struggling along. I don't want to rest on 'I Want You to Want Me.' We always strive to do what we think we can do best. We've never tried to make the most money or play the most dates or anything. I worry about what's going on around me but being in a band is what I always wanted to do."

Carlos has learned to separate a lot of bull-shit from reality. "If you start believing it when they tell you you're great, you're a goner." On the other hand, "I take some things for granted now. I walk offstage and I scream if there's not a towel there. I wouldn't have done that four years ago." He pauses and adds with a slightly embarrassed smile, "but we didn't pay a guy to handle our towels four years ago."

"The band is rejuvenated. We've got a new album, a new musician, a new tour and a new stage show all coming up at once. It's finally coordinated; it's all going to happen together, instead of happening in bits and pieces the way it has for the last four years."

Nielsen: "We've always set our sights and goals with ourselves — not what Boston does, or what Van Halen does, or what Led Zeppelin does. We're in competition with 'em, but we're not the only band in the world. Some bands believe they are, but it's not true."

"This is glamorous, yeah: you drag your butt all over the world. It's a regular job. The good points are obviously better than anything else I can imagine. I've got the best job in the world. But," he adds with a determined look, "it *is* tough work." ∎

FRANK ZAPPA

TP 37, APRIL 1979

By David Fricke

"*What is all this shit in the newspaper if we got such a big name? We're starving, man. This fucking band is starving, and we've been starving for three years. I realize it takes a long time, but goddamn, does it take another five, 10 years from now? ... If we'd all been living in California, it would have been different.*"

"*If we had all been living in California, we wouldn't work at all.*"
—From a dialogue between a disgruntled Jimmy Carl Black and the voice of reason, Frank Zappa, on the state of finances in the Mothers of Invention, as recorded on *Uncle Meat*.

FRANK ZAPPA HAS always had problems with musicians. As the present-day composer who refuses not only to die but to give any quarter whatsoever, the 38-year-old is constantly suffering criticisms and complaints from the people he employs, many of whom openly describe him as an authoritarian monster, dictator, asshole and all of the other derogatory things one might call a guy who wants something done his way, right and right now. And Zappa — who's gone through more Mothers, ex-Mothers, Zappaites and sessioneers than [Savoy Brown leader] Kim Simmonds can count — insists it's not just the young punks he employs now. The elderly Mothers are just as liable. Take the band that recorded *Cruising*

With Ruben and the Jets, the greasy '50s celebration of so-called "cretin simplicity."

"It was fuckin' murder to make that record," relates Zappa with a coldness suggesting he's still a bit pissed off. "There's only two songs on that record that were easy to do — "'No.No.No'" and 'Cheap Thrills.' I wrote them, recorded all the instruments and vocals and mixed both of those songs on a Sunday afternoon. It took about seven hours, and I did both songs from top to bottom.

"But everything else on there was just murder. For one thing, the guys in the band didn't want to do it because they thought it was square. Ray Collins and Roy Estrada knew about that kind of music and Jimmy Carl Black, too. But it was not up Ian Underwood's alley or Art Tripp's or Bunk Gardner's. They thought it was moron music. 'Hey, I can play jazz. What do I need this shit for?'"

Zappa is really rolling now: "And you can't argue with these people. All you can do is say, 'I'll play it myself,' and a lot of times that's what I end up doing. When a guy has a certain amount of musical skill, he can't always see that the thing that matters is the song. That's the net result, the completed thing the audience wants to hear. They're not so impressed that you can play your instrument fast or loud."

It has never been easy for Frank Zappa to be Frank Zappa, whether he's leading a band ("It's more like being a referee among a bunch of playground psychotics"), fending off and/or instigating the lawsuits he seems to have going all the time or defending his music/fans/reputation against the typewritten barbs of critics who say he just ain't got it no more. The fact is, he's still got it — and in abundance. At Zappa's Halloween shows in New York last year, the audience (SRO every night) was nothing short of fanatical, exhibiting a rabid enthusiasm rarely seen at your average "rock" concert, much less one four hours long (Halloween proper). When the costumed crowd wasn't parading around the hall scaling new heights in outrage, they shamelessly begged Zappa for autographs in mid-song and mouthed the words to latter-day epics like "Dinah Moe Humm" (from *Over-Nite Sensation*) — the same song a *Rolling Stone* reviewer dismissed as "in-

sistent, almost depressingly professional backing accompanies recitation of doggerel porn." Even if the kids — for the average age was indeed 17 — could understand that they wouldn't care. Nor does Zappa.

"There are plenty of other groups to entertain people who need reinforcements of their lifestyle. They're all out there, freeze-dried and shit, who wear space masks and cat whiskers, groups who play like a typewriter hooked up to a pentatonic scale generator. There's plenty of those, plenty of everything for everybody. I just do mine for me and people who happen to like it."

As early as *Freak Out*, Zappa knew who those people were. Based on the mail requests for the "Freak Map" advertised on the album and assorted scribblings sent to the Mothers' United Mutations PO Box, he surmised that the Mothers of Invention audience was 90 percent male, between the ages of 16 and 20, and of Jewish suburban middle-class birth — the very same social strata that attended the New York Halloween shows.

"We were obviously saying something those kids wanted to hear."

IF THE MOTHERS OF INVENTION had been around in 1956, when Francis and Rosemary Zappa moved from Baltimore to Lancaster, California, they would probably have been just as attractive to Francis Vincent Zappa Jr., an impressionable young kid happily indulging polar opposite interests in sleazy R&B and avant-garde composition. Zappa has never made a secret of his contempt for California and the comfortable middle-class hypocrisy it fosters. "If it sucks," he says affectionately, "it's in Los Angeles." But it was probably the threat of suffocating on the poisoned psychological candy handed down by mums and dads throughout the state which forced him to develop even further his innate wit and musical interests as a high school student and junior college grad. Gigging with the Blackouts (copy band rock and roll) and Joe Perrino and the Mellotones (copy band lounge'n'roll) didn't fatten his bank account, but always the cultural absorber, Zappa certainly took note of what went on around him. His music is full of cross-references from

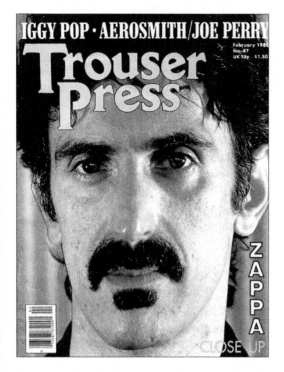

that period, including out-and-out parodies like "Go Cry on Somebody Else's Shoulder" (doo-wop melodrama) and "America Drinks and Goes Home" (lounge lizards on the loose).

A 1962 soundtrack to a movie entitled *The World's Greatest Sinner* and a Steve Allen TV appearance hyping "cyclophony" — playing music on a bicycle — were only two early manifestations of Zappa's early compositional interests in Stravinsky, Edgard Varèse and their 20th century crew. When, in 1964, Zappa bought an old, dilapidated recording studio in Cucamonga, California for a thousand dollars (renaming it Studio Z), Zappa's plan for world musical conquest began in earnest. Unfortunately, the record companies of the day didn't share his enthusiasm.

A 1974 Zappa press kit littered with informative and amusing clippings includes some of the rejection letters the composer received for his songwriting and production efforts. Dot Records politely said no thanks to a tape of "Any Way the Wind Blows," an instrumental version of "Take Your Clothes Off When You Dance" and a master take of Don Van Vliet (a.k.a. Captain Beefheart) singing Little Richard's "Slippin' and Slidin'." The last item, according to Zappa, was rejected by the

Dot A&R man because "the guitar was distorted." Other submissions that came bouncing back included a script for a television rock opera called *I Was a Teenage Malt Shop.* To this day, Zappa refuses to admit that this stuff was too advanced for the psyches of the day.

"I don't care whether the record companies were ready for it," a theme he sounds whenever given the chance. "I knew there were people out there who would love it if they heard it. That's why I did it. Just because there's some bimbo at the record company who doesn't understand it is no reason not to try and push it through. Why should a guy in a middle management position be the ultimate arbiter of taste for the American public? What does he know? What does he care?"

In Frank Zappa's case, the answer is no and no again. But apparently the San Bernadino County Vice Squad cared, because they busted Zappa at Studio Z in 1964 on a trumped-up porno charge involving a minor (19 years old) and for manufacturing pornographic materials for a used-car salesman who turned out to be fuzz-in-disguise. He eventually did ten days in the slammer, bailing out the 19-year-old with royalties on a song ("Memories of El Monte") he wrote with a singer named Ray Collins and recorded by the Penguins.

Collins was a member of a group called the Soul Giants. With Zappa as a new recruit, Collins, bass guitarist Roy Estrada and drummer Jimmy Carl Black became the Mothers — Zappa's creative vehicle for the next five years. (The Soul Giants' sax player, suspecting Zappa's motives, got out fast. Guitarist Elliot Ingber later filled the space.) Some of the original four-piece band's early tapes recently surfaced on a bootleg of material apparently slated to appear on Zappa's unreleased ten-record Mothers anthology. The studio jams are only of historical note, although there are some classic moments — the band trying to remember the words to "Rock Around the Clock" and singer Collins soulfully warbling that "Once I had some cheese." The live stuff has Zappa soloing his moustache off before degenerating into a raw blues and finally segueing into a rousing party-powered jam. Good 1964 bar band shit.

That's actually the kind of stuff MGM staff

producer Tom Wilson heard when he caught the Mothers playing one of their residencies at the Whisky a Go-Go in Los Angeles later in '64. Reportedly taken by Zappa's Watts riot song, "Trouble Every Day," Wilson investigated further, liked demos of "Any Way the Wind Blows" and "Who Are the Brain Police," and got Verve Records (then an MGM subsidiary) to put the Mothers of Invention (MGM made them add "of Invention") under what Zappa calls "contractual bondage." Only recently has Zappa been able to extract himself from that bondage and the lawsuits that followed. But, with all due respect to Zappa and his lawyers, the 1965 release of *Freak Out* — a satirical collage of barroom rock, musique concrète and pointed social commentary — was worth the bother.

"After *Freak Out* was released," Zappa explains, "it sold terribly. In the first year, it didn't do shit. It cost so much money — $20,000 — an unheard-of amount of money for that day and age. An album in those days cost $8,000 and this was a double album!"

Naturally, MGM went after Wilson, who Zappa admits really did produce *Freak Out* and "pretty much was producer on *Absolutely Free*. So, when it came time to record *Absolutely Free* in 1966, MGM got tight with the bucks, giving Wilson and the Mothers $11,000 and, according to Zappa, "one day with 15 minutes per tune to do all the vocals on that album. That's right. It's called 'sing or get off the pot.'"

During this time, Zappa's reputation as a wily gamester, the rock and roll Rasputin, increased thousandfold. He described "freaking out" to a *New York Times* reporter in 1966 as "a process whereby an individual casts off outmoded and restricted standards of thinking, dress and social etiquette in order to express creatively his relationship to his immediate environment and the social structure as a whole." But he knew damn well that when America orders a last round and goes home, such sociological doubletalk gets left at the bar along with the salted peanuts. America — in all its jaded glory — only understands shock treatment. So it was that the Mothers of Invention, their ratty hair, outlandish third-rate hippie dress and stage shenanigans, became the visual mani-

festation of Zappa's attempts to reach an audience with his music, much of it defiantly serious. It was pop electrolysis of the highest voltage.

The Mothers' extended New York stay at the Garrick Theatre in 1967 was one such jolt. Like a drop kick in the crotch, the band hit New York with two shows a night, six nights a week, for six months with Zappa's freewheeling soundtrack for the Great American Abomination. Zappa explains that the Mothers first went to New York because they were literally kicked out of Los Angeles. This was the time of the Sunset Strip riots, when property owners along the Strip attributed falling real estate values to bands of freaks cruising up and down Sunset Boulevard and got City Hall to do something about it.

"The net result was illegal police roundups, with no warrants, of people on the street. They'd show up with a bus and just herd 20 or 30 people in a bus, arrest them, take them downtown and let 'em go. It was pure harassment."

Subsequently, Sunset Strip clubs stopped booking the bands which attracted the crowds, the scene dried up faster than a prune in the sun and the Mothers tried New York as an alternative. After a pair of gigs at the old Balloon Farm off St. Mark's Place, the band happened on the 300-seat Garrick, moving in for a two-week Easter vacation gig in '67. The Garrick shows — originally titled "Pigs and Repugnant," later changed to "Absolutely Free" — did turnaway business for those first two weeks. Flushed with success, Zappa decided to stick around, snaring a lease at the Garrick through Labor Day in the hope that the rest of New York was dying to witness the Mothers mix-master their own unique combination of metaphorical stage violence, Top 40 avant-garde sounds and underground rock oratorios.

"Of course, after Easter vacation, the crowds dwindled to zilch. Some nights there were three, maybe five people in there and we'd still play. But we would do it just for them. In fact, there was one night when there were just a few people in the audience. Now the Garrick Theatre was located right above the Cafe Au-Go-Go, and there was a connecting passageway down to the Au-Go-Go. So, all the guys in the band went downstairs and got some hot cider and coffee and stuff, put little napkins over their arms, and each guy in the band went up, sat down next to each person and served them a drink, talking with them for an hour-and-a-half. That was the entire show."

Zappa's shows still retain that spark of dynamic dementia. Last Halloween, Zappa invited a member of the audience onto the stage. The guy turned out to be a Garrick Theatre regular who, if memory serves correctly, was fond of jumping up on stage, only to lay down in front of Zappa who, in turn, would pour soda over him in a weird baptismal rite. The Mothers, naturally, would play on.

"Yeah," says Frank of the possibility that the Garrick spirit is alive and well at least in New York. "But at the Garrick, it was small enough that you didn't have to exaggerate your movements because of the size of the place. You could actually behave in a normal manner — be normally weird."

During the band's New York residency, the Mothers recorded their Sergeant Pooper parody *We're Only in It for the Money* and Zappa polished off his orchestral opus *Lumpy Gravy*. Both works were held up for release because of lawsuits — the former because of a discussion between Zappa and Beatle reps on his satirical piracy of the *Sgt. Pepper* cover design. *Lumpy Gravy* — an extraordinary unfinished ballet that forced pundits to reassess Zappa's compositional abilities — became another corporate thorn in Zappa's side.

"Right after the completion of *Absolutely Free* in '66, the basic tracks were cut for *Lumpy Gravy* in Los Angeles. This guy Nick Venet — a producer at Capitol — heard I could write orchestra music and asked me if I'd like to do an orchestra album for Capitol because my MGM contract didn't preclude me from conducting. I wasn't signed as a conductor and, since I wasn't performing on the album, there didn't seem to be any problem. He gave me a budget for a 40-piece orchestra, X number of studio hours and said go do it. And I did."

But as MGM's legal department would have it, a problem did arise. When Zappa brought the orchestral tapes to New York for mixing, MGM complained about it — after Capitol had spent over $30,000 on the album. Capitol was even ready to release it.

"In fact, if you're looking for rare collectors' items, there are 8-track tapes with the Capitol label of *Lumpy Gravy* that have a different *Lumpy Gravy* than the album. Those have only the orchestral music and they do exist."

MGM eventually gave Capitol their 30 grand back for the master *LG* tapes, and Zappa added "all that talking and stuff" later. But the litigation cost Zappa and his album 13 months before it could be released. Even now, Frank Zappa's legal problems are not over. Are those first three Mothers albums on Verve still in print? "As a result of the settlement of the lawsuit with MGM, they no longer have the right to repress those records. Those masters have reverted back to us."

Which means we can see *Freak Out*, *Absolutely Free* and *We're Only in It for the Money* on local record racks — where they belong — before long? "Yes, as soon as the lawsuit between me and [former manager] Herb Cohen and [former label] Warner Bros. and all that stuff is settled."

Translated, that means don't hold your breath. Here's something that might take it away, tho'. Apparently, *Apostrophe* is not Zappa's biggest selling LP, despite the fact that the single "Don't Eat the Yellow Snow" chased the album into the Top 10, a first for the formerly uncommercial Frank.

"The album sold very fast and the speed with which an item sells determines its position on the charts. It's not the numbers. *Apostrophe* is not the biggest selling album we've ever had. Just the fastest. Probably the best-selling album was (get this) *Freak Out*. But there's no way to prove it because of the way the financial records were kept at MGM, which was shoddy to say the least. It wasn't criminal, but hey, they weren't gonna do us any favors."

ANY CONVERSATION of some length with Frank Zappa will touch on a variety of subjects, if only out of deference to Zappa's flagrantly diverse interests. Some of those subjects don't necessarily follow in chronological or topical order, so what follows are some of the bits and pieces not covered in the preceding narrative...

In your ten-plus years as a bandleader and performer, is there any one concert or show you consider to be the ultimate Zappa show?

"There were a lot of them that were pretty funny. But you have to consider them in context. What might be the ultimate show one year might be a bomb the next. The differentness of the show is the product of the contrast between it and the surroundings — the incongruity of doing a certain thing in a certain place at a certain time. During a year's touring season there may be quite a few incongruous events. And, well, they're getting harder and harder to pull off because of the attitudes of the musicians. Most of them don't have the historic sense of why it is aesthetically good to perform something incongruous. They're worried about other things on their minds, these young guys."

Would you say the age difference between you and the younger players contributes to that?

"Oh, definitely. It's sometimes difficult for me to talk to some of the guys in the band because there's whole eras of musical experience they don't know anything about. They might have heard rumors about what rhythm and blues was in the '50s. All they know about it from personal experience is hearing Sha Na Na records. Besides that, most of the guys in the band don't bother to listen to our records. They don't like them."

As leader of the band, how do you differentiate, say, between material appropriate for Zappa the bandleader or Zappa the solo artist?

"Those distinctions are no longer applicable because it's not the same thing anymore. When there was the Mothers, I distinguished those things — if the group that was making the record was the same group that was touring, then it was a Mothers of Invention album. If it was basically a studio situation where I used a variety of players, then it was solo album."

How about the difference between producing your band and producing somebody else? Grand Funk, for example?

"In Grand Funk's case, what they were looking for was somebody to help them get a sound on record that was what they actually sounded like at the time — not a cheap imitation, but something that revealed they could actually play their instruments. So, that's what I went for."

What about somebody like Wild Man Fischer?

"He needed some structuring, someone with an appreciation of what his craft was, to sit through the problems of making the album and then have the patience to put it together in the continuity the listener could pay attention to. That was a completely different story."

When you recorded Wild Man Fischer, did you think he had something people could relate to?

"Yeah, I thought so. Don't you think so?"

"Listen, the people who bought the *Saturday Night Fever* album probably won't like *An Evening With Wild Man Fischer*. But that album was made for the people who like that kind of stuff and all the rest of the albums I make are for people who like that kind of stuff. If they like it, fine. If they don't, there's other stuff."

You have a penchant for coming up with some perfectly bizarre song and album titles (e.g., "The Chrome Plated Megaphone of Destiny," "Poofter's Froth Wyoming Plans Ahead," Weasels Ripped My Flesh*).*

"It helps people remember your records. Actually, if I called an album *Frank Zappa Sings for Lovers Only*, that would be absurd enough to be remembered."

Well, remember this. Frank Zappa's latest album is called *Martian Love Secrets*, it's on his new Zappa label, it's real good and it's only phase one of a renovated master plan for world pop domination. Also keep your eyes peeled for a feature film of the 1977 Halloween shows in New York. The present-day Zappa indeed refuses to expire.

One more question. In the liner notes to Ruben and the Jets, *you refer to yourself and the Mothers as "just a bunch of old men with rock and roll clothes on ... mumbling about the good old days. Ten years from now, you'll be sitting around with your friends someplace doing the same thing, if there's anything left to sit on." Now it's over ten years. Are you surprised that there's anything left to sit on?*

"No. Just remember liner notes are for amusement purposes and not intended to tell the future or create inner turmoil. The liner notes on *Ruben and the Jets* were also talking about Ruben's three dogs, Benny, Baby and Marthy. I'm surprised you didn't ask me about them, too." ∎

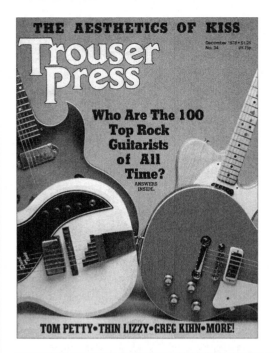

Trouser Press' 100 Greatest Rock Guitarists of All Time was selected and written about by Ira Robbins, Dave Schulps, David Fricke, Kurt Loder, Jon Young, Jim Green, Jim Kozlowski, Scott Isler and John Paige.

Rather than include the whole thing (which ran to 15 pages in the magazine), here's the introduction and a list of the honorees.

Clearly AWOL from this unabashedly rockist list: Sister Rosetta Tharp, T-Bone Walker, Elmore James, Eddie Hazel, Muddy Waters, John McLaughlin. And, as our readers recommended, Richard Lloyd, Roy Buchanan, Henry McCullough, Wayne Kramer, Ron Asheton, John Martyn…

100 GREATEST ROCK GUITARISTS OF ALL TIME

TP 34 AND 35, DECEMBER 1978 AND JANUARY 1979

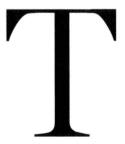

Throughout the history of rock and roll, from the early blues-oriented Elvis days to the latest new wave next big thing, the guitar has substantially dominated the field as the single most important instrument. In a large percentage of rock bands, the guitarist is the leader, and very often the guitarist has shaped and defined the sound of his group. Of course, this is not the case with all groups, and the importance of singers, keyboard players, and songwriters can't be downplayed, but guitar has always stood out in its domination. And not coincidentally, guitarists have long been a topic of discussion, reverence, disgust, and intrigue.

There are, by our guess, about 150 absolutely essential rock guitarists. But we decided to stick with 100, choosing only those who have either contributed to the world of rock and roll by setting a style that influenced others, or who have themselves been so totally unique and original as to have defined a new approach, or those who have definitively typified a discernible style. We started with a list of everyone we could think of, and then narrowed it to the 100 who we felt deserved recognition the most. We know that there'll be lots of dissension regarding those we've excluded, but we feel confident that this selection is fair and sensible.

The guitarists are arranged alphabetically. Each entry shows the birth (and death where applicable) date, groups played in, noteworthy sessions, a selection of the guitarist's best recorded solos (or playing in general, where applicable) and favored guitars. ∎

THE COMPLETE LIST:

Jan Akkerman
Duane Allman
Syd Barrett
Jeff Beck
Chuck Berry
Ritchie Blackmore
Mike Bloomfield
Marc Bolan
James Burton
Glen Buxton
Randy California
John Cipollina
Eric Clapton
Eddie Cochran
Steve Cropper
Dave Davies
Buck Dharma
Bo Diddley
Duane Eddy
Dave Edmunds
John Fogerty
Peter Frampton
Robert Fripp
Fred Frith
Rory Gallagher
Jerry Garcia
Lowell George
David Gilmour
Mick Green
Peter Green
James Gurley
Steve Hackett
Ollie Halsall
George Harrison
Jimi Hendrix
Steve Hillage
Steve Howe
Wilko Johnson
Mick Jones
Steve Jones
Danny Kalb
Jorma Kaukonen
Robby Krieger
Paul Kossoff
Albert Lee
Alvin Lee
Nils Lofgren
Phil Manzanera
Steve Marriott

Hank B. Marvin
Brian May
Jimmy McCulloch
Roger McGuinn
T.S. McPhee
Scotty Moore
Bill Nelson
Rick Nielsen
Ted Nugent
Jimmy Page
Carl Perkins
Joe Perry
Eddie Phillips
Mick Ralphs
Johnny Ramone
Lou Reed
Keith Richards
Robbie Robertson
Mick Ronson
Francis Rossi
Todd Rundgren
Carlos Santana
Tom Scholz
Andy Scott
Chris Spedding
Jeremy Spencer
Leigh Stephens
Stephen Stills
Mick Taylor
Richard Thompson
Johnny Thunders
Pete Townshend
Robin Trower
Tom Verlaine
Henry Vestine
Dick Wagner/Steve
  Hunter
Joe Walsh
Leslie West
Clarence White
Charlie Whitney
Alan "Blind Owl"
  Wilson
James Williamson
Johnny Winter
Steve Winwood
Ron Wood
Roy Wood
Link Wray
Zal Yanovsky
Neil Young
Frank Zappa

HELLO IT'S ME

TP 36, FEBRUARY 1979

A fairly comprehensive list, but what on earth would one use it for, except to mail Christmas cards? Two glaring omissions, however:
1. Where is Alex Chilton?! Remember *Radio City*?
2. Where in the hell is Henry McCullough? Infinitely more important than Messrs. Gurley, Rossi, Scholz and Williamson. Also, why Tom Verlaine and not Richard Lloyd?

Peter Holsapple
New York, NY

TP 37, APRIL 1979

I was disappointed that Gary Richrath of REO Speedwagon was not mentioned among your top 100 guitarists. People far less talented and/or notorious were mentioned. I sing for and produce REO; Gary has played outstandingly on eight albums and deserves mention in my view.

Kevin Cronin
Chicago, IL

The absence of Black Sabbath's Tony Iommi is most aggravating. You said guitarists were chosen if they typified a discernible style. Few have done this more than Iommi. I'm not really pissed off, just slightly baffled by some of your choices.

Bruce Schafer
Eau Claire, WI

I give up. How come Bruce Springsteen wasn't included in your list of the 100 top rock guitarists of all time?

Lou Cohan
Cypress, CA

When are you going to do a list of the best 100 violin players?

N.L. Slaughter
Bellaire, TX

"HI, I'M RITCHIE BLACKMORE. AND I WANT TO TELL YOU WHAT I'VE BEEN DOING FOR 15 YEARS..."

TP 30, JULY 1978

By Jon Young

As Dave Schulps and I rolled along in the darkness to our impending interview, we were filled with apprehension. After all, Ritchie Blackmore has never been known as a pussycat. In fact, most accounts of his years with Deep Purple emphasize his moodiness, sullenness, even outright hostility. The Teutonic severity of Ritchie's current group, Rainbow, does little to suggest that time had mellowed the guitarist one bit. We didn't even know where we were being driven! What if Ritchie got annoyed with our questions and had us "silenced"? Paranoia strikes deep.

As it happened, there was nothing to worry about. After a circuitous drive, we pulled up to a suburban bar in Greenwich, Connecticut (Ritchie lives nearby) and parked ourselves in a greasy-looking swinging singles place. Over a typically giddy barroom roar, interrupted occasionally by notes from an "admirer" who asked things like "are you Deep Purple?" we had our talk.

Ritchie Blackmore turned out to be a genial model of decorum and was fully prepared to dis-

cuss anything and everything. Indeed, when we got over the surprise of discovering him to be a pleasant fellow, he even fielded borderline tactless questions, unthinkable to ask of someone with his image. My only complaint about the thoughtful and open Mr. Blackmore was that he insisted on keeping his juiciest comments off the record.

Rainbow had that evening finished a rehearsal prior to their multi-month tour in support of a new album, *Long Live Rock 'n' Roll*. Seeing as how this was the band's fourth album, why the long wait to try and make a mark on America?

"The other markets came first, Europe and all that. We took advantage of it rather than just playing around America as a small-time band. Now the only market left is America, and we're the underdog. Most of the time we're sharing the bill with REO Speedwagon; Foghat is topping the bill in other places. It's not like starting again. A lot of people feel that, but it's just something you do. I'm quite looking forward to it. It means I can get back to the bar afterwards. If you're a top-billed act, you get back to the hotel and everything's closed."

Did Deep Purple audiences get too big? "Sometimes. It was moving too fast. It's funny how sometimes it will escalate and turn into something that big, when you know you're just the same as any other band. All these people are turning out to see this band, and next year they'll be turning out to see some other band equally as bad or as good, whichever way you look at it. The way it's been going I think it's been getting worse. In America you have some very strange big groups."

Like Kiss?

"No, Kiss I like because they don't care what people think of them. They take a chance and it's worked. They're the first ones to admit they're not good musicians. I'm talking about middle-of-the-road bands that turn out that lethargic laid-back cocaine beat. The DJ's love it, and they play and play it all the time."

Oh, Fleetwood Mac?

Laughing, "Funny you should mention them. Nice people, but I have reservations about what they're doing. But the rest of America doesn't seem to have reservations. It's gone into this mellow thing, and I'm not keen on that. I like intense music that comes across as drama, as acting."

The new wave has that excitement, doesn't it?

"Well, that's got the impetus, the energy, but it hasn't got the music. That's wrong as well. I don't quite know what I prefer to listen to, the new wave or Fleetwood Mac. I think I would play Fleetwood Mac because I can't take the other stuff."

To go back to square one, when did you start guitaring?

"When I was 11. It mostly was my idea along with my father. He made sure I went along to proper lessons, because if I'm gonna have a guitar, I've got to learn it properly."

Did you have it in your mind to rock? "Yeah, because there was a guy called Tommy Steele prancing around with a guitar, and Presley and all that lot. I wanted to do that just like everybody else ... Duane Eddy, then Hank B. Marvin, then Django Reinhardt, Wes Montgomery, James Burton, Les Paul. I bought all of Les Paul's records up until I was about 17, but after that I didn't have any idols. Then I was mostly practicing. I listened to rock via Buddy Holly up until 16, 17 (1962). Then I was on my own. I didn't have any inspirations from guitarists, it went more into inspiration from violinists.

"I really don't listen to too much rock and roll. Jimi Hendrix was good, and I liked Cream. I wasn't really getting off on people like the Beatles and the Hollies, all that vocal business. The Stones? I considered them idiots. It was just a nick from Chuck Berry riffs. Chuck Berry was OK. I don't have any time for the Stones. I can see where they're respected and their rhythms are very good, very steady on record. I respect them but I don't like them."

And the blues?

"It might sound condescending but I find them a little too limited. I like to play a blues when I'm jamming, but then I want to get on to other things. I listened to B.B. King for a couple of years, but I like singers more than guitarists. I thought Albert King was a brilliant singer. That depth, which comes out in Paul Rodgers, too. I do like a blues base to some things, that can be

s very interesting with classical overtones."

So, what was your earliest professional gig? "My first band was with Screaming Lord Sutch. He had amazing publicity stunts — he would go up to the Prime Minister and stick his hand out and say hello. The Prime Minister's first reflex was to shake his hand and suddenly he's thinking, 'Who is this man?' He's got pictures of him about to shake hands with everyone in the business. He used to copy Screamin' Jay Hawkins.

"From there I was onto a group called the Outlaws. I did sessions for three years. They were known as a very steady band, good for session work, so we used to work together for sessions (besides putting out a number of singles of their own). You were just given the music to play, sometimes it was just the backing tracks. It wasn't our job to know who we were playing for, it was just to get the money and go."

Did you read music?

"Yeah, but not well. It was more like chord sheets. Pagey was in all those sessions. Sometimes you'd get complete rock and rollers who could play but wouldn't be able to read and others who could read but wouldn't be able to improvise. Sometimes they'd want rock and roll sessions and that's what we'd do."

You and Jimmy Page both played in Neil Christian's band, right?

Blackmore laughed and mused a second before answering: "I was with him on and off for about a year. Chris, that's his real name, was a slightly bizarre person to work for. In fact, Jimmy Page played with him for about three years. That's when I first met Pagey. I was 16 years old. He was good then; I rate him as a three-dimensional guitarist. He has a range, he has ideas, but he can't be everything, so sometimes he lacks on improvisation a bit. He's so caught up with producing and everything else concerned with being a top band. Whereas someone like Jeff Beck is entirely in the opposite direction. Jeff can extemporize really well, but I don't think he can write a song. It's always somebody else's tune. He doesn't have many ideas, but he's a brilliant guitarist."

Our brief search for other three-dimensional guitarists failed to turn up any more that met with Blackmore's approval. We asked Ritchie to evaluate himself.

"This is gonna sound very cocky, but I think I can improvise better than any rock guitarist. My failing is composing, I really fall down in composing. I can come up with riffs and I'm good at improvision, but I'm not very good at putting a song together. I have done, but there's nobody else around to do it anyway. I feel very frustrated in my songwriting, I think it's terrible half the time. But improvising for me is no problem — in fact, it's something I could do all the time. That might sound slightly weird."

So, you tend not to memorize your parts. "No, that's partly my downfall. I have a very bad technical memory, so I can't remember, if I write a tune, exactly what the notes are. It's really exasperating, 'cause I'll write one and 'That's great, I'll play it again and record it.' And I'll play it again and, 'Oh dear, I've forgotten it. What did I play?' It's really annoying. I don't like to write. It's a chore for me. I do it because there aren't a lot of other people around me who do it. It's not knocking the people around me ... songs are a letdown half the time."

But didn't you do most of Purple's music?

"I did most of the riffs and progressions. We had so many arguments in the first two years of Purple, and I was sick of it, so I said let's split it five ways, because everyone was bickering about 'I wrote that one note' ... 'Include this song which is a bunch of rubbish, but I wrote it.' Every band goes through that. There's one thing today we haven't got over with modern technology. We haven't found a way to fashion a computer to take the information and tell you who's written the song. That would be very nice.

"People said to me, 'You were silly to split it five ways for most of it,' but I said Purple wouldn't have been together at all if I hadn't done that, because they were very strong-minded people. It would have died out in 1970 if I hadn't done that. They did (write) to a certain extent, but not to the extent that they should have gotten a fifth share on every song. Jon (Lord) would have written what would have been one song an LP, but he would get out of eight songs a fifth share on each song. It's the only way to work. But to give him his due,

the drummer (Ian Paice) gave his enthusiasm. Jon was always there for stability. He wouldn't come up with the ideas, but he'd remember them when I forgot them. Ian (Gillan) would write the lyrics, and Roger (Glover) used to write some."

How did Deep Purple get together?

"I saw Ian [Paice] with another band in Hamburg in 1967 and I said, 'When I get something I'll let you know.' When this Purple thing came up, I said, 'Right, we've got something here. We had a millionaire backer (Chris Curtis, of Searchers fame). It's very hard to start without financial backing. He just wanted a very good group. As far as he was concerned, Jon was the best organist he knew and I was the best guitarist ... but once we all got together, he kind of fell out. I told Jon about Ian and then we got the other two. Jon knew [bassist] Nick (Simper) and I knew [singer] Rod (Evans).

"We were all living in one big mansion in England which we used to rehearse in. There were a lot of things happening there, psychic phenomena. For the first few years Purple had no direction whatsoever. If anything, we used to follow what Jon wanted to do, which was OK, because nobody else had any ideas."

Be that as it may, Deep Purple roared into the American Top 5 in the fall of 1968 with an acidy remake of Joe South's "Hush." Yet that original band never seemed capable of capitalizing on it. How come?

"Jeff Wald (Mr. Helen Reddy) was our manager on the road and we did a lot of gigs that didn't mean anything. They were ballrooms, they weren't on the circuit to make it. The only time we really made it was when we supported Rod Stewart. We'd be playing around headlining all the wrong places. Nobody knew where to put us. We played with Cream at the Hollywood Bowl, but they never really knew who we were.

"I really admired Jimi Hendrix and I really loved Vanilla Fudge, so we just tried to integrate the two. We did 'Hey Joe' and a lot of standards because we didn't have a lot of writing going on. I'd never written a tune before '69, when I started feeling my way and came up with a few ideas. But at the time we were just so over the moon about playing with good musicians, because we'd had such a hard time finding good musicians. We were just so pleased to be playing with each other that we didn't really care which direction we went in.

"Until about '70, when we decided we should replace the singer and bass player. The singer wanted to go anyway, and the bass player was asked to leave." Ritchie's friend Micky Underwood (now with Strapps) was in the soon-to-be-defunct Episode Six, and he invited Ritchie to come down and check out their singer, Ian Gillan.

"Ian was amazing, his voice, the way he looked and everything else. Stupendous. We took him right there. We didn't know who to have on bass but Ian recommended Roger.

"Why we thought we had to change singers was because of Robert Plant. We were playing at Mother's in Birmingham and Robert got up to sing with Terry Reid. We thought, 'Christ almighty!' He was so dynamic. And the next two weeks we were looking for a singer, people who had Robert Plant's dynamic approach. It was thanks to him."

IN ROCK WAS the right formula: agile musicians playing with a tidal wave of force. But not a Zeppelin steal; the textures were much more varied, the sound more flexible. Suddenly escalating popularity soon led to "supergroup" status. That must have been a little surprising.

"I *was* surprised, because I was happy to be working."

Did you like the Yardbirds?

"Well, Jeff was always brilliant. Yeah, I did like the Yardbirds very much. They were an exception. Jeff was one of the first to use distortion. There's quite a few guys before Jeff that used distortion but you wouldn't have heard of any of them. Like Bernie Watson with Lord Sutch. In 1960, he made a record with Cyril Davies which had an amazing solo, all distortion. It was like Hendrix on a good night. He now plays for the Royal Philharmonic."

Ritchie said he was motivated to try something like that himself in 1963. The results ("I just freaked out") can be found on the B-side of the Outlaws' version of "I Hear You Knockin'." From there, via "You Really Got Me" ("The solo was too bad to be Page. It had to be Dave Davies."), the talk drifted to stealing.

"Everybody steals. It's healthy to steal. The thing is to disguise who you're stealing from. I used to steal a lot from Jimi Hendrix."

But "Rainbow Eyes," on the new album, sounds especially like Jimi.

"What it is, is the inflection of playing in fourths. Jimi used to play a lot of fourths. Several single notes he'd play a fourth above and that gave him the effect. On *Axis: Bold As Love*, it's all fourths."

Digress, digress. Some albums and many converts (and bucks) later, Purple found itself in a state of chaos after the recording of *Who Do We Think We Are?*

"I wanted to leave with Ian (Paice) at the time because we'd both had enough. I am a very sensitive kind of person, believe it or not. I was working too hard and couldn't take the strain. I had hepatitis and was in the hospital for a couple of months, which was a good rest for me; I needed it. I said the only way I would stay was if we completely changed the band. 'Get a new bass player and I'll stay.' Ian and Jon said OK. Glenn (Hughes from Trapeze) came in, so I stayed. Ian and I were gonna form another band with Phil Lynott from Thin Lizzy, actually."

What did this aborted group with Lynott sound like?

"It was like Hendrix number two. He looked like Hendrix, sounded like Hendrix. He was just singing, Roger was playing because he was a better bass player then." (More than a little odd to ask Glover along considering Blackmore insisted on throwing Glover out of Purple...)

With the guitar boom in full flower, wasn't there a temptation to do a solo LP? (This question came the closest of any to making Blackmore blow his cool.) Scoffing a little and raising his voice, he said: "My solo LPs were Deep Purple! Because, off the record..." The gist of his comments was that he felt he was doing too much of the work.

To kill off the Purple era (that drew a snicker from Ritchie) we asked him to rate the group's albums.

"My favorite LP would be *Machine Head,* followed closely by *In Rock* and then *Burn. Fireball*

I didn't like. *Who Do We Think We Are?* I haven't heard for ages. I didn't like it when we did it. We were having a lot of friction at the time, a hell of a lot. Ian (Gillan) was about to leave. I was sick to death of Ian, Ian was sick to death of me. Girlfriends were involved. I thought, 'Here we go again, another LP.' We'd had one week off the road then we were told to go into the studio and make another LP. It was just ludicrous, we didn't know what to do. I felt great about *Burn* (the first one with the new group) because we'd had a year to write it.

"When we did *Stormbringer* I thought it was a very cold LP."

Had you decided to leave by that time?

"Yeah. I thought, 'I wanna see what everybody else is doing, I'm tired of pushing the band.' Seven years is long enough. I though the band was on the decline. There were other bands coming up. Jon was into drinking, wining and dining. Ian was into cars, expensive things."

But the new lineup had worked … at first. "It worked for the first year and then it started getting a little bit shaky. It started getting into this funky music. I can't stand it. I like it vicious."

Come Taste the Band, which featured Tommy Bolin on guitar and was the only post-Blackmore LP, seemed to lean in a Stevie Wonder direction.

"That's exactly where they were going, and I wasn't interested in being around for that! I thought it was only proper of me to say, 'Look, I'm going. I don't want to break up the band but I'm off. Get another guitarist and do your thing.' I just didn't want to be around for all that cool pseudo … They were shocked. My music was up-front music, hate music. Their music was becoming much more like 'If you don't like it, just click your fingers.'

"I wanted to get out gracefully if I could. I thought, 'Now it'll be interesting to see because I'm not pushing my ideas. Let's see your ideas.' Whenever I said that in the studio, they'd say, 'Oh, we don't have any ideas' or 'We're waiting to see what you think so we can collect the twenty percent.' But it sounds bitter to say that.

"I took a gamble because at that time I'd acquired enough money to say I'm gonna take a chance and go out gracefully and maybe make a crash landing in something else. But I'm certainly not gonna go down with a big-name band. I could have stayed with Purple and earned a good living for five years, a steady kind of decline (laughs). But I wasn't interested. It was very cushy the last two years of Purple, everything was financed. They said, 'Do the *California Jam*.' I said no. 'You'll make half a million.' 'We'll do it.'"

There were some stories of you demolishing cameras there.

"When I'm on stage I feel very hyper anyway, and it was a combination of that and being very annoyed because they'd given us hell. They'd been so conservative about the whole festival. Everything was built around the fact that this was gonna be a festival for the benefit of the camera people from ABC. The kids that paid ten dollars each will not have any fun, but we don't care if they won't be able to see the band. That's beside the point as long as we get the money."

"I said to my manager, 'I hope they're not gonna have a press enclosure.' I looked the next day and, sure enough, there was about a hundred feet of just press, who were bored stiff. The audience was about a hundred yards away, so I insisted that they let the people who had paid into the press enclosure. I was getting madder and madder. All the kids were in the distance going, 'Yaaaa yaaaa,' and the press were going, 'Oh, boring, another loud metal rock and roll band. Where's the beer?' You don't need that.

"I hate the business. I love the fans and I love the music. But I don't like the radio, I don't like the DJ's, I don't like the press."

So why are you talking to us?

"Yeah, right. Well, you're buying this round, mate." (Gulp!)

Exit Purple and enter Rainbow, dominated by the twin howitzers of Ritchie and Cozy Powell, once with Beck, on drums. (Ronnie Dio is a good enough singer, but it would take the Mormon Tabernacle Choir to stand up to the volume of those two.)

"Cozy and I, we're always trying to outsmart each other. He's a very fast person, him with his cars; me with my medieval music. He hasn't got a clue where I'm coming from. We have our differences, but when we're on stage we click because he wants to be the best drummer and I want to be the best guitarist.

"It works to a certain degree. Sometimes we do tend to get a little carried away with being very aggressive when we should slack it off. I find to record we should tone down everything. We have to mush it up a little, put some icing on it to make it sell.

"In Europe and Japan, they're more into adrenaline, but in America they wanna hear safer things. I've never really studied American culture as far as music goes, but I've been listening more and more. We're gonna concentrate more on a back beat. We'll be playing more slow songs. I know what the American people are looking for. I don't really care what the American DJ's are looking for; they piss me off no end."

Jeez, shades of "Radio Radio"! Just how far would you compromise?

"Not very far. I cannot play anything which is not in me. I could never play like Fleetwood Mac. I could play like that if I was fast asleep [*chuckling*]. I'm not trying to be derogatory, I just can not play that way. Lucky for them it's worked, because they were going through some hard times about six years ago. So, I'm glad for them as people. They're very nice people."

How do you feel about your audiences, seeing as how they tend to be so wild and crazy? It's hard to imagine that they catch too much of the music.

"In Purple I was happy to have any audience. In Rainbow I come off stage quite confused sometimes. There are certain numbers we do that are very intricate and I know they've missed them. But I can't expect them to catch on. They're not musicians, it's Friday night, they've finished their work, they want to have a good time, they want to see someone break a guitar [*which he often does*]. I can't expect to educate people; if they'd wanted to become educated, they would have become musicians themselves. At the same time, I do like to listen to certain quiet parts that we play and get on to the party at the end. I don't understand an audience that's stomping all the way through and saying, 'Let's boogie man, let's get it on.'"

So, you *do* get upset.

"Yeah, I do a bit. I'll just stop, or I'll go through the motions. We'll give you what you want, four-to-the-bar-stomp-stomp-stomp.

Ever consider playing another kind of music?

"Yeah, I have thought about that, but I'm very interested in extreme rock and roll. At the other extreme, I'm interested in medieval modes, quiet 15th century sitting in a park playing little minuets ... I don't like to mix the two. I haven't reached the stage where I can play classical the way I'd like.

"I think I would miss the masses. Those type of people, they're extremely brilliant players, but they play in front of 20 people. There is that self-esteem thing that comes in, too. You do like to be proud of yourself and play in front of all these people, sharing something. If you're playing in front of 20 people you think it's a bit strange what you're doing. You need a certain response. Five-to-ten-thousand people is great, after that it becomes..."

What if Rainbow got really big?

"Well, I'm self-destructive. I would knock it on the head and start again. I love to play in Europe because they have seaters over there that are no bigger than eight thousand, ten thousand, and that's just right. You can still become intimate with the audience. In America things can get out of hand, as with Purple playing stadiums. I don't think I would want to do that again.

"You've got a manager coming along saying, 'Look, this is worth a lot of money. Think of what you can buy.' And you're thinking, 'Yeah, that's true.' You do the gig and you think, 'Oh dear, all those people have just heard me play a lot of nonsense.' But when you're faithful to the people and you say, 'Look, I've got something really honest to play to you, listen,' they won't. When you're in front of 100,000 people and you're playing utter shit, because you're a cult figure or a name, they'll listen, because they've been told by their friends to listen."

Does it ever bother you that you don't get more respect?

"In a way. I'm good. Some people know I'm good. I'm not into being a personality, a Johnny Carson, a Rod Stewart. I'm very thankful for as far as I've got, and I really don't think I should have any more than I have. If I hear other bands and I hear how bad they are, I get a little bit upset that people are buying their records in the millions. But I know my limitations. I think this is more than I deserve. I can't believe that people take as much notice of me as people do, I just think there's such a poor standard in rock and roll. I think it's disgustingly low."

Rock isn't a musicians' medium.

"No, but it should be."

So, whatever happened to original Rainbow members Tony Carey (keyboards) and Jimmy Bain (bass)?

After a mysterious laugh: "Tony was a bit of a raver. He was asked to leave the first time, and he was asked to come back. After a while, he left of his own accord. He couldn't take the pressure. We were coming into contact with unforeseen psychic phenomena, which is kind of another story. It's just kind of a hobby of mine, psychic phenomena. He couldn't take that, 'cause we were playing at the Chateau in France. It got very heavy spiritually, and he backed out. He thought I was completely mad. He thought I was trying to kill him. I don't know why he thought that." (Said with no irony.)

"Jimmy Bain was a great guy, fantastic person, but his bass playing left a little bit to be desired."

How do you feel about your music being called heavy metal?

"It's better than punk, which means inferior. It suits us fine. I know I can play a bloody concerto any day, so it doesn't bother me at all. It would bother someone who was sensitive and knew their limitations."

The hour was late and things were getting decidedly less businesslike. The pursuit of musically relevant info was soon abandoned for more speculative matters…

"Sometimes I feel like I own the stage completely, on my own for an hour. I'm just going crazy. The adrenaline is so much that all my musical upbringing is thrown into intensity on stage rather than being a musician. After 22 years of playing, it goes instead into a mood and comes out as an aggressive bulldozer. I often wonder why. I'm not an aggressive person offstage, I don't know why I am on."

You used to say how rude you thought Americans are. Does that still hold?

"I've accepted America for what it is. The older I get, the broader my outlook on life gets. I can see why someone thinks this way or that. The one thing I think about Americans, I wish they would bring up their kids with a bit more discipline. Stop giving them hamburgers and shit like that. Stop pampering them. The mother and father seem to lay down the whole life for them. The kid takes over the whole family. I think it's disgusting."

What about the times we live in?

"We're going through a period now where nobody knows what's really going to happen in 25 years. This era will be written off as a group called the Rutles, or should I say the Beatles, and that's about it. We're just bordering on being invaded by UFOS, which I think certainly will come in the next five to ten years. Which could coincide with the Earth being taken over by Satan. But who knows.

"The last 36 years we've had UFO sightings. They're right here now, so it's just about ready to happen, I think. They're obviously watching us now. Otherwise, it's gonna be bombs from Russia or arrows from the east. One clairvoyant actually said that about 15 years from now fiery arrows would come from the east. It was Edgar Cayce, maybe. But he predicted the earthquake in California that didn't happen…"

Ship to ground! We've lost control of the interview!

Ritchie Blackmore obviously displayed a great deal of himself in this interview, and I'm not gonna be dumb enough to try and summarize him with some slick closing remark. He may have said the most about himself when discussing his reputation as a heavy: "I have a bad reputation, but I don't mind. My good friends, people who really know me, know what I am." He said he got his image "by being very moody, being very sincere, telling people to fuck off when I shouldn't have done. But I don't care, not at all. I quite like it."

And that's the way it is. This is Jon Young, signing off from Connecticut, U.S.A. ■

THE GLORY OF GLAM

> 66
>
> *I have lovely shoulders, knobbly knees, good balls, a terrific vibrator, a false hand and five pairs of identical trousers, three cats, fifteen tape recorders. I like girls with brown hair, Chinese food and rock music.*
>
> 99
>
> —BRIAN ENO

The glam era was on its way out by the time we entered the picture, but we were hardline fans of the New York Dolls, Alice Cooper, Roxy Music and Iggy, so we were primed for the music that was engulfing England — even if we didn't get to experience much of it in the flesh. Older than the average fan, we latched on to what was left of the era before it died out. We never did write about Slade, Gary Glitter or Suzi Quatro (other than some of their records), and we never gave a toss for Alvin Stardust (probably a mistake) or Mud, but we did cover T. Rex, Bowie, Mott the Hoople, Sparks, Roxy, the Sweet, Cockney Rebel, Wizzard, Queen and some of the lesser lights.

The late Kathy Miller attended Catholic school in Queens, New York, with Linda Danna; together, they discovered the New York Dolls (running the band's fan club) and glam rock. While Danna took up photography, becoming the prime shooter for Trouser Press in the magazine's early days, Miller — under the tutelage of Lillian Roxon — began writing about the music they dug. Lester Bangs was an early fan, and she was contributing to Creem (album reviews, features about Roxy Music and Brian Eno, that sort of thing) by the time TP came along. We loved having her freewheeling, opinionated prose in our pages, but she only did a few things for us before hanging up her typewriter.

Although Bolan was no longer the svelte sex god of a few years earlier, the rude headline of this piece wasn't her doing.

T. REX: ROLY POLY BOLY

TOTP 8, APRIL/MAY 1975

By Kathy Miller

I like T. Rex. I can hear a tidal wave of groans and moans and "he sucks" and the ilk, but I reiterate. Even at this late date, I like T. Rex. I also like rye and ginger, Ring Dings, Wise Bar-B-Q potato chips and lots of other things that aren't good for me. And, furthermore, I am sick of defending Bolan from the slings and arrows of outrageous fortune. This article is my last vindication/interpretation of T. Rex's quagmire of a career — all other such meanderings will be reserved only for dearest and closest friends. So, if by the end of this you still cannot fathom Marc Bolan's role in rock, and do not understand or appreciate it, then park it, Chester, kindly get off the express and take the local.

Marc Bolan has the worst timing in the world. He has never toured the United States at the right time with the right songs or the right band. Whereas Bowie surrounded himself with the most brilliant sidemen, with Ronno surfacing as an ace producer/arranger who, in retrospect, seemed to curtail David's worst excesses, Bolan played with nitwits. I have always felt — and still feel — that he needed another guitarist in the band.

To continue, Marc is erratic. He has wallowed in superstardom so long that he really can't conceive of fighting for an audience. He tries, but by trying to win an audience, he seemingly gouges out his throat by doing less. Solid, simplistic riffs start disintegrating into eerks and ear-shucking screeches as he lets the guitar dangle in order to start posing and mugging as Britain's most photable notable. When the sound system blew at his February 1972 Carnegie debut, he wiggled his rumpus, but America wasn't buying cute little rear ends that year, and one by one, the scribes felt gypped. The music was the same as it was, but the image that had been so roundly hyped wasn't jiving. [Rock critic] Barry Taylor verbalized it succinctly: "I thought he'd be the new Eddie Cochran, but he was just a twerp." The basically enchanted, but disoriented, public gave him a second go-round in September of that year, at his gig at the Academy of Music (Swamp of 14th Street, the once high spot of Victorian glam nightlife, where Sarah Bernhardt made her American debut, with a wooden leg). The first show went splendidly, the audience gyrated and yelled, and the only thing they threw during the acoustic set was a little plastic dinosaur, which Bolan used for a pick.

But the *late* show — urp! A catastrophe. Bolan literally staggered onstage not drunk, mind you, but *sleepy*. "I need some ENERGY!" he yelped. ZZZZZZZ. ENERGY (action, action, we want action a-c-t-i-o-n!). The soporized mob roused itself blearily to catcall (pre-Hawkwind) — spurred on by an entire first row of Argent fans. "Iggy Pop," "Gimme head," "Get off, faggot," "We want blood" and the last tickler, "DAVID BOWIE!" "David Bowie?" Bolan spit out with disgust. (Remember, Marc said he was bigger 'n Bowie the way Lennon was bigger 'n Christ.) "The KING OF ROCK AND ROLL!" "The King of Rock and Roll?"

The din mounted and threatened to raze the corroded Academy foundation, splitting the beams and bringing the roof down on our heads. Bolan cut the acoustic set short and pulled out all the stops in a feeble attempt at winning an audience which had come not to praise but to bury him. Perhaps, for the first time ever, people walked out on him — first one, then three, then dozens. When Bolan walked off, it was five-thirty. He had won the rest of the audience over — they were dancing and screaming, and in the last gasp of "Bang a Gong," they had rushed the stage. They stomped and mooed for an encore, but Bolan didn't come back — *never* came back. He hasn't played this metropolis since. Oh yeah, this was the show the critics caught — they missed the early show to see Helen Reddy's debut.

It was the start of something big. The reports came drifting back — L.A. was half-filled and, in San Francisco, two thousand people in a sold-out hall of five thousand took a powder during the acoustic set, flouncing out of the exits in streams.

Slade, who ironically debuted in the same Academy two days after Bolan flopped, met the same resistance. This pair of less-than-stellar impacts scared the up-'n'-comers at home shitified, and if you've ever wondered why Gary Glitter and Sweet haven't toured when their singles went gold/Top 10 here, or why Mud stays home to play tiddlywinks, put the blame on Bolan's greased fall from grace via American rejection.

The difference between Bolan and Slade is the difference between lazy and industrious. Bolan lounged about in England, cutting and recutting hundreds of songs, pulling a Brian Wilson, fiddling while Rome burned. Slade began touring these United States non-stop, playing dinky little clubs in the Midwest that held 400, building a rapport so that the next time Slade played cities like Milwaukee, they had jumped from hundreds in attendance to thousands. While Bolan came on as a headliner, the much-prattled-about new Beatles, Slade, were workin' class mugs, never too proud to bust a butt as an opening act. As Nelson Rockefeller has often said, "America loves an underdog."

Evidently so does England. Bolan's roots have the earmarks of an English Horatio Alger. Born a humble Jew, Mark Feld, son of fruit vendors, was introduced to rock and roll when he sent his dad to buy a big band record by a fellow named Bill Hays. Instead, Dad returned with Bill Haley's "Rock Around the Clock," and Feld/Bolan was struck like a lightning bolt, whap. He wanted to shimmy, but his parents were poor, busted, flat broke, so Bolan constructed his first guitar out of fruit crates and wires. (The Pretty Things constructed amps out of orange crates with speakers stuck inside. Fruit vendors must have done booming business selling wood.) Like a good mum, momma Feld scraped nickels and dimes [*well, shillings and pence*] together and bought him a real axe, which set him practicing until his fingers were bloody.

Touched by mom and dad's dedication and their poverty, Bolan, like Ragged Dick or Oliver Twist, took to the streets, and became a face, a glamour-boy-cover-boy smeared across the glossies, a quintessant mod in three-piecers. Old pics show that he looks like Prince Charles, a royal arrogance surfacing and triumphing over the dinge of back alleys.

The arrogance in those open doe eyes is even more apparent as Bolan began penning material for, and performing with, mod cult band John's Children. Lines urging Desdemona to "lift up your skirts so that I may see you" blew the competition (still holding hands and eye-gazing) stiff dead. J's C became minor legends, and after Bolan left them, Kit Lambert and Chris Stamp tackled him, pleading with him to sign with their management, saying that they'd do it up, push him over the top and go to town. Bolan, with characteristic verve, asked, "Are you gonna let me get bigger than the Who?" Lambert and Stamp were aghast, they were mortified, they gagged and gurgled and screamed no, no, a thousand times no! (Actually, they just said uh-uh.) Well then, recalls Bolan, you can take your contract and stuff it — "because I *am* gonna be bigger than the Who!" Lambert and Stamp made one more go of it and were rebuked again. (Obviously L & S's needles were stuck in the same groove, because Bolan remembers that they approached the earliest incarnation of Cream and pulled the same frothing deal, with Clapton querying, "Are you gonna blahblah the Who?" Lambert and Stamp wagging their hangdog heads side to side nope, and Clapton raising a finger of destiny repeating those immortal words, "Well, we're gonna be bigger 'n 'em!" and striding out into the Anglo fog. "And they were bigger 'n 'em, weren't they?" Bolan smiled. "The whole idea is preposterous, something, something bigger than US? US? THE WHO!")

Boly rolled along gathering fern, along with legends — living with a wizard (*really* — he swore it was true). Until he decided, like Christ, the time was right to strut on into the public limelight. The earliest form of Tyrannosaurus Rex was a five-man electrical band playing that scuttlebutt r&r akin to more modern Bolan music, a form that Bolan returned to on the *T. Rex* and *Electric Warrior* albums. They lasted about a week and never left the rehearsal studio, namely because they couldn't afford the type of equipment an electric band needs to go professional. Breaking his solid rocker's heart, he had to fire the band, retaining only the acid poster boy, Pink Fairies-mutant-conga-drummer-and-burned-out-Tolkien-overdose Steve tada! Peregrin tada rumpity rum! TOOK (Yay)!

If you don't know the rest of the story, then what are you doing perusing America's Only British Rock Magazine? Bolan and Took began playing unearthly folk music, indigenously Celtic —

but so antiquated that it predated even Beowulf and Sandy Denny, like Bolan had a mainline to his Celtic/Hebraic forefathers, the mythic Beltanes. They moved into the UFO club and, along with Pink Floyd, created a spiritual/psychedelic hoohah, a little chunk of Haight and a big stir when John Peel began spinning his tapes on Radio Caroline. Cultists began flocking, they were moving the gigs out of sweltering UFO and into Hyde Park, Bolan was an egghead sensation and probably would still, to this day, have his dignity intact if he had starved and stayed obscure — like Syd Barrett and Kevin Ayers and the slew of his contemporary cultist avant-gardists.

But, to quote the man himself, "Bolan likes to rock, yes he does." He kicked Took out after three albums (*People Were Fair* etc., *Prophets, Seers and Sages* and the awesome *Unicorn*, wherein Bolan gets his brand of Middle Earth folksy warble to mate with Kinks rinkydink) and made the subtle move to electrolysis via Mickey Finn's Nureyev good looks (and makeup by Pierre LaRoche) and plugging in the ole gittah.

Jeez, it must have been like Dylan at Newport or Forest Hills, amp power as the audience raspberried and screamed SELL OUT! *A Beard of Stars* was his *Bringing It All Back Home*, a long electric regurgitation graced "Elemental Child," mating with his visionary mythology. Electric T. Rex (losing the yrannosaurus) attained perfection in the truly amazing *T. Rex* album on Warners. (Try and find it, kill for it, it's the best.) Bolan's command is subtle and true from the romping recut version of "One Inch Rock" to the long, almost Motownish "Wizard" (it's a riff from a Four Tops song, I used to know which one, but I'm getting on in years) and the "Beltane Walk," whereby the people who ride white swans do the trucking stroll. The *T. Rex* album seemed to be a beginning realization of the promise Bolan had hinted at all along — avant-garde vocalization (does Ferry's warble seem *so* new now? And Sparks are dead ringers for that larynx shuffle — listen to "Equator" or *Woofer* and try and deny it), visionary poetry and a rocking bottom you can dance to.

Then something happened. Not at once. But enough so that rarities. such as the *T. Rex* album, were impossible ever after. Bolan wanted to conquer America, he thought he could rewrite ole rock standards better than anyone else and went full speed ahead with a regraft. *Electric Warrior* was fully devoted to the new ethos, and his mythic people died. *Electric Warrior* was a skillful blend of car imagery and metal, of dancers and vampires and never-never land — its lyrics were brilliant as they stretched over taut simplistic strum-strum. Warner Bros. had paid a cool million for Boly's band, and then, like always, let them wither on the vine for the *T. Rex* album, didn't promote their first acoustic-cum-electric tour (where they opened for Mountain at the Fillmore East) and were sitting twiddling when *Electric Warrior* came out. The record debuted in late summer '72, and radio stations, such as the then-free WPLJ, began playing "Bang a Gong." Slowly, then surely, the record began selling 100,000 copies a week. The Carnegie debut sold out; Warners gave a late, impotent thrust for publicity. He almost had it. Then blah. The concert, not entirely Bolan's fault, bombed. Warners said too bad and went to sleep. (Roxy's sax symbol, Andy Mackay summed up WB the best: "I don't blame Warners …They just aren't very good.")

Slider, the last brilliant album by Bolan, came, went and died bargain-binned. Then *Tanx*. Bolan opened for Three Dog Night, who cancelled more than they played, and Bolan churned out formula singles, sometimes exquisite forays with his old knack, sometimes not. *Melody Maker* was reporting every time he blew his nose, and, to this day, his [UK] gigs sell out with screaming little girls. The *Born to Boogie* fantasia/documentary, the movie he made with Ringo that would level the U.S., will never be shown, not here, not anywhere. He's not interested in it anymore and can't be bothered showing it, even as history, because "It's too recent to be history."

Zinc Alloy, supposedly his departure album, wallowed in excesses up to his snout, enough to asphyxiate him, and enough to send long-time producer Tony Visconti out [the door], so that Bolan had to clean up the mess himself. It taught him something. When Casablanca signed him up, he asked Neil Bogart not to release *Zinc*.

He set himself to produce *Light of Love*, the first album that captures his *Electric Warrior* stance with some Celtic TexMex. He plans to release his EMI collection of *Great Hits*, including the Stooges-oid "20th Century Boy," which Warners wouldn't release "because it wasn't commercial. I fucking wrote it for America, and they said it wouldn't sell. Those songs have been hits in several continents, they're great." (No bravado, they are.) His collection of books are being published, and he's polished up the band — starting with axing Mickey Finn, who wanted more money and more limelight.

Bolan is toying with the notion of returning to a bit of the old mythology as well. "You really liked the old stuff?" he asked disbelieving. "That's the way it happened in England, we never planned it, it just did." (Maybe too much planning for America? Maybe a misinterpretation of our values?) Now a return to more visionary subjects, like the created world of Beltanes and Dworms and Kings of the Rumbling Spires. (Bolan convulsed with laughter when we told him we tried to look his characters up in various mythological volumes. He had to come clean [and admit] that, like Tolkien, he made it all up out of *his* head, not borrowed from Bullfinch's book. He stopped laughing when we mentioned that we thought he wrote like William Blake, believing that poetry is an action that comes from the soul, through the body, and cannot be controlled, the mind can't be bridled or forced and that the experiences of hundreds of generations and lives pass through into print. "Yeah, Blake, he saw a tree of angels. I could get into that — I have, too.")

Most people, to this day, don't realize that Bolan views his artistic dilemma with a great deal of wry, tongue-in-cheek humor. *Zinc Alloy* is brimming with allusions to his career as a hits-bound tunesmith. "The Groover" could be Bolan's theme song, with comeuppance to the critics and a doff to his fans and a laugh on his lips. "It hurts me when critics say I'm obscure, of course it hurts, but as long as people as intelligent as yourself understand me, then that's my reward." (Bolan throws more bull than a cowboy steer roper at a rodeo.)

Yeah, he's erratic, a baloney artist, a huckster — Bolan has taken hype-cum-press manipulation and made it into an artform, a rocker, a poet, self-indulgent, excessive, a visionary, lazy, sensitive, as tough as brick. Yet, recently, at the Joint in the Woods, he made me believe in him again. Yeah, the Joint in the Woods, in Parsnips, New Jersey, which looks like a swank Coventry hybrid with a dingy Bottom Line. (They've got the gall and pomp to forbid jeans.) By the end of the gig, the Joint had turned away 2,000. (Bolan, typically, mispronounced the number on Scott Muni's WNEW-FM English Hour so that it came off like 200,000.) The resurrection was awe-inspiring for those whose faith in T. Rex had disintegrated into oblivion, like dust in a sun ray. The space in front of the stage got smaller and smaller and tighter 'n aunt Bessie's Playtex girdle, and the mob of anglo-philiac-cum-weenybops who got in with phony ID's catcalled all through Chelsea Warehouse, a roto-rooter hackster's dream band. (Mr. Chelsea looked like a cross between Sonny Bono and a knish; Ms. Warehouse looked like a porpoise somebody had decked out in Mary Quant vintage '65 — they sang the entire Delaney and Bonnie songbook — *twice*.)

When a star catapulted Boly onstage, the audience made a sound like an SST in your ears. This blonde next to me let out a yelp that shot her diaphragm down to her Achilles heel, then propelled her upward so that her hip grazed my ear. Just when Bolan has written off hysteria and is sniffling about how he doesn't want mass acclaim with nymphets gumming up their bloomers, now it seems like he has them, American fans who yelled for oldies pre-*EW*, who yelled "The Wizard," and for only-English singles and his latest, not then even out in Angleterra, "Zip Gun Boogie." Now, when Bolan looks like the Weinstein that Leslie left back in the Vagrants when he moved West, Bolan, sag-jowled in a Hamlet shirt — black and baggy like a budget floor Lane Bryant fat lady special — *now* they're dancing and caterwauling and reeling in giddy delirium.

"It hasn't felt like this in five years, in England," Bolan yelled, so happy he could giggle. Like I said. Piss-poor timing, but sometimes so good. ∎

There was no Marc Mayco: the pseudonym, a tribute to the washing machine manufacturer, was trotted out occasionally by whoever on our staff wanted their authorial identity hidden for one reason or another (e.g., a conflict of interest, the possibility of subsequently thrown drinks, possibly a disguised collaborative effort). Who actually wrote this piece has been long forgotten, but the original byline acknowledged Jim Green and Richard Grabel, who added sidebars (not included here). It's likely that photographer Linda Danna Robbins, who was an early and enthusiastic supporter of the band, had a role in preparing this article as well.

NEW YORK'S FINEST: THE DOLLS

TP 44, NOVEMBER 1979

By Marc Mayco

The date is October 3, 1972. The place is the Oscar Wilde Room of the hip Mercer Arts Center. On the tiny stage are the New York Dolls — David Jo Hansen, Johnny Thunders, Sylvain Sylvain, Arthur Harold Kane and Billy Murcia — and the small crowd is packed in tight and loving the show.

Seven years later, David Johansen, promoting his second solo LP, is on the road somewhere, wowing the locals with an energetic rock and roll that leans towards the tight and brassy. Syl's in the studio, putting finishing touches on his first solo LP. Jerry and Johnny still occasionally play with/ as the Heartbreakers, the band they formed in

1975 after walking out of the Dolls, but they also have had other commitments: Johnny with whoever's handy and Jerry with the Idols along with Arthur, who is still in the ozone after wandering through a series of go-nowhere outfits.

In the time that's passed since the Dolls were the most terrifying group threatening the heartland, the rock world has undergone some major events that have changed the context in which groups now exist. In the wake of the new wave — which the Dolls preceded by a full three years — and the outrageousness of the Sex Pistols, the Stranglers and the Snivelling Shits, the Dolls seem almost tame in retrospect. However, as one. of the very few American bands to attack the rock behemoth without conceding a thing, they displayed the courage of their convictions to be themselves to a fault, and thereby unalterably changed the course of what followed them.

Things that are now acceptable — mediocre technical expertise, violent/decadent posturing, club orientation, androgynous imagery — all caused much more than raised eyebrows at the beginning of the '70s. At the time, new bands looking for a record contract and a shot at the big time had no upper hand to deal from. Record companies held all the cards, and a band that wanted to get in the game had to accept the rules. It wasn't until record sales had become a tangible asset that any sort of balance between company and artist could be achieved. The idea of a bunch of no-talents dressed in women's clothes and wearing glitter and makeup, playing R&B-tinged rock and roll at unbelievable volume in clubs where the opening act didn't go on until well after midnight hardly caused record executives' hearts to glow. The translation of such a phenomenon — a band without a record that could draw fantastic crowds to seedy dives on weekday nights — into a salable commodity must certainly have seemed an unlikely proposition at best.

However, through the efforts of the group's management — Marty Thau and Leber-Krebs, the folks that later brought us Aerosmith and Nugent, plus Paul Nelson (then an A&R man for Mercury, now the reviews editor of *Rolling Stone*) — the New York Dolls did get a record contract and created two tremendous landmark albums that became the prototypes for all punk bands that followed.

But the very same factors that made the Dolls what they were — a bunch of crazy kids from New York's outer neighborhoods acting just as free as they felt — also destroyed them. Drugs, chronic chaos, over-extension and ultimately too much jerking around brought the Dolls grinding to a messy but indefinite halt in the middle of 1975 — despite a late attempt by Malcolm McLaren to revive the group's sagging momentum following the commercial failure of its second album and the waning interest of the record company.

As soon as Dolls' carcass was ultimately laid to rest, the various members, (by this point an extended family that included road manager/occasional bassist Peter Jordan, former Leber-Krebs employee and drummer Tony Machine and two keyboardists, Bobby Blain and Chris Robison) set about straightening out their musical careers. Thunders and Nolan, fading from the good-time depravity of the Dolls into the abyss of the drugged-out Heartbreakers, made an album in England that just seemed an exercise in misery and sarcastic self-abuse. Sylvain, always the professional, put together a nice little band to work the New York club scene. The Criminals, including Tony Machine and Bobby Blain, did pretty well for themselves, but the big payoff came when David Johansen (new spelling) finally sorted out his contractual problems, hooked up with Steve Paul and the Blue Sky record label and put out a solo album.

With real industry support and money, Johansen went out on the road in early 1978, taking Syl with him; the Criminals fell apart within the year. With David's career on the uprise, Syl was able to rustle up a solo deal of his own, and his first LP is imminent. Arthur Kane, always the least musical of the bunch, has been in and out of the spotlight and seems destined to become the forgotten alumnae. On the whole, for a band not generally expected to live out the first half of the '70s, they've managed to stay involved enough to benefit from the scene they were years ahead of.

The Dolls' first gig was at the end of 1971.

Johansen recalled it for us recently. "It was in a welfare hotel, The Endicott, across the street from this bicycle shop on Columbus Avenue [*on the Upper West Side of Manhattan*] where we used to rehearse. The guy that owned the shop used to stop renting bicycles in the winter. He had some old drums and amps, so we used to plug into them and put a mike in with the bass and rehearse. He would lock us in so we couldn't steal the equipment and come back at dawn to let us out. These people from the welfare hotel said that the band didn't show up for their Christmas party, so we went over and played some Otis Redding and Archie Bell songs. We had a great time doing that."

The lineup for that momentous occasion was somewhat different than the group that finally surfaced on vinyl 20 months later. The rhythm guitarist (later replaced by Sylvain) was a fellow named George, who later helped form the Brats, and the drummer was Billy Murcia. Billy, Arthur, Johnny and George had been together in a group, with Johnny switching from bass to guitar due to Kane's poor guitar work. Johansen was added as vocalist, George was ejected for not showing up at rehearsals, and Syl joined a few weeks after Christmas.

From an old press packet, Johansen continues the early saga: "We played at the Hotel Diplomat (a sleazy joint on West 43rd Street) and got bomb reviews. Then we got a gig with Eric Emerson and the Magic Tramps at the Mercer Art Center. We went on first and they freaked out. Then the Magic Tramps came on, and then we came back after them and we ended the show. After that, we got our own room at Mercer."

Back in the present, David recalls further: "We got the Oscar Wilde room on Tuesday nights. That was our first steady gig. We started playing at the Coventry in Queens — then we started playing at Max's as sort of a house band. They had acts like Waylon Jennings and Bob Marley, but we started playing there once a week. Also, we did gigs at Kenny's Castaways, up on the East Side.

"We started going around to places that didn't particularly have music. A lot of places started opening up because we had a following that would go where we played. We used to play places in Long Island and New Jersey, branching out, so pretty soon we had a scene going on."

The following developed by the Dolls during their first year of operations, 1972, was unprecedented in New York's rock and roll circles. This was before the era of cult bands really took hold. A traveling pack of regular fans willing to show up anyplace anytime to see the band play made them a very bookable outfit to local club operators. The glam rock underground, such as it was, revolved (at least in part) around the Dolls. Everybody from Bowie, Lou Reed and Alice Cooper to the Warhol crowd hung out with the Dolls, and their retinue regularly included the "hippest" folks from the avant-garde. The Dolls became the darlings of the post-Velvets crowd, who had made the back room at Max's into the Casbah of the scene. Photos of the Dolls with all manner of celebrities were frequent in the press.

SOME DOLLS QUOTES [*both poignant and prescient*] from early 1973:

David: "The record companies are very interested in us. They know we're the New Wave [*!!!*], but instead of taking a chance, they'll pass, they won't take the responsibility. There's a whole lot of people who want to make a lot of money off rock and roll, but they're not prepared to take rock and roll for what it is and stand behind it."

Jerry: "I suppose, in a fad kind of sense, everyone will be like the Dolls in a few years. The public and people in general always pick up things from leaders… I've worked very hard in this business. I hope I've still got a little time left — someday I'm going to snap behind them drums. I don't take drugs. I'm not into drugs at all, I'm into my music. I drink a little bit and every once in a blue moon I'll take a down just to mellow off… I think the Dolls will last a good decade. If the world don't catch on to it, I'll be surprised."

Arthur: "I'm a latent Puritan. I used to be an altar boy and all that stuff, Lutheran, and I still have some sense of right and wrong… I would really prefer to be an IT as opposed to being a he or a she. I guess it's one of those LSD hangovers…"

In the midst of this high-velocity world, the

Dolls got their big break, and it almost ruined them. A huge, complimentary article in England's *Melody Maker* by a writer who had been checking out the New York rock scene attracted the attentions of the Faces, who invited the Dolls to come over and be the opening act for them at an important Wembley Pool gig — an amazing feat in itself for a band without a record label. While in London, they played high fast games, and drummer Billy Murcia drowned in a bathtub as a result of an unwise mixture of drink and pills. In one sense, it took the steam out of the Dolls' sails — a realization that life (and death) weren't all fun and games and fooling around — and on the other hand, perversely, it raised them to the status of do-anything-for-kicks psychos. What could possibly be a heavier trip than having your drummer die? Death was a luxury reserved for the ultra-successful rock giants with no sense of reality, nothing left to try for kicks. But Billy Murcia?

The Dolls survived Billy's death, enough so to be able to dedicate their first album to him ("Billy Doll") less than eight months later. They held auditions on their return, and eventually settled on Jerry Nolan, a club band veteran who had been in bands that opened for the Dolls. At his first gig with the band, faithful fans waited in the street afterwards to tell Jerry that he had been okay, that he was accepted.

The group, also, was becoming accepted. The publicity they had attracted in a few months was more than established bands could hope for in a year, and the companies were starting to come down to the shows and try and entice the band to come home with them. The person who succeeded was Paul Nelson, an important rock critic who had gotten a job with Mercury Records.

Johansen: "He had been a big fan of ours because he's very sociological, and he wanted to get us on Mercury. One night we had ten record companies in the audience, and a lot of them were going, 'What is this?' The kids were going crazy, having a wild party. Paul kept on trying to get us on Mercury, and eventually he succeeded.

"We made our first album with Todd [Rundgren] — we had a lot of trouble getting a producer. Todd used to hang around Max's in those days, so I just asked him one day if he would do it, and he said, 'Yeah.' We recorded it in six days and mixed it on the seventh [in about eight hours]. We didn't have a very big budget. I haven't really got any regrets that we did it so quickly. I prefer to make a record quickly. I don't like to be cooped up in the studio."

The album came out in July 1973, and the band went on tour with Mott the Hoople, who were then in their prime. I remember an early August date at New York's Felt Forum. The Dolls, minus David, came out and started playing "Personality Crisis." Then Johansen, resplendent in a silver silk top hat and tails, came running out with a magnum of champagne, swung it over his head three times and exuberantly let the first two rows have a Moët shower. The Dolls were on their way!

Or so everyone thought. Despite a tour that lasted most of the year, covering all points west (including four nights at the Whisky in L.A. and a couple of television tapings), sales of the LP fell short of expectations, giving both the hip press and the record company pause. The glow was off and the cold reality of commerciality began rubbing raw spots all around. Johansen again: "The record company was so straight, working out of Chicago, that they had a different sensibility than anybody in New York. If we had had a New York company it wouldn't have been like that. The fact that you had long hair made them think you were crazy. They exaggerated stuff a little bit — we would come late, or fall asleep during interviews sometimes, but I think most companies would have capitalized on stuff like that."

That first album stands as a true monument to what rock and roll, played at full tilt with no regard to convention, can amount to. "Personality Crisis," "Looking for a Kiss," "Private World" and "Bad Girl" delivered the goods — and more. David's lyrics were certifiably dangerous — just like Lou Reed's had always been, but the music had an energy — powered by Johnny's utter garbage guitar sound and Jerry's tom-tom heavy backbeat. Left off the record (except for Bo Diddley's "Pills") were the band's huge repertoire of cover versions — "Don't Start Me Talking," "Seven Day Weekend," "Showdown," "Daddy Rolling

Stone," "Stranded in the Jungle" — many of which showed up on the second album. Certainly, the sound of the LP was a revelation — noisy, just barely in tune, with Johansen's nasal growl wandering all around the melody. But those background vocals — Johnny and Syl teaming up for a near-California sound on songs like "Trash" and "Jet Boy" — gave the album just the touch of class it needed to avoid the pit of sameness that has plagued lesser-quality punk bands in recent years.

In early '74, the Dolls returned to the studio with '60s producer Shadow Morton (Shangri-La's, Dixie Cups, Ad Libs) and made *Too Much Too Soon*, which certainly was a fair characterization of the way things were going. With only six of the ten tracks originals, the band was reverting to its roots a bit, going back to Morton's era and their faves of the past. A couple of quotes from various Dolls in a Pete Frame chart in *ZigZag*: "One album was produced by an acid freak, the other by a drunk." By the summer of '74, the Dolls were back in New York clubs, "a wrecked monument to pill-popping, booze-swilling, multi-sexual wasted teenage America."

The spring of 1975 brought drastic change in the Dolls camp. Malcolm McLaren, a friend of the band's through basically fashion work, became their manager briefly, relocating to New York for a change of scene. His bright idea consisted of giving the Dolls a Red Chinese fashion motif, and he dressed them all in red plastic and leather, putting up backdrops of Chinese flags. With very little left to hold the band together, the shows of this era were inconsistent, although sometimes really incredible. But by April, Johnny and Jerry had become a faction in the band, and they split during a tour. They soon formed the Heartbreakers with Richard Hell (ex-) of Television and floated over to England a year later to support a tour with the Sex Pistols and the Clash. Despite immigration problems, they stayed on, signed to Track Records, and cut an LP (*L.A.M.F.*) with Speedy Keen. The Heartbreakers (sometimes with Jerry, sometimes without) continue to exist to this day, playing one "farewell" gig each month around rent time, while the various members do other things the rest of the time. Thunders, signed as a

solo artist to Real Records last year, made a fairly interesting solo album, *So Alone*, that seemed a bit more on the mark than the Heartbreakers' joyful self-destruction ("Chinese Rocks," "Too Much Junkie Business"), but late last year he appeared third on a Blondie-headlining bill in New York and was such a pathetic, depressing sight that I could have sworn off rock and roll right then and there. Watching rockers sink to Bowery bumdom is not a pretty sight.

The Dolls reformed a few times between '75 and '77, basically because legalities prevented Johansen from going off under his own name. With the previously detailed sidemen, the band toured Japan and played around New York, marking time until something better came along. For Johansen, that happened when Steve Paul signed him up and launched his solo career. Speaking to *New York Rocker* in mid-'77, Johansen put his new attitude about things into fairly cogent form: "What I hope is that people who liked the Dolls will know it's me, and I hope that the general populace of America, especially those who hate the Dolls, will not think of the Dolls."

As for how the new band came into existence, "I met this guy, Frankie LaRocka, on the Staten Island ferry. I remembered him from years ago, so I got together with him and Tommy Trask, and jammed in somebody's garage on Staten Island just for the hell of it. We built it up from there and then I went to Steve Paul and said, I want to make a record now, because I had wrangled out of my contracts. I had asked Steve a year before to manage me — I've known him since the old days at Max's — but he had been putting me off because of my old contracts.

"We made the record in the winter, and it took a long time." Originally begun in late '77 with Jack Douglas and Joe Perry of Aerosmith producing, the project devolved to Richard Robinson and the artist himself when Aerosmith's recording schedule ran a few months over. With a basic band ("The Staten Island Boys") consisting of Johnny Rao and Tommy Trask on guitars, Buz Verno on bass and LaRocka on drums, the album also featured appearances by Perry, Felix Cavaliere, Scarlet Rivera and Syl Sylvain.

The press went wild, and the band hit the road.

"First, we did a swing through the Midwest, all those great places to play in the Midwest. It's like rock and roll out there — hard rock. Then we came back to New York and did six shows at the Bottom Line, and then we just took off. We got this great tour for nine months. We went all over the States, Canada and Europe." For that tour, Sylvain joined on keyboards and guitar, putting the Criminals on hold while he was away. "He was getting tired of the Criminals. I asked him to come along until he could decide what he wanted to do. He was one of the best pals I ever had in my life, so it was great to travel with him, because we can do a lot of things together. First, he was going to come for three months, then it became six months and then nine months. I didn't particularly want him to leave, but I certainly didn't want to stop him from pursuing the goals he set up for himself. Syl's last show was New Year's Eve at the Palladium, and then I got Ronnie Guy in the band. Then Buz Verno and Johnny Rao went into Syl's band, and I got Freddie G and Charlie Pipp, who were in a Jersey band that used to play with us a lot."

The second album, produced by David and Mick Ronson earlier this year, features the bass playing of labelmate Dan Hartman and the keyboard abilities of Tommy Mandel in addition to Ronnie Guy. "I made the album without Charlie and Freddie because it was time to do it and I didn't have time to go hunting around for people and work them in. We recorded it at Dan Hartman's house in about three weeks."

Strangely enough, the fast and dirty approach makes *In Style* a vastly superior album to its predecessor. A fuller sound, harking back to Motown more than anything else, the LP takes a soulful bent, not a disco/funky one.

At the Palladium in July, opening for Rockpile, the band was tight and professional, spotlighting Johansen as New York's first white soul singer of the '80s. His singing is still pretty much as it was seven years ago, but the songs are a bit different — slower, subtler and more carefully put together. In deference to his past, Johansen includes a couple of Dolls songs in the set: "Personality Crisis" and "Girls," which the Dolls introduced towards the end of their existence.

Sylvain's album, unheard as of this moment, should be pretty interesting. Always underrated as a Doll, his work with the Criminals showed a real feel for both R&B and jazzy uptempo numbers, with a creative ability far beyond anything obvious in the past. His new band, named Teenage News after an old Dolls tune, isn't the Criminals, but one supposes that whatever Syl does bears his own imprint.

Johnny, Jerry, and Arthur may never recapture their former abilities unless they can overhaul their personal lives. While David and Syl have managed to reenter the American record business in a positive manner, benefiting from the lessons of the past, the others have managed to stay outside, still working in the "underground" circuit of clubs, independent labels and self-management (or lack thereof). The Heartbreakers' live album (and there's another in the can) was as good as the band, although Jerry Nolan's presence might have helped. Artie's single (as Killer Kane) and his various bands — L.O.K., the Corpsegrinders, well...

In summation, the Dolls more than did their bit for the state and development of rock and roll. They went way out on a limb and paid dearly for their daring. But without them, there never would have been a new wave. Carri on... ∎

QUOTES OF THE DECADE

"I would never consider myself a musician: I'm just an entertainer."
—JOHNNY THUNDERS (1980) TP 57

"Pop music isn't by any means the central issue of my life; it's hardly a peripheral one." —BRIAN ENO (1982) TP 76

"In New York or L.A. you can go out and get anything at any time, as long as you get your shots afterwards."
—ALICE COOPER (1980) TP 52

"*As obnoxious a twit as Harley may be, he has written a brilliantly engaging, thoroughly unique set of songs, given them excessively affected vocals (which are perfect) and produced the whole affair with the tracks running together in such a fashion that the album consists of two coherent sides, neatly bound up with a refrain that both ends and begins the album.*" (Ira Robbins in Phonograph Record Magazine, *February 1975*)

This interview (and the above LP review) were strongly colored by overindulgence in, and slavish acceptance of, the British music press, which found Harley absurd and risible. He spotted the prejudice right off and was rightly irked about it. He may well have been a cocky egotist with towering pretensions and no fear of sounding the snob, but his frustration at being seen that way, even by a fan of his music, was completely understandable.

COCKNEY REBEL: STEVE HARLEY INTERVIEWED

TOTP 8, APRIL/MAY 1975

By Ira Robbins

Ever since the first rumblings came across the Atlantic about Cockney Rebel, they've generated quite a bit of curiosity and debate among American Anglophiles who know only what they read in the papers. Their two British albums (actually three, with the recent release of *The Best Years of Our Lives*) have been argued over in Britain, but the usual upshot is an article which appears to be serious as it tirades against Steve Harley. Like Roxy Music, they have been treated as a public joke by several of the major rock papers in England, despite very successful tours and records.

It was in the interest of finding out for ourselves that we met and talked with Steve Harley, the voice and brains of Cockney Rebel, now billed as Steve Harley and... The band had played a few assorted gigs in the States (late February), so

Steve made a quick stop in New York on his way back to London to film a TV show the next day. The interview took place in his room at the Waldorf-Astoria.

I'm afraid your reputation has distinctly preceded you to America.

I'll be really honest with you, Ira, I'm surprised that someone who's writing so intelligently and so rationally should have believed what the press said. As a former journalist, I know better than to believe what I read in the newspapers. You see, in England it's very bigoted — they're more bigoted than I am. They're very silly little boys — very hung up, the reporters, very hung up.

I'm more familiar with American journalism and I more or less turned to British writing because I find it vastly superior to what comes out of America. There have been good writers and publications in America, but generally the writing is self-indulgent to the point of not caring about the music. The redeeming feature I find in British writing is that no matter how much they slag an artist and call Bryan Ferry "Brant Ferrari" or call you "Cocky Rabble" or whatever... [I wonder where I was going with this thought…]

There's only one comic you're talking about, believe me that's a comic.

The New Musical Express?

This is sixth form schoolboy sense of humor, it's regressive. It's backward, it's retarded. The whole of that staff is still into cheap rock and roll boogie. They don't understand modernism in any way at all. They're very behind the times. They're into being the paper you love to hate. They're more image-conscious than most rock stars. They don't prevent me [from] selling records or selling out concerts. They don't help me, but they sure don't prevent me.

Wasn't the NME *one of the first papers to write seriously about Rebel?*

It was, but the guy who wrote it was a freelancer, Austin John Marshall. He wrote a whole page about how brilliant and wonderful we were. A month later they fired him. I don't know if it was political or by coincidence. Maybe it's paranoia, but I get the impression that there's a definite policy at the *NME* about Cockney Rebel. It probably hurt their feelings quite a lot to have to put us at number-one in their hit parade this week.

You've had your jabs at them. There have been a couple of songs in which you lyrically attacked them.

Yeah, because my songs are my chronicles, they chronicle my life. If I'm going through a period of hating the press, which I've been in for maybe a year now... I probably hate them more than they hate me. They don't understand me, and you know when you don't understand something, there's this human fear of the unknown, you attack it. These whole little Freudian hangups — they're the least important thing in my whole life.

I doubt that [press criticism] really affects either the audience's opinion of you, your opinion of music or your opinion of yourself.

It doesn't affect anything in any way.

That's probably the best attitude. But, as you can see, in America, there's not very much that we know about Cockney Rebel except what we read in the British press. It's difficult to say "I know better" because you don't. Subjectivity is unavoidable.

But you were very objective. Even though you bought this bullshit, you didn't let it cloud your view of what you were listening to.

I think [The Psychomodo] is a great album.

And I appreciate that, 'cause it's something I'm not used to. In England, it's total subjectivity. You were objective even though you'd been subjected to their bullshit. Maybe what they say is true. When you leave here you might be thinking they were dead right. This is your chance to find out. I just don't like it when the word spreads, people start believing it. I arrive at the airport, first time I've been in a country, and someone confronts me

with, 'Even though you're an obnoxious bastard, how do you feel about being in America?' Well, I could do without it. Let them find out for themselves. Let them write the truth, then I'll respect them. In England, I haven't got a chance.

What do you think about the influences on your songwriting? "Sling It" is obviously taken from "All Along the Watchtower."

Oh yeah.

Did you sit down and say, "I'm going to write a song to nick 'All Along the Watchtower'"?

I meant to. Deliberately, consciously. I wouldn't have done it so blatantly if it wasn't conscious. I'll tell you why I did it. I had a story. "Sling It" is obviously just a sustained metaphor, the metaphor being the ship sinking, the struggle for the shore, people being trampled, the voice in the sky, the whole thing is just a frantic little metaphor. I wrote it as a piece of poetry and I said, "This is 'All Along the Watchtower,' only you're saying it entirely differently." Lyrically, it's nothing like the way [Dylan] said it. His was a sustained metaphor, his was far more religious, I think, mine is more political. I said, "Look, I must parody 'Watchtower,' which is such a wonderful song anyway, one of the best songs Dylan ever wrote." "Sling It" is one of the best songs *I* ever wrote. It's one of my favorites because lyrically it says everything I wanted to say. I just didn't want to be bothered with finding an original tune, 'cause why should I? It's like if Ginsberg writes a poem in '75, he might say the same thing as Keats said in 1875, or earlier, of course, but he'll maybe think to himself, because it's the same theme, let me use the same meter that Keats used, or Shelley used. Lennon wrote "Yer Blues" on *The White Album,* "even hate my rock and roll," things like that he was saying, and deliberately wrote a twelve-bar blues to express the emotion. This frantic "Watchtower" three-chord rhythm was the only way I could express that emotion. It was deliberate, conscious not nick but parody.

Before forming Cockney Rebel, were you interested in rock? I've read you saying that rock was a challenge you wanted to face one day, not particularly your life or anything.

I went to both big *Isle of Wight* [festivals]. I saw the Dylan one and the following one, Hendrix's last concert. I was at the *Bath* festival, which was the American invasion — three days and nights. I sat through all the festivals when I was 18, 17, so it was in my blood, but it was a phase I was going through. The poets and the novelists were more the way I spent my time. The standard of rock isn't very high.

I'm curious because there's a lot in the character of Cockney Rebel that's derivative of things that preceded it. There are a lot of comparisons that have been made that are just too pat to be useful, but you can't get away from the fact that there's a relationship between Cockney Rebel and bands that preceded it.

Only because they represent the same thing ... which is a good thing. The bands, the people you're thinking of are, like Cockney Rebel, part of the third generation of rock. Their influences aren't apparent. The influences that they derived or took from the first and second generations aren't obvious, so they're all part of the third generation that doesn't seem to have any roots — they all appeared out of nowhere; Ferry was a schoolteacher, Steve Harley was a journalist. They are a new movement in rock — the way they dress, the way they talk, the way they look, the way they write — it's like an artistic movement which is good for the '70s. Deep Purple and Black Sabbath will probably always pull 30,000 people wherever they play. But the more artistic side is opening up in the '70s 'cause we're not ashamed of it anymore.

The Times sends critics to the Rainbow. And artists are playing looking like roadies. Not me. I don't want to look like a roadie on stage.

Do your roadies still dress up?

No. [laughs] I went through a lot of funny things in those days. I'm very much into modernism. I'm just a great modern.

But a lot of your influences are a good 60, 70 years old.

Oh yeah. But thank god they're not ten years old. Yeah, they are 60, 70 years old. My influences are far more from Dietrich's acting and Busby Berkeley and Alfred Hitchcock. I studied their work, was flabbergasted. And the same as the writers — I know more about Hemingway and Steinbeck than I do about Deep Purple and the Rolling Stones. There's some of us that are trying to be artistic. There's some of us that are trying to modernize it. Art changes. We're not painting like *that* anymore [he points to a dusty, but evidently prized, member of the Waldorf's collection]. We have Dali now, the surrealists. There's schools, you know, schools of painters, we have schools of poets, schools of novelists ... what does rock have? They're still trying to tell me that rock is the music of the streets, of the revolution, that we are the revolution. It's the music of the anti-establishment, but we are the establishment! We've had our Bill Haleys and Little Richards, our Jerry Lee Bloxes, we've had all those people. They were the wall-kickers. We went through the second generation with the Beatles and the Rolling Stones, through Led Zeppelin and Cream, Purples of the world. Suddenly someone said, "Look, rock should evolve as an art form, the same as art and poetry, acting. The cinema's evolved over 50 years so much. Where's this modern art called rock music?" Still in the '60s, it still lives in Woodstock, in America. *Woodstock's* still going on all around us. So, the biggest bands in America are morons. Millionaire morons. They haven't got any real talent. I'm not saying that I don't care — I think there are a lot of people out there — a lot of various tastes — some people like cabbage, some people don't like cabbage.

There's a band I'd like to ask you about. I sense a certain similarity in spirit — the band is Be-Bop Deluxe. I know there's been some incestuous personnel changes that have been going on. It was rumored that Bill Nelson was invited to join Cockney Rebel.

No chance. Milton Reame-James [keyboards] and the bass player, Paul Jeffreys, played with Bill Nelson. They soon split; it was a mistake all along. I didn't know anything about it. We lost contact, I didn't care for them very much. We weren't very friendly.

You didn't like the band?

No, I mean the old Cockney Rebel. We weren't the greatest of friends when it split.

What do you think of Bill Nelson and/or Be-Bop Deluxe?

Bill's a pretty neat guitar player. I took them on tour with us in England. That's how come you heard of them. Best publicity they ever got. The guys playing with him, Christ, all-time losers. He woke up to that one night and he couldn't do anything about it 'cause he's such a nice boy, so EMI sacked 'em for him. He had no chance with the guys he was playing with. He's just putting a band together now with better musicians.

What do you think of your audience in Britain? You must appeal to 15-, 16-, 17-year-old kids, right?

Up to 30. They're wonderful, really incredible.

Don't you feel that you go over the heads of a lot of people?

Oh sure. When a whole auditorium stands up and applauds at the end — they usually end up singing, "Look what they've done to the blues." It's pretty amazing when the band just stops and walks offstage. I just wish I could believe that they knew what they were singing, the words that I was putting into their mouths. I don't believe they do. I don't care, 'cause I enjoy so much being on stage. I enjoy working on an audience and manipulating them over two hours. "Manipulate" is not the right word, it's a nasty thing, but I think working on them, building their emotions and taking them up and down. I enjoy it so much that I really don't care if they understand. I'm not hung-up about it. I'm not going to claim to be the misunderstood poet.

Don't you sometimes worry that there's absolutely no explicable reason why you're so popular?

I came on pretty strong in the beginning. There's something that happens [when we play live] I can't describe because it would sound terribly egotistical. It's hard for me to explain without sounding self-opinionated. In the most humble way I can, I'll show you what it's like. I'm doing this for your benefit. I'm not sitting here trying to sell me, because I don't have to do that. I'm just doing it to explain to you. It's not egomania, get that right.

Something very funny happens at a Cockney Rebel concert. It's funny enough, funny-strange, something happened in Detroit, Cleveland — this is American people that I was told it wouldn't happen with. Something very strange, when, for someone totally unknown, which I was, in Detroit, Cleveland — well, not totally, they'd bought the record — we'd sold out the hall on curiosity value, not because they were crazy about Cockney

Rebel. Cleveland was three-quarters full, about two and a half thousand, and I'd say 2,000 of them came out of curiosity. But they still stood up at the end, at my command, and without the group playing, total silence from the stage. I don't stand around going, "Yeah, yeah, let me hear you sing, lemme hear you say it one more time, lemme hear you say it, put your hands together!" I don't do that shit. I just quiet my band down, I kind of have a rap, like it's a living room, just three or four of us in a living room, talking to 3,000 people. Somehow, I make them feel guilty. I seem to have this knack of making a person sitting there think, "If I don't sing to him, I'm being very selfish. He's given me his whole life, his heart and soul for two hours. He's given me everything he can possibly give me, and he looks totally wiped out and exhausted" — which I invariably am. "If I don't give it back to him, I'll be very selfish." And suddenly they'll start singing. Then suddenly they put their arms up. Then suddenly they're standing up. These aren't 15-year-olds, and I'm not Goebbels, it's just this knack I've got where somehow, up there, He gave me something that's hypnotic. Maybe it's the shape of me nose. Maybe it's because I limp. Maybe it's because I've got blue eyes, I don't know. And I don't take credit for it — that's the difference between egomania and the fact that I've got the habit of opening up to people like you and telling you the truth. It's a funny thing — it's very strange, like a spell where the band isn't even playing, they've maybe walked off stage even. It isn't the Faces. It isn't everyone singing along with "Angel," with scarves in the air, it isn't that. It isn't James Brown committing suicide on stage, whipping people to death. It isn't the Osmonds getting them to scream, this is someone whose whole two-hour act is like a surrealistic look at life, which, we've agreed, goes over 90 percent of the audience's heads. So, how can you explain it? It's just that somehow I make them feel guilty. I don't mean to, I don't go out there saying, "I'll make you bastards feel guilty," I don't do that, but some of that comes off me. That's the vibration they get.

[Harley pages through an issue of *TOTP*.] What are these people? Idle Race, Patto...

We mostly write about British bands.

But they're all dead! Animals... What is it? Why do you want to write about the Idle Race? Are you kidding? You're putting me on. Is this serious?

Oh, definitely. Very serious. In fact, we've been accused of not having a sense of humor.

I look forward to having a good look at it. I won't ask you anymore, because it would sound silly. Cream? They're not just not well known anymore, they don't exist anymore.

But the music exists. It does.

Not in many people's homes. Not Patto. Certainly not Idle Race.

There's just no point in disallowing the existence of anything before today.

I'm a great modern, a great progressive. As an individual, I'm more interested in tomorrow, because that's our savior. Yesterday is our disaster. I have to believe in modernism. It's probably the only chance I have of being accepted as a writer. ■

LOU REED IS "ALIVE" AND, WELL, IN CLEVELAND: A REPORT FROM THE FRONT

TP 14, JUNE/JULY 1976

By Janet Macoska

No one conducts a "normal" interview with Lou Reed. In fact, we didn't do any kind of interview with him. His publicist informed us on the scheduled day that Lou was in one of his moods, being "testy" and not at all cooperative. Instead, your *Trouser Press* reporter (and photographer) followed Lou Reed and his RCA entourage throughout Cleveland on a recent promotional trip to the city to plug his latest album, *Coney Island Baby*. The day proved to be more revealing of Lou's character than any interview could have been.

You can get out now if you prefer, or come along for the ride...

With the wind-chill factor lowering the temperature to below zero, I was in no mood for conflict with the Lou Reed born of imagination, rumor and innuendo. You know the one you've read about, the ozoned maniac ... the killer shark with razor-edged teeth who gnaws on rock critics like a dog with his favorite bone.

Three Hare Krishnas were beating on their tom-toms, pushing their strawberry incense and religion outside the May Co. A Black woman was screeching "SINNER" at the top of her lungs, clutching her Bible and tambourine, instilling the fear of God into the double-stamp-day shoppers.

You know, there's a possibility for a rock and roll band here, but no, Jethro Tull's already done all this before — and plus they've got that damn vaudevillian zebra for laughs. Anyhow, the only salvation I wanted was from the agonizingly numbing cold.

When I reached the Bond Court Hotel (Cleveland's newest and ritziest inn), I found the editor and photographer of the leading free rock publication in Cleveland standing in the lobby, scowls covering their faces, mumbling nasty things under their breath. They had just come from an encounter over breakfast with Lou Reed. It had obviously spoiled their appetites.

Louie was, I learned, being uncooperative, though stronger language was used to describe it. He was "playing games," and the paper threatened to trash their whole article. The record company anxiously tried to soothe agitated emotions.

This just might not be the best day of my life.

It was quietly suggested that, in lieu of a regular interview, I might agree to follow the star around for the day. A dream date with Lou Reed? Wow!

After a little uneasiness (no one is ever completely comfortable in Lou's presence; he almost always sees to that), the entourage piled into a car. The local promo man started spinning the radio dial, searching for a station, any station, that might be playing a Lou Reed tune. He didn't find one. Not very impressive. The first stop was to be the largest record wholesaler (one-stop, as they are called in the business) in the area. We freeze time for a moment (not difficult in this weather) to make a few observations.

Lou Reed, you see, is actually a chess master. He could stump Bobby Fischer blindfolded. Life is a game to him, and the people he meets are his pawns. He's always testing, always pushing to see how far you'll let him go. Some people consider this cruel treatment and detest him for it, while others ignore him and still others unassumingly fail to realize that they ARE part of Lou's private contest. Most are just not prepared for Lou Reed's "mind games."

We now return to exciting tournament action in Cleveland. *TP* is at ringside, bringing you the first matchup. Lou Reed is in all four corners.

RCA's reason for bringing Lou to the one-stop was so that he could meet and spur on the salesmen who'd be pushing his disc to record shops and chain stores throughout the area. Lou Reed's reason for agreeing to visit the one-stop was to test RCA's generosity and see how many records and tapes he could abscond with.

As the RCA staffers hyped the salesmen and employees, Lou Reed drifted through the warehouse, pulling albums and cassette tapes at whim, putting them all on RCA's tab. Occasionally, they'd glance over their shoulders to see how bad it was getting, then turn away and grimace as the dollar signs danced in their heads.

During his shopping spree, Reed stopped to pose for a photo or two. A dozen albums, eight or nine cassette tapes and two packages of Memorex blank tapes in exchange for a couple of snapshots. A fair trade? No one said a word.

The area's second largest one-stop (they try harder) was next on the list. The routine began again. As the RCA promo man piled a second load of records and tapes into his trunk for Lou, he begged, "When we get to the radio stations,

Lou, please leave the turntables!"

His lust for freebies still hadn't been satiated, however, as we reached the first radio station, an FM Top 40 outfit. Lou performed all the perfunctory niceties, allowing himself to be introduced to the program director. He even said hello. Then he spotted a crate of Polaroid Colorpak Cameras that the station was awarding as prizes over the air to listeners.

"Can I have one of these?"

"No, I'm sorry, they're all spoken for."

"Are you sure I can't have just one?"

In desperation, the program director looked pleadingly at the local promotion man, who shrugged and handed Lou the new Bachman-Turner Overdrive album that had also been pegged for giveaways by the station. Lou was satisfied. He'd won again; a consolation prize, but a victory, nonetheless.

The next two stations proved to be different kinds of conquests.

The city's newest FM station — the second most popular (they play album cuts and singles, semi-free form) — is located in the spacious and luxurious Park Centre complex in downtown Cleveland. The studio is smack-dab in the center of the shopping mall so that passersby can observe the jocks performing on the air in a glass booth, an amusement second only to visiting the Cleveland Zoo.

No sooner had we reached the station's office upstairs than Lou got himself embroiled in a polite argument with the program director … about music, groups and the labels placed on artists. Queen was a heavy-metal-bubblegum band, the program director insisted. Reed disagreed. The program director cheerfully tried to drop the subject.

Reed wanted to continue. He wanted to know if he could appear on the air with the jock in the booth downstairs.

"It's against station policy, I'm afraid."

Reed was adamant. The DJ had asked him at a promotion party the night before and it was only courteous to be permitted to do so. Right?

Upon reaching the studio, a microphone was provided for Lou to say a few words ("a first for the station" it was announced).

Could he play one of the songs off his new album, say a few words, then play a second song? He was testing again.

No, station policy, only one song permitted. Reed cursed. "Have you heard the album yet?" he asked the program director. Well, no…

Okay, then, could he say a few words and introduce "Kicks" off the new album?

All right.

The program director left, feeling that he'd enforced his authority and controlled the situation properly. Reed grinned, did the intro to "Kicks" and walked out of the studio.

In the car, Reed bounced enthusiastically. "That guy doesn't know what I just did to him. Boy, is he going to be surprised when he hears 'fuck' come over the air. I can just see his face."

Even before Lou's ecstasy had died down, we arrived at Cleveland's dying Top 40 station, a decade ago the most powerful radio station in the entire country. The program director was a fixture in Cleveland radio, a middle-aged woman with considerable influence and power. Lou Reed was ready for her.

The program director apologized for being late, sat down at her desk facing Reed and attempted to initiate some small talk. "How long did it take you to record *Coney Island Baby*, Lou?"

"A week and a half."

"Oh, c'mon, seriously!"

"Really. Two weeks at most."

"I mean, writing all the material, the recording and final mixing."

"Two weeks."

An expression of disbelief, a look of he's-pulling-my-leg, crossed her face.

"Look, I can answer this question any way you want me to, if you'd rather believe another answer, but it was two weeks," insisted Lou.

Conceding, she offered, "You know, you're lucky if you can do it that way. Why, I was talking to Andy Williams and Henry Mancini about recording recently…"

Lou's eyes lit up. That was just what he wanted. Was this lady leaving him a beautiful opening. Reed launched into a nonstop tirade about mod-

ern recording methods and "obsolete artists" like Andy Williams and Henry Mancini. The program director could only sit and nod, barely getting in a word edgewise. At the first opportunity, she stood, thanked everyone for coming and excused herself.

Back in the car, Reed commented, "I hope she got the message. It's her and her station who are the ones that are out-of-date."

The main event Lou had been waiting for all day was next… his bout with The Kid, Cleveland's top jock on the city's most influential FM station. Lou had insisted on The Kid and wanted the day's schedule arranged accordingly. His reasoning: "He's the one with the most power, isn't he?"

It was strictly one-on-one for this match. Clear the studio, no hangers-on, no writers or photographers, no RCA staffers. Just The Kid and Lou. Everyone else would have to hover around the monitors to catch the on-the-air action.

The Kid, who could be Mr. Cool with all the other celebs he'd interviewed, was clearly intimidated by Reed and the psych-job he was performing. Verbal jabs right and left. The Kid was coming unglued. He didn't know whether to be serious or humorous with Reed, and Lou kept him off balance.

By this time, I'd really had enough. The Kid–Lou Reed confrontation seemed to be just a repeat of the day's events. I entered the studio (cautiously) to say my goodbyes. Lou looked at me, almost hurt, "Aren't you gonna take my picture with The Kid?"

I returned with my camera and was permitted to play the role of audience and impartial referee to this private contest. The off-the-air tactics were even more interesting than the on-the-air comments. While the records played, Reed never let up, never let The Kid take a rest or get the advantage, never let him score on points. Perhaps Lou Reed is the Jimmy Connors of the rock world?

The psych was working. The Kid was sweating and looking for encouragement from anyone — me — or anything — the wall — (almost one and the same). I followed the action from court to court, and half expected Curt Gowdy to break in at any minute with a play-by-play.

Reed would periodically remove his shades and stare at The Kid with those eyes that looked as if they'd seen hell on alternate weekends. The Kid would shrink into his chair, then try to get back in Reed's favor by comparing experiences with various brands of drugs and booze.

On the air, the repartee imparted a small portion of information to the public, none of it really vital.

"*Coney Island Baby* is my first LP since the Velvet Underground. I walked through the rest of them.

"*Metal Machine Music* cleared the air. With *Metal Machine Music*, I was saying, 'Hey, I'm still here and I'm saying hello.'

"Nixon was beautiful. If he had bombed Montana and gotten away with it, I would've loved him.

"I have no fear … of anything!"

Okay, the end was in sight. The Kid could relax and brighten up the conversation a little. So, he thought.

"Hey Lou, is it true blondes have more fun?"

"Is it true you're an idiot?"

Match point. Lou Reed wins the trophy.

Though I didn't hear it (I was on my way home at the time), listeners report The Kid was just not the same cocky jock the rest of the afternoon. Someone or something had spoiled the day for him.

Oh well...

Meanwhile, Lou Reed was giggling and cackling as he rehashed the event in the car on the way to the airport. "The Kid had the fear in him. Didja hear him? If he wasn't paranoid before, he certainly is now."

Never mind the ravaged psyches strewn in his path, for Lou Reed, Cleveland had been a success. For everyone else Lou Reed had been, at best, a trying experience. ∎

QUOTES OF THE DECADE

"I thought the Velvet Underground stunk."
—IAN HUNTER (1980) TP 53

SPARKS: RON & RUSSELL AT HOME, AT WORK, AT PLAY

TOTP 9, JUNE/AUGUST 1975

By Ira Robbins and Dave Schulps

On the occasion of their first tour of America, we got a chance to speak to Ron and Russel Mael of Sparks before their New York date early in May. Like several other top pop bands in Britain, they are articulate, intelligent and totally convinced that they have no equals, musically, in the British charts. Although we wouldn't go that far, they are definitely a unique and talented group, a fact confirmed by the thoroughly enjoyable show they present.

IR: As Britain's only American rock band, what is it like to become British pop stars after looking up to British pop stars?

RON: One thing, just to clarify, is that us looking up to the British pop stars was only a part of it, 'cause we liked all the people like the Who, the Move and the Kinks, but then we liked a lot of other people, too. So, it wasn't our ideal to be a Los Angeles British band, and the reason for us going to England was just out of frustration and desperation that the situation was not making it in Los Angeles. It was terribly exciting, and still is, for us to be playing in England and receiving all the buzz that goes on and having hit singles and being on *Top of the Pops*, it's just that that isn't the end.

DS: Who are some of your other influences?

RON: I really like the Beach Boys and all that L.A. sort of flair to it.

RUSSELL: Jan and Dean.

IR: What was it like being Halfnelson?

RON: That was just an artsy-craftsy sort of situation where we weren't concerned about playing in front of people and we just did things.

RUSSELL: We didn't know what we were doing at all. We still don't know what we're doing.

RON: We were not knowing what we were doing in front of a lot less people. It's more fun not knowing what you're doing in front of more people than less. We always thought at that time that, all things being equal, we had elements that were incredibly commercial, so we were just waiting for the time to come along when it would click on that sort of level, but meanwhile we just kept going.

IR: You really thought that Halfnelson could have been a major American band?

RON: One problem with it that we saw a while later was that the execution was not as assured as it might be. In the present format of the band, the playing is more assured, so that it can't be knocked as a band, whereas you might hate Halfnelson or you might hate guitars being out of tune.

IR: Why was it so much easier to make it in England than in America? In America you were really starting to build a very strong little cult.

RON: One thing, the audiences there are younger and more receptive to new things, I think.

RUSSELL: It's not as Beatle-oriented there. Here, we found out to our dismay, that the Beatles are still a pretty big band, and that's really amazing. We've driven around a lot, and you turn on the radio and they're still having Beatle competitions and Beatle giveaways and Rolling Stones weekends. In England, it's not that way at all. There's a new generation of kids that hasn't been brought up on the Rolling Stones and the Beatles, and Eric Clapton isn't a hero anymore. Clapton's still a figure to be reckoned with in the States, but in England the kids don't really care about Eric Clapton that much. They're really open to new things, and it really gave us an opportunity to be one of those new things.

RON: There are a lot of limited-appeal bands in Britain which still flourish a bit. People have asked how we're gonna change what we're doing for the States, thinking that maybe we were one of

those limited-appeal bands. We haven't altered anything for America. It's the same band you'd hear in England, only playing in the States. The reaction has been almost unwarranted at times and really exciting for us.

RUSSELL: We played in Los Angeles, the Santa Monica Civic Auditorium. It was the best concert we've ever done, including any English concert, any European concert, and it was in the United States, in our hometown. The reaction was exactly as it's been in Europe when there's people yanking at your leg. We were really shocked. In America, before our TV appearances, I don't think the band was something to be reckoned with. It really put Sparks on the map.

DS: You said you really like touring, but when you were in America you really didn't tour extensively.

RUSSELL: No one wanted to have us.

DS: You originally started as a studio band.

RUSSELL: Yeah, originally it was just three people: Earle Mankey and the two of us. Earl had a tape recorder, and we had some songs. We didn't really care about playing live, but after we made tapes and found out we couldn't get signed with those, we decided that the only thing to do was to play someplace. We couldn't just play with the three of us, so we added Jim Mankey and Harley Feinstein.

DS: What's happened to the Mankey brothers?

RUSSELL: Earle we just saw a couple of days ago in L.A. He's the head engineer at the Beach Boys' studio. Jim's gone back to university, and Harley's gone back to university, he's gonna be a teacher.

IR: Do you listen to any bands that have records which might exchange places in the charts with yours?

RON: We listen to the radio; it just isn't that interesting. A lot of people trying to cause a stir as personalities where they don't have any music to back it up. It can work a lot of times in England because they kind of go for that sort of thing. But then there comes a time when you have to release a record, sad to say, and that either holds water or it doesn't.

DS: Are you planning to record anything while you're here?

RUSSELL: No, we're being produced by Tony Visconti, and he's got a studio in his house. We've finished two songs already, and when we go back to England, we're going to finish the LP.

RON: He's really a good person.

RUSSELL: One of the two new songs we recorded lasts four-and-a-half minutes. The idea was to release that as the next Sparks album, just that one song, because it's got so much thrown in. We put everything into it. We're thinking of retiring after that.

IR: Did Alice Cooper steal "No More Mr. Nice Guy" from you?

RUSSELL: Yeah. It's a totally different song, but they had seen us play a lot at the Whisky in L.A. as Sparks and Halfnelson and we always did that song, and it was always the one song that went down the best, sort of the only song that got any reaction at all, and that's 'cause it has a really moving chorus and we didn't flub that one up too badly. That was one thing people really remembered the band for. They really liked the band, and they just took it. They took the whole idea of the chorus [but] they changed the melody and all.

IR: Who are the women on the cover of the *Kimono* album?

RUSSELL: They're from Stomu Yamashta's Red Buddah Theatre. A lot of people wondered if it was us, but it definitely was not.

DS: There's a rumor that you sang backup vocals on "Waterloo Sunset."

RUSSELL: No, that wasn't true. Anything else?

RON: Trevor White is not joining the Rolling Stones.

DS: What got Adrian Fisher fired? Was he into too heavy a thing?

RUSSELL: Asshole. The other was that he wasn't too concerned with being in Sparks. He's a really good guitarist, but he's from "de blues skool." You can't fool people into trying to be excited about what you're doing.

IR: Would you like to clear up the ultimate all-time Sparks rumor?

RUSSELL: You've got a better one than the Kinks thing?

IR: That your mother is Doris Day and your brother is Terry Melcher.

RUSSELL: Yes, I'm Terry Melcher.

RON: No, we actually mentioned that just as a giggle when we first went over to England, not thinking that anyone would take it seriously. We were in Copenhagen, and I got a call at the hotel from a lady saying, "Is Mr. Melcher there?" I said, "No." She said, "We have on our records that you're Doris Day's son..."

RUSSELL: "...and we've been trying to get in touch with her because we've got publishing royalties for her songs in Denmark and we've got all this money sitting in the bank and we're trying to give it to her but we can't get in touch with her. Do you want to pick up the money?"

RON: If you want to be Terry Melcher you can go pick up a very large sum.

DS: How long does it take to write a typical Sparks song?

RON: Well, it takes a long time because you have to go through a lot of stuff you don't use. You sit down for ages and ages and then something will pop up, maybe rather quickly.

DS: They don't seem like the kind of things you just knock out.

RON: I really wish there was a fast way, because it's really boring. But when one comes up, then it's all worth it. When it's not coming up, then it's not worth it at all. Each song is its own reward. ■

November 1977
No. 23 $1.25
UK 75¢

Trouser Press

FREE GRAHAM PARKER STICKER!

BRYAN FERRY:
Has the fizz gone out?

PAGE on ZEP
STONES RARITIES
DWIGHT TWILLEY
BLONDIE

Gentle Giant   AC/DC
Brand X   Elvis Costello

BRYAN FERRY AGONISTES

TP 23, NOVEMBER 1977

By Janet Macoska

It came as very little surprise to anyone when the five members of Roxy Music (six, if you want to count the revolving bass player) went their separate ways last year.

Bryan Ferry released a single, "Let's Get Together," and an EP in Britain, both hits, which were stretched into an album in America. Guitarist Phil Manzanera released the *801 Live* album and produced an LP by New Zealand group Split Enz. Andy Mackay got involved with *Rock Follies '77*. Keyboard player/violinist Eddie Jobson joined Frank Zappa's band and went on tour, while drummer Paul Thompson played with anyone who asked him.

The split, incidentally, was never officially announced. It simply happened. And … it was expected. Throughout the lifetime of Roxy Music, controversy and rumors of discontent amongst the members were reported frequently. The subject of most of the rancor was the leader, singer-songwriter, image-maker and undisputed (at least in his mind) creator of Roxy Music, Bryan Ferry. He was considered by some to run the band like Captain Bligh on the Bounty; his work and policy decisions were final. Many, including members of Roxy, thought Bryan ran too tight a ship, stifling personal and creative freedom. Thus, the dissolution of Roxy Music.

Recently, Bryan Ferry embarked on his first tour of America without Roxy Music, as a solo artist with (excuse me, but I've fallen into the Ferry brand of thinking) another backup band (everyone's replaceable). Interestingly enough, this new but transient band contained various former members of Roxy. In Bryan's touring band (and appearing on his last album, *In Your Mind*) were Phil Manzanera, Paul Thompson and part-time Roxy bassist John Wetton. New characters in this sterling cast were legendary guitarist Chris Spedding, keyboard wiz and arranger Ann Odell and ex-Crimsonite Mel Collins, who led a three-piece horn section. Admittedly, Roxy Music were one of the primo bands of the '70s; but this lineup certainly rivaled the original in many ways.

Despite such a seemingly positive beginning for an all-out attempt at a solo career, all was not well with Bryan's first tour of America. It, and the corresponding *In Your Mind*, were not the successes they deserved to be. Record company support was nil, and Bryan was keeping public and press discussions to a bare minimum.

Cleveland being possibly the hottest spot for Roxy Music in America (several hundred fans once converged on the airport to mob the band as it arrived in town, and Roxy filled 10,000-seat halls here easily), Bryan softened his stand and consented to do two interviews. One was for WMMS radio, the powerful FM station that first played Roxy Music in America: the other was with this reporter for *Trouser Press*.

The interview covered a good many aspects of Bryan's career with Roxy and as a solo artist. The best way to present it, I thought, was as it happened. You are there!!! The questions and answers are related as they happened, as verbatim as possible, with a few editorial corrections (even Bryan doesn't speak correctly all the time; I don't most of the time).

The scene opens, and you are sitting on the sofa in the luxurious (for Cleveland) suite at Swingo's Celebrity Inn, across a glass table from Bryan Ferry, infamous lounge lizard, who sips his tea and engages in a sometimes-not-so-elegant discussion about everything you always wanted to know but didn't have the nerve to ask.

Bryan is staring blankly into space, answering the first question almost by rote, reciting a well-known speech about life with Roxy and life as a solo artist. Through careful prodding, Bryan's conscious attention is gained and finally we start getting specific answers to specific questions.

There are conflicting reports as to the past, present and future of Roxy Music. Some reports say that Roxy is merely on sabbatical and will one day rise again, while others state that Roxy is dead and that everyone is happy and content with their own solo careers. Why is the whole matter so vague?

It's vague because it is vague. There aren't any plans to get together again. The next Roxy thing that is going to come out is *Roxy's Greatest Hits*, believe it or not [laughs]. It makes me chuckle whenever I say it. That is later this year. Whether there will be another Roxy studio album ... I don't really think there will be one, but it is slightly possible, which is why there was never any kind of official statement saying, "Roxy is finished." It is possible there will be another album called Roxy Music, but it probably wouldn't be the same lineup as before. After the *Siren* album, everyone got down to doing their own individual projects.

A lot of people speculated that the breakup of Roxy occurred because of discontent and arguments within the group, but that apparently is not one-hundred-percent true, because Phil Manzanera and Paul Thompson are playing in your current band; so is John Wetton.

Well, John wasn't a member of Roxy as such. He's always played with me on my solo albums. And, yes, Paul played on the album, of course. Phil didn't actually play on the album as much as I'd intended originally. In fact, he only plays rhythm guitar on one track. There were some hard feelings between me and Andy, but that was something that had been brewing for years until it finally got to the point where I didn't want to record with him anymore. It's one of those things that happens in groups. People can't stay together forever, and if they do, they usually stay together for all the wrong reasons. Groups that stay together for ten years, I think, are under pretty severe handicaps artistically as to how much fresh stuff they can get out of each other. and as to how much electricity they can spark off each other. I felt that five albums was a long run for me to be with more or less the same number of people under the right conditions. To me, it all worked out perfectly for everyone. The live album, *Viva!*, came out right after that. If we had been in the position where we had to do a studio album together last year, it would have been boring, for me anyway. If it would have been boring for me to make, it probably would have been boring to listen to. Whereas making *In Your Mind* was a delight because every day there was something different happening. One day it would be the string section, the next day it would be the horn section, the guitar overdubs coming in on the next day and so on. It was really enjoyable.

What struck me about In Your Mind *was that it seems to be less a typical solo album of yours, and more a natural progression or follow-up to* Siren.

Well, it is, in terms of the songs.

Right, it is the first solo album where you've recorded all your own songs rather than someone else's material. I also wanted to ask you about the previous solo album, Let's Stick Together. *You released a single and an EP in England, then somehow stretched it into an album for America, including redone versions of old Roxy tunes to fill it out.*

They were recorded years ago; one in '73, one in '74 and '75. I gave Atlantic Records the four tracks and the single, which were put out in England as an EP and a single. I didn't want those four tracks on the album, and I didn't want them to be singles, so I thought, why not revive the EP? We did that, and it worked incredibly well. The EP went on the singles chart. I'd wanted to [release an EP] before, and when we finally did do it, it was for a very genuine reason ... four tracks make an EP, you see? I brought the EP back into vogue, and now one after another are pouring out. The American record business, on the other hand, is too inflexible to allow for the EP. It doesn't fit; everything has to be so categorized and simplified in this country. Atlantic wouldn't put it out. They said, "Well, can't you make it into an album?" So, we found all these tracks that hadn't been released in America before, most of them B-sides, and put them together. There was only one track specifically recorded for the album, "Casanova." It was a bit weird album, but I think it was quite interesting in that in unintentionally became a bridging point, with half my songs and half other people's songs. Strangely, it was the biggest-selling album I've ever had in some places. It was the biggest selling album in Australia all last year — double platinum or something. Also in Holland and Sweden. It made the English charts as an American import. It didn't do anything in America, needless to say. The single was the biggest thing I've ever had, "Let's Stick Together," and we really thought that it would be the big hit for me in America. It is the second most disappointing thing that ever happened to me ... the first being the failure of *In Your Mind*.

It hasn't been a failure yet. Aren't you going to give it a chance?

The record company gave up on it after four weeks, which is a very short time, and gave up on "Tokyo Joe" [the first single off the album] after one week. They haven't supported our tour at all. Certain things are not well in the state of Denmark.

You wouldn't happen to be considering finding yourself another label, would you?

[*tongue deeply in cheek*] No, we'll stick with Atlantic forever. [*Strangling noises are emitted from the elegant one's throat.*]

Tell me about Chris Spedding. You've been featuring his guitar on the last couple of solo albums and on this tour. Where did you learn about him?

Oh, I've known about him for a long time; I always thought he was a jazz player. For the last ten, twelve years, he's gained a reputation as one of the most notable session guitar players in England. He used to play with jazz-oriented bands like the Mike Westbrook Band. The peo-

ple in the studio, the engineers, who see a lot of musicians coming through, recommend to me some of the new ones just for the buzz of playing with different people. They recommended Spedding, and I used him on a few tracks and he really knocked me out. I got on quite well with him, so I featured him quite heavily on the new album, along with another guitarist, Neil Hubbard. On "All Night Operator" [Neil]'s got a very beautiful solo. He used to be in Kokomo and the Grease Band. He's got a very different style than Spedding: that's the beauty of it. I go to Spedding for a part I want done very heavy metal. For something more delicate, I go to Neil Hubbard. That's the nice thing about having an infinite pool of musicians to choose from.

Has Spedding's punk image conflicted in any way with your well-known refined image onstage, or does it help make a nice contrast?

Not really, because I've been wearing leather on tour as well! [*Bryan breaks into hearty laughter. Interviewer is taken aback. Bryan is usually not this jovial, and he is really opening up, more so than in any other interview I'd done or could remember.*]

I started off the tour, the English part, with a brilliant silver-grey Harlem kind of suit from the Philippines, made by the same guy who makes all of my clothes. It was incredible, but it just didn't seem to go with this band, so we moved onto Costume Two, which is just leather trousers, with a shirt that looks a bit like the one I wore on the *Country Life* tour. Anyway, the whole idea on this tour was to make a heavier, more direct, musical statement. What we wear onstage is meant just to complement that. It's definitely a musically oriented show, which is a nice change. Besides, Chris's leather outfit was stolen a few nights ago, and he's not wearing that outfit now.

Do you concentrate mostly on your solo material in your show?

Yes. Since it's the first solo tour, it's been a cross-section of all the albums, really. There are bits from every one. I would have preferred, in retrospect, to have done more with the current material. Since this is the first tour, I hope we managed to get all those early albums out of the way and make some reference to them throughout the set. If this were the second solo tour, for instance, I wouldn't do any of those numbers at all. I would only be doing all of my own songs. Because I think that has been one of the problems for us in America, that there has been too much diversity and not enough concentration on a specific musical image. I think the usual image has outgrown the musical image in America, or at least it has had more attention paid to it. People just don't give one much credit for being a musician at all. And now, when you consider that we [*again this "we" business — he means "I", you know*] have done ten albums, and they've all been fairly contrasting. There is a thread that runs through them all, but there seems to be variety to them that has confused the people in America.

In the past your solo albums have served as a kind of escape for you, a definite change of pace from the Roxy albums.

Yeah, it was a holiday from my own writing.

Did it serve mostly as a self-indulgent kind of thing? Were the solo albums mostly for your benefit than anything else, because you needed a holiday from what you were doing with Roxy?

That's one of the reasons. I was just curious to see what an album of that nature would sound like. I thought it would be interesting. Take the second solo album: If I'd had 24 songs of my own, enough for a Roxy album and a solo album, the second solo album might have been all my own work as well. But I don't write that quickly. I have to work very diligently to write ten songs.

The second solo album (*Another Time, Another Place*) was to me a logical extension from the first (*These Foolish Things*): just bigger production numbers, more involved, getting more into the style of the thing as opposed to the content. The content of the songs was very important on the first solo album because they're all such great songs: everyone's favorite song is on that album. The second album features songs that were slightly more obscure, but the treatment became more important.

What about the selection of material for your solo albums? The songs were obviously favorites of yours, but you had to take into consideration what would sound good coming out of your mouth. You can't sing every favorite song you've ever had.

Not only that, there are some songs you steer away from because they're so perfect as they were originally recorded that you can't think of any other way to do them; or you think that if you did do them they would sound really bad in comparison with the original. I still believe, however, that if a song is good, there are millions of ways of doing it.

"These Foolish Things," for example, has been recorded, I suppose, hundreds of times by different people. "A Hard Rain Is Gonna Fall," on the other hand, has probably been recorded only once; and a lot of those songs from the '60s and '50s weren't thought of as songs but more as recordings. There was just one (accepted) version of it. I thought it might be interesting to apply the technique, use the idea of the standard which is recorded by everybody — usually terrible middle-of-the-road artists. I thought, for someone like me, who really isn't considered a middle-of-the-road artist by any means, to record an album in that way would be quite funny. And it worked in various countries. In America it fell flat.

The solo albums were less demanding than your work with Roxy.

Oh, yes, much less, because it was fun to do them. You didn't feel the responsibility; you didn't feel the pressure of, "This is my musical statement for this year ... this is my work."

That doesn't make you any less proud of that recorded effort, does it?

Oh no, not at all, because there are some great things on those albums; especially instrumentally there are some great bits. I'm not ashamed of any of the records I've made. I could see now that there are certain things I've done on record which weren't a good idea commercially, but I'd still stand by all of them.

Speaking of commercialism, some of your fans who have followed you and Roxy from the beginning and your more experimental days during the first couple of albums now say that you led Roxy to become too pop and too commercial. It's offensive to some of them because they think you've lost sight of the original intentions of the band which were innovative, avant-garde.

I still think my records are innovative.

They are the breed that feel that if four or more people discover a band, they're not worth listening to anymore.

To me that's narrow-minded and silly. That's like the whole punk rock scene at the moment. If the parents of the kids who are aficionados of it said, "Well, that's really nice," they would drop it like a hot potato; they'd hate it! I'm not really interested in fans of that nature. There was never one narrow vision at the beginning of the Roxy Music story anyway. I can't submit to the whims of fans as to what they think my destiny ought to be.

But did you intentionally modify what you were doing with Roxy somewhere along the way? Long about the Stranded *album your music became more accessible to more people and therefore more commercial.*

It became more musical because I found it the easiest thing in the world to make things that were experimental. I could go into the studio tomorrow and make what I think would be a very weird album and which would be interesting for me to make and very self-indulgent and I could make it all myself with various machines. But to me that's too easy, especially after doing *These Foolish Things*. I was so impressed playing with all those musicians whom I hadn't played with before. I was amazed at how interesting it was to make things musical. That kind of sold me on the idea of Eddie Jobson. He's very musical and was the most technically accomplished player that was ever in Roxy. Though he wasn't that experimental, he was a brilliant musician. That's why *Stranded* became more musical, for those two reasons, though Eddie hardly played on the album.

I did *These Foolish Things* after finishing *For Your Pleasure*, and by that time every other band in the world had added a synthesizer to the line-up. At that point, there was little more Eno could do — I'm not trying to put him down, don't get me wrong, I've got a lot of respect for him — but I thought there was little he could do in the context of Roxy at that time. I can't stand those people who come up to me and say, "Oh, the first album was the best," because I know it wasn't the best. It made the most impact because it was the

first and there wasn't anything around like that at the time. The imitators hadn't come out of their closet yet. I understand what they're saying, but it doesn't really make a lot of sense. I'm still doing experimental work. There are a couple of tracks that I haven't finished yet which easily could have gone on the new album. One of them is one of the most experimental things I've ever worked on. It's just that I was so careful not to rush it. It will probably go on the next album.

Can you say anything about it, a preview?

No, not really. I never do that. It spoils the pleasure for me if I do that. I hate to talk about things until they're done, otherwise it is just so much hot air.

[*Back to the previous subject, which has almost become an obsession to Bryan:*] I know it's difficult for those people to grasp it. I suppose it's like "Re-Make/Re-Model" or something like that. I enjoyed doing that ... there's no difference ... I can't really figure out their mentality, why they can be into that and not be into any of the tracks on the new album.

There are people who do sell out and make records simply for money. All you've got to do is pick up any copy of *Billboard*, go through the charts and you can spot them a mile off. On the other hand, there are great records that become great commercial successes, and I don't think there is anything wrong with that. I think it's great for an artist to be able to do something without compromising, and then it is shared by everybody as well as making lots of money, which is highly important to me. You also get through to a huge audience, which is what I got into the business for — one of the reasons was that I wanted to share my talent with a lot of people and try for a big audience. Otherwise, I might as well be recording very off-the-wall records up in some attic somewhere and playing them for ten or twelve people every year at some kind of private showing or private listening, which is what I escaped from. Phil Spector is a good example of someone who made a definite artistic statement which was a huge commercial success. That is the sort of success that I would like to have, where he's his own man all the way through.

Yes, but when things weren't working out the way Spector wanted, back in the '60s when he released his classic, "River Deep, Mountain High" by Ike and Tina Turner, and it wasn't accepted on a mass scale, he just couldn't handle it. He retreated and became a hermit rather than fight back. He was totally frustrated.

He just had to stop. Yeah, that's what happens and that's terrible, but I can't blame him for it. I understand him taking that attitude. I've had to at times, in disgust.

Has America's reluctance to accept your music with Roxy and as a solo artist been that frustrating?

Just about. I mean, "River Deep, Mountain High" was the peak of Phil Spector's art as far as I'm concerned and was a huge hit in England and nowhere else.

Especially in America, which is what hurt the most.

I didn't know that until a couple of years ago.

What do you do about America, then? It is frustrating for you, but there are hot spots like Cleveland where you are accepted, where your records sell, and you play to large audiences.

The funny thing is, on this tour we've had such incredibly enthusiastic reactions everywhere we've played. It's been delirious to have done that without any kind of advertising or support … In America, I think the record company has to put its money where its faith is, which is sad. In England, we don't have to do that sort of thing, at least not to the same extent.

[*Again, a return to that subject:*] I don't think there is anyone making records today who wants to have an audience of ten very loyal people who have fixed ideas about what you ought to do and throw their hands up in despair if you veer one inch away from what their preconceived notion is about what you should be doing.

You've always kept people off balance anyway, either with your music or the image. For instance, for Viva! *you selected more obscure material, instead of the so-called hits, which most "live" albums seem to feature. I wondered why you did that.* Frampton Comes Alive *and most other live albums creeping up nowadays mostly serve as a "greatest hits gone live" type of album.* Viva! *wasn't.*

It is nice to make something different. Rather than set up the mikes for just one night, one concert, which is usually what's done — most live albums, I think, are a rip-off — we recorded five concerts during a period of three years towards a live album which we knew we were eventually going to do and just went through all the tapes and chose what we thought were the best performances from each period. I thought because Roxy had changed through the years it would have been wrong to have chosen material from just the most recent taped concert; that would've been the one that "Both Ends Burning" came from, which had Johnny Gustafson on bass, the girl singers and all.

Did it do well commercially?

No, it didn't. It was the least successful of all the albums we'd done.

This tour is almost over now. What is next for you?

I'll press on regardless. I'm probably going to finish the next album in America and sell out [*laughs*].

Bryan Ferry will put out a disco record?

Yeah. I don't know. I just want to spend more time in America, so I'm going to be spending a lot of time in L.A. and New York and probably will be working with a few American musicians. I don't know who yet 'cause I don't really know any. It's going to make the next album interesting for me. As I said, some of it was started last year, but it will be interesting to see how it turns out.

You're leaving the comfortable confines of your country to go to a strange new environment and work with American musicians you don't know. Does this kind of adventure cause you any anxiety?

Stress? I think it's good for me to force myself to do it. All the albums that I've done have been recorded in the same studio in London, and I feel it's time to branch out and see how it sounds. Maybe just the fact of working in a different studio will — it's not that I'm dissatisfied with the old one but I think of it as an adventure, something I haven't tried.

[*Bryan sits back in his chair and speaks somberly.*] Of course, the only place where we haven't had the success we wanted has been in America.

I think that maybe by spending more time here it will make one's presence felt more, at least to the record companies. That's really the whole story.

WITH THAT, Bryan lets out a sigh, the tape recorder is clicked off and he resumes his search through *Trouser Press*, amused and delighted each time he comes across the mention of a "rare" Roxy or Ferry solo side. An ad lists "Sultanesque" for sale and he chuckles. I mention that it is considered valuable because it is a B-side not available on any album. Then another Spector story comes to mind, and I tell Bryan how Phil used to put throwaway instrumentals (two-minute jams really, like "Tedesco and Pitman" on the flip of the Ronettes' "Be My Baby") on his singles, so that stations and jocks would be literally forced to play Spector's chosen "A" side if they played the record at all. He was the decision-maker. He picked the hits, and no upstart was going to foul up his plans, his preconceived destiny.

Bryan hadn't heard that story before. He turned the page and remembered "Sultanesque" as "rather a good tune, really." Yet one almost had to flinch, seeing in Bryan many of Spector's traits: the determined single-mindedness and desire for success on his own terms; the limited but high-quality output; and the frustration when expected success wasn't forthcoming.

One hoped that Bryan's unconscious emulation of an idol was limited to the man's more positive characteristics and success. I can't really imagine Bryan, five or ten years from now, hiding behind security guards and electrified fences, wielding a six-shooter and diving off the deep end all because of a few frustrating setbacks.

Bryan has too much class to allow for an epilogue like that. ∎

QUOTES OF THE DECADE

"Punk is just something that's been created by the musical press to sell papers."
—CHRIS SPEDDING (1977) TP 19

Although he never appeared on our cover, Eno was a favorite of Trouser Press. *In 1974, we ran a Kathy Miller profile of him ("Being born was the last mundane thing Eno did…") that repurposed an interview she did in Eno's hotel room on assignment for* Creem. *Before they got down to the business at hand, publicist Simon Puxley asked photographer Linda Danna, impromptu, if she would take some test shots of Eno for a nude photo spread he had been offered in Bob Guccione's* Viva *magazine. He stripped off and she obligingly took the pictures, but they never appeared in* Viva.

Miller recounted the experience (including Eno's threat to break the unnamed photographer's glasses if the photos ever ran in a gay magazine) in Creem *(December 1974), but we actually ran some of them, accompanying a Q&A by Greg Allen in TP 32 (October 1978 if you're keeping score), wherein Eno enthused about Wire, XTC and the Buzzcocks. The photos were tastefully cropped and (intentionally) omitted any photo credit. Some of them are now available from Getty Images. (Two additional Eno features ran in issues 61 and 76.)*

BRAIN WAVES FROM ENO

TP 20, JUNE/JULY 1977

By Paul Rambali

B

Brian Eno's distinct eclecticism has gathered, over the years, a coterie of fans sufficiently large to enable him to pursue his singular artistic ideas. *Here Come the Warm Jets* and *Taking Tiger Mountain* were, after all, hardly your usual commercial fare. They were oblique collections of unlikely and absurd images. Eno's dry, humorous but humorless voice contrasted with the inventive, compelling and diffuse sound textures.

I would have expected to meet a very strange fellow indeed, but Eno turned out to be gracious, self-effacing and slightly nervous. Deliberately clear and precise in his speech — occasionally even sprightly — his demeanor and the tidiness of his demurely furnished North London flat both seemed to reflect the calm, quiet mood of *Another Green World* and *Discreet Music*. In fact, one of Eno's main preoccupations at the moment is creating homogeneous, somber and calming music. I doubt that there will be any return to the mellifluous chaos of his earlier albums.

In a recent interview Eno noted, "What I've been interested in is having this texture rippling along, with a few tasteful, nice events taking place. I want to have something that *Discreet Music* hasn't got, which is that, at particular moments, a beautiful, complicated little ornament would happen and then it would disappear. It wouldn't happen again. A while later, another little thing, like a jewel in the desert sort of thing." More perspicacious readers will have noticed that the first side of [Bowie's] *Low* owes quite a bit to this idea. As Eno pointed out, when music was performed but not recorded it was necessary to repeat themes for people to become familiar with them. However, a lot of people are going to buy a Bowie album and listen to it, so you can depart from that, which is what they did.

Much of *Low* contains isolated musical events that happen once and don't recur. Many British reviewers have given Eno most of the credit for *Low*, something which he was anxious to disclaim when I spoke to him. His ideas had an undeniable influence on the album's direction, but listen to "Golden Years," "Word on a Wing" or Kraftwerk's "Kometenmelodie" and you'll see that it wasn't as strong as one might think.

The marked difference between *Tiger Mountain* and *Another Green World* (and Eno's current orientation) came as a surprise to me. The latter LP seemed much more personal, devoid to a great extent of whimsical humor and mechanized mania. Instead, it is a careful, subtle collection of sound pictures. For the first time, Eno seemed to be making an album not because it was time to make one, but because he had something to say.

"I got myself prepared for *Another Green World* in the normal way that I use; which was that I had written a number of pieces and they were all demoed on tapes I made here at home. I had a fairly good idea of what they were going to be and how they were going to come out, but about a week before I just abandoned them all and decided to go into the studio without a single pre-organized idea. I was just going to go into the studio and start working and just follow whatever started happening, and that's what I did. It was a nerve-wracking way to work because I had no guarantee that anything was going to come out of it. The reason I started working like that was because with the old method you shut out a lot of possibilities, you're not responding quite in the way I wanted to to what's going on now; you're responding to a mixture of that and what you want to happen.

"I made 36 pieces of music and put 14 of them on the record. There are still some from that time that I shall use again. I also started working with musicians in a different way. I gave them as few instructions as I could to make them do something. I didn't want them just to jam, and I didn't want to tell them exactly what to play. I tried to give them just the right level of instruction so they would do things that are very much their own and yet things that I can use as well. Little exercises like, "This piece is going to be ninety seconds long and you must only make ten noises in it." These experiments are quick to do, and that allowed me to have a lot of material to choose between. I had chosen the musicians very carefully from different disciplines so that they wouldn't be able to predict what the others were going to do and something odd would happen.

"In the old way of working, the surprises were in the material rather than in the execution and I wanted to move my focus into the studio, which is now the way I work."

One of the interesting things about *Another*

Green World is how precisely controlled the over-all flow of the album is, right down to the unusual time gaps between tracks. "It took a very long time to put that together. I had 22 different versions. My approach is that I want albums now where a whole side is very similar."

Like [the 30-minute title track of] *Discreet Music,* a long, quiet synthesizer piece of slight variations on repeated themes, endlessly woven together and deliberately recorded at near inaudible volume?

"Yes, I made that for myself originally, just because I like that kind of mood. That kind of slightly melancholy, slow mood. I like just sitting down, reading something and having something very, very slow and gentle going at the same time."

BIONIC ENO

Brian Eno has a quirky fascination with systems. Systems and methods. Possible ways of arriving at conclusions interest him far more than possible conclusions. "Arts of process rather than arts of product," is how he puts it.

The clearest manifestation of this interest came in 1975 when he collaborated with painter friend Peter Schmidt (responsible for the *Tiger Mountain* cover) on an unusual concept called Oblique Strategies. It was a set of cards; not conventional playing cards but plain white cards printed with succinct instructions applicable to any situation. "Strategies" is designed to provide the impetus towards solving problems by opening up avenues of thought.

"It's a way of foiling that situation you often get into when you're working — just having a very fine focus. When you're concentrating on something, by definition it means you're blinkered to other things and the point of Oblique Strategies is to suddenly throw you outside of that so you could watch yourself in there and see what other options were still open to you. For me they still work; I still use those cards, use them quite often." When I told Eno that some enterprising souls are selling them for the better part of fifty dollars (they originally cost five pounds), he was annoyed but I suspect not a little flattered.

BACK TO THE BEGINNING

It was, in fact, this interest in methods of working that motivated his entry into the world of rock music, though not entirely the main reason.

"I was involved in experimental music, if any kind of music. That started at art school, first in Ipswich, then at Winchester. I spent five years at art school altogether. At that time the art schools in England were the cradles of experimental music. There was no other place that it happened really. I was at art school from '64 to '69. Music colleges weren't — and still aren't — interested in contemporary music of any kind and had a very snooty attitude about it. I got into it almost by accident. My intention was to become a painter but whilst at school I became progressively more frustrated with two things about painting. First of all, it was part of the art world, which meant that it was subjected to a whole lot of restrictions, quite a lot of which were to do with the marketing difficulties of painting. The second thing was that painting wasn't a social art; it's something you do on your own and I've never been very good at things like having an idea and struggling through with it, then presenting it to a fairly unsympathetic world, which you do with painting. I got more and more interested in collaborations, in things that you do with other people. My music thing started with working on scores for painting, ways of involving lots of people in visual events."

Scores for painting?

"Yes. For example, I would give a specific set of instructions to four different people who each had a canvas exactly the same, and they weren't allowed to look at each other's pictures. They would each do a picture, following the instructions as closely as possible. Then I would fix all four of them together, often with quite interesting results.

"Since I was working with groups of people, it became obvious to me that music was an art that dealt with groups of people and there was a whole mechanism that already existed for doing that. I had always been affected very strongly by music, but I had never even considered it as a possibility because I couldn't play any instruments. However, partly as a result of the technology that was around, it was just becoming possible to get tape recorders that multitracked — it seemed very easy to move into music. One could actually start to do things with tape recorders without having to go through this period of learning notation and learning to play things.

"Another thing was that I began to get frustrated with the slowness of painting, whereas music is a very immediate art form. What you're doing now is the piece and as soon as you've done it, it's gone.

"Also, I was interested in arts of process rather than arts of product, arts that dealt with periods of time. First of all, I tried all kinds of things to integrate these ideas into painting. It took quite a lot of time for me to realize that all these things I was doing were quite similar to what musicians do, what composers do. So, the transition was fairly slow; after about four years of dabbling with music I realized that this was what I would probably end up doing — but I've always had this thing of not having a long-term view of what I'm doing.

"Back then, I think I was probably doing more talking than listening. I had a sort of gap in my listening habits. In the early '60s I was very into the U.S. girl group syndrome: Shirelles, Mary Wells, that sort of thing. The thing that impressed me always was the production. But I wasn't conscious of it because I didn't know anything about how studios worked. Spector and all those kind of things were very formative.

"When I went to art school I got very snobbish about rock music because I was still suffering under this distinction — which I think is a false one — between the fine arts and the low arts, and so, for a couple of years, I wasn't really listening to rock music at all, or I was listening to it grudgingly. I liked the Who very much at that time; I was a big fan of theirs and used to follow them around. But that was partly because they had the sanction of the art department — two of them studied under the same teacher I studied under, so it was alright to like them.

"The next big breakthrough musically for me was the Velvet Underground. That was when I suddenly realized that there wasn't a distinction, that the two things could and would come together. There were lots of reasons that made them im-

portant, one of which was that their music was very uncompromising and obviously wasn't part of the commercial world in the strict sense that I considered rock music to be. Also, they were connected with Warhol. The third thing was that they were non-musicians — they weren't making a premium of being great players and I found this very interesting."

Of course, Eno must have heard people like Terry Riley and John Cage...

"Yes, a great deal. In fact, that's about all I was listening to for about three or four years. I used to go to all the concerts of experimental music. I was very devoted to it and used to travel around the country going to these concerts. I used to spend all my grant money traveling around art schools finding out what was going on musically."

A ROXY ROLLER

Which should bring us around to Roxy.

"Not quite. What happened was that I did this concert of experimental music at Reading University. They asked me to play, and I met Andy [Mackay] there, who was also interested in experimental music. We didn't see each other for a couple of years, until I met him again at a Cardew concert at the Queen Elizabeth Hall and found out that we were both getting quite interested in rock music. About a month after that he met Bryan Ferry, and they both approached me. That's how Roxy started — that was in January 1971."

Roxy Music's existence has been sufficiently well charted elsewhere. Suffice it to say that, when Roxy burst into the media eye back in early 1972 with their decadent time warp stylizations and avant-garde sax solos, nobody was quite ready for the group, much less [for] Eno, looking like some kind of androgynous waif with his long blond hair, make-up and emotionless expression. What really confounded people, though, was that he only played synthesizer and tapes. In those days, nobody just played synthesizer; some keyboard players had mellotrons and maybe a few had synthesizers, but nobody played only synthesizer. On top of that, he claimed to be unable to play any instrument, not even keyboards. His entirely novel approach has since become almost a trademark, but at the time it caused a great deal of surprise and confusion.

"With Roxy, any time anyone heard a sound that they couldn't identify they assumed it was me. I actually got credit for a lot of things that I didn't do. [Guitarist] Phil Manzanera was very interested in the electronic possibilities of his instrument, and so he had an independent array of things as well. I had all the instruments linked to my synthesizer so I could switch an instrument through and fiddle around with it, but it was very rare that I had more than one instrument going through at any given time.

"When we first started playing, I wasn't even onstage. I would be at the back of the hall with my synthesizer, mixing and playing. When I got on-stage we had an external mixer and there would be two things going to him: the instruments direct and another feed from me.

"Phil joined the band by a very strange route because he came along first of all to mix. We had auditioned him as a guitarist sometime before; it was between him and Dave O'List [originally with the Nice], and we chose Dave. We wanted a mixer and Phil came along and mixed a couple of gigs for us. Then Dave left for various reasons and we invited Phil to play guitar.

"On Roxy's first album, we used an old-fashioned way of working, playing live and then over-dubbing one or two things. Ever since that time I've done most of my work in the control room because I like to be close to the desk, which I regard as an extension of what I do anyway. But we were quite naïve really about recording studios. None of us had spent any time in the studio, and we didn't really know the possibilities. Also, we were keen to get the album done cheaply because we didn't have any money.

"The second album was done in a more standard style. You put down a backing track — bass, drums and rhythm guitar — then add all the other instruments later. Towards the end of that we got more into the idea that the addition was the interesting thing, the overdubbing. So, we put quite a lot of attention on that aspect."

POST-ROXY ROVING

Since Eno's departure from Roxy in July '73 he has been involved in numerous projects, both on his own or in collaboration with others. His first venture after leaving Roxy was the *(No Pussyfooting)* album with Robert Fripp, followed in February '74 by the release of his first solo album. In the latter half of '74 Eno attempted a short-lived tour with the Winkies as a result of what he calls a "standard rock decision."

"I was quite confused after my first album. I didn't really know what direction I was going in. I thought I would take the album on tour — something I've never thought since.

"Some time after I had made my album, I saw the Winkies playing in a pub. They were very good, and I was keen to get away from all the shit and over-sophistication that characterized a lot of music, so I decided to go on tour with them. I collapsed a lung on the fifth concert, so the tour got cancelled anyway. It was the only project I've been involved in during the last few years that I would say was abortive. And it wasn't their fault at all. I must give them all credit because they were very, very good. It was my fault for not thinking straight about it, not thinking the thing out. I don't like touring and I don't have any inclination to be the leader of a group, it's just not my role. I was the lead singer, the focal point. What I enjoy very much if I am on stage is setting up a context for other people to work in. That's what I did with Fripp, for example. When I worked with Fripp [a European tour, late '75/early '76] I just had all these tapes and loops and synthesizers and so on and it was just a very interesting bubbling undertone that he could play in, something for him to jump off from. I like that role, but as it's something which isn't recognized by the rock press — there isn't a name for it. Someone who normally likes setting a foundation for other people to work on top of."

Eno also appeared live in '74 at the Rainbow with Kevin Ayers, John Cale and Nico; with Cale at the end of '75; and at the 801 concert (and subsequent live album) of '76, a project he was not very enthusiastic about. He has also, of course, contributed to all of John Cale's Island albums and also to the Nico album [*The End...*] which Cale produced.

"John Cale influenced me quite a lot. The way he works with musicians is very interesting. If you do a session for John, it's the most harrowing experience because you get in there, you've just got yourself set up and the tape's suddenly rolling! You're playing and you don't know what the number is, you don't know what's going to happen; you finish, he says 'great,' and that's it, that's your take, finished, done. Because, and this is something I've picked up, if you catch someone on their first time through, they do some very odd things, before they start getting to know and polishing it up. You get this kind of liveliness to it which is a mixture of a sense of danger and excitement. I also picked up Cale's sense of arrangement. I started listening to the kind of instruments he uses; he uses a lot of orchestral instruments and he's one of the only people who uses those instruments in a way that doesn't sound trite and sloppy."

Eno has also played on Phil Manzanera's *Diamond Head* album and with Quiet Sun, Manzanera's pre-Roxy band, who reunited to record *Mainstream* on Island. He contributes "direct inject anti-jazz ray gun" to Robert Wyatt's *Ruth Is Stranger Than Richard*. He produced Bob Calvert's *Lucky Leif and the Long Ships* on UA in '75 and recently finished producing new band Ultravox!'s first album. The peripatetic Mr. Eno has recorded unsuccessful demos for New York's Television (in '74) and worked in Germany with the Neu!/Cluster circle of musicians. As befits such an inventive individual, his sphere of activities has often taken him outside of the traditional rock world: he is increasingly involved in soundtracks (he wrote music for *Sebastian,* a soft-core gay film of the saint's life with Latin dialogue); he once did a lecture tour of universities and still occasionally gives lectures; and, of course, there is the Oblique Strategies project.

Finally, there is Eno's own Obscure label, a vehicle for him to expose similarly unusual musicians and give them a chance to put their ideas onto vinyl.

Eno intends to be prolific over the next year, releasing, he hopes, around ten albums: a couple

with Fripp, another one with Bowie, some more on Obscure and whatever else his fertile imagination can concoct. So far, though, the only certain one is his next solo album. Due this spring and tentatively titled *Natural Science* [but released as *Before and After Science*], it was recorded with the same musicians he used for *Another Green World*, but with the addition of Fred Frith (from Henry Cow) on guitar.

Balding and diminutive, Eno makes a most unlikely rock musician. I get the distinct impression he is just beginning to feel comfortable with his chosen means of expression. The feeling of self-consciousness which marred his earlier albums bums to a certain extent has now vanished, replaced by a lot more confidence and a clearer view of what his aims are. While his music occasionally sounds pretentious, it certainly no longer sounds contrived. That he is more comfortable with his music is borne out by the fact that he is now less afraid to experiment and attempt new means, methods and types of music; in other words, progression. In Eno's case, his fascinating eclecticism makes that process of continuous refinement and redefinition well worth the attention. ■

QUOTES OF THE DECADE

"If Roxy Music were starting now, perhaps we'd all be playing keyboards."
—PHIL MANZANERA (1982) TP 74

"I can't submit to the whims of fans as to what they think my destiny ought to be."
—BRYAN FERRY (1977) TP 23

"I know your type. This is the worst nightmare ... If you weren't a journalist you'd never be invited to anything hip."
—LOU REED, to an interviewer (1979) TP 36

"Nowadays, everybody's in tune. everybody can play great. I want to hear a band that can't play."
—ALEX HARVEY, SENSATIONAL ALEX HARVEY BAND (1975) TOTP 11

Return of Son of Rock Write-In

The following twenty lucky souls have been awarded the special TP bag of goodies as the result of a random drawing of all the entries received before the deadline. Thanks to everyone that replied, and better luck next time to the losers.

Lisa Rosenberg, Spring Valley, NY
Michael Oldford, Whitestone, NY
Gary Young, Walla Walla, WA
Melanie Steele, San Bruno, CA
Donald Murk, Brooklyn, NY
Carole Leitle, Smyrna, GA
Jeff Battis, Seattle, WA
Brad Hawkins, Cupertino, CA
Dennis Di Crescenza, Drexel Hill, PA
Gary Cipollini, Newark, NJ
David Beckereich, Bronx, NY
John McGraw, Austin, TX
Don Lawrence, Flushing, MI
Sa'ad Shallal, Oak Park, MI
Kevin Walsh, San Rafael, CA
James Vincent, Fairfax, VA
James Fisher, Kent, OH
Steven Grant, Madison, WI
Scott Hendricks, Kupsville, PA
Luanne McDuffie, Rockingham, NC

• • • • • • • • • • • • • • • •

Here are a few choice quips sent in by readers on the questionnaire:

I fear that someday I'm going to walk past the magazine rack in my local supermarket, and see the new Trouser Press...with that little Orwellian 'international pricing code' in the lower left corner of the cover. I shall be afraid to open up that issue. —*Steven Greenwood, Lawrence KS*

Do you really think the Sex Pistols are going to make a lasting impression on rock music? Lasting value? Oh well. —*Kathy Ebreter, Bellevue, WA*

How can we get the Fucking Industry Assholes to give the New Wave more attention? The radio promo people etc. are probably all over 35 and don't give 2 shits about anything except the Billboard top chart stuff —*Neil Hubbard, Seattle, WA*

TP is certainly a rock collector's bible and I hope it will keep its serious attitude towards rock music and continue with its fine discographies and interesting articles. Don't let TP turn into a capitalist/pseudochic piece of garbage like Rolling Stone. Yecchh! —*Mark Bozen, Andover, MA*

I personally don't think you've sold out at all. You have continued to cover music that is ignored by most major publications and you do so in depth and fairly comprehensively. —*Don Ferko, State College, PA*

The thing I really enjoy are the times you let the Artist the freedom to speak intelligently about his art, dealing with the private and potent symbols of his life and culture. E.g., Kevin Ayers' revealing rap on his banana obsession. —*Tom Butt, Oshkosh, WI*

An English mag was inevitable in the splintered 1970's; but the fact that you've done it with almost impeccable taste and instinct, decent art, and growing imagination is a great surprise. —*Blair Helsing, Saratoga, CA*

readers' ToP 99

Pos. Group/Artist	Votes		
1 BEATLES	290	49 Blue Oyster Cult	33
2 Who	270	50 Steve Harley/	
3 Rolling Stones	266	Cockney Rebel	32
4 David Bowie	181	51 Moody Blues	31
Led Zeppelin/		Sparks	31
J. Page	181	53 Traffic/	
6 Kinks	180	S. Winwood	30
7 Roxy Music	178	Steely Dan	30
8 Genesis	134	Bonzo Dog Band	30
9 Eno	129	Free/P. Kossoff	30
10 Jimi Hendrix	116	57 Flamin' Groovies	29
11 Iggy/Stooges	110	Neil Young	29
King Crimson/		59 Eric Clapton	27
R. Fripp	110	Peter Frampton	27
13 Yardbirds	106	61 Bad Company	26
14 Yes	95	ELP	26
15 Jeff Beck	93	Ted Nugent	26
16 Bob Dylan	74	10cc	26
17 Move/Roy Wood	72	65 Byrds	25
18 Todd Rundgren/		New York Dolls	25
Utopia	71	Paul McCartney/	
19 Pink Floyd	63	Wings	25
Queen	63	68 Black Sabbath	24
21 John Cale	61	Deep Purple	24
22 Patti Smith	60	70 Pretty Things	23
23 Van der Graaf/		Soft Machine	23
P. Hammill	59	72 Small Faces	22
24 Mott the Hoople/		73 Family	21
I. Hunter	58	Henry Cow	21
25 Sex Pistols	56	Rush	21
26 Doors	55	76 John Lennon	20
27 ELP	54	Procol Harum	20
28 Rod Stewart/		Elton John	20
Faces	53	79 Clash	19
29 Bruce Springsteen	52	MC5	19
30 Velvet		81 Hollies	18
Underground	51	Jefferson	
31 Jethro Tull	50	Airplane/Starship	18
32 BeBop Deluxe	47	Badfinger	18
33 Bryan Ferry	46	Blackmore's	
34 Aerosmith	45	Rainbow	18
Frank Zappa/		Television	18
Mothers	45	Thin Lizzy	18
Peter Gabriel	45	T. Rex	18
37 Ramones	44	87 Jackson Browne	17
38 Cream	43	Kiss	17
39 Graham Parker/		Heart	17
Rumour	42	Van Morrison	17
40 Fleetwood Mac	41	Renaissance	17
Gentle Giant	41	Mick Ronson/	
Lou Reed	41	Spiders	17
43 Robert Wyatt/		Tangerine Dream	17
Matching Mole	38	Tubes	17
44 Dave Edmunds	37	95 Alice Cooper	16
45 Kevin Ayers	35	Dictators	16
Gong/ D. Allen	35	Little Feat	16
47 Elvis Presley	34	Strawbs	16
Beach Boys	34	UFO	16

I like your attitude. Your magazine is very open-minded, but sometimes a little too open-minded. Your critics seem a little too willing to give every artist the benefit of the doubt. —*Amy Fernandez, Syracuse, NY*

America Underground is a fine feature since it recognizes that home grown rock talent is not something confined to New York. —*Joseph Kapus, Evergreen Park, IN*

Attention Ira—Keep it up. As an impartial (?) observer, it's one of the best and getting better. The New Wave as it pertains to signed and unsigned bands needs credibility to survive. The typical New Wave fanzine often lacks credibility. Your magazine, because of its professionalism and objectivity does more for the cause than dozens of N.W. zines. For this we remain grateful. —*Nick Nicholis, Akron, OH*

I think Dave Schulps and Ira Robbins are two of the best writers I've ever followed. With a little effort, they could be to British rock what Jann Wenner was to American rock 'n' roll. —*Sharon Goodwin, Jackson Heights, NY*

I love critical record reviews which cleverly attack recordings which are inferior or otherwise undeserving of praise. —*Mark Rudnick, Brooklyn, NY*

Your (plural) levels of writing are quite high except for Mr. Robbins' consistent ramblings on. Other than the fact that he sometimes 'acts' like a child, I'm quite pleased with his magazine. In fact, I recently cancelled my subscription to Circus due to boredom. I don't love all the news about punk rock, but I don't want to keep a closed mind either and who knows—tastes change. —*David Shur, Union, NJ*

In my opinion, the writers are given too much freedom in their praises and their put-downs of groups and/or albums. It appears this magazine has no editor. I don't like Ira Robbins' immature ego trips. —*Steve Schindler, Downey, CA*

Please leave out all 'punk', so called 'new-wave' shit, and anything else which does not advance the state of music. I want to be kept in touch with those creative musicians who are seriously pushing forward and extending music to new heights. —*Layne Gulleridge, Houston TX*

Not everyone who reads TP is a 14 year old punk rocker. TP leaves a bit to be desired. Seems to be in existence solely for those of p.r. persuasion. —*Alan Kayser, Cornwells Heights, PA*

Quit writing about the fucking punk rock shitheads. —*Scott Seegert, Fullerton, CA*

From *Trouser Press* December 1977

PROGRESSIVE AND ART ROCK

Before things got out of hand and the genre succumbed to the exaltation of virtuosity, endurance and stadia, "prog rock" was a loose catch-all for bands that were some (or all) of the following: spacey, largely instrumental, non-guitar-based, jammy (but not blues-based) or arty without decadence or irony. (Weirdly, bands like ELP that embraced classical music were somehow thought of as "progressive" as well. Go figure.) If an album had Roger Dean art on the cover or a Mellotron in the credits, chances are it would eventually wind up in the overly inclusive Rhino box set called *Supernatural Fairy Tales.*

When *Trouser Press* got going in 1974, prog was one of the prime musical exports of England (and Germany). Since we valued imports for their lack of mainstream awareness in the U.S., we were intrigued by some of those bands, starting with Genesis, King Crimson, Gong, Gentle Giant and Van der Graaf Generator.

It wasn't really what we were into, and we never committed fully to covering prog rock (Archie Patterson's magazine *Eurock* did a good job), although we did institute a column (*Across the Channel*, TP 16 – TP 25) to keep up with releases from the continent. And we fell happily into the gutter of punk rock when it arrived a few years later.

THE GENESIS OF GENESIS: ART ROCK IN EXCELSIS

TP 20, JUNE/JULY 1977

By Jim Green

"I see the band as sad romantics..."
—PETER GABRIEL, *Melody Maker*, 1971

Peter Gabriel's off-the-cuff assessment of Genesis was uttered at a critical point in the band's evolution, in the midst of the greatest period of flux the band was ever to experience. Yet, Genesis's melancholy romanticism has been one of the genuine constants of the group, from its schoolboy beginnings to the present.

Genesis have produced nine albums in as many years. They've gone from fairly straightforward pop-rock to more complex progressive rock, from neophyte levels of musicianship to being themselves musical inspirations, from teen dreams of success to Madison Square Garden. Their talents have matured, both in their technical prowess and in the songwriting which is the self-professed basis and core of the band.

Genesis's history is a checkered one, beginning in 1966 at the Charterhouse school in Surrey. Tony Banks, Peter Gabriel and Anthony Phillips formed their own pop group, the Garden Wall (with Chris Stewart on drums), joined shortly thereafter by Michael Rutherford. Their raison d'être was songwriting; little know-how but lots of enthusiasm.

"We were really raw writers and unprofessional players as well," remembered Anthony Phillips.

"Tony was the only one who could really play. I could play some guitar, but Mike could hardly play anything, believe it or not. Tony used to sit down at the piano, Peter would sing and the rest of us would do harmonies and later take turns hacking out bits on the piano." The demos that attracted the attention of youthful pop wiz Jonathan King were done with such a lineup, Phillips and Rutherford adding some guitar.

"We were really one of those typical Carnaby Street gear, young, bouffant-haired pop bands in 1966, just dreaming that we'd get on *Top of the Pops*," recalled Phillips. "It's a bloody good thing we didn't get on it, because we'd never have recovered from it. We had all the delusions of grandeur that everyone had —we were 16 then, you know."

King signed them to Decca; the selection of the name Genesis came about then (although memories are a bit murky as to how). They released a single, "The Silent Sun," in '67 and one called "A Winter's Tale" in '68. On a school holiday that year, the band cut their first LP, *From Genesis to Revelation*. The title had to do with the band's discovery that there already was an American band with the same name, prompting a change to Revelation — only to find that name was taken, too. At least so say the original liner notes; Anthony (or

"Ant," to friends) hinted that King was behind the name-changing or the choice of the second name, suggesting a conceptual framework for the LP.

King believed the songs were good and liked Peter Gabriel's voice, but his production, aided and abetted by arranger Arthur Greenslade (soon to be renowned for "sweetening" many an album, like Chris Farlowe's *Paint It Farlowe*), was inappropriate and overdone, while the playing, by Anthony's own account, was appalling. A second single was released from it, "Where the Sour Turns to Sweet" ("The Silent Sun" was included on the LP), but King lost interest, neglected to promote it and little commercial mileage was made. Nowadays, those in the group at the time remember King as a "funny guy" who was "great to work with."

The band made its first proper public appearance as Genesis in 1969 at Brunel University in Uxbridge. John Silver, who'd replaced Chris Stewart in time to record the first record, was replaced in turn behind the traps by John Mayhew. Inside of a year, they had attracted the attention of Tony Stratton-Smith at Charisma, and with a good bit of playing under their belts, the lads entered Trident Studios to record what they regarded as their "real" first album, under the direction of producer John Anthony.

Melody Maker hailed *Trespass* as an album of "lyrical depth ... flawless technique ... a minor masterpiece." This bombast certainly goes too far; the lyrics often take themselves too seriously, the arrangements tend to ramble rather than unfold and, on occasion, the band resorts to clichés that are just a wee bit embarrassing. Nevertheless, everyone was starting to take large steps forward: Tony Banks and Anthony Phillips were exerting classical and pre-classical influences on the arrangements, Tony with his organ and Anthony with his distinctive use of the 12-string guitar. Michael Rutherford was developing into a true musician, providing incisive counterpoint on bass.

Even if the lyrics occasionally bore traces of just-out-of-university poetic license, the general themes were more engaging than the simpiness on the earlier disc. While all six songs, especially "Visions of Angels" and "White Mountain," stand up to repeated listenings, the band hit on one

enduring classic, "The Knife," a dynamic aria of a demagogue camouflaging his dictatorial ambitions amid incitements to destroy evil and fight for liberty. Live, it helped build an enthusiastic following for the band, was released as a single in 1971 and remained in the repertoire as an encore number until Peter Gabriel left the band.

Yet, at this point Genesis was to take some drastic turns. John Mayhew and Anthony Phillips left before the album even came out. Phillips wanted to avoid heavy touring, which would remove, for him, all sense of occasion from each concert, giving each gig an assembly line feeling. He went on to study classical music and teach but maintained his ties with the band.

This is the juncture at which Phil Collins enters the picture. As a child prodigy of sorts, he'd starred as the Artful Dodger in the West End production of *Oliver* for ten months. At the time of Genesis's upheavals, Collins was in his first proper band, Flaming Youth, as drummer and one of the featured singers. Also in the band were guitarist "Flash" Gordon Smith, bassist Ronnie Caryl and Brian Chatton (later with Jackson Heights and the *Rock Follies* backing band) on keyboards. Chatton had been in the Warriors with Ian Wallace and Jon Anderson, the latter going on to form Yes, and Flaming Youth were not so very different from early Yes (although originally formed, under the name of Hickory, as a back-up to a soul act).

Both bands did originals, but the prime focus of each was careful rearrangements of other people's material. Collins recalls that Flaming Youth did songs like "Carpet Man" by the Fifth Dimension and a 15-minute "Norwegian Wood," "with a drum solo and everything, our counterpart of Yes's *West Side Story* medley." Then the hit-making team of Ken Howard and Alan Blaikley came along. They'd written hits for Dave Dee, Dozy, Beaky, Mick and Tich and the Herd; the Herd had just split up, so they were on the lookout for a new set of teen idols.

"We were rehearsing in Eel Pie Island in 1969 when these two guys came down with an idea for a record." It was to be called *Ark 2*, a bunch of pop tunes loosely limning the flight of a neo-Noah's spaceship as it escapes the "fiery flood" that ignites "the funeral pyre of Earth." "It was all a bit cosmic, and much more commercial than we were, but it was a concrete idea and looked like a flamin' fortune. They sent us tapes, just guitar and voice, and we arranged and recorded it. Looked like it was going to be the album of the century, but it went nowhere. It was immature music," Collins allows, "but it was 1968, so you've got to make allowances." Perhaps not so bad as all that, it simply couldn't live up to *Melody Maker*'s ecstatic notice. "...superbly done. The lyrics are adult, bitingly witty and sophisticated." "We got a lot of press, good reviews, but it sank without trace," he says.

"Bands like Genesis and Quintessence were the big gigging professional bands at the time. We were somewhere in the middle of the road, no one knew quite where to put us, so we did television spectaculars in Holland and Germany but gigged once in a fortnight while Genesis was working all the time." In 1970, Flaming Youth threw in the towel.

"One big reason is 'cause I answered an advert in *Melody Maker* which said, 'Tony Stratton-Smith is seeking a drummer sensitive to acoustic music and a lead guitarist who also plays 12-string.' I went in the first place largely because I knew Stratton-Smith very well and thought I could get it without a try-out." No such luck, but he was hired.

Ronnie Caryl had gone with Phil to the audition and hadn't made the grade; unfortunately, there was no one else who had, so Genesis went out as a four-piece, Tony doubling the guitar lead lines on his electric piano. By this time the album was out and garnering great reviews, and the band performed the material with "more balls than on the album," because Mayhew was rhythmically limited and Collins packed much more punch.

Genesis made their television debut in November 1970 on the *Disco 2* show. It was a disaster. Gabriel took the blame for being too nervous, but apparently he wasn't the only one. For a band that eventually emphasized its stage presentations, Genesis must have been rather unimpressive. Peter later said, "When we first went out on the road, we thought we'd just get the music out and play behind a black curtain; now we have to perform a bit, but it's just a means to an end."

By this time, they'd picked up a guitarist named Mick Barnard. "He was good," said Phil, "but he didn't have that fire, so while he was in the band we started looking for someone else." Meanwhile, a guitarist named Steve Hackett, anxious to find a band but disenchanted with auditions, put his own ad in *Melody Maker*. "We answered it, and he came down to Tony's bedsit in Earl's Court. He brought his little six-inch speaker and a couple of fuzzboxes, and when he played he seemed to have something original, so he joined the band."

By the spring, Hackett had begun to integrate his idiosyncratic — though Fripp-influenced — style into the fabric of Genesis's music. More importantly, Gabriel, who'd only in January reluctantly agreed that perhaps playing behind a black curtain was not suitable stagecraft, was now regaling audiences with between-song patter and drum juggling! His drily delivered, morbidly witty stories and intros went over quite well, as did his antics with the drum, which was actually played at strategic moments. "I used to be a drummer, you know. Not a good one; I could do simple stuff, like Simon Kirke bashing, but not much else," he admitted. Good enough reason to be allowed only one drum on stage.

Also, he'd taken to playing flute on certain numbers. He managed to escape comparison to Ian Anderson, but his singing came in for some criticism. "I'm supposed to be a Roger Chapman copyist," he told the press at the time, and not without some vexation. Chapman was the vocalist for Family, a group with a loud and loyal following: in some ways it was a compliment to even be compared with this unusual and well-respected figure, for Peter's vocal style had a ways to go before becoming as distinctly personal as Chapman's.

The next year, the entire band made significant progress towards a more coherent and immediately recognizable style. They went back into Trident with John Anthony and recorded *Nursery Cryme*, which contained two lengthy masterpieces, "The Return of the Giant Hogweed" and "The Musical Box," the latter being the source of the LP's title. Both songs relied on Peter's performance as singing narrator/protagonist and begged to be illustrated by his theatrically inclined imagination. He began experimenting with onstage characterizations and costuming; first, making up in white-face, eventually shaving his hair to enlarge his expanse of forehead. The release of *Foxtrot* in '73 was marked by his use of a fox's-head mask; he subsequently adopted various other headdresses and facial disguises to become an old man during "The Musical Box," a flower during "Supper's Ready" and a bat for "Watcher of the Skies," the opening track of *Foxtrot* (subsequently the set-opening number from then on). Peter's thespian prowess was further displayed when, at Brunel, the site of the band's debut, Genesis premiered the 25-minute "Supper's Ready" from *Foxtrot*.

Both albums were impressive if uneven. *Nursery Cryme* was quite unbalanced, "Musical Box" and "Hogweed" filling side one, separated by the brief (1:44) "For Absent Friends." The material on the second side was necessarily a letdown after the brilliance of the first, its highlight the sprightly three-minute "Harold the Barrel." *Foxtrot* has no clinkers either, yet the sheer, almost superhuman intensity of "Watcher" and the awesome reach of "Supper's Ready" tend to overshadow even fine material like "Get 'Em Out by Friday." Another problem is the dead sound, giving the impression of being filtered through an old sock.

Phil analyzed the situation:

"There was this incredible wedge of sound: Tony with all his keyboards, Steve with his fuzz-boxes and octave divider, Mike playing 12-string and bass and me thrashing about on the drum kit. Big thick chords, and Peter had a big, thick voice — there was no room for anything. Live, it worked great, a big, exciting sound, and I suppose if we'd had a really top-notch producer, we could have gotten it on record, but we were struggling to re-create a kind of live atmosphere in the studio, and it just didn't happen."

The "summery feel," as Phil termed it, on *Trespass* was replaced by a doomier, broader, busier sound, and John Anthony was unable to cope with the shift. *Foxtrot* ran into further difficulties. "We weren't going to use John Anthony again — of course, he's done very well since, with Ace and so forth — so we started off with this Nashville guy named Bob Potter, who was Bob Johnston's right-hand man. Johnston [who'd produced

Dylan's *Nashville Skyline*, among others] had just produced Lindisfarne and consequently had a close relationship with Charisma, and Potter was around, so we thought, 'Well, in for a penny,' tried him for a couple of days, and got some backing tracks down. He said, 'It ain't happenin', is it?' and we had to agree, so we had to use one of the house engineers at Island, Tony Platt. Now, there's a breed of engineer we don't get along with, and he was one, and we had a particularly difficult day with him. Then we got another Island engineer called John Burns, who seemed to hit it off with everybody. The end of "Supper's Ready" and the end of "Willow Farm" onwards is with him."

Non-stop touring helped make Genesis one of the top live attractions in Britain, where they were acclaimed in polls in the music weeklies, not to mention the fanatical followings they developed on the Continent. They even made a brief jaunt to the States, the highlight of which was a benefit concert in New York sponsored by WNEW-FM. While Peter was convinced it was an awful concert, the fans loved it, and waited with bated breath for their next Stateside appearance.

The band next put out *Genesis Live*. The sound quality is not inspiring, but it is a valid document of the band's best-loved live songs. However, the group's lack of decisive sales success in the States delayed its issue here until after their next studio effort was released.

With *Selling England by the Pound,* Genesis's star was most definitely on the rise, at least in England; this album gave them a boost both there and here. Once more joining forces with John Burns, the band turned out their most satisfying work yet, superior artistry from start to finish. In Burns they'd found someone capable of getting the sound they needed. Also, the group's writing had not only developed an identity, but also the consistency to go with it.

An insight into Genesis's growing self-awareness may be gleaned by their apparently reaching an understanding of the difference between good live songs, songs too good not to preserve via recording and songs by which they'd want to make themselves known on their albums. [The non-LP single sides] "Happy the Man" and "Twilight Alehouse" were both onetime mainstays of their live act. "Happy," with its goofy lyrics and acoustic arrangement, was probably a crowd-pleasing change of pace, and "Alehouse" is the closest Genesis will ever get to boogie; neither comes near the quality of Genesis's best (although "Alehouse" could easily fit in with the material on *Nursery Cryme*). Curiously, they put out "Happy" as a single in '72, backed with "Seven Stones" from *Nursery Cryme* — a totally unwarranted choice for an A-side. On the other hand, by the time *Selling England* came out, they knew that something from the LP was most appropriate to put out as a 45, and thus "Alehouse" appeared as the flipside of "I Know What I Like (in Your Wardrobe)" as a fillip for the fans.

After a concert in Nottingham in the fall of '73, in the midst of the UK *Selling England* tour, Phil and Mike dashed into the studio to cut a 45 with Anthony Phillips, Phil handling vocals as well as the traps. They worked straight from lunchtime till five the next morning on what was, especially for Anthony, a good commercial pop tune ("The Silver Song") and its flipside (working title: "Only Your Love"). It was thought to be a fine reentry for Anthony into the pop arena after having acquired classical guitar and orchestral training (and a teacher's credential), and all were pleased with the result — except for Stratton-Smith, who declined to issue it on Charisma.

(Shortly thereafter Anthony took part in an anthology of Charisma artists doing modern hymns, a pet project of Stratton-Smith's. *Beyond an Empty Dream*, with Anthony and Mike's contribution, "Take This Heart," was issued just as B&C, Charisma's distributor, was going out of business, Nevertheless, Anthony was floored when, on a recent trip to the U.S., he attended a Peter Gabriel concert in New Jersey; he was approached by a fan who declared that that song had changed his life!)

In December, Genesis traveled to the States once again, this time for a slightly more extensive sojourn. They were showcased in venues with no other groups on the bill, including a marvelous and well-received gig at the Roxy in L.A. This set the stage for a return visit just a few months hence, playing more and larger halls. Extensive touring, the change-over of Charisma distribution in the

U.S. from Buddah to Atlantic, and the more uniform quality of *Selling England* made it Genesis's most commercially successful venture yet in the States, not to mention its success in the UK and on the Continent.

The band then took some time in gearing up for the task of assembling their double concept album — and an ambitious multimedia stage presentation — called *The Lamb Lies Down on Broadway*. Peter ran through props and costumes acting out the tale of Rael, a New York street punk on a surreal journey, assisted by slide projections and other special effects.

Suffice it to say that the success was limited. It was expensive to produce, the initial pressings in the U.S. and the UK were defective, and the tour in the States followed so hard on the heels of the album's release that few people had had enough time to assimilate the four sides in their entirety before seeing the show, which could not be fully appreciated without some familiarity with the lyrics and scenario. Critics and audiences alike felt overwhelmed by the presentation, like seeing an opera in Italian with no libretto. Even fans left the shows impressed but confused.

There are indeed criticisms to be made of the concept and execution, but, as Phil was quick to point out, and as the passage of time has revealed, the songs are good by themselves. "They almost all stand on their own as good compositions." Unfortunately, the size and timing of the project worked against them.

Then, too, there was the problem of Peter leaving the band. It's not easy to play grueling shows on a long tour knowing that your success hangs on your lead singer, essentially the lyricist behind the vast presentation and the focus of the entire production, and that he is leaving after the tour. It couldn't have been easy for Peter, either. But they kept it a secret until afterwards, then made an amicable — if slightly traumatic — split.

Both Gabriel and the band were in rocky situations, but to many it seemed it was mainly Genesis that was done for. How could they replace him as a singer? Worse, people took for granted that Peter was the genius behind Genesis; that he wrote all the songs by himself. Without him, then, Genesis would continue as just another shallow "progressive" band until they gave up. As Phil put it, Peter was imagined to be some sort of "mysterious traveler" instead of "just another lad from Surrey"; the departure of that mystique undercut Genesis's future credibility.

Until, that is, they put out *A Trick of the Tail*. Phil, who'd sung on "More Fool Me" on *Selling England by the Pound* (as well as his warbling with Flaming Youth), took over the vocals. His voice was thinner and less multi-purpose than Peter's, but how remarkably similar he did sound! On some tracks one would hardly realize Peter had left.

Any doubts that the band could compose without Peter were stilled by the title track, "Robbery, Assault and Battery" and "Squonk"; some even spun about and questioned whether Peter could compose without Genesis. To surmount the problems of properly enunciating the lyrics while manipulating the drum kit, another drummer was needed to go on tour. Phil managed to catch Bill "Have Drum Will Travel" Bruford in between engagements. The former Yes-man undertook to learn the parts arranged and played on the records by Phil during the vocals, leaving the stage or working in tandem on the instrumental sections.

The combination of slide projections (and a neat film clip during "Carpet Crawlers"), laser beams, Phil's uncanny Artful Dodger-like stage posing and the bonus of Bruford on drums brought amazing responses wherever they played, but Genesis didn't play everywhere.

"Some areas we've played enormous halls and filled them; but we played Memphis on our first tour to 400 people, and we've never been back since," said Phil. "The States are inconsistent for us; some areas are out of touch with others."

When *Wind and Wuthering* finally came out, people were wondering if *A Trick of the Tail* hadn't been a fluke, whether they could do it again. Commercially, it was indeed a success, rising into the Top 30 on *Billboard*'s charts; a truncated version of "Your Own Special Way" (Phil calls it "butchered") slipped into the Top 50. They played big halls again, in certain places moving up into arenas and stadia. In New York, they played Madison Square Garden, nearly (though not quite) selling out.

The band had a new drumming problem. Bill, busy with Dave Stewart's National Health, couldn't make it. They needed someone, Collins says, with a "heavy foot, a heavy hand and a lot of imagination," and listened to loads of records to find someone. "I asked Roger Pope, of Elton John's band, 'cause I know he's heavy as shit, but he said if Elton called he'd follow, so he was out. Then I thought of Chester Thompson.

"I didn't think that he, having worked with Weather Report and Zappa, and being a Black American, would want to work with us, a wimpy white rock group. But I'm friends with Alphonse Johnson, who is also Black, in Weather Report, and in fact a Genesis fan for a long, long time. He told me to call Chester and gave me his number, and when I rang him up, he was very interested.

"Chester is a lot better for the group than Bill. A lot more solid. Bill puts trip wires in front of himself, he'll try things so hard that there's no way they can work, just for the sake of trying them. On some of the things we needed a bit heavier stuff and Bill doesn't play like that, like John Bonham, but Chester can. Bill plays more like me, but I'm also a bit of a chameleon; if I have to bash away, like on 'Squonk' or 'Los Endos,' I can, whereas Bill just plays himself. Which is fair enough — he's one of the best British drummers there is, and a good friend — but not what we really had to have."

Be that as it may, Chester didn't seem to be easily adaptable to the material and sort of playing necessary in this type of rock. Perhaps it is what the band wanted from him, but he seemed, comparatively, to be a plodder. Also, while on the previous tour the band did a wide range of older material, including "White Mountain" from *Trespass*, the emphasis now was on the new, "Lamb" and "Musical Box" thrown together for the encore. Some of it may have had to do with Chester adjusting to Genesis, but much of it was probably motivated by the band wishing to distance themselves from Peter's former involvement.

What did Genesis lose when they lost Peter Gabriel? A difficult question to answer with total certainty, but it may reasonably be surmised that they lost a bit of the bite and ineffable intensity he brought to the songs. He was not merely a stage presence, but a significant component of the group personality. It is certainly true that he was, and is, a "sad romantic" as he pictured the group in the quote at the head of this article, but his romanticism had, it would appear, a darker, more convoluted side to it than that of the others, also a sharper, wittier side. Tony and Mike are good storytellers, but perhaps the added ingredient which would make them great is Peter, or someone of his artistic temperament. Steve primarily writes music, if anything; his compositional tendencies may be glimpsed in the solo album released in late '75 (U.S. in early '76), *Voyage of the Acolyte*, an eclectic collection of tracks based on different Tarot cards (Phil and Mike assisting, among others).

Phil, the man with the best sense of humor in the band, does very little writing, save for his pet band Brand X. Started in '74 as a jam band (comprising former Liverpool Scene bassist Percy Jones, guitarist John Goodsall and Robin Lumley on keyboards), Brand X has released two albums. A tour seems probable for this summer, featuring Phil himself (or, if touring with Genesis conflicts, Simon Phillips, Bill Bruford or "this guy who used to play for Stevie Wonder"). Phil also has made tentative plans to record and even tour with Alphonse Johnson and Percy Jones, Allan Holdsworth on guitar, and an unknown keyboard player. "Lots of Black musicians want to find out why white rock groups are making so much money and are discovering that it's a radical difference to play in the English way, instead of pure funk."

Doesn't this moonlighting distract him from Genesis? "Well, at one point, when Peter quit, I was going to leave, too, and join Brand X permanently. I didn't, and I'm glad. We are getting into things more the way I like them, although I'd still rather be playing the kind of thing Brand X does.

"We're still a group of songwriters, basically, just writing what we like, however we like." True, but is the romanticism losing its bite, or was that Peter Gabriel? Is the flabby pop of "Your Own Special Way" Genesis's new direction? Or the lightweight instrumental, "Wot Gorilla?" Or the shallowness of "One for the Vine" or "All in a Mouse's Night"?

I don't believe it's the loss of Gabriel alone, because some of the lyrics do indeed hold up; but where they do, the music seems enervated or irrelevant.

Yet the band are closer to the top of the heap than they've ever been before, in terms of material success. It's a mighty long way from where they were five years ago: £14,000 in debt. The band is becoming more recognizable as individuals to the punters, especially now that they've come out from the shadows. Where once they sat in a semicircle around the back of the stage with Peter at the center, now they all stand to the fore. Steve, in fact, has shaven his beard, come out from behind his hornrims, stood up and donned rockstar togs to look like a younger, near-sighted Alex Harvey. He even introduces a song! Mike, too, sways about out front, chiming in with a harmony or two, and Tony sits conspicuously enthroned amid his keyboards. Superstars to be? Like (heaven forfend) Yes?

That may be stretching it, but there are tendencies of which the band may not be aware. What they sought in Steve Hackett, that "fire," is mostly missing. I don't refer to brimstone and hellfire, but to encroaching complacency and, in Phil's case, a lack of interest which threatens to choke the artistic life out of the group while the commercial corpus is kept alive artificially. What is most encouraging is that, if any band has the ability to rise to the challenge, it is this bunch of sad, romantic songsmiths.

And whatever happened to Anthony Phillips? He's just put out *The Geese and the Ghost*, that's what. In 1974, with the help of Mike Rutherford, who co-wrote two of the longer suites on it, Anthony began piecemeal recording at home on private equipment. It took almost a year to finish, since Mike was continually going off to record or tour with Genesis, and slowly became less and less involved. It's pastorally idyllic music, for the most part, with much medieval English influence. The duo, particularly Anthony, play a wide spectrum of instruments, although perhaps the single most prominent is the 12-string guitar which Anthony introduced to Genesis's music — and which is why the LP brings to mind early Genesis. ∎

This unique and disarmingly frank dialogue between King Crimson leader Robert Fripp and a New York engineering student takes many surprising twists and turns, not the least of which is the number of questions asked by, rather than of, Fripp. For some reason long forgotten (possibly sloppy trafficking of typeset galleys, or just the way the interview was conducted), topics come, go and return haphazardly. In addition to some reordering of sections, a few weeds have been cleared away.

WHO'S ASKING THE QUESTIONS? ROBERT FRIPP INTERVIEWED

TOTP 6 – 8, DECEMBER 1974 – MAY 1975

Interview by Ihor Slabicky

This interview was held in the New York City offices of Atlantic Records on the afternoon of October 18, 1974. Before the conversation began, Robert Fripp played "Starless" from the latest King Crimson release, *Red*. As the last notes of the song faded, we began…

PART ONE

RF: King Crimson is completely over. For ever and ever.

IS: *That's sort of hard for some people to bear. When I first heard it, it was like someone dying in your close family.*

But why?

I grew up on King Crimson. I was 15 when your first record came out and I bought it then and I've been buying every single one since then. I enjoyed it and now the thought of not having it anymore … you have the old records to listen to, but you know what they're like, where every note is, just about, so a stopping point would be terrible. But if you say things will go on, that's great.

They're not.

What will happen?

I'm mixing a live album [released in 1975 as *USA*], recorded over a period of nine months from the end of last year until this year, with John [Wetton].

What's going to be on that?

Probably "Easy Money." "Exiles" will probably follow "Easy Money" followed by a blow or something like that from Asbury Park. Side two, probably "The Talking Drum" into "Larks' Tongue Part II" into "[21st Century] Schizoid Man." Something like that.

That leaves "Doctor D." out.

Yes. "Doctor D." was never a complete piece. We were never fully satisfied with it, so it won't be used.

Is there anything in the studio from the other bands or from this band which is left over? When you went into the studio, you just recorded enough for an album?

Just recorded what we needed, yes.

Well, besides "Groon"…

That's it.

So, there's going to be another Crimson album and then what?

I'll then do two composite albums, personal selections. Although there will be nothing new, it will be presented in a way which isn't done normally in best-of albums. And it will include "Groon," which of course most people don't have.

You've got Robin Miller and Marc Charig on the new album [Red]. They were on the second and third albums.

Yeah. Robin is co-principal oboeist with the BBC Symphony Orchestra under Pierre Boulez. An amazing musician, quite frightfully good, in a different way than Mel [Collins], who is also good. I was rather — put out isn't the word — flabbergasted, awestruck if you like, by just how good Mel was on that cut. He just came in and did it and then went next door and did a session for Humble Pie. They were in the next studio. He's in Alvin Lee's new band, which is rehearsing at the moment. Ian MacDonald, shortly before our session, was tearing up tickets in the cinema, and who is now at this moment in New York.

I suppose what I'm doing is wiping out anything which prevents me from having relationships with any people I've worked with. I wouldn't like to think there is anything within me, any failing of personality which … I wouldn't be able to work with anybody again. I went to see Boz [Burrell] at Central Park and Bad Company was good. I was so impressed and so pleased. His bass playing was fabulous, really nice. We've gotten really, well, happy to see each other again. I'd love to play with him, love to get him on an album.

[Violinist] David [Cross] left Crimson after you played in New York in July.

Well, it was mutual, I suppose, as in all these situations. No uptightness or unpleasantness involved. Sensitive musicians can't work in the situation in which we were working. But a few, from time to time, do get as far as that. With David it was, I think, affecting his health, as it was with everyone who was involved with it. But David was too sensitive and gentle a personality for the rock business.

What's it like on the road?

An awful lot is travelling. You have rehearsing, you have practicing, writing and the actual playing comes last of all. That's for free. You play for nothing. You get paid for travelling. And we were doing from 80,000 to 100,000 miles a year.

That's quite a lot.

I mean, I must have done a quarter of a million miles in the past five years.

Have you ever played anywhere besides Europe, England and America?

No. We had plans for next year to go to Japan and Brazil. One of the fundamental facets of the personality of King Crimson was that the people involved, the personalities involved, had no consideration of anyone else involved.

You mean, in the band itself?

Yeah. Individuals would do their things regardless of what other people were doing.

How can you keep something like that together when everybody wants to do something differently?

It involves the discharge of a lot of energy, far more than I'm prepared to lose again.

Did you ever play "Red" live?

No. One of my two main regrets on Crimson ceasing is that we'll never play "Red" live because it is primarily a live number.

Every one of your albums has a song like that which is sort of violent, in a way.

Side One is the heavy metal side. It's very definitely heavy metal. But I think it's well done, actually.

On your first album you had "Schizoid Man" and then…

Yes, the iron. It's the iron, isn't it?

Right. I heard this and I thought this was very brutal, as if you'd get hurt just listening to it.

[laughing] I wonder if they'd play that over here. I'd be surprised.

[As published, and without notice, the conversation abruptly turns to the song "Starless" from the Red *album.]*

The ending is very moving.

The ending? Actually, the beginning, the song part, is my favorite.

The beginning was sort of very...

Ephemeral.

The mellotron would be playing and it would be very quiet and the low bass gives a very sad feeling...

It's very resigned. Very resigned. Do you want to hear any more?

[I understand you] played on Peter Hammill's album Fool's Mate.

Yep.

And John Wetton plays on...

Everything.

On everything?

John's on everything. Every time he goes over for a drink, a major band offers him a gig. Really. John is forming a trio at the moment.

Who's going to be in it?

The drummer is a heavyweight, but I can't tell you who. John is looking around for a good guitarist who's heavy enough to take on the drummer and himself. That combination is difficult.

WHAT ABOUT [The Cheerful Insanity of Giles, Giles and Fripp]?

[laughs]

How do you feel about that album now? I guess that was six years ago or so. Do you still look back at it and say, "Well, I didn't like it" or "I did"?

It has some very good things on it. I played guitar in those days.

Your style sounds to me like a Wes Montgomery type.

You've got to appreciate that I didn't like a lot of the music on that album. I didn't even want to play on it. Most of Side One is nonsense. Pete Giles, for example — the only guitar sound he liked was Barney Kessel's. Side One was Pete's side. First half of Side Two was Mike [Giles], and the second half of Side Two was me. That's sort of a very rough guide.

Was Giles, Giles and Fripp *a big success?*

Oh, no. We sold 500 and something in England. I still get royalty statements. It sold one in Sweden, 40 in Canada.

It was released in the U.S.

Yes, it was. Greg Lake managed to find a copy. It has a different cover to the English one. He threatened to have it blown up into a huge poster. I reminded Gregory that I had, and still do have, a few of his early publicity photos, which include Greg holding a huge two-foot diameter plastic rose with a crown of thorns. I threatened reciprocal action with these.

What's on the American cover?

I'm wearing a hat, a cap which looks like a Salvation Army cap and, well, it's just different.

Now normally, I don't talk about history with anyone, but I appreciate that you're a special case, you've taken a deeper interest in the band.

Who discovered you?

No one discovered us.

How did you manage to put out the album?

When I turned professional in the beginning of 1967, I was told that the Giles brothers had left Trendsetters Limited, which was their group, and were looking for a singing organist. Since I was a guitarist who didn't sing, I went along for the job. After rehearsing for a month and doing tape recordings in the Beacon Hotel in Bournemouth on a Revox, I said to Mike Giles — this is a bit of a joke, since I'd been working with him for a month — "Well, have I got the job?" He rolled a cigarette in his mouth and lit it and puffed on it and said, "Well, let's not be in too great a hurry to commit ourselves to each other." From which you can gather that Mike never made his mind up about anything in his life. Anything that involved accepting responsibility was not really for Mike.

In September — this was about July — we moved to London. I knew that as a professional musician I had to go to London. It was the only place to go. And the Giles brothers, being professional for some four years, they knew the ropes, really, and I needed their experience, so we went to London. I got us a gig at an Italian restaurant. (You're not going to find this in many places, you know.) I got us a gig with Douglas Ward, a piano-accordionist, at an Italian restaurant in Jermyn Street near Piccadilly.

But we had a week before that when we were in the Dolce Vita and at the end of that week the accordionist was beaten up and carried off to the hospital, where we visited him. He was burned up in a roundabout by these three louts, and he stopped his car and went back and sought them out and realized that he, little man with no muscles, white and puny, was no match for these three large oafs, who proceeded to duff him and kick him and make somewhat of a mess.

Anyway, we no longer had an accordionist to play with and we were suddenly thrown on our own in a situation that would not have normally been of our choosing, backing an Italian singer called Moreno, who I christened "Hotlips" Moreno.

He came onstage and he would say, "Please, please, you do not call me Hotlips." We would go through his numbers, and he'd write some of his own, and they were appalling. Peter and I used to alleviate the situation by doing steps and swing guitars and make a very big to-do about some of the sequences which were really hideous.

I remember one diminished chord which came in as if by chance and I would do this lovely rippling diminished run finishing on the most inappropriate chord conceivable to man. And at the same time as this, we would swing our guitars in perfect unison, combining to narrowly miss Moreno's head as he was singing.

There was a girl group, I think it was a quartet. They would sing; organ, drums, the whole lot, Italian ... and the idea would be that one of them would go off, we would play "Blue Moon," they would play "Blue Moon," and we would play "Blue Moon" [laughing] and one of their people would go off and I would start ... the organist would stop, for example, and I would start to play the tune and then the drummer would quickly move and Mike would come in, so that no one would realize that the band had changed! This was a great idea, but frankly, the difference in Mike Giles's drumming and the Italian girl's drumming was significant.

In order to get to the stage, we had an awful lot of people to go by, and we would get snagged along the way. So, Pete and Mike would get to the stage, but I wouldn't. I'd still be stuck in the back, struggling through a crowd ... and all the girl singers, all the girl musicians, would come

off, leaving a sort of faltering "Blue Moon" or just "Blue Moon" played on drums or something like this, and I'd eventually struggle on and play "Blue Moon," having completely blown the mood.

When we went off, Mike would go into some amazingly naughty times, which would be impossible for any of the Italian musicians replacing us to actually take over. Good fun. But, anyway, we got back from Mike's warning that we were tempting fate a little too much with Hotlips by our brand of humor, and we broke into Hotlips' set. Except there was no drumming, the drums suddenly weren't there. We turned around and there was Mike [laughter] with a maniacal, twisted smile on his face ... going through exaggerated motions of playing drums, but not actually hitting any of them. It was one of the funniest things I've ever seen. That was just the end for Hotlips. He walked off there and then. We had to finish off the week as a trio, with the girl Italians backing Hotlips Moreno, the Italian singer.

That was probably more appropriate for him.

Yes, I think it was a lot better. We, meanwhile, got on with a set of beguines, for example "The Breeze and I" and "Spanish Harlem" beguines. The only difficulty was that we did them both in E, which was very nice as a trio where I could play open chords and spread out the sound. But Mike used the Italian girl's kit, and the bass drum was tuned to E flat, a wholly inappropriate note. The root note for both "The Breeze and I" and "Spanish Harlem" was E, which Pete was playing in the same register as the bass drum, but a semi-tone away. The clash was hideous. It was really horrible. And we used to do "Mellow Yellow" with Mike singing.

We then realized that we were being rooked. Now, bear in mind that the Giles brothers were probably two of the most cynical musicians one could imagine, having been through so much nonsense and dishonesty in the preceding four years that they didn't have faith in anyone. In fact, Mike remains to this day the most suspicious man I've ever known. We realized that we were being robbed by the agent. We were being paid £30 a week when in fact they were paying £40 a week.

So, I wrote the agent a letter and stated that he was being dishonest. I've always been rather to the point in situations like this. Where other people would consider my actions tactless, I would consider them forthright and responsible. The upshot of it was that at the end of the week we lost our job, and I didn't work for a year and a half, with very few exceptions and odd gigs.

Mike, meanwhile, got a job playing with the Mike Moulton Five and Pete Giles did sundry things, including collecting supplementary benefits with me on a Friday in Camden Town, and did a few independent gigs with the Italian pickup band at the Dolce Vita. This left me free to practice up to 12 hours a day.

Did you enjoy practicing?

Oh, very much. Very much.

What did you practice?

Scales, chords, techniques, different solos. My sort of background as a guitarist is not one that is ever likely to be very widely known, which is a rather fortunate thing. I heard Roy Clark on the radio today playing "Twenty-First Street Rag." That's all the things I used to do: "Orange Blossom Special," "Zarda's," "Nola," all those kinds of things.

My guitar teacher was an old banjoist from the '30s. He also played guitar and mandolin. My background was what you call "corny," sort of Nick Lucas, Eddie Lang acoustic guitar pieces. Some of them are very difficult.

The acoustic guitar, especially the plectrum acoustic guitar, is a completely different thing from rock and roll guitar. They're two instruments, electric and acoustic guitar, and I suppose there must be very few people who have a background in the classical period of classical guitar, which was in the '30s, with Eddie Lang, and the end of the '30s, Django Reinhardt and so on. But that was substantially my background, which is completely and wholly inappropriate for life as a rock musician.

I developed an interest in playing classical guitar pieces with a plectrum, the Cárcassi "Etudes," the "Recuerdos de la Alhambra," this sort of thing. If any of your readers would like to find out how good their plectrum technique is, I suggest they have a go at "Recuerdos de la Alhambra" by Tárrega, and I think they'll have a shock. Or Cárcassi "Etude No. 7," which is quite simple and straightforward, nowhere as difficult as the "Recuerdos." Nevertheless, it sorts the men from the boys.

Do you still play that?

Yes, I'm practicing those pieces at the moment because it looks as if I might play an acoustic guitar onstage for the first time in my life.

I met someone recently who said there were two singles actually released from Giles Giles and Fripp: "One in a Million" and "Elephant Song." What was on the other side of "One in a Million?"

The back of "One in a Million" was called "Newly-Weds." The version was different than the one on the album. Similarly, the single of "Thursday Morning" was different than "Thursday Morning" on the album because Ian MacDonald was on it, both singing and, I believe, playing clarinet.

We also recorded three more tracks for Decca as Giles, Giles and Fripp with Ian MacDonald that were never released. One was called "Under the Sky," which Pete Sinfield did. It was fabulous. And "Talk to the Wind" is with Mike Giles on drums, Pete Giles on bass, myself on guitar, Ian on flute and the singing by Judy Dyble, who is on the first Fairport Convention album, and Ian. Those are the definitive versions of "Under the Sky" and "Talk to the Wind."

"Under the Sky" is on Sinfield's solo album, but you say these are much better?

Oh yes. Also, the "Talk to the Wind" is far better on the home-made tape I have than on the King Crimson album.

How did you record it?

At home. We did it on a Revox. It's good stuff. But Judy left. She found me hard to work with apparently. You seem still interested in acquiring the single "One in a Million." There's no point in getting the singles because they are on the albums…

Well, if they're different versions…

But why bother? These aren't important, these are just small details for the collector, and you're wasting a lot of good time getting into these small details. You're taking it too seriously.

PART TWO

There was another track we recorded as Giles, Giles & Fripp. There were the three sides for Decca which weren't released. One was "Under the Sky," which was nice. The other was one by Pete Giles. What you need on this is the tape of the television show we did, the Giles brothers, Ian MacDonald and myself for *Color Me Pop*, a 25-minute television show in England. We recorded the music at home ourselves because it was better doing it that way. And there's some good music there, let me tell you. It was a series, and we were one of the groups. After we completed the show, I think, I told Peter that I didn't want to work with him anymore. But the music is of interest. It also has one track called "Drop In," which was the third one we recorded for Decca that wasn't released. It was meaty rock and roll, with me writing the lyrics. The lyrics were dreadful.

Really? You haven't written any other lyrics...

Apart from the Giles, Giles and Fripp album and that, no. Other than the punchline in "The Great Deceiver": "Cigarettes ... Chocolate cigarettes, figurines of the Virgin Mary," which was mine.

There's a line which I heard you do live once, "Camel hair, Brylcreem ... some stores full of antiquary." What is that line?

That sounds like it comes from "The Great Deceiver."

Right.

Maybe this was in the early days of the song and John was just trying a few lyrics to see which felt best.

He would actually improvise onstage?

No, but he might have...

... or he had an idea of what he would do.

Yes, yes. Your words are never complete till you've just sung them. In the studio, Peter [Sinfield] would be ferociously rewriting up until the last minute. "Court of the Crimson King," for example, went through many, many different versions. I happen to like some of the earlier ones. The finished one's also superb.

That was put out here as a single.

It got to number-98 as a single. But it's just an abbreviated version of the album track.

Also, "Schizoid Man" appears on...

Nice Enough to Eat [a 1969 bargain compilation released in the UK by Island].

Right. I guess that was abbreviated, too, because it doesn't have the introduction.

I don't think they've got the wind on it. Has it got the wind on it?

No, it just starts off with the music. Is that supposed to be the wind or factory noises?

The wind at the beginning? We had this pedal organ, which shows up at the end of "Crimson King," and I said to Mike, why not just get the wind noises out by pressing the keys but not pushing far enough to get a note, so you just got the wind.

WHAT'S GONNA HAPPEN now? King Crimson is finished and you say you're going to be...

You haven't even asked me why it's finished.

Well, why is it finished?

Why didn't you ask me?

I'm asking you now.

No, I'd be interested to ask why it didn't occur to you. I want to know if that was the first question.

I don't know, King Crimson breaking up, it occurs every couple of years.

You didn't think this was the final one?

Not really.

I see.

When David Cross left, I heard you were going to tour as a trio, and I figured that would be exciting because I've seen you perform as a trio onstage. At one show, towards the ending of "Schizoid Man," David Cross actually walked off the stage and he wasn't missed. The sound was sufficient, so I thought that should be interesting, playing those two albums as a trio. Then I heard that you had broken up, and it was sort of expected.

All right, let me put the history, King Crimson and all the changes of the past six years into perspective. I've been experimenting with different ways of living and doing many things, and I'm continuing to do so. King Crimson ceased to exist for three reasons. The first is that it represents a change in the world. Second, because the energies involved in the lifestyle and the music are no longer appropriate to my life as I live it. And thirdly, because the education that was King Crimson, the finest liberal education I could receive at that time, is no longer the best liberal education that I could receive.

First reason: it represents a change between the old world and the new. The old world is characterized by the unit of organization that has a very large body and a very small brain, is unwieldy and incapable of adaptation, and is wholly inappropriate for the conditions relevant to modern life.

Examples of this unit are huge corporations, and the obvious example in the music business are groups that carry lots and lots of roadies and lots and lots of equipment. Unbalanced.

Or a supergroup that isn't accessible?

When you get into inaccessibility, that's not really the point.

Can I give you an example? At the last Bowie concert in New York, I think there was only one photographer for the whole show and he was hired by MainMan.

Well, I must say how reasonable and civilized that is, having spent most of my professional life in America having to fight off the irritations, the insensitivities of photographers who were quite happy to click away throughout the most delicate and difficult moments without any regard at all for the people on the stage. May I therefore laud what Bowie did. But I say that the organization which was surrounding David when I saw them in England was very large and unwieldy.

The characteristic organization of the new world is small, independent, mobile and intelligent. By intelligence, I mean as a measure of adaptability to circumstances. You have a period of stress and tension when the transition between the old world and the new becomes most marked. For example, Atlantic [Records] here is a perfect example of the old way of doing things. No one knows what's going on. Really breaking apart at the seams, don't you think? Lots of people, lots of rooms, no one knows what's really going on. Lots of graft, you know, going out and having drinks on the firm, wasting time, wasting money, which should presumably be the artists'. All this kind of nonsense can't make it.

I think I've been in that kind of situation. I worked for IBM, which is a worldwide corporation.

That's exactly it.

I didn't feel very lost in it because where I worked there was a department and there were about a dozen or 20 people, everyone pretty much knew each other, and it was sort of one group.

And how many other groups are there?

Thousands.

And how many…

Our number was 42A and there was obviously a 42B and an 89J and all the other numbers in there.

What I suggest to you, essentially, is that that is really an unwieldy organization and it can't adapt at all.

That's true.

This system is breaking down, I mean you couldn't disagree with that, you only have to go out in the streets of New York to realize that this city, a large, unwieldy unit of organization, with no brain in command, is just not going to make it.

What will happen?

There will be a period of breakdown, which will be most marked in the year 1990 and be most critical in the decade from 1990 to 1999. Sixteen years away. In an extreme situation, you could get the complete breakdown of social, political and economic order, which you're going to get anyway, but it may not be final, if you like. Once again, in an extreme situation, you could have a nuclear war.

America is going to collapse completely because it is so large and unwieldy. The only things that are going to get through are small, independent, intelligent, mobile small groups, units. In the '80s it will be, I think, a continuation of the drive towards spiritualization, but in a real sense. Getting out of your brain and saying, "Yeah man, that's really groovy" doesn't really take you very far, but what it does do is create a situation where a population is sympathetic towards those who are working in a certain area. For example, the majority of conservative Americans would not let certain things take place. Liberal maneuvers could not take place with the consent of much of American popular opinion. However, in ten years' time, the heads of the '60s will be in their forties and will be forming the backbone of America. If they are open to and sympathetic to people who have a more real interest in changing America, then you will have a situation which, although it may not help actively, is nevertheless passively open to it.

Liberal things won't happen because America is mostly conservative now. The people who were radical in the '60s will have become moderately radical or liberal in 20 years.

What I'm suggesting is that they will be more aware that there is more involved in living than satisfying purely immediate needs and desires and gratifications.

IF YOU KNEW that tomorrow you were going to be dead, wouldn't you do something today?

I don't know what I'd do today.

I suggest, whatever you did do, you live to the full. If you were going to have a hamburger and you thought "Christ, this is my last hamburger," you'd cherish every bite.

Right.

The majority of the people are not going to make it through.

But you can't live as if you're expecting to die.

Have you read *Don Juan*?

I have.

Death lives on the shoulder. This is what I'm talking about. Have you read the New Testament?

Not really.

Where Paul talks about dying daily. Exactly the same idea.

Dying daily could be going to sleep.

Dying daily has to do with breaking out of sleep. It's an assertion that man lives his life in a condition of sleep and dying daily is where man actually wakes up. One can only live fully if one knows that tomorrow one will be dead. Puts things in a completely different perspective.

We have to make believe that we are going to live.

That's nonsense. We don't have to make believe at all because it's not necessarily true. In fact, for a lot of people, it isn't. This is a vital point. Because when you do live with that realization that tomorrow you will be dead, your life takes on a totally different character. You see, nothing is guaranteed.

WHERE DO YOUR parents come from?

From the Ukraine.

Yeah.

Do you know where that is?

Well, out there.

PART THREE

The last gig you did in New York here, did you know that that was going to be the last one?

Well, I knew it would be the last one for David, but at that point I had considered touring with the band. We considered experimenting with a number of different forms, as a trio and as a quartet with Ian MacDonald. But four weeks ago yesterday [*that would be 9/19/74*], I decided that was it. And, I have no real regrets other than not playing "Red" live, and not going to Brazil and Japan, I suppose. That sort of thing. But no real regrets because the decision was a right one.

I don't think you'll hear very much from me.

What do you mean?

I think you'll find that I might just disappear.

And just have albums appear in record stores every so often?

Maybe not even that.

Wow.

You must wait and see how much is wanted. I respond to people who want something. You see, if you do something like the Fripp & Eno album [(*No Pussyfooting*)], and Atlantic turned it down, I don't think I have very much in common with Atlantic. In fact, I have nothing in common with Atlantic.

Are they required to put everything out?

No, they're absolutely not.

So why...?

Well, if they don't want to, I don't want them to put it out. The album has a meaning for me.

I was under the impression that you went into the studio and made it very fast.

We made Side One at home. We just took a lady friend around to Eno's, had a glass of wine and a cup of coffee, plugged in and did Side One in 45 minutes. Two guitars, that's all. No amplifier, just me, my pedalboard, direct-injected into two Revoxes. Side Two in a studio, recorded in an evening. Took it right into another studio, mixed it, put it together, there you go. That was the album.

I was thinking that to have some meaning you have to work on it for a while.

I worked on it all my life. It was the most perfect expression of whatever I've done or thought or felt. In other words, if anyone doesn't like Side One, they won't like me. So, when Atlantic turned it down, in fact, they turned me down. Which doesn't make me uptight, or bitchy, or cheesed off or anything like that. I just appreciate that for what I will be doing in the future, the appeal will be limited to people of certain types. I don't feel the need to bang my head against a wall, to rush around America again. If the people want me to come to America, I might, because I've got a lot of things I want to do as well.

ONE OF THE FIRST advertisements for the King Crimson album was this ad [headline: "What Pete Townshend Thinks About King Crimson"].

Oh, right.

How did you get him to write that?

Well, I had this idea for an advert, which was to ask Pete Townshend, to give him a record to review. And he really liked the album. And this is what he wrote, unsolicited. That's just his reaction to it. It's difficult to tell you the kind of excitement there was in England when the band came out. It only really got to that pitch in America afterwards, when the group broke up, but in England, the feeling was quite amazing.

And since it was my first professional rock group, the first time I played live on stage in a rock group, I didn't know how rock groups did anything. Ian had been in the Army for five years, was suicidal, neurotic. As we all were, I suppose. Mike Giles came from the Orchid Pearly and cabaret bands. Greg Lake was the only one who had any experience as a professional rock musician, and that was with the Gods, who eventually became Uriah Heep. So, if you like, think of Uriah Heep as Greg's rock background.

YOU WERE GOING TO make some point about Trouser Press?

Oh, that's right, yes. Where you refer to me as a "cold unemotional genius" in the star system. Well, look, this is complete nonsense. I mean, do you realize that? Do you realize, first of all, that I am not a genius and second of all that I am not emotionless? [*He's referring to a throwaway line in the TOTP 4 explanation of our ill-conceived LP rating system: "2. Technical Musicianship: Ever since Alvin Lee grew his silicone fingers and began playing sterile speed guitar, the possible dichotomy between feeling and competence has existed. For an example of this we have the Dolls, who mean it but can't play it, versus an emotionless genius like Fripp."*]

That's the sort of impression that one gets of you.

Well, surely you can see a little more than that.

I don't know. I think I came in here pretty openly, I don't know how I'm going to come out.

Fff … well … ehh … Well, whenever someone has a mind and uses it, I suppose there is a tendency for him to be regarded as calculating. However, not only am I not my body or my feelings, I am also not my mind. To regard me as a genius is nonsense. To regard me as emotionless is somewhat lacking in observation and penetration.

I think that observation arose from watching you onstage, where you're just very intently playing and you just barely look up to see the band and you hardly ever look out into the audience. If you were in a bell jar of some sort, it would create the same impression. You seem distant, in a way. But the other day I was reading some article in Melody Maker: *"Robert Fripp Super-Stud," and they said you were trying to change your image.*

That reflected me as I was then. It was also great fun to see how many people, personal acquaintances as well as people along the way, were quite surprised, quite shocked, to find that I was a young man with developed carnal interests, which were not held in perhaps as great a check as they should have been. It is also interesting how many young ladies, having read the articles, were interested to find out a little more.

What are you now?

That fashion of living is no longer appropriate to my life as it is now lived.

Can you tell me something more about what your fashion is now?

I've already told you.

All right.

If you want the handy sentence, here it comes again. It's the harmonious development of all the parts of my being simultaneously and in a hurry.

Do you think you can do it in a hurry? I mean, is the reason why you're doing it in a hurry because you're worried about what will happen?

There are some techniques to do it in a hurry. Yes, that's exactly right.

How does one find out about these techniques? Does one just simply have to look for them or can you tell me now?

When you spend a sufficient period of time looking, but looking in a certain way, which is more than a casual interest, you find yourself presented with an opportunity, which you then take or not.

So, the analogy would be my looking for a copy of Giles, Giles and Fripp *and finally getting one.*

Yeah.

It eventually comes around.

You have to actually work.

I'VE DECIDED to give some guitar lessons.

To musicians or non-musicians?

To guitarists of medium and advanced capabilities. Not beginners. Whereas the King Crimson idea represented an attempt to influence and to reach a lot of people, the ventures for the future, the Eno situation, the guitar teaching and other activities will seek to influence a smaller number of people but nevertheless will have a greater effect in time. In other words, instead of striking at the base of the pyramid, I'm striking higher up. I would rather give guitar lessons to a half dozen guitar teachers than 60 of their pupils. I'm working on a guitar technique that doesn't seek to give the player control of his guitar as much as control of himself.

You have an interesting style of playing. You pick strings with both hands.

The distinguishing feature between myself and most other guitar players is that I have two hands and have worked hard over a period of 13 years to develop my right-hand technique, my plectric skill. Most electric guitar players, in fact, have no plectrum technique, and most of the movement is done by the left hand. Which is very good for

phrasing and so on, but it means that the player is not in control of his instrument.

When you were playing onstage what did you put your guitar through? Did you have it directly into the amp?

It went through a Fripp pedalboard.

What's on that?

Oh, these things aren't important.

THE KIND OF FEELING I've got from other musicians is that they rather envy what they see as, well, my courage. I'm not saying that. I'm not considering it courage; I just continue to consider my action wholly sane and appropriate to the time. But there are a number of musicians I know who wish they could do the same — and, of course, they can.

That's true. King Crimson, speaking from a record industry point of view and an audience point of view, reached, I guess, a high point, or re-reached it. I thought that the first album was excellent and from there it went down a little until you reached Islands, *which was very different, and then you had* Earthbound, *which showed what, maybe, American touring was like, but then…*

Earthbound *wasn't King Crimson.*

I think in a way it was because it sounds like an awful bootleg.

It's King Crimson's own bootleg.

Right, and it sort of, it sort of represents, well, this is what it really is like, it's just sort of really bad, it's, I mean…

It wasn't King Crimson.

I think what the album stands for…

The album was released to show why the band broke up.

Yeah, right. I guess that's what I was trying to say.

Well, you succeeded in saying it then. ∎

QUOTES OF THE DECADE

"[Fripp] wasn't the main influence in King Crimson, however much he cared to think he was."   —GREG LAKE (1978) TP 28

Thank you, Stranger Things, *for making this one relevant. I was 26 at the time of the interview, but she was barely 20 and seemed like a kid to me then, albeit an extremely poised one. I suspect she was well on her way to becoming jaundiced about the interview game, although she was pleasant and forthcoming during our talk. At one point, she asked me if I needed a copy of her album (*The Kick Inside*), which struck me as strange — I wasn't very experienced at the time, but I already knew enough to have done my homework and listened to the music beforehand! I interviewed her again in 1993 (probably for* Musician*) in conjunction with the release of* The Red Shoes, *and it was like meeting a totally different person. Professional and polished. (JY)*

KATE BUSH GETS HER KICKS

TP 30, JULY 1978

By Jon Young

All of a sudden, Kate Bush was at the very top of the UK singles charts. "Wuthering Heights," her first 45, was number-one and her album, *The Kick Inside*, wasn't doing badly either, sitting in the Top 5 LPs. Whoosis? I wanted to know.

So, I got a hold of the album. On the cover, which could easily pass for a *Vogue* photo session, a spooky young woman with gigantic almond eyes clutched at her head as if trying to keep her odder thoughts from rising into public view. No matter if she succeeded, the album turned out to be unusual enough. Bush's songs are based on simple piano chords utilized in clever variations that nag at you much the way Bryan Ferry's do. The lyrics are striking, even at a casual glance, just because they are about things (rare) and because they avoid clichés (rarer still); many tunes are about sex, but with none of the "consuming bitch" or the "submissive lady" so often in weary evidence. Instead, Kate espouses the view that, blush, sex can be fun, maybe even a good idea. Other numbers concern strange phenomena, outlaws and Emily Brontë, but through all of it comes a loopy immediacy that distances Kate from your average creaky balladeer.

Very well, but big deal, right? Well, as anyone who has heard even a few seconds of Kate Bush knows, the real kicker is ... her voice! Depending on your reaction, it's either Minnie Mouse or the Heavenly Host. Kate sings Up There where Laura Nyro and Joni Mitchell have sometimes tried to reach, but with an important difference: she's not striving, that's where she's at home. And it's not an affectation, feminine or otherwise. The conviction with which she sails along at that stratospheric pitch makes the music seem eerie, driven and finally tough, despite its aerial quality. It didn't take me long to conclude that Kate was one of those genuine originals that may not be destined for mass acceptance (most people I know dislike the record) but should be reckoned with on the basis of her creative uniqueness alone.

Enough ranting. When Kate Bush sat down to talk, I was curious to know about her roots.

Born in Kent in 1958, she said she'd started out taking violin lessons, but "couldn't get on with being taught it." So, the rebellious 11-year-old began fooling around with the family piano, writing songs. That turned out much better.

"Every night for a couple of hours I'd sing and play. When I was 14, my family thought it would be a good idea to maybe meet some people in the music business and see if I could get some response from my songs ... I think they were pleased to see I had something I could release myself in. They neither encouraged me or discouraged me, they just let me be myself, which is something I'll always thank them for."

They sound like progressive parents. Enter

Kate's brother, who "had a friend who'd been in the record business for a couple of years. He came around to listen to me. I put 20 to 30 of my songs on a tape, and he'd take it to record companies. Of course, there was no response; you wouldn't be able to hear a thing, just this little girl with a piano going 'yaaaaa yaaaaa' for hours on end... [The songs] weren't that good. They were OK, but..."

Usually, the only musicians who disparage themselves are vets who have had time to acquire self-confidence. I wondered how the artiste of the early days differed from the current one.

"I could sing in key but there was nothing there. It was awful noise, it was really something terrible. My tunes were more morbid and more negative. That was a lot of people's comment: they were too heavy. But then a lot of people are saying that about my current songs. The old ones were quite different musically, vocally and lyrically. You're younger and you get into murders..."

Rejection was merely a small delay, though. Along came David Gilmour of Pink Floyd. "Dave was doing his guardian angel bit and scouting for talent. He'd already found a group called Unicorn in a pub and was helping them. He came along to see me, and he was great, such a human, kind person — and genuine. He said, 'It looks as if the only way you can do it is to put at most three songs on a tape and we'll get them properly arranged.' He put up the money for me to do that, which is amazing. No way could I have afforded to do anything like that. EMI heard it and I got the contract."

Indeed, so good were the Gilmour demos cut in 1975 that two of them ended up unchanged on the LP. Remember that in '75 Kate Bush was 17.

The Kick Inside was produced by Andrew Powell in the summer of 1977, showcasing really hot-slick playing from some then-Cockney Rebels and Pilots. The rest is chart history; chart history that would seem to have happened a little too quickly. In response to a question about future plans, Kate sounded weary: "I'm actually pretty heavily committed until late autumn. The trouble is that the records moved so quickly, and I don't think anyone expected it. I found there are commitments already that are going on and

on." How about her reception here in the U.S.? "The only people I can talk about are the people in the company and the interviewers. They're all great. I figured they would be anyway, because when you're talking to someone about themselves, you're usually nice." Jaundiced so early on?

The last three songs on *The Kick Inside* seem the most personal. "Room for the Life" comes across as a sort of "I Am Woman" glorifying childbirth. She feels women have "a much stronger survival unit than men," since they can bear children, and thus should use their advantage to help men rather than play games with them. I don't really understand what she's talking about, but it can be dismissed as a Heavy Philosophical Matter, since she admitted to being in no hurry for a baby herself.

When we turned to spiritual matters, she seemed to be on firmer ground. "Strange Phenomena" suggests that she believes in Other Forces.

"Oh yes, I do. The thing about us humans is that we consider ourselves it, that we know everything. I think we're abusing our power and are guided by things we don't know about that are much stronger than us. But you can't label them if you don't know what they are. Also, it tends to sound a bit trendy like 'the cosmic forces,' and it's cruel to do that, because most religions have been exploited. As long as they're not misinterpreted, they're good because they give the individual something to hold onto."

A cynical view of faith for someone who regards herself as a believer. Later she would make a similar response when describing Gurdjieff as "the only religion I've been able to relate to" and then quickly ending her sketchy account with, "I don't wanna say much because I don't really have the knowledge to say it." At no time did she feel the need to justify herself to anyone else; she must get enough moral support from her own instincts.

The last song on the album is the title cut, which contains opaque lyrics. *Qué pasa*, KB?

"That's inspired by an old traditional song called 'Lucy Wan.' It's about a young girl and her brother who fall desperately in love. It's an incredibly taboo thing. She becomes pregnant by her brother and it's completely against all morals.

She doesn't want him to be hurt, she doesn't want her family to be ashamed or disgusted, so she kills herself. The song is a suicide note. She says to her brother, 'Don't worry, I'm doing it for you.'"

One of the best ways to look silly is to make predictions. Still, I suspect Kate Bush is going to show a lot of staying power. Her LP is so fully realized and so distinctive that if her music progresses at all, she may well come to be one of those creative voices that everyone, pro and con, must take into account. Her unapologetic self-assurance never wanes and looks like the thing that will allow continued exploration.

Musicians can reveal a lot about themselves when giving their opinion of the new wave, but Kate Bush did so intentionally. Professing an admiration for the Stranglers and Pistols and the way the status quo had been shaken up, she went on to say, "Maybe it's ironic, but I think punk has actually done a lot for me in England. People were waiting for something new to come out — something with feeling. If you've got something to tell people, you should lay it on them." ∎

LAURIE ANDERSON

TP 78, OCTOBER 1982

By Moira McCormick

"I'm afraid it's just going to be like this," Laurie Anderson sighs as her dressing-room door opens for the fortieth time to admit yet another person on last-minute business.

The diminutive performance artist takes care of said business and smiles apologetically. She picks up her damp black jeans and spreads them on a counter. "Need anything ironed?" she quips, setting the appliance's control for "cotton."

In less than an hour, Anderson will make her fourth appearance in Chicago. It's something of a homecoming, since the 35-year-old spent her formative years in the Second City's exurbia. Her previous performances, however, had been viewed only by a comparative handful of local art cognoscenti in gallery settings; this two-night stand, while sponsored by Chicago's Museum of Contemporary Art, takes place at the city's swankiest new-music showcase club, the Park West, and is overflowingly attended by new wavers and North Shore art patrons alike.

How did this Barnard/Columbia-educated, world-traveled, highly respected performance artist become a pop star? Primarily on the strength of her eight-minute ditty "O Superman," a minimalist, vocoderized, mesmerizing composition exploring life in a technocracy. A runaway hit in Europe and an underground hit at home, "O Superman"'s success led to a Warner Bros. contract, a full-length LP (*Big Science*) and sudden hipness in the pop music sphere.

After a decade of performances on the art circuit, being a pop star all at once must be a bit surprising, no?

"No," Anderson says, her softball-sized dimples deepening. "I planned it from the first day I saw Elvis Presley, and I thought, god, I wanna be a —"

"Come on, Laurie!" expostulates a nearby band member. She grins even wider.

"'O Superman''s success? That was planned, too." She giggles, then decides to give the interviewer a break. "I was surprised that it didn't do very well here, after it did well in Europe," she owns up.

Anderson is primarily a visual artist but had dabbled in recording before her fateful single. Given the ephemeral nature of performance art, "I wanted a record of my performances," she explains simply.

"O Superman" was recorded last year for New York's One Ten Records, with an initial pressing of 5,000. It's long, weird and you can't dance to it — some people even find it maddening — but that didn't stop it from zipping up to the number-two position on the British pop charts.

"It came into England as an import about which nobody knew anything, so it had a certain odd mystery to it at the beginning," Anderson says, pondering the single's appeal. "I have to assume that people bought it because they liked it, because it was an alternative to the pop love song." (It also makes you feel like a jerk for owning an answering machine.)

Though "O Superman"'s lyrics are peppered with banalities and catch-phrases that punctuate life in these United States ("Smoking or non-smoking?" "Come as you are." "Hi Mom!"), Anderson feels its relevance is universal.

"I don't think it's particularly unique to the United States," she says, "especially since there was more response to it out of the U.S. I think it's a very American song in a lot of ways. It has a lot of clichés; it's about any high-tech society. German audiences in Berlin probably understand it even better than American audiences."

The punk-coiffed gamine is bemused with her newfound fame in the rock world, and not unexpectedly has had to endure cries of "sellout" from fellow performance artists, whose works will probably never be seen outside of SoHo galleries.

"I can understand that," she says kindly. "The politics in the art world are really ... byzantine. Artists can say, 'The icky record world, how could you do something like that?' But at the same time, I think the commercial record world is *clear*.

"In the art world, it's grants and who you know, what kind of parties you're at, whose collections your work is in — really complicated stuff. But the terms on which you get a recording contract and the terms on which you maintain your career in a commercial situation are very clear-cut. If you sell records, you can make more. If you don't, you don't make any more." Anderson laughs delightedly. "I like that!"

Big Science is a collection of spoken pieces, instrumental passages and stripped-down songs with a rock sensibility, if not language, culled from Anderson's monumental work in progress,

"United States I-IV." She sings and plays keyboards, vocoder and violin (which she studied for 15 years), assisted mainly by co-producer/musician Roma Baran, avant-rock's Most Valuable Drummer David Van Tieghem and reedmen Bill Obrecht, Perry Hoberman and Peter Gordon. It isn't an easy album to listen to, initially (Anderson's publishing company is cutely dubbed Difficult Music), but is gradually addictive — sometimes spellbinding, sometimes grating, ultimately very affecting.

Anderson's own reaction to *Big Science* is mixed. "I'm always disappointed in everything I do, so it wasn't any exception to that. I always feel it could be so much better.

"What I didn't like about it was the ... talkiness," she decides. "I want to learn how to make songs where the words are more integrated with the music. Not choruses and verses and all that, but linked in a different way than I've linked them."

She describes her songwriting process: "In general, I start with some kind of digital line electronically produced, or maybe very simple claps or metronome — real basic. The words usually dictate the rhythm.

"I don't really like guitars. They're irritating; they have a lot of association for me with rock band machismo. I don't like electric guitar sound, with the exception of Glenn Branca — the kinds of things he's getting are really beautiful."

Anderson's next album will probably be a videodisc. "My main media is pictures. I assume that's one of the reasons Warner Bros. is interested in working with me. Nobody knows what to do with video. The technology is way ahead of the art. It's awfully hard to do one without making it seem illustrational or just promotional."

Anderson's artistry with pictures is dazzlingly apparent in her Park West performance of "United States I-IV." The mixed-media presentation utilizes slides, film, taped and live music, electronic tricks and Anderson's singular, dynamic presence. It's art without pretension, like the woman herself — pyrotechnics leavened with humor, open to interpretation but rife with messages for those who care to find them. For the rock crowd, it was a revelation.

Does Anderson think her current high profile is a shot in the arm for performance art in general? "Could be," she muses. "A lot of artists are doing things that are real interesting and completely accessible. It's just that American artists are off in their corner of avant-garde snobbism and want nothing to do with pop culture. They feel if something is entertaining it can't be good."

Anderson, on the other hand, intends to utilize pop's mass communication to further her work.

"I'm most interested in getting people to see my work, and I'm also conscious of the incredible privilege of just being able to pursue what I'm doing."

Sincerely, Laurie Anderson. ■

GONG

TOTP 9, JUNE/AUGUST 1975

By Danny Cornyetz

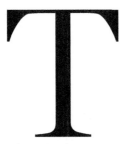

To enjoy Gong's somewhat unusual sound, you have to know something about Daevid Allen's unusual version of reality, as embodied in the mythology of a planet called GONG.

Daevid Allen (aka Dingo Virgin) came out of Melbourne, Australia in 1960 and landed in fair Canterbury, England, where, by 1963, a number of interesting things were going on. Specifically, during the following few years, Daevid became involved with a circle of friends who have since achieved prominence in their own rights. Kevin Ayers, Pye Hastings (Caravan), the Sinclair and Hopper brothers (David and Richard, Brian and Hugh) and others used to populate Robert Wyatt's

house. Canterburians remember seeing Nick Mason and Roger Waters in town during these times. Daevid was a teacher at this stage and a jazz fan to boot. Wyatt remembers him as "the first bloke with long hair. It seems trite now, but at the time that seemed important." His interest in jazz is also known to have influenced Wyatt and others.

It was some years later when Kevin and Daevid accepted an invitation from writer Robert Graves to stay on the French Riviera for a spell. Undoubtedly influenced by the French jazz scene, on their return to England, Daevid and Kevin formed a musical group. The abortive Mr. Head became the original Soft Machine, composed of Wyatt (drums, vocals), Ayers (guitar, vocals), Hopper (road manager, bass) and Daevid (guitar). Name copped from William Burroughs, the Softs were the first British band who set out to explore jazz-rock.

They recorded a classic single, "Love Makes Sweet Music," which aroused British interest, and then split for St. Tropez. Playing clubs in the south of France and experimenting with new sounds and ideas, the Softs became a popular European band (people still take them very seriously in Italy). When they returned to England, however, Daevid was refused entry by British customs and chose to stay in Paris while the Softs continued without him.

Although this must have been a great disappointment to Allen, he did not remain idle for long. During this period, he began to evolve the mythology of the planet Gong. Befriending a Welsh poetess and adventurer named Gilli Smyth and later a French Dharma Bum named Didier Malherbe, Daevid assembled a band of European gypsies.

Actually, Gilli and Didier had been guests of the Graves' on the Riviera, but until a reunion in Paris, Gong remained dormant. Didier had been playing sax since his early teens. A veteran of French clubs, he travelled to Tangiers and eventually India and took up the flute as well. Thus, with as much influence from poetry and free jazz as American or British rock, and a conscious blend of Eastern influences and contemporary music, Gong was born.

In the fall of 1969, this nucleus, joined by French session men, recorded the first Gong record for French BYG records (ACTUEL 529305), which has since been deleted. It previews all the directions later taken by Gong. Recorded at Europa-Sonor, *Magick Brother* was unfortunately a budget production, and the overall sound is not what it could have been.

However, with its acknowledged influences from "Le Plink Floy," "Mr. Mingus," "M. Satie," "Terry O'Really" (Riley), "Thelonius Sphere" (Monk) and, of course, the "Oft So Machine," it represents the originality and durability of Gong's sound. Although the content is typical of Allen's later compositions, albeit zanier, all tunes were written by Gilli, who was obviously the prime mover in early Gong, although she seldom appears in person with the group anymore. At any rate, the record remains refreshing, even today, with its alternately serious and loony outlook characterized by political and social messages mixed with proto-hippie rhetoric (peace/love).

The record shows Eastern influences and includes odd hypnotic repetition, primitive but original electronic sounds and decidedly weird stereo effects. Some cuts approximate the sweeping, gliding sound which Gong later polished and supplemented. Snatches are in French, but the majority of the album is in English.

In addition, the first thing one notices upon opening the rather straightforward cover is a sleeve drawing by Daevid depicting bizarre figures in the Gong mythology such as Fred the Fish, Captain Capricorn or one of the numerous Pot Head Pixies. Almost all of Gong's subsequent records bear these line drawings of mythical beings. Also, just below a nostalgic photo of Robert Wyatt, Daevid is credited with "Guitar Bass Guitar Semprini Crystal Ball & Vocal." If you can imagine an Anglo-French Frank Zappa whose cynicism was somewhat muted, there you have it.

The following year, 1970, BYG released *Bananamoon*, the original European super-session, with Daevid Allen, Gary Wright (Spooky Tooth), Maggie Bell (Stone the Crows), Archie Leggat (Soporifics), Robert Wyatt, Pip Pyle (Gong), Nick Evans (Centipede, among others), Christian

Tritsch (Gong) and others. It is also now deleted (ACTUEL 529345). Featuring liner notes by Daevid and a colorful illustration on the cover by Didier Leon depicting "the temporary eclipse of the planet Gong by an alien banana," Daevid explains each track's progress and gives the total mixdown time (TMT) for each cut. On Allen's "Stoned Innocent Frankenstein and his adventures in the land of flip" (TMT 11 hrs.), "White Neck Blues" (TMT 13 hrs.) and "Codeine Coda," the players jam at length. "Memories" is an old Hopper-Wyatt Soft Machine track which Robert has recently re-recorded as the flip of his "I'm a Believer" single. Although plagued by its directionless mixture of eclectic music, *Bananamoon* has extremely bright spots and, as an experimental grouping, is a success.

Giorgio Gomelsky first aided Gong during this period — he later produced their records — by promoting the group in various French clubs. Gomelsky owned several Parisian nightspots, and playing in these clubs, Gong developed a cult following in France. (Gomelsky has released various early Soft Machine tapes with Daevid without the artists' permission on a *Rock Generation* series and *2001* series.)

Next, Gilli wrote the music for a film called *Continental Circus*, which was about a champion motorcycle racer, collaborating with the filmmaker J. Laperrousaz. Gong performs the soundtrack (French Phillips 6332033); even stripped of the visuals, it is a captivating and mood-evoking record. "What Do You Want?" previews the next Gong album, originally released in 1971.

Camembert Electrique was recorded at the Château d'Hérouville (of *Honky Chateau* fame) in suburban Paris. Improved sound and an exciting new lineup proved the necessary ingredients for this excellent record. Re-released (the original ACTUEL 529353 is deleted) in England by Virgin in 1974, the record obviously still has appeal. The original featured a double-folded sleeve with a color photo of the group looking for all the world like continental nomads. Pip Pyle was on drums and Christian Tritsch on bass. Didier Malherbe, saxes and flutes, was called Bloomdido Bad de Grasse, and Robert Wyatt's three-and-a-half-year-old son appears in the photo. Gilli Smyth, who uses the name Shakti Yoni, co-wrote several cuts with Daevid, who has assumed the bulk of the writing chores, while Tritsch contributes here and there.

Also, mention must be made of the group's "switch doctor and mix master," Venux de Luxe. Artwork is again provided by Daevid. While "Radio Gnome," "Wet Cheese Delerium," "Squeezing Sponges Over Policemens Heads" and "Gnome the Second" are strange electronic fantasies à la Stockhausen, the gliding sound which was becoming one of Gong's recognizable trademarks is evident on "Fohat Digs Holes in Space" and "Mister Long Shanks." Daevid is credited with Local Vocals and Lewd Guitar, using his somewhat hoarse voice well on soft tracks like "Selene."

Following *Camembert Electrique*, Gong contributed to the *Glastonbury Fayre* album. The band snuck into Britain with gear and pixies to appear at a free concert held in late 1971 in Glastonbury. This live performance, which fills an entire side, is comprised of a 22-minute piece not entirely recorded at the Fayre.

Here the personnel of Gong has changed again. Including Laurie Allen (Lawrence the Alien) on drums, the new Gong was more experimental than ever before. The cut is entitled "Glad stoned buried fielding flash and fresh footprints in my memory," and the plan for its performance along with lyrics and story line appear on one of the numerous inserts furnished with the three-record set.

It starts out with a pedestrian beat, but soon begins to warp and bend, using Glissando guitar (a style Daevid claims to have lifted from Syd Barrett) and mellotron. Then, suddenly, as if lightning has struck, the music halts and over the loud hum of amplifiers an announcer apologizes, "The generator's gone out, but now it's fixed and we'll continue with Daevid Allen and Gong as soon as we can find the members of the band." It seems absurd, but abruptly it begins again and the band tries some electronic voicebox foolery with HA-HA's directed alternately to the left and right channels.

This leads into a musique concrète section that settles into a slow gliding beat suitable for the ethereal closing "sun chant." The succinct ending typifies Gong's tight sound. Listening to Gong live, it is apparent that they'd developed into a fully professional outfit.

A year and several months later, Daevid was allowed to reenter the United Kingdom. Gong migrated across the channel and became the first artists to be signed to Richard Branson's infant Virgin Record label. Starting out as a mail order record business, it grew into a chain of retail shops and is now an asylum for some of the most creative and avant-garde British musicians. *Radio Gnome Invisible, Part I* (Virgin V2002) is a full statement of Gong's individualistic music. With the added breadth of mellowing jazz influences, the zany, almost Syd Barrettesque vision of Daevid Allen reaches its current maturity.

Each side is composed of a complete story/trip, starting with a kind of telepathic pirate radio emanating from a flying teapot, introducing Planet Gong's most amenable inhabitants, the Pot Head Pixies and the Octave Doctors, following the presumed adventures of one Zero the Hero as he meets the Witch Yoni for some fish and chips. The recording production, handled by Giorgio Gomelsky in the Virgin Manor Studios, is excellent, and the amateurish qualities of *Radio Gnome*'s predecessors are gone.

At last, a Gong album released in England! *Camembert Electrique* had been a best-selling import in British shops, and although far from a commercial smash, *Radio Gnome* earned Gong the right to wax more madness. After touring Britain as a support act, Gong headed for the south of France with the new Manor mobile studio (purchased by Virgin thanks to Mike Oldfield's success with *Tubular Bells*).

They recorded *Angel's Egg* (Virgin V2007) in August 1973 under the full moon, like all Gong's work. *Angel's Egg* contains a full libretto booklet (whose frank language held up the French edition for several weeks) which explains Gong's peculiar mythology better than many pages of interpretive speculation could.

On *Angel's Egg*, increasing instrumental dexterity makes for a slicker sound as Zero continues to experience the wonders of Planet Gong. One of the nicer features of the sleeve is a visual barometer of the musical topology.

In 1973, another live Gong concert made it onto plastic, filling an entire side of the second Greasy Trucker's package. Although titled *Greasy Truckers Live at Dingwalls Dance Hall* (Greasy Truckers GT4997), that doesn't necessarily explain where the disc was recorded: "General Flash of the United Hallucinations" was supposedly recorded in Tunisia (?), while "Part 32, Floating Anarchy" is really several songs from *Camembert Electrique* combined in a new way live. "General Flash..." is actually "Zero the Hero and the Witch's Spell," with mellotron filling in where Gilli Smyth used to spacewhisper. The exquisite synthesizer squiggles that follow the lazy intro to "General Flash..." are the live set's highlight. Unfortunately, the side includes a boring, if unusual, drum solo.

The final step in Gong's trilogy, *You* (Virgin V2019), released in the U.S. months after its British counterpart, both strengthens Gong's mythology and returns to Daevid's Eastern roots. A scandalous mandalous (mandala) by Allen appears on the back of the sleeve, setting the mystical tone for the album, along with the cover depicting a Mayan step pyramid immersed in a field of stars. Promising a full-color illustrated booklet complete with all you could ever wish to know about the planet Gong, the liner notes provide lyrics and the new personnel of Gong 1974. With the notable reduction of the usual lyrical humor, the Terry Riley influence comes to the fore here, and the album flows effortlessly from start to finish.

The personnel for the three British studio efforts remain essentially similar. Steve Hillage joins Gong on lead guitar on the first of the trilogy and has recently done a solo album, *Fish Rising* (Virgin 2031), which is really Gong minus Daevid. The result is amazing, and the lyrics are more meaningful than anything Gong has recorded.

It seems that Pierre Moerlin (a.k.a. Pierre de Strasbourg) is back with Gong for good after brief stints by Laurie Allen (no relation) and King Crimson's estranged Bill Bruford on drums. Christian Tritsch was replaced on bass by Francis Bacon, who in turn was supplanted by Mike Howlett (a.k.a. Mista T. Being), while all three British studio albums were augmented by Tim Blake (a.k.a. Hi T. Moonweed) on keyboards and VCS3 extraordinaire. Miquette Giraudi has replaced Shakti Yoni (Gilli) on vocals and spacewhisper. She is also known as Bamboloni Yoni.

Critics are prone to dismiss Gong as a holdover from the days of psychedelia, sometimes on the basis of their lyrics alone. Perhaps this tendency to regard Gong as pretentious art-rock is as superficial to Gong's progress as their lyrics are to most listeners' enjoyment of the music.

At one level, the lyrics make sense; at others, ultimate nonsense. Much of Allen's imagery is erotic; while Steve Hillage has been quoted as describing Gong's music as essentially feminine, it is interesting that Daevid distinguishes between masculine and feminine instruments and tries to balance their contributions. Perhaps we'll have to wait for Daevid's official explanation, but I for one prefer ambiguity to neatly tied packages. Meanwhile, I'm trying to figure out how to become an Octave Doctor, so I can change my name to something more exotic.

Latest Developments:

Daevid Allen has left the group. He is in Spain writing a book and doing solo recordings.

Tim Blake has left Gong and moved to France.

Pierre Moerlin has been replaced by Brian "Blinky" Davison from the Nice/Refugee axis. ■

QUOTES OF THE DECADE

"As a cultural contribution, all [the Twist] did was help chiropractors ... but it did make it possible for people to admit they liked rock and roll."

—*AMERICAN BANDSTAND* HOST
DICK CLARK (1981) TP 63

"It's an actual fact that I'm a better cook than I am a record producer."

—ROY THOMAS BAKER (1982) TP 69

REGGAE

I taught Bob Marley music, seen? Eighty percent of the songs that Bob Marley wrote was co-written by me and never credited. And not only co-written, but musically architected by me. Because I am the music, and I was the music.

"

—PETER TOSH

Truth be told, our inclination to cover reggae was less encouraged by the global impact of Bob Marley than the enthusiasm for it by the British punk groups we followed. With the Clash featuring Mikey Dread, Generation X doing dub mixes of their songs, the ska revival leading more rockers back to Jamaica and even the Police dabbling in it — plus the unique punk–reggae hybrid of America's Bad Brains, who we covered in the same issue as Peter Tosh — there was good reason for us to write about Black artists who were creating and shaping the music.

TOUGH TOSH

**TP 92/93,
DECEMBER 1983/JANUARY 1984**

By John Walker

"The heir to Ras Tafari?"

Peter Tosh lets the phrase fairly drip off the tip of his tongue. Imagine sarcasm with the consistency of honey. "Madness... It's pure bullshit."

What has brought forth this burgeoning irritability? The notion, bandied about in Timothy White's Bob Marley biography *Catch a Fire*, that the late singer may be the spiritual/cultural successor to Haile Selassie — Jah.

"I'll tell you, I just heard about the biography. But these guys obviously intend to promote Bob Marley. They want to promote Bob Marley even more than Emperor Haile Selassie. And that's why Bob Marley is where he is today, seen?"

Suddenly Tosh's emotional temperature bubbles over.

"They don't realize that Bob Marley IS ONE OF MY STUDENTS! I made Bob Marley 'Bob Marley.'"

Peter Tosh understands the value of drama. Most people do. Sometimes, though, we neglect the drama of values. It isn't always an issue. But when a Rasta man meets the press, it ought to be. It's very easy to be absorbed by the novelty of Peter Tosh's culture — and forget that he has his own ideas.

For years we've been getting the dub version of Peter Tosh: that booming foundation of Rasta, the angry kick drum, the heavy echo of injustices from long ago. Basic tracks. Undisputed essentials of the Tosh personality. But as you read on, listen for the A-side. Peter Tosh is worth it.

Before our meeting, everyone I'd spoken to shared a vague sense of discomfort about Peter Tosh. He was too full of himself. A tough nut to crack. Even the publicist arranging the interview gave me a mildly distracted pep-talk about how, OK, Peter may come off a little spacey, but he's really a lovely fellow. Dub version, dub version. But what if I told you the secret of secrets? For every minute you spend with the Stepping Razor and the Bush Doctor, you get two with Ward Cleaver in dreadlocks!

How else to describe a man with a dry, easy wit — a man who patiently frees your head from the bars of cultural contrariety ... and follows up the whole thing with a lecture on good eating habits? Peter Tosh was born to keep the butcher's thumb off the scales of justice. Well balanced? The man travels by unicycle! But when his sense of justice is ruffled, the floodgates tend to open and give the situation a good washdown. These outlashes are not the Armageddon of personality some people take them to be. Tosh is just weighing all the factors and distinguishing them with emotion. For purposes of illumination.

Now sit up straight and pay attention.

"I TAUGHT BOB MARLEY music, seen? And when my student is promoted and reach a potential of acceptance ... well, it's very good, but at the same time, *remember the teacher*. And they *always* tend to forget the teacher. They pretend as if the teacher never existed, seen, and pretend as if the student's potential is bigger than the teacher. And that is wrong, totally wrong.

"Eighty percent of the songs that Bob Marley wrote was co-written by me and never credited. And not only co-written, but musically architected by me. Because I am the music, and I was the music. When I met Bob Marley, Bob Marley wasn't playing no instrument, so he did not know how to design a song. He could only sing out of his mouth. But the world don't want to accept that shit, seen? They want to keep me in the back, keep

Bunny Wailer in the back, like we weren't doing NOTHING, like we were just baggages. THAT'S WHY I HAVE TO WRITE MY BOOK! And when my book is written, then they will know."

There will be a lot to tell. It has been 20 years since the Wailers — forever, principally, Marley, Bunny (Neville Livingston) and Tosh — came together to become the cardinal reggae aggregation in the music's history. It has been nearly a decade since Tosh "left." Since then, he has survived: survived a devastating automobile accident that killed his girlfriend; survived more than one brutal beating at the hands of the Jamaican police; survived the animosity of politicians and businessmen; survived the death of Bob Marley. His faith and philosophy have helped him to cope with these most tangible tragedies and disappointments. His solo career has finally established him as perhaps the reigning reggae representative outside of Jamaica. But Tosh still seems concerned with the nebulous forces that disrupted the Wailers.

Ten years' passing haven't clouded the issue. The '70s were the era of the front man, and Bob Marley was the obvious choice for the Wailers — just as you'll never see the phrase "Keith Richards and the Rolling Stones" outside of bootlegs.

Tosh, who to this day sings, "I don't want peace, I want equal rights," clearly balked at this development. Although he recorded solo while still a Wailer, he clearly did not regard this as a conflict of interest. To Peter Tosh, "the Wailers" was a rock-solid entity unto itself.

A PERTINENT DIALOGUE

Was there animosity between you and Bob Marley?

"No. No animosity. The shitstem designed the animosity, seen?"

Was Marley affected by the emphasis on him? Did he believe the promotion, or was he just swept along with it?

"Well, it's like he wasn't concerned about that. Maybe that was his *intention*, because nothing was said after he saw what was done, seen? I wouldn't know if he helped them to create it, but he *accepted* the fact that they divided us, seen? [*A hint of pain in the voice.*] And he said nothing about it, so ... silence is consent."

We all know the ego is a strange bird. What if the shoe had been on the kicking foot? Ponder the concept: *Peter Tosh* and the Wailers. You might as well indulge yourself, because Tosh sure as hell won't. As if he were teaching arithmetic to an extremely dull child, Tosh leadenly reiterates: "It was *the Wailers*, seen, it was a *group*, seen. The power of we three come together to make the power of the group *the Wailers*." Seen, seen.

"Me and Bunny used to be the harmony of the group, and we sang harmony like birds. We two sing harmony, sound like five. Bob Marley never sing harmony, no time."

Harmony was Bunny's middle name. More mystic than egotistic, he apparently felt the jagged vibes between Tosh and Marley like a blast of Santa Ana wind. When Wailer recording sessions started to resemble episodes of *Divorce Court*, Bunny quietly skanked away.

While no less prolific than his brethren as a recording artist, Bunny has not pursued stardom with commensurate gusto. Reggae connoisseurs consider his to be the sweetest of the Wailers' three voices; the combination of talent and reputation should have guaranteed Bunny stardom. Instead, he has maintained the lowest of profiles.

"He is doing what he is doing," Tosh reports of his former bandmate. He pauses for a split second, as if silently contrasting Bunny's lifestyle with his own. "And ... he's cool. He's making music and intending to make a move. Which could be Africa, anytime.

"Plus, you know, we are working together to make an album and keep the name of the Wailers alive."

WELL, *NO*, I DIDN'T know. The notion sounds dazzling, but Tosh's voice dips into the portentous range. He's not known for his sentimentality; nor would Tosh keep the group's name alive only for posterity. This "reunion" shows he has not resolved the issue of the Wailers. There are still factors to be weighed, evidence to be reintroduced.

New testimony: "When we left *as* 'the Wailers,' Bob Marley took unto himself some other people and called *them* 'the Wailers.' And that is what is now causing the animosities."

Tosh's tone is like fast-hardening cement. For him, the furor over "the Wailers" is not just a matter of clinking egos, but a case of stolen identity.

The real issue is unity. In discussing competition within the reggae community, Tosh displays a healthy perspective. "Anything that is more than one always becomes competitive. It's not a matter of direct competition, but people are trying to do their best ... and people who are weak in this world many times are controlled by ego. And they many times get carried away, seen? They begin to put all confidence and trust in themselves, not knowing from whence inspiration cometh. And one or two years later they fade away, they've lost all inspiration. They don't remember how to create."

Between Tosh and Marley, then, was the natural competition of two people trying to do their best. They were stirred up by outsiders who related to competition only as a win/lose situation.

THE DEPTH OF Tosh's perspective becomes intensely apparent when asked if he felt a sense of loss when Marley died. The question begets a small explosion.

"No, I never lose *NOTHING*. When my woman die, I never lose nothing, so when my brother die, I lose nothing. I don't fret about it."

Perhaps he'll see them again?

"No! If them come back here, I will see them, but if them still out there, I won't."

But when Tosh goes "there"...

"*I won't go there*. I have been there so many times, mon. *You think it is joke-business I am talking — I AM NOT. The gift of Jah is eternal life.* Everyone who goes to Sunday school will read that the wages of sin is death ... so the preacher say. And he says the gift of God is eternal life. So, what does *that* mean? What does 'eternal life' mean? Go in the coffin and come out back?! I will be *HERE*. Who are going to die will die ... and they will never see who live. I'm not going anywhere, I promise you that."

Tosh's Rastafarian foundation supports him, though it may confuse others. "I was born Rastafarian," he asserts. "You cannot turn a Rasta man, you have to be born a Rasta.

"What makes you confused is when you try to be influenced by too many things. But if you keep your eyes on one thing and keep moving towards this one thing — you may stop by the way to pick up something and to look at it, but you say, 'No, this is not it,' and you keep going."

Is he open to the possibility that somewhere down the road something he never conceived of will show itself?

"I don't go down the road, I go *up* the road," Tosh laughs. "I don't like 'down the road'; I've been come from 'down the road.'

"My psychology teaches me to expect the unexpected, seen? So, I'm always prepared."

NINE OUT OF TEN people would call Peter Tosh arrogant. Roger Trilling, a friend of mine immersed in the reggae culture, thinks Tosh obscures his most important accomplishments — influencing a generation of reggae guitarists, for example — with his boasting.

Tosh sure seems to fit the bill. When I fail to grasp a rather esoteric religious point, he gestures toward the lager in my glass and concludes, "You cannot understand that and drink beer ... Michelob, seen." Soon after, he states (albeit the quote is out of context), "I live higher spiritually than you."

But I wasn't offended. When looking at another's culture, it's easy to misjudge the intensity of a statement — to hear nothing but the dub throb.

Peter Tosh likes to argue. Coming from a country where a national pastime is debating scripture, he could read aloud from the Brooklyn phone book and sound like he was spoiling for a fight. Don't forget the A-side: the man who will break down the components of an argument like the squares of a Rubik's Cube just to clarify his position.

It's not easy to build a bridge to such a personality. People who try often weave one from the most convenient material: hemp and dreadlocks.

"Yeah, we know that. But, then again, it's just as far as we have people whose minds are lower than people, and people who see deeper than people, people who hear deeper than people, seen? But we know that irrespective of how high or low they see or hear, we still have to teach them, we still have to awaken them. And musically is the easiest way to get across."

The situation is different, if not much better, in Jamaica. Back home, Tosh is a celebrity on the receiving end of adulation that can cross over to harassment.

"I am a diplomat, so I know how to move amongst the people. You go to the fish shop, you go here, you sit down, then you go here, now we don't know where we are going..." He giggles at the effect of his comings and goings.

"'Here, *here*, Peter, he *was*.' That's the way I love it. I come and go freely. Me move like the people.

"Most people don't want to deal with me because most people say I'm hostile, some people say I'm arrogant. Them have all different kinds of names to class me and most people who hear these things are in fear to even talk to me. So, with that, I get around."

When people connect to the star and not the person, Tosh says, "I teach them. My duty is to teach them. And I am always successful, because when they see me *that* way, I see the level of thought and mind they function off.

"Psychology teaches you everything. When you know psychology, you can deal with any kind of situation, any kind of people anytime, anywhere. I think that my psychology teaches me to do that, and I think that I am doing my best, seen? I have learned to live through all situations. I have learned to be *absent in my presence*. So, I am able to cope."

How does he compare his experiences inside Jamaica and out?

"I've been respected more outside of Jamaica than in Jamaica. And I have been treated better outside of Jamaica. I don't go to jail out here, first thing. I'm not being brutalized by the police out here, second thing. And I don't see too much bad-minded people who don't want to see our progress but want to see our destruction."

I suggest the latter batch of folk are all over the place, and Tosh only notices them more in Jamaica, where he's in the thick of it.

"Well," he concedes drily, "I prefer where I'm not in the thick of it."

THAT MAY EXPLAIN Tosh's various ploys to break into the rest of the world — like the Rolling Stones fiasco. To be fair, Tosh got a lot of expo-sure in their spotlight, dueting with Jagger during a hip, hot tour. But apart from "Walk and Don't Look Back," his three records on their label didn't click. Some of Tosh's most enduring fans now regard those albums as sub-par. Tosh himself sees the failure as symptomatic of his relationship with the Stones.

"I was inhumanely treated. But, as I told you, I am always prepared. Because if I was not prepared, I'd be exhausted and frustrated."

He feels the records were, willfully or accidentally, under-promoted and incorrectly marketed. Considering the Stones' reputation as a corporate steamroller, didn't Tosh anticipate the inevitable wane of their attention?

"I do not judge a man by his looks until he do what he does. It is not to say that I would not have *known*, but if I had told the world before it had happened, that would be libel, seen? I know it is a tragedy, but I know I must be compensated. My trust is in the Almighty. I leave all these cases that are difficult to him." Tosh smiles. (Cut to the Glimmer Twins in purgatory, sweating.) Then there's Tosh's recording of "Johnny B. Goode," "as seen on MTV." Rumor has it he was less than enthusiastic about *that*.

"Well, it's all in the business. That's the way the whole music business has been designed — not to cater for cultural music, but to depreciate and destroy the presence of the music. I was asked, I wasn't compelled to do 'Johnny B. Goode.' I wasn't interested much — not to say that I'm not interested in the song, it's just that I'm not interested in doing other people's things. I like to create my own things, seen?"

AND NOW IT'S TIME FOR *LIVE AT FIVE*

Tosh races from the interview to appear on the local NBC-TV news. Lightweight in tone and heavy on the ratings, *Live at Five* tosses Tosh into the conversation pit with newscaster Sue Simmons. The two of them create an allegorical tableau worthy of off-Broadway. Simmons is Black, but she isn't about to ditch her plum co-anchor spot for repatriation. This is New York. This is bright lights show business.

The spot opens with a short clip from the "Johnny B. Goode" video, but something sounds peculiar. Was there flamenco guitar in this production? The mystery is solved when the camera opens up on Tosh. Eyes hidden behind ever-present darkers, he's in possession of an acoustic guitar, which he strums and plucks throughout the interview. Musical worry beads.

Sue Simmons is, as a rule, very good at these snack interviews. Her questions are thoughtful, but, by necessity, very *Live at Five* basic. Tosh goes on automatic pilot, punctuating stock recitations with an occasional (and decidedly non-deferential) "Yes, my dear." As he works the bugs out of his flamenco run, one wonders whether his distance is motivated purely by boredom. Could it be the habit of a culture where an anchorwoman looks after the anchorman's children? Or is it shyness?

In the last seconds of the interview, Tosh deadpans a line about the destructive qualities of the "shitstem," and Simmons bids a brisk and formal farewell to the Not Ready for Prime Time Punster. She, too, has the deadpan expression of a weary professional.

SHOWTIME! And — uh, oh. Talk about being an outsider!

At the very moment Tosh hits the stage at New York's open-air Pier 84, about 20 of his countrymen attempt to crash the gate. It's a drastic move, but what can you do when the show of your dreams is sold out and the ticket you intended to buy was snapped up by a spliff-smoking preppie for a scalper's ransom?

The tiny mob storms past a small guard of freckle-faced ticket-takers, who freak out and slam shut the huge section of cyclone fencing that passes for a gate. This move proves very unpopular with the remainder of the ticketholders. After a long and cautious appraisal, the powers that be decide to reopen the facility. I am caught, literally, between the reggae and the hard place. By the time I get through the gate, Tosh is well into his set. At least I *think* it's Tosh. An entire audience standing on their chairs — the giveaway of a headliner in progress — makes it a certainty.

The last time I saw Peter Tosh perform was a good seven years ago. Back then, he had the presence of a crocodile, trudging across the stage with a very ominous and deliberate motion, as if the air were water.

But *this* Peter Tosh dances about in the garb of an African emissary. He ends each song with a flourish of synchronized arm waving like Elvis of Vegas and fronts an extremely cranked-up band.

This Peter Tosh could almost be called an *entertainer*. A purist next to me complains to his friend. Hundreds of college kids in topsiders and alligator shirts, pudgy from non-ital diets of institutional food, shout "Jah!" like their elder siblings shouted "Yeah!" They crane their necks as Peter races through "Walk and Don't Look Back." Maybe Mick is here...

MY PETER TOSH INTERVIEW did not begin on a sensational note, nor even an historical note. As Tosh sat behind somebody's desk, distractedly peeling a lichee, I asked if he was happy. It seemed the obvious thing to ask someone who looked so damned miserable.

Tosh looked slightly taken aback. He gazed out the window. Then he spoke quietly of learning to make the best of a situation. He voiced a sweet, sad hopefulness that conveyed the reality of being Peter Tosh. I would convey it better to you, but I had forgotten to release the pause mechanism on my tape recorder. (It is only thanks to the eagle-eye of Tosh's traveling cook that the rest of the interview made it onto tape.)

I will compensate, though, with a quote that does equal justice to Peter Tosh's wisdom, that indicates the drama of values may serve some purpose after all. The question was if he'd been approached by any political factions for his endorsement. Tosh allowed that the intent was clearly afoot, but the futility of garnering his support was virtually a given.

"They know I don't support politricks and games. Because I have bigger aims, hopes and aspirations. My duty is not to divide them, my duty is to unify the people, 'cause to divide people is to destroy people. And destroy yourself, too." ∎

EUREKA! UHURU! BLACK UHURU LEAD THE NEW REGGAE WAVE

TP 80, DECEMBER 1982

By David Fricke

The first rule of Rasta mind combat is "keep Babylon waiting." In the lobby of a midtown Manhattan Howard Johnson Motor Lodge this fine sunny morning, local press hounds cool their heels in frustrated anticipation of scheduled interviews with the hardest of reggae's hard — dread harmonizers Black Uhuru.

Initially, this comes as no great surprise. In Jamaica and other Caribbean islands, the sun beats down with a ferocity that demands a slower, more savory pace. Lateness is a way of life. "Soon come" is roughly the Rasta equivalent of "the check's in the mail."

But this is beginning to take on the air of a guerrilla action. Lead singer and lyricist Michael Rose is over 40 minutes late; he apparently hit the subway near his part-time Rego Park, Queens apartment right around the time when he was supposed to be here chatting. The day before, he blew out his first interview of the day with barely an apology. Derrick "Duckie" Simpson and Puma Jones, the male and female vocal backing

to Rose's impassioned roots rants, slipped out of the hotel earlier this morning and haven't been heard from since. The only member of the Black Uhuru entourage to keep the press engagement is drummer Sly Dunbar, half of reggae's crucial Riddim Twins with bassist Robbie Shakespeare. Dunbar shows up ten minutes *early*; he's a session player, and, to a session player, time wasted is money lost.

Rose, 25, finally saunters into the HoJo lobby dressed in a tracksuit and tall cap jiggling with the barely suppressed energy of the knotted serpentine dreadlocks inside. He sits down in the coffee shop and proceeds to treat our interview like an itch that needs to be scratched. He dispenses one-sentence answers and Rastafarian doctrine. ("Rasta music is militant to shake up Babylon," he whispers conspiratorially at one point. "I see even the Pope a Rasta number-one enemy. You know that?") Occasionally he dives into thick Jamaican patois. After 20 minutes, he signals the end of the interview by getting up and walking away. Peculiar behavior for a man who declares, "What's important is we get our message across."

YET, BLACK UHURU'S message — like the late Bob Marley's, a hardline Rasta manifesto of freedom from Babylon's oppression through love and unity — is getting across through the sheer force of their rhythm and conviction. Underground college radio and commercial Black-oriented stations alike are disseminating Black Uhuru not just to the growing white/collegiate reggae crowd but to America's mainstream Black audience. The Police and the Rolling Stones, booking Black Uhuru as opening act in arenas and stadiums, have further introduced them to white rock hordes.

"Those who want to listen, listen," Rose shrugs philosophically. "Those who choose not to, they are not forced to. Music is open. You can take it or leave it."

But Black Uhuru doesn't let go that easily. If the one-two punch of the Dunbar/Shakespeare rhythm section doesn't get you, Rose's hypnotic vocals will. (Follow the tortuous melodic turns on the title track of the new *Chill Out.*)

Simpson and Jones hardly play second and third banana, either. Simpson, a lean, bearded figure who dresses in layers of red and black leather and often hides behind pitch-black sunglasses, founded the group in the early '70s. His strident, uplifting harmonies are offset vibrantly by the American-born Jones' alto. In a music where women work as solo acts or anonymous backup singers, Puma Jones — diminutive yet vibrant, with a master's degree [in social work] from Columbia University — is Black Uhuru's wild card.

"Having a woman in the band," Rose notes, "I and I know this music needs one good sistren [sister]. She can bring certain things together. She is a lady, and we accept her. She brings something special to the song.

"That is what gives us the identity as Black Uhuru. We have a different sound. If you check our albums, it is a different type of music from what's going on around. People would say, 'It's rock' or 'It's soul.'"

What it *is* is uncompromising, militant and as angry in its despair as it can be loving in its hope. Contrast the opening blast of last year's *Red* — "Youth of Eglington," an unnerving portrait of ghettos awash in guns and blood — with the joyous erotic bounce of the succeeding "Sponji Reggae." Rose's hoarse wail has an ominous bite that suggests Uhuru even takes its fun seriously.

"I and I not a singer who sing of love," Rose declares with a glint of fire in his dark brown eyes. "I and I am more militant. That mean we don't force you to listen to our music. But when reality catch up on you, you will understand what's really going on.

"It's strictly liberation to us," he continues, working himself into an atypically intense passion. "Africa, I and I deal in. I say, the Chinaman wants China, the European wants Europe. The African wants Africa.

"That what is causing war and strife. You come in my yard and say you own this. No! What's yours is yours. What's mine is mine. You can visit my place, I can visit your place. No problem. But the people have to know themselves. And playing and listening to reggae, it can help."

MICHAEL ROSE'S musical upbringing suggests militants are made, not born. As a teenager, he worked the hotel lounges and tourist traps of Jamaica's north coast singing "all that stuff — dinner music, club music, American music, calypso. One has to listen to all music."

Thus, Black Uhuru's topical ferocity is laced with Motown harmonies and echoes of other American soul forms in the group's vocal blend. Listing his favorite singers, Rose checks off Sam Cooke, Jerry Butler, Smokey Robinson and even Johnny Mathis. But the only vocalist he cites as a direct influence is Jamaican roots crooner Dennis Brown, whose pop charm and velvet tenor represent the apex of reggae's commercial sub-genre, lover's rock. "When I first started, when I would play the talent shows and entertain tourists on the north coast," Rose explains with a hint of disdain for his naïveté, "I used to sing like Dennis Brown. Then I stopped."

By the time Rose joined Black Uhuru he had embraced Rastafarianism, the outlaw Jamaican religion which proclaims Haile Selassie, the late emperor of Ethiopia, as lord, marijuana as sacrament and return to the African homeland as salvation. Because the Jamaican media long refused to acknowledge reggae as anything more than the subversive mumblings of "herb" zombies and religious fanatics, Black Uhuru's early recordings made the rounds on traveling sound systems set up by enterprising DJs at parties or just in the streets. "General Penitentiary," "Love Crisis" and "Guess Who's Coming to Dinner" (the answer, of course: the symbolic Natty Dreadlocks) electrified ghetto and poor back-country audiences with their aggressive beat, cutting instrumentation and vocals and uncompromising Rasta pride.

UNFORTUNATELY, what success Uhuru enjoyed at the time was undercut by rampant thievery in the Jamaican record industry. The all-male Uhuru never saw any money from the only album they recorded (*Love Crisis* from 1977, recently released here as *Black Sounds of Freedom*). Fortune smiled, though, when Rose met Sly Dunbar. As Rose tells it, Dunbar was playing the same north coast clubs, hotels and recording sessions — no doubt with Shakespeare — when they met. Rose, who was already turning Rasta, offered the drummer some herb; Dunbar, much to Rose's surprise, declined. (Dunbar and Shakespeare, more business than Rasta, don't smoke at all.) Yet the two kept in touch. After Black Uhuru's debut album rip-off, Dunbar took some of the band's singles to a label for distribution.

"At this other record company, it was a one-man thing. Sly gave him some of our songs to distribute and he comes around for payment, but the man run away with the money. But," Rose insists, "we didn't get discouraged though. We keep working. The man run away with our money, but we didn't take it to heart."

As rhythm section producers and owners of the highly successful Taxi label, Dunbar and Shakespeare helped transform the new Uhuru — now including Jones — from a cult reggae sensation to a visible, militant force in Jamaican music. "That some genius works," Rose sighs with almost mystic admiration of the Uhuru/Sly-Robbie combination. "I and I bring in the songs, and Sly and Robbie find the chords to fit it." The description does little justice to the way Dunbar and Shakespeare underline Rose's smoldering lyrics. With guitars, synthesizers and dub studio tricks, they create an atmosphere clouded not just with the smoke of marijuana but of the emotional fires burning in the world's Trenchtowns.

BLACK UHURU APPEARS to be leading a new reggae wave (including black British bands like Steel Pulse and Aswad), but Rose emphatically denies that he covets the king-of-reggae crown worn by Bob Marley.

"The next Marley is Bob's son," he cracks, only half-kidding. "I know Bob is militant and a great singer. But I don't know Bob Marley the same way I sit here and talk to you. I know him from his works, works I see and works I feel. I don't know enough about him to say I take his place. I live my life and make my music. Seen? Leave to the public to say that. I and I don't think about what *happened*, but what can be *done*."

To see Black Uhuru live is to see Marley "works" in action. Jones swivels her body and waves her arms in a Salome-like dance, heightened by the flow of her rainbow robes and scarves. Simpson plays UltimaDread at stage left, doing a stiff martial shuffle at his mike. Rose takes off into high-stepping sprints, dreadlocks whiplashing around his head. The dramatic ritual dances, hard dub chop of the band and dark blend of voices have the same mesmeric effect as Marley's most expressive shows. And they work toward the same end.

Maybe that's why the Police and Rolling Stones chose Black Uhuru as an opening act. "You know what a Stones crowd is like," Rose grins. "They throw things if they don't like you. And they didn't throw nothing at us.

"You see, Black Uhuru is on a journey. Everyone must try to see what they can do for each other. Without unity, the people suffer. You get that? One has to be together. Black Uhuru bring people together."

And, Rose adds, before abruptly getting up from the table and strolling away, it will happen only with "more work. Our music works hard." ■

QUOTES OF THE DECADE

"There is quite a tradition in music, as well as other arts, of looking to other cultures for things to steal... The principle of theft — with respect —should be encouraged."
—PETER GABRIEL (1983) TP 81

"I see myself as a white European, but I'd like to restate the black values of the '60s."
—ANNIE LENNOX of EURYTHMICS (1983) TP 90

"I think working with Chic is probably one of the most radical steps we could take. Contemporary Black music is not considered safe by white audiences."
—CHRIS STEIN of BLONDIE (1981) TP 62

"I live a kind of normal life ... for a New Yorker."   —MICK JAGGER (1980) TP 54

To TP's way of thinking, 1977 has been a truly ace year for rock 'n' roll. In years gone by, the age-old tradition of compiling Top 10 lists has been a painful challenge; it was often impossible to find 10 singles or albums that had spent more than a few dubious moments on the turntable. This past year, for a change, has been good enough to make it tough to whittle our lists down to 10 (witness IR's top 12 LP choices). In any case, here they are: the particular preferences of the TP editorial staff, excluding confusion like "Anarchy in the UK" (actually released in December) and a few singles that qualify more as LP tracks than 7" wonders. So now, for your edification and entertainment, we are pleased to present (a little fanfare please) the

BEST OF SHOW 1977

IRA ROBBINS
ALBUMS
1 **The Clash**—*The Clash* (import)
2 **In Color/Cheap Trick**—*Cheap Trick*
3 **The Boomtown Rats**—*Boomtown Rats*
4 **IV Rattus Norvegicus/ No More Heroes**—*Stranglers*
5 **Vibrators**—*Vibrators* (import)
6 **New Wave Sampler** (Vertigo import)
7 **Animals**—*Pink Floyd*
8 **Get It**—*Dave Edmunds*
9 **Heroes**—*David Bowie*
10 **Rocket to Russia**—*Ramones*

SINGLES
1 "God Save the Queen"— *Sex Pistols* (import)
2 "Go Your Own Way"— *Fleetwood Mac*
3 "Sheena Is a Punk Rocker"— *Ramones*
4 "Your Generation"—*Generation X* (import)
5 "London Lady"/"Grip"— *Stranglers* (import)
6 "Remote Control"/"London's Burning"—*Clash* (import) "Complete Control"/"City of the Dead"—*Clash* (import)
7 "2.4.6.8 Motorway"— *Tom Robinson Band* (import)
8 "Lookin' After No. 1"— *Boomtown Rats* (import)
9 "Neat Neat Neat"—*Damned* (import)
10 "Jet Airliner"—*Steve Miller Band*
Honorable Mentions: Elvis Costello (**My Aim Is True**), the Kinks (**Sleepwalker**), Ramones ("Swallow My Pride"), Television ("Venus"), Sex Pistols ("Liar" and "Pretty Vacant"), Jam ("Away from the Numbers" and "In the City"), John Cale (**Animal Justice EP**), Hot Rods ("Do Anything You Wanna Do" and "Quit This Town"), Talking Heads ("Love Goes to Building on Fire"), Roger McGuinn and Tom Petty ("American Girl").
Thanks for Helping '77 swing: Nick Lowe, Horslips, Pete Townshend, Graham Parker, Queen, Blondie, Jackson Browne, Motors, Jon Richman and Little Bob Story.

JIM GREEN
ALBUMS
1 **My Aim Is True**—*Elvis Costello*
2 **In Color**—*Cheap Trick*
3 **Rough Mix**—*Pete Townshend and Ronnie Lane*
4 **Marquee Moon**—*Television*
5 **Sleepwalker**—*The Kinks*
6 **Get It**—*Dave Edmunds*
7 **Twilley Don't Mind**— *The Dwight Twilley Band*
8 **Cheap Trick**—*Cheap Trick*
9 **Ramones Leave Home**—*Ramones*
10 **Blondie**—*Blondie*

SINGLES
1 "God Save the Queen"—*Sex Pistols* (import)
2 "Father Christmas"—*The Kinks*
3 "2.4.6.8 Motorway"— *Tom Robinson Band* (import)
4 "Summer Sun"—*Chris Stamey*
5 "Holidays in the Sun"—*Sex Pistols* (import)
6 "Hold Back the Night"— *Graham Parker & the Rumour*
7 "Down on the Boulevard" (EP)— *The Pop!*
8 "Mongoloid"—*Devo*
9 "Do Anything You Wanna Do"— *Eddie & the Hot Rods*
10. "Lookin' After No. 1"— *Boomtown Rats* (import)
Honorable Mentions: Too many to name 'em all. Tops include (for LPs) Robert Gordon with Link Wray, Mink DeVille, Frankie Miller, the Clash, Ramones (**Rocket to Russia**), Kiss (**Alive II**), Split Enz (**Mental Notes**), Sherbet (**Magazine**), Deaf School and **Bionic Gold**. Singles include Split Enz ("Another Great Divide"), Kiss ("Calling Dr. Love"), Queen ("Long Away"), Generation X ("Your Generation"), Gentle Giant ("Turning Around"), Peter Gabriel ("Solsbury Hill") and *every* Ramones single. Album that should've been Top 10 (but wasn't): Dictators' **Manifest**

Destiny. Top 10 album that never was (but might be next year): The album the Planets should have been signed to record. Special mention to Stiff Records for thumbing its nose at the vagaries of the Biz, and the Residents for thumbing their noses at the vagaries of the music.

DAVE SCHULPS
ALBUMS
1 **My Aim Is True**—*Elvis Costello*
2 **In Color**—*Cheap Trick*
3 **Boomtown Rats**—*Boomtown Rats*
4 **The Clash**—*The Clash* (import)
5 **Sleepwalker**—*The Kinks*
6 **Marquee Moon**—*Television*
7 **Rough Mix**—*Pete Townshend and Ronnie Lane*
8 **Super Active Wizzo**—*Roy Wood's Wizzo Band* (import)
9 **This Is the Modern World**— *The Jam* (import)
10 **Rocket to Russia**—*Ramones*
SINGLES
1 "God Save the Queen"— *Sex Pistols* (import)
2 "Pretty Vacant"—*Sex Pistols* (import)
3 "Sheena Is a Punk Rocker"—*Ramones*
4 "Summer Sun"—*Chris Stamey*
5 "2.4.6.8 Motorway"— *Tom Robinson Band* (import)
6 "Complete Control"—*The Clash* (import)
7 "Gary Gilmore's Eyes"— *The Adverts* (import)
8 "Whole Wide World"— *Wreckless Eric* (import)
9 "Lookin' After No. 1— *Boomtown Rats* (import)
10 "Hold Back the Night"— *Graham Parker & the Rumour*
Honorable Mentions: LPs: Sex Pistols, Dictators, Blondie, Dave Edmunds, Graham Parker, Rubinoos, **Chiswick Chartbusters**, first Cheap Trick and Bowie. Singles: The Pop! ("Down on the Boulevard"), Generation X ("Your Generation"). Unexpected pleasure of the year: Paice, Ashton and Lord's **Malice in Wonderland**. Most overrated group: Talking Heads.

From *Trouser Press* February 1978

ROOTS OF PUNK

66

I do business like a barbarian. My word is gold and I split everything with everybody. The best way to lick rock and roll is to be a savage.

99

—IGGY POP

Straddling the historical fence, the first two pieces in this section — about artists widely viewed as pioneers of the music and attitude that enabled punk to happen — were written well after their stylistic effects had been felt. The third concerns a reluctant leading light of the UK movement that, in its selection of venues and rejection of pretense, got things ready for a new generation of more aggressive bands.

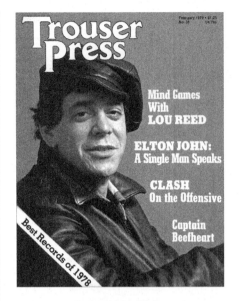

To illustrate this article, we commissioned a punk artist who called himself Banger to do a collage. We didn't really know him; it was his first and only contribution to the magazine. But Henry "Banger" Benvenuti made headlines later that year when he walked into the offices of the Soho Weekly News and chopped off two of his fingers. The Washington Post called him "an artist with a message: He was tired of the runaround." The paper quoted staffer Donna Frost: "Nobody screamed. He didn't make a sound. You can still see where the blade cut into the counter. There wasn't much blood, just a few drops. He left behind a rat trap with a dollar bill in it, his briefcase and his hatchet. He walked out of here so calmly that I thought it was a piece of theater — until I saw his fingers lying on the floor."

TRANSACTIONAL ANALYSIS WITH LOU REED

TP 36, FEBRUARY 1979

By Scott Isler

Imagine the burden of being Lou Reed. A certifiable (if erratic) rock genius since at least 1966, Reed should be a dignified, respected BOF by now. Sadly, this is not the case. Aside from some polite intelligentsia, the Lou Reed fan (as evidenced on his *Live: Take No Prisoners*) is a slobbering moron who probably enjoys watching his hero tie up on stage; this fan may even have been with Lou all the way since "Walk on the Wild Side." The less sympathetic public simply dismisses him as a backfired joke. This is how we treat artists in America?

The real shame is that, despite this mis- and under-appreciation, Reed has been on a winning streak lately. Future generations will probably rank the savage *Street Hassle* on a creative par with the first Velvet Underground album; it sold about as well, too. Next was the double live *Take No Prisoners*, a breakthrough both in its sound — Reed is captivated by Manfred Schunke's binaural stereo process — and its personal revelation of Lou as bitter comedian. He himself has stated, "This is as close to Lou Reed as you're probably going to get." Count your blessings.

FORMER VELVET Undergrounder Doug Yule was reassuring. "There's a great deal of normalcy about Lou Reed," he had counseled prior to the interview. "His biggest problem with reporters is when he's feeling paranoid."

Your Reporter felt confident. Hadn't he been following Reed since early 1967, when "Heroin" amazed him with an expressive power then unknown in rock? Didn't he possess a Lou Reed guitar pick from the 1970 Velvet Underground gigs at Max's? A legendary terror at interviews, Reed had been portrayed more than once as the classic punk-schmuck. But who knew the other side, when Lou had opened up, only to be rewarded by a journalistic boot in the back? Your Reporter was sympathetic; he understood. This time would be different.

Unfortunately, one factor not reckoned with

was Lou himself. He seemed calm enough, seated behind a desk at Arista Records' New York offices like a mischievous child visiting his father at work. Customary Lou Reed attire included a custom-made black leather cap, black leather jacket over grey plaid lumberjack shirt, tight St. Tropez jeans over black boots and (thankfully) no shades. Despite puffiness and discoloring under the eyes, there is still a youthful (or maybe impish) quality to his thin face topped by tousled hair. Then he starts to talk.

In fact, he takes the initiative, carefully enquiring about his interviewer's name, sexual preference and religion. This last item — more specifically: "Are you Jewish?" — is scrupulously traced through a couple of generations to Reed's satisfaction (his antisemitic remarks always make good copy). Isn't Lou Jewish himself? "Of course. Aren't all the best people?"

The voice is the familiar Reedian monotone, pitched a little above a whisper. Combined with a weary expression and a habit of rolling his eyes up into his head and shutting his lids upon completing a sentence, Lou succeeds famously at giving the impression he would rather be anywhere than here.

After a little more probing (how much rent Your Reporter pays, for example), Reed suffers himself to be interviewed. Somehow, though, the session isn't going quite the way Your Reporter envisioned. When he's not injecting random comments ("Reginald Dwight ... sucks hair"; "Best of luck to the dead worms") or interrupting questions ("I want to talk to you ... about gay rights," he announces at one point, then drops the subject), Reed provides the briefest of answers — or non-answers. Asked about "I Wanna Be Black" — the song was a few years old before finally turning up on *Street Hassle* — he replies, "It was transmogrified — that's a big word that means Catholicism."

"You want to know the real Lou Reed? Turn around. Now bend over." Perhaps it's all insecurity over a two-day-old haircut. How would Lou describe himself? "Medium height, dark, sexy, emotionally retarded." He seems to take delight in brandishing the cigar-shaped tape recorder

microphone in front of his mouth and stating, "Say the magic woid: the duck comes down and gives you a hundred dollars." (He does this more than once.) The humor is indeed Groucho Marx from the other side of a black hole.

All the while Lou is keeping up a regular stream of verbal abuse: "I know your type: a typical downtrodden Jew ... A make-believe hippie ... This is the worst nightmare. I've dreamed of this on the subway ... If you weren't a journalist, you'd never be invited to anything hip." The only dent anything has made on him has been a suggestion that *Take No Prisoners*, more than previous albums, exposes Reed's personality. "*What* personality?!" he growls, in a rare leap up from his barely audible speech level.

In view of this failure to communicate, Your Reporter takes a different tack: fighting fire with fire. Maybe this is how Lou likes to be dealt with. The plan fails quickly as Reed turns defensive ("I'll come on any way I want. You're here to be annoyed," he charges); subtle hints at negotiation are ignored and the interview is brusquely declared over by Lou.

At this point Reed is delivered to the photographer (who has been quietly apoplectic during the preceding match). Your Reporter steps outside with an Arista publicity honcho; he tries to explain Reed's method, which essentially boils down to "Lou is ... just Lou."

What Your Reporter doesn't know is that, immediately upon my leaving the room, Reed has turned into Mr. Nice Guy. "I'm not normally that much of a horror," he confides to photographer Mitch Kearney. "I'm amazingly easy to get along with." He expounds upon the inherent moral superiority of photographers over writers ("They don't have any pride"), runs through his repertory of off-color jokes and is indeed charming in a withdrawn manner. After the picture-taking's over, Reed greets Your Reporter with a terse "C'mon, let's talk," and the interview begins in earnest.

ANYONE WHO'S LISTENED knows that *Take No Prisoners* alone justifies the spate of exploitative double-live rock albums that was 1978's curse. The album captures small-club atmosphere with astonishing accuracy and features Reed extensively reworking his material, sometimes (as on the 17-minute "Walk on the Wild Side") junking songs entirely for bitingly funny monologues.

"I wanted to have a live album that was something *I* would have liked. There'd been previous live albums, but I hadn't liked them. I thought I was the minority stockholder."

The new album's title has been subject to interpretation. "When we were in Montreal, before we went on, somebody out in the audience was yelling, 'Take no prisoners, Lou, take no prisoners!' Then the guy would just bash his head against the table. 'Lou Reed, take no prisoners!' — *smack!* I thought the phrase was great. It couldn't have been more appropriate: Don't take us prisoners; beat us to death. Shoot us. Maim us. Kill us. But don't settle for less. Go all the way! That's what I took it to mean."

More than one reviewer has suggested *Prisoners* is more a comedy than a music album.

"It *is* a comedy album: Lou Reed talks and talks and talks. Lou Reed, songwriter, is dried up — ran out of inspiration."

Could he be serious? Lou has been collaborating with Nils Lofgren lately. Post-photo session, Reed still drones quietly but the weariness is now tinged with a martyr's patience; he even mumbles "excuse me" after clearing his throat.

Besides *Take No Prisoners*, most of *Street Hassle* was recorded live — in Germany. "They didn't understand a word of English — like most of my audience. They're fucked up, assholes. What difference does it make? Can they count from one to 107?

"What must be remembered is Lou Reed is at least as smart and hip as you are." Lou is addressing the world as well as Your Reporter; he likes referring to himself in the third person. "At least. Minimal. I mean, that; I really do. I don't think the people who listen to rock and roll for a minute think that the guy who's making music or singing is as hip as they are. One of the reasons I put out *Take No Prisoners* is to let 'em know I'm at least as hip as you are — and maybe just a little bit more." Your Reporter tries to remember Doug Yule's comments about paranoia.

The technical success of *Take No Prisoners* rests with binaural stereo, whereby microphones modeled after human heads simulate human hearing response; playback (especially over headphones) yields a startlingly lifelike sound. Reed first used the process on *Street Hassle*; who else has used it?

"One or two people but they don't announce it. They don't want to get the flak their mother gets. Your mother has taken all kinds of horrible abuse for this." He pauses. "You know who your mother is, don't you?"

Reed's interest in sound extends even to his helping master his records; the new live album uses dynamics as virtually no other rock LP does. Musician Reed has been using a guitar built to his own specifications. It's some distance from the Velvet Underground days of Gretsch guitars and Vox amplifiers. "We didn't know better."

Although he likes '50s doo-wop/rock and roll, Reed has no room for personal nostalgia. "Are you gonna throw my past up at me?" he asks rhetorically in another rare outburst. "You can't confront me with me! I'll say he was well-meaning but miserably off base." These days he listens to Richard Pryor and disco: Exile, Candi Staton, Grace Jones. No rock? "No." It has nothing to say to you? "No."

His own music swings back and forth between the accessible *Coney Island Baby* variety ("I like a lot of those commercial sappy-sounding things. I like trash...") and a more anarchic avant-gardism (*Street Hassle*, the dreaded *Metal Machine Music*). The day after the interview, Lou was off to Germany to begin production on his next album, a self-described guitar symphony. "Everybody's been instructed to think symphonic; delusions of grandeur." Lest anyone scent a son of *Metal Machine Music*, Lou reassures that it's all songs.

Although he now records in Germany — Schunke's studio is in Wilster — Reed is unswervingly loyal to New York City. "I can't imagine spending the bulk of your time anyplace else. Packing, customs, flying — I don't like that. I try to get fucked up before I go on a plane." He sees no virtue in travel, no broadening of experience. "A guy with a 12-inch cock — that's a new experience. Other than that..." The voice trails off.

Despite his urban creature image, word leaks out that Lou has just bought a getaway retreat in rural Blairstown, New Jersey. As he enthuses about fishing and shooting basketball hoops, a more rounded picture of Lou Reed emerges.

The interview winds down. "Anger is something that shouldn't be wasted," Lou observes in a philosophical moment. "Ah! A bon mot! It should be used for what? Garbage delivery, restyling a haircut, shooting a paramecium. How do you shoot a paramecium? Carefully." One hesitates to interrupt this tortuous train of thought, even when Reed next recites a textbook definition of "paramecium." He is sharp — as a razor blade.

He asks to see Your Reporter's notes ("I want to make sure we covered everything") and the meeting is over. Next is a phone interview to Los Angeles. The connection is horrible, but Lou characteristically keeps his voice at minimal level.

This, then, is Lou Reed holding forth from behind a desk at Arista Records: addressing his friends there as "faggots," inviting them to "come in and be abused; we need some Lou Reed humor." Your Reporter feels he has learned something about human behavior, but he's not sure what. After a parting (firm) handshake, he asks Lou's forgiveness for any untoward aggression during the interview's opening rounds.

"Sure," Reed replies, meaninglessly, and walks out. ■

QUOTES OF THE DECADE

"I find it very tiresome to be famous."
—NICO (1979) TP 40

"The best way you can prove responsibility for what you do is to go out and live it and not get killed doing it."
—IGGY POP (1980) TP 47

"If people expect me to do any one thing, fuck 'em."
—GRAHAM PARKER (1978) TP 25

IGGY POP: IT'S A LONG WAY BACK TO GERMANY

TP 47, FEBRUARY 1980

By Scott Isler

Of course you like rock. But chances are you haven't bled for it, starved for it, suffered literal slings and arrows (or at least beer bottles) defending your musical taste against an outraged populace. Jim Osterberg has.

Perhaps his professional alias, Iggy Pop, is more familiar. Ten years ago, both names were equally obscure addenda to the rock register; today, at 32, Jim/Iggy's place in history is assured. He has reaped the fame of those so out of tune with the cultural mainstream that they anticipate future trends — the prophets without honor. Osterberg will never be a superstar, selling out arenas or releasing triple-platinum albums. He merely has the satisfaction of knowing that the music and attitudes with which he provoked early-'70s audiences became the blueprint for rock's new wave several years later. And one more achievement: he has survived.

THE PASSION OF IGGY is one of the great rock legends. Our hero grew up in Ypsilanti, Michigan, a suburb of Ann Arbor; his parents lived in a trailer park. The teen-aged Osterberg took up drums, performing with local mid-'60s bands like the Iguanas (hence his sobriquet) and the Prime Movers. The former cut an amateur single, recently bootlegged (to Osterberg's wonder but not acute embarrassment). The drummer wasn't singing yet, though. In late 1966, Osterberg went to Chicago; he stayed through the spring of 1967, playing with bluesmen like J.B. Hutto and Walter "Shakey" Horton. When he returned to Detroit, he formed the Stooges.

The Stooges (sometimes the Psychedelic Stooges — everything was psychedelic in those days) comprised Osterberg — now Iggy Stooge — on vocals and school chums Ron Asheton (guitar), Dave Alexander (bass) and Scott Asheton (drums); Iggy later claimed he practically taught them how to play their instruments. At a time when bands were trying to prove how "serious" and respectable rock could be, the Stooges blasted out of a middle-American void like Tasadays [*a tiny indigenous population resident in the Philippines*] dropped into a Rand think tank. Their musical philosophy consisted of getting ripped on every ingestible substance at hand, then going on stage and churning out a couple of riffs for 30 minutes while Iggy did his inimitable thing — of which singing was only incidental.

Whatever it was Elvis Presley started, Iggy Pop finished. His cardinal sin was to violate the dividing line between artist and audience. Iggy clambered into his crowds, demanding involvement; confrontation replaced stimulation. Perhaps the original Stooges' finest hour came during a 1970 broadcast of a Cincinnati rock festival. In between Traffic, Grand Funk Railroad and pre-Vegas Alice Cooper, Iggy walked on outstretched palms, smeared his chest with peanut butter (shirts are too confining; he often dispenses with pants) and flung himself into spectators. Announcer Jack Linkletter provided running sports commentary.

The Stooges were great theater but obviously too raw for mass consumption. They released two LPs on Elektra to general indifference; by 1971, Iggy was into heroin and the group disbanded.

IT PAYS TO have friends, and Iggy had an influential fan in David Bowie. Fresh from salvaging Mott the Hoople's career, Bowie may have hoped

to do likewise for the Stooges. Iggy had cleaned himself up by 1972; a year later he was a MainMan artiste (just like Ziggy Stardust), had reformed the Stooges and released a new album for Columbia.

In its combination of amphetamine-driven music and existential lyrics, *Raw Power* predicted the new wave yet to come. New Stooge James Williamson's crackling lead guitar runs complemented Iggy's manic intensity; songs like "Search and Destroy" and the title cut spoke for a generation who didn't know what they wanted but knew how to get it. Despite Bowie's imprimatur on the back cover, the album barely crept into the Top 200. (Even the first Stooges LP almost reached number-100.) Iggy later excoriated Bowie for his part in mixing down the tapes, but it's doubtful that sound alone kept *Raw Power* from topping the charts. "Death Trip" and "Your Pretty Face Is Going to Hell" were just not what most people would admit identification with.

The Stooges were back on the road, and Iggy was back on a crash course with disaster. Having split from MainMan, he was trying to manage the band himself; downs provided escape. At a New Year's Eve concert in New York, Iggy left the stage only when he stumbled off it. He also sang lying down on his stomach and announced songs as upcoming after he'd finished singing them. In 1975, after a period of bumming around Los Angeles, he committed himself to a hospital to shake his barbiturate addiction. Bowie made a visitation; after his release, a newly renovated Iggy accompanied the Thin White Duke on 1976's *Station to Station* tour and then (with a little help from his friend) wangled an RCA record contract.

This third coming of Iggy Pop was undoubtedly the most triumphant. The new wave was now in full flower, and Iggy was hailed as its spiritual forefather. Three RCA LPs (*The Idiot, Lust for Life* and *TV Eye Live*) didn't sell appreciably better than earlier recordings, but Iggy Pop concerts (there were no Stooges now, only backing bands) drew rapturous young audiences paying tribute — a far cry from the abusive crowds of yore.

Now with Arista, Iggy's music has matured from moronic, one-chord Stooges days without losing its roots in jackhammer rock. The freak-show attraction has become an artist.

SO MUCH FOR THE LEGEND. What about the individual?

The first thing that usually strikes people who meet Osterberg is how small he is (5'7"); it's testimony to his aggressive onstage dynamism. The next surprise is his articulateness. As opposed to the monosyllabic Iggy of stage and disc, Jim Osterberg is a quite fluent and funny conversationalist. (His father teaches high school English.)

The disparity between Jim Osterberg and Iggy Pop has been commented on by more than one rock scribe. The temptation is to construct a Jekyll-Hyde theory around nice Jim (who even wears glasses) and monstrous Iggy. Osterberg's occasional moodiness no doubt encourages such ideas, but truth is never that simple.

Iggy is very much a conscious creation, the "world's forgotten boy" (of "Search and Destroy") who slashes himself with broken glass and throws up on stage — the self-described "king of failures." Osterberg strives to give the impression of always being in control, knowing exactly what's going down. He is brash and contradicts himself fearlessly.

I encounter Osterberg horsing around with manager Peter Davies on a landing at New York's Iroquois Hotel. He is wearing black cords, sneakers and argyle socks; a white T-shirt with rolled-up sleeves exposes brawny arms. (Iggy's physique has varied widely in the past from scrawny punk to muscular Adonis.)

Seated inside his hotel room, Osterberg plays monologist with a Midwest twang, entertaining and expansive. He seems more interested in hearing himself talk than getting feedback from his interviewer, possibly the result of lunchtime sake at a Japanese restaurant. The rubbery, animated face often breaks into the smile on the cover of *Lust for Life*. Osterberg is nothing if not at ease, occasionally smoking, at one point continuing a stream of conversation while he gets up and strolls out of sight into the bathroom. A real pro.

As is to be expected, Osterberg is excited about the band he is currently touring with. Allowing for hype, though, this is a new wave All-Star team: Brian James (ex-Damned, now with the Brains) and Ivan Kral (Patti Smith Group) on guitars, Glen Matlock (ex-Sex Pistols and Rich Kids) on bass and Klaus Kruger on drums. Osterberg runs them down: He picked James by "looking for a guitar player so good you couldn't hear him." Kral, "from Czechoslovakia, plays 'boy by the lake' music, the balalaika parts." Kruger, who had drummed previously with Tangerine Dream, "taught me about American music. He's also the first German that would speak to me" after Ig relocated to Berlin three years ago.

This voluntary exile is at the core of Osterberg's self-image. Analysts must have a field day speculating why Jim/Iggy lives in a divided city. Asking why Osterberg prefers Berlin to the U.S. brings an abrupt halt to his volubility.

"It's not what I prefer," he resumes, speaking more slowly. "It makes sense for me. I've got nothing against the U.S., outside of California, which I wish somebody would obliterate quickly. But here there's no place for me — a person who's been tromped on by the fucking cretins of this country for so long — except professionally. There's a place for me there. On the block where I live, I go downstairs, I have little cakes and coffee in the morning, I like black bread — I don't like white bread, I've always liked black bread."

His voice rises ominously. "You can check back ten years; I was talking about black bread. I like strong bread, I don't like weak bread. I like strong people, people who come straight to the point, not this wishy-washy shit I encounter here. I could get very vehement, but I'm not gonna put down this country because I believe in it. But there they love me; here they're just out to grab, see what they can suck off rock and roll artist number 999."

The Nietzschean outburst having passed, Osterberg recounts the facts behind his final RCA album — the amazingly shoddy *TV Eye Live* — and his lacuna before turning up a year later on Arista.

"I made *TV Eye Live* because I was short a few bob and wanted to make as much money in as short a time as possible — bleed the record company like they bled me. My contract called for an enormous budget for each album. I made *TV Eye Live* for about $2,500; it was not very much money. I said, here, give me the rest before I hand you the tape; then I said, here's your tape, fuck off! If you want to blame anybody for that album, blame me. I think it's justified. The cover's lovely. It was an honest portrayal of myself on stage at that time. That's exactly what I sounded like. I should know because I recorded it on a machine just like this" — he points to a nearby portable radio/cassette recorder with a broken glass dial covering — "and those were the good tracks. Four other tracks were recorded professionally; I didn't like those.

"I was at the end of my rope with RCA. I bought my way out with the money I got from the live album. I also brought Fred Sonic Smith's Rendezvous Band to Europe. At that time, my credibility had sunk to an all-time low there. People had gotten sick of me flouting my music with these fucking rhinestone cowboys from the West Coast [*apparently a reference to Osterberg's band with Tony and Hunt Sales*]. I wanted to show people what real Detroit rock was about. I lost a ton of money on their tour, and it was glorious; I regained my credibility, and it turned out to be a very smart business move.

"The next thing I did was sit home in Berlin, eat beans, hock my rugs [recovered later] and play guitar 18 hours a day — till my fingers bled. I learned to write songs so I'd never have to depend on some shitty guitar player whom I thought wasn't as talented as me anyway. I don't play on stage 'cause I'm too good a lead singer, but I'm excellent when I play by myself. I'd get up in the morning, buy German diet pills and chug 'em, and play all morning pretending I was Keith Richards. Then I'd go to a local winemaker, get drunk, come back home and practice all over again. Over and over and over for six months. It made me feel really good."

These new songs became last year's *New Values*. Manager Davies (lured away from RCA: "he was the only one there who didn't have his head up his asshole") scouted around London for an attractive record deal. Arista filled the bill; its

American division picked up the album a few months after its English release.

As is evident from his live LP anecdote, ethics is a subject close to Osterberg's heart. On his new album, there's even "a lovely song ["Play It Safe," written with Bowie] about my desires for criminality, to deal with the world in an organized criminal manner. That's as good as anybody deserves" — he chuckles — "that I've ever met. My motto is cheat others before they cheat you. I try very hard to overcome certain ideals I was taught in my youth. I don't see any percentage in playing straight with people 'cause they'll just walk all over you anyway. Crime implies victims, and I'd much rather be on the top than the bottom." Much as he hates the subject, Osterberg says he talks about it because a couple of his songs refer to it. "That's only fair!"

His bitterness doesn't seem directed at the world in general so much as the music industry in particular. "I'm not very thrilled about this side of the business." He adopts a macho basso: "'Hi, I'm Iron Man. I'm gonna lay some really green shit on ya, put it in a heavy metal package and sell it up your asshole.'" Besides amateur bootleggers, Osterberg has to live with legitimate but unauthorized LPs like *Metallic KO* (a late Stooges concert) and *Kill City* (a scrapped project from his down-and-out days). The latter in particular is "just an outrage; I'm ashamed it's out with my name on it."

OSTERBERG ON OSTERBERG is probably most revealing — in both direct admissions and mutually exclusive statements. He admits his highly theatrical style is derived from Jim Morrison, but also names as formative influences the Rolling Stones, John Coltrane, Howlin' Wolf, Sun Ra and "all the rockabillies from whom I borrowed song structure: Carl Perkins, Dale Hawkins, Jerry Lee Lewis. After that I don't think I had another influence until Bryan Ferry, from whom I borrowed my *Idiot* haircut. It's nice to have a contemporary influence, especially one so tacky.

"The beauty of my songs, of course, is that they're so simple. You can play my songs on a Jew's harp, an autoharp, a synthesizer, a sitar —

or you could play them on a symphony orchestra because they're such good music.

"I don't have an idea in hell who might enjoy what I do. I just make my music; my fun is to see who might like it. I'm not so interested in acceptance. All I want out of music is: can I eat, can I have constant activity, can I learn, can I have a challenge? I guess my popularity is due to my energy — certainly not the content of what I do. It's the heat, the warmth. As opposed to light without heat, this is probably heat without light.

"I think I can be really good someday and I'm nowhere near it. I'm just getting decent. I want to play guitar better, to write nice songs everybody can sing and understand. I want to live up to the responsibility of my songs. The best way you can prove responsibility for what you do is to go out and live it and not get killed doing it. Then people will know it's an honest expression.

"You get jerks like the New York Dolls; they try to live what they do, and they last about 12 minutes. I've managed to last 12 years already and I don't look so bad for my age, as I well know. I make sure I can back anything up with action. I try to give people a little excitement, some sex in their lives, and someone to question — someone to say no when they're sure yes.

"In the past, my music has put forth propositions which were totally indefensible. When I tried to live them I would utterly fail. That meant my music was wrong. My lyrics are now more responsible."

Faced with this intense self-scrutiny, one hardly knows whether Osterberg is letting it all hang out — from all viewpoints — or is perpetrating another hustle. Nerviness alternates with self-deflating humility; referring to the abrasive crowd-baiter on *Metallic KO*, he comments, "I listen to that guy and it's like, 'Do I know him?' You've gotta laugh at anybody who'd say, 'I am the greatest.'"

Between talk of smart business moves and percentages, chinks in the fortification let light through.

"One of the thrilling things about being a solo performer — not tied to a group — is that you can exchange roles between management, peo-ple, record companies, bands, girlfriends, fire escapes, catastrophes and triumphs. Turn into anything — like alchemy — at will. You're still in the same test tube but you're like a little piece of horseradish in mercury. You're a floating unit. My thrill in life is to get a chance to work with that guy you always used to meet but his band wouldn't talk to your band." His voice takes on a wistful breathlessness. "You always wanted to talk to him but little details like who's screwing who used to get in the way."

What is this man — who once claimed as a major achievement that he helped destroy the '60s — proudest of? Osterberg thinks for a bit and replies, "My mother and father."

"We're very proud of Jim," Louella Osterberg replies in kind. "We get along very well. We're just a small, very close-knit family." The Osterbergs have indeed always stood behind their only child, including those periods when he was battling drugs (which he now claims he's "not too thrilled with anymore"). "We golf together whenever we can; we go to his shows when he's in the area. We call him Iggy only jokingly."

Osterberg also dotes on his ten-year-old son, Eric, in the mother's custody. His own mother isn't disturbed by the variance between Osterberg's image and personal statements: "That's show biz, I guess."

New Values indicated a shift in personae; the album is emblazoned "A James Osterberg Production." Will there ever be an Osterberg LP — his name on the front cover?

"No, no," he protests. "I think Iggy is fucking important — so important that if you call Iggy's name across a room people still wince. Girls go, 'Ooh, what kind of name is that?' Anything as good as that deserves a place, and I'll stick to it. I really like Iggy and I'm gonna keep him right where he belongs. Jim Osterberg can make albums — I make 'em but I wouldn't want to" — an internal struggle is taking place — "no, I'm Iggy Pop, man, I'm not Jim Osterberg, I'm Iggy Pop, and I'm proud of it." The voice has become sullen, slurring over words. It's true! Jim Osterberg is Iggy Pop! "I don't want to be like everybody else." ∎

The music world, at least the pieces of it that we chose to cover, was going every which way in 1976. This very down-to-earth article was inside an issue with Queen ("Superband Analyzed"), who played Hyde Park that fall, on the cover. TP 16 also contained interviews with Kevin Ayers, Peter Bardens of Camel and Steve Hillage of Gong, three men who would never reach such mass acceptance, along with profiles of the Finnish group Wigwam and a young New York band called Blondie.

The issue before this had a cover story (two, actually) on Dr. Feelgood, whose frantic R&B roots rock provided a crucial stylistic bridge to the future and became the inspirational table-setter for British punk.

GRAHAM PARKER: DON'T CALL IT PUB ROCK!

TP 16, OCTOBER/NOVEMBER 1976

By Dave Schulps

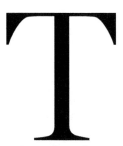

They'll tell you themselves: for a rock band, they look pretty ridiculous — like parts of the wrong jigsaw puzzle stuck together.

For a start, there's Graham Parker: songwriter, lead singer, sometimes guitarist and bandleader. From the publicity shots and album cover he looks a bit menacing, but meet him and he's short, small, frail-looking and a bit nervous and fidgety. But you can't blame him, really; a year ago he was pumping gas in Surrey, today he's touring America as the front man for some of London's most respected musicians. They call themselves the Rumour.

Onstage, though, Parker totally transcends the somewhat shy figure whom we interviewed. It's as if some Dr. Frankenstein were lurking somewhere in the wings to pull a switch marked "electricity." Graham Parker comes alive. The nervousness is transformed into stage energy, the quiet into coolness.

Then there's Martin Belmont. Martin is tall. Standing alongside Parker, he looks positively awesome. The contrast is amusing: Mutt and Jeff. A year and a half ago Martin was playing guitar in Ducks Deluxe; today, he adds fuel to Parker's fire, contributing both burning lead guitar and searing rhythms to Parker's gut-wrenching, soulful singing. He moves about the stage mouthing all the words to the songs, occasionally stepping up to his microphone to help out with a backing vocal.

You sense commitment in Martin. He's enjoying what he's doing and, dammit, he wants you to feel the way he does. "Thank you for dancing," he tells the customers at the Bottom Line. "If you're not too tired, you can dance to this one, too." Martin is being sarcastic. He doesn't realize that the audience is made up mainly of record company people and journalists. Dancing is verboten. If they like you, they will applaud loudly at the end of the set. I wonder if they all caught the sarcasm. Probably not.

Brinsley Schwarz plays guitar. And organ. And saxophone. Brinsley used to have a band called (no points for guessing) Brinsley Schwarz. A lot of people loved and respected Brinsley Schwarz. Not enough, however, to keep them together. About a year and a half ago (weird how everything seems to begin at about the same time), they broke up after six years, six wonderful albums and one "Greatest Hits" (sic) treasury.

Brinsley Schwarz were the first well-known British band to associate themselves with the pub rock movement of the early '70s. Because of this, Brinsley became known as "Mr. Pub Rock." This bothers him no end. In this band of extremes, Brinsley is Mr. Normal. He concentrates on his instrument and exudes a quiet flashiness. He looks neat but doesn't move around too much. He lets his fingers do the walking. Chalk one up for the wonders of amplified guitar.

Bob Andrews was another Brinsley. He is the Rumour's fair-haired boy (blond), but he seems to be losing some of this valuable commodity. Martin describes him jokingly as "blobbish." This isn't because he's fat, but because the rest of the band are so godawfully thin. He's equally at home on piano or organ, and, as if to prove it, he constantly switches instruments during the course of a song. It's not uncommon to see Bob finishing an organ lick with his left hand while getting ready to come in on piano with his right, his body situated somewhere between the two keyboards until the organ part ends and he can slip quietly onto the piano bench and commence two-handed boogie-woogie. His are the most prominent vocal harmonies behind Parker.

Bassist Andrew Bodnar and drummer Stephen Goulding are a rhythm section that sticks together. The least-known members of the band for their prior musical excursions, they both played with a band called Bontemps Roulez which did not survive long enough to immortalize itself on vinyl. Andrew is tall and thin and would look tremendous standing next to Parker if he weren't also standing next to Belmont.

"Stephen," says Brinsley, "is a mod. He looks like a failed RAF pilot. Very, very English." Like the RAF, Stephen supplies the heavy firepower to sustain the efforts of the troops. His "semi crew-cut" is indeed a throwback to the "mod" days of the mid-'60s. Like most drummers, he's a bit of a loon.

This unlikely looking band has put together one of the year's best albums. Those who haven't heard it yet should do so soon, because *Howlin Wind* gives a good picture of where this talented bunch are coming from — and where they may be headed in the future. It's a blend of Parker's own songwriting and influences with some stylings that fans of the Brinsleys or Ducks won't be totally unfamiliar with. For instance, "White Honey" could easily be the Brinsleys were it not for Parker's uncharacteristic lyrics; "Soul Shoes" could be the Ducks in their most Stonesish moments.

Most of the other songs lie somewhere in between and tell us a great deal about Parker's musical background. There are touches of Van Morrison (especially on "Gypsy Blood" when he sings the word "caravan"), the Stones, Dylan ("You've Got to Be Kidding" is, both in sentiment and overall feel, a reworking of the "Positively 4th Street" theme), the Band, Little Feat, Eddie Cochran, Bob Marley, Allen Toussaint and Bruce Springsteen, but what emerges is in every way a statement by Graham Parker and the Rumour.

Onstage, Parker's debt to '60s soul music is also brought out by the band's rendition of the Supremes' "You Can't Hurry Love," Aretha Franklin's "Chain of Fools" and the Trammps' "Hold Back the Night."

By and large, the influences are almost all American, yet coming back at us through these British musicians, they somehow are given a renewed life and power and a totally distinct style. This idea seems to be one of the main forces behind most of the bands that have become connected in one way or another with the pub rock movement. Among the best-known bands to have regularly played pub rock gigs in London were the aforementioned Brinsley Schwarz and Ducks Deluxe, as well as Graham Parker and the Rumour, who began on the pub circuit last year, but have since graduated to bigger and better bookings.

The problem with pub rock is that no one

seems to be able to pin down exactly what it is, or even if such a thing exists at all; least of all Americans who have grown accustomed to reading about it but have little or no firsthand experience with either the pubs or the bands that play in them.

So, aside from our curiosity with Graham Parker and his quick rise from obscurity, the *Trouser Press* thought there'd never be a better opportunity to talk about the whole pub rock phenomenon than the day we assembled Graham Parker, Brinsley Schwarz and Martin Belmont at Mercury's New York office. The following interview helped satisfy our curiosity about both Parker and pub rock, as well as taking a few interesting turns in the process. ∎

A CHAT WITH GRAHAM PARKER, BRINSLEY SCHWARZ AND MARTIN BELMONT

TP 16, OCTOBER/NOVEMBER 1976

*Interview by Dave Schulps
and Ira Robbins*

Until a year ago you were pretty much unknown. Where were you all these years?

GP: Hiding. No, I was just working ordinary jobs, not as a musician. I was working part-time and writing a lot. The gas station was the last job I had. I had an R&B band when I was about 15 which used to play youth clubs around the area where I was brought up in Surrey, which is about 30 miles outside London, but a long way in terms of music.

In what way?

GP: London is the only place in Britain where it happens — where you can get an understanding of what goes on by playing pubs and things like that. Outside of London, it's all very middle-of-the-road type entertainment apart from a few discos and clubs. There's no place for musicians to play together.

Did you have to come to London to be heard?

GP: Yeah. Well, that's how I met these guys, just by establishing some contacts in London.

Did you go to London specifically to try to make it as a performer?

GP: I left home and travelled around a few times, vaguely looking for bands in obscure places like Morocco, Gibraltar. I was into the Incredible String Band at the time. I had an acoustic guitar and was writing quite a bit. I joined a band in Gibraltar, and when I came back to England about four years ago I was getting to the point where I had to find musicians who wanted to play songs, as opposed to solos and suites that people were writing then. To find musicians I had to come to London unless I wanted to go to America, which is like another planet to me.

Is that what you've found since coming over here for this tour?

GP: It's still like another planet. I knew the music I was doing was more American-oriented, though, because I was getting into more American artists. I knew I was going to have a difficult time getting the right band. It worked out though because there were some people in England who had some idea of what I was doing.

How did you meet up with the band?

GP: The first thing I did was to put an ad in the *Melody Maker*. I met a slide guitarist named Noel Brown who knew a few people. He plays on the album, on "Back to Schooldays" and "Not If It Pleases Me." I played with him in a cafe in London, doing my material and just working things out. He knew the bass player from Chilli Willi and the Red Hot Peppers [Paul Riley] who knew [manager] Dave Robinson and Brinsley.

I guess your influences are fairly apparent, but

who are some of the people you'd name?

GP: The Stones, really. There are so many people I've dug. I used to idolize Peter Green at one time. Jack Bruce — there was a time I used to sing just like Jack Bruce, it was on a shallow level because my voice hadn't really developed. It only really developed two years ago. I'm into Bob Marley now ... Little Feat ... Staple Singers.

I think the person you've most been compared to is Van Morrison.

GP: Well, more Bruce Springsteen since we've been in America.

MB: We kept a list for a while. We had a table going with the names we'd seen Graham compared to. We had Van Morrison, Bob Dylan, Bruce Springsteen and Nils Lofgren. Lofgren fell behind pretty quickly. Right now, Van Morrison and Bruce Springsteen are neck and neck.

GP: I've also heard Neil Young comparisons; some guy named David Blue, who I've never heard; and Southside Johnny, who I haven't heard either.

Do you consider yourself R&B-influenced?

GP: Yeah. My early influences were Sam and Dave and Otis Redding.

What do you feel about the whole recent British return to R&B? Do you consider yourself part of it?

GP: I don't feel like part of anything, really, because I feel much more soul-oriented than a lot of those bands. I feel that the songs I'm writing cover more ground than straight R&B.

Do you like the Feelgoods?

GP: Yeah, but I'm not listening to that stuff really. I'm buying Aretha Franklin records that I couldn't afford when I was really into them. I'm looking for odd singles that I really like. I also like some of the early rockabilly stuff, I'm getting into that now.

Have people compared you to Eddie Cochran? The emotions you express are similar.

GP: Yeah, I've found that listening to Eddie Cochran.

Are you writing any rockabilly-type songs?

GP: I think "Back to Schooldays" is pretty much rockabilly.

MB: Wait'll you hear Dave Edmunds' version of that, he's done one that sounds like it's straight out of the Sun recording studio.

GP: You should hear the Tooting Fruities, Noel Brown's band; they play rockabilly.

How does the Rumour fit in with the pub scene? In this band you have two of the most important bands ever called pub rock represented. The pub scene is pretty much forgotten, at least from reading about it over here. Is the Rumour a pub supergroup, or a continuation, or something totally different?

BS: It's not an ultimate pub rock super group. It's a continuation of what five individuals were doing. We're not like Brinsley Schwarz, we're not like Ducks Deluxe and we're not like Bontemps Roulez — the people were in these bands and something was there, but it's been had and gone.

Are people in the Rumour happier with this band than they were in their previous bands?

BS: I couldn't really tell you that. This band is a lot easier going than other bands.

MB: It's hard to answer a question like that because when you're in a band now you've got all that you've done before as an example of either what to do or what not to do. It's an entirely different situation. When I was in Ducks Deluxe, I thought it was the greatest thing in the world, now I think this is.

Do you think Ducks Deluxe was as good as you though it was then in retrospect, or do you think it's a step behind what you're doing now?

MB: It's just different. From a purely personal point of view, the Rumour is more satisfying for me because it's broader than Ducks Deluxe ever was. I can see a difference in my own playing, there's a logical progression.

I'd like to talk a bit more about the whole pub rock phenomenon...

MB: Thought you might...

I get the idea that pub rock has taken on a sort of derogatory meaning in England.

MB: Not derogatory. We're all a bit wary of being labeled because it must be very different from what you know about pub rock, what actually went on in England. You read about it as if it were a musical movement, yet it wasn't a particular kind of music, it was a particular kind of venue. A way for a small band to play without breaking their backs financially.

BS: In the big gig era, all the little gigs got phased right out. At the time, the early '70s, it got into a rut where you played colleges until you were ready to play town halls, so all the clubs just faded out.

MB: A couple of bands eventually started playing in pubs, and it caught on. People were getting off on those places because it was such a different vibe from the average club or college gig. You could just go there and drink. When they first started, nearly all the gigs were free. The pubs used to pay the bands £25 or something like that and you would go in and the atmosphere was really good."

It seemed a tight circle in every way and there were, you'd have to admit, some similarities in the bands which were labeled pub rock.

MB: You mean musical similarities? Well, there were in a way because you couldn't go into a pub and play "The Seasons Suite" or "my latest composition" whatever, because it's just not on with a crowd of people drinking beer and wanting to have a good time. In that sense, there was an area of music, but it was as different as Brinsley Schwarz was different from Dr. Feelgood was different from Ducks Deluxe.

BS: I know what you mean about it being musically connected. When it started in 1971...

MB: It was Eggs Over Easy, they were the first.

BS: That was '71–72. That's a long while ago. At the time what we were doing was festivals. We had played so many times for free. It was the end of that wave of heavy groups and underground music, which is where the clubs were at.

Brinsley Schwarz weren't ever really like that though.

BS: We played simply but we were similar in that we were doing all our own numbers religiously, every night. If the audience didn't like us, we just played for ourselves, which is what all bands were doing at the time. The thing about pub rock was that it didn't matter what you played. It didn't have to be your own material and you didn't have to wear high heeled boots. It was just you and the audience standing next to each other.

Were the pub bands playing more to provide music for people who were drinking, or because people wanted to see a band?

BS: We were the first English band of any renown to do it. We did it because we saw an American group called Eggs Over Easy playing at the Tally Ho and it was purely by accident that we saw them. We just happened to be in the area. It just seemed like more fun than anything we had been doing 'til then. I guess we did it for selfish reasons. It looked groovy, so we wanted to do it. That was what Brinsley Schwarz did most of the time, we went through loads of phases.

Do you think there was a danger of getting stuck on the pub circuit with either Brinsley Schwarz or the Rumour?

BS: What the Brinsleys did was to do it for such a long time that at one point we just had to stop completely. That was after we started charging money.

The current New York scene is really very similar. Bands come out of nowhere with no real reputations and play around hoping to get recording contracts.

BS: That's kind of what it's for. There was nothing like it in England and that's why it started. We happened to be in on the beginning of it, but it didn't have to be us. It changed all the time. The fact that my name was the name of the group so that I'm labeled as "Mr. Pub Rock" is ridiculous. I've got as much to do with pub rock now as you have. People who want to do it can do it as a start or whatever, but it's got nothing to do with me.

Getting back to the musical similarities, most of the bands seemed very American-influenced. That seemed to be the common denominator.

BS: Yeah, but Dr. Feelgood, for example, are very British in their approach.

They're doing American material, though.

MB: But, of course, R&B is American music...

BS: Dr. Feelgood are so American in their approach, though. Wilko plays like Mick Green who played with Johnny Kidd. That's essentially British. Mick Green was one of my heroes, too. They're also very Stones-influenced. The rhythm section is much more like the Stones than any American group.

The Stones were the ultimate British band doing American material.

MB: There is no indigenous British music, that's why. There is in terms of folk music, but not rock.

BS: We always figured we could do American music better than you can.

Graham, how have you found American audiences as opposed to those in Britain?

GP: I think they're the same inasmuch as if they've gone to see the headlining band, they're not really prepared to listen to the support band. It's the same in England.

Do you write mostly for danceability, for lyrics, or both?

GP: I never think about what I want to write. I just write what I'm forced to write by what I'm going through. If you want to think about them, that's great, I don't mind.

Your lyrics aren't the usual "ooh baby" rock and roll lyrics. They always seem a bit vague, like "Don't Ask Me Questions."

MB: I feel that it's a mistake to look at anybody's lyrics and ask what they mean, because if you're doing that, you're missing the whole point. The thing is just to listen to it and make of it what you will.

That's true of Bob Dylan or anybody else. It's just what it means to you when you hear it. If it means to you the secrets of the universe, that's fine, but if it means to somebody else, "Oh, that's a good rhyme," that's fine as well.

GP: The point is that the lyrics should be good enough to do that. I take a lot of care with the lyrics. I rewrite them a lot, but the main feeling I started with is what comes through in the end. You start off with the feeling of a song and you work on it and work on it and eventually you're trying to get back the original feeling.

Mercury is presenting this image of you as a mysterious, shadowy figure, an artful dodger in a leather jacket... Do you think image is important? Do you think it fits?

GP: It's just the way I look, I think. The photographs just come out the way they do because I don't smile and say, "It's great to be a star," or sit cross-legged and say, "Here I am, the center of the universe."

I just say, "This is it, here I am." It's become an image when they've presented it because there's really no other way to present me. That's about it, really. It is a bit mysterious, maybe a bit elusive. ∎

HELLO IT'S ME

TP 13, APRIL/MAY 1976

This letter from a pub rock icon was in response to an article about his band, Ducks Deluxe.

I have just received a copy of TOTP 11, sent to me by our devoted French manager, Marc Zermati, a man of impeccable taste. I was impressed by the somewhat flamboyant obituary to the Ducks, ambiguity unintentional, but by Peckinpah's standards, a rather terminal piece. Indeed, Silvester's real humdinger of a sock-dolager shattered me throughout, opening some nasty wounds, which he intermittently dressed with candid expositions and an embarass de richesses. Alas, it is a shame that such a good piece of journalese should be spavined by a few crossed wires.

It was Nick Garvey, not I, who had the dubious pleasure of working for the Flamin' Groovies; I was going 'down the road again' with Help Yourself. I do not wish to reprimand the solitary transatlantic pub-rock paladin, on the contrary, I applaud his sense of histrionics; he just left me feeling a little disturbed. So much for the Ducks.

If I can be forgiven for running off at the mouth, you may wish to hear the latest news from the Tyla Gang. My brother left the band a long time ago, consequently, we have permanently operated as a four-piece. We have a new album finished, recorded at Rockfield, and titled *Rangoon Rusty and the Botswana Beach Rats*. I produced the album myself, with assistance from our engineer, Pat Moran.

Nick Garvey has a band by the name of the Snakes, who I really like, and Martin and Brinsley are known as the Rumour. They have Bob Andrews on keyboards and they are fast becoming a notorious outfit. They are touring England with Ace at the present time. Billy Rankin is one-third of a supergroup along with his fellow alcoholics, Nick Lowe and Dave Edmunds. I do believe there is going to be a revolution this year.

Sean Tyla

EDDIE AND THE HOT RODS ARE SO BORED WITH THE USA

TP 27, APRIL 1978

By MT Laverty

One couldn't help but wonder whether the patrons at Max's Kansas City weren't frozen to their seats. Onstage were Eddie and the Hot Rods, one of the tightest, fastest, most successful live bands to come out of England in the past few years, but only about 30 kids in the packed house at Max's bothered even to stand up and cheer them on, much less dance. As guitarist Dave Higgs complained later, "You'd think they were watching television rather than watching a band."

At the end of the tour, which lasted seven weeks and spanned 35 cities, the Hot Rods agreed to talk about their first (close) encounter with the United States. As the first English new wave band to complete an extensive tour of the country, they have achieved moderate success. Boston's WBCN radio gave their excellent anthem "Do Anything You Wanna Do" lots of airplay, and even New York's WNEW noticed the record. Yet the Hot Rods seemed confused and disappointed over their reception here.

Gathered in manager Ed Hollis's hotel suite, the Hot Rods watch the *Gong Show* on TV as they joke about the position of their second album, *Life on the Line*, in the American charts. "It's 189 with a feather," laughs guitarist Graeme Douglas. An Is-

land Records publicist corrects him: "No, it's 174."

Hollis joins in the joviality when he's not mockingly complaining about how everyone in the group takes advantage of him. Meanwhile, Dave Higgs squats in the corner with his friend Mandy, amused at the two-headed-man singing act on the tube. He is aloof from the others in the room, who include wasted-looking bass player Paul Gray, a roadie nicknamed Meaty (short for Meathead) and several young women.

Higgs doesn't talk a lot. His speech and movements have an incisive edge to them; at one point, just when the interview is about to get under way, Higgs gets up and leaves the room with no explanation. He is shy. And he is also rumored to be just a little bit upset over the amount of notice newly added guitarist Graeme Douglas is getting in the band.

Across from Higgs sits Douglas, a former Kursaal Flyer who has been with the band since February. Graeme likes to socialize more than Higgs does. He'll talk about most anything and seems to take pride in being articulate.

As the *Gong Show* comes to a close, Higgs, Douglas, Island publicist Margret Lapiner and I filter down to the hotel bar in search of a quiet place to talk. Alas, there aren't tables in the bar. We are thus forced to Graeme's room, where the two Rods clam up the moment the tape recorder is switched on. Higgs is suspicious of the press in general and Douglas dislikes tape recorders in particular.

What was your favorite city of all those you visited on tour?

Dave Higgs: I can't remember where we were.

Graeme Douglas: I don't know, Frisco, maybe.

Where were the fans best?

GD: New York, I suppose. They were a little more into us here than other places.

DH: Playing America was like going backward two years.

What impression of American fans did you get from your first couple of nights at Max's?

DH: Well, the kids just sat there. They didn't stand up or move or anything. The first night we thought, "Oh, another night. We'll play better tomorrow." But after about a week of playing here, we decided it was the audience that was the problem, not us.

But they were warm to you, in comparison with how they are to a lot of the bands. You should see how cold the fans are to most acts.

DH: We have seen it. We've seen bands come onstage and everyone just sits there, not standing or anything. It's got something to do with the New York way of life, I think.

One of the English journalists who was over here to see you at Max's said that the kids in America aren't "sufficiently bored" to get into rock and roll. What do you think of that?

GD: I think it's a load of shit. You've got to put something into rock and roll to get something out of it. Someone who's bored is certainly not going to get into rock and roll. They'd just as soon watch *Charlie's Angels.*

It looks as though some of the people who go to rock concerts in New York would just as soon be watching Charlie's Angels. *Do you have any idea why this is so?*

DH: No. All my illusions about rock and roll in America have been shattered. I don't think America would know a good rock and roll band unless they were advertised on TV.

GD: I'd like to go on record as saying I'm totally freaked out by the whole tour. You have all these visions of what America should be, and when it's not like that it's hard to understand what it is. There have been times on this tour when I've hated America as much as you can possibly hate anything, and other times when I loved it as much as you can possibly love anything.

Do you care that you haven't knocked over American audiences as you have English ones?

DH: Well, we're quite concerned, 'cause there's a lot of money over here.

How do audiences in other places compare?

DH: French audiences are crazy. Before you start, you know you've got a bunch of lunatics on your hands. It doesn't take much to spark them. We've played Finland, too, which was strange because they've hardly ever seen rock and roll there. They didn't react at all to us. They didn't even clap. And we played a gig in the north of Holland where not one person clapped through the whole set. They just sat there. So, we got offstage and went back to our dressing room. Then two guys go up to our sound man at the mixing board and say to him, "What do we have to do to get the band back?" So, he told them to clap. They went back to their seats, started clapping and within five minutes the whole house was clapping. So, we came out and did another number; after that they just went wild, started breaking up chairs and all.

What did you think America would be like?

GD: Any kid can grow up to be President. There is as much myth-making about America as there is about rock and roll.

DH: We thought all the New York bands were going to be as good as Eddie and the Hot Rods. But when you come over here, you find out they're rotten. The English bands that are worth seeing — like us, the Stranglers, the Jam, the Pistols and the Clash — are much better than the New York bands. But I don't think America could really get off on a band like the Clash. They're too English, I think. They're too political. I don't even know how long they'll be around in England. The punk thing is sort of withering right now.

Do you think some of the English bands' politics will keep them out of America?

DH: The politics are entirely different over here. In England you've got a lot of 18-year-old kids who can't get a job and don't see that they ever will. They think that their generation is different from the ones that went before. But in America everyone's satisfied, aren't they? Every time you turn on the TV, there's someone saying how wonderful things are.

Did people here think you were going to be a punk band?

DH: Americans don't even know what a punk band is. And until they've seen some English bands, they won't. New York bands are just New York bands. They're not punk. Over here, they seem to use the label to talk about musical ability. Like, "Oh, that band can't play their instruments. They must be a punk band." But Eddie and the Hot Rods don't have anything to do with punk, and they like us and come again. But other kids, when they find out we're rock and roll, they leave.

GD: Some of the kids have to be told what to

like. They have to be told what to do. The punk thing is like any scene. You've got some people who understand the concept — they do what they want to do. Then you've got the people who don't realize that they've got it in themselves to decide. So, they look to other people.

What do you think of the American clubs you've visited. How about CBGB?

DH: I don't think CBGB's is a punk club. It's just a rock and roll club.

What American bands have you liked?

GD: Uhhh...

DH: Ask us about the ones we don't like. Actually, I think most of the bands are quite amusing. The New York bands — I think they've totally got the wrong end of the stick.

What do you mean?

DH: I don't know what I mean. And I'm not sure they know what they mean, either.

Did you like any of the bands that played support for you on the tour?

DH: I can't even remember the names of them.

What did you think of the Ramones?

GD: The Ramones are scared shitless of us. We can play and they can't.

DH: It's like comparing a Cadillac to a dustcloth. I suppose for a New York band the Ramones are good. But none of the New York bands can play.

What are they lacking, as far as you're concerned?

GD: Insanity. Real insanity.

DH: New York bands don't realize they all have to play the same song together. They don't realize you all have to tune your guitars with one another. They don't realize that the drummer has to be playing in time with the bass player, that the rhythm guitar player has to play in time with the rhythm section, or that the singer has to sing in the same key the band is playing in.

Aren't there any bands you saw here that you liked?

DH: Well, there was a terrible band in Washington. They came onstage and played the second side of *Abbey Road* note for note. Then they ended their set by doing rock and roll.

GD: That was the band we were throwing peanuts at.

DH: We did see a little blues band in Pittsburgh, though, that could wipe any New York band. And we saw another band in California — Leila and the Snakes. They were like the Tubes. They were good.

Were there any surprises on the tour?

DH: One gig we got to and found out it was an Italian restaurant. I think it was in Philadelphia. Or maybe Pittsburgh.

What good came out of the tour?

DH: I'm glad we came over here. Because now I'm sure what I always thought was true. And that's that the best rock and roll bands came from England.

Success came pretty quickly to you in England, didn't it?

DH: Yes, maybe because we didn't want it. In England there's a lot of bands who just want success; if they don't get it after three or four months, they go and form another band. And they'll go on doing that all their life. They don't realize that you have to stay together for a couple of years, usually, before anything happens.

What do you think is going to have to happen before you get the kind of success you want in America?

DH: We've just got to come over here a couple of times, get people to know us. We're not going to judge from one tour.

What will have to happen before people get up and dance at your shows here, as they do in England?

DH: They'll have to stop being afraid to be normal. They've got to stop thinking, "What's the person next to me thinking?" Our whole thing as a band is to make the punters think they're just like us. They could do what we do onstage if they were willing to serve an apprenticeship at it. We don't want them to be afraid to have a good time. We don't want them to sit there and idolize us as if we're some rock stars or something. Of course, America is a big place. I'm not confident that when we come back to tour again we'll be a smash hit in America or anything.

Is there anything you are confident of in regard to America?

DH: Yeah. That's that we'll blow all the New York bands right off the stage. ∎

AMERICAN PUNK AND NEW WAVE

The dumbest mistake we ever made, editorially, was to allow our ambitious self-image as a national (or, heaven forfend, international) magazine cloud our recognition of the editorial significance of what was going on in our backyard. All of us were regular clubgoers and enthusiastic fans of many of the bands playing CBGB and elsewhere around town. But we got it in our heads that we had no reason to write about bands who didn't have records out and were unlikely to range much further from the Bowery than Queens to play shows.

On paper, it made sense: it felt elitist to tell readers around the country about music they had little or no chance of hearing or seeing. Add to that the misguided (but not entirely unrealistic) conviction that our beloved local bands had little or no prospect of mainstream success that would necessitate things like record contracts, radio play and *American Bandstand*. How wrong we were! Fortunately, our friend Alan Betrock started *New York Rocker* (subsequently run for many years by another pal, Andy Schwartz) to treat our hometown heroes with the same enthusiasm and depth of coverage as *Mersey Beat* had done for the Liverpool groups a decade earlier.

WE FINALLY HIT ON A WAY that *Trouser Press* could show some love in its pages for the bands we loved seeing and hanging out with on the Bowery night after night. With an issue 12 cover line promising "NY Rock," we launched a monthly section called *New York Notes* in early '76 (virtually the same month Alan launched *New York Rocker*) to present short profiles of local acts.

From the introduction to that issue: "Inspired by rave letters we received on Scott Isler's Planets article in TOTP 9 and the daily-growing New York music scene, we've decided to feature a 4-to-6-page section each issue including articles on several bands of merit. Non-natives need not feel left out since our goal is to inspire national interest in these bands. If tape trading of underground groups becomes the next big thing you can thank us later."

With more personal prejudice than clear-eyed editorial vision, we kicked things off with the John Collins Band (who were favorites of Karen Rose's), Ian North's Milk 'n' Cookies (who had connections to Knickers, a band that included Ira Robbins and Linda Danna) and a longer look at Television.

Although subsequent issues gave ink to the Marbles, Mumps and the Fast — as well as Talking Heads, Blondie and others — we shuttered the section in issue 17, explaining, "We feel that the New York scene is no longer as local an affair as it was when we began this column last summer. It's hard to believe that things change so fast, but in the past few months several local bands have been signed to national contracts (with several more to follow suit soon), two local albums have been released (two more are on the way) and the national press has begun to explore the bands as a phenomenon, not as unique musical organizations. Our feeling now is that local talent is finally getting the break it has been waiting for, and it's time to turn our attention westward to the rest of the country. This past year has seen an enormous proliferation of local bands everywhere recording and releasing their own records, a truly heartwarming development. So, from here on, *TP* will begin covering any local band that needs or deserves the exposure and/or attention in a new section, *American* [sic] *Underground*."

The lengthy interview that was done for this article offers a fascinating view of what Tom Verlaine was like before he became famous beyond Manhattan. The full transcript is available at https://bit.ly/3H9rpuB.

TELEVISION

TOTP 12, FEBRUARY/MARCH 1976

By Dave Schulps with Bruce Bauman (a.k.a. A. Mindswallow)

[*All puns unintentional]

Television. Their name conjures up a million images (ha, ha*) and, yes, a lot of bad puns too. Right now, though, to anyone seriously looking at the New York rock scene, Television are the band to watch (*). And it's not necessarily because they're the best (I happen to think they are, but I don't want to turn this into another ridiculous hype job — we've all had enough of that this past year), but because they are (FACT!) the most widely known, most talked-about, biggest-drawing still-unsigned band in town. When CBGB sells out its New Year's Eve shows three days in in advance, when their locally produced single gets played on WNEW-FM, when Eno has produced their demos and John Cale wants to produce their eventual album — you know something's gotta be happening. But if you've never seen or heard them, you don't know what it is, do you...?

Television is Tom Verlaine (né Tom Miller) on guitar and lead vocals; Richard Lloyd, also on guitar; bassist Fred Smith and drummer Billy Ficca. To some they're reminiscent of the Velvets, to others they sound like the IRT during rush hour. Maybe they're just sophisticated punk rockers. Seeds of the '70s. Whatever they are, it's hard to deny their power.

Tom Verlaine is a powerful figure on stage. He is the focal figure of Television. He looks the total antithesis of the typical New York rocker. Maybe he should have called himself Tom Sawyer instead. Or Huck Finn. He comes from Wilmington, Delaware, but he looks further west than that. He brings a maniacal intensity onto stage. Under the right circumstances, he could be downright scary. The desperation is everywhere in his voice, in his face, in his eyes, in his guitar playing, in the way he wrenches his neck to sing into the microphone. He seems at times to be on the brink, teetering dangerously close to the edge. He resembles Keir Dullea in *David and Lisa*.

Television opens shows with "Fire Engine," originally recorded by the 13th Floor Elevators, a mid-'60s Texas punk band whose tragic end rates an article in itself. Why "Fire Engine"? "I love the singer's voice, he sounds like a white James Brown. I couldn't make out the words though, so we only used the first line. Do you know what the real lyrics were? It's not 'Let me take you to the empty space,' it's 'Let me take you to DMT space!' These guys were the only drug band in Texas at the time, so all the songs had stupid things like that thrown in. The lead singer's [Roky Erickson] just released a new single. The A-side is a dumb ballad, but the B-side sounds like six horribly produced Les Pauls on 10 all playing the same chord. It's on Mars Records. I don't know where you get it."

The rest of Television's material is original. Verlaine writes it. His best songs are "Prove It" ("Jes' the facts ... confidential"), a snarling accusation, and Eno's favorite, the witty, dreamlike "Venus de Milo" ("I fell into the arms of..."). There are more, some better than others. I wish I could hear all the lyrics, those I've been able to make out are unusual and challenging. I'll have to wait for an album to really say how great they are.

On the recording front, Television have a limited-edition single out on the privately pressed Ork Records, "Little Johnny Jewel (Part 1 & 2)." As a song, it's not one of their best. It was chosen mainly because they probably wouldn't want to put it on an album, and because, "It would sound different from the usual single." That it does. It serves quite well as an introduction to the Television sound and keeps sounding more and more accessible each time I hear it on the radio (sounds great tinny!). Against a repetitive three-note bottom laid down by Lloyd and Smith, Verlaine plays some of the most bizarre lead guitar imaginable, sliding up and down the strings of his Fender like they were greased. Herky-jerky, stop and go leads; weird, trebly tones; the return of "ostrich" guitar? Billy Ficca's drumming, too, doesn't fit into the usual rock and roll mold. Strange, syncopated rhythm; lightly, sparingly played. A subtle pop-gun barrage. Very complementary.

The only other recorded Television is Verlaine's stellar guitar performance on Patti Smith's "Break It Up," for which Tom wrote the music and "semi-coordinated" the lyrics. Verlaine's powerful lead guitar work on the song contrasts well with Lenny Kaye's simpler punkish chord attacks on the rest of the album and makes "Break It Up" the most unique song on the record. In fact, I think Verlaine's guitar work steals the show from Patti on "Break It Up." Just listen to the last half minute, where Verlaine's guitar begins to wail and screech like a pack of wild horses. It's positively spine-tingling.

Verlaine said Clive Davis really liked the song. I asked him if Arista was interested in Television. "He doesn't really know what to make of us... he doesn't know what to make of Patti, but he realized that there was somethin' that she was gettin' all this attention in the press and that someone must want to hear her record. I guess we haven't gotten enough attention for him yet."

Television's history probably goes back eight years ago when Verlaine left Wilmington for New York. "I wanted to do it down there... I'd always loved New York, so I figured I'd come here and give it a try." That was in 1968. In December 1972, Verlaine called Ficca, an old friend from Delaware then in Boston, and said he'd like to put a band together. "I said, 'Look, nobody's doin' anything. All there is is this crappy folk-rock and country shit.' So, Billy came down and we looked for a second guitarist, but we couldn't find one who could play either a good lead or strong rhythm. Then I asked my best friend, Richard Hell, if he wanted to learn bass and he said, 'Yeah, OK,' but things didn't work out eventually. That first band was called the Neon Boys."

Verlaine then played alone for a while to totally unenthusiastic audiences. He remembers having water thrown on him at Reno Sweeney one night. "Things were looking pretty bleak until one evening Terry Ork and Richard Lloyd came down and saw me. We then decided to reform the Neon Boys with Richard Lloyd on rhythm guitar and change the name to Television, which Hell thought up."

The new lineup gave Verlaine a chance to play both lead and rhythm guitar and really develop his unique style of playing. I asked him about his influences. "I love playing rhythm guitar. I could play rhythm for an hour. When I was a kid, I grew up on Wagner, so I've got that kind of sense of melody. Then, when I was in from seventh to tenth grade, I really got into [John] Coltrane and [Albert] Ayler, and I'd read everything about them. Like Ayler would say, 'I've got to get out beyond the notes' and stuff like that. I think they might have influenced me. I never liked guitar then. Then '19th Nervous Breakdown' came out and 'You Really Got Me' and 'All Day and All of the Night,' they were the first rock songs that really grabbed me. Those Kinks guitar solos were the first that really whammed me out."

Television first began receiving attention in '74 when they landed a job opening the shows at CBGB for Patti Smith. At the time they were a lot less musical then they are today. In fact, much of the show was spent with the audience wondering whether Richard Hell was going to fall down backwards and break his head. He seemed like he was always so precariously balanced that if someone should move in the tenth row he would topple. For all that, Hell wrote one of Television's best songs, the sorely missed "Blank Generation." However, Hell's bass playing and singing left something to be desired and he left to join Johnny Thunders' newly formed Heartbreakers.

Fred Smith was brought in to replace Hell and the current version of Television got under way. With every performance, Verlaine and Lloyd seemed to play better and better together. There were still off nights, but when they were both playing well, they were nothing short of incredible. I remember one night last summer at CBGB, at four in the morning, fighting sleep to catch what was for me one of the most exciting sets I've ever heard. They were "on," and everybody in the place knew it. You had the feeling then that things would begin to happen for Television, and slowly but surely they have, as evidenced by the recent sell-outs at CBGB. With the enormous success of Patti Smith, can Television be far behind? One thing is for sure, the association won't hurt them, even though it would be an injustice if their closeness with Patti became a basis for success. Television are unique unto themselves and deserve to be recorded regardless of whom they know.

Go and see Television while the intimacy of a small club is still available. You may love them, you may hate them, but you won't forget that you've seen them. ■

HELLO IT'S ME

TP 19, APRIL/MAY 1977

I have a few gripes ... the artists you cover are too much above ground, so to speak. Who needs to read about Bowie? Who cares? I'd rather read an in-depth article on the Residents (though you do give less popular groups plugs here and there). I'm glad to see that you've put less emphasis on the NY bands because all they have turned out is commercialized, stagnant garbage; i.e., Television LP is total dullsville; Ramones second LP is no different from the first. Also in your British Punk Discography you didn't include the Saints, "(I'm) Stranded" (PX 242). Even though they're from Australia the 45 was released in England and they would knock Eddie and the Hot Rods on their asses.

I also liked TP better when the cover mentioned "... and no disco."

Gregory Patrick Prevost
[*future founder of the Chesterfield Kings*]
Rochester, NY

IN SEARCH OF ADVENTURE WITH TOM VERLAINE

TP 28, MAY 1978

By Dave Schulps

It has been over a year since Television's debut album, *Marquee Moon*, and for the band's American fans most of that time has been a complete blank. After all, since the band's initial U.S. tour supporting Peter Gabriel, Television has had next to no Stateside activity. Even the New York club circuit, which TV was instrumental in developing, has not seen the band during that time.

Where have they been? What have they been up to?

Well, to start with, there was the recording of their second album, *Adventure*, in the test-pressing stage as of this writing (and probably in your local spin-joint by the time you read this), which kept the band occupied for nearly five months. Prior to that, Television had spent most of their time working in England and Europe, where acceptance has come far easier than in their homeland.

Obviously, then, Television are looking forward to making more of an impact in America after the release of *Adventure*. Although I was only able to get a couple of listens to tapes of the album, it's apparent that the band have stuck close to the sound of *Marquee Moon*, proffering refinements in the general direction charted on that album, rather than making any great leap forward into new areas. Still, those refinements should create ample distance to avoid criticism of *Adventure* on the grounds of lack of progression. Fortunately, it is the album's first two cuts which show the greatest movement into unexplored territory. Probably in the band's favor is that these songs are probably the most "commercial" they're ever recorded.

"Glory," which opens the album, is as catchy a song as Tom Verlaine has written, sporting a strong hook which should get it lots of FM airplay. Yet, far from sterilizing their sound, the added accessibility of "Glory" does nothing to diminish the gut-level emotional appeal which, to my mind, made *Marquee Moon* such an incredibly stunning debut. "Days," which follows, is something altogether different still. Reminiscent of nothing if not the Byrds circa *Younger Than Yesterday* / *Notorious Byrd Brothers* with its jangling guitars, lilting harmonies and crisp, clean sound, it, too, could find favor with radio programmers. It also is as far as *Adventure* strays from the *Marquee Moon* "sound."

Next up are two songs TV used to play back in the days they were appearing regularly at CBGB. "Careful" and "Foxhole," which sounded quite horrifying in its evocation of a battlefield, but which Verlaine said he thought was "really funny." Side One ends with a slow, keyboard-dominated number called "Carried Away" on which Verlaine shines on both piano and organ.

The songs on Side Two all sound like they could have come straight off *Marquee Moon*. Verlaine calls "The Fire" "this album's 'Torn Curtain,'" and it certainly does recall that song to a point. "Ain't That Nothin'" was "originally inspired by someone in rock and roll," but Verlaine isn't telling who.

Finally, "The Dream's Dream" is the album's major work, at least length-wise, clocking in at nearly seven minutes. Structurally, it recalls "Marquee Moon," as it builds on a repetitive guitar figure in much the same way. "The Dream's Dream," though, has an even more beautiful sonar quality than "Moon." Carried initially by the sturdy backbeat of drummer Billy Ficca (who turns in another superb performance throughout *Adventure*), the song builds through a series of stop-and-go guitar blips, harmonics and the usual contrapuntal interplay between Verlaine and Richard Lloyd, until Verlaine comes in with a lengthy solo — also strikingly reminiscent of the one on "Marquee Moon," although he sounds less frantic and agonized here.

All in all, Television have probably accomplished what they set out to do with *Adventure*. They have made an album that is not only as hauntingly beautiful and uncompromisingly emotional as their first, but which is also more accessible to new ears and, very possibly, radio programmers, who have the power of censoring anything new and different from the airwaves. Let's hope so, anyway.

TOM VERLAINE SITS by an enormous conference room table at Elektra Records' New York office, one which looks like it came out of one of those great "boardroom" scenes in movies like *Sabrina* or *Putney Swope*. He has been busy coordinating the final mixes of *Adventure*, which he produced with help from engineer John Jansen, as well as approving the artwork and taking care of various last-minute details that accompany the release of any album. He gives the appearance of being very much in control of whatever it is that Television is involved in.

When I walk in to start the interview, bassist Fred Smith is also sitting in the room, but he declines my invitation to join in the discussion. Verlaine is to be the spokesman for the band.

We start off by discussing the switch in co-producer/engineers from Andy Johns to John Jansen, and whether that move was meant to alter the sound in any particular way on *Adventure*.

Verlaine leans back and expounds: "I just wanted to work with somebody different. It's nothing against Andy or anything. Everybody's got different ways of doing things, so you learn more by working with different people. We actually did the basic tracks on a couple of the songs with a guy I know at the demo studio, Craig Anderson..."

"Bishop." Smith corrects him.

"Yeah, see I don't even remember the guy's name anymore. That was just to work with a guy who I knew and had some rapport with. Alan Lanier of Blue Öyster Cult told me I ought to meet John Jansen, that he liked the group and he had two months off that he wasn't doing anything. Alan thought I'd get along with him really good. As far as the sound goes, generally, we aim to get a different sound on each song."

Did he accomplish that on *Adventure*?

"I don't know. To me every song sounds different on it, but I don't know how much it does to anybody else. To me, the songs themselves don't sound that far away from the material on the last album. There aren't many overdubs on this album, just a little bit of this and that, lots of guitars, some keyboards."

It should've been a quick album to record if that's true. How long did they actually take to record it?

He laughs. "Years. Actually, it took all of September and October, half of November and December, January and a week of February — four, four-and-a-half months."

Why so long?

"Mainly to try out different ideas; different guitar solos, this and that. Some things that got on are first takes and some are fiftieth takes. Some guitar solos were just shot off and they sounded good, others we worked on a little more."

The topic at hand switches from the album to the band's experiences on their first tours of America and Europe, respectively. How did he assess Television's reaction on the Peter Gabriel tour early last year, and why hadn't they toured here since?

"The band wasn't badly received," he comments on the Gabriel tour, "but being the opening act, you're playing for somebody else's audience, so they're bound not to be really into you. I like to play on big stages, though. I'd rather go out on a big stage than play a club where it's so cramped all the time. Basically, the tour was a no money thing just to go to those towns. We went over better — really good, in fact — in Midwestern towns like Kansas City, where people hadn't heard of us and didn't know what to expect."

What did people who had heard of Television expect them to be?

"We went to a couple of towns where people thought we were a punk rock group or something like that," he chuckles.

Did he feel Television had been unfairly classified as a new wave band, especially in England?

"I don't think they call us new wave over there anymore. They may have before we got there, but they didn't afterward." He pauses a second for thought. "We may be new wave, though," he adds, laughing. "We may not be punk, but we might be new wave in a sense, I guess there's something new about us. I don't know what it is, though. Maybe it's that we don't use Les Pauls and Marshalls. I think that's the difference, really."

When asked about how successful the band had been in Britain, Verlaine points out that *Marquee Moon* has sold more records there than it has here — amazing, considering the relative populations of the countries. The British tour was really successful, as well, he mentions, with sell-out shows every night in front of excited audiences.

Does this mean Television would be concentrating on Europe more in the future?

"We'll go to Europe 'cause we can make money there. The first time we didn't, but now we can. Plus, I like Europe, too. It's neat to be in a foreign country, to have record company people buy you dinners in Paris. That's the real attraction of it — to go to these great European restaurants and not pay for it. Also, the audiences — it's so amusing, because you know they can't possibly understand what you say. It doesn't matter, though, it's communicating a certain kind of energy that isn't present in that country. It's bringing something that's foreign to them. That varies from country to country. Germany is like what it must be like playing in Alaska or something. It's very, very slow and serious — weird. Places like Belgium and the south of France, Sweden and Copenhagen are really alive. They really love rock and roll, they really respond."

Where were the best gigs to play?

"England was the best by far. Brussels was good. Sweden, too. The West Coast of the States was good. Texas was really good — really fun. Texas was like New York in a way, because like a New Yorker you wouldn't call a Texan an example of an American. They're all very individual about what they like, and they don't care if nobody else likes it. They apparently really love guitar music. I think that's why we went down so well there."

TELEVISION HAS certainly traveled an odd path over the course of the past four years, since they became the first band to play CBGB on a regular basis. At this point they seem to have totally abandoned the Bowery circuit; Verlaine has always had his gripes with the New York "scene," anyway. At this point, they can hardly be considered a "New York band," although they're still based [in the city]. Verlaine admits to not having seen a band this year but doesn't say whether it's because he's too involved in his own projects or he's just decided to abandon the scene. The other members of the band, however, do seem to be keeping a considerably higher profile than TV.

I wonder if the reaction to the band from the public and press in Britain — *Marquee Moon* was *Sounds*' Album of the Year — had not caused Television to become more oriented toward Europe than the States. How does he feel about the press's reaction toward Television?

"It's nice to get good reviews and it's interesting to get reviews that are so bad that they're good. Some good reviews are so off the wall that they're funny and some bad ones are the same way, but I've never seen a good or bad review that I thought the reviewer had his head on straight..." He giggles at his statement.

"Seriously, the good reviews and the bad reviews both seem like the reviewers express their own personalities more than they express any general truth about the group — which is fine, in a way."

Does he think there are any general truths about groups?

"I think you can write about music in a way that illuminates your audience. There was this classical guy in the 1920s, Paul Rosenfield, who was great. If you read one of his pieces, it totally turns you on to wanting to hear a Ravel record. And when you hear it, you know what he was talking about. In rock journalism, you don't. Also, LeRoi Jones, before he changed his name to that African name, used to have a column in *Downbeat*, and the way he used to write about stuff really put across what the people sounded like and made you want to hear them. Now the criticism doesn't seem to be related to the music.

"There's a piece in the [*Village*] *Voice* about politics and punk rock. I mean, what is all this stuff? There's a guy smashing 16th note chords —

there's no politics in that. There might be a snotty vocal, but you can't be political when you're 17, it's impossible."

So, he isn't any more impressed with what's happening in England than here?

"I didn't really see anything there, either. I heard some of the records — people were giving me records left and right. They all sounded the same to me. The sound was copped from the Ramones, and the lyrics, the attitude, were taken from Patti Smith. Not the manic side, but the 'fuck off' side. I know what her style was like at the time she first toured there. I think a lot of people were struck by her attitude — especially bands."

What about Richard Hell's album? Had he heard *Blank Generation*? Considering that the title cut and its author were both once part of Television, I figured Tom would've been interested.

He does his best to sound blasé and offhand. "I heard a side of it — or maybe whole thing — once. I didn't think much of it. There were a lot of old Tom Verlaine chord changes on it, but I don't care 'cause we're not doing them anymore anyway. I don't say that out of conceit. I just heard it right away — I don't even think he's aware of it. Actually, I don't care."

Verlaine is obviously not particularly interested in pursuing the subject of Richard Hell, and we turn instead to discussing the records he's been listening to, a topic which seems to stir his interest more than anything else we've talked about so far. Verlaine has extremely eclectic musical taste, ranging from early Kinks and Stones to obscurities like 13th Floor Elevators through to avant-garde jazzers like Coltrane and Albert Ayler. He's an ace bargain-binner and seems to know where to find all kinds of odd and interesting records cheap.

"Right now, I'm listening to a lot of really weird stuff," he says. "The soundtrack from the TV show *Twilight Zone* is one. It's really nifty — all sorts of weird effects. What else... a record of Dervish music, some modern jazz. I listen to Duane Eddy quite a lot lately. Then there's this Scotty Moore record [*What's Left*] — it just sounds like a jam session album, just really nice playing. The group really turned on to each other.

It's all rockabilly stuff. The whole record has a great tone to it."

Does he listen to such a wide range of music in order to widen the spectrum of his own writing? Does he find himself incorporating ideas from them?

"No. It's just a question of finding records that have some real feeling to them. I can't listen to Boston, I don't think there's a real feeling on those records. I don't get any vibe out of it. Maybe it's me — it's a hit record and it must be getting to a lot of people, but it doesn't grab me."

Thankfully, Television is able to convey the kind of emotion you can't get from Boston or Kiss, etc. They many never make a platinum record (or even a gold one), but there's something in Verlaine's strangled vocals and the truly individual instrumental style Television has developed that makes this band penetrate so much deeper. Life is not always fun, not always easy to take and neither is Television. Ultimately, though, both can be extremely rewarding.

The future?

Says Verlaine: "Well, as soon as we get some money to buy a couple of amps — we had to hock ours — we'll go back on the road. We've gotten a few calls from theatres in the U.S. — places in the Midwest. It's basically a question of seeing who calls in and wants to book us. After that, well, I'm sure we'll go back to England." ■

QUOTES OF THE DECADE

"I won't make any friends saying this, but if Americans like something it's probably crap."
—STEWART COPELAND of THE POLICE (1981) TP 59

"[New wave and punk] is very similar to what we were doing: being as obnoxious as possible to a large segment of the population." —PAUL KANTNER
recalling THE JEFFERSON AIRPLANE (1983) TP 83

Buy this kitten or we'll kill this rock star.

Patti Smith by Linda Danna

The Trans-Oceanic Trouser Press
P.O. Box 2434
Grand Central Station
New York, New York 10017

I'm
I bought the
kitten myself

We were hanging outside of CBGB in 1975 when Patti Smith scooped up a kitten running down the Bowery. We used the photo on the back over of issue 10 to parody the 1973 *National Lampoon* cover and somehow got Smith to autograph the issue. Despite her claim, according to our late friend Duncan Hannah's 2018 memoir, *20th Century Boy*, he adopted that cat and named it Nick.

Nobody didn't like the Ramones, and we — like many others in the rock press — kept seeing their well-deserved commercial breakthrough right around the corner. Of course, that never happened, but you can read (and perhaps weep over) the unfounded optimism in this Phil Spector-album moment.

Trouser Press *did four major features (plus a guest singles review column) on the Forest Hills Four. The first, in TP 33, was written by Lester Bangs — his only appearance in our pages (as a contributor). We had a bit of a misunderstanding over that article ("Ramones Go Depresso!"): offering double our usual feature pay rate (so, 2X peanuts), we assigned it and arranged the inter-*

view (Johnny: "We wouldn't have girlfriends if we weren't in the Ramones" and "...people are offended when they see swastikas, but swastikas are a little more camp than hammer and sickle buttons. The Nazis lost the war, and there's no threat right now of any Nazi thing, but there is a communist threat."). But Lester also sold the story to the NME, which — having the advantage of a weekly publishing schedule — ran it before we could, which made it appear as if we were reprinting their piece rather than the other way 'round. We were miffed, but Lester's need-to-earn-a-living defense was hard to dispute given our rates, and our good relations with the Brits survived a pissy letter sent to the paper's editor warning them not to resell it to Creem.

THE SHORT AND LONG OF THE RAMONES

TP 50, MAY 1980

By Scott Isler

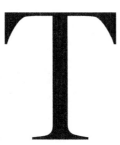

The Ramones "are a band with obvious commercial potential, and one imagines that potential will start being realized very soon."
—John Rockwell, *New York Times*, 1975

"John Rockwell's a shithead. Nobody should read the *New York Times*." —Johnny Ramone, 1980

The above two statements are a condensation of the Ramones' life story, thus saving you the time and effort to plow through the following article. Study the contrast in attitude, content and (especially) dates. If they still mean nothing to you, a refresher course in the Ramones' LP catalogue is definitely in order (and also a lot of fun) — or you could read the following. But don't say we didn't offer you a short cut; it's more than anyone has offered the Ramones.

Joey Ramone has just moved into a sun-drenched studio apartment in a 21-story doorman building. *Just* moved in: the total decor consists of a chair, a sofa bed (on loan from the super), a night table with lamp on top, a full-length mirror leaning against a wall, a dolly, a box of Nilla Wafers perched on the window ledge, a toy model London transport bus (companion piece to the Nillas) and, propped up against another wall, a large poster announcing a Ramones concert date with the Boys. The last two items are mementoes of the Ramones' just-completed British tour (their fifth), and the apartment is Joey's welcome-back present to himself. Although located in a nondescript buffer zone between New York's East and West Villages, the building is a vast improvement over the Bowery loft Joey and cohabitant Linda had been sharing with the band's lights operator.

Joey's betterment of his living arrangements is no sudden whim — he's been trying to get into this building for a couple of years (his mother lives here) — but it does come at a fortuitous moment. *End of the Century*, the Ramones' fifth LP (not counting an import-only live double-album), has just been released, and — hold your breath, everybody — it appears to be the record that will finally establish the group as more than leather-jacketed lunatics with cult appeal. As of press time, the LP has charted in the 40s — higher than any previous Ramones record — and is still rising: a just-issued single track ("Baby I Love You") is sure to add some fuel to the fire.

Despite (or because of?) their importance as new wave standard bearers, the Ramones have been overlooked consistently by the general public. After six (!) years of blaring in the wilderness, most bands would be content to sell their gear and go into the construction business. But the Ramones couldn't even achieve total failure. They always had that margin of significance and a bedrock following whose purchases kept them in that embarrassing limbo of the record charts: too high to write off entirely, too low to take seriously.

In the last few months, though, the vast MajORity [*2024: you'd be forgiven for missing this typographic allusion to Middle Of the Road culture*] would seem to have caught up with the Forest Hills Four — and the Ramones themselves have met them halfway. Producer Phil Spector must be credited for a good deal of *End of the Century*'s popularity; he has sanded down the rough edges and still delivered a thunderously raucous LP. There's no future (not to mention royalties) in being musical prophets without honor. The 1980 Ramones are definitely looking up — and at more than Joey's new digs.

THROUGH SOME UNDERGROUND communications network — only Joey and Dee Dee have telephones, and the former's was installed the day of the interview — Johnny and Dee Dee Ramone have agreed to rendezvous at Joey's gleaming new domicile (stark, but a nice echo) for an interview. (Marky was incommunicado in lower Manhattan.) It's a blustery winter day outside, and although the apartment is not cold, there's not a T-shirt to be seen. Johnny wears a long-sleeve red pullover, new jeans and clean white Adidas; Joey, a red zippered sweatshirt, faded jeans and dirty sneakers; Dee Dee, a denim jacket (alright, it's probably covering a T-shirt).

Before a tape recorder can even be switched on, Dee Dee announces that he thinks he'll be going. He says he doesn't feel well, but one can't help thinking he feels self-conscious in this situation. In contrast to Joey and Johnny's stream of conversation, Dee Dee speaks in slow, halting phrases, although he can come up with penetrating insights. The others prevail upon him to stay, at least temporarily.

Johnny's voice is a pleasant baritone which squeaks upon the slightest provocation. His tone, surprisingly polished diction and charming smile are in sharp contrast to the pouting lout he portrays onstage. Gangling Joey sounds pretty much the way he sings: heavy on the Forest Hills. He punctuates his speech with "likes" and "y'knows," is quite affable and kibitzes when the others talk. The awkwardness he displays onstage is not much in evidence; as we gather around, Joey pulls up the dolly and collapses onto it, his legs splayed on either side. Although Joey claims the band doesn't socialize much offstage, he and Johnny appear to have a compatible relationship (and now live around the corner from each other).

Besides the charge of a new album, the Ramones are flush with the success of their European tour. In addition to England, they played Paris, Belgium, Holland and — a first — four dates in Italy. Until recently this country was considered off limits to rock bands due to a political situation that regularly turned concerts into riot exercises. The Ramones' Italian concert promoter hired the Red Brigade to provide secu-

rity, and there was no trouble. The band had to modify its comic-book Americanism, however. The huge backdrop flags (suggestive of the Great Seal of the U.S.) weren't permitted. Neither were any songs that mentioned communists; a line in "Commando" was changed from "don't talk to commies" to "don't talk to swamis."

The militant Italian rockers "don't like big groups, 'cause they're capitalists," Joey explains, and everyone laughs ironically at the Ramones escaping that classification. The band played to audiences of six or seven thousand a night and found that (Joey continues) "kids are the same just about anywhere." Dee Dee interjects: "I felt that in Italy they were more average than normal. They're less jaded; they were more into rock than fashion."

The Ramones' concern with fashion seems surprising until one realizes they've returned from England, a land where "correct" tastes in rock are as important to social well-being as political opinions are in the Soviet Union. It's a good question whether the entire new wave would ever have gotten off the ground if the Ramones hadn't made an epochal British debut in London's Roundhouse on July 4, 1976; even the date cries out with significance. Before that watershed gig, Dee Dee states, English bands "wanted something but they didn't have direction. They went more into R&B, where we went into something totally original." Joey is more direct: "We kicked it off there. When we left, that's when it all started." Johnny comments, "We had hoped the kids would see us and feel they could do it, too." The British scene quickly took on a political cast, and the Ramones have been slagged in the UK press for their passivity ever since. (Johnny shrugs that this time around coverage was "bad, as usual." "They love us," Joey adds.) For all its bitching, the English music papers haven't been able to affect the Ramones' popularity; during the last tour, "Baby I Love You" went into the Top 10 there.

The Ramones' remake of the Ronettes rondo has also been released as a 45 here. Since Joey is the only recognizable band member [*2024: in fact, the only band member*] on the track (and even he sounds like Ronnie Spector, struggling under Phil's syrupy string arrangement), how does the band feel about being represented by this cut?

Joey, for one, has no compunction. "I think it's great," he says with firm conviction. Johnny agrees, although more guardedly. "Yeah, y'know?" he smiles, his voice soaring indeterminately. "Your single has to be played on the AM radio." "Middle America counts," Joey affirms.

Middle America — or whoever wasn't listening to the Ramones before — is apparently taking notice now. "The audience has broadened," Joey notes. "Now we're getting young kids — like 12-, 13-year-old girls — and we're getting the hardcore 17-year-old kid who's into Kiss, Ted Nugent and Aerosmith. You don't wanna play for a bunch of old rock critics, you wanna play for kids."

"You need that audience," Johnny says. "When we started, we thought, 'Those are the kids that are like us.' But they weren't yet. They were still stuck in the heavy metal bag. Now I think those kids are growing up and starting to become interested in new wave."

"I think they're disgusted with the old sludgy bands," Joey continues. "They want some real excitement geared towards them personally rather than their mothers and fathers." He cites Meat Loaf and Foreigner as artists with parental appeal.

Radio, of course, has long been the Ramones' big stumbling block. Joey credits "the breakthrough of more middle-of-the-road new wave" — the Cars, the Knack, Blondie (who did "a disco song to make some quick bucks"), Joe Jackson — with opening up the airwaves. The subject is an obvious pet peeve, and *End of the Century* even contains a song about it: "Do You Remember Rock 'n' Roll Radio?" reflects Joey's view that "radio in the '60s picked up on everything" and that people have to demand change to turn anything around. Who said this band wasn't political?

"When we started, the industry was trying to kill us 'cause they wanted Billy Joel and the Eagles. I guess we were too extreme at the time; it had to take a softer core. We did an interview at a radio station that at the time didn't play us — but you have to plug away. They told us, well, if you guys would sound more like Boston or Queen or Toto then we could play you. The radio program director was pulling a power trip on us, like, 'Your

future's in my hands.' Fuck him!" "That station's now playing us heavily," Johnny adds as a moral.

PHIL SPECTOR HAD WANTED to produce the Ramones since *Rocket to Russia*, their third LP, came out in 1977. In a *Melody Maker* interview at the time, Joey related that Spector had invited the band to his house when they were in California. "But he was really negative to us all... He said that we'd gotten as far as we were going to get... He wasn't very encouraging."

Encouraging or no, Spector pursued the wary group. "We didn't know if he was serious," Johnny says, "or if we could work with him. We didn't want to jump into any album with anybody and lose our say in the matter — lose us. It's very important that we maintain control over things." The Ramones tested Spector by allowing him to remix "Rock 'n' Roll High School" for the film's soundtrack album before committing themselves to a full LP.

Joey claims that while he never quite idolized Spector, he was certainly excited about his producing their album. "There hasn't really been anything for him to do. The stuff he did with Cher and Leonard Cohen is a joke. That's not what his services should be called for."

Spector's phobias and neuroses are only slightly less fabled than his productions, but the Ramones seem to have hit it off with him. Joey was a frequent guest at Spector's mansion, although he only saw three rooms all the time he was there. He describes something out of *Sunset Boulevard*: an uncared-for house, a front-yard fountain choked with weeds, signs warning of electric fences and killer dogs on the loose. Spector gave Joey marathon private singing lessons for "Baby I Love You," accompanying him on piano.

"He taught me about timing, pacing right. He would stamp on the floor, and I'd sing to the beat. Some days I'd be doing this till five in the morning: he'd say, 'Tired already?' He's a perfectionist; he's crazy. One night he made me listen to 'Danny Says' about a hundred times. He really cares."

This care slowed the Ramones' usual whirlwind recording schedule to a virtual crawl. *End of the Century* required two months for the band to lay down tracks and another four for Spector to assemble them. The pace wasn't helped by Spector's philosophical arguments with engineer Larry Levine that kept the group waiting in the studio for hours. They used no less than five studios; one of them, Gold Star, was the site of Spector's original triumphs. The producer kept the thermostat so low that the Ramones recorded wearing coats and scarves. And yet, to listen to the album, it was all worth it.

The Ramones' image facelift didn't stop with their new producer, as anyone who's seen *End of the Century*'s cover can attest. It's the first to depict them without black leather jackets and is studio-lit to perfection. "Ehhh" is Johnny's less-than-neutral reaction. "We had no pictures to choose from." "The guy that we used was a real asshole," Joey says. Johnny adds, "We've had a lot of ideas for covers but [the record company] says, look, you're not making a comedy thing."

THIS LEADS STRAIGHT to Ramones dilemma #438: their sense of humor.

"We're not a comedy band," Joey says flatly. "We're not Frank Zappa — or the Bonzo Dog Band." [*Does he mention them to all his interviewers? —Ed.*]

Johnny runs with the ball: "You read reviews that say, 'When are the Ramones gonna grow up?' You don't know what to do so you put on a couple of songs that are serious. We never try to write funny songs."

"We all have that sick wit," Joey explains, "and we like to stick it in there, but it's not like you try to write a funny song. We have a lotta taste."

This *is* the band that performs "Teenage Lobotomy," "Pinhead" and "Cretin Hop," isn't it?

"Taste is a thin line," Johnny concedes. "We sing about glue and all that; we feel that's within taste. You can sing a song about pinheads because there are no pinheads; you don't see any pinheads. But to sing about retards would be in bad taste. Cretins?" He puzzles that one over.

Joey to the rescue. "Cretins are fun."

"It seemed like a fun word," Johnny resumes. "It doesn't seem to be as touchy as 'retards.'"

"Everybody uses the word," Joey rationalizes. "There's a band from L.A. called the Cretones;

they write for whatshername [Linda Ronstadt]."

Why don't the Ramones write for whatshername? Joey (sadly): "She doesn't like us." Johnny: "She ran out holding her ears when she saw us somewhere."

As a sidelight, Joey relates how, riding through St. Paul, Minnesota, the Ramones passed Cretin High School. At that evening's show, Joey made a dedication to anybody who went there. "They all cheered, so it's real popular there."

"What's funny, though," Johnny says, "is that Cretin High's a military school." (Johnny attended several military schools himself.)

While on the subject of taste, *End of the Century* includes "Chinese Rock," a ditty about heroin previously recorded by (Johnny Thunders') Heartbreakers. The Heartbreakers shared composer credit with Dee Dee Ramone, but their claim didn't make it to the Ramones' LP.

"It was our song originally," Joey says. "It seems in the last six months everybody in the world's been doing it, so we decided to show them the right way." Dee Dee apparently gave the song to the Heartbreakers ("which he wasn't supposed to do"—Johnny) before the Ramones decided to record it. It was written at the same time as "Commando" and "53rd & 3rd"; the latter appeared on the first Ramones album, so "Chinese Rock" dates back quite a ways.

"At that time in our career we didn't want to have any reference to heroin," Joey says in explanation of the song's delayed appearance. "We care; we're not a junk band. We've got prestige."

1980 IS SHAPING UP as the year the Ramones reap the benefits of their tumultuous activities over the last 12 months: a Phil Spector-produced album, their appearance in *Rock 'n' Roll High School* ("We're gonna do a Hitchcock film next," Joey deadpans), and — last but not least — a new manager.

Danny Fields, the band's original pilot, had been unashamedly in awe of them since first seeing the Ramones in 1974. After four years of his tutelage, though, the band felt it was time for a change; they certainly hadn't taken over the world. They emphasize there are no hard feelings, and even immortalize Fields on *End of the Century*'s "Danny Says," a good-natured tribute written before the split. (The title is a spoof on "Caroline Says." Explains Joey, "Danny was involved with that Lou Reed crowd.")

Joey reiterates, "We like Danny, we like Danny," but the Ramones' allegiance now belongs to Gary Kurfirst, who also manages Ramones labelmates Talking Heads. What can Kurfirst do that Fields couldn't? "Everything," Joey mutters under his breath, to a round of laughter.

"[Kurfirst] felt he understood us best and had the right temperament," Johnny says. "He's aggressive and answers to things." "The old fight, fight, fight," Joey butts in.

Johnny: "He has integrity."

Joey: "He eats dirt!"

No one can question the Ramones' integrity. For all their fans' enthusiasm, this band seemed Least Likely to Succeed; now they're on the verge. "I'm really excited about things now," Joey enthuses. "Working with Phil was great. We got a new manager. Things are looking up." Even some of those padlocked radio station doors are finally giving way.

Joey candidly admits, "We want to be successful, and we want to be a little richer than we are now. But we care about our crowd; we want to give them everything we can give 'em." For that reason, the Ramones' initial four-song sets (Johnny: "We gradually worked our way up to 25 minutes") now run an hour and a quarter. "You can't charge kids nine dollars and play 20 minutes," Johnny states.

A chorus of "nah" greets the idea that the Ramones might ever go mainstream. "We play live the way we always have," Dee Dee says. Joey concurs: "We've kept all our ideals. We've stuck to our guns. We believe that the more you keep banging, the more things are gonna change. We ain't normal." Johnny: "Hopefully we'll become less normal if we become more popular."

Joey: "After five and a half years in this business you're gonna go crazy anyway."

They're aware they still have to prove themselves nationally and are banking on *End of the Century* to do it. Johnny has memorized the week's chart positions in all three trades. He knows from experience what the Ramones are dealing with.

"Our years in the business have managed to take a lot of fun out of things. It's still fun playing, but they made us miserable. Maybe it was naïve of us to think it was gonna be a little easier than this. Nobody did anything for us."

"We got treated like shit until a few months ago," Joey says. "We're taking the fall for starting off when we did. We took the fall for everybody."

"Sire [Records]'s been nice," Johnny adds hastily, "but nobody ever got anything we needed: no TV shows, no radio play. I guess the industry just wanted to keep new wave down." Joey mentions that the Ramones never even used the term "punk." "You used it on us," he says half-accusingly.

Even if/when *End of the Century* earns the Ramones their due, it's unlikely they'll cut down on their heavy tour schedule. They're currently winding up a three-month U.S. tour, then it's over to Japan (another first) and back to Europe for the summer. Joey sounds like a gratified proselytizer when he talks about the band's experiences in culturally deprived areas.

"We're spoiled in New York City. In most states, forget it. We were touring Louisiana, and I was dying to hear a Foreigner song just to hear some rock and roll. All the radio was playing was Olivia Newton-John, John Denver and disco. You gotta play everywhere; people in Louisiana are dying to hear a good rock and roll band. We played Birmingham, Alabama and they tore the place down. We did four encores."

How can you fault a rock band doing missionary work? ■

QUOTES OF THE DECADE

"We thought we'd always be a cult band."
—SLIM JIM PHANTOM of THE STRAY CATS
(1983) TP 91

"I don't mind being a cult band, but I think rock and roll is meant for the masses, not for a few weirdos."
—LUX INTERIOR of THE CRAMPS (1984) TP 94

BLONDIE: PROGRESS REPORT FROM THE POWER STATION

TP 42, SEPTEMBER 1979

By Jim Green

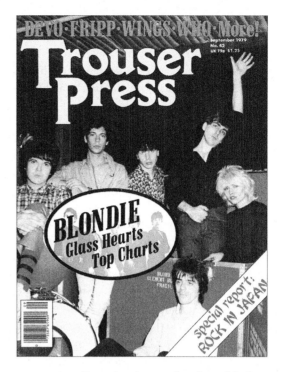

A A brassy orchestra plays a Grand Guignol gurgle. A deep voice ominously intones, with a faint echo, "The time: early spring, 1975, The place: a dank and dingy bar called CBGB, on the Bowery in Manhattan. A young man, in search of musical adventure, has dared the depths of this urban jungle. Little does he know what is in store for him: Blondie and the Banzai Babies."

Of course, now would be the proper instant for an organ sting, except that the sextet now on stage doesn't have one to sting with. What it does have is a guitarist, a bass player and a drummer, desultorily pulling and pushing at their instruments while a front line of two brunettes and a blond are hully-gullying, frugging, singing and exuding a rare mixture of innocent exuberance and raw, kittenish energy.

"Good grief," thinks our hero, "they can't do that!" What they're doing is an unholy hybrid of raunchy, almost Velvet Underground-ish instrumental work backing up '60s "girl group" pop tunes and vocal stylings. But then again, they are indeed doing it, and in no time at all our hero has to admit he's impressed, even excited by it.

He watches the guitarist, who somehow seems like a maestro, conducting it all while casually strumming distortion-heavy chords on his Stratocaster. But more often, his eyes are on the girls, particularly the blonde. She sings more than the others, but that's not why. It's not even because she sings better than they do — with this sound system it's hard to tell. She has the most extraordinary face — like a cross between Tuesday Weld and Sandra Dee, he thinks. And there's something intangible about her, an attraction, that he can't quite put his finger on...

...Four years later, our selfsame protagonist is seated in front of a recording mogul whose credentials, in terms of sheer success, are phenomenal. In a clipped, mongrelized Australian/English accent, this musical magnate is saying things like, "The music industry was waiting for something like us to come along. They were hoping that each thing that came along would be the next Beatles, and all that bullshit, but what they overlooked was that the next Beatles could actually be a group with a girl in it."

Our lad is sitting trying to keep his eyes from bugging out, listening to these grandiose proclamations and remembering that night at CBGB, marveling that the embryonic band he'd seen four years ago had now evolved into this, and that the two members on whom he'd first focused are the only ones left from that original model.

Kind of corny, right? But this isn't some hokum excised from a grade-B late, late show. This is reality: I am the listener, attempting to assimilate these weighty words from the mouth of producer Mike Chapman. Chapman scored a coup last fall when his productions of Exile ("Kiss You All Over") and Nick Gilder ("Hot Child in the City") held down the number-one and -two spots, respectively, at the same time, two weeks running, in the trade singles charts. ("Hot Child" then went to number-one as well.) The same thing very nearly happened to singles he cut with the Suzi Quatro/Chris Norman team-up ("Stumblin' In") and Blondie's "Heart of Glass," both of which topped the charts within weeks of one another.

The Blondie album that spawned "Heart of Glass," *Parallel Lines*, is about to pass the platinum mark in sales (one million units) and is still selling like ice cubes in the Sahara. At the same time, the LP's follow-up single, "One Way or Another," which was released just before the conversation at hand, is making noises like it'll be another mega-hit. Chapman and I are seated in the control room of the Power Station, the New York recording studio where he's getting ready to begin another long day (and possibly night) pursuing the next milestone in Blondie's campaign, cutting the group's fourth album, *Eat to the Beat*.

What a way to start such a day: Chapman neatly sums up the thrust of his discourse by saying, "Blondie are the superstars of tomorrow."

Fairytale come true, rags to riches, la-de-da ... except it's not that simple. The success wasn't overnight, in fact the rags are only just beginning to show signs of golden stitching, and, yes, Virginia, life can be very taxing on the way to the top, to say the least. Personality conflicts (the Artist vs. the Label, vs. the Manager, vs. Themselves), huge debts incurred, the mounting pressures of accelerating commercial expectations, and an often unsympathetic, even hostile press.

Which last point brings us to the genesis of this piece. After initially welcoming the prospect of a Blondie story with open arms, the representative of the independent publicity firm hired by the band suddenly became less than encouraging, speaking in a language of ifs, maybes and I-don't-knows. Soon after adding a few we'll-sees and I'll-have-to-get-back-to-yous to her conversational repertoire, she announced that the band was not doing any interviews. Something about trouble with *Rolling Stone*, and they weren't talking to *Newsweek*, either, only to people that they know, sorry. I know them, I protested to no avail.

So, I called up Blondie guitarist Chris Stein, and he said, "Yeah, sure, we're gonna be in the studio, come on over."

At the Power Station, Chris said he saw this article as an opportunity to set the record straight on a few things and to get an in-depth profile of the band without having to fence with a self-serving journalist harboring *a priori* antagonisms and licking lips at the thought of shooting the band's image full of holes at the twist of a phrase.

I hadn't just caught Chris with his paranoid tendencies showing, either. I'd heard this before from him (not to mention several other bands). The British music weeklies have seemed as eager to take potshots at Blondie — apparently, mainly because they've become successful — as they are to print photos of Debbie Harry. Certain members of the American press have been less than friendly also, and Chris was particularly peeved with the group's encounter with the man from *Rolling Stone*. The piece ["Platinum Blonde"] had yet to come out at that time, but Chris knew it would be a disaster: the guy [Jamie James] knew little about rock and roll or the pressures it can bring — hadn't even seen the band play — and, demanding his interview at an unexpected juncture, was evidently armed with eager skepticism. "We gave him a hard time."

On the other hand, I knew Blondie, and they know *Trouser Press*. I'd been in a band for a short while with Jimmy Destri just before he joined Blondie, and have been on casually friendly terms with Chris, Debbie and drummer Clem Burke after having done an article on the band for another magazine when they were recording their first LP. Since then, I'd done a pair of pieces on them, including one for *Hit Parader* about which Chris and Debbie had been particularly enthusiastic. So, I had the stamp of approval — but while I wasn't out to dig up dirt, this wasn't to be for *Hit Parader* — no facile, glossy puff piece this. Chris acknowledged as much when I told him so.

The idea was to go into the studio and talk with everybody in the band and soak up what I could of what making an album — specifically a Blondie album, this particular Blondie album — entailed. I entered into their schedule, the limits of which, while testing the stamina of various members at various times, were determined chiefly by the necessary work foreseen by Chapman, whose endurance was astounding. Most of the basic tracks (i.e., drums, bass and some guitar and/or keyboards) had been done; remaining were overdubs on most of the lead and background vocals, more guitars and keyboards, extra percussion and so forth. The band, then, was working under the pressure that playing for high stakes can bring to bear. Adding to the pressure-cooker situation was the wear and tear of overdubbing, usually a tedious and drawn-out process in which many parts are built up into dense and deep textures. The manifestations of the resultant annoyance and ennui were many, both large and small.

Even as Chris explained the *Rolling Stone* debacle to me, after I'd just arrived at the studio for my first look-see, he sat there tossing a small razor blade at the wooden wall of the recording chamber. Inside the control room, the air was thick with talk of the trials and tribulations of arriving at a working understanding with Terry Ellis, the head of Chrysalis Records.

At moments like these, a bit of light diversion helps dissipate the tension for those in whom it is amassing in intolerable increments. So, when Jimmy Destri walked in with his latest acquisition, a digital delay sequencer, he was met with playful jeers of, "Oh no, a new toy!" and — this from Chapman — "Manny's [the city's top musical instrument and accessories store] must be making a mint out of you guys!" Jimmy had everyone in stitches as he related the group's business manager's "Oh no, what next?" response to Jimmy's call to requisition funds and showed Chris how the gizmo worked. The sequencer was

to see a good deal of use in the coming days of keyboard overdubs.

Chris had some time before he was needed for his next overdub, so we retired to a mini-kitchen alcove to talk.

"We were gonna do Jack Lee's greatest hits this time, but we decided not to," he cracked, alluding to the author of "Hanging on the Telephone" and "Will Anything Happen?" from *Parallel Lines*, and possibly to the eyebrow-raising in some circles over the inclusion of two songs on one album by someone outside the band. But that was nothing, especially compared to the cries of "sell-out."

"One thing I really resented was all the people who said we'd sold out because 'Heart of Glass' was disco." In Europe, they'd already ascended to near-superstar status on the basis of a string of huge hits, of which "Heart of Glass" was merely the next in the series (which had kicked off a year prior with "Denis"). "I know full well that, if it hadn't been a hit, nobody would have said anything negative about it — maybe, 'Oh, Blondie did a disco song, isn't that cute.' The reason it's a hit is because it's a good song. We used to do it a long, long time ago as a funky song.

"It also has to do with the sound, which is a sophisticated, Eurodisco sound, a little like Kraftwerk and some Giorgio Moroder stuff — it's kinda novel here. [Friend and former mentor] Marty Thau said he was at this disco convention and he heard the song and thought, 'This is cute, really hip, it's punk-disco,' not having realized at first that it was us."

We spoke of the specialization of rock in the '70s, Chris referring to the "egocentric consciousness of the '70s as opposed to the socialistic consciousness of the '60s." This past decade has spawned groups who watered down rock and roll, removing it further from its former spirit and energy, diluting, over-intellectualizing and departmentalizing it. "Everything is bullshit in the '70s," Chris added morosely.

Jimmy, who had wandered in, interjected, "I think our band will probably be responsible for bringing everything — like disco, heavy rock, everything we do — into just one genre, a pop genre. In England and in Europe the kids just look at these as parallel aspects of one overall form, but they don't here.

"A lot of people think it's hard to crack America because of its size," he continued, "but the real reason is that it's the only country in the world where every art form is just a backdrop to sell a product; all of it, including rock and roll, is there to sell Ivory Soap on the radio."

"Anyway," said Chris, "I don't think we're gonna release another disco single here." There will be a disco song on the new album, with the tentative working title "The Spaghetti Song" (so called because it reminds Chris of the movie soundtrack music used in Italian-made Westerns), but it simply doesn't sound like a single, at this stage.

Talk wandered to the last album, and I suggested that *Parallel Lines* seemed somehow too disparate, the individual parts strong but, taken as a whole, not fitting together well. Chris agreed, and said he thought that that would be remedied with a more unified sound on *Eat to the Beat*. "The last album was so technically perfect, everybody executed their parts very well, but I think there was a lack of personality..."

Destri: "I was sort of absent while we recorded the album. It's a very, uh, technical album, and Mike pulled it out of us. Personally, I was going through the trauma of asking myself whether or not I wanted to be a pop musician anymore. It was a difficult period for all of us, though; we were under management we didn't feel comfortable with..."

Chapman wandered past, towards the men's room, and broke the mood by tripping over the tape recorder, picking it up and yelling "Fuck fuck fuck" into it. Everybody broke up laughing (Clem Burke had stuck his head in by now).

Back to *Parallel Lines*. Chris commented that he thought its cover "stinks." Clem, he reported, had had an idea for a montage which Chrysalis had simply not found acceptable. Clem and I got to talking as Jimmy and Chris drifted off to the control room after Chapman emerged from the men's room.

"Sometimes we're so unhip that we're hip; iconoclastic, in a way. When we did 'Heart of Glass' it wasn't too cool to play disco, at least not in our social set, but we did it anyway 'cause we wanted to try it." But what for the group was somewhat of an experiment could not be handled casually, if indeed anything could have been at that time. "Mike was conducting me as I played, there was a lot of eye-to-eye contact. The emotions were different, more intense, on that album than on this one," said Clem.

Chris had said that Chapman had been more involved in creating *Parallel Lines*, sacrificing some energy perhaps, but "getting it right, more mechanically perfect." Clem explained that the band was building confidence in itself as a working unit and in its identity as a band. "I think we look at our stuff now more like, 'Is it good as a Blondie song?' rather than, 'Does it sound good?' We've found our own little niche, we've got our own standards now, instead of using the standards of what others do.

"We're not as inhibited now about playing or songwriting in that regard," he continued. The old "We've-done-it-before-so-we-can-do-it-again" philosophy? "Yeah. And, also, we're more aware — I certainly am — of how a drum roll or a guitar lick will translate onto record, how it'll sound when I put the record on six months from the time it's done. I've gained a kind of looseness; the only thing I'm worried about these days is trying not to repeat myself.

"I'm into the idea of being as good as I can be — the regeneration of the mod thing is like that, the opposite of the original punk ethic of 'I can't play, but I don't care.'

"We've never wanted to be 'underground.' People toss around terms like 'sell out' about us, but in my eyes we never have. I don't want to get into defending the band," he said, in a fairly matter of fact tone. "What we always wanted was to be pop-oriented and have hit records. What I've always liked about the group is that focus, and now other things can rise to the top, too," he said, referring to crossbreeds of various pop forms, like Chris's artier tendencies.

But Chris, who'd wandered back in, made sure to differentiate experimentation from "sterile, over-intellectualized groups like ELP." "Some people are arty," responded Clem, "some people are pop, some people try to imitate Jimmy Page."

I recalled that, after the period of flux four years ago which left only Chris and Debbie from the original band, fleshed out by Clem and Gary Valentine, I'd seen them and thought that their reach exceeded their grasp. Chris and Clem chorused in agreement, with Clem citing "Man Overboard" and "Attack of the Giant Ants" as two numbers that were more ambitious than the band could handle properly at the time — exactly the ones that had come to my mind. "I've always sensed that Debbie is a great frontperson, singer/stylist, songwriter, and I've always had faith in the band," Clem continued. "Chris is a little more the avant-gardist and I'm more of the pop type, and his interest rubbed off on me and I got him to like the Bay City Rollers — who I don't like anymore, I like Rosetta Stone [*a band from Northern Ireland who had an ex-Roller in the lineup*]."

I further ventured that at that time an awful lot of people were putting down Blondie as hopeless — and worse. Chris remembered it all too well. "That we got a negative reaction was better than none at all, but on the scene, there was a feeling of conspiracy against us—all kinds of fucking cliques. What happened in the New York scene was that, for a year or so, it was great, everybody shared their amps, their guitars, we were palsy-walsy. As soon as the first record company, the first dollar, showed up at CBGB, the whole thing began to change — the whole scene was blown, everybody was dead competitive, and that was it. Everybody was in a rush to sign a record contract."

"It's really hard to get started now," said Clem, "with so many bands imitating and emulating everything and one another. Thank god, nobody sounded like us, nobody did what we did, or what Talking Heads did, for that matter."

"We were innovative in being a synthesis," said Chris. But Blondie had a tough time convincing people that their synthesis was worthwhile.

THE NEXT DAY WAS the Saturday of Memorial Day weekend. The Blondies — as they're referred to by people around them — were off on Sunday, but would come in on Monday, Memorial Day, and Chris was the main man in the studio with Mike Chapman and Dave Tickle, Chapman's wunderkind engineer and production protégé (he's only 19). Chris was dubbing guitar parts until every note was just right, and then going back over each again to double them up. The song primarily receiving the benefits of this labor was "Shayla," a quiet, lullaby-like track. After sitting and watching and waiting for Chris to take five for a quick chat, I was amazed that hours of this careful, painstaking repetition, dubbing increment by tiny increment, didn't put them to sleep! Especially on such a quiet number. Little was I prepared for the final result, as the track evolved a gentle force of its own.

Memorial Day was strange, as friends and ladies of people connected with the studio had the day off and came to visit. The Kinks, who were hurrying through their own sessions in the next studio (Power Station has two control room/recording chamber units) in order to meet their deadline, were unused to alien bodies sitting and flitting about while they cut their tracks, being used to the privacy of their own Konk Studios. Even a seasoned veteran of rock and roll writing was put slightly on edge by being in the studio at the same time with both a group that has long been a legend in its own time and one that soon may become one.

Chris again was doing a lot of overdubs, this time for an obvious standout track, "The Hardest Part." Chris was layering guitar riffs over Frank Infante's basic rhythm guitar. These layers would intertwine with Jimmy's keyboards and another Frankie riff. Debbie's vocal and Chris's solo would sit over this foundation, the end result containing all the quintessential funk licks, and calling to mind "Fame" and "Miss You" and "Superstition." This, however, ended up as a hard, chunky rocker, driven by the inexorable force of Clem's bass drum and tom-toms, as unstoppable as the "25 tons of hardened steel" armored truck which the tune's singer is urging her compatriots to hijack. All of the guitar and keyboard parts eventually would be doubled, a device Chapman believes gives richness to Blondie's trademark sound — superficially unnoticed yet subtly effective. "Union City Blue," a melodiously evocative uptempo number, got the same treatment next.

With Chris having done his fill for the time being, Jimmy and Mike Chapman took a listen to a playback of "Die Young, Stay Pretty," a reggae tune that's been on the shelf since Blondie's early days (about as old as "Heart of Glass," i.e., dating from early to mid-'75). Mike got a flash: "Let's do backing vocals for it!" So, leaving Tickle at the controls, he and Jimmy went into the sound chamber and, trotting out their best Jamaican yes-men poses (Jah-men?), "sang" (the word is used lightly) answers to Debbie after lines like "deteriorate in your own time" and "dilly near senility." Mike subsequently experimented by — having put the heavily echoed voices on a separate track — removing the actual voices and keeping only the echoes. These will later be redone, but they will be recut after this fashion, an idle amusement becoming a recording reality.

I snuck off to have a few words with the newest member of Blondie, British-born bassist Nigel Harrison, who confessed he had done few interviews and hadn't thought of himself as the "interview type." Harrison's first major band was Silverhead, and his tenure with them started on a rather strange note:

"When you're looking for gigs in the back of *Melody Maker*, if it's a large block advert, then there's money behind it. I'd answer any of those, even if it was for a topless go-go band or whatever and there was one that wanted 'erotic relaxers.' I didn't know what that meant, and it turned out to be Michael Des Barres" — previously best known in the States as an actor for his portrayal of the class punk in *To Sir With Love* — "getting a band together. There seemed to be a mysterious godfather figure behind it, and after a week, it came out that it was Andrew Lloyd Webber and Tim Rice [of *Jesus Christ Superstar* and *Evita* notoriety] backing it."

The band's music was ballsy rock and roll just this side of heavy metal, and the image was très glam — "but it wasn't glitter, it was 'cock rock,' that was our thing. We'd go on tour with Deep Purple and steal all the girls from 'em... It was a good band, but after two albums it hadn't really made it." Silverhead continued after Des Barres left, working on a third, more blues-rock album (Nigel's previous background was bands in the blues boom, "Y'know, Savoy Brown, Chicken Shack, Fleetwood Mac-type bands").

Nigel wound up playing with ex-Doors keyboard man Ray Manzarek, who he'd gotten to know during Silverhead's L.A. days. He played on *The Whole Thing Started With Rock & Roll Now It's Out of Control* LP and stuck with Ray through the well-intended but misconceived Nite City band. After that folded, Manzarek and Nigel put together a band with Iggy Pop, who backed out, evidently feeling he was coming too close to doing a resurrection of the Jim Morrison persona.

After the Ig allied himself with Bowie, Ray and Nigel went to see him perform. Blondie was the opening band for Iggy on that tour, and Nigel was knocked out. Through mutual friends, he was contacted and asked to come down to the Whisky to play with the band at a soundcheck, where he found out that they were interested in his joining on bass. "But I'd seen Frankie [Infante] onstage playing bass with them, and he looked so cool, and I thought, 'What do they need me for with someone like him?'"

But things happened so fast that there was almost no time to think. He was back in New York with the band before fully realizing he was going to leave Manzarek and join Blondie. Then, before he knew it, he was flying to England for the start of Blondie's European tour, even before he knew any of the material. This all happened in a matter of days, and somewhere in there he and Frankie realized that they would both stay, with Frankie shifting over to guitar.

It was a bit of a shock to realize his first gig as a Blondie would be in Aylesbury, near where he grew up. "It went great — the papers said, 'Local Boy Makes Good.'"

Despite the fact that he wrote very little prior to joining Blondie, he penned the music for "One Way or Another" and the new album's title song. Perhaps it's because he hadn't previously envisioned himself as a creator, but the fact of his creative blossoming isn't to be denied, though he spoke of Blondie's outpourings in general terms: "The ultimate thing to me would be to have an album out every month and a single every Friday — it used to be that way almost, in England, in the '60s."

THE NEXT DAY I spoke with Chris briefly while the Kinks blasted away in the background, pulling together a track that eventually became "Captain America." "There's volumes of shit about Blondie in the press, and reams of it are superficial drivel and misinformation," he said disgustedly. I mentioned that there was a bottleneck of sorts: now that the person in the street was beginning to know Blondie, more than ever his/her conception of the name meant Debbie. Debbie was the spokeswoman for the group, yet people focused on the "dumb blonde" image, and how could a dumb blonde speak with words instead of body language? Plus, often Debbie was not the perfect public personality; she hadn't developed the aplomb to be a glib Merv Griffin talk show guest, and that only confused things further.

"People aren't really willing to take her seriously and accept it when she talks straight to them. Everybody thinks what she is publicly [both the "dumb blonde" and the straight talker] is an act. Debbie's a genius. When she gets into it, she's great to talk to, but she's also very natural and can't turn herself on and off." We chatted about Marilyn Monroe, a bright woman doomed by the public's non-acceptance of her as anything other than a "dumb blonde."

The Kinks were still blasting away, people were coming and going, there was a television on and Chris got up to make sure his presence wasn't required in the control room (all of his overdubs were done with him sitting by Chapman at the board, playing either through the amps in the adjacent chamber or straight into the board itself).

Chris returned, and we went back to discussing Debbie and the group's image. "People say that Debbie gets all the money in the band, but it's just not true. All she gets extra is on the merchandising of stuff that's only Debbie Harry stuff,

like posters of her alone. Otherwise, she gets the same as me and Clem and Jimmy. Frankie and Nigel get a little less because they joined much later."

Chris went on to say that, besides, Blondie owes a huge amount of money in addition to the amount still owed Chrysalis. "Chrysalis — Terry Ellis — got the money together to buy us from Private Stock." (Some rumors placed the price tag in the seven-figure bracket.) "The band has to repay Ellis." This led into a discussion of the band's management situation, which was sticky, as the band wanted to cut loose from Peter Leeds, who still managed them on paper but was no longer involved in the day-to-day affairs.

We spoke of the possibility of a concept album (which he, Debbie and Jimmy had mentioned at various times) that will have to wait due to time commitments and commercial considerations. We talked about writing songs and how writing hits had to do with tuning in to a collective cultural consciousness. We didn't get too far into any of these due to interruptions, and eventually gave in and drifted off to check on what the rest of the Power Station was up to.

In the control room, Frankie and Jimmy were listening, with Chapman and Tickle, to a playback of Frankie's solo, or rather solos, on Jimmy's tune "I'm Not Living in the Real World." Confronted with the task of coming up with a solo on the spot, Frankie had first been bewildered as to which tack to take, but after some experimentation, he came up with a satisfactory solo, a chaotic Pistols-y raver and was promptly told by Chapman to double it. "I didn't know what I was doing, I just played it," said Frankie, so Chapman told him to do more or less the same thing again, and not worry about the variation. When played together, they sounded fabulously wild.

But for Chapman, that wasn't enough — he wanted to put a huge electro-metallic crash at the end of the solo, which he proposed to do by simply banging the echo amplifier at the end of the final feedback note of the solo. Everybody had a laugh, Mike included, as he repeatedly struggled to drop the amp head at the exact moment. Nigel grinned, and said, "For this we pay a fortune per hour?" Jimmy's comment: "Look what they done to my song, Ma."

At some point, I spoke to Jimmy at length. We avoided distractions by camping out on the stairs and then in an unused office upstairs. Before settling on keyboards, Jimmy had tried and dropped drums, bass and acoustic guitar, driving the Destri clan nuts in the process. When his father bought a piano, he'd jumped on it, surprising his family, who intended the instrument for younger sister Donna ("I was gonna become a doctor or a lawyer, right, but the cute little one should learn how to play the piano.") Donna became a classical musical prodigy of sorts, while Jimmy tried to teach himself rock solos off records. Donna's own interest flagged; in spite of some academic approval, she lacked confidence in her playing and "clammed up." She did, however, stay with it long enough to instruct Jimmy in some of the basics. He never did learn the proper way to play, though, which is why he uses the synthesizer so much ("I don't have a good, independent left hand").

This, of course, didn't deter his interest in playing in bands, and he went through the usual neighborhood combo scene, but was soon hanging out with an older crowd. He acquired an old Farfisa organ, but it soon went into disuse; he became intrigued by visual arts and threw himself into that academic world. He flirted with the notion of playing in several New York club bands, but it wasn't until he saw Blondie for the second time that he was knocked out. Watching Blondie (then Chris, Debbie, Clem and Gary Valentine) intently, it was love at second sight.

"They remembered me because I was the only one in the audience with short hair and a black suit," said Jimmy. "I was standing at the bar drinking, and Debbie came up and said, 'We heard you're quite a piano player.' I said, 'I don't have a piano, all I have's this tinny old organ.'" But she persisted, asking him down to rehearsal. "It wasn't an audition, it was, 'Would you like to try it?'"

We touched on the subject of Gary Valentine, and it was an emotional one for Jimmy. Gary'd been a friend of Clem's who was picked to re-place Fred Smith when the latter left to join Television, not because he was a good player — he could barely play bass at all — but because of his attitude: charming, exuberant, very "up." But although he and Jimmy became close friends, "I was the reason Gary left the band. We were going through another tough period, all of us fighting with one another. But Gary is such an idealistic nut, brilliant as he is, he would never bend like we all did toward one another to solve a problem. He was just driving me crazy, so one day I walked into Peter Leeds's office and said, 'It's either him or me.' They fired him the next day."

Before heading out to L.A. and forming his own trio, the Know, Gary left the band with a parting gift, "(I'm Always Touched by Your) Presence, Dear," which became a huge hit for Blondie in Britain and Europe.

Jimmy offered a shrewd assessment of the contrasts of the band's components: Frankie, who approaches guitar from a musician's point of view; Chris, who is more "picturesque" and concept-oriented; Clem and Frankie, who love the road and playing out all the time; Nigel, who enjoys that but has other interests as well; and Chris, Debbie and himself, who enjoy performing immensely but would stay in New York to pursue outside projects when not recording or gigging. "But, as Clem says, and we all know it, Blondie has at least two more years of heavy touring until we determine whether or not we've reached the point where we can afford not to tour frequently."

Before Jimmy got up to go add some keyboards, he made a final statement about the work at hand: "What makes me proud of this album is that when the kids hear this album, after 'Heart of Glass' being number-one, when my friends hear it, when Gary hears it, they'll say, 'Thank god, they haven't lost it, they still have the feeling.'"

CATCHING UP WITH CLEM proved difficult. His father had been ill, and he was spending as much time as possible with him. When I did manage to sit down with him, he seemed a bit lethargic and perhaps distracted, thinking about his father, the work to be done, and various other band problems. Clem, as Destri had observed, is a realist in his own right. "We're only now learning some of the things that the kids on the street still don't realize — the truth of the Kinks' 'Tops of the Pops,' where they say, when you've gotten to number-one, 'Now you can make some real money.' I'm concerned with selling records now where I wasn't before, not so much in terms of real financial success, but in terms of artistic survival. However many records you sell, you have to sell more, or by industry standards you're slipping." Asked about his playing, he had little to say other than that perhaps he was helped by the open-minded structure of the band; his "exaggerated style" (his term) was developed by having to fill holes in the sound while Gary was learning to play. His striking visual stage persona was laughingly ascribed to his sense of "show biz." "I always liked showmanship, but I have to sit down."

Frank had even less to say. He doesn't share a lot of the others' concerns and hasn't had what he considers a colorful past. He knew Clem and Gary; used to hang out with them when they played CBGB. One time, when calling to see when they were playing next, Clem told him Gary'd left the band and they needed somebody to play bass on the album. Frank volunteered. Period.

"Nothing was definite, there were no heavy commitments. Even then I sometimes switched off on guitar and bass with Chris on stage. When Nigel came, it all sorta worked out, even though no one told me what was supposed to be happening." Frank just went with the turn of events.

Frank wasn't able to describe how he'd gotten the inspiration for "Defectors," an incredible mix of a heavy metal rondo and Cossack music; but when I heard it, I didn't think to ask questions — I just sat in the control room with my jaw on my chest. Phenomenal!

ON WEDNESDAY, Chapman was prepared to start at noon, but no Blondies had arrived yet, so I took the opportunity to get him into the act, which he welcomed. He was brimming with optimism and energy; little did we know how much of it he'd need to get him through the day.

Chapman had known about Blondie for a while before he met them; having been tipped that he ought to see them, he caught them at the Whisky in Los Angeles and was enchanted with their songs. "I went right out and bought their first album on Private Shock" — his term — "and within three or four plays, knew every song; it's a classic album." On meeting Jimmy and Clem for the first time in London, his first words shocked Jimmy, who'd idolized him: "Oh, you wrote 'Look Good in Blue.'" Chapman then sang him a snatch of it. "Some Blondies came down to the studio when I was in with Suzi Quatro, and I was trying to suggest a producer for them, throwing out all these names, when all the time I wanted to say, 'Can I work with you?'"

"Nicky Chinn and I have, in the last nine or ten years, written 50 or 60 hit songs; I've produced about as many hit records — we've sold 300 million records worldwide." But working with Blondie is a learning experience; their whole artistic outlook is fresh and new to him, "an invaluable experience, and I'll continue to produce them as long as they want me."

Blondie's songs, he feels, are classic pop, which the public desperately needs. "Blondie could sell 15 million of one album; not this album — it'll probably do six to eight million — but the next one. New wave's been an art form that's a little too abstract for the general public to understand. The basis of Blondie is their songs, which are totally accessible; what we've done is to take that art form and not tamper with it, just make it a little cleaner, a little more accessible, put Blondie's ideas in. And the public loves it." He admits that it's just starting, "but it'll take off to astronomical heights. These kids are brilliant... Never in my life have I come across a group that has such amazing expression. I know all of their frustrations and all of their ambitions and I'm able to use that by helping them to put all their feelings on their records." What works stays on the record, what doesn't, comes off. He admitted that *Parallel Lines* was "an album of discovery ... the sound is too precise," and he wouldn't do it quite the same way if he had it to do over again. "But the concepts were correct," he maintains.

If Blondie succeed, contends Chapman, they'll

open up a door in the industry that many other groups will be able to pass through — a hope and a belief shared by the band. "Somebody has to kick the industry in the ass," Chapman vows. And he has the hits to back up his judgment. And the seemingly indefatigable energy too — in that session he worked with various Blondies from around 1:00 p.m. until 8:00 a.m. the next morning with only a few brief breaks.

DEBBIE COULDN'T do the vocal she was scheduled for. There'd been a mistake in the recording of the track, so while Chapman and Tickle tried to work around it, Debbie and I took off for one of the sitting areas.

Debbie is shy sometimes and doesn't speak freely unless she's relaxed. However, she warmed to the discussion fairly easily this time, as we touched on the film she had acted in, *Union City*, a high-budget underground production based on a short story by the fellow who wrote *Rear Window*; it's a psychological suspense drama in which Debbie plays opposite an accomplished "legit" actor, Dennis Lipscomb.

"I'm not really an actress," although, as Jimmy and Chris had mentioned, she very much wants to be, "but I have a good sense of timing, which the cameraman remarked at. It's like an automatic instinct. I photograph well" — even in motion, on a movie set — "and I was able to project a certain personality. At certain points I really felt like the scenes were happening to me, and it was a rush, just like doing a good show."

Having broken the ice, I suggested that I wanted to go over some historical background, and Debbie agreed. "Those were hard times," she says of the days she spent struggling, with the Stilettos and the early Blondie. Patti Smith and Television were the attractions, and Blondie was "at the bottom of the barrel." Not that there was even much of a barrel in 1974–75; Blondie played CBGB frequently for seven months, and the audiences consisted mostly of "a few friends and three Hell's Angels at the bar." Then, all of a sudden, there was competition, and as tough as it had been to make ends meet, "everybody [in the various groups] was supporting one another

and digging this very private, small, clandestine rock and roll world." The new climate of money and rivalry was somewhat of a shock. "I didn't have a career motivation, I had a personal motivation. I had fantasies of becoming a pop star, but that was so removed from what I was doing. I just wanted to write good songs and perform good music."

The band almost broke up at one point, but Clem wouldn't let the group waste away. "He kept calling us up and saying we had such a good start, and he kept prodding us to continue." Chris and Debbie got a break when they got a deal on a loft they could move into together and use for rehearsals as well, and Clem supplied the keystone to those rehearsals by enlisting friend Gary to play bass. "We got banned from CBGB for eight or nine months. Hilly booked us in and then threw on four other bands, and Gary yelled at him. But I admired Gary for it, not taking anything from anyone..."

But Blondie weren't getting any more gifts after that loft. They had to play out-of-the-way places with poorer drawing power. Recalling that edition of Blondie, Debbie could only say, "We were really a mess."

Later, the acquisition of Jimmy began to have its effects, as did the growing sense of stability among the rest of the group. As the band developed material and tightened up, their enthusiasm rose. "We were so excited, in such a rush to do our songs," said Debbie. Of course, when they went into the studio to record their first LP with Richard Gottehrer, they were still amateurs. "We were so unprofessional — we discovered that we'd never stopped to break down what we'd been doing, and sometimes we were all playing different chords!" But they started learning fast.

Debbie only wished she'd gained more from her earlier experiences in Wind and the Willows (however meager they may have been: "I just wasn't paying attention") and the Stilettos ("We were without a real manager and blew possible deals with RCA and Bearsville"). Blondie's had to come a long way, the hard way.

The album will be out a few weeks after you read this. Meanwhile, the band, on tour, hit Central Park's Wollman Arena. Oddly, they seemed more unsure and less powerful on both the newer material (understandable) and even on songs from the second and third albums (hard to figure) than they did on the numbers from the first LP, which seemed to dominate the second half of the set. By the time they got to their last encore ("Bang a Gong") however, they were smoking hot. The crowd had risen to a fever pitch and didn't want to let them go. Add to this the fact that local newspapers blasted Blondie's triumph in drawing 20,000 in the Toronto indoor arena playing the same night as a bill down the street of Ted Nugent, Aerosmith, Nazareth, Johnny Winter and the Ramones, all of whom put together drew 50,000 in an open-air stadium. And Blondie just packed 52,000 fans into Belmont Raceway. Somebody out there must like them...

Perhaps, one way or another, Blondie will be superstars. Was their recently found U.S. stardom merely the result of crass marketing of a disco crossover single hit, or is America finally ready to embrace a great '70s pop band? Only the resounding success of the new album will silence their critics and any remaining self-doubts the group may harbor. Alright, everybody: Eat to the Beat! ■

HELLO IT'S ME

TP 24, DECEMBER 1977

Thank you for mentioning my departure from Blondie. It was nice to note that it was newsworthy. Incidentally, I was "fired" after I had announced my plans to leave the group upon completion of our second album. (Sour grapes? ... No.)

I am currently in Los Angeles, formulating my ideas into what will hopefully be my own group. Thank you for all the wonderful things you've written about Blondie and I hope you'll keep an eye open for my activities.

Gary Valentine
Los Angeles, CA

END-GROOVE AREA MESSAGES

TP 24, DECEMBER 1977

"The very first thing I do when I buy an album is check it for messages," writes Maggie Echazabal. "Is that like playing them backward? I'm worried."

The two messages cited most often seem beholden to their artists' popularity. "Have you found.../the lost Hawiians [sic]!" on Adam and the Ants' *Prince Charming* refers to the grass-skirted version of "Los Rancheros" heard briefly at the LP's end. "In space no one can hear you Clash!" is spread out over *Sandinista!*'s six sides.

"Tear down the walls!," similarly distributed on the Clash's *London Calling* was another popular message. But most were considerably lighter. Still, a two-record retrospective of Joy Division (a band not known for its sense of humor), has "The chicken won't stop" on its first side, followed by two sides of tiny fowl footprints, and finally "The chicken stops here" on Side Four. ("Is this their way of calling Ian Curtis's suicide cowardly?" wonders Dave Sheridan.)

The Go-Go's *Vacation* asks, "Is this record a pencil or a beer can?" "Personally, I can't tell the difference and don't care if they can either," writes Adam Bradshaw.

Earliest scratching proffered was "Do what thou wilt shall be the whole of the law" ("From Aleister Crowley's favorite fortune cookies" — Susan McLaughlin), appearing on both Led Zeppelin's "Immigrant Song" 45 and, in truncated form, the *Led Zeppelin III* album in 1970.

Other groovy messages: "Elvis was murdered" (Cramps, *Psychedelic Jungle*); "What we don't know we make up" (Go-Go's, "Our Lips Are Sealed" 45); "1984 happened in 1930 and we're just finding out about it — Black Randy" (Dead Kennedys, *Plastic Surgery Disasters*).

The R.E.M. boys were a pleasure to talk to, unfiltered and unpretentious. Peter Buck was definitely the one who already had his act together; Michael Stipe still seemed to be figuring out who he wanted to be and wasn't ready to project too much, not unlike their earliest music. Their comments about people assuming that folks from the South were ignorant rednecks really struck a chord with me, being a transplant from Atlanta myself.

The hotel where we did the interview was a fleabag in Manhattan's West 40s, which I think was familiar to plenty of other impoverished bands. At one point in the interview, one of them (I don't recall which) left the room to make a bathroom stop and didn't close the door, so I could clearly hear him peeing. "How relaxed," I thought, and kept talking.

I ran into bassist Mike Mills again on a different day at the A&M Records (which distributed IRS at the time) office, where he seemed to be scoring promo LPs. I loaned him a little change— maybe 25 cents — to help make bus fare downtown, which he has yet to repay. With interest, I figure he owes me at least two dollars now. (JY)

R.EALLY
E.XCITING
M.USIC

TP 88, AUGUST 1983

By Jon Young

Are you tired of constantly being told how this or that band is the new greatest wonder? Of course, you are. Unfortunately, superlatives have a way of spreading like germs.

But, if you will, suspend disbelief for a moment. Here's a band truly deserving of the most elaborate praise: R.E.M. Anyone who's heard this Athens, Georgia quartet knows their attention to melodic detail and punk-derived enthusiasm make for a pretty exciting combination. R.E.M.'s "Radio Free Europe" single and *Chronic Town* EP showed a group with impressive songwriting abilities and much technical promise.

Murmur, their first LP, fulfills that promise on one well-executed track after another.

Enough gushing! It's hard not to go overboard when describing this band, so, on with the interview. I met with Peter Buck (guitar), Michael Stipe (vocals) and Mike Mills (bass, vocals) in their Manhattan hotel (drummer Bill Berry was out shopping) and came away marveling that such unreasonably good music could be made by such reasonable people. They're frank but civilized, matter-of-fact but very confident. No wimps here!

Here's what Buck, Stipe and Mills (good name for a law firm!) had to say about...

THE ORIGINS OF THE BAND

Peter Buck says he was never a musician. "This is the first band I've been in. But I've always been arrogant enough to think that if I was in a band, it wouldn't matter that I couldn't play. If you have good enough taste, you don't have to be a great musician to make great music. When the band started, I knew about five chords and a Chuck Berry lick. I didn't even know bar chords."

Army brat Michael Stipe recalls, "I accidentally [?] got a subscription to the *Village Voice* when I was 15 and living in Illinois. I read about what was going on at CBGBs, bought the first Television and Patti Smith albums and then picked up on all the people that influenced them: the Velvets, Stooges, Dolls and so on. Before that time, I had virtually no musical background. My parents listened to Gershwin, Mancini, Wanda Jackson and the soundtrack to *Dr. Zhivago*. That's all I heard."

Buck and Stipe met at the University of Georgia in Athens when musical winds were beginning to shift — even in Georgia. Atlanta's Fans and the Brains, and later Athens' B-52's and Pylon, made the mid-to-late '70s a hot time for the hip South. The Fans, best known for a recording of the Tornadoes' "Telstar," were a special favorite of Buck's. "They were one of the all-time great bands as far as I'm concerned. They were everything a band should be: great songwriting, unpredictable stage shows and different types of music. I saw maybe 50 dates they did over a two-year period. If I ever get a lot of money, I'm going to have a label and put out a Fans LP. A&M owns a live album that they never released."

The two first played together in an Athens cover band. As other members drifted away, bassist Mike Mills and drummer Bill Berry entered the fold. "We'd all been at school in Athens for four or five years, more or less," Buck recalls. "In 1980, we started playing for fun at parties, then at benefits. Then people started offering us money to play. We got $250 to open for the Brains on our first professional date, and I was thrilled. Then Pylon canceled a date in North Carolina, and we played that. Pretty soon we were playing every weekend.

"For the first year and a half we made our living as a bar band that played originals. We'd play three sets a night at bars or pizza parlors, and just hope that some of the people who showed up would have a handle on what we were doing. It was weird."

THE SINGLE

"Radio Free Europe"/"Sitting Still" was released in 1981 on Hib-Tone Records. R.E.M. doesn't like it much, according to Mills: "It has a muddy quality that isn't very good. It got garbaged up in the transition from the studio to being mastered and pressed. Originally the record was a lot cleaner-sounding."

"All the nice subtleties were lost," Stipe adds.

"Radio Free Europe" garnered R.E.M. a lot of first-time attention, despite spotty distribution. "The single was only marginally available," Buck says. "It did well for an independent record, but only in three cities: Atlanta, Athens and New York. Sales totaled 5,000. It sold 4,000 initially and then went out of print for eight months."

THE EP

Like "Radio Free Europe," 1982's five-song *Chronic Town* was recorded with producer Mitch Easter at his Drive-In Studio in Winston-Salem, North Carolina. They don't like this record much, either. "We just did it for our own pleasure, as a learning process," Buck notes. "We used lots of backwards guitars and weird sound ideas. We tried anything we'd ever wanted to try, so a lot of things on there are too busy. We didn't edit ourselves the way we did on the album.

"The instruments were recorded on Friday, vocals on Saturday and it was mixed on Sunday. We didn't have the money to take any longer. The EP was mastered and the cover ready to go while we were negotiating to sign with I.R.S., and it didn't come out until six months later. So, it wasn't very representative of us."

THE LP

At last, they're happy! "The idea was to make a strong record with no filler," Buck says, "like *Aftermath* by the Stones, where every song is different but it sounds like a group effort."

Murmur, produced by Easter and Don Dixon, is hallmarked by a dense yet easy-to-follow sound. "Most of the basic instrumental and vocal tracks are very simple," Stipe says. "Then there's a lot of other stuff buried in the background that occasionally surfaces."

"Little things were added on to distinguish one song from another," Mills adds. "We like that, the more you listen to it, the more you hear things that didn't pop up the first few times, especially on headphones. It'd be horrible to hear a record once and pick up everything on it. That wouldn't be any fun."

One of the more exotic buried sounds occurs on "We Walk": pool balls colliding, slowed down to half-speed.

Stipe explains the album title came about because "murmur" is "one of the six easiest words in the English language to say." He doesn't cite a source.

THE SOUTH

R.E.M. hails from Dixie. If that amazes you non-Southern aesthetes, don't forget that all great American music — blues, jazz, rock and roll — has roots below the Mason-Dixon line.

Buck is accustomed to the "problem" of being a Southerner. Still, it doesn't make bigotry any easier to take. "People think that everyone from the South is a racist hick," he says wearily. "We go to big cities elsewhere and people say, 'How can you be from the South? Isn't everyone stupid there?' It does gall me sometimes that people have such a backward image of the South. Our best audiences are there, because they have no preconceptions."

"There isn't the musical segregation you find in Los Angeles or New York," Stipe says, "where you get the ska crowd, the hardcore crowd, the techno-pop crowd, the art crowd. If a band is halfway decent, it doesn't matter what tag they have. People will go see them."

"I like New York," Buck appends, "but the South is one of the last places where you can live as a human being. People in Atlanta still nod to each other on the street and say, 'Excuse me' if they bump into each other."

INFLUENCES

R.E.M. is generally regarded as a classic '60s-style pop band, i.e., descendants of the Beatles, Byrds and that ilk.

"That's not invalid, but it's not very valid, either," Buck remarks. "There's no conscious '60s influence. The idea that you can do whatever you want with pop songs and play around with structures, as we do, is more punk to me than anything else — not that we're a punk band. Maybe it's because we're melodic rather than buzzsaw that we come across as a '60s band."

As for frequent comparisons to the Byrds, he declares, "I probably listen to people that stole from the Byrds more often than the Byrds. I've got one Byrds album, and it's the one that doesn't sound anything like them — *Sweetheart of the Rodeo* — because I love Gram Parsons. The Byrds are OK, but none of us ever paid much attention to them.

"Early reviews compared us to the Cure, so I bought their first album to try to figure that out. I can see the comparison a little bit on 'Boys Don't Cry' and 'Jumping Someone Else's Train.' But then I got their second album, *17 Seconds*. We don't sound like that a bit — a nihilist in a leather jacket moaning over a blah tempo!"

"Nobody compares us to the Velvet Underground," Buck continues, "and that's probably the one group we all love. I think a lot of the things we do sound like the Velvets — not to the extent of the Dream Syndicate, but a lot of my guitar parts are real Velvety— droney but melodic." (The cassette of *Murmur* contains an extra track: a version of the Velvets' "There She Goes Again.")

You can also discount any Beau Brummels influence. "I don't know if that's a man or a band," Stipe says.

"No one's picked up on our country thing, either," Stipe says. "My vocals are influenced by early country singers, mostly women: Patsy Cline, Skeeter Davis, Kitty Wells, Wanda Jackson." (Insert expression of editorial disbelief.) "A lot of country guitar playing is really neat," Buck says. "It's melodic and pithy and not chord-oriented, without being jerk-off guitar solos. I stick things in all the time that are real country. That's a country lick right before the chorus in 'Catapult.'"

"In one interview a guy asked what I listened to. I said the Ink Spots," Stipe laughs. "So, in a review, he worked in the Ink Spots as one of our main influences, which is pretty weird. We don't sound a thing like the Ink Spots!" No kidding!

VOCALS AND LYRICS

It's impossible to figure exactly what Stipe is singing most of the time. He claims that's unintentional. Perhaps his gruff singing style is due to the unfiltered Camels he smokes heavily. Concerning his lyrics, "I don't have any great message to give out. Subtlety is a virtue and something you don't see very often these days."

Buck: "The music carries the weight of the message. A lot of times it's not what you say but the way that you say it."

Stipe: "The words are written in the context of the song. God help us if someone misconstrues them as poetry. A lyric sheet isn't necessary."

Buck: "I never listen to lyrics unless they're really up front. I couldn't tell you what a single one of the songs on Van Morrison's *Veedon Fleece* is about, but I think it's one of the greatest albums ever made."

OTHER BANDS

"I'm sick of DOR [dance-oriented] stuff like Flock of Seagulls," Buck offers. "They don't write a song, they just write a hook. Actually, we've been slagging off other bands far too much. It makes us sound like arrogant assholes, which we're not. We just have a healthy contempt for a huge segment of what now passes for rock and roll."

THE MUSIC INDUSTRY

Buck observes that in "the last six months, commercial radio has become a lot more open to new bands. Our record has had something like 27 adds [to radio station playlists] in the last five days."

"If we get mass exposure," Stipe says, "it'll be because radio bent to us rather than the other way around. The state of the record industry is such that people are grabbing at straws trying to find something new to play."

Consequently, "A lot of weird things are slipping in the back door," Buck notes. "Record companies know they're screwed, because people haven't been buying their records. Five years ago, Warner Bros. would never have signed Slash. It's just like 1957, when the big companies were scared by Specialty, Ace, Federal, Chess, Sun, all those little labels.

"It's all very well to sell 20 million copies of *Led Zeppelin IV*, but you're killing off any new music by loading the airways with bullshit. Now the big companies are bending over backwards to let in new stuff, but with a few exceptions all the people in marketing and sales hate it. You can't market something with contempt and do it well.

We would never have signed with a bigger label. "Companies like Slash, I.R.S. and Twin/Tone are going to be the wave of rock and roll future."

HOME TAPING

Buck: "R.E.M. endorses home taping."

MUSICAL PHILOSOPHY

Buck again: "The greatest music has always been made by individuals from unique standpoints, without commercial considerations. It doesn't matter how good or bad they are as musicians."

Stipe cites the Cramps, "basically a cover band, but they've made the best records of the last five years."

"They're an example of a strong, unique band that didn't try to make it but has nonetheless," Buck says.

The guitarist feels R.E.M. has made it, too. "To me, 'making it' means being able to play and make records, having people appreciate your music and enjoying what you're doing. Right now, we've made it. If we went on like this forever, I'd be happy."

So would we, pal. ∎

AMERICA UNDERGROUND

TP 72, APRIL 1982

R.E.M.: "Radio Free Europe" b/w "Sitting Still" — Hib-Tone HB0001. Here's yet another band from Athens, Georgia; whatta they do, grow 'em in Petri dishes in the high school chemistry lab? Like predecessors the B-52's and Pylon, R.E.M. has a choppy/jangling guitar sound and walloping backbeat. Whereas the B-52's revel in surf riffs and Motown, and Pylon opts for almost PiL-style sparseness, however, these people are wholehearted popsters — of both Anglo ("Europe") and California ("Sitting") persuasions. Three cheers for tuneful Georgians! (Robert Payes)

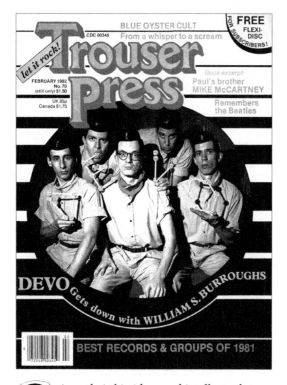

having conceptual imagination and felt a bit of satisfaction later on when other music magazines paired up oddly matched characters to interview each other for articles.

The New Musical Express, *with whom we regularly traded pieces, reprinted the conversation with our blessing. Twenty-six years later, it turned up without warning, translated, in the Italian* Rolling Stone. *They got it from an Italian book publisher who — despite never seeking our permission — included it in a 2008 collection called* William S. Burroughs: Rock'n'Roll Virus.

DEVO MEETS BURROUGHS

TP 70, FEBRUARY 1982

By Scott Isler

At last count there were 16 godfathers of punk/new wave. William S. Burroughs is the great-godfather. Ever since his novel *Naked Lunch* made its controversial debut in 1959, Burroughs has pioneered literary techniques and introduced subject matter whose daring (the former) and outrageousness (the latter) have assured him of a youthful audience. Now 67, he is hardly of the rock world yet commands its respect. David Bowie went through a Burroughs phase about the time of *Diamond Dogs,* and more than one group [*e.g., Steely Dan*] has named itself after a Burroughs book title or phrase (such as "heavy metal"). Burroughs himself used to have a column in *Crawdaddy* magazine; more recently he has been giving readings in rock clubs, and even appeared on *Saturday Night Live* (with a considerably cleaned-

G iven their big ideas and intellectual sophistication, we came up with our own big idea for a Devo cover story: to have them interviewed by a famous person rather than a rock journalist. We were surprised when, after they suggested futurist architect Buckminster Fuller, their second choice was porn star Marilyn Chambers (or was it Linda Lovelace?). The former wasn't available, and the search for the latter ended with a threatening phone message. On a whim, we proposed William S. Burroughs, setting up a Midwestern match of Missouri and Ohio. Devo greenlit the idea, which put the onus on Trouser Press *editor Scott Isler to sell the idea to Burroughs.*

Several dozen phone calls later, the event took place in "Bill's Bunker," a loft in a derelict section of Manhattan's Lower East Side. It's not certain who was talking at whom, but the conversation, which Scott witnessed and documented, sure was bizarre. (If memory serves, there was a discussion of cocaine — as in the obtaining of — that was left on the cutting room floor.)

We might have been disappointed at the results, but we were pleased with ourselves for

up text). His most recent book, *Cities of the Red Night*, finds him still flustering critics and delighting others with his cataclysmic imagery.

Devo needs no introduction to *Trouser Press* readers, having been profiled here on various occasions. For this encounter, though, we thought we'd see what would happen when the band's glimmer twins, Jerry Casale and Mark Mothersbaugh, met someone who was staring into the abyss while they were watching TV sitcoms in knee pants. (It goes without saying that Casale and Mothersbaugh are Burroughs fans.) What follows is hardly your standard rock interview. But these are not standard rock subjects.

WILLIAM S. BURROUGHS: One thing that's been very encouraging in the past 30 years is the worldwide cultural revolution, and the fact that the generation gap is getting wider. A lot of pressure to decriminalize marijuana is coming from congressmen and judges whose sons were getting busted. That apparently is all over the world, even in the Far East, which is usually so conservative, and the Moslem world. One of the big factors in that has been pop music. It's everywhere; it gets behind the Iron Curtain and all through the Orient and makes these changes.

Jerry Casale: [Devo chose rock as a medium for its message] because it's the most hideous area there is. It's exciting because it's filthy — nauseous yet erect.

WSB: Wait a minute. You chose it because you like music.

Mark Mothersbaugh: That's not true.

WSB: No? Don't you feel some aptitude for music? The reason I write is because I have always had some natural aptitude with words.

MM: Well, the equipment was just inexpensive. We couldn't be filmmakers because we couldn't afford the equipment.

JC: On an immediate, unguarded level there's no doubt about it: There's some drive to do it because you can do it. But then when you add to that the consciousness, the willful use of this innate ability, that's where it gets into "you do it because you hate it," because you hate what's being done.

The arena is so complex and vulgar; it's filled with the worst con artists, the most bizarre people, the biggest amount of bucks, the most mass dissemination. It deals with electronic innovations, it deals with TV, theater and dance, it deals with the immediacy of performance itself, so it's packed full of nuances. The limitations are what you place on it. You could certainly go into that area and twist it, do anything you want with it, and your success or failure is largely on your own lack of or inclusion of vision over a sustained period. As soon as you forget what you want to do, it's over.

But what most of 'em want to do is exactly what the zombies who run everything want 'em to do, because there are plenty of lackeys out there that are happy to be voluntary robots and get paid for it. Their particular hack imaginations synch up with those who want to give 'em bucks to do it.

So, Devo enters the scene knowing all that, but knowing also there's no choice but the basement or that. Now what do we do? We let all the demons come out. All the horrible supermarket themes and elevator music and TV theme songs and MOR ballads on radio that filled us up while we were growing up become twisted. If anything, Devo is on a performance level the enactment of a mutation aesthetic.

William, you and David Bowie had a discussion in *Rolling Stone* in 1974 about whether to use sonic warfare onstage. Bowie said he was not interested in doing that to people. He said he would never turn it on a crowd and make them shit their pants. I suppose we would. I think to send a whole crowd in, give 'em Kimbies at the door and inform them as part of Devo's performance they're gonna get to shit their pants *en masse* at the end of the night — that we probably have that tendency to do it, whatever you want to decide about that.

WSB: In a sense, if any artist is successful he would do exactly that. If you wrote about death completely convincingly you'd kill all your readers.

JC: What's going too far, though? Making them shit their pants?

WSB: Would it be going too far to kill them? I'll ask that question.

JC: Well, I suppose there's still some liberalism left in Devo; we'd say yes. We want 'em to come

AMERICAN PUNK AND NEW WAVE

back and shit again.

WSB: If your music or your novel isn't fun, nobody's gonna read it or listen to it. Showbiz!

JC: We base our aesthetic on self-deprecating humor. We include ourselves in it. But obviously there's something behind it. We have that sense — maybe that's the Midwestern part — that sense of shame about being human.

WSB: Everybody does. That's part of being human.

JC: But dealing with it and admitting it is rare. The masses are bad spuds who resort to defense mechanisms like fundamentalist religion and other psychotic values, far-rightists who deny it because they cannot deal with it. They've worked themselves into a constipated corner where to admit it is threatening to the rigid order they created. Good spuds have the ability to make fun of themselves.

JC: THERE'S NO QUESTION in our minds that humans are Devo. We've stated our case. I don't even see how you can disagree with it.

WSB: I feel there are too many of them.

JC: Too many humans.

WSB: It's intolerable.

JC: It seems like humans have always taken care of themselves like any other organism; there's a self-defeating gene that makes sure they wipe themselves out in the right numbers. Possibly that's all going on again. In other words, the artificial manifestations of that basic urge would be Reagan's politics and the far right; environmental manifestation would be the very strong death wish to allow pollution to take over like, fuck it, here we go. Maybe this stuff is all perfectly in keeping with human existence on the planet. Maybe we shouldn't bitch about anything or be appalled. Maybe we've got some erroneous ideas about enlightened human beings that could live in a different manner.

WSB: There's no way that things are. Things are changing with such rapidity.

JC: We wish!

WSB: They are.

JC: Well, changing but staying right the same.

WSB: Not really. Remember, 40 years ago the word "fuck" couldn't appear on printed paper. It was a whole different world then. No one questioned the Depression. No one questioned the right of a cop to beat up a n----r. All that is gone in the last 40 years. The only way it could come back would be with an out-and-out fascist takeover — a real police state. We talk about fascism here but we don't know what we're talking about.

JC: I know that, but there are different forms of it.

MM: There are new ways to do the same things they used to do. They aren't beating them over the head with clubs, they aren't stopping you with gunfire. But there are new, more subversive, nastier ways to control people.

WSB: Yeah, but just compare that with living in Argentina, where 4,000 people are dragged out of their beds and shot every year just for nothing, just for any liberal association. I've talked to people who've just gotten out of that. I'd rather have this than that, wouldn't you?

JC: That's a mature attitude. [laughter]

WSB: You don't want to starve to death, either.

JC: No.

WSB: Well, that's what I mean. Some things are a hell of a lot worse than others.

JC: More immediate and more crude, maybe.

MM: There's a good chance 4,000 people are gonna get dragged out of their houses in New York and shot each year. It just won't be by cops.

JC: Those things are all on the continuum; there's no dichotomy there.

WSB: None whatsoever. And the reason we aren't dragged out and shot is probably because other people are. We pay the price of other people starving. We buy our relative freedom. That's the whole CIA policy: Let it happen somewhere else.

WSB: EVERYTHING IS political in a sense. You can't say "politics stops here."

JC: We think everything is political anyway. We're in a vulgarity/mass arena. It's like an inverted aesthetic 'cause we're dealing with subverting sickness — taking what *you* know about society and people and what we agree with and applying it to an aesthetic to make the very sick people buy it.

WSB: It's always been my feeling the very sick

260   ZIP IT UP!

are *not* going to buy it. They're not gonna buy anything — except more sickness. You can't tell anybody anything they don't know already. It's only people that are in your areas of synchronicity that are going to respond.

JC: But what do people know?

WSB: You make people aware of what they know and don't know.

JC: We're just trying to put out information. You can't tell people what they don't know; that's why mass education is a joke. We know the world's upside-down.

WSB: It's obviously completely ill-intentioned so far as our species is concerned. There's something behind the whole scene — any scene, if you see chaos, ask yourself who profits in this. Somebody does. Of course, in a situation of chaos one group who's going to profit are the very rich. Not the fairly rich — I'm talking about a very, very select club. They can weather anything. Inflation's to their advantage because they can buy things nobody else can buy.

"Pessimistic" is a meaningless word. The captain says the ship is sinking; is he a pessimist? If the ship actually is sinking, no!

JC: That's exactly it. We're accused all the time of pessimism; we're maligned for being cynical, and it's frankly disgusting because all we're doing is reporting the facts. Because we question popular mythologies about progress and the value structure it's all based on as being absolutely rancid, then of course we're accused of having sour grapes. It's ridiculous; all you have to do is look at Jerry Falwell and Ronald McDonald and Ronald Reagan and start putting it all together. What we see, then, are born-again Christians dressed in double-knit pilgrim suits with particle guns that look like blunderbusses gettin' in station wagons and searching out people who aren't Christian enough to eat Thanksgiving turkey.

WSB: The born-again Christian thing is advantageous to the very rich, to keep people in line. It isn't an accident at all.

JC: Possibly we're even as popular as we are because we're misperceived as sickness. We didn't put things together quite the same way somebody else would, being from the Midwest and being

raised in mindless eclectic filth. We responded to it and received all the information, but what we chose to do about it was kind of aggressive in a malign way. Not really malign; we can see how it's perceived that way. Because we're pissed-off spuds with a plan; we aggressively take the case to those who make life hideous.

We'd like to make Devo a Church of De-evolution — legally, seriously, a cable franchise same as Oral Roberts, Garner Ted Armstrong, all those evil fuckers. Not pay taxes, like them. Not be presented in the rock and roll arena as labor for a corporate record company but rather the Church of De-evolution. Then, whatever you're presenting is suddenly appearing in a whole new context. We'd probably be assassinated if we could pull it off.

JC: DE-EVOLUTION is basically an extended joke that was as valid an explanation of anything as the Bible is, a mythology for people to believe in. We were just attacking the ideas humans have that they're at the center of the universe — that they're important, that they must be immortal, that there must be a Guide. The whole (what we think of as inverted) valued system that precipitates every cultural/political form follows from it.

WSB: Essentially monotheism — Christ and Muhammad. Incidentally, Muhammadan fundamentalists are fully as bad as Bible-belters; in fact, I think they're worse.

JC (to Mark): See, we've been leaving them out.

WSB: They're more used to killing, for one thing; it comes more naturally to them. In Egypt they have seen these people as a political mass, and the same thing could happen here. Fundamentalists are seen in Egypt as subversive, as a political danger to the regime. They're the ones who killed [Anwar] Sadat. It's as if Jerry Falwell's boys had assassinated President Reagan.

JC: If there's anything important about history, it's that stupidity wins. We're paranoid for good reasons: hundreds of years where assholes take over, knowledge is lost and things go backwards. We question the whole theory concerning progress, and the middle-class idea of a "better life."

WSB: You must remember this is a modern idea. While it completely permeates America and a good deal of Western Europe now, progress is a new concept; it came in with the industrial revolution. Another idea that came in there that we are really suffering from now is "the more the merrier" — more producers, more consumers, more people and therefore more pollution, depletion of resources, etc. Inflation's a direct result of overpopulation: less and less for more and more.

I think the concept of progress is pretty much devaluated in respectable intellectual circles. I mean, it's a pretty primitive person — although god knows there are millions and millions of those — who really believe in progress at this time. We've seen where it goes; we've seen places like Hawaii stopping progress saying, "We don't want any more hotels built here. The ocean's gonna be so polluted you can't go in, so what do they come to Waikiki for?" That's a very simple illustration of how the whole idea of progress is breaking down.

JC: We totally agree. We're attacking the idea that there is progress, the whole mythology of the last 300 years, the industrial revolution, which we feel has gone nowhere. We're at the end of it. You see exactly what consumerism has done, you see exactly what sin, guilt, work and disease have wrought as cornerstones of culture, and it's still operating. That's why we thought "Working in the Coal Mine" was so funny: "Lord, I'm so tired; how long can this go on?" The answer is it can go on as long as there's one guy to swing a pickaxe.

WSB: Most of the trouble we have now was quite predictable at the beginning of the industrial revolution because nothing was done to control it — the same way they don't do anything about pollution until it's too late. Many scientists say that the cumulative effect of the radiation level already is lethal. We can go so far as to say we don't have more than a hundred years.

JC: When you consider how this happens, it becomes obvious to us that it's inherent in human design — that humans are unfortunately very predictable in their response patterns.

WSB: It's not an either/or position. There's no doubt that there isn't a damn thing you can do about a lot of what's happening. It's like the fall of the Roman Empire: people knew that the currency was going, and the barbarians were moving in from the north, but life went on: people wrote poetry, played music. It almost becomes like the weather; there isn't anything you can do about it, so why keep yourself in a state?

JC: DEVO deals with people who eat McDonald hamburgers and wear Jordache jeans; that's our dilemma. We're almost fed by the things we hate.

WSB: Everybody is. Can man exist without enemies? Well, the answer is he never has.

JC: We're looking at the planet, pretending we're hovering in the Starship Enterprise observing the planet for a month. You can tune in anywhere.

WSB: I would say, "I want to see the manager! Who is responsible for this mess?" ∎

RALPH RECORDS: SURREALISM A GO GO

TP 54, SEPTEMBER 1980

By Jim Green

California: state of extremes, land of endless promise and fractured dreams. Where else could one find a disparate lot like Tricky Dick, Timothy Leary, I.M. Pei and the SLA? Or — more to the point — the definitively mainstream rock of Fleetstadt MacEagles around the corner from the nose-thumbing inventiveness of Zappa's Mothers? And the widescreen Warner Bros. homestead just a (relative) hop, skip and jump downstate from the sanctum sanctorum of the enigmatic Cryptic Corporation and its recording arm, Ralph Records?

This hand-drawn one-third-page ad was the first one Ralph Records ran in *Trouser Press* (TP 18). We had a great relationship with the label, whose implacable sense of doing things their way we greatly admired, even though they never would tell us who was inside those eyeballs.

The Golden State is only beginning to spawn its own; on close inspection its distinguished/notorious indigenes turn out to be transplants. So, the following scenario comes as no surprise: a bunch of artistic malcontents, figuring they can't get no satisfaction in Shreveport, Louisiana, migrate to that cradle of creative non-conformity, the San Francisco Bay Area. They whip up their own brand of musical mayhem, and, inspired by Captain Beefheart, attempt to capture the attention of the Warners marketing director who handled the good Captain. Predictably, little comes of their efforts. Not having left a name with their return address, the group receives a reply from the record company addressed to "residents." They not only begin calling themselves the Residents, but also beget their own record label (Ralph), the initial step in their campaign to make a jagged mark on the world.

In ensuing years, Ralph has issued a dozen albums (not to mention assorted singles and EPs) by the Residents and like-minded artists attracted to the label, including a sampler released in Britain by Virgin Records. The Residents themselves have accrued an impressive heap of press clippings from *Record World* to *NME* to *Creem* (but you read it in *Trouser Press* first!), all raving about the Residents' vicious vivisection of pop music and irreverent reconstruction of its entrails. The catalogue also includes the Rozz-Tox Manifesto, which deals with the creation of a "broad-based art movement" and "a pseudo-avant-garde that is cost-effective." Pretty neat, huh?

That's what Ralph/Cryptic and the Residents have been laying foundations for: self-sufficient artists who don't have to rely on music industry mechanisms to promulgate their creations. As the *Complete Residents Handbook* asserts, their records are not documentary but art objects in themselves. Touring is almost a dirty word; the Residents have performed live only once. They shun identification and its attendant personal charisma. At that singular concert, they were swathed in impenetrable mummy costumes. According to the *Handbook*, "The Residents look the same in color as they do in black and white. Invisible."

The mystique of anti-identity has been almost as responsible as the music for spreading the Residents' name far and wide. Who are these masked men, and what are they really up to?

"SNAKEFINGER GOES absolutely apeshit over mee grob." Nope, that's not an obscure formulation in Residents language. "Snakefinger" is the nom de vinyl of Philip Lithman, an expatriate Englishman best known as a Residents collaborator and solo artist in his own right on Ralph Records. Mee grob is a noodle appetizer served at Thai restaurants (there are many in the Bay area); if people can be maniacs for Big Macs, why not mee grub?

The speaker is Jay Clem, a tall, polite, clean-cut fellow. As one quarter of the Cryptic Corporation — the other three are Hardy Fox, John Kennedy and Homer Flynn — Clem has evolved his efforts on behalf of the Residents into the role of spokesperson/publicist; he also handles the bulk of the Cryptic Corporation's business deals, as befits his college background in business administration. Thus, he's the most "visible" of the Cryptic clan.

Clem's genial Southern drawl is the Residents' prime link with the world beyond their studio-warehouse-office complex on San Francisco's Grove Street. Nonetheless, at a Thai restaurant in New York prior to flying to London on business, Clem's post-grad dress and demeanor are disarmingly unweird.

"Heck, you'd be surprised at how 'normal' the Residents are," he says with an ironic grin. "Nothing in their appearance would tell you that they're engaged in any sort of bizarre musical ventures. Strictly not posers!" Sounds like he's talking about himself. The Cryptic officers are often rumored to be the Residents.

"Two years or so ago, *NME* almost came out and said it; the guy posed the probability. *Sounds* has published our names as bona fide members of the Residents. Based on the prima facie evidence, I'd have to say that's, um, a fair assumption."

Clem won't cop to it, but his answers are loaded with qualifications meant to avoid any self-implication. "People tell me, 'I listened to this stuff closely, and I really think this could be the work of one or two people.' I am never — I say never, I mean 99 percent of the time — around, meaning in the studio, when this happens, but I do know that they construct things one track at a time. By and large, I don't think they're all in the studio at one time."

Clem, Kennedy and Flynn were mates in the same Shreveport, Louisiana high school. Flynn went off to Louisiana Tech (followed by Kennedy the next year) and wound up rooming with Fox; Clem attended the University of Southern Louisiana but was already slightly acquainted with Fox.

Kennedy tentatively recalls arriving in San Mateo, 25 miles south of San Francisco, in 1966 after leaving school early; the other three drifted out during the next two, three or four years (by various accounts). Around the turn of the decade, the Residents were holding jams every Sunday. Before he'd been in the Bay Area two weeks, Clem was introduced to the men who would be Residents at one such get-together:

"They were playing some weird shit. I was intrigued. I didn't have anything much else to do." Clem got involved with the quintet's activities. (The fifth member left in '72, and no one wishes to divulge any whys or wherefores.)

As with Fox, Flynn and Kennedy, Clem's participation was for some time quite casual and marginal. They were still amateurs — yes, the Residents had to work day jobs, although no one will say what kind — and their projects in music, film (later videotape), silkscreen and even sculpture were in a raw state of conceptual development.

"By the time I got there," Clem remembers, "they'd recently acquired their first tape recorder and were making tapes of jams. They had no formal music training; it was more like, 'Let's turn on the recorder and see what happens.' They had a complete arsenal of instruments, all of which they'd gotten as gifts or from thrift shops. It didn't matter if they were in tune or not or missing a string or a button or a key."

What *did* count was ordering and organization into sequences. An interest in sonic texture and timbre came later, though that's never been too conventional either. "It's a natural progres-

sion," Clem says slyly. "Now they're to the point where they can make melodies."

It's not quite that simple, but these notions coalesced in earnest following the arrival of Snakefinger and the mysterious N. Senada. The two worked with the quintet for roughly half a year, including a performance at San Francisco's Boarding House. Snakefinger opened as a solo and was then joined onstage by the Residents and other friends, more or less as accompanists for the crazed poetry and sax playing of the punningly named N. Senada.

The band didn't have its moniker yet, but they had started recording and editing their music into "album" formats. The first two were called *Rusty Coathangers for the Doctor* and *The Ballad of Stuffed Trigger*; a third was sent to Warners with a multiple-choice coupon ("Would you like to sign us?" etc.) and returned addressed to "residents."

The Warner Bros. Album was the first of the tapes to have album-style packaging and graphics; the second, *Baby Sex*, included supersonic Snakefinger soloing on Frank Zappa's "King Kong." (Snakefinger was so christened when a picture snapped of him playing guitar on his wedding night showed him to possess a decidedly snakey finger.)

The Residents' first vinyl product was *Santa Dog*, a seven-inch double-45 intended as a 1972 Christmas card; the "season's greeting" message was signed "Residents, Unincorporated." An aborted feature film, *Vileness Fats*, took up much of the Residents' time in 1973.

After Snakefinger went back to England to play blues and R&B and N. Senada had supposedly retired to the Arctic to poke around among the Eskimos, the Residents continued to work on their debut LP, and released *Meet the Residents* in 1974.

Despite the do-it-yourself raunchiness of the sound, *Meet the Residents* is far more engaging and accessible than descriptions of early jams might lead you to believe. N. Senada's theory of phonetic organization was modified to cope with a "more Western style of music," such as "These Boots Were Made for Walkin'." Catchy tunelets sounded spooky in alien musical sonospheres.

The Residents then went through an artistic crisis (the story goes), remedied by their recording *Not Available*. This work was intended to live up to its title but came out in 1978. It blends what sounds like Schoenberg scores for *Looney Tunes* with doomy musical madness.

What emerged next for the world to hear (two years after *Meet the Residents*) was *Third Reich 'n' Roll*. It presumably dealt with the cultural fascism of pop tastemakers: the cover depicted Dick Clark as a Nazi general holding a carrot. Both sides of the album ("Hitler Was a Vegetarian," "Swastikas on Parade") consist of familiar refrains from '60s rock and roll radio inverted, perverted and distorted by the audio equivalent of funhouse mirrors.

Later in 1976, the Residents released a single of the Stones' "Satisfaction," a milestone in their history. A distillation of *Third Reich 'n' Roll* into one song, this frighteningly intense and wildly humorous version makes Devo's cute, out-of-kilter rendering sounds as tame as Mantovani. It provoked extreme reactions and got the Residents what they claim to be their first substantial American review, in *Trouser Press*. Snakefinger had returned from England, where he'd been rocking the pubs as a member of Chilli Willi and the Red Hot Peppers, to live in Los Angeles; he flew up to San Francisco to play prominent ear-bending guitar.

Around the time of the "Satisfaction" sessions (June 1976), the Residents — along with Snakefinger, vocalist Zeibak (a.k.a. Pamela Wieking, who'd helped out on *Meet the Residents*) and assorted other friends — made their only public appearance as the Residents at a party for Rather Ripped Records in Berkeley, the first (and, for a long time, the only) store to carry Residents records.

RALPH RECORDS was formed in 1971 ("to call ralph" is Southwestern slang for "to vomit," but Fox isn't sure this has anything to do with its choice as a name), and things had escalated considerably since then. The newly formed Cryptic Corporation's first release was *Fingerprince* (retitled at the eleventh hour from *Tourniquet of Roses*). The record contrasts the Residents' short compositional style with what the liner notes term "their better known 'train of consciousness' format."

Purported difficulties within the group were resolved prior to (perhaps because of) the next undertaking. In need of an ambitious project, the Residents considered the Eskimo connection. Only one new recording emerged in 1977: "Beyond the Valley of a Day in the Life" is a powerful single on which the Beatles play the Residents via doctored, embroidered and looped Beatle bits. You never thought the Fab Four could sound so scary.

The *Eskimo* sessions were quite heavyweight, so for a breather, the fellas cut their *Duck Stab* EP, which was pressed — and sold — in unprecedentedly large quantities for the Residents (probably due to its atypical accessibility). It was reissued on the *Duck Stab/Buster & Glen* album, the "Buster & Glen" side recorded in an attempt to fill out an album's worth of the catchy Residentalia that *Duck Stab* had begun. Perhaps these diversions took too much time away from *Eskimo*, or they were done to avoid coming to grips with a project that had gotten out of hand, but *Eskimo*'s long heralded October 1978 release wasn't to be. Instead, Cryptic issued *Not Available*, another stopgap. After recutting a track from the *Santa Dog* EP (pressed as a 45 with the original on the flip and sent out to Residents supporters), the Residents settled down to finish *Eskimo*. The album finally came out late last year and proved itself worth the wait. *Eskimo* is chilling and otherworldly, yet compelling in a way the Residents had rarely been before — with, of course, a few strategically placed snickers, too.

Meanwhile, Snakefinger and the Art Bears (a British band, descendants of Henry Cow/Slapp Happy) each had a single and following album released on Ralph, proving the label was more than an in-house plaything for the Residents.

(Art Bears drummer Chris Cutler had helped out on *Eskimo*.) Ralph also reissued the *Subterranean Moderns* sampler, featuring the Residents plus Bay Area bands Chrome and Tuxedomoon and Bloomington, Indiana transplants MX-80 Sound. The latter two bands have since put out their own exciting albums on Ralph, accompanied by singles with non-LP B-sides. The company's first 12-inch 45 is the Residents' "Diskomo" backed with a send-up of Mother Goose ("Goosebump").

THE CURRENT Residents project, due out in September, is a single album of 40 songs, each exactly one minute long. Fox is at work mixing the LP. It's his self-taught role, just as Clem's is being the public face and biz wiz, Flynn's is handling the art department (alternatively called Porno, Pore No or Poor No Graphics) and Kennedy's is riding [herd] on the pressing, inventory and films.

Two more have recently joined the company's staff: Helen Purdum, who stage managed the '76 Berkeley show, has taken over the sales department (otherwise known as paying the bills!), and Graeme Whifler, who directed a segment of *Vileness Fats*, now works with Flynn in developing promotional visuals, such as the "Hello Skinny" flick which premiered at SF's rock disco, the City, on "Diskomo Night" last May. "Diskomo Night" attracted a huge crowd, and many people were turned away at the door — including the Residents. Why can't they start letting people know who they are?

Clem patiently explains, while continuing the masquerade: "The Residents never as much as gave me a reason, but I know why from working with them. First of all, from about '72 to '76, they were getting something of a reputation as filmmakers in the Bay Area film set — the artsy chic crowd — and that was under their own names. They were given a certain amount of attention and were uncomfortable with it. Secondly, they all have large egos, but everything they do, whether individually or collectively, comes out as the Residents, since most of it is a result of their interaction anyway and changes vastly while they're doing it. They're aware that the whole is more than the sum of its parts."

Can Clem tell who does what? "Well, obviously one guy does most of the vocals, and I happen to know that another does more electronics. But in all sincerity, beyond that I don't know who plays what. They're all very much of the same mind, point of view, direction... I found out five years ago that there's no point in asking about it any further. Besides, they're as pure a group as I'm aware of."

So, there's the story, believe it or nuts. The artistic notions behind it are admirable in this day and age, and the Residents have a large body of work to look back on and be proud of — whoever the hell they are.

As the *Complete Residents Handbook* puts it, "The Residents are here to stay, and apparently need no one's permission to do so. Their place in history is already assured, just because no one knows what else to do with them. For sure a sign of greatness, if there is one. But, of course, there isn't." ∎

HELLO IT'S ME

TP 24, DECEMBER 1977

I hope you realize the power of your medium! Following that beautiful expounding on the Residents' "Satisfaction" and "Aphids in the Hall" in *TP* 17, we are pleased to announce that both records immediately sold out! (No accounting for taste!) Also, four or five other magazines have picked up on "Residentmania," not to mention that KBDO-FM in Portland, Oregon totally bridged the gap of public decency with a six-hour special on the fab four.

We are working on a single that will probably be the most sought-after collectors' piece of the year. I can hardly say anything more about it at this time as it will be sold underground in hope that it won't be confiscated as quickly. We're proud to live in a country where anyone can grow up to be (a) Resident.

The Residents
San Francisco, CA

RIGHT ON, SISTERS! THE GO-GO'S HIT PAYDIRT

TP 79, NOVEMBER 1982

By Scott Isler

Trouser Press answers the question all America is asking: What do the Go-Go's eat for lunch?

For someone who wears a crucifix around her neck, lead guitarist Charlotte Caffey is doing a good number on a bagel and lox. Weight-conscious bassist Kathy Valentine nibbles away at a salad. Both are eating out of aluminum take-out plates.

Wait a minute. Where's the elegance? The *savoir faire*? The other Go-Go's?

The rest of the band is across the continent in Los Angeles, tackling press there while Caffey and Valentine pacify New York newshounds. The duo's two-day marathon of non-stop interviews is part of a well-orchestrated campaign to make the most of the Go-Go's' just-released second album, *Vacation*. When your first album sells over two million copies, there's going to be a lot of excitement in the air about its follow-up — and also a degree of nervous tension from those with something at stake in the enterprise.

As for the band's chi-chi, almost camp aura — don't be fooled by album covers. The five women who comprise the Go-Go's have a flair for fashion, but it wouldn't get them anywhere without a commitment to solid American virtues: hard work, team effort and a willingness to eat out of aluminum take-out plates.

EVERY YEAR HAS its success story, and 1982 looks like the Year of the Go-Go's. Their long-playing debut, *Beauty and the Beat*, hogged the number-one chart position for two months. (The last group to hit number-one with a debut album was the ill-fated Knack three years ago.) The Go-Go's also scored two Top 10 singles in "Our Lips Are Sealed" and "We Got the Beat," the latter selling a million copies.

It's an impressive showing by any standard, especially given the contracting universe of radio airplay. But the Go-Go's triumphed under the handicap of belonging to the country's only oppressed majority group: women. They're just the second all-female band to top the U.S. album charts, after Diana Ross and the Supremes — and the Motown trio didn't play their own instruments or write their own songs. "The other day, a friend of mine said to me that after 25 years of rock and roll there's not a whole lot of history left to be made," Valentine, 23, relates. "The Go-Go's have done it."

It wasn't easy. Far from being an overnight sensation, the Go-Go's slowly fought their way to the top. *Beauty and the Beat* bobbed around the charts for well over half a year before coming to rest at number-one. As a result of their long haul, the band takes nothing for granted.

"It probably sunk in that we had done something when we got our platinum albums," drummer Gina Schock, 25, states matter of factly. Singer Belinda Carlisle, 24, says she was sure the Go-Go's made it only after hearing that the LP had gone double-platinum. For rhythm guitarist Jane Wiedlin, 24, the acid test came sooner: when she heard "Our Lips Are Sealed" played on Los Angeles' KRLA — "the station I listened to when I was growing up." (Wiedlin, who we spoke to separately, was born in Wisconsin but moved to California as a child.)

Carlisle and Caffey, 28, are also from the Los Angeles area. The former just missed making history of another sort when illness prevented her from becoming a founding member of the

Germs, a notorious L.A. punk outfit, in the mid-'70s. ("Plus I was too lazy to play drums.") But she did notch up some pre-Go-Go singing experience with the theatrical Black Randy and the Metro Squad.

By 1978, Carlisle knew Wiedlin from hanging out at "underground" rock clubs. "Everybody knew each other — it was a very small scene," she explains. "Nearly everyone we did know was in a band, so we decided why not form one, too?" "We" included Margot Olavarria and Elissa Bello. No one knew how to play. Anything. Literally.

"I wanted to play bass or sing," the soft-spoken Wiedlin now confesses. "Margot had already decided she was going to play bass, and Belinda said she wanted to sing, so what's the next thing? Guitar." Bello ended up on drums.

"We weren't very good, but we still did it," Carlisle says. "We didn't even know how to plug our guitars into the amps. We really started from scratch." Thus, the unpromising beginnings of the Go-Go's (not to be confused with the 1964-vintage Go-Go's, a male trio who recorded for RCA, of course). [*Of course. —Ed.*]

They soon received help in the form of Caffey, another Angeleno. She had plenty of musical background: classical piano training, a degree in music (which she downplays — "anyone can do that"), former keyboard player in Manuel and the Gardeners and former bassist in the Eyes. The Go-Go's must have been impressed. Caffey signed on as guitarist.

Back in Baltimore, Gina Schock had been pounding drums since she was 15. "They were the easiest instrument for me to play," she admits. "I always knew I wanted to be a musician. I tried bass and guitar, and it seemed like I'd have to take lessons. I didn't have the patience. Drums were so easy and natural that I continued to play them."

Schock's professional career took off when she made a four-city tour with Edie Massey, a habitué of John Waters films like *Pink Flamingos*, in 1978. The following year, her taste for travel whetted, Schock decided to relocate. She loaded her belongings (including drums) in her father's pickup truck and struck out for the West Coast. Fame and fortune awaited: a job in a grocery store while playing in two different bands. Then she met the Go-Go's at a party, and the band asked her to join.

"I thought they had a lot of potential," Schock says in safe retrospect. "The songs were good; they just didn't know how to execute them properly. I'd been playing drums longer than anybody else had been playing their instruments, so I felt like a real pro!" She quit her other two bands the same day she enjoyed a trial session with the Go-Go's; the band fired Bello the day after that.

The Go-Go's personnel now seemed stable. Another important element added that summer of '79 was manager Ginger Canzoneri, who had first seen the band a year earlier. "There was something there," says the 31-year-old former graphic designer at CBS. "I wanted to get involved in it all, it seemed so great." Canzoneri had no more managing experience than the Go-Go's had musical chops, so she fit right in.

"Their energy, their ambition — they're just so persevering." Canzoneri could also be talking about herself. "Whether or not they were good wasn't the issue. It was that they wanted to succeed. They all had day jobs. They'd work all day long, then go straight from work to rehearsal and work every night until 10 or 11. They put effort into it. Otherwise, they never would have improved as vastly as they did."

THE GO-GO'S held onto their day jobs, but they made some influential friends in the music field. Among them was the British group Madness. The Go-Go's opened local shows for them in December, 1979; Madness then invited them along for a UK tour the following spring. To raise money for the trip, Canzoneri borrowed from friends, pawned jewelry, took out a loan on her car — and the group had to quit their day jobs. It was the Moment of Truth.

They stayed in England three months, touring with Madness and another British band they'd met in Los Angeles, the Specials. Audiences "didn't really go crazy," Wiedlin says drily, and the Go-Go's led a hand-to-mouth existence. But they were honing their music all the time, and achieved a breakthrough when UK Stiff released their first record — demo versions of "We Got the Beat" and "How Much More." The single didn't even dent the British Top 100 but became a dance-floor favorite in U.S. clubs. The Go-Go's returned to Los Angeles and an uncertain future.

They now had a solid local following yet couldn't get to first base with record companies. Canzoneri grew used to hearing the corporate wail: "'We've tried it before with other female acts that have failed.' They liked the band, but nobody wanted to take the risk. It was real hard for me to stomach the fact that I couldn't get them signed."

John Guarnieri, in charge of production and A&R at I.R.S. Records, had seen the Go-Go's before they went to England; "they were still learning to play their instruments." He was more favorably impressed after the band got back and attributes the lack of label interest to bad timing. "People were recovering from the Knack attack. Record companies were (and still are) pretty cautious."

Guarnieri was intrigued, however. He became friendly with Canzoneri and introduced her to I.R.S. president Miles Copeland. Copeland loved the band and finally signed them in spring, 1981 — presumably after Canzoneri gave up trying to attract bigger fish. I.R.S.'s biggest sellers at the time were the Buzzcocks and Oingo Boingo.

The Go-Go's I.R.S. signed had a new bassist. Olavarria had taken sick before a big New Year's engagement; the others, dissatisfied with her attitude, used the opportunity to look for a permanent replacement. Guitarist Kathy Valentine had left L.A.'s Textones and was "watching TV a lot and trying to work up some songs" when Caffey approached her at a club and asked if she played bass. After an intensive four days of rehearsal, she did, and knew the Go-Go's repertoire as well. "I have a very good memory. That's how I got through school."

Although the youngest member of the band, the Austin, Texas-raised Valentine was hardly an amateur. At age 17, while visiting London with her English mother, she answered a classified ad and found herself briefly a charter member of Girlschool, the all-female heavy metal band. ("They were called Painted Lady then.") Back in Austin, Valentine started the Violators, which she claims was the city's first punk band. The big time beckoned. Valentine moved to Los Angeles; she was 18 and miserable. "I didn't have any money. I'd gotten my hair cut really funny and couldn't get a job." She did sing, play guitar and write with the Textones for a year and a half, cutting two singles with them. (The Textones also recorded but didn't release "Can't Stop the World," which turned up on *Beauty and the Beat*.)

HAVING WON the elusive record contract, the Go-Go's got to work on their debut LP. Production chores went to Richard Gottehrer and Rob Freeman. Gottehrer, who produced the first two Blondie albums and co-produced the Angels' "My Boyfriend's Back" (when girl groups were girl groups), had work to do. "They were a live rock and roll band," he says. "When we got into rehearsal, I realized some of their songs were really good. I slowed songs down and simplified their arrangements, had them play a little less — made it so it sounded more unified to me in terms of a commercial sound."

The band had mixed feelings about *Beauty and the Beat* when they heard the results. "It was a polished version of what they thought their crowd was expecting of them," Gottehrer admits. "They might have been a little uncertain whether they really were a pop act or a new wave band."

"From the very beginning, we wanted to be a pop band," Carlisle counters. "We just didn't know that many chords. As we get better our abilities match our ideas." Wiedlin agrees. "We started out punk 'cause we didn't know how to play. We wanted to be a sort of punk-pop band. We certainly don't sound like any of the punk bands I hear now."

If the Go-Go's had any doubts about their album, Gottehrer didn't — especially about one particular song. "I thought the whole album was good," he says, "but I thought 'Our Lips Are Sealed' was amazing. It had handclaps, claves, shakers, tambourines — I like tambourines and shakers. I was sure it was a number-one single. I wanted the whole record to sound like 'Our Lips Are Sealed'; I just didn't have enough time to do it." Gottehrer's intuition was slightly off; "Our Lips Are Sealed" stalled at number-20. But the single served its purpose in calling attention to the group, and *Beauty and the Beat* began its eight-month hegira to the top album spot — an eminence that left even Gottehrer "flabbergasted."

WHO DECIDES WHAT bands will be popular? There's no easy answer. The pop process is a long chain of events rife with factors interacting in infinite combinations.

"The Go-Go's had street support," says Guarnieri. "The kids loved them. They had a lot of support from retail [stores]. There was a lot of resistance from radio; that was the final stumbling block." I.R.S. hired independent promotion people to help break the airwave barrier.

"I like to give ourselves credit that we were really on top of it," he continues. "We acted fast in getting the band into the studio after we signed them, getting the right producer and getting something out to capitalize on that street buzz. If we hadn't been kicking [distributor] A&M in the butt every day to get 'em going on it, it could easily have slid by."

"I think the main thing with their success are the songs," Gottehrer maintains. "They write terrific songs, and that's what people buy. They play well enough and make good music, but you can't make hit records out of lousy songs." (Caffey agrees: "This is a songwriter's band more than technical virtuosos.") Surprisingly, Canzoneri has a rather casual attitude. "Anytime someone is successful it has to do with being in the right place at the right time. There are other female bands out there but maybe they're not as polished yet. We were just fortunate enough to be more accomplished." Perhaps to maximize their chances of being in the right place at the right time, the Go-Go's conspired to be in as many places as possible. Over the space of one-and-a-half years, the band had only five weeks off from touring. Most observers (and band members) agree the big break came with an opening slot on a Police tour early this year.

"We didn't want to do it," Wiedlin recalls. "Luckily, Ginger and Miles Copeland [whose brother Stewart is the Police's drummer] talked us into it."

Beauty and the Beat had already reached the 20s — dizzy enough chart heights for a new band — when the Go-Go's set out with the Police. The mass exposure in arenas gave their album a new lease on life. It also created some embarrassing problems.

"Towards the end, the tour got a little funny because we were selling more records than the Police," Schock laughs. "But those guys were so happy for us — which I think is pretty cool." (Unlike the Go-Go's, the Police have yet to score a number-one album in the U.S.)

SEX. Or rather *SEX*. Any discussion of the Go-Go's phenomenon inevitably gets down to the naked truth that these women have made it in a male-infested cultural milieu without getting screwed.

"A lot of our audience consists of young girls who find a role model in us," Carlisle says. "Before us, everyone was either too glamorous or too butch. I guess they can really see themselves in us. We get letters from girls pouring their hearts out."

"I never thought of us as symbols, but we really are," Wiedlin adds. "I think we've given a lot of girls encouragement. Everybody grows up wanting to be in a rock band. When you're a girl you realize how 'unrealistic' it is and you give up that dream, which is what I went through when I was growing up. But now it's not unrealistic."

"Girls have come up to us and said, 'We started a band because of you guys,'" Schock says. "When you go to our shows, you see the first ten rows of girls dressed like Belinda, so I guess we do have some influence."

"These girls made a serious contribution to popular music," Gottehrer sums up. "They're gonna create a whole generation who're gonna have confidence in themselves. There's a deeper point to the Go-Go's than some girls in underwear on the cover of *Rolling Stone*."

Even discounting the benighted days of "girl groups," the Go-Go's are far from the first all-female rock band. Their predecessors, however, look manipulated by comparison. The Runaways, closest in time and place to the Go-Go's, are archetypal. "That's one case of not concentrating on your playing and writing," Valentine notes. "Plus, they were pre-packaged," Caffey says; the Go-Go's "just grew together as a band." Caffey was asked to join the Runaways as bassist in 1976 but declined. "I knew I wouldn't be happy."

Wiedlin remembers seeing the Runaways during their blaze of media glory. "Even then, their look was real dated, and their songs were regular-sounding. I'm not sure it helped that the Runaways went before us. I don't think they made that much of an impact."

So, who *do* the Go-Go's themselves look up to? Not other women.

"I never really had any heroines," Carlisle admits. "Maybe Patsy Cline [!] I had heroes — typical teenage heroes like James Dean."

Wiedlin admires Bryan Ferry, whose lounge-lizard cool would seem to be the antithesis of what the Go-Go's are about. She states he's the "best" songwriter but denies Ferry has influenced her own material. "I wish."

Off the top of their heads, Caffey names the Beatles and Valentine the Stones as idols/influences. On reflection, however, they do come up

with a female role model or two. "When I first saw Blondie, I was impressed," Caffey says. "Debbie Harry inspired me, gave me a push when everything was going rotten with the Eyes." Valentine: "I never cared for her music much, but I have to admit it never occurred to me I could be a musician until I saw Suzi Quatro. I can't say she's a heroine, but she's the one that made me realize it wasn't out of the question."

Only Schock has an immediate response: "Joan of Arc!" She might be kidding.

The opposite side of the sex issue is the topic of feminism. "Actions speak louder than words," Wiedlin believes. "A woman can't just sit there and go, 'I'm equal, I'm equal.' You can only prove yourself equal by being as good as or better than men. A lot of times we didn't get cooperation or respect from people working at clubs or halls before they saw us play. They would just dismiss us as a bunch of dumb go-go-dancing girls. But after the show it would be another story because they'd realize we were musicians."

Schock concurs — "What we're doing is enough of a statement for me" — but Canzoneri is more outspoken: "I do feel I'm a feminist. My definition of a feminist is not a woman who is independent in that she doesn't need somebody else, but independent in that she can support herself and do proper work. There's no reason a woman should be restricted from doing certain things she's capable of doing.

"What I have the hardest time dealing with is people saying, 'Oh, the Go-Go's are such a novelty act!' What's so hard to accept about an all-female band? That should be no different from an all-male band. What does that mean — that women are novelties?"

Guarnieri, however, feels the "overall novelty" of the Go-Go's helped put them across. "They're cute; they have personality; they're girls."

"YOU GOTTA KEEP proving yourself [with each album], especially if you're an all-girl band," Gottehrer says. In the record business, an isolated smash LP is good news but a consistently top-selling group is something to treasure. *Vacation*, the Go-Go's' second album, will determine whether they're one-shot wonders or here to stay on the pop scene. "Our attitude is different than it was on the first album," Valentine says. "We're a lot more confident. When you've had some success, you know it's attainable."

Gottehrer, producing the band again, noticed the difference. "They had a better idea of what it takes to make a record: how you have to play, what to do with arrangements, what to leave out and put in. They were a lot closer to finished arrangements than they were on the earlier songs." Schock feels the new record isn't as "sweet" as the first; "it has a rawer sound." "It sounds more like we do live," Carlisle adds. "It sounds fuller to me — and the vocals don't sound like the Chipmunks!"

Finding new material is the root problem behind "second-album syndrome," but the Go-Go's had a stockpile. "I never thought 'Beatnik Beach' would get on an album when we started it," Caffey says. "We recorded it for the first album; it didn't work out." It did this time around. "He's So Strange" is another oldie, partly written by Leonard Phillips of the Dickies, Caffey's ex-boyfriend. Valentine's "We Don't Get Along" first appeared on Phil Seymour's 1981 solo album; Seymour, who considered it his "token punk song," picked it up from a Textones demo tape.

Vacation's title track bears a slight resemblance to a B-side [of the same name recorded and released in the UK] by the Textones. The difference bespeaks the amount of work the Go-Go's put into their music. Wiedlin added lyrics, and Caffey went over the music with Valentine, the song's original author. They overhauled a "real rough" song with "no hook" (Guarnieri's opinion) or chorus into a Top 10 pop tune worthy of being the first single off the album.

Wiedlin, the band's main lyricist, takes a modest view of her talent. She finds inspiration in "things that happen to me or friends — a good story I can elaborate on. I'll take a circumstance and make it more dramatic than it really was." "Lust to Love," on *Beauty and the Beat*, stems from an affair Wiedlin was having. "While I was writing the song, I really did think I was in love with the guy. Once the song was over, I realized I wasn't."

AMERICA'S LOVE AFFAIR with the Go-Go's seems to be a more lasting relationship. *Vacation*, released appropriately this summer, barreled up the charts; in August the band embarked on their first major-venue U.S. tour as stars in their own right. It's quite a change since Caffey and Canzoneri swapped sleeping shifts guarding their equipment in a van parked on a New York side street.

Even the Go-Go's' parents have come around. "My dad kept telling me I was wasting my time," Valentine says. "He said being a musician was a lifestyle of little substance." Now Pa Valentine keeps his Go-Go's records proudly alongside his Merle Haggard.

"They pleaded with us to get normal desk jobs," Carlisle remembers, "but we never did — fortunately."

The band's attitude is a mixture of genuine camaraderie and clear-headed responsibility. "All songs are a team effort," Schock notes. "Nobody feels left out. It's very democratic." Schock and Carlisle's writer credits on *Vacation* indicate increasing participation — a move Valentine encourages: "A lot of writers come out with their best material when they [first] start writing. On the third album I think they're gonna come out even more."

That's confidence — to be talking about your third album when your second has just been released. But at present there aren't any clouds on the Go-Go's' horizon.

Caffey takes an almost mystical view of the band's success. "I feel like the girls in the band that have been in bands before — Gina, Kathy and myself — were all leading parallel lives, working hard at being in bands and failing. Then we got together; it's like fate."

They all agree they'll stick together until they stop having fun. "Who knows how long that is?" Wiedlin asks. "I'd like to keep it going another five years."

"If you don't enjoy what you're doing no amount of money makes it worth it," Schock says. But, she adds hastily, "I don't mind the platinum records."

Only the dourest of party poopers would look

for cracks in the Go-Go's' façade. The band exhausted its back catalogue of songs on *Vacation*, conceivably delaying the second-album crisis until the third album. More concretely, Valentine has done some non-Go-Go writing with Carlene Carter for Carter's next album. The fecund Valentine also contributed a tune to the Rockats' repertoire. Textones manager Saul Davis, who shares in Valentine's song publishing, hints that "Kathy doesn't look to the Go-Go's as being something that's necessarily going to last as long as the Rolling Stones. She's also the youngest one in the group and has a lot of ambition."

For now, though, the band presents a united front, reveling in their commercial clout. "In the old days I could manipulate those girls more," Canzoneri laments. "I think a little bit of rock-star syndrome has gone to their heads; they're beginning to think they're as fabulous and foolproof as they can be. But they deserve to feel special. They've paid their dues. It's not like they had it handed to them on a silver platter."

"I used to dream of being able to play guitar and jump around at the same time," Wiedlin recalls. "That was what I worked on. I don't know a lot of fancy licks, but I play my parts well — and I can jump around." She bursts out laughing.

"We're really serious about what we're doing," Schock states. "Music is our main concern. We're not just dressing up and going onstage — although everyone [in the band] likes to dress up. 'Cause we're girls, y'know?" ■

HELLO IT'S ME

TP 72, APRIL 1982

Trouser Press puts "let it rock" on its cover, but never has and never will "let it rock" because it refuses to recognize where real rock is coming from. TP is not new, hardly ever features new bands and, to put it bluntly, sucks.

Lou Barlow [*of Deep Wound*]
Westfield, MA

---

*W*e were not big supporters of hardcore punk; that was the first fissure in a generation gap opening up in our musical outlook. We were all around 30 years old, and the idea of slam-dancing to speeding tuneless guitar rock did not hold the appeal it might have done a decade earlier. None of us (save for* America Underground *columnist Tim Sommer, who hosted* Noise! the Show *on the New York University radio station) were going to CBGB's hardcore matinees.*

As New Yorkers, we scoffed at the L.A. scene depicted in Penelope Spheeris's Decline of Western Civilization. *Maybe it was a case of "if it's too loud, you're too old": metal had never been our thing, either. We consigned coverage of that genre to a pair of desultory roundup articles, one of them cheekily coverlined "The problem that won't go away."*

So, while we were late to the "TV Party," we recognized that it was a genre and a scene we needed to cover. Fortunately, we found a knowledgeable writer from D.C. willing to get in the pit for us.

BLACK FLAG: WANNA DANCE?

TP 86, JUNE 1983

By W. Vann Hall

A little over midway through Black Flag's first set, Henry Rollins takes a break to dedicate the next song. For a half-hour Rollins, 23, has presided over the slamming crowd packing Washington's Nightclub 9:30, hurling himself about the tiny stage, fighting back dancers trying to climb up beside him, and bellowing a dozen songs spanning six years of Black Flag releases. Now, gasping for breath, he manages to say: "This is for all the girls I've ever loved... and some even loved me."

What follows is the most tortured rendition of "Nothing Left Inside" imaginable. Rollins staggers around the stage, clawing at his face and chest, hoarsely shrieking his vocals over a rumbling "Peter Gunn" bassline and guitars sounding more hard rock than hardcore. The song doesn't so much end as slowly strangle; guitarists Greg Ginn and Dez Cadena strum aimless chords while Rollins, stabbing his finger at the audience, howls a lover's soliloquy:

"You can laugh, it's OK — it's not your fucking heart, it's mine! You can laugh... Sometimes I laugh. Sometimes I get so mad! And sometimes the tears just roll down my face."

The crowd, grounded partly by the dirgelike music, partly by the onstage spectacle, stands and stares. Meanwhile, Rollins has fallen to his knees, then thrown himself backwards across the floor, where he lies, moaning. The natural urge, of course, is to laugh — until you realize that, in some twisted way, Rollins really means it.

THERE ARE TIMES when it's nearly impossible to take Henry Rollins seriously. It's hard to take anyone seriously who's given to saying things like "Pain is my girlfriend," or wears a tattoo reading, "Life is Pain," or perversely revels in his every moment of mental desperation. But Los Angeles's Black Flag has elevated the public dumping of one's emotional cargo into an art form, and Rollins is merely that form's most enthusiastic practitioner.

The band starts with a worldview that makes Joy Division's look rose-tinted by comparison; mixes in a generous helping of impotent, self-indulgent anger; then sets it all boiling to a nonstop, hardcore thrash. The energy, wit and talent Black Flag's displayed in seven years of playing and on a dozen or so records have earned them nearly as many fans as detractors.

At the same time, though, a refusal to compromise either their assaultive musical style or fiercely personal, almost solipsistic, subject matter has cost the band listeners. And recent changes in direction threaten to alienate the hardcore contingent, weakening support from the movement Black Flag helped found.

Ginn started Black Flag in late 1976 with vocalist Keith Morris; the band quickly found a place in the then-nascent L.A. punk scene. Their first release, 1978's *Nervous Breakdown* EP, had something of a British feel, not unlike the Vibrators. As they became more proficient, however, and as styles changed, their music became harder and faster. Morris left in 1979 to form the Circle Jerks and was replaced by Ron Reyes (Chavo Pederast). Reyes stayed for a year, long enough to record the *Jealous Again* EP and — more importantly — to appear in *The Decline of Western Civilization*, the Penelope Spheeris documentary that introduced hardcore to much of America. Reyes was followed by Cadena, who vented his pipes on the *Six Pack* EP and the band's rave-up of "Louie Louie." The latter's B-side, "Damaged 1," showed Black Flag's sound becoming heavier and darker. Cadena elected to move to second guitar, and Rollins, then singing with Washington's S.O.A. (State of Alert), was tapped as a fifth member. The expanded line-up gave Black Flag the chance to explore what bassist Chuck Dukowski calls the "mantra-like effect of certain riffs"; Cadena's droning guitar also gives Ginn a broader base against which to play breaks. (Dukowski has been with the band nearly from the beginning. Longtime drummer Robo left last summer, replaced first by Emil Johnson, then Bill Stevenson.)

FREQUENT PERSONNEL CHANGES haven't been the band's only problem. Although they tour constantly — Black Flag played over 150 shows in 1982 — L.A. clubs are loath to book them, worried by hardcore's (exaggerated) reputation for violence. Countless headlining West Coast concerts have been shut down during the opening acts; their most recent hometown gig was accomplished only by playing a Mexican club whose manager had never heard of them.

In addition, their first album, *Damaged* — co-released by Black Flag's own SST label and Unicorn Records — was refused by MCA, Unicorn's distributor. The band and Unicorn have since become entangled in a legal dispute, still in the courts, which blocks the release of any recordings made after "TV Party."

But the biggest challenge may come from their own conviction to remain true to their music. Although they decline classification, the hardcore elements of Black Flag's sound discourage some listeners; non-aficionados won't penetrate the surface noise and density to discover, say, the quality of Ginn's playing or the band's songwriting ability. At the same time, their refusal to stay safely within hardcore's bounds and "reiterate" themselves, as Dukowski puts it, has brought cries of dismay from thrash-happy fans worried that Black Flag is losing its edge.

But mainly it is a stubborn obsession with their hindbrains, writing song after song concerned only with dark emotions and personal terrors, that has earned Black Flag the most criticism. Accomplishing nothing but the act of speaking up, the band seems an experiment in pointlessness to many. What exactly does Black Flag want?

ROLLINS HAS the answer. "Impact. We definitely want to have impact. No matter whether you go, 'Fuck these guys' or 'Wow!' or 'Eh, so what?' If you don't walk away with something, it means we didn't get to you. And we *want* to get to you."

Once you've been gotten to, of course, Rollins wants you to react: "What we're trying to get at is a personal, emotional, physical release of energy and emotion." "Personal" is clearly the operative term, for band as much as audience. Onstage, Rollins wants to experience what the lyrics are describing; he wants to *mean* it. Which is one thing for Donny and Marie singing "Puppy Love," but something very different when your set list includes "Depression," "Dead Inside" and "Life of Pain." But you have to give Rollins credit: he tries.

"Pain is my girlfriend; that's how I see it. I feel pain every day of my life. When you see me perform, it's that pain you're seeing coming out. I put all my emotions, all my feelings, and my body on the line. People hurt me, I hurt myself — mentally, physically."

It may be a bit sick watching a grown man pick and pry at his mental problems like a kid wiggling a loose tooth — but it sure as hell is fun.

Onstage, Rollins appears to be in perfect health, sweating through almost hour-long sets that require nearly constant singing and motion. Dressed in gym clothes, with the body of a weightlifter (which he is) and his once-shaven head covered with a couple of inches of curly hair, he looks more like a successful ROTC candidate than one of the country's most infamous hardcore vocalists. It's only up close that one sees the scars and cigarette burns on his face and chest.

The 9:30 crowd obviously loves Rollins, and welcomes him home with stage dives, chicken fights and non-stop slamming. (Rollins's mother has brought some relatives for the first set; later he says she thought it was "by far the best Black Flag show she'd seen.") A consummate showman, Rollins focuses the band's energy and directs it to the audience. Dukowski says the band has trouble playing enthusiastically when the singer sits out some instrumental numbers.

Rollins's treatment of "Rise Above," hardcore's transcendental anthem, is masterful. As for "Nothing Left Inside," the crowd has largely stopped slamming and presses up against the stage to shout the lyrics in unison. Playing off this, Rollins "conducts" a skinhead chorus. With one hand beating out the rhythm, he whips the microphone from one face to another, each fan blurting out a syllable or two: "We." "Are tired." "Of your." "Abuse." "Try." "To." "Stop us." "It's." "No use."

The band is amazingly tight, considering the speed at which they're playing. Ginn manages to drop a compact but effective break into nearly every tune. The songs themselves are surprising, as well. One rarely thinks of hooks when describing Black Flag's music, but they are there — especially the infectious guitar fillips in "I Love You."

AFTERWARD, Rollins is pleased with the show; for him, Black Flag is a performance band.

"Personally, I feel I'd have to see it to really get it. The record — the record's all right, but OK, that's a record. When I see it live, I go, 'Whoa. So, *that's* what they mean.'"

He hopes the songs have universal appeal. "I think our songs can get to anybody who is open-minded enough to take them. It's not a question of agreeing or disagreeing, 'cause we're not about topics as such, like Afghanistan or El Salvador or churches. It's just emotional stuff, like 'Depression.' Who can't identify with that?"

But Black Flag cares more about being heard than enlightening its audience. The resulting music is — to be kind — very self-interested.

"Every Black Flag song is a variation on one song: 'I am, I am, I am, I am.' That's the only song. When you write a song, what else are you saying but 'I am'?" Even the band's seemingly topical songs, like "Police Story" or "American Waste," deal with potentially political problems on a personal level. "American Waste," for example, is a song of frustration, not rebellion; the singer rails against regimentation and limited opportunities but accepts his situation.

Rollins adamantly stresses the band's apolitical nature. "There are no songs telling you to do anything. There are no political songs, there are no songs that speak out on some topic. I'm not into songs about the fucking six o'clock news." He has little love for such "commentary" bands: "I read an interview with the Lords of the New Church [in TP 81]; I thought that was the most hilarious crock of shit I've read in so long. They were saying, 'Even Black Flag is growing their hair long in order to rebel against the military.' I thought, 'Jesus Christ. The guy's got his head up his ass.' I grow my hair 'cause I fucking feel like it."

Fighting words, but then Rollins is down on a lot of bands, especially British punk groups. During Black Flag's UK tour last year, he says, "I found the music to be bad, the Exploited — all those bands — to be very, very tame. They didn't have any impact on me. I thought they were really lame — no anger, no ferocity, no emotion, no soul, no energy. They just played boring shit and sang about World War III and bombs. World War III doesn't scare me a bit, doesn't have any emotional impact on me." (Rollins does speak well of the UK Subs and the Damned, both as people and performers.)

AS MIGHT BE GUESSED, that tour was far from an overwhelming success. Black Flag found British punks too concerned with styles and fads.

"People were a little too afraid to trust their own judgments," Rollins says, "their own instincts, their own feelings. We didn't look like anybody. I didn't have a leather jacket, and neither did the rest of the band. People didn't like it. They were coming up to us and saying, 'You guys were great, but why don't you get some studs or something, some leather?'"

Unfortunately, the fans expressed their displeasure [*Or pleasure? —Ed.*] in ways other than giving fashion advice. "We got into a lot of fights with skinheads. I got knocked out cold at the 100 Club — someone just punched me out. They jumped us here and there, tried to wreck our van. Everyone spat on us, tried to burn us with cigarettes. And we had no money. We ate one meal a day, we didn't have anywhere to live. This was for two and a half weeks... I don't know, it got me a little depressed."

Dukowski agrees the tour was a fiasco but is a bit more heartened by it. "They weren't ready for us, and they didn't like us, but we blew their pants off. When the Exploited were here, they made a big deal out of slagging us off. That makes me feel good, that we can present a threat to someone like that, that they can't take the competition. I'm looking forward to what happens when we go back." (Two days after this interview, Black Flag left for a four-week European tour.)

ALTHOUGH THE LEGAL hassles with Unicorn have prevented any further recording, Black Flag has just released a double album on SST. *Everything Went Black*, which has been out for a while in Germany, is compiled from previously unreleased material dating back to the band's early days. There is a side of Morris vocals, a half-side of Reyes and a side-and-a-half of Cadena; the fourth side is a collection of Black Flag commercials recorded for KROQ and the like. Even though he doesn't appear on the album, Rollins approves of it: "It's a cool record."

But a new album is his top priority for the future. "We've got a lot of new songs — we sure would like to do an album. And probably another, real soon after — we've got *lots* of new stuff."

Their "new stuff" is a bit different from the

razor-sharp hardcore that made Black Flag famous. Even though their live sets still contain plenty of out-and-out thrash, a lot of the newer material derives from *Damaged*'s second side, with its tortured phrasings and guitar-heavy, hard rock sound. The hardcore beat is there, but punk's harsh minimalism has ceded to the drone of scratchy guitar and feedback-ridden solos.

Whether or not this new direction in Black Flag's music will find new listeners, or even retain the ones they have, it has already made one influential convert. "Some of our songs might challenge your values," Rollins says. "Some challenge my values. That's fine — everybody needs a little shove now and then. I like all the new songs. They test me, they really make me dig. And that's something I'm more than eager to do. Until I drop dead."

Rollins isn't laughing. He means it. ■

X: STAND BY YOUR BAND

TP 94, FEBRUARY 1984

By John Leland

"If we were true artists, we'd be like Leadbelly or Woody Guthrie — just wandering around the country and playing for whoever would listen." With characteristically clumsy sincerity, bassist-singer John Doe (real last name Polish and unpronounceable, he says) reveals the American folk reverence and populist motives of L.A.'s new traditionalists, X.

From its formation in 1977, X has grafted chunks of folk, blues, rockabilly, country and punk into a jagged synthesis that's more like a car crash than a smooth blend. The band's sound and image have always been strikingly American. Its sources hark back to the days when rock and roll was a purely American phenomenon "before that British Invasion ruined everything," croaks Exene (Christine) Cervenka, Doe's better half and X's other mouthpiece.

If X holds a unique place in the tradition, it's because the band's disparate ideas clash with a violence that benefits each. Doe, Cervenka, blonde bombshell guitarist Billy Zoom and indomitable drummer DJ Bonebrake embrace (often at each other's expense) the resignation of rural blues and the flashy exuberance of rock and roll. "Woody Guthrie sang about b-e-E-t-s, not b-e-A-t-s," Doe and Cervenka sing in "I Must Not Think Bad Thoughts," a ponderous think piece from the band's new album, *More Fun in the New World*. The glory of X's music is that it is about both.

"Our strength is that our lyrics mean something to us and to the people we sing them to — and then the music is loud and fast and fun," Doe says. "The lyrics are introspective, and the music is uplifting. That's the difference between us and, say, Joy Division, or the Ramones."

This split reflects X's seemingly incompatible personalities: Doe and Cervenka, beat intelligence wavering between arty pretensions and poetic vox populi; and Zoom and Bonebrake, keeping the artistes honest with a kick in the ass.

"Me and Exene will get real analytical sometimes," Doe admits. "Billy's got to tell us that we're full of shit."

Zoom does most of his talking from the business end of a gold Les Paul, wringing out rapid-fire slabs of traditional guitar noise. He comes to X from a journeyman career in rockabilly, R&B and black soul bands — even a brief stint (in 1971) in Gene Vincent's last band. Onstage, Zoom stands stock still, grinning from ear to ear and not breaking into a sweat even at tempos that threaten cardiac arrest. His speedy guitar runs propel X out of the mire of self-absorption.

"If the music matched the lyrics, people like me and DJ would probably never go see the band," Zoom says.

Happily, Doe and Cervenka agree with this

musical philosophy. "I see that as our biggest strength," Doe says. "Otherwise, X wouldn't be as rock and roll. It would be more introspective and probably more arty." "God, I'd hate to be in a band like that," Cervenka adds.

THE FOUR X-PONENTS came together in 1977. Doe and Cervenka met at a poetry project a few months after she came to Los Angeles from Tallahassee, and have been together (through stormy weather, to judge by their records) ever since. Zoom entered the picture after he and Doe placed nearly identical "band wanted" ads in the paper. The guitarist then wanted to find a drummer who used a marching snare. When Doe caught Bonebrake at the Masque torturing just such a tub, the quartet was complete.

At first, the band's eclecticism was a stumbling block. "To create a sound, a band has to put aside its influences and just work on what it's doing," Doe says. "Billy knew about all kinds of rockabilly, blues and rhythm and blues from playing in soul bands. DJ had been in orchestras and marching bands. We decided not to deal with those things at first — to be totally narrow-minded and pin our sound down."

In 1980, that sound became the careening noise of *Los Angeles*, X's disturbingly acute dissection of Hollywood Boulevard funk. Over a jarring loud-and-fast attack, Doe and Cervenka examined L.A.'s decadent-chic society with an insider's ambivalence between pride and disgust.

"Johny Hit and Run Paulene," "Sugarlight" and "Sex and Dying in High Society" detail the escape hatches of a self-annihilating society: violent sex, heroin, social climbing. The album's title track reeks of urban claustrophobia. The knotty awkwardness of X's Chuck Berried punk barrage befits its struggle to fight off this hatred and make sense out of the debris.

Doe says X formed "as a reaction against people like Peter Frampton" — the bland FM sounds of the mid-'70s. *Los Angeles*'s eerie "The Unheard Music" protests that there are "no hard chords" on the car radio and ends up celebrating the city's budding underground. Similarly optimistic, the album's closing "The World's a Mess; It's in My Kiss," fueled by a reeling guitar riff, poses the possibility of finding insane love to match insane times.

LOS ANGELES, released on the fledgling Slash label, sold an incredible 100,000 copies and catapulted X to national status. On the strength of this success, the band started to branch out musically. "Once we got our sound," Doe explains, "we moved a bit to the right and left. We applied our sound to our influences."

The band's 1981 follow-up, *Wild Gift*, sanded down some of the debut album's ragged edges. Lyrics became more personal, and the music more country (!), without sacrificing any horsepower. *Under the Big Black Sun*, released in 1982, showed even more pronounced country underpinnings.

"I love country music," Doe declares. "I grew up with it. Not that I lived in a shack in Arkansas."

Cervenka says the influence was always there. "It took a while for everything to come out, and to realize that no one was going to yell at us for doing a song like "The Have Nots," a populist tune from *Under the Big Black Sun*.

But X has not become a country band, nor is it likely to become one. "We use our musical knowledge indirectly," Doe says. "It's stuff we love, but we don't want to say, 'OK, X is going to do a country and western album.' Elvis Costello did it, that's fine." Like Creedence Clearwater Revival, X is a rock band that draws on folk sources.

THEIR LOVE of country music has exerted a sobering influence on Doe and Cervenka's lyrics, however. They've tightened the reins since earlier high-falutin' talk and sharpened images to hard-edged specifics. This straightforward writing is more affecting, and more personal without being confessional. "We listen to [country] music because it applies to us as people," Cervenka says. "That music goes along with our lives; then we write about the same things."

What things? "Cheating, drinking, fussing, fighting," Doe drawls. "They're able to write about all that stuff. We do have songs about cheating. That came along in our lives, and we said it was all right to write about it, because somebody else did, too."

So, have the punk traded in their berets for Stetsons? Absolutely not. For X, country music offers a perspective, not a vocabulary.

Under the Big Black Sun, recorded shortly after the death of Cervenka's sister Mary, is a depressing record. The dark cloud hanging over the band dissipates some of X's customary energy. The album is moving at times but misses a lot of what is so special about the band.

By contrast, *More Fun in the New World* comes on like hellfire. Zoom and Bonebrake make a joyful noise, and Doe and Cervenka record with gripping honesty the slurred voices of lower America. Instead of straining to make a Statement, as on "The Have Nots," *More Fun* relaxes its grip for a more objective look at the world.

X WILL ALWAYS BE a literary band. But its literary models are becoming less obscure and more personal and more populist.

"Sometimes the themes are too personal for people," Doe concedes. "But I like that. To me, that's what writing and poetry are all about."

Like *Los Angeles*, *More Fun* looks at people living on the fringe: assorted misfits, outcasts, slobs, losers, alcoholics, lowlifes and underachievers, facing the day bleary-eyed and disoriented. It takes place in cheap hotels, bars, bus terminals and coffee shops across industrial America. It's as seamy as the first LP, but more sympathetic and less moralistic.

The album's most memorable character is the barfly in "New World." Doe and Cervenka don't ennoble the lush or make him a symbol; they consider him interesting enough as he is. "I wish we were simple enough people to be able to write something like Hank Williams," Doe says. "We know too much for our own good. When media bombards you all the time, you have to learn the stuff. You can't help but know the ins and outs of what happened in Beirut, El Salvador or Grenada."

Both sides of *More Fun* close with a departure from the narrative vignettes. "True Love Pt. #2" sets a series of one-liners over a funk riff.

"That was just fun," Doe explains. "Exene had the line 'True love is the devil's crowbar.' Billy and DJ and their wives Dinky and Denise just started adding lines like 'True love is the devil's lapdog.' We just did it as a fun take-off on '"True Love."'

In the brooding "I Must Not Think Bad Thoughts," Doe tries to shout down a list of doubts and fears about American society with the title motto. "It's like what a crazy person tells himself to keep from going over the line," he says. "The song is bitter, but it's really about salvation. There's no success in bitterness."

BITTERNESS? X's American identity and punk roots haven't exactly endeared them to the FM behemoth. "New music" formats tend to pass the band up in favor of faddish British acts. "Cute English boys will always be more popular than talented American bands," Cervenka grumbles. After four years of touring and rapturous press, Doe estimates X's audience at 100,000 — the number of people who bought the first album.

All the band members blame a lack of exposure. To radio and its advertisers, X is "a hardcore band from Los Angeles, and at our shows people get hurt really bad, and it's real violent," according to Cervenka. But they insist the audience is out there. Zoom: "If they played our records on the radio and MTV as much as Duran Duran, I think they'd sell like hotcakes."

The band will continue to stick to its guns. "Our goal is to mean something to a whole bunch of people, without compromise in any blatant form," Doe says. But that's not stopping them from pursuing outside projects. Zoom produces and plays live with rockabilly bands. Bonebrake works with producer and artiste Geza X. Cervenka teamed with Lydia Lunch on a book of poetry, *Adulterers Anonymous*; both she and Doe appear on *English as a Second Language*, a double-album compilation of young L.A. poets. The couple also perform with Dave Alvin of the Blasters in an acoustic trio called the Knitters.

X's inarticulate fumblings put their message across by the strength of their sincerity. These people with the funny names display their souls — gawkiness intact — with everything they do. And what is the real name of the aspiring folk hero who calls himself John Doe?

"Samuel Clemens," he quips. ∎

WHAT MADE MILWAUKEE FAMOUS ... MADE WINNERS OUT OF THE VIOLENT FEMMES

TP 88, AUGUST 1983

By Cary Baker

They're the first band they can think of in Milwaukee history to be signed by Warner Bros. Well, OK, Slash/Warner, but they still get a computer bar-code on the album cover. Suddenly, everyone in Brew City can say they knew the Violent Femmes *when.*

When... the city's new wave saloons barely took this semi-acoustic trio seriously enough to book them. Where were their amplifiers? Their synthesizers? A drummer playing a wash basin with brushes? This isn't rock, it's hokum. Worse yet, these ... *Femmes* ... didn't always spend their (numerous) nights off sudsing it up in the same establishments.

When... they played in front of the Downer and Oriental theaters, their acoustic instrument cases open for spare change like any self-respecting French Quarter bagpipist. When they couldn't get a wink, not to mention a nod, from the majority of passing streetfaces, it took one James Honeyman-Scott to trumpet his "find" and have the Violent Femmes open for the Pretenders at the Oriental that night. The Femmes, who claim they'd never previously listened to the Pretenders, had been serenading ticket-buyers on Farwell Avenue.

Milwaukee knew them, all right. And today, 24 hours before heading east for a tour, the Violent Femmes have vaulted the final hurdle of household legitimacy. *P.M. Magazine*, TV courier of topics middle-American, is taping a segment on the band, but the crew doesn't have all afternoon. The TV reporter recalls he "may have said something potentially defamatory to koalas" in an earlier Milwaukee Zoo shoot. "The station's deficient in total adult male koalas, ages 18-34," jabs a crew member as the production van full of Femmes and cameramen wends through a barren city park.

No sweat — koalas won't go extinct before nightfall. Besides, the Femmes don't need all afternoon to set up or tear down. Gordon Gano brings his acoustic guitar and Telecaster with minimal amp; Brian Ritchie, his amplified acoustic bass guitar; and Victor DeLorenzo, an equally high-tech trap kit, which on an elaborate night might contain a snare, a small bass drum, a cymbal and a tranceaphone (his invention: a metal washtub mounted onto a floor tom).

For on-location atmosphere, the band has tapped a tiny neighborhood shot 'n' beer joint just around the corner from DeLorenzo's house. "They've got the best drink policy in town for musicians," the drummer foams. "You have to have ten free drinks or they won't let you leave." The Femmes are clearly loyal to the seven Johnson brothers who own the Gordon Park Pub and not to some of the other club owners in town.

WHETHER THE Violent Femmes are part and parcel of anyone's Milwaukee "scene" doesn't matter much now. Hardcore punks and techno freaks, neo-psychedelics and mutant funksters have all been known to join them onstage. There's even an occasional horn section, formal enough to bear a name (the Horns of Dilemma), informal enough to show up as a threesome or a solo with instruments like sackbut and cornetto.

"We're always putting ourselves in danger," Ritchie says. He's so tired of trendiness that he hasn't cut his hair in a year and dons a chasuble for the TV shoot that makes him look like a white Blood Ulmer. "Most bands have their little song list taped to their monitor, and say, "This is a tune from our EP... 1, 2, 3, 4...." The Femmes rarely if ever board the stage with a set list, preferring to call them out as the spirit strikes.

A lot of this comes from their street band roots. "We decided to play out on the streets because the idea of busking was attractive to us," DeLorenzo explains. "It got us in touch with really playing, instead of hiding behind a shroud of electricity. Besides, none of the clubs wanted to book us at the beginning."

Perhaps because they're so in touch with each other, the Violent Femmes court musical danger. Their use of jazz improvisation as a model makes sense with their repertoire. One night in Madison, DeLorenzo and Gano spontaneously walked off a club stage mid-set, leaving Ritchie to fend for himself on bass for a while. Thank goodness he was well-studied in Mingus. "Rock has gotten so ... *stagnant*," DeLorenzo moans.

THE FEMMES' SOUND has been dubbed "punk-folk," further bloating the hyphenated-genre ranks. The band itself neither perpetrates nor decries this horrendous handle. "We didn't want to be called new wave-folk," says the demure Ritchie, who previously played in Plasticland, a psychedelic outfit, "so we figured we'd prefer punk-folk."

What this boils down to is that the Femmes are the newest, and possibly the truest, scholars of both the sanguine and ribald periods of Jonathan Richman. Add an acrid aftertaste from sitting out many a sock hop to an antipathy to the modern world matching that of Jim Skafish or any other rock "outcast." Embellish with a skiffle sound windburned on the diagonally intersecting Milwaukee streets and dynamics from a whisper to a scream. The rest is open to suggestion. Got a harmonica? A koto? C'mon up. Wanna rile 'em into writing about you? Outstay your welcome.

THIS WORLD — variously vindictive, euphoric or merely thwarted — is that of Gordon Gano. The quiet 20-year-old wrote all the band's songs practically out of high school, and he was reportedly expelled from the National Honors Society for performing one of his songs at an awards ceremony. Gano's expressionism previously found an outlet

in acting: he auditioned for the guilt-ridden teen played by Timothy Hutton in *Ordinary People*.

Violent Femmes' ten songs ooze confession. "Why can't I get just one fuck?" Gano seethes in "Add It Up," the album's most stirring song. But wait — is the singer addressing his mother? He's grown now and ready for the kill in this thinly disguised Oedipal fantasy.

"What we're saying is, 'Here's romanticism thrown back in your face without frills or $500 costumes. Here's raw, gut emotion. Can you deal with this?'" exclaims DeLorenzo, at 28, the eldest Femme. "Can you warm up to it or will you be totally repulsed? Either reaction is fine with me."

DeLorenzo, an ex-jazz drummer, is serious when he talks about the Femmes' "element of free jazz." The band's bon-voyage Milwaukee gig takes place at the Jazz Gallery. (Like the Gordon Park Pub, it's steps from DeLorenzo's house.) The small lounge has knotty pine walls, a minuscule stage and a backdrop portrait of Charles Mingus.

DeLorenzo says the Violent Femmes are "trying to express something more emotionally volatile than the mass of what's happening in the music scene now, which is packaged to fit onto MTV's playlist."

Will radio ever come around to such bludgeoning, unadulterated honesty? "It depends whether they want to show any intelligence," notes a dry-lipped Ritchie.

"I'm not going to force this record down anyone's throat," adds DeLorenzo. "I'll simply go out and promote it by playing the best I can every time we perform."

IF *VIOLENT FEMMES* becomes this year's black sheep hit, it will be a tremendous blow to the idea of producer domination. The album's nominal producer is friend and manager Mark Van Hecke of New York, who DeLorenzo had known from his theater days. Van Hecke knew what the Femmes were about and didn't set out to extract *Toto IV* from a blister in the sun. They recorded most of it on 8-track in a Lake Geneva, Wisconsin studio capable of 24-track.

"He coaxed us into doing good live performances in the studio," DeLorenzo says. "Sometimes we'd end up doing a song about 20 times. If Brian didn't feel particularly good about a bass part for some reason, we'd do the whole song over; we wouldn't overdub the bass part. It was a very meticulous production in that it succeeded in capturing our spontaneity. We left some mistakes on it — a track that's perfect can often be lifeless."

Perhaps this *modus operandi* will apply on the Femmes' second LP. Perhaps not. They plan not to get locked into a concept, nor pandering to an audience by compromising.

"The only thing we'll pander to," DeLorenzo states, "is our own desire to grow and amaze ourselves through our progress. We may not remain totally acoustic."

"The best artists of recent years," Ritchie says, "the Clash, Talking Heads and Elvis Costello, went out on a limb. I think we're going to be that way."

But much roadwork looms ahead before the band will see the inside of another recording studio. Ritchie has compiled travel tapes of Tyrannosaurus Rex, Cecil Taylor, John Cale, early Stones, Balinese gamelan, blues and Indian folk music. The Femmes will remain Milwaukee rent-payers, however, and they have a pre-concert compilation cassette of Milwaukee bands to spread the word.

"Milwaukee has the feel of a European village," DeLorenzo says. The city has remained fairly true to its Germanic foundation. And its art community, perhaps due to the city's ideal size, is closer-knit than that of Chicago, which is ten times as populous and only a hundred miles south. Commercial rock radio spearheads nearly every Milwaukee musician's list of grievances, but the station once rated the country's most neanderthal now integrates U2 with Styx. Would a choleric "folk-punk" band down the computers?

"A friend of mine is a DJ at that station," Ritchie says. "I called him this morning. He said, 'Everybody keeps calling for "Mr. Roboto" and it's driving me crazy.' I told him his association with that radio station is causing his subliminal, spiritual decay."

But will they play the album? "If not," says one violent Femme. "I'll whack my friend upside the head." ∎

HOLLY AND THE ITALIANS

TP 66, OCTOBER 1981

By Karen Schlosberg

Album cover shot: A young woman in a flowery '50s party dress, pink tucked gloves, Fender Stratocaster slung over her shoulder and electric pink lipstick on a "come-hither" punkette pout. What's wrong with this picture?

"The bra strap, which was not intentional," Holly Vincent laughs. "I just thought [afterward] that was perfect. The picture of the girl standing there in this pink party dress with her bra strap showing reminded me of the music itself. It's almost right, but there's something about it that's just a bit tacky."

If there ever were a rock version of Peter Pan, Vincent would be a front-runner to play the title role. Holly and the Italians' lead singer-songwriter-guitarist and bassist Mark Sidgwick are seated at a long conference table (littered with miniature candy bars and soda cans) in their manager's New York office. The 25-year-old Vincent wears a white middy blouse and tight black pants and sports a short, boyish haircut that emphasizes a small, finely featured face. The look would be androgynous but for flat gold shoes, big yellow earrings and a touch of lipstick.

The pair are in town to search for a new drummer and to talk about their debut album, *The Right to Be Italian*. (They have since settled on John LaForge and added guitarist Colin White, both of whom toured with Vincent and Sidgwick in England.) There has been a buzz about Holly and the Italians for a while now, and anyone who has kept up even marginally with the English music scene since late 1979 has heard about Vincent and her band.

(Holly Vincent is her real name, by the way — though she says a friend once tried to convince someone that Vincent's mother had been a groupie for Buddy Holly and Gene Vincent. Holly's father changed his surname, a long Italian one, to his more succinct given name.)

Vincent, who is from Los Angeles (via Chicago and Lake Tahoe), formed the band there in early 1979. She then moved to England, where, her manager at the time assured her, the trio (with drummer Steve Young) could get a record deal more easily than in the States. After a personal falling-out, the manager left them with no record deal and very little money.

"We knew it was going to be all right in the end," Vincent says, "so it was just a matter of sticking it out. Everything we did was building toward something. We could see there was going to be an end — or a beginning, rather — that was much better than what we were going through at the time."

They managed to secure a one-off deal with [Charlie Gillett's] Oval Records for a single, "Tell That Girl to Shut Up," which was released in the UK at the end of the year. Virgin Records signed them about a month later, right in keeping with the Italians' plans.

"We went to smaller labels with the single" — Vincent's soft, British-inflected accent mixes a bit oddly with a mellow south California drawl — "but that was really just a tester to get a larger deal. We didn't want to be a cult band; we wanted to be big."

WHY ITALIAN? Vincent and Sidgwick have a fairly well-rehearsed rap on the meaning of "Italian" and the requirements for being one.

"Disliking Italian food," Vincent says.

"It's the art of acting and not reacting," Sidgwick says. "You've seen *Raging Bull*. You take the offensive as an Italian. You don't just sit there and wait for things to happen to you. Italian is just a front for individualism. Most people can't take being Italian for very long."

The Italians' own experience bears that out.

Sidgwick is the group's third bassist. Percussionist Young, although drummed out for "non-Italian behavior" (according to Sidgwick), was a high-school chum of Vincent and helped cultivate her musical tastes. "He virtually came over, took me down to the record store, sold all my fusion rock and progressive albums, and made me buy Love Sculpture and Rory Gallagher records."

The moniker itself came to Vincent, she says, while drunk. "I was just sitting around trying to think of names. I'm a bit Italian, but [basically] I just liked the name. It was funny in a light-hearted, humorous way. I had no idea how far I wanted to take it at the time. It's easy for a record company. The publicity department has a field day with it."

That's for sure. Virgin packaged her "Miles Away" single in a red, white and green sleeve, with peel-off stickers bearing slogans like "The Day the World Turned Dago," "Wop Rock Rules" and "Never Mind the Bolognese." In the more ethnically sensitive U.S., though, Vincent worries about offending people. "We don't make fun of anything," she's quick to point out.

THE ITALIANS' music does indeed have nothing whatever to do with race, religion or ethnic background. *The Right to Be Italian* celebrates — what else? — the trials and tribulations attending youth and adolescence. The band has the energy of the Ramones and the spirit of Phil Spector-era girl groups. Vincent's lyrics can be endearingly snotty or sensitive, her voice alternately tough and tender and the music is generally pert and sassy. A re-recorded "Tell That Girl" (written about a male friend with a "really bratty girlfriend ... whenever I'd call him, she'd slam the phone down") is the album's centerpiece — exuberant, wonderfully cocky and irresistible.

It doesn't match the first version's raw energy, however, and its faults are symptomatic of the album as a whole. Producer Richard Gottehrer (Blondie, Joan Armatrading, Robert Gordon) allowed Vincent to go overboard with her loud, fuzz-laden guitar and layered instruments almost to the point of suffocation.

"Considering the chaos and circumstances," Vincent says (Young's mid-session departure stretched out recording from summer 1980 through December), "I really like the album. It's different from what I would have expected us to make," she allows, pausing. "I would have preferred us to sound more the way we do live, which is much more powerful."

For her own part, Vincent admits she's "the Gerald Ford of guitar-playing. It's really terrible. Every time we do a video or television I fall over."

While taping a video in Belgium, for example — in that pink party dress and stiletto heels — she got carried away with her miming and next thing she knew she was on the floor. Then there was the time, while supporting the Clash in England, that Clash drummer Topper Headon threw his snare drum across the stage to attract the attention of a roadie. Vincent backed up, fell over the drum and fractured her leg. Even today she is accompanied by a cane, having newly injured her ankle (same leg). "It's a standard joke, my falling over," she says.

But Vincent is going to keep jumping until she gets the pose right. "I haven't learned the guitar," she insists. "I never practiced. I just pick it up and play." She says it's all in the attitude — and being confident.

"You just think, I can play in a band, I can do this. I imagined so hard for so long that when I went to pick up the guitar I knew what to do. It's a bit sloppy occasionally — sometimes I miss notes — but the excitement is there and the attitude is there. And I think that's what counts."

The "cool" to which Vincent aspires (and which she says Sidgwick has naturally, probably because he's English) involves her onstage persona. She refers to the latter in the third person as someone who can live out the rock myth and at the same time make the stage a safe place for Holly Vincent.

"I've had to divorce a bit of myself away from the music just for my own good. If you go onstage being totally yourself all the time you're too vulnerable. It's great if they love you, but if they don't it's too difficult to handle. I've done it" — notably on the English *Right to Be Italian* tour, in which the Italians' rock was sandwiched roughly between the Selecter and the Bodysnatchers' ska and reggae.

"I've learned to define the person onstage. She's just a kid — a real tomboy. Loves attention, loves the spotlight, lives to be noisy and boisterous. I usually end up onstage in jeans and a T-shirt, very boyish, just because of the way I play and move. There's no place for stiletto heels, as I found out. I like wearing dresses, but if I went onstage in a dress I'd feel stupid with a guitar. As a grown-up, mature adult, I would not even want to be onstage with a guitar in the first place," Vincent laughs. "Everything's written from the point of view of this adolescent kid. That's the part that is onstage."

Afterwards, Sidgwick says, "The roadies come on and put it in a flight case."

Let's hope that boisterous little kid never has to grow up. Just like Peter Pan. ■

RAVING FAVES

SONG SWIPES

TP 68, DECEMBER 1981

Self-plagiarism is seemingly rampant in this hit-obsessed business. Besides the Knack nick cited below, chronic repeaters included Ted Nugent, the Buzzcocks and Graham Parker, who "simply swiped *Squeezing Out Sparks* from himself and renamed it *The Up Elevator*," according to Paula Carino.

1. Doors: "Hello, I Love You" (from the Kinks' "All Day and All of the Night")

2. Kinks: "Catch Me Now I'm Falling" (from the Rolling Stones' "Jumping Jack Flash")

3. Jam: "Start" (from the Beatles' "Taxman")

4. Beach Boys: "Surfin' USA" (from Chuck Berry's "Sweet Little 16," although they had the decency to credit it)

5. George Harrison: "My Sweet Lord" (from the Chiffons' "He's So Fine")

6. Knack: "Baby Talks Dirty" (from the Knack's "My Sharona")

There was a lot wrong with this ambitious article. Attempting a taxonomy of bands, many of whom were in the process of evolving, was a recipe for confusion and rear-view-mirror ridicule. The only purpose for including it here is to show that Trouser Press, *like* Bomp!, *was an early champion of power pop as a genre and to list off who we thought qualified at that particular point in time. We wanted to plant a flag and did it with a six-page extravaganza, designed to look like a spiral-bound book, that even included a ridiculous rating system. Instead of reproducing the whole sorry escapade, these are the introductory sections.*

(Historical precedence: Ken Barnes used "Slade power-pop punch" in reference to Nazareth in '76 and Gene Sculatti called the Blue Öyster Cult song "Debbie Denise" "a totally novel brand of power pop"; the following summer, reviewing a Pezband LP for Crawdaddy!, *Toby Goldstein put it in quotes.)*

Artists covered in the article: ABBA, Bachman-Turner Overdrive, Bay City Rollers, Blondie, Boston, Eric Carmen, Cheap Trick, City Boy, Clash, Dictators, Eddie and the Hot Rods, the Flamin' Groovies, the Jam, Kiss, Kursaal Flyers, Nick Lowe, Tom Petty, Pezband, Piper, the Quick, Radio Stars, Ramones, Rubinoos, Todd Rundgren, Shoes, Slade, Sparks, Chris Stamey, Michael Stanley Band, Sweet, Dwight Twilley Band, Vibrators and Wings.

The postscript to all this is a chapter critiquing the article in Go Further: More Literary Appreciations of Power Pop, *edited by Paul Myers and S.W. Lauden (Rare Bird Books, 2021).*

POWER POP PRIMER

TP 27, APRIL 1978

By Ira Robbins

If one may hazard an absurd guess based on no real information, it will probably be around November of this year when some smart punk rocker will wake up and realize that a change has occurred since the inception of the new wave. In place of similar sounding four-piece noise machines, groups that used to be called punk are replacing hoarse shouts with melody, volume with a sense of dynamics. Not that groups have abandoned their instruments or ideals, just that a new influence has been taken on. At that point, the renaissance of power pop will have officially occurred.

Not that power pop is anything new. A few groups have always managed to hold on, even during the roughest trend, to the notion that ideal music blends songs, lyrics and energy into a form where catchy hooks find the strength of blaring guitars a help, not a distraction. That's power pop: rock with hooks. Not tepid chart stuff like Gary Wright that uses studio musicians to lend rock credibility. Not Led Zep riff rock. Not overblown, gas-filled balloons like ELP. Not wimpy ballads like Debby Boone. Just hard rock with a beat and a melody — something you can sing on the subway or rehearse with your band. Music that'll stay with you a while, but not too long.

Already, in fact since the beginning, there have been new wave bands devoted to power pop. Although a large segment of the bands is more blam-blam oriented, the general trend so far has been towards power pop, not away. Groups that were unheard names in the British press a year ago are turning out to be, with fair regularity, more or less pop groups that joined in the fun and got swept along by the excitement before they had a chance to explain what they were about. Generation X, Advertising, Yachts, Gorillas and Motors are all incipient pop bands. Larger names like the Clash and Vibrators are forging strong pop-punk connections, and in America

the Ramones are becoming young Beach Boys in leather jackets.

With any luck, 1978 will be the ultimate power pop year, and may prove to be a means by which new wavers and old farters will be able to realize that music is music, regardless of fashion styles or the posturing of performers. It may seem surprising that some of the groups presented here are power poppers but give it some time and some thought and you may find out something you didn't already know.

What we're doing here is running down the groups of 1977–78 and judging them for their relevance to the world of power pop. By no means is this a complete list; T. Rex and Tommy James and the Shondells have been left off because they are no longer around. Many other groups are missing for the same reason; this does not purport to be a history of the genre.

PRE-HISTORY

Some of the best all-time American pop groups have broken up. but their influence and persever-ance (especially during a period in rock when pop was generally dismissed as garbage) warrant their All-Star Power Poppers status. Big Star, led by Alex Chilton in Memphis between 1971 and 1974, released two monumental albums before breaking up. Milk 'n' Cookies, who almost made it in England during Sparks' reign, posthumously released an album of pure power pop marred only by the unfortunate choice of vocalist. Then there was Nazz, Philadelphia's contribution to the world. Still nonpareil in their blend of rock and Rundgren, their LPs are collectors' items worth paying for.

Between 1970 and 1974, the Raspberries were THE power pop band: not only did they continually strive to recreate sounds of the '60s, they actually succeeded in getting their records on the radio and in the charts. Their unwavering commitment to a style of music finally killed them, as the confusing issue of nostalgia plagued their artistic credibility. But, still, they probably encouraged a lot of beginning groups who might otherwise have given up and practiced playing "Dark Star."

Going back ten years, the origins of power pop lie somewhere between *Revolver*-era Beatles and the bubblegum bands of 1966–67. Despite the fuzzing of distinctions, U.S. psychedelic bands — the Strawberry Alarm Clock, Blues Magoos et al. — were basically playing power pop with some modification. But this is all getting too complicated and arcane: the groups that follow are those who are still functioning and have released an album. Not all of them currently produce power pop, but they've done so in the past and might do so again. ∎

1981:
THE 10 BEST

Some people make resolutions when a new year rolls around; others make "10-best" lists. Those of you who keep track of such things will note that this is the third time in four years that Elvis Costello has topped TP's honor roll. [*Now will you give us an interview?—Ed.*] Half of our overachievers are no strangers to TP's Top 10, with Squeeze making the most dramatic gain in popularity. Of the others, U2, Go-Go's and Holly and the Italians unleashed impressive debuts; the dB's' long-awaited album delivered as their 45s promised; and hardy perennials the Dictators proved there's life in the Bronx yet. Drop-outs from last year include Talking Heads (missing in solo action), Rockpile (busy licking wounds), the English Beat, Gang of Four and Public Image Ltd.

1
ELVIS COSTELLO
Trust
A confident show of force from Mr. Reliable before plunging into Nashville terra incognita.

2
U2
Boy
Raw, quivering messages from the heart. Defiant expressionism at a time we could use it.

3
THE CLASH
Sandinista!
Overblown, overambitious and only this bunch could pull it off. Still the only band that matters?

GO-GO's
Beauty and the Beat
Refreshing dose of pop insouciance. Also the new wave chart invaders of the year.

5
SQUEEZE
East Side Story
Craftsmanship needn't be dull. Someday their songs will get the recognition they deserve; don't wait.

6
HOLLY AND THE ITALIANS
The Right to Be Italian
More polished than the Go-Go's, but just as breezy and tuneful. (Subscribers: Play flexi-disc for details.)

7
THE PRETENDERS
II
Derivative? Sure! But Chrissie Hynde can still charm your pants off (*sic*) when she wants.

8
THE dB's
Stands for DeciBels
Thanks to an amazing timewarp, this band is with us right now—and almost singlehandedly saving power pop's reputation.

THE UNDERTONES
Positive Touch
Derry's finest grow up without growing old. Refined yet rocking, and true to its title.

10
DICTATORS
Fuck 'Em if They Can't Take a Joke
Our first cassette-only selection. Rock will never die as long as bands like this are around to give it a swift kick in the pants.

RUNNERS-UP: KID CREOLE AND THE COCONUTS, **Fresh Fruit in Foreign Places**; SHAKIN' PYRAMIDS, **Skin 'Em Up**; SHOES, **Tongue Twister**; SPLIT ENZ, **Waiata**; ALAN VEGA.

From *Trouser Press* February 1982

BRITISH PUNK AND NEW WAVE

> " *I like punk. I'm not that into it ... I regard it as another style with good fashion and a good attitude.* "
>
> —PAUL McCARTNEY

Given how excited we were to read the British weeklies' coverage of the punk scene exploding there, we were incredibly lucky to attract London correspondents who could report on it in our pages. Pete Silverton, Paul Rambali, Harry George (Robinson) and Pete Frame, the zen master of family tree rock genealogy, gave us exactly the sort of vicarious authority we craved and allowed us to share it with our readers. This was history in the making.

*P*aul Rambali, who wrote this clumsily (cleverly?) named monthly column for us (TP 15 – 23), went on to a staff job at the New Musical Express *and then became the first assistant editor of* The Face. *He later wrote television documentaries, two novels and a number of fine books on diverse non-music subjects around the world, including Brazil, an Ethiopian marathoner and his relocation to France. Paul died, after a long illness, in January 2024.*

ENGLISH RAMBLINGS

TP 16, OCTOBER/NOVEMBER 1976

By Paul Rambali

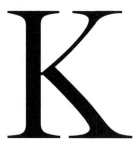

Kicking off this time with news of a very interesting little record company that has just begun operations over here. The label is called Stiff and it's run by Jake Riviera (formerly Andy Jakeman), who used to work for the Feelgoods (in fact, the Feelgoods are providing part of the funds for the venture.) The aim of Stiff is, according to Jake, "releasing three-chord songs lasting three minutes, as well as collectors' item discs and possible chart records." However, they intend to have the maximum amount of fun doing it, witness the name — "Stiff Records: the most flexible label in the world," and the sleeve logo — "if it means everything to everyone ... it must be a Stiff" and "Today's sound Today."

The most interesting part, though, is the music, by Nick Lowe, Chilli Willi, Brinsley Schwarz, the Pink Fairies (with Martin Stone, formerly of Chilli Willi) and Eggs Over Easy. At the moment, the main man is Nick Lowe; the rest of the stuff is old material, Chilli Willis' first LP (not the *Bongos Over Balham* LP; before that and very obscure), the Brinsleys from '73, all being mixed by the artists involved. Nick's first single, "So It Goes"/"Heart of the City" (BUY1) should be in Discophile (New York City) by now, so you can all find out for yourselves what it's like. (I think it's great.) Jake intends to start looking for new bands to sign, but no news as yet of any names. There is talk of Richard Hell (formerly of New York's Television) doing some things with Nick and Tim Roper (Ducks Deluxe's old drummer) and also a possible tie-up with the Beserkley label.

Nick Lowe has been very busy lately; he has just appeared on the new Dave Edmunds single "Here Comes the Weekend" (Nick and Dave worked together on a single called "Let's Go to the Disco"/"Everybody Dance" on British UA earlier this year). "Here Comes the Weekend" should have been released in the U.S. by now, so you should be aware of the fact that he has been signed by Swan Song for a princely sum, I'm told. The album, which is almost finished, should be well worth the wait. Edmunds sounds as if he has finally learned/absorbed what he wanted and is ready to give us some first-class music. Nick Lowe has a hand in the album, too.

The music papers here are giving a lot of coverage to the Sex Pistols at the moment. It's a very mixed response though, as nobody is sure what to make of them yet. Sex Pistols is a great name; you can imagine kids bringing home their records and causing parents further anxiety. It's difficult to pigeon-hole them. The blend of influences is obvious, but their own ideas meld the sources into something individual. If you imagine something halfway between the Stooges and the Who, both at maximum potential, then add *Man Who Sold the World*, *Hunky Dory* and *Ziggy* plus what Ronson/Bowie were heading towards, you'll have a (rather intense) idea of what they're up to. The guitarist, Steve, is like a young Townshend. He windmills his arms, screws up his face and pours out some of the most punching, intense and inventive guitar ever — even if he stole the opening chords to "Fireball" from the Ducks. The only non-original song they do is "Substitute," and it has just as much power as the original (hard to believe).

However, what's causing the most reaction is Johnny Rotten, his stage stance and the lyrics. He comes on completely blank, his face emotionless throughout, apart from occasionally looking as if he's desperately trying to get some kind of emotion across. The lyrics, or what I could make out of them when I saw them, sounded more original than anything I've heard in ages, but we'll have to wait to find out. It would be pointless attempting to describe them. Chris Spedding has been in the studio with them recording a demo LP. They aren't signed yet but lots of people are after them. They are in an odd position at the moment, because the audience they attract seems more interested in looking fashionable than in watching the group.

Since my last missive, Eddie and the Hot Rods have been going from strength to strength. They've been getting an amazing reaction from audiences in France and have played to packed houses all over England.

Barrie Masters describes it thus: "It's like being at a football match, they're waving scarves about and shouting for us and they're young kids too; at first we were getting all the posers who just came to see us because of the publicity, but now we've got our own following." Musically, they have begun to define themselves a lot more clearly. The "Wooly Bully" single was a disappointment to most people here, including the Rods, who felt it didn't have enough drive. They don't intend to go back into the studios until early next year, when they start work on an LP.

In the meantime, an EP, *Live at the Marquee*, will have to do. It's made up of non-originals: "Gloria," "Satisfaction," Bob Seger's "Get Out of Denver" and ? and the Mysterians' "96 Tears." "We tried not doing any oldies for a while, but it didn't work, 'cause everyone would just be shouting for them at the end, so we had to play them. We're putting out the EP for the kids, really, because they like the songs so much." The Rods at the moment look all set to follow the footsteps of the Feelgoods (both bands hail from the South-end/Canvey Island area, and Dave Higgs was in the Fix with Lee Brilleaux and Wilko) and move out of the pubs and into the college gigs and bigger halls. They've got what it takes, but you're going to have to wait until next year to find out whether I'm right or not. ∎

THE BRITISH NEW WAVE (WILL THERE ALWAYS BE AN ENGLAND?)

TP 18, FEBRUARY/MARCH 1977

By Pete Silverton and Paul Rambali

Sgt. Pepper might have been a great album, but it also killed rock and roll. It wiped out the singles market and marked the beginning of a period dominated by album sides filled with pretensions and indulgences.

In London, the first signs of a reaction against this was pub rock in 1972. The phrase itself was only a journalistic cliché, but at least the music returned to short sharp songs clocking in at under three minutes. Brinsley Schwarz's Nick Lowe was a great songwriter (and someone who'll crop up later in our story). Ducks Deluxe marked the first, if balding, awakening of a "punk" consciousness, and Dr. Feelgood was just a helluva fine rock and roll band.

But, because it never reached a large audience (the Feelgoods didn't hit the UK charts until late '75/'76), pub rock was a false dawn, and it wasn't until January 1976, when Nick Kent wrote an article in the *NME* lauding the New York punk explosion, that things started moving again. Then in April came the mercenary fiasco of the five-day Stones bash at Earl's Court. They were no more than the shell of what was expected, and a sizable section of the audience felt like animated puppets at the end of strings joggled by the music industry hierarchy. If Kent's article showed there were alternatives, the Stones' gig gave a lot of people the impetus to go out and find them nearer home. To wit, the Ramones came over to tour.

Suddenly (or not so suddenly, actually) a whole new wave of bands were upon us. They drew shamelessly from the teen-oriented attack of the mid-'60s English bands and the over-the-top naked energy of Detroit heavy metal, added their own songs and produced a form of rock and roll that was an expression of frustration with current English social conditions. With the highest level of unemployment since the '30s (especially severe amongst kids just leaving school) and widespread uncertainty about the future economic stability of the country, that frustration takes a stance of antagonism towards the powers that be (even if the highest expression of that is often only heaving half a brick through the window of the nearest rock star's Rolls).

Not that the bands themselves would always put it that way. The Clash might. But Sex Pistols vocalist Johnny Rotten says, "We're not into music. We're into anarchy." Taking that as a founding statement of the movement, the English rock press went overboard with extensive coverage, varying from gratuitous slurs on the bands' musical abilities and personal morals to low-grade post-[Herbert] Marcuse sociology to "this is the only future of rock and roll" gush. The rock press has settled down to a more balanced view in the last couple of months. The national [papers], however, are something else again — as you'll read about in the Pistols' piece.

Most of the bands are truly new wave, having sprung up out of nowhere in the last six months, though some of them have been around longer. Eddie and the Hot Rods have been playing for a couple of years. Joe Strummer was the founder

and leading light of the seminal 101'ers. And the semi-legendary London SS spawned Mick Jones (the Clash), Brian James (the Damned) and Tony James (Generation X) — the band never got off the ground but they're supposed to have had a wild version of "Slow Death."

Bands that have just sprung up are Siouxsie and the Banshees, Eater (average age 15), Subway Sect, the Slits, the Wet Lepers, Slaughter and the Dogs and Manchester's Buzzcocks. They have spawned their own fanzines, notably *Sniffin' Glue* and the brand-new *Bondage*; even their own club (as so many venues are closed to them), the Roxy in Covent Garden.

In case you must know (and why not?), the dance craze currently "sweeping" the town is, I kid you not, the Pogo. The dancer's purpose is, as someone else so beautifully put it, to launch himself or herself vertically towards the ceiling with maximum velocity and let everything else take its natural course. Chris Spedding, trend-spotter extraordinaire, even put out a record about it ("Pogo Dancing").

Once you've got your dance steps together, it's time to start thinking about your threads. If you want to be the star of the night, you'll be sporting some sort of S/M gear from Malcolm McLaren's King's Road shop Sex (preferably stolen) and odd bits and pieces picked up from jumble sales, all held together with bondage straps or safety pins (although they're probably a thing of the past by now) and topped off with enough make up to hide Mae West's age. If you want to be truly original, it's only a matter of inventing your own clothes. Fancy a "Chuck Berry Is Dead" T-shirt, anyone?

All these bands are singles-oriented, the single having become once again a viable force. No small thinks for this are due Nick Lowe's "So It Goes" and the surprising success of the other Stiff and Chiswick releases (and also, to be more cynical, due to the fact that nobody can afford to buy albums on impulse anymore — they're too expensive).

Don't believe these bands are no more than CBGB copyists. Beyond the superficial lunacies of their names there's some real rock and roll.

SEX PISTOLS

Would you believe me if I told you that, towards the end of last year, one band managed to make themselves known to almost the entire populace of Britain, a feat probably achieved by no one since the Beatles? The Sex Pistols did it, got themselves branded as corrupters of youth on the front page of every national daily. It wasn't deliberate, though, and they probably regret it, as it caused the virtual collapse of their first national tour. The Pistols appeared for a short interview on a current affairs TV programme hosted by Bill Grundy. That they appeared at all was surprising, considering they didn't have a record in the shops at the time. They were, and still are, the spearhead of a whole cluster of punk rock/new wave bands that have been given widespread (and possibly premature) coverage in the rock press here.

Bill Grundy has a sarcastic tone at the best of times, but he was really on form that Wednesday. He set out to make the Pistols look like a bunch of stupid kids, being as condescending and sardonic as possible. The group chose not to be fodder for him, and he was looking progressively more foolish. Then someone in the band muttered "shit" under his breath. Grundy seized his chance.

"What?"

"Nothing, a rude word, next question."

"No, no, what was the rude word?"

"Shit."

"Was it really, good heavens, you frighten me to death."

The rest of the interview was reduced to goading by Grundy and more swearing from the band.

The following day everybody knew who the Sex Pistols were. The dailies had taken "Anarchy in the UK," the odd fight at Pistols' gigs and the TV debacle and turned "punk" into a fascist teen army with violent Nazi overtones — cheap sensationalism, but nonetheless uncomfortable topics in England.

What's this got to do with rock and roll? It's beginning to sound like politics. It *is* politics. The Sex Pistols have chosen an inflammatory political statement as their first release. Some of it is just shock tactics; it contradicts itself, and the political theory behind it is questionable. But it is a force-ful statement, driven by volatile, adrenochrome rock like you haven't heard in years; a reaction to the decadence and apathy that has infected a lot of other things besides music recently.

Whether the Pistols will be catalysts for any social change remains to be seen. They've come on stronger than anyone has ever dared and been rewarded so far with being unable to play — most promoters won't book them. The single entered the charts at 43 (quite an achievement) and didn't show the following week because EMI (their label and one of the three biggest) suspended it for a while following the TV appearance. Onstage, the Bowie influence is less discernible, but they still sound like the Who when Daltrey was a Young Man. Steve Jones' guitar is pure rock and roll energy and getting better, Glen Matlock (bass) and Paul Cook (drums) provide the pumping rhythm and Johnny Rotten the twisted, snarling voice. Do anything necessary to lay your hands on the single; it's the most important British record of '76. And one of the best. (PR)

THE DAMNED

If you like the Ramones, the Damned will be a treat. The Ramones know their limitations and stick well within them. The Damned might be aware of theirs but don't appear to let it worry them. Play loud, hard and fast, the criteria is "the attitude." "The kids see us and they think, hey, that could be me up on that stage, I could be as good as that," says Brian James, founding member, guitarist and main songwriter. Formed at the beginning of the summer from the debris of a band Nick Kent was mentor to, the Damned are Rat Scabies on drums, Captain Sensible (Ray Burns) on bass, Dave Vanian on vocals and James. Their rise to fame came suddenly on the night of the near notorious "punk rock festival" at the 100 Club. They had the dubious honor of being the band on stage when the fighting broke out, which they were in no way responsible for. At that time, I felt and wrote that they were the nadir of an uninspiring evening.

Since then, I've had an attack of remorse; giving the Damned another chance, I went to see them at the Hope and Anchor, and they were entertaining, noisy and showed lots of spirit. Rat played powerful drums, Captain Sensible and Brian James played appallingly, and Dave Vanian stalked about the stage with the required menace. But I still wasn't persuaded to think of them as anything more than an amusement.

Trouble is, their single "New Rose" vastly exaggerates them; its infectious chorus kicks like hell. This could be explained by the presence of Nick Lowe as producer and would be borne out by the fact that they mimed to it for a promo film being made that night at the Hope.

If the Damned ever make it to your town don't let good taste stand in your way, go out and have a laugh. (PR)

EDDIE AND THE HOT RODS

To paraphrase Barrie Masters, second encore time at an Eddie and the Hot Rods gig is like being at the Stretford End when Denis Law puts the lads 3-2 up in the 89th minute of a cup-tie. Hot and sweaty band. Hot, sweaty, and jumping crowd. Maximum R&B 1976 style.

The Rods are definitely a force to be reckoned with. They've got their own nigh-on-fanatical crowd. Their album is supposed to have shipped 20,000 in the first week. The Roundhouse was sold out for their first large-venue London appearance (which, unfortunately, was severely marred by an atrocious PA that cut in and out like the vocals on a slice of dub reggae — no matter, their crowd went wild anyway).

And they're such nice boys. The acceptable face of punk. Especially singer Barrie Masters. He's a Canvey Island Tom Sawyer, the cliché of the bad boy with a heart of gold. If he ever wants, or has to, give up rocking he could probably still pull the birds working out in a gym or become a PT teacher and flash his muscles to impressionable nymphoids. With his onstage headsprings, forward rolls and daring-young-man-on-the-20-foot-PA-stacks leaps, it's a bit like watching someone practice for a Scout jamboree.

Paul Gray (bass) and Steve Nicol (drums) make up a competent rhythmic skeleton fleshed out by rhythm 'n' lead axe-man Dave Higgs, who's straight-ahead powerful but should relax a bit; his playing sometimes topples over into

flashy Wilko Johnson nervous-breakdown frenetics.

Probably the last band to rise out of the London pub circuit, their roots were the same Thames estuary wasteland that produced Dr. Feelgood (Higgs used to play with Wilko and Lee [Brilleaux] in a local band called the Fix). They spent the first year or so of their existence playing dead-in-the-hole Essex clubs, developing a manic stage show as a reaction borne out of frustration with audience apathy.

With a bit of help from the Feelgoods, they got a gig at the Kensington, a London pub, and moved onto the regular metropolitan pub and club circuits roundabout, eventually being rewarded for their energetic determination by copping a contract with Island Records.

As each of the Rods' releases sold more than the company expected, release dates were brought forward and — after two successful singles, a brace of *Top of the Pops* appearances and an EP recorded live at the Marquee — they schlepped out the best front cover of '76 wrapped around their album, *Teenage Depression* right at the butt end of their super-successful *Winter Freeze-Out Tour* of Britain.

Personally, I can't get too excited about the Rods, but they are a pretty fine rock and roll shake-your-ass band, they've got stage presence (Barrie sported an Invisible Man wraparound bandages mask for "On the Run" at the Roundhouse), and I ain't about to knock anybody that brings their degree of energy and enjoyment to music.

Even more importantly, I like 'em because their dance, sing and stun the audience stance certainly helped pave the way for....

THE CLASH

...who not only had Patti Smith jump up and "play" with them at one gig, and prompted the comment from Lisa Robinson that they'd rejuvenated her faith in rock and roll, but also happen to be the best band in the world right now.

Okay, so I'm biased. I'm a long-term fan of Joe Strummer (voice and coarse-as-coarse-can-be rhythm guitar). I'm also biased by natural temperament towards any aggregation which has "three people who all wanna be the star and have such big egos they all bust a gut trying to outdo each other," as Mick Jones (lead guitar, complementary vocals and third place in the *Sounds* annual Keith Richard lookalike contest) put it.

The Clash are London late '76 boiled down into a one-inch concentrated stock cube. Tapper Zukie tell his bredrin it's "Ten against One, Natty 'gainst Babylon"? The Clash come right back and replay it a few days later from the point of view of a white kid on the dole or just holding down a scumbag job in "White Riot."

They've got a lot of other great songs which also creatively mirror the dead-end-street-kid universe, like their already neo-classics "Janie Jones" and "1977."

The band's lyrics serve to prove that Joe's still the great metaphysical imagist he was when he wrote the 101'ers' concluding statement, "Clang, Clang, Go the Jail Guitar Doors," and on to the one true kitsch masterwork in the band, Paul Simonon's bass. It's black with a perspex back, flecked with paint like a corporation urinal wall and he's got the notes painted on the frets (in pink! — the color of '76) in case he forgets which notes are which. He's only been playing a few months, you see, and claims he achieved his fresh originality by playing along to reggae records because "they've got interesting bass lines."

The drummer's a moot point. They haven't settled on one full-time yet. The early standby, Terry Chimes, was replaced (by mutual consent) for the Pistols tour by Rob Harper. But all that really matters is that in Joe, Mick and Paul you've got a front line that'd put to shame the 1925 Muscovite troika for aggression and ability.

They've not yet got a record contract, but they're being assiduously wooed by Polydor and should have signed by the time you read this. Their garage-owning manager, Bernie, and Pistols manager/safety-pin-and-general-schmutter-salesman Malcolm McLaren are reportedly intent on conquering the world by having their bands sign to two different major labels and then setting the labels at each other's throats, Beatles vs. Stones style. (PS)

THE VIBRATORS

The Vibrators are only a punk/new wave band by dint of an insidious process of self-adoption. Formed from the remnants of the good-timey Bazooka Joe and bits of what has since become the Lee Kosmin Band, they played an early residency at Holloway Road's Lord Nelson (that's where Dr. Feelgood got their first break) with a solid, enjoyable set of rock and roll classics, the Stooges' "1969" and a few of their own numbers.

Feeling their age (a disgusting, for London late '76, average of 29 years old), sensing the possibilities of the up 'n' coming bands and genuinely liking the music, they tightened up the act, joined up with Chris Spedding (mostly by chance) and got a record out.

It's the *de rigueur* punk hip chic thing to slam their single ("We Vibrate"), but to me it's a more than passable piece of Mickie Most (he produced it) class pop with some added basic raunch courtesy of the band: Knox, lead guitar; John Ellis, second guitar; Pat Collier, bass; Johnny Wheels, drums.

The Vibrators got themselves stuck amidst all the Pistols TV furor and have also been banned from various venues — for no other reason than the fact that they have claimed, perhaps ingenuously, to be a punk band.

Do they deserve it, you ask? I don't think so, because their shows are still innocently fun, and they play some good songs. But then again... I'm open to arguments. (PS)

GENERATION X

Generation X are worth more than a passing mention because they're certainly the best of the very latest wave of bands (class of December '76). They used to be called Chelsea until they junked the singer, Gene October, and reformed with a new guitarist, Bob Andrews, the other band members being singer Billy Idol, Tony James on bass and John Towe on drums. They've played two or three gigs so far and have in "Ready Steady Go" a song that'll make Greg Shaw cry his eyes out. Definitely a band to watch out for, the only obstacle in their way being the ridiculous advance they're apparently asking from record companies. (PS) ∎

THE CLASH: GREATNESS FROM GARAGELAND

TP 26, FEBRUARY 1978

By Pete Silverton

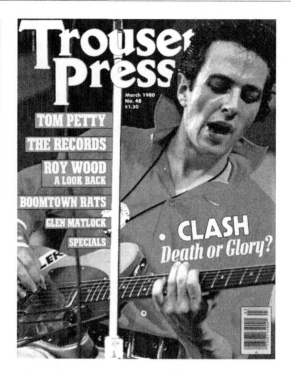

Unannounced to say the least, a kid in boots, suspenders and short cropped hair clambers through the photographers pit and up onto the stage of London's Rainbow Theatre. Benignly ignored by band, stage crew and security alike, he wanders around the stage a little drunkenly, uncertain quite what to do now that he's made it up onto the hallowed, sacrosanct boards, and is not making quite the impression he thought. Decision flickers across his face, lit by the giant spots, and he grabs hold of the singer's mike and prepares to join in on the harmonies. When the singer wants his mike back, the kid's frozen to the stand in fear-drenched exhilaration, so the singer has to shout the lines over the kid's shoulder while the kid pumps in the response lines on perfect cue.

The encore over, the band leaves the stage, and the kid's stuck there in front of two-and-a-half-thousand people, unsure what to do next. With the merest jerk of his head, the bass player motions the kid to join the band backstage and everyone goes home happy.

Sounds like some fantasy of what rock and roll should be about, or at least a case of a cunning audience plant, doesn't it? It wasn't. It was the Clash. And it happened just that way at the first

of their three nights at the Rainbow in December.

That's the thing about the Clash; they can break rules you hadn't realized existed till they trashed 'em. That's why, in a year, without any kind of Springsteen-like hype — except from zealot journalists like myself — they've gone from empty college and club halls to three nights at a major London venue. Like the Pistols, they're so special that they've created not only their own style but also their own rule structure. Only the most carping would say that the Clash are like anybody or anything else.

Because of events like the one just described, the Clash command an awesome respect, even adulatory deification from their fans. Some of them really do seem to expect the Clash to slip 'em the meaning of life in a three-minute rock and roll song. Mind you, full-grown rock writers have been known to make the same mistake. And to think, all that was achieved with only two national tours of Britain and but one album and three singles (in total 17 songs, 19 tracks) in general circulation.

And I still don't think the Clash realize themselves what kind of position they're in. It's as if they're (very understandably) scared of facing up to the fact of that worship and its implications.

Here's another little scene which might help explain what I'm getting at. A few days before I sat down to tap this through my crappy little Smith-Corona portable, I found myself at a gig, competing with Clash meistersinger Joe Strummer for the bartender's attention. (I won.) Having known Strummer for almost two years, I wasn't too surprised when, after exchanging the usual pleasantries, he turned on me a little drunkenly and demanded to know who my favourite English band was. More than a little embarrassed, I told him: "Your lot."

"Nah, come on," he replied, "Tell me who you really think's the best."

"The Clash," my voice getting louder, "Honest!"

Joe didn't believe me. "I bet you'll tell the Hot Rods the same thing tomorrow."

So, here in cold type, let's set the matter straight with an open letter.

Dear Joe,

The Clash are not only the best band in Britain. They're the best band in the world. (I think that for a magnitude of reasons I'll explain in good time.) For me, you're the latest in a straight three-act lineage: Chuck Berry, the Stones, the Clash. No one else comes near. The Beatles may have written better songs but... The Pistols may have been a bigger force of change but... Fercrissakes, if I didn't believe all this stuff, you don't think you'd catch me spieling out all these cascades of yeeugh-making praise, do you now? There's a whole lot more becoming things for an adult to do, you know.

Yours,

Pete

P.S. But I still don't believe that you're the saint, let alone godhead that some of your more impressionable fans crack you up to be. I know you're just as big a headcase as the rest of us.

Good. With that out of the way, I can move on to telling you good and patient — you must be if you've got this far — readers just how and why the Clash have come to occupy such a prominent place in my — and a lot of other people's — affections.

The Clash at core are three people. Mick Jones on lead guitar vocals and Keef lookalikes. He was in the London S.S., about whom the myths outweigh the facts at least tenfold. Paul Simonon plays bass, smiles a lot, lopes around like a grossly underfed gorilla on a vitamin B and methedrine cure for malnutrition and catches the fancy of more women than the rest of the band put together — Patti Smith, for example. Joe Strummer sings in a manner that some find so unmusical as to be repulsive (you find those kinds of philistines everywhere) and others reckon is compulsive and entrancing. Joe was the leading light in the "world famed" 101'ers and still plays the same tortured, demonic rhythm guitar that was the highlight of that band.

And then there's the fourth man. Nicky "Topper" Headon, the drummer. He gets left out of the central three because he's the last in a long line of skin-beaters with the Clash — Terry Chimes (a.k.a. Tory Crimes) plays on the album — and, although Nicky's occupied the stool longer and deservedly so than anyone else, he's still relatively unimportant in the overall image of the band. But who knows, a year from now, he might be as important as Ringo was to the Fabs.

How did they come together? Well, not to put too fine a point on it, the line they usually hand out to gullible journalists is a heap of shit. They claim that Paul and Mick were trotting down Portobello Road one balmy Saturday, already intent on forming their own band, when they chanced upon Joe Strummer and, knowing him from the still-in-existence-at-this-point 101'ers, asked him to be their lead singer. After a couple of days to think it over, he junked the 101'ers and threw in his lot with Mick and Paul. That's the fantasy. The reality, as usual, is both more complex and much less romantic. To explain for the benefit of future historians of the social mores of the '70s, I must backtrack to the first time I encountered Mr. Strummer.

I'd been writing for this rag [*He means us. — Ed.*] for a bit and I'd decided I wanted to do a short piece on what it was really like for a struggling band in London, the supposed Mecca of rock and roll. On the recommendation of a friend who'd known Joe since schooldays, I went down to a truly scummy college benefit to check out the 101'ers.

At this point (two years ago), I was just emerging from a five-year period where I was so disgusted by the rock and roll scene that I spent all day in bed listening to Chuck Berry and reading Trotsky. [*Glad he wasn't listening to Trotsky. —Ed.*] I'd come to like quite a few of the current pub rock bands, but however much I enjoyed them, I knew in my heart of hearts there was something lacking. And, although, if pressed, I'd say it had something to do with lack of stage presence, it wasn't till I saw Joe that night that I realized just what was lacking — full-blooded desperation to become a star and communicate with your audience, and the sense to realize that not only is that a far from easy task, but that, if you don't find your own way of doing it, you might as well junk the idea right there and then.

The 101'ers were an immensely lovable but generally pretty ramshackle bunch who'd rip through Chuck Berry and old R&B numbers with not a trace of genuflection at the altar of the greats. What they — or rather what Joe — took was theirs/his.

I became so enamored with the 101'ers that what had started out as a short article ended up as a veritable thesis which *TP* still has on file (and I hope they don't dig it out, even if it is the definitive work on the subject). [*Read it here*: https://trouserpress.com/letsagetabitarockin/] The day I mailed the piece off, the band broke up. The rest of the 101'ers dropped into the limbo of obscurity, but Joe, with much flourish, hair-cutting and clothes-altering, hooked up with Paul and Mick.

I'd suspected that something of the kind had been in the offing since I'd been with Joe watching the Pistols (who were at this time supporting the 101'ers). As someone else put it, he saw the light and the Sex Pistols simultaneously.

Meanwhile, Mick Jones, Brian James (later of the Damned) and Tony James (now in Generation X) had been sorting out their chops in a basement under the name the London S.S. and the tutelage of future Clash manager Bernard Rhodes, a close pal of Sex Pistols manager Malcolm McLaren.

The London S.S., unable to locate a suitable drummer, never actually played a gig but, according to the few who've heard them, their tapes were very impressive.

When Brian James walked off/was pushed off to form the Damned, the rest of London S.S. faced up to facts, chucked in the towel and went their separate ways.

This is when Mick joined forces with Paul — who'd never even touched a bass before ("I used to be an art designer till I discovered the Clash") — and Keith Levene, who only stayed long enough to do a few early gigs and cop a co-credit for "What's My Name" on the album. He was a great guitarist but... well, just check out "Deny."

Masterminded by their hustler-manager with tertiary verbal diarrhea, Bernard Rhodes, the three of them persuaded Strummer — over a period of time — that he was exactly the vocalist they needed. When Joe was finally convinced, the four of them moved into an enormous (but very cheap) rehearsal studio of their own and began to audition drummers. Getting the name was easy enough. After an initial flirtation with Weak Heart Drops (after a Big Youth song), they plumped for the challenge of the Clash. But getting a drummer wasn't so easy.

They searched with an unusual but understandable (and probably correct) attitude toward drummers. To wit, drummers can't drum because they all suffer from a Billy Cobham complex and want to play as much as an egocentric lead guitarist. Therefore, drummers have to be taught to drum. And drummers, being by and large nutters, don't take too kindly to such condescension. Also, at this time, while the rest of the band were outwardly convinced they'd be an unqualified success, under the surface they were stone scared that they couldn't live up to even their own belief in themselves. The tensions in the Clash camp (late summer '76) were running so high that just sitting around the rehearsal studio could be an exceedingly uncomfortable experience.

But after rejecting various drummers who were more in tune with the band's commitment but couldn't really hack out the relentless trip-trap bottom line, they settled on Terry Chimes, who didn't give a flying one about the politics (in the widest sense) of the Clash but made up for it by being one of the best drummers this side of Jerry Nolan.

Anyway, that's how they'd shaped up to the point of their early gigs, so that's enough of this hagiography. That's not nearly as important as why the Clash are the CLASH.

SCENE ONE:
Bernie Rhodes holds a Clash preview for the press in the studio, subtly paralleling Paris schmutter previews. Giovanni Dadomo of *Sounds* is suitably impressed and reports that the Clash are the first band to come along that look like they could really scare the Pistols.

SCENE TWO:
The reaction sets in. When the Clash support the Pistols at a London cinema gig, Charles Shaar Murray [in the *NME*] says that they're a garage band who ought to get back in the garage and leave the car motor running. (This prompts them to write "Garageland").

SCENE THREE:
The sides settled, every Clash gig becomes an event. When Patti Smith comes over, she sees the Clash at the Institute of Contemporary Arts and is so knocked out that she jumps up and "jams" with them. Some kid in the audience does a mock-up of biting off someone's ear (with the aid of a tomato ketchup capsule), and the picture gets in the weekly music press. By the time they play the Royal College of Art (Arty lot, aren't they? Still, what do you expect? They all went to art college and wear some of the flashest clothes imaginable), emotions are running way too high. They play a set under the rubric "A Night of Treason." (It was November 5th, the night that honors the burning of Guy Fawkes, the bloke who tried to blow up the Houses of Parliament.) Some of the audience, when not lobbing fireworks around, take an extreme dislike to the Clash and start bunging bottles at the stage. The rest of the audience is split between Clash fans who already think their band can do no wrong and the uncommitted, whose prevailing attitude is "Well,

they are playing violent music, and if you play violent music, well, you know what they say about what you sow..."

The band are certain how they feel about playing in a rain of bottles. Strummer lurches off stage and tries to sort out those responsible ... personally.

THE CLASH STYLE has been set. It's a straight case of being ruthlessly certain about how you feel and what you want to do and making sure that no one gets in your way. Like the man said, "We ain't looking for trouble, but if someone starts it, it ain't gonna be us that's gonna be on the losing side."

Remember this is back in 1976, when punk was still overwhelmingly seen as being political. More than anyone else, it was the Clash that everyone held responsible for putting down a party line. Now they've all pretty much retreated from that position (except the Clash, they just smile Highway 61 smiles) and say aw, we're really only into having fun, *maaan*. But then, you've no idea what a relief it was to have songs about something else than falling in love with some acne-infested adolescent or what a drag it is to be slogging our guts out "on the road" and staying in all these faceless hotels (when most kids in England have never even stayed in a hotel) or pathetic dirges about let's have a little more rock and roll.

I know rock and roll is supposed to be about the banalities of the pubescent dream, but it had pretty much got to the stage where the average rock and roll song was indistinguishable from moon/June bilge. If the Clash have done nothing else, they've given a big help to kicking out all that garbage (of course, many others have been working to the same end).

Strummer certainly didn't come from any poverty-stricken background (on the other hand, he never really pretended to) but his songs were like a well-aimed boot plonked straight into the guts of an overfed and complacent music business.

And Mick Jones was no slouch either. "Career Opportunities" for example. [*lyrics removed*] Okay, so it ain't gonna cop him a poetry prize (who wants 'em?) but it displays both a savage understanding of the demands for immediacy in a rock and roll song and a large helping of witty comment on what it's like to be given the choice of one shitty job or another shitty job. Of course, the Clash never thought they could really change things. They're only (only!) a rock and roll band, not a political party. But, if you're gonna sing about something, you might as well sing about something that doesn't usually make it onto pop singles. Unfortunately, while they handled it, lesser talents came along and decided that they'd have to write "political" songs and, as a matter of course, mostly came up with insulting simplicities like Chelsea's "Right to Work."

And then, even more important, there was the music. Even early on (and especially after Small Faces addict Glen Matlock got the boot), the Pistols were very fond of heavy metal drones. I don't think the Clash even listened to HM. Joe only cared for '50s rockers (especially bluesman Clarence "Gatemouth" Brown, believe it or not) and reggae. Jones was deeply into Mott, which shows in the Clash's attitude. toward their fans both in their songs and their stage demeanor. And Paul Simonon was into football (listen to the chant on "Janie Jones") and painting (look at the clothes, stage backdrops and all their visual presentation.)

By the time they'd done the *Anarchy Tour* with the Pistols, the Clash were in an unrivaled second position. They began to get the kind of press eulogies and fan worship that'd turn anybody's head. How could anybody fail to react to them?

Onstage, Strummer is so obviously a natural star, forcing his body and Telecaster to ever greater heights of pain/pleasure, grabbing the mike and screaming lines like he really does care.

Mick Jones bopping around like a younger Keef (yeah, that comparison again), doing a military two-step and sending out shards of steely guitar licks.

And Paul lumbering around, looking looser and more relaxed, but thumping his bass while indulging in perverse, arcane calisthenics.

And the clothes. Obviously paramilitary in origin — zips and slogans featured very heavily — but whoever heard of an army splashing paint all over their tunics?

All this combines to make sure the Clash, even at their worst, are never mere music. I am absolutely convinced that it's not only me that feels that they're the '70s answer to the Stones. If asked, Clash fans will say they love 'em so much because "They're good to dance to" or "I fancy Mick Jones" or "I just like 'em, that's all." If that is all, why do they shout out for "White Riot" all the time at gigs? It's not one of the Clash's best songs, but it is the one that most represents where they're coming from, what they stand for and, by extension, what particular fantasy they're enacting for their audience. If the kids just wanted to dance or screw, they could go to a disco or home to bed. They want and get more, but their lack of articulacy prevents them from explaining what. Where success and even the music are subordinate to the stance — they're saying not we play rock and roll but we *are* rock and roll.

If Chuck Berry represents for me an idealized adolescence I never had and the Stones were an adolescence that I lived through once removed (because, like so many kids, I was too busy studying), the Clash are as good an excuse as any for me to live out a perfect adolescence ten years late. Hell, why else be a rock and roll writer — there's more to it than freebie albums, you know.

Which is also why — just like the Stones — while the Clash will fire imaginations, they'll never become a grandiosely successful band. Some reckon they won't make it in the States at all. I don't agree with that. Judging by the recent Rainbow shows, they've got enough classic big stage rock and roll choreography worked out to handle any auditorium. And their newer songs, like "City of the Dead" and the as-yet unissued "(White Man) in Hammersmith Palais," are played at a pace that even ears used to the Eagles can handle.

Also, by slowing matters down a trifle, they seem to have upped the energy level — too much speed becomes nothing but a fast train blur. They learned their lesson on the first English tour. The set started out at 45 minutes. By the end of the tour, it was down to 29 minutes — and that included all the album plus "1977," "Capital Radio" (only available on a limited edition giveaway — which is a pity because it's one of their best songs), their truly awful version of Toots and the Maytals' sublime "Pressure Drop" and "London's

Burning" twice. It gave their roadies something to boast about, but if you wanted to keep up with it, you had to snort at least two grams of amphet.

This drop in speed/rise in intensity is obviously partly a result of their smoking a lot more dope and listening to a lot of very spliffed-out rasta roots reggae. They realized you ain't gotta run at full throttle to give out the necessary power.

Nonetheless, the Clash have come in for a lot of criticism. Ignoring the early jeers about unmusicality, the most hurtful has been that they're a kind of punk Bay City Rollers, programmed to do just what their manager tells them to do. Quite simply, that's like saying that the Stones were only Oldham's puppets. Of course, Bernie, being some kind of weird conceptual artist, lams in a fair share of the ideas but, at the last resort, it's Mick, Paul, Joe and Topper that cut the cake onstage and on record.

Anyway, I reckon that carping like that is just more proof of the Clash's importance. Nobody gets into the same kind of polarizations about, say, Slaughter and the Dogs or 999. People only get into heavy duty arguments about bands that really matter.

Look. If you already like the Clash, you'll like 'em even more live (if they play a good show — which admittedly, they don't do as often as they should). If you hate the Clash, you'll either learn the error of your ways when you realize what great little pop songs they write or continue to hate 'em. The choice is yours.

All I can say is that any band that can bring a relatively cynical scribbler like myself to gush like a besotted fan, has got to be one of the most special things to have ever happened. ■

QUOTES OF THE DECADE

"There is no doubt in my mind that the Sex Pistols were England's greatest contribution to rock and roll, well over and above the Rolling Stones or the Beatles."

—MALCOLM MCLAREN (1983)

We had good relations with two of the British weeklies — Sounds and NME — that we read assiduously and looked up to in many ways. They ran some of our stories, we ran some of theirs; our UK stringers ended up with staff jobs at them; and when they needed someone in New York to cover a concert or report a news story, they occasionally reached out to us. Dave Schulps reviewed the Sex Pistols' concert in Memphis and the Vibrators in Toronto for Sounds; Jim Green covered a Cheap Trick show in New Jersey for the paper.

We knew Giovanni Dadomo, who died in the late '90s, because he wrote for Sounds. He also led a satirical punk band of journalists called the Snivelling Shits, who released a memorable single, "Terminal Stupid," in 1977. This was his only contribution to our pages, but it was an important profile that we ran just a few months before the Pistols finally arrived in the U.S.

SEX PISTOLS: NOT SO ROTTEN AFTER ALL

TP 22, OCTOBER 1977

By Giovanni Dadomo

Right now in London, late August 1977, there's not a single sliver of doubt about it: this is the year of the Sex Pistols. They are, in a word, ubiquitous. In the last couple of weeks no less than four separate poster magazines have appeared, vast, glossy technicolor teenage bedroom wallpapers which originated in the now-so-distant era of the Rollers and Gary Glitter, dallied for a while in the side streets of *Kung Fu*, *Star Trek* and Hammer horrors and now, in this latest incarnation, pause to focus full frontal on Johnny Rotten, Sid Vicious, Steve Jones and Paul Cook, Open any of Britain's four major pop weeklies and you're face to face with the same quartet, if not in person then via the countless scores of groups who have sprung up in their wake. Open virtually any daily newspaper and it's the same story — punk-rocker this, punk-rocker that, punk-rock fashions from mail order to haute couture, news of punk-rock movies in the making, of the punks vs. Teds battles which have now become a regular Saturday afternoon feature in the King's Road. It's just about everywhere; even skin mags offer "punk sex." It's a phenomenon, one that can stand easy comparison with mods and rockers, swinging London, flower power, glitter; a phenomenon that's slowly but surely changing the dress and listening habits of a whole generation of British kids.

The music papers have room for little else and mail order punk fashions are big business. The letters pages of the pop press mark the changes; where even six months ago the cons far outweighed the pros, the opposite is now the norm. It's the year of the Pistols, alright.

Events are supposed to look obvious in retrospect. Maybe it's too soon to look back and see it all clear as crystal, but obvious is one thing the rise and rise of the Pistols still doesn't seem.

First time I saw the Pistols was some 18 months back and, yes, I was transfixed. Strange one that, being scared of a pop group. I only had it happen once before, and that was the Who the first few times they played the Marquee. Johnny Rotten and the Pistols, they were just kids armed with scowls, glared and arrogance, all taunt and threat.

Plus, they had some great lines: "We're into chaos," they told the first reporter they met. "Don't waste my time," Rotten would spit, his voice a mixture of scrawn and whine every bit as bloodcurdling as Peter Lorre's. It wasn't funny.

That first time was a stunner. Seen again within a matter of days the shock began to wear off and, as the bravura diminished, they were just a bunch of kids again, more petulant than dangerous.

From the start, though, they had their camp followers, an odd collection of seemingly hand-picked eccentrics: women in bondage outfits, wasted young boys in ragged T-shirts and swastika armbands, the whole crazy crew bouncing up and down madly in a dance-travesty labeled "the pogo."

Rotten said, "We want more groups like us," and all the musicians in bands laughed at the Sex Pistols' obvious lack of technique. But smiles froze when the ever-present undertow of bottled anger and violence began to erupt into the real thing.

It was all good copy, though, and the music press gobbled up every snide one-liner, every attack on old farts, and scrabbled in its thesauruses for new and more effective ways of describing this weird new brood's mastery of the art of spitting.

One by one the Sex Pistols said goodbye to all the major London clubs. At the Marquee they reportedly threw chairs into the audience and smashed up the equipment loaned to them by Eddie and the Hot Rods. At the Nashville the group joined an audience brawl which was transmitted nationwide via the cover of the next week's *Melody Maker*. At the 100 Club, *New Musical Express* writer Nick Kent was beaten with a chain.

And so on.

Astutely managed by one Malcolm McLaren, a style-conscious boutique owner who'd gone from greaser gear to pornographic T-shirts and S&M fashions for the masses, the Pistols received enthusiastic publicity from quickly established music press champions, publicity the volume of which record companies couldn't ensure except for their most grandly successful artists, and even then, never with such satisfyingly incessant regularity.

Public demand was inevitable, even if most of it was probably the result of pure curiosity. That's what selling's all about.

But here's the unpredictable part: somewhere along the line the Sex Pistols became a very powerful rock and roll band. Sure, they continued to owe a lot to the Who, Stooges and a handful of other rebel heroes; but you'd had to have been around a long time to suss that one.

Sides were taken. There wasn't much middle

ground. One camp dismissed the group and their followers as self-conscious egomaniac nihilists and berated them for their lack of technical know-how. The Pistols' supporters toasted their youth, energy and the coolly natural way they embodied the anger and frustration of a new generation with no hope and no future.

By autumn, the group had secured a hefty advance from EMI and quickly invested part of same in putting the entire circus on the road. The Pistols headlined over the Damned and Buzzcocks ("more bands like us") with a little transcontinental flavoring from Johnny Thunders' Heartbreakers (thanks to McLaren's previous dabble in management, a last-ditch attempt at salvaging the New York Dolls).

It was about this time that the Pistols began to make an impact beyond the safe confines of the rock world. First, EMI chickened out and aborted the group's "Anarchy in the UK" 45. Next, the Sex Pistols did a TV interview at teatime during which they were repeatedly goaded. They replied as required, delivering a string of four-letter words which guaranteed outraged reactions on the covers of nearly every national daily the next morning. England rediscovered the generation gap right there and then.

The "Anarchy" tour never got too far after that. All over the country municipal officials turned their shock into repression; one by one all the gigs on the itinerary were scuffled. Among the more extreme reactions was that of one small town where a hall close by the one the Pistols were playing was taken over by a priest and his congregation. The evening was spent singing hymns to fend off the no-doubt contagious evil of this self-confessed teen anti-Christ and his horde.

The Pistols' second record deal with a major company lasted less than a week. Following an astonishing press conference at which 50 or so members of both national and European press sat speechless before a rightly disgusted Sex Pistols (including the first public appearance of new bass player Sid Vicious), A&M dropped the band like a hot coal. There were various explanations: tales of the group destroying toilets and attacking young secretaries in the record company office, a

violent scuffle involving a leading DJ at London's Speakeasy Club, even a petition from the label's major established artists insisting that the Pistols contract be immediately terminated. Pick and choose; if there was a truth in there somewhere no one who knew it was telling.

Once the Pistols were front-page news, there was no halting the forces of righteousness. In 1977's first six months, the group made exactly three public appearances: one at a sympathetic London cinema, news of which was circulated by word of mouth alone; one for the benefit of a U.S. TV film crew before a strictly limited audience; and the last on a chartered boat trip down the Thames during Jubilee Week, abruptly terminated by the arrival of hordes of police and ending in a series of scuffles which left Malcolm McLaren among the party-goers awaiting trial on various assault charges.

Meanwhile, the group were back on wax again, this time on the Virgin label, the first deal with which the band themselves claimed to be happy. Hence, "God Save the Queen," a Top 10 hit despite a near-total radio and TV blackout, and the following "Pretty Vacant."

Time to take sides again, right? But it's not that by becoming public whipping boys the Sex Pistols have revealed just how reactionary and repressive contemporary Britain can be; that the liberation fantasies of the '60s haven't changed anything at all — that's not what makes the Sex Pistols worth cherishing. The truth of the matter is that when it came to the crunch, they rose to all their detractors' challenges and produced some of the best rock and roll singles of the decade.

All the same, one couldn't help but sympathize when both Johnny Rotten and Paul Cook were beaten up on London streets within a matter of days. They still couldn't find anywhere to play.

Europe was less sensitive, it turned out, and at the beginning of August, Virgin revealed that the group had the quit the country for a brief Scandinavian tour. So, the first time I saw the Sex Pistols in 1977, I had to fly all the way out to Stockholm, Sweden for the privilege.

It was worth it. The band was sturdy, exciting, all the best things. And Rotten? Quite simply one of the most compelling and original frontmen I've ever seen. He moves like a white ragamuffin Bob Marley, eyes burning from a face which takes on a pallor close on blue in the glare of the stage lighting. And he sings — yes, sings — as only Johnny Rotten can, an indefinable mishmosh of phrasings and accents as uniquely strange and English as Bowie, Hunter and any other of a handful of stylists you'd care to mention. The records are great, but live the Sex Pistols are better. That, too, is something worth cherishing.

Rotten's gone through a welcome period of humanization in the last few months, both on and off stage. His brief audience raps in Sweden were warm and friendly, a million miles removed from the venomous droog who, 12 months before, had featured such unnerving displays of public self-abuse as putting lighted cigarettes out on his wrists.

Off stage he's still sharp-tongued, but recent press interviews and one radio broadcast in particular revealed more of what he's probably really like than ever before. Gone is the intolerant antagonism, replaced by a reasonable, intelligent, likable individual with a broad knowledge of rock and roll coupled with a proud (even courageous) individuality.

The aforementioned radio broadcast, for example, featured a goodly helping of reggae, sandwiched around which were all manner of less predictable likes, John Cale, Kevin Coyne and Peter Hammill among them. "I've always told them," says Rotten now, blaming the press for the more grotesquely painted character excesses of old. "But they're not interested in things like music, they only print what they want to see printed."

Where early write-ups had Rotten hitting out in all directions, regardless of target, he now treats his followers with equal lack of compromise. "I don't like walking the streets and seeing 30,000 imitations of me. That pisses me off, quite frankly. I always used to laugh looking at all the Bowie imitators, all the Bryan Ferry imitators. It was just a joke, people without minds of their own, or directions or anything. The great unthinking majority."

Running parallel to this, though, is a down-home faith in common sense, the great British grass-roots leveler.

"You don't need no fucking education to be clever, to suss things out. It doesn't take much to realize what's wrong and right." An opposite example is offered in the form of one particularly reactionary British politician who'd recently made some cheap capital thanks to his attacks on the group.

"For him, he's probably dead right. But he shouldn't try to take away from others. His attitude is one worse than keeping up with the Joneses. Only it's like, 'Oh, look, they've got a garden mower — shoot them,'" says Rotten in mock upper-class twit accent. "Eliminate them — I can't afford one!

"Everybody should have it," says Rotten, returning to the subject of common sense. "It's there in their brain somewhere if they'd only bother. But most people don't use it, for one reason or another. Usually because it's easier not to."

A really surprising revelation, considering the new wave's contempt for all things hippie, concerns Rotten and hallucinogens, one highly popular late-'60s brand in particular.

"God ... that stuff..." He almost sighs, suddenly brightening with a typical spot of parody; "Terrible, man," this last delivered with just the right amount of weary ennui. "I'd just as much rather have a bottle of brandy than all that junk."

Musical criticisms are no longer reserved for the obvious targets of old. It's difficult to know how to take Rotten when he sideswipes the Clash; Clash-bashing has been such a popular sport for all the Pistols recently that it could just be an in-joke. Patti Smith, though, gets a definite thumbs down.

"I laughed when I saw her. I couldn't believe it. It was like 1967. It would've been alright then, I suppose, but now..."

Nor does much else on the current New York scene emerge unscathed. Rotten disputes the recent *New York Rocker* claim that London stole the essence of its current style from Gotham, but didn't have the musical competence to do much more than pose.

"I like the Ramones, but that's about it," he says

dismissively. "I mean, what else has come out of New York since we've been going?" Television is afforded a brief-but-lethal demolition.

"Jonathan Richman I do like, though. I think he's got a great sense of humor. If he's joking, that is. We asked him to tour with us, but he couldn't do it because he was into religion. I thought that was great," he laughs. "What a way to turn someone down!"

Two things frighten him: water and prison. One Pistols song, "Sub Mission," is about drowning. "That really frightens me. I'm a really strong swimmer, too. But the thought of drowning is really frightening."

And prison?

"I think that's really vile, locking people up. That would break me. I couldn't stand the thought of being locked away."

I last saw John Rotten one night last week huddled in the corner of a bar with a pint of beer, surrounded by half a dozen mates, most of whom didn't look in the least like punks. There was an old-fashioned blues band on stage. He didn't seem bothered by that; he was busy enough trying to hold onto what little privacy he could. Then someone recognized him and a crowd started to gather. He slipped away into the darkness.

Latest reports from the Pistols' office have U.S. and Japanese tours penciled in for early '78. The album's all but finished and should be ready for October release. Meanwhile, McLaren's busy sorting out the finances for a film autobiography of sorts, to be directed by Russ Meyer. A video collage of various live and TV spots is already in the can. Future plans are nebulous, but the tape may well cross the Atlantic before the group does. I can't wait to find out what America makes of the Sex Pistols. Or what the Pistols do to America. ■

QUOTES OF THE DECADE

"I get a religious experience when I have a crap."
—HUGH CORNWELL of THE STRANGLERS (1981)

X-RAY SPEX TAKE A SHOT AT THE U.S.

TP 29, JUNE 1978

By MT Laverty

P oly Styrene is not a cliché. And, despite the claim on her upcoming single, "I Am a Poseur," she is not just another soulless new wave screamer. In fact, Poly Styrene is totally unlike those dippy, dayglo, crap consumers who populate the song world of her and her band, X-Ray Spex. Perhaps that is what makes her music so enjoyable, what makes Poly Styrene so appealing both as a personality and as the leader of a five-man band.

Like Poly herself, X-Ray Spex's music is totally guileless. Which is not to say that it's beautiful, or ethereal, or even tight, or anything like that. It's not: the group's Virgin Records debut single, "Oh Bondage Up Yours!," may have sold a lot of copies for a relatively obscure new wave record (35,000 units, by Poly's count), but it is undeniably one of the most amateurish and incompetent cuts that the genre has suffered through thus far. Based around the raspy warblings of Ms. Styrene's untrained voice and the inconsistent and limited saxophone meanderings of a youngster who's been playing the instrument less than a year, the record is notable for its potential to make unsympathetic listeners scream in pain.

Produced by the band's manager, Falcon Stuart, the record is absolutely awful, on the one hand.

But, on the other hand, it is absolutely wonderful. Poly's obvious joy in performing makes both the sound and vision of her almost beatific.

On record, the exhilaration in her voice undercuts the harshness of her lower register and the shrillness of her upper ranges. In concert at CBGB the last two weekends in March (the band's only U.S. shows), Poly displayed the same exhilaration, whirling about dazedly onstage and gesturing comically. She laughed robustly while singing such ironic commentaries as "I Am a Cliché," "Artificial" and "Genetic Engineering." When she sang "Germ Free Adolescence," she was effectively both dead serious and deadpan.

In person, Poly Styrene is the most winning of all. Conducting the following interview in her bedroom at New York's Century Paramount Hotel, she apologized for being too sick to entertain more cordially — the breakneck pace of the band their first weekend in the U.S. had left her hoarse and slightly weak in general.

Nevertheless, Poly was jovial as she answered questions about her band's short, flashy career. A demure young woman at heart, she invariably begins answering questions, in her thick Brixton accent, by saying "I don't know" before she pauses and then proceeds with a perfectly good response.

How did X-Ray Spex get started?

The band got together about a year ago. The Roxy club was our first gig. Before that, there was nowhere to play. I'd always been singing, just knocking around, not with a band or anything. But then I saw the Sex Pistols, and they were really the first band I liked. Well, I suppose I quite liked the Rolling Stones and the Beatles, but mostly I just thought they were good for their time. I don't like them too much now. For our generation, mostly I like reggae bands.

Why reggae?

I like heavy dub because you can dance to it. *Columbia Colly* by Jah Lion is my favorite album, I guess, but I like different records for different reasons. I like Big Youth because I like his voice. And some of them I like because of the words, the Rastafarian attitude. I don't own too many punk albums, but I do like the Sex Pistols. The Sex Pistols are like reggae — you can dance the same way to them as you do to reggae.

When you started singing, you got a reputation for flamboyance.

It wasn't flamboyance, really. I used to wear the tablecloths and all sorts of horrible plastic things as a statement, I used to have really short hair, too, because I wanted to be like a boy. And all the dresses I wore were really straight, so they'd hide my shape. All you could see was arms and legs.

Did Virgin Records take you seriously at that point?

No, I don't think so. In fact, I think they were surprised when "Oh Bondage" did so well. It didn't get played on the radio. It didn't get any promotion, hardly anybody knew it was out. But it spread by word of mouth. I don't think Virgin knew how to promote punk bands when they first started out doing it. They're getting better at it now, though.

But you're not with Virgin anymore?

No, we just had a one-off deal with them. We didn't want a long contract because they wanted to tie us up too much. I think they wanted like fifteen albums. So, our next single, "The Day the World Turned Day-Glo" and [*B-side*] "I Am a Poseur," will be on our own label — with no name, just the X-Ray Spex logo — that will be distributed by EMI International. That way, you don't make any money until you sell a few records, but that's only fair. And that way, you've only got to sign up for three years.

What's the makeup of the band?

Well, there's five of us, and we're all age 19 or 20. I write the words and melodies to the songs, and the band writes the music. Jak Airport plays guitar, Paul Dean plays bass, Steve "Rudi" Thompson is on sax, and B.P. Hurding is on drums.

Are you responsible for the "message" of the band?

I don't like the idea of having a message. It's a bit pretentious, kind of like you're fooling someone or something. I just like the idea of the songs being a reflection of what's happening, nothing more, nothing less. People can make up their own minds.

Haven't you been written up a lot for your attitudes on racism? (Poly is mixed race.)

Yes, but color is really not a big thing for me. I just accept it. You've got to remember that with Rock Against Racism and magazines like that who have interviewed me, most of the people who support it are white, and they can't get through to black people, so they try to get me to do it for them.

What are your plans for an album?

We have plenty of material; we have about twenty songs, thirteen or fourteen that we do in our regular set. And the album is ready. It's just a matter of getting it pressed. There are a lot of contract things to get out of the way, too, before we can do an album.

Who handles the contract stuff?

Falcon Stuart. But he always asks the band before he does anything. We know about it.

Do you make enough money to live?

[Beginning to laugh even more boisterously than usual] No, not really. I suppose we owe a lot of money. And I think we lost a little bit in coming to America.

That's all right, as long as you don't have to pay it back.

Well, Falcon did mortgage his house for us. That's where we all live. Paul Dean stays with his parents, and Jak sometimes goes back to his mom's house. But the rest of us stay with our manager. I live in the basement.

How have you liked your stay in New York?

I've just walked around the streets, getting a general impression. I haven't done much sightseeing or anything like that. But everything's interesting when you haven't seen a place before. I don't think New York is more dangerous than London, like they say it is. It's just more out in the open. People say things to you that they would never say in England. One guy came up and told me he was writing a book on sex, and what did I think? I told him that I didn't have any opinions, that I don't like sex. I just wanted him to shut up. And some of the taxi drivers must have thought I was a hooker or something, because they would say, "Oh, you really look sharp today. Looks like you're going to earn a lot of money today." They would take it for real, the way I dress, the stilettoes and everything. And they would ask me if I was a showgirl, or if I was in one of those live sex shows.

Didn't that upset you?

No, because I just look at all this stuff and study it. I don't take it seriously. I just laugh it off. ∎

RAVING FAVES

BEST DRESSED

TP 67, NOVEMBER 1981

David Bowie's lead in this competition shouldn't surprise anyone. He's certainly been classiest longest. The runners-up all have made recent sartorial splashes, with the exception of Strangler Hugh Cornwell; "basic black is always in style," advises Alyssa Dellaria. Bryan Ferry, despite impeccable taste — "What other rock musician has been featured in *Gentleman's Quarterly*?" asked Debra Faust — may have been too low-key (and inactive musically) to compete against the new peacocks.

Rock females in general didn't fare too well. Lene Lovich rated for a "Spanish K-Mart wardrobe" (Mary Essig). Votes for Plasmatic Wendy O. Williams as best undressed were not counted.

Karen Blocher thought the Clash trade off four sets of clothing between them. ("Here, Paul; your turn to wear the leather wristband. I get the bondage pants today.") Or, as Dave Sheridan noted, "Wouldn't you think that Robert Fripp could afford more than one suit?"

1. David Bowie

2. Lene Lovich
   Steve Strange (Visage)

4. Hugh Cornwell (Stranglers)
   Kate Pierson (B-52's)

ELVIS COSTELLO: I FOUGHT THE LAW

TP 24, DECEMBER 1977

By Dave Schulps

Rarely has mystery surrounded the arrival of a new rock performer the way it has Elvis Costello. Totally unknown a year ago, courtesy of Stiff Records, Costello burst forth onto the British music scene. His debut album, *My Aim Is True*, quickly became the largest selling import of 1977 and led in short order to a contract with Columbia Records in America.

If Elvis's name alone wasn't enough to make you do a doubletake, the album cover, featuring this unusually plain-looking bespectacled chap striking a knock-kneed Presleyesque pose, was certainly enough to garner a raised eyebrow and second glance from any dedicated rock and roller. But it was the music inside that provided the most complicated mystery of all: 12 songs of revenge, guilt, jealousy, humiliation and rage written and sung by Elvis, who also supplied his own lead guitar work in tandem with an unnamed backing band, spartan arrangements and minimum-frills production by Stiff stablemate Nick Lowe.

In fact, prior to the release of the album, Elvis was keeping such a low profile that some suspected Lowe himself, recording under this strange pseudonym, had made the record, and that our boy Elvis was just a figment of Lowe's and the inscrutable Jake Riviera's collective imagination. Gradually, it came to be known that there was indeed a real live Elvis lurking about London, and that he and band would soon be unleashed on an unsuspecting public, gigging around London in the near future.

By the time the reviews were in on *My Aim Is True*, Elvis was already hot property on his way to stardom. Not only was his single "Less Than Zero" climbing up the British charts, but American FM stations were hooking onto the album almost as if it were an American release. The race to unscramble the Elvis mystery was on, but nobody was saying a whole lot, least of all Elvis, whose interviews were as oblique as most of the lyrics on the album.

It wasn't until Nick Kent of the *New Musical Express* managed to get Elvis drunk and (for him) talkative that a picture began to emerge from the blankness. It turned out Elvis was really one Declan (D.P.) Costello hailing from Whitton, Middlesex, and was, as his lyrics strongly indicated, not just a little bit hung up on the idea of revenge and guilt, even going so far as to carry a little black book around with him containing a list of people to be dealt with when the propitious time arose (presumably after he had achieved some degree of notoriety in the pop music world). Admission to the list seemed to be tied to rejection of Elvis in one way or another, and quite obviously, Elvis had known some rejection in his time.

Other interesting tidbits included Elvis's prior employment as a computer operator in an Elizabeth Arden plant (the "vanity factory" of "I'm Not Angry"); his annoyance at being compared to Graham Parker; the fact that he had recorded a demo for Dave Robinson (now director of Stiff) two years ago under a different name (rejected!) at the same time that Parker (accepted) and Willy DeVille (recording under his real name, William Borsay, also rejected) were doing the same; that he had once been a member of a bluegrass band called Flip City who had opened at the Marquee for a while; and that he was married and had a child.

Aside from that and whatever could be gleaned from the seemingly autobiographical nature of his lyrics, the Elvis Costello story is strictly a game of fill in the blanks. And Elvis doesn't seem too keen on helping. The story was going around that a journalist from *Sounds* had been stuck into a corner of Dingwalls (a club in London where Elvis was appearing) by Jake Riviera, Elvis's manager, and told to wait there for Elvis to join him for an interview. Over an hour later, the writer was reportedly told that Elvis had left the building long ago.

Fortunately, Jake likes *Trouser Press*, so when we asked him for a crack at Elvis, albeit from 3,000 miles away — hardly the proper circumstances for dragging anything out of a tough interviewee — we weren't left holding the phone. No, Elvis called at the appointed time (thanks!), but — as expected — proved a tough nut to crack. Not that he was hostile, or even particularly evasive, but he made it clear that he felt his past was for the most part irrelevant, that he wasn't too crazy about people analyzing his songs and certainly wasn't going out of his way to help them. That didn't mean there was nothing to talk about, but it did limit things. Still, so much had happened to Elvis in the year since he had joined the Stiff stable that we were at least able to put Elvis's recent doings in some kind of perspective.

How long had he been writing songs and trying to find a label before coming to Stiff?

"I suppose I've been writing for seven or eight years now, since I learned to play lead guitar. I started writing soon after that, but it doesn't mean the songs were any good. You just start writing for a bit of fun and then you find it means something. I started taking my songs around about three or four years ago after I moved back to London from Liverpool, where I'd been living for two years. From then on, I tried to get various things going without much success. About a year before I signed with Stiff, I was actually taking tapes around to all the other labels and not getting very far with anybody. In fact, I wasn't getting anywhere. That's about it, really."

Why did he think they had passed him up then? Was it just too different from what was around at that time?

"I'd say it was down to lack of imagination on the part of the people at most of the other labels. They can't hear something unless it's put on a plate for them. I didn't think it was all that different; maybe they did. I think it was their ears that were at fault, not mine, and fortunately that's the way I kept thinking about it. I did sometimes wonder whether I wasn't mad and that maybe it wasn't any good, but I kept on thinking it was they who were wrong and not me. It turned out to be the best way to think about it."

For sure. But then Dave Robinson, who eventually was to sign Elvis at Stiff (at this time Elvis is no longer with Stiff, having been caught in the internal breakup there and choosing to stick with Riviera, who has left the company for undetermined points), was one of those who'd rejected Costello back then.

"Funny about that. He was quite surprised when I turned out to be the same person. When I submitted the tapes to Stiff, he didn't realize that it was the same person who'd done the earlier tape, because I used another name then. It turned out he already had over an hour of me on tape and didn't know it. None of it's of great interest now except historically. It doesn't interest me in the slightest. Whether it'll ever get used is another matter."

An inquiry into the name Elvis used to record those earlier demos, however, brought out Elvis's defenses. That was digging too deep. "I'm not going to go into all that," he stated flatly, "because I don't like to dwell on the past. I don't see that as important now, that's gone. It's just a matter of irony, really, that they happen to have those tapes, but I don't want to talk about them that much."

Anyway, Elvis's reunion with Robinson took place because he answered an ad by a new record company who were looking for artists to submit tapes. "I believe it was one of the first they received," he recalled, "They just reacted to one of the songs and said, 'Yeah, we'll make a single,' which was the policy of Stiff in the early days. It just developed from doing a single to doing an album as we cut more and more tracks."

The album. It hit me right in the gut the first time I heard it. The compact, straightforward delivery, the pure simplicity of great rock and roll songs, the words. Songs for losers, for anyone who's ever felt like they were being hurt or humiliated. Maybe not each and every song, but the feeling pervades the LP.

Not angry? Sounds positively furious to me. Why, Elvis? Why so bitter?

"Because I'm an extraordinarily bitter person. I don't like to sound as if I'm too obsessed and can't feel any other way, but it just happens that those songs evince that kind of feeling and, therefore, the album is like that. The next one could be very, very different, although I don't think it's necessarily going to be any kinder. In fact, if anything, the way I feel at the moment, it's going to be a lot crueler.

"People have noticed that a lot of the album is about being rejected, but I don't like the idea of getting too analytical about it. It's just what the songs are about, I don't think about them too hard. I think people will see the next album as being a little different. I hope they do, anyway, because I don't want it thought that I'm totally obsessed with one theme, because I'm not. Just like everyone else, I have good days and bad days. The things that mean the most to you or affect you most you write songs about."

But Elvis, isn't that a reason to get analytical? Precisely because the songs affect or move the listener, they'd want to know more.

"I think that's maybe journalists' job, if they choose, depending on the nature of the paper or magazine. Sometimes it's on a very superficial level — asking me what I eat for breakfast or something — other times they want to know

what books of philosophy I've read so they can determine something about my soul. It all depends on the complexity of the analysis."

I protested that it wasn't as a journalist, but as a listener who was moved by what the songs said or implied, that I wanted to understand his motivations better. Personally, I didn't feel it had anything to do with my job. I was touched by the songs, identified with some of the feelings he was expressing.

"I suppose you try to make people think a little bit," proffered Elvis. "You intend to have people identify with what you're writing. Not to be crass about it and say, 'How will I write a song which will go to the heart of every kid in the land?' or, on the other hand, be like Cat Stevens and write these terribly introspective songs that only have meaning to yourself. That's it, really. I don't really plan these things. I just write them, and they come out as they are."

Did he have any particularly favorite songwriters, or people that he felt were influential on him?

"Yeah, but they change so rapidly that I tend not to itemize them and say, 'My favorites are...' because they change from day to day. Somebody asked me last week and looked at me kind of surprised when I said Dusty Springfield was my favorite singer. Right at that moment, she was. Right now, George Jones is my favorite singer, because I happen to be listening to his album a lot. The same thing happens with songwriters, they just float in and out of my head. I'm not particularly obsessed with any who would bear down on me in any way."

Elvis has put together a backing band since he started doing concerts. The Attractions consist of ex-Chilli Willi drummer Pete Thomas, ex-Quiver/Moonrider bassist Bruce Thomas and Steve [Nieve] on keyboards. Elvis says the band is meant to be permanent, "or until it goes wrong," but adds that he's not thinking about anything going wrong. "We're thinking about it going right," he adds for emphasis.

Questions about the band members' past history, however, meet with the same response as questions about his own.

"They're not particularly interested in talking about the past, either. We don't like to dwell on the past in general. They're the Attractions now and I'm Elvis Costello and we're not bothered whether people talk about the past or not. We just generally encourage them not to, because I don't feel it's very interesting and they feel the same way. We think it's polite of people if they don't talk about it, and we usually think a little less of them if they dwell on it too heavily."

I wondered if that was a subtle warning. Anyway, when did he start calling himself Elvis?

"A while ago."

Why?

"Why not?"

So much for motivation. But couldn't people just hearing about him now get the wrong idea and think he was jumping on the Elvis bandwagon? Did he feel Elvis's death hurt him?

"We did lose a bit of press, but it's not any big deal, it's just a name. It wasn't meant as an insult to Elvis Presley, and it's unfortunate if anybody thinks we're having a go at him in any way. I don't really comment on it at all, usually — it's really irrelevant. It's just because it's such an unusual name that anyone would even bother asking me about it. If John Lennon died tomorrow, people wouldn't ask John Miles about it."

Come on, Elvis, that's ridiculous. If Elvis was your given name, I could understand, but you did take it on.

"Yeah. It's rather like wearing a crown, because people expect something of you. I don't mind that; I'm prepared to give them all I can. I don't think any feelings on it are relevant, though. I'm not prepared to be quoted about it."

ONE VERY AMUSING incident made headlines in the British music papers recently. It involves Elvis's getting arrested for playing music in the street without a permit, an incident which took place in front of London's Hilton Hotel in ritzy Park Lane where, inside, CBS Records was holding its annual international convention. Jake and Elvis thought it would be a laugh if Elvis went outside and played for the company staffers when they went outside on their lunch break.

"We were playing a gig at Dingwall's that night and we went down to let them know that the gig was on," Elvis explained. "We had guys walking around with placards advertising the gig and I was playing through a battery-powered amplifier. They came out on the pavement and quite a big crowd gathered very quickly, including quite a few of the big guys at CBS. All these guys were actually standing there and applauding, but the Hilton didn't see the humor in the situation and called the police. The police didn't see the humor in the situation and arrested me. It wasn't a big deal. It was just a crazy stunt." Elvis is now signed to CBS in America.

Getting back to *My Aim Is True*, there were two songs I felt Elvis might be willing to shed some light on (not analytically, of course), because their subject matter stood out from the other songs. One is "Waiting for the End of the World," the album closer, which seemed to be some kind of fantasy story, with Dylanesque images; the other is "Less Than Zero," which also appeared on *A Bunch of Stiff Records* and refers to British Nazi spokesman Oswald Mosley in its lyrics.

"'Waiting' was just the result of a particular feeling I had. At the time I wrote it I was working a day job. It was written on a train where several incidents had occurred to spark off this frame of mind. It's rather the way I feel, more resigned than angry. The whole album is pretty much that way because I feel that, particularly in England, people don't go shooting each other in the streets — if they get fed up with their neighbor, they don't go and kill him. It's probably just that we can't buy guns so easily as you can in America. We read a lot about people getting shot over trivial things there just because there's a gun handy when somebody gets angry, but it's different here. It's not that we're any better because we don't actually kill people — the feelings are still there — it's just under the surface, very close to the surface, and it breaks out quite easily. It's just that we don't have these tools at hand.

"Some of the songs are about those kind of feelings, but I don't like to put it in grand terms. I just like to put it in the way I feel about it myself, maybe from one person to another. That's why some of the songs have got violence in them or elements of violence. Those things are very close."

It seems a repressed violence, though, quite masochistic.

"I'm not sure I'd like to get so analytical about it. I tend to shy away from words like that because I'm not sure of the implications of using those kind of words, but you could look at it that way, I agree.

"Briefly, 'Less Than Zero' is about Mosley's being allowed on TV during the evenings. I really don't feel like itemizing these things though, because there's no point writing songs if I have to explain them.

"Uh, listen, I gotta go, my wife's on the other line."

A face for '78? Definitely. The album should've already been released here by the time you read this, and Elvis says there are plans for some U.S. dates before the end of the year. Whether or not he plays here, get the record; listen to Elvis. The guy has something to say, and his record has touched me like no other album this year. Make Elvis king once again. ∎

ACCIDENTS WON'T HAPPEN
THE PREMEDITATED RISE OF ELVIS COSTELLO

TP 39, JUNE 1979

By Pete Silverton

A couple of days before Christmas, trying to make it home on the London tube before I dropped the bottle of tequila and the *Times Atlas of the World* I was balancing in one hand while attempting to flip over the evening paper with the other so I could skim the Third and Fourth Division football results, I heard a voice somewhere say "Hello." More a surreptitious rasp than a warm greeting, the disembodied voice could, if my mind had been working that way that evening, have made me think I was being contacted by some especially devious MI5 operative.

No such fun. When I turned around (slowly — tube etiquette demands vigilance against ex-professors asking ten pence for a cup of tea and friends of the Maharishi trying to "give" you copies of albums with "George Harrison" in big letters on the front and "Guaranteed 100% Tortoise Turds" in invisible ink on the back) I was staring at Elvis Costello wrapped in a dark wool overcoat and sporting the inevitable shades. Seated next to him was one of the Attractions, Bruce, Pete or Steve, I forget which; seeing Elvis on the tube temporarily scrambled my powers of perception.

"Hi, how's it going?" We exchanged all that kind of embarrassment-easing small talk. We spoke for a bit about his show earlier in the week. I'd caught the first of his six nights at the Dominion. It's a 3,000 (or so) seater, a Greco-Roman cake decoration cinema usually used as the major London showcase for the latest piece of multi-million-dollar slop that's about to do the rounds — *The Wiz* is there right now. I'd found his show distant, lacking in real passion or contact with the audience (who admittedly did look like they'd come down to check out the latest soundtrack for a Habitat sofa) and told him as much, only in more euphemistic terms. He agreed and seemed to express slight unease about playing the place at all, preferring to look forward to the unseated venues later on in the tour.

He and his Attraction got off at Leicester Square so they could change trains to get to work; one stop on the Northern Line and they'd be at Tottenham Court Road station, right outside the Dominion, ready for the final show of their six-night stand.

Don't read too much into that brief encounter. I'm not about to claim I'm some special friend of the man — I've met him maybe 10 times — we are in the same business, more or less. Nor am I about to twist his received image through 180 degrees and pump him up as some closet friend of the people.

What I am trying to convey is that, like all the rest of us who ain't had our allotted 15 minutes of fame yet, Elvis is a mess of contrary emotions, counterclaims on his psyche and all-purpose messed-up confusions. Only, being a famous pop star and all that, everyone wants to KNOW ALL. Swiftly scanning press revelations about Rod or Bianca's bon mots about "life with Mick," what the general public secretly wants to read about is the night Rod or Mick COULDN'T GET IT UP, i.e., they want to gloat over the star's charmed life, then find those feet of clay, smash them to dust and smilingly prove that he or she is really just like us.

With Costello, this neo-cannibalism manifests itself in one of three forms: those who've heard that *My Aim Is True* is a collection of chansons à clef about the break-up of his first marriage and wanna know every last kitchen-sink detail so they can "understand" the songs; those who picked up on the little-black-book-of-revenge and photographers-having-accidents stories (they want the portrait of the artist as a young psychotic masquerading as a "rilly sensitive individual"); and those who are obsessed by Costello's borrowings — they wanna be able to point the finger ("Hand in Hand" tiptoeing on the trail of Booker T and the MGs' "Time Is Tight" or "Pump It Up" neatly filed under "Interstellar Overdrive" via "Neat Neat Neat").

More accurately, this last category again divides into two. Those who get upset by it and those who don't. The former can check out of this page right now — you patently never saw that the best thing about "Subterranean Homesick Blues" was that it was Dylan owning up to how much he wanted to be Chuck Berry by rewriting "Too Much Monkey Business" in too-much-junkie-business slang, or that the finest moment of Ted Nugent's entire career was when he copped the lick from Hendrix's "Third Stone From the Sun" in the middle of the Amboy Dukes' cover of "Baby Please Don't Go."

You that don't get upset and are still with me can now have the perverse reward of a few randomly ordered sartorial facts about Elvis to help you get laid on wet Tuesday nights.

The red shoes in the song of that title are cherry red Doctor Martens. Calf-high work boots with soles designed for cripples, they were the favorite footwear of skinheads when they were kicking the shit out of passing hippies. Also much favored by scuffling rock stars affecting the common touch. Elvis is supposed to have lost his pair at an early pub gig. No, I don't know whether the Angels were there that night.

The owner of the green shirt was Angela Rippon, a BBC newsreader, kind of Britain's answer to Barbara Walters. Elvis caught a glimpse of her in the green shirt on the way out of *Top of the Pops* one evening. Hence all the red, yellow, orange and green turning into black and white.

"So what?" I hear you whine. So that crummy bunch of disjointed facts is what landed me with this crazy assignment, which has got me up till Clapton-knows-what-time of the morning — with 12.5 milligrams of Durophet playing pinochle with the crevices of my cerebral cortex, and two or three gallons of orange juice dyeing my tongue the color of a pumpkin. I daren't look at the clock.

LIKE SO MANY before them, *Trouser Press* had shafted themselves straight into the Elvis Costello bear trap. They'd scheduled a cover story on the man. He deserved it, they'd been the first American paper to put him on the cover, they'd always been behind the lad, made *This Year's Model* the *TP* fave album of the year, plus *Armed Forces* was suddenly big business. So, there it was. Deft Kantian reasoning of unarguably symmetrical beauty. One problem. Elvis don't do interviews, even with old friends. Ask *NME*'s Nicholas Kent.

[Dave] Schulps got me on the phone first. Calling collect, he asked if I'd be up to rattling out an Elvis Costello "think piece" — man, myth and music ... that sort of thing. Sure, I said. How can you refuse a man you let freeze to death on your floor each time he manages to blag his way over the ocean and inveigles you into showing him where to get a pair of genuine red suede Beatle boots made?

Obviously doubt raised its seductive head in the *Trouser Press* office that afternoon, as next morning, Ira Robbins — Publisher-in-Chief, no less — called up. "Hey Pete," he whined in that wonderful Noo Yawk accent of his, "Hey, look, y'know, this Costello piece. It's not gonna be one big slag-off, is it?"

"What, me say something nasty about those truly delightful people of rock and roll?"

He wasn't having any of that so, winging it by the seat of my pants, I rapid-fired him on the origins of the red boots and the green shirt. Suitably impressed, he told me to go ahead, take care and be sure I mailed it by March 26.

It's now April Fool's Day.

Welcome to the alternative Elvis Costello bear trap — writing this damn story without the standard fallback of 90 minutes of inconsequential tape or a ten-year history to spice up with a few unstartling personal observations.

Not that there's a shortage of things to write about the man. If they ever set up the Elvis Costello Memorial Archives, my notes for this piece [*Can we see them? —Ed.*] could be Exhibit Number One — Elvis Doesn't Meet the Press.

No, it's the originally shielded but unavoidable fact that to attempt to put down on paper something more than yet another facile piece of gush or bile about Elvis puts you right face to face with the big one.

Right now, commenting on Costello or the Clash, you're not talking about just another artist, you're confronting rock and roll as a whole form as it stands now. They're both state-of-the-art, the living embodiments of more than a score of years and the linchpins of most probable futures. Who else is there? The Boomtown Rats are great fun, and Geldof gives great mouth but us dumb lunkheads always thought rock and roll could be more than brilliantly executed flash'n'tacky egocentrism. Springsteen is OK, but why all the fuss about a low-rent Holden Caulfield with great taste in oldies and sax players? John Lydon and his "experimental cancer music of the '80s"? C'mon, who really wants old Can riffs regurgitated, even if they do come with astonishingly bad lapsed-Catholic poetry? Sure, he's brave, but so was Gary Gilmore. So, c'mon, who else is there? Dire Straits?

Please pass the smelling salts, nurse.

So, you're back to the big two Cs, Costello and the Clash. And the Clash are real easy to write about. All that dynamite copy but genuine (if sometimes slightly forced) rude boy chic. Piece of cake.

But Costello, he's so, so tricky that anyone with any sense would stay at home, keeping clear of tapping out theories for a paper that'll scarcely pay me enough for the results of this piece to keep my cats in the manner to which they're accustomed for a week or two.

Ask any honest writer who's tried. I've certainly yet to read a memorable long piece on him. (Nick Kent's original interview doesn't count. That was the drunken occasion that Elvis chose to launch his bitter-twisted-guilt-and-revenge image. With gorgeous copy like that how could it fail to make for gripping reading? And I'm not belittling the fustian grace of Kent's writing.)

If you're still in doubt, ask *New York Rocker*. Their original cover story was meant to be by Kent. He offered them a piece which had already appeared in *NME*. They rejected it — it finally turned up as *Creem*'s cover story. Then they contacted my fellow *Sounds* writer Sandy Robertson. Duly telexed at the last minute, his story was also dumped — too negative or something. Finally, Andy Schwartz hacked out something and called it "Elvis — The Story He Won't Tell." Won't tell? My grandmother could have told him, and she's keeping the maggots company.)

STILL, A CHALLENGE is a challenge, and, like most others, I can't help but be drawn like a voyeuristic moth to the panache of the Costello *Blut und Eisen* [*That's "blood and iron," folks —Ed.*] assault on the consciousness of the Western world. And the problem is that it's often difficult to pinpoint the precise reason for the success of that campaign — leaving aside, that is, the sheer hard work that's gone into it.

For starters, while everyone else around was heeding the rallying call of "Anarchy in the UK," here was this four-eyed squirty gimp whinging on about some lost love named Alison. Worse, the American version of the single even featured that horror of horrors — synthesized strings.

Again, he's rarely struck me as anything more than a diffident performer. It's as though some innate traces of crippling shyness surface every time he straps on his Jazzmaster and faces a braying crowd with only the microphone there to shelter his sense of inadequacy. So, operating on the reaction-action principle, he tries too hard to project an image of mean moodiness laced with the odd piece of blather which is sometimes fatuous — like bothering to lower himself to slagging that St. Louis radio station on the air (a basically jejune gesture — why did he agree to the show in the first place?) and sometimes not ("Everyone get up and dance!").

The only times I've ever seen him really cut it live — cut it so sharp to the bone that for a scant 50 minutes or so you really do believe — was once in Belfast, where he was plainly terrified, and Pawtucket, Rhode Island, where he spent the whole of Mink DeVille's set sitting at the side of the stage sucking on a bottle of wine. When he finally had the mike in his grasp, he was so deeply wired that he got so honest, his emotions were so nakedly displayed, that it verged on the embarrassing. Kind of like looking at photographs of battlefront casualties.

The rest of the time, though, he seems to fall too easily into what's wanted rather than what's needed (there's a nice rehash of a Dylan/Costello paradox for you). Play the hits, keep the record company satisfied. And he plainly hates doing it. Sometimes, maybe, his brusque treatment of audiences has its roots in disgust at himself.

And, while he started out with that whole bagful of exquisitely crafted songs, *My Aim Is True* still sounds like everything was made to suffer grievously at the hands of Clover. Lovely blokes probably (although my sources indicate otherwise), but they still sound like the proverbial Marin County cowboys on Valium. Even the burgeoning talents of Nick Lowe couldn't salvage the likes of "Sneaky Feelings" from their grip. Anyway, that was the least of Lowe's problems. If reports are to be believed, he kept on nipping back to the Stiff offices during the recording sessions for a spot of rest and recuperation and a few large Pernods, moaning, "Gawd, I can't take all this gloom and despondency much longer." Since *Aim* and the arrival of the Attractions, though, it's

been a whole different story, of course.

And finally, the most telling chink in his armor is his habit of sometimes reaching for the first facile phrase, metaphor or paradox that comes his way. Balancing the terse precision of "Pump It Up" (the perfect phrase describing doing it all to death), there's the glib and inane couplet in "Accidents Will Happen" pairing a made-up mouth with an "undone mind." Sometimes he ladles on the menace so deep and so thick, as in "Hand in Hand," that it becomes almost laughable. (Really, Elvis. You sound like a little boy threatening to bring in his dad 'cos he's bigger than the other kid's dad.)

And yet, even taking all those Achilles tendons into account, Elvis is still one of those destined to carve out his name large in the history of rock and roll. He's a sly, sometimes deceptively casual, songwriter. He's got passion, guts, aggression, compassion, insight, all those things which on the printed page can look so much bullshit but are in fact the lifeblood of any worthwhile artist, no matter whether it's paint he's daubing or strings he's plucking.

So far so good; but the same things could be said of quite a handful of rock and roll performers. What makes Elvis more compelling than the rest is the scope of his vision and the breadth of his ambition. Like the Clash, he's gonna use every last drop of his wit to ensure that his work is never treated as mere music.

And, at the moment, he's on a winning streak of almost awesome momentum. Like Dylan around the time of *Highway 61*, he's running before he's learned to walk and rubbing that uncomfortable fact in the face of anyone who dares to doubt.

Two years ago, he was still the unhappily married computer clerk with a kid trying to hustle his way into the big time on the back of some country demos that he got DJ Charlie Gillett to play on the radio. First the deal with Stiff, then the overnight putsch which ended up with him, manager Jake Riviera and Nick Lowe striking out on their own. It was around this time that he tried to interest Columbia by busking on the pavement outside their conference at the London Hilton. They ignored him. He got busted. And, as in all good fairy tales, they finally signed him. (This, incidentally, has not always been the smoothest of relationships. Mr. Riviera was reportedly asked to restrict himself to conducting his business over the phone after he accused one of the employees in the Columbia art department of being a defenseless little cripple. Unfortunately, said employee was a…)

LESS THAN TWENTY MONTHS gone by. Three albums. Clutches of singles — last time I looked I had eleven of the blighters and that wasn't counting "What's So Funny" or the odd promo-only 12-incher. Wide-ranging tour after punishing tour — only now he doesn't have to squeeze the band and their guitars in one station wagon like he did on the first visit to the Americas. The wife's gone. She got the house and, I should imagine, the kid. He's got Bebe Buell. Such is the price of fame.

And still he wants more. As the man says, world domination.

Once upon an innocent time, I used to think that EC was satisfied with merely wishing he'd metamorphose one night — like a rock and roll version of Kafka's creepy crawly — and wake up as Joe Strummer. That way he'd have real credibility. Now I realize this kid Costello don't stop at no petty aims like that. He wants to go the whole way. Consumed by the romanticism of the Prometheus myth, he wants to plunge deep into the realms of the untalked-about and capture the fire single-handedly for the rest of us less determined souls … before lunch, preferably. And all that in full knowledge that, on his return, he stands a good chance of having a load of messy birds passing the time of day by gobbling lumps out of his kidneys. Of course, like Dylan, who had similar visions, he'll probably be satisfied by a couple of years playing Faust, after which he'll settle down and write a book.

Still, world domination. Now there's a worthy concept. Personally, these days I don't trust anyone who isn't bent on their own trail of world domination. Since the Great American Novel dream started going down the pan the day Kerouac got treated as a serious novelist, and finally gave up the ghost when it caught the Beatles on the *Ed Sullivan Show*, since the idea of making the perfect rock and roll album got lost soon after the twentieth tab

of acid, what else is there for a poor boy to do?

In this Indian summer of a society, what hope of survival is there other than making sure you're the one that's calling the shots?

So, Elvis has opted for bare-faced hubris, screaming at the gods to just dare to come and waste him. Which means, when all that's squeezed into song form, he's just as quotable as Dylan used to be when he was still patron saint to literate speed freaks. What else is "bite the hand that feeds me" but the one true epigram for a generation that doesn't have the confidence or the misguided imagination to push "it doesn't take a weatherman" to its ultimate conclusion?

And I'm sure that aura of overweening ambition is just what makes Costello so appealing to the wide, wide world. Above all else, rock and roll is melodrama. The chants, the lights, the violent jerky moves, a good part of the whole rock and roll live experience is a late 20th Century variant of the "died and never called my mother" school of art. Which is fine by me. Better that than an unceasing diet of Samuel Beckett.

With Costello, that melodrama shows itself in many ways. The surly but aggressive wit of his ad campaigns; the spindly fountains of white light that he used as a backdrop for his Dominion Theatre gigs in London; his hunched, tense postures at the mic; the Garboesque approach to interviews (in fact, he's probably better off avoiding them; while generally pleasant enough, he's rarely said something quotable that someone else hasn't already said better); the occasional step into pure hamminess like "Hand in Hand"; the global sweep of *Armed Forces* (from "Goon Squad" to "Oliver's Army" via the authoritative sounding "Moods for Moderns" — you can get a fair idea of where those songs are coming from without even listening to the music) and beyond all reasonable expectations, he's produced unsullied masterpieces like "Watching the Detectives."

The [song's] sheer eerie impotence is positively suffocating in its harrowing evocation of domestic disharmony: wife watches *Starsky and Hutch*, husband squirms in his chair wishing he could be up there with the big boys, telling it all to the world from behind his guitar instead of being stuck here in his safe West London home in front of the box with wifey.

Then Elvis started to sell enormous amounts of *My Aim Is True* on import in America, I expressed my bewilderment to Dave Schulps. "Oh, that's easy," he blithely told me. "I got that one all figured out. All his songs are neurotic. All Americans are neurotic. They suit each other like Liz Taylor and Richard Burton in *Who's Afraid of Virginia Woolf?*"

I believed him at the time. But, honestly, neurotic? That's like saying a suicidally inclined manic depressive has problems with his nerves.

"Two Little Hitlers" is a cunning and witty song for sure, but way beyond mere neurosis — these days even his private rage takes on an epic form. Which can be seen in the history of the song itself. Elvis thought of the title "Little Hitler" and mentioned it to Nick Lowe, who promptly — such is the morality of the man — nicked the idea for himself and connected a lot of nonsense around one of his invariably quirky tunes.

That's the difference between Lowe and Costello. While Lowe trumpets on about pure pop, it's Costello who actually does it. Lowe's own songs — despite the radio reassurance factor of containing references to everything from Bo Diddley to Abba — are far too oddball in their construction for easy assimilation between, say, Gloria Gaynor and Showaddywaddy: pure pop for people with encyclopedic memories and a fair grasp of what the future might bring is more like it.

Elvis, however, is both more devious and more straightforward. He might be denied an American hit single by the innate conservatism of American radio (not that British radio is any better — just that he *is* homegrown talent), but the suppleness of his melodies are invariably a decoy for the sharpness of the lyrics. "Oliver's Army" has been both his biggest British hit (number-two) and one of his most directly targeted lambasts of a power structure which recruits its killers in uniform from this year's tired poor wretched rabble. True subversion from a master of his past who's still fresh enough to be forcing himself to his own limits.

Maybe one day he'll even learn to tune his guitar. ∎

The headline was ridiculous, sure, but it kind of rolls off the tongue, no? Jim Green's equally odd encounter with a gratuitously hostile Jake Riviera either explains (or merely provides evidence of) his rancor toward the magazine after we had enjoyed a very positive and friendly relationship with the Stiff staff in its first year. "Always up to something"?

CLOSE ENCOUNTERS OF THE IRISH KIND: BELVIS IN ELFAST

TP 29, JUNE 1978

By Jim Green

These days it's a big deal for me to take a train down to CBGB and a major odyssey to get into a record company bus to zoom out to, say, the Nassau Coliseum. So, imagine my surprise at finding myself, not 48 hours after arriving in London for the first time, on the road in Northern Ireland. Picture it: I'm looking out the window of this gorgeous Austin Princess limousine at the picturesque Irish countryside. I coulda sworn I went to sleep and awakened in a movie.

"Cripes, lookit those rolling hills! Those quaint old farmhouses! Check out those cows! Those — those SOLDIERS?!?" Sure enough, there was a British Army Land Rover at the side of the road, a soldier leaning out the top, aiming his automatic rifle at us as we approached the checkpoint. A distinct contrast to the winos cadging quarters outside CBGB. What the hell was I doing there?

I was on my way to see Elvis in Belfast on St. Patrick's Day.

When I'd gotten into London, the album had just come out and his name was on everyone's lips as usual, but he'd only begun his British tour and would reach London after I'd left England. However, I hadn't counted on Glen Colson.

Colson is the one-of-a-kind rascal who taught me what "ligging" means ("hanging around and grabbing all the freebies that come your way although you've done nothing to deserve them whatsoever"). Glen wound up working for the crafty, if off-the-wall, manager of Nick Lowe and Elvis Costello, Jake Riviera. No sooner had I called to say hello than he said, "You are, of course, coming to Belfast with me to see Elvis, aren't you?" How could any sucker refuse?

Not this one. Which is why I wound up at a delightful little hotel outside Belfast (delightful except for the parts that had been blown away by bombs), drinking the afternoon away with my colleagues from the English papers and then whisked away to the concert in Belfast, in a large old hall distinguished mainly by small wedges of seats behind the stage on either side of a mammoth pipe organ. The less-than-stupendous Mickey Jupp Band were on first, so I nipped up to the dressing room.

The band were chatting with the press and drinking orange juice or a revolting excuse for beer in cans showing briefly attired young ladies. Elvis nervously moped about, and I took the opportunity to ask him about his touring plans in the States. I mentioned the gig at a 600-capacity room at Rutgers University in New Jersey that I'd last seen him at, and he spoke earnestly about doing high schools next time instead of playing for "college students with their notebooks" and academic orientation. He was just getting into it when the five-minutes-to-go signal was given and he had to break it off.

We journalists had no seats, so we stood at the back, which afforded us a panorama of the audience. The band was strong but obviously still limbering up as El interspersed older material like "I'm Not Angry" (taken at a slower pace, as he projected a quiet bitterness-beyond-rage) with

newer things like "Living In Paradise" and "Radio Radio" (an odd choice since it's not on the UK pressing of *This Year's Model*). The audience was enthusiastic but politely reserved, only showing signs of real excitement as Elvis launched into "Chelsea," the newly released single from the LP.

It was almost an omen that at this point I noticed that Elvis' shadow loomed large against the wall behind him, like some gigantic specter. But regardless of such metaphysical speculation the performers and audience were warming to each other; a couple of kids got up to leap about frantically, and then a couple more. The standing contingent edged up a few rows toward the stage.

And then, late in the set, it happened. Three or four kids strolled up to the stage. I decided to join them. The other standees joined me, and before I reached the foot of the aisle, people were streaming into the aisle, and I was caught up in a vast pogoing tide. There was no way not to pogo — otherwise you couldn't see and would likely be mashed by your flying neighbors. Besides, the excitement was infectious, and the music intoxicating as only great rock and roll can be.

After a few minutes my endurance ran out and I hopped on top of a seat. But I kept bouncing as I watched Elvis lead the final charges. He was less reserved than I'd seen him in America, interacting with the audience, moving about with a fire even manifested in half-windmill guitar strums. And the band followed close at his heels, sweat pouring off the lot of them: Steve Naive ranging over his keyboard, Pete Thomas masterfully pounding his drumkit like a man possessed and Bruce Thomas looking cool from behind his sunspecs, despite his perspiration, as he lunged about gracefully. Suddenly it was over, but the crowd wouldn't let go. Not even after four encores; it took quite a while to disperse them. I marveled at their reaction, and as we passed some more soldiers in the street on the way back to the reception at the hotel, I pondered what this must have meant to them.

The reception was dullsville until Jake and the band arrived, at which the festivities began in earnest. Highlights: Pete Thomas searching for a hash pipe and, failing to find one, using a device concocted from my Hawkwind badge and an up-side-down glass; Jake searching in vain for rolling papers ("Now come on now, all you mob in 'ere was once hippies, long hair, Earth shoes, listened to Grateful Dead records, so where's the skins, eh? Christ!"); Colson, Naive and a roadie having a beer fight; Jake and I having a verbal sparring match —

"Oh, Jim Green from *Trouser Press*, what are you doing here?"

"Well, I'm just on holiday..."

"Nonsense, you Trouser Pressers are always up to something."

"Well, while I'm on vacation I still gotta do some stuff, but here I'm just along for the ride."

"Jim, did anyone ever tell you nobody likes a smartass?"

"Sure. Did anyone ever say that to you, Jake?"

And so on. Allan Jones in *Melody Maker* the next week mentioned "an unfortunate American journalist" whose "first mistake was talking back" and who, despite "a valiant rearguard counterat-tack ... lost on points" to Riviera. Ya can't win 'em all, but when we meet in Vegas, I'll kayo da pug.

I did manage to speak to Bruce Thomas about the Elvis tour strategy. "Sure, we could avoid doing gigs like these, slogging around on trains and in vans, but these kids, especially a place like Belfast" — many a band has pulled out of gigs in Northern Ireland for fear of getting caught in the midst of a violent situation — "don't get too many concerts, and they deserve it. We may never play here again, or not for a long time, and these kids are the ones who buy the records, who put you on top." We spoke of what Elvis had said about playing Ameri-can high schools, and he said, "We'd like to do that. They've offered us huge venues, but we'd like to play for the kids more directly. Maybe that means more gigs, but..."

I interrupted: "Doesn't that mean diluting your strength each performance?"

"Not so much if you give 110 percent each night. The technical thing may vary, but the feel-ing will be there, and that's what counts."

On the way through the checkpoints and de-tention-camp style airport facilities, I realized he was right. If this Belfast show is any indication, Elvis may well one day be King. ∎

NICK LOWE'S WONDERFUL WORLD OF POP!

TP 75, JULY 1982

By Scott Isler

"T

"Too Many Teardrops" extends its 16-bar structure with a rising two-bar extension.
—From the *TP* review of *Nick the Knife*

"You mean the bit after the other bit."
—Nick Lowe, correcting
the reviewer's terminology

The Nerd is around, and Columbia Records is in a panic.

The Nerd is a New York rock columnist, and he sniffs Nick Lowe in Columbia's offices. He's right, too; Lowe is chatting away with an interviewer while his publicist worries about getting him to Brendan Byrne Arena, across the river in New Jersey, in time for soundcheck. Being waylaid by the Nerd could be disastrous, as Lowe is too affable to know when to pry off his admirers. A Columbia staffer strategically buttonholes the Nerd for small talk while the publicist hustles Lowe out of the building and into a waiting limousine.

The singer/songwriter/Pure Pop exponent is dressed for intrigue. Lowe wears a wrinkled raincoat that looks closer to dirty-old-man garb than *Nick the Knife* chic. A small yellow rose, harbinger of spring, is stapled to his lapel. Lowe absentmindedly left the coat in a Houston restaurant three weeks earlier and is overjoyed with its near-miraculous return. Rumpled but comfortable,

T echnically, this was Basher's second cover with us: Rockpile was featured on the front of TP 59. Continuing the trainspotter tally, our multiple cover stars parade begins with the Who (eight covers, counting a Keith Moon solo and one little headshot of John Entwistle), then the Rolling Stones (five, ditto), Elvis Costello, the Kinks, Ramones, Beatles, Blondie, Clash, Cars and Adam Ant (three each, although two of Mr. Ant's were small inset photos) and Jeff Beck, Roxy Music, David Bowie, Peter Gabriel, John Lydon, Cheap Trick, Talking Heads, Police, Pretenders and Devo (double-timers all).

Lowe inhabited a unique place in '70s music: a singular bridge between the ramshackle sincerity of pub rock and the raging archness of punk/new wave. Meanwhile, the launch of Stiff Records by his manager encouraged his sardonic creativity as a pop artist and put him in the studio with the Damned, Elvis Costello and others as a producer.

the coat might bear analogy with Lowe himself. Before leaving the interview, he carefully places an open, half-full bottle of Heineken — one of several adorning a desktop — in his coat pocket.

It is the day after Lowe's 33rd birthday, and the final night of a seven-week tour opening for the Cars. To escape the euphoria backstage at Byrne Arena, Lowe selects his band's parked tour bus for an interview location. The wood-paneled, compartmentalized interior resembles a Victorian railway carriage. A small white cake on a table toward the front carries the legend "Happy Birthday Basher" around an anatomically impressive female figure in high relief. "That's from last night's party," Lowe remarks. It is untouched.

A moptop of hair, spilling over his collar, is almost as devoid of color as Lowe's eyes. He stares out a window as darkness falls and hordes of kids troop by, oblivious to the bus or its inhabitants. While he talks, he idly shuffles a deck of cards, doodles on a matchbook cover and fools around with a wind-up toy. This nervous agitation also suffuses his conversation with witty remarks, comic accents and a plethora of profanity.

As it turns out, Lowe and his new backing band, Noise to Go, don't get a soundcheck at Byrne. Such is the peril of opening-act status. The last time Lowe was in the U.S. he was headlining venues as one-fourth of Rockpile, but he doesn't seem perturbed by his change of fortune.

"I like being the damned opening act," Lowe protests in nasal British tones. "If I got in a position where I could fill up any of these damn barns we've been playing I'd do it differently. I wouldn't go to see the sermon on the goddamn mount in one of these places. I wouldn't go see the fucking Beatles if they got back together in a place like this. I think it's horrendous; how can anyone watch a rock and roll show in a horrible gap meant for ice hockey?"

But he has no bad words for the Cars. "They're paying us a lot of money to be on this damn tour with 'em, and I'm very pleased about it. They've been bloody good to us as well, the old Cars. They're sports. [Sports cars! — *Bloody old Ed.*] Their road crew has been really good to us as well. Road crews can make your life absolute hell.

You hear all these stories: They only give you a candle to light the stage, and about three watts of power." Is Lowe himself, then, a big Cars fan? "Big cars, well, yes, I like big cars," he harumphs distractedly, and it's time to change the subject.

NICK LOWE WAS a forces brat. Although he was born in a village 25 miles west of London, his father's career in the Royal Air Force took young Nick to Cyprus and Jordan before he was carted off to a British boarding school. "I spent most of my life on RAF camps when I was a kid," Lowe reminisces. He pauses. "That doesn't make any sense, does it?"

Lowe enjoyed singing as a child. His mother taught him to play guitar. "She knew a few chords. We used to sing harmony to Kingston Trio songs, quite harmless stuff." Lowe's first record purchases were equally unprophetic: "Magic Moments" by Perry Como and "Sink the Bismarck" by British cover artist Don Lang. In common with most of his generation, Lowe was profoundly affected by the double whammy of adolescence and the Beatles (and the groups that followed in their wake). "I realized I wanted to be in a band when I saw these groups getting fucked so much and taking tons of drugs. I thought it would be a far more exciting way of earning a living than what I had going for me."

Before turning pro, Lowe traveled the usual emulation route: "I was in a number of bands that used to imitate West London groups like Creation and the Birds (with Ronnie Wood). They were like the Who: three-pieces with a singer, R&B-based with a bit of Motown but a wild guitar sound. Every group used to do 'Heatwave.' I wanted to be in Creation; we used to do all their numbers.

"I was in some bands where I knew only the first names of the guys in them. In those days it was like, 'Let's form a band. I know a bloke who's got a guitar!' You'd ring a doorbell and say, 'Uh, have you got an electric guitar?' 'Yeah.' 'You wanta be in a band? I know a bloke who's got an amplifier.' It was just getting people who had some equipment."

One of Lowe's schoolmates was Brinsley

Schwarz, who had an electric guitar and was putting a group together. "He'd only let me join if I got a bass. I did a bit of singing — I thought I was Wilson Pickett for a time — but mainly I played bass. No one wanted to play bass because you had to have a group to go along with it. You couldn't just sit at home and get off playing bass."

Lowe's professional fortunes (the term is used loosely) then followed upon Schwarz's for the next decade, first in Kippington Lodge and then the eponymous Brinsley Schwarz. Turning solo artist of necessity after the Brinsleys broke up, Lowe signed aboard Stiff Records in 1976. For once he was in the right place at the right time. As Stiff rode the crest of Britain's new wave, Lowe gained a reputation for his warped pop sensibilities and production know-how on albums by the Damned and Elvis Costello, among others.

BY 1978, LOWE WAS juggling his solo career with membership in the shadowy organization called Rockpile, including guitarists Dave Edmunds and Billy Bremner and drummer Terry Williams. Due to different record company affiliations, Edmunds and Lowe released their own solo albums and played back-up on each other's, with the other Rockpilers in tow. After the contractual problems were resolved in 1980, Rockpile released a "debut" album and toured the U.S. to much press hoopla. A couple of months later the band broke up.

Lowe is tired of answering Rockpile questions even though the split has never been explained consistently by the parties involved. Warning that he is about to rattle off a stock answer ("but it's the truth"), Lowe proceeds:

"We used to hate rehearsing. It was all simple stuff we used to do, and the air of spontaneity was part of the 'Pile's act: It looked like friends having a good time, which we were. Especially over here, people liked the fact that we were under-rehearsed and kind of scruffy. But whereas a lot of bands who are better rehearsed and have a slicker show can stay together even if they hate each other because there's a dollar bill in it, when we started losing it, we really noticed. Maybe we could have done another tour and pulled the wool over

people's eyes, but we were all such good mates that we couldn't lie to each other. We'd just done it for too long.

"It happens to all bands. You get carried away with the euphoria of starting a group. Then there comes a time when you get stuck and stale and you have a choice of either jacking it in or working at it, ironing out what's going wrong. Frankly, we were never committed enough to Rockpile. I rehearsed more for this tour than Rockpile did the whole time we were together. That's why we were good, although it brought about our eventual demise. We knew we were losing our vibe. Our philosophy was, as soon as it stops being fun, we tell each other, 'Sorry, fellas, I'm not grooving. I'm off.'

"Dave [Edmunds] and [manager] Jake [Riviera] were always having little arguments. Dave's a bit of a businessman — he knows about contracts, which I have no clue about at all — but I felt he engineered this argument with Jake to get out of owning up, so he could leave in high dudgeon or with dignity. I got annoyed with him because I didn't think he was man enough to own up to the fact that it was all over. Another group is breaking up, big deal. I'm not angry with [him] anymore; it was a goddamn year ago. The only sad thing about it is I've found I don't miss Edmunds. I'm sure he doesn't miss me either, but I thought after that time we spent together and how close we were — obviously I was wrong. I was thinking one thing, and he was thinking another. That does actually break my heart.

"Dave's a real showbizzer. He was the first one to start talking to people after we split up, and I couldn't believe it when he said, 'Oh, yes, we're still great mates.' I thought, you cunt, how can you possibly say that? Of course, we're not mates! I can't be bothered to stonewall people. He's still the fucking best at what he does; there's no one to come near him."

Would he consider working with Edmunds again?

"Probably, but I can't see it in the near future. We've just got no reason to. That's the short answer. It's all over now anyway. Bollocks."

Even if the wounds Rockpile left have yet to

heal, Lowe remains proud of the band. "We were a straight-ahead rock and roll band that related to the '80s. We never sat around talking about it, we used to play cards and go to boxing matches. It annoys me when people who play rock and roll feel they gotta grease their hair back and dress like a fucking clown. I don't see why you've gotta walk around to demonstrate to people 'I'm dressed up as the sort of music I play.' There's no need for that at all. The old 'Pile weren't exactly oil paintings, but we were a country-rock group in the proper sense — not like the Eagles or some drippy guys in cowboy shirts singing wimpy songs about Colorado. And we were the only damn ones at one point."

NICK THE KNIFE was recorded over a long period of time. Lowe downplays any ideas about its cohesiveness or continuity.

"I kept on recording until someone said, 'You've got enough for an album now.' Then I just stopped. I didn't really think it out. I'm extremely uncommitted to music. It's like a hobby to me — 'something I do in the evenings' is what I always find myself saying."

In keeping with the grab-bag approach, "Queen of Sheba" dates back to at least 1973, although Brinsley Schwarz never performed it. "Heart" appeared on Rockpile's sole LP, *Seconds of Pleasure*, but *Nick the Knife*'s spare arrangement is the way Lowe originally conceived it. "I did a demo of it ages ago, overdubbing everything and with a tape loop for the drum part. And that's how I recorded this. A lot of stuff on this record was done with just me, engineer Aldo Bocca and tape operator Neil King in the studio. Aldo can play lead guitar, which I can't. Neil played a lot of keyboards."

Elsewhere, Lowe used Martin Belmont (guitar), Paul Carrack (keyboards), James Eller (bass) and Bobby Irwin (drums). These musicians also comprise Noise to Go. Lowe didn't have a hard time recruiting them.

"They were all bloody out of work! Bunch of fucking scoundrels. They were playing with Carlene [Carter, Lowe's wife] on some gigs; when she stopped, I just swung in and picked them up.

Martin, of course, I've known for years. He was a roadie for Brinsley Schwarz; I used to employ him to carry my equipment! [Belmont, who was in Ducks Deluxe, achieved greater fame more recently in the Rumour, Graham Parker's late backing band.] Paul I know from his pub rock days with Ace in the early '70s. Bobby Irwin played on a lot of things I did with Stiff and was with Lene Lovich and the Sinceros."

Two *Nick the Knife* cuts, "Zulu Kiss" and "Stick It Where the Sun Don't Shine," were recorded with ex-Rockpilers Bremner and Williams. Some people think "Stick It," a bitter put-down, refers to Lowe's falling out with Edmunds. The song predates Rockpile's split, however; Lowe and Edmunds even used to sing it together before it assumed final form. Its composer describes it as an "inverted love song... It's not about anything, really. None of my songs are about anything!"

Lowe fans will certainly disagree. *Nick the Knife*'s preponderance of love songs ("I never was an angry young man") seem to have edged out an earlier predilection for bizarre subject matter. Lowe's infamous "Marie Provost," for example, relates the [semi-]true story of a down-and-out Hollywood actress whose corpse is nibbled on by her pet dachshund. After a pro forma denial of conscious intent, Lower nevertheless admits some things have changed.

"'Marie Provost' was then, and now is now. There comes a time when you can beat up this fucking smart-ass doing a glib little tune. The number of tapes people have given me and said [adopting a greasy American accent], 'Listen, Nick, ya're gonna love this man, it's about a kid who got run over by a train and lost both his legs, man, it's gonna kill ya!' — I think, what the hell do you think I am? I thought 'Marie Provost' was a sensitive song — a bit tongue in cheek, but it's a sad song."

Lowe can't be blamed for favoring love songs these days, considering his marriage to Carlene Carter. He paints a picture of domestic bliss; the couple have even been collaborating on songs.

"We find it very easy to write together. I vibe her up and she calms me down. Carlene and I are very similar in so many ways. We both like to —

how can I explain it — live life to the full!"

One of Lowe's increasingly rare outside production credits was for Carter's last album, *The Blue Nun*. He claims her American label, Warner Bros., turned down the R&B-inflected record because it was "too sparse." ("They wanted a surrogate Linda Ronstadt.") He recently worked with the Moonlighters, a San Francisco band formerly with Commander Cody, and will produce the Fabulous Thunderbirds in Austin, Texas this June. "I only work with people I like," Lowe says of his lowered production profile. "I almost don't care if I don't like their music."

IDIOSYNCRATIC? No doubt Lowe wants to sound that way. A similar openness about his eclectic compositional methods gave him a reputation he's still living down.

"Everybody steals riffs; it's all been done before. That I cheerfully owned up and admitted it shocked people when I first came over here. Now everyone looks into every fucking note I play. It annoys me when people think I've nicked some song I've never heard in me life.

"After I did 'Breaking Glass,' Elvis Costello came to the studio. I said, 'Listen to this,' turned it up really loud and it sounded fantastic. He said, 'Well, that's great but you're gonna run into a lot of trouble, aren't you?' And he told me to my horror that David Bowie had a song called 'Breaking Glass.' I'd never heard of it. It was just an incredible coincidence. It's such a weird title for a song; I'd never steal something as obvious as that.

"There's a difference between the way I plagiarize and copping someone's act, wrapping yourself in someone else's persona. That's why the music business is in such a state: There are too many wankers about sounding like something that's gone before."

Uh-oh. Lowe on the music-industry warpath is not family entertainment. "People go on about how awful radio is over here. It's not radio's fault, it's the witless bozos who make the records. Musicians are the stupidest bunch of people; the record company makes them feel they're on top, but they're ripped off blind. They ought to do something original, that has a spark of personality, in-

stead of saying, 'Hey man, we really wanta get a hit.' They go out to make a record which sounds like it will get on radio; that's why no one is buying records, and I'm fucking glad. If it gets tougher to get a record deal the music will get better, not blander."

THE BYRNE ARENA looks considerably less than sold out as Nick Lowe and his Noise to Go hit the stage at 7:35 p.m. Those who are there know who they're seeing, and they try to make up in enthusiasm what they lack in numbers.

The band delivers a no-nonsense package of Lowe favorites: "Breaking Glass," "Switchboard Susan" and, of course, Lowe's one genuine U.S. hit single, "Cruel to Be Kind." Lowe strums an electric guitar. "I hit it every time I hear the snare drum — exactly the way I used to play bass."

Oddly enough, on this tour Lowe is performing "Shake and Pop" instead of the revised "They Called It Rock." Both songs are essentially the same, but Edmunds had converted the stompy "Shake and Pop" beat to a smoother shuffle and come up with the new title. Perhaps Lowe still does hold something against his former guitarist buddy. "They Called It Rock" was the first recording Rockpile made.

"Heart of the City" is played slower than Rockpile's breakneck pace, with Carrack's rolling piano figures replacing the Edmunds/Bremner guitar spitfire. Carrack also takes soulful lead vocals on a new Lowe song, "It's Always Better With You," and "Tempted," from his short-lived Squeeze membership. The latter number receives a round of cheers even as it's announced.

Lowe's casual stage banter veers toward self-destructive. "That sound in tune to you?" he asks the audience as he strums his guitar between numbers. Turning to his band, he remarks, on-mike and laughing, "They're all deaf." A humorous reference to Bruce Springsteen brings boos. You don't joke about the Boss in New Jersey. Lowe modestly introduces "(What's So Funny 'Bout) Peace, Love and Understanding" as "a song Elvis Costello recorded" — he himself only wrote it — and the band quits the stage after 35 minutes. There is no encore. Afterwards, a rather placid Lowe sums up the performance: "That's the longest film I ever sat through."

THE CARS TOUR is over but the next night Nick Lowe and his Noise to Go headline at New York's Palladium. Lowe seems correspondingly up for the occasion. "Story of my life!" he blurts out during "Shake and Pop"'s cynical scenario, and he clearly relishes the lyric's naughtiness ("Someone in the newspaper said it was shit-tuhh!"). Somebody in the audience throws a toothbrush at Carrack; "good idea!" Lowe retorts. He trots out some rarely performed oldies ("Marie Provost," "Nutted by Reality") and converts "Switchboard Susan" to her English cousin, "Switchbox Susan." He tells the crowd how well he was paid for touring with the Cars, whose name elicits a mixed response. (Stone-faced Elliot Easton, the Cars' lead guitarist, joins Lowe onstage for encores.) This time, when Lowe introduces "Peace, Love and Understanding," he mentions that he wrote it.

It's a good show, but more than one observer misses Rockpile's freewheeling synergy. If Lowe does, he's not saying. "I think bands are really quite dull. I don't know if there's such a thing as bands anymore. Rockpile was one of the last, where each person was as important as the other one. There was never any question of substitutions. But Rod Stewart hasn't got a band, he's got a bunch of geezers he's fuckin' hired to play with him. I had a terrific time on this tour, the way Rockpile used to."

So, Lowe won't be sublimating his ego to a group effort anymore?

"That time's gone, it's all over."

Although *Nick the Knife* finds Lowe as winsome as ever, the album stalled in the record charts. It failed to beat *Labour of Lust*, Lowe's previous album, or Rockpile's *Seconds of Pleasure*. But the coiner of the term "pure pop for now people" ("It's now a cliché, which I suppose is a high compliment") isn't the type to get upset over losing the slippery grip of the American masses. His solid following cuts across many post-new wave duchies. "I don't know if I have particularly succeeded," Lowe muses. "I get away with it. I make a living." ∎

The year after we published this one-pager by our precocious rising teen star America Underground *columnist, it was reproduced on the back cover of the Soft Boys'* Two Halves for the Price of One *album. Not sure if we were asked permission for the usage, but we thought it was very cool in any case.*

SOFT BOYS

TP 57, DECEMBER 1980

By Tim Sommer

During a photo session in a cluttered downtown studio, someone asks the Soft Boys if there's any particular music they'd like to hear while their pictures are being snapped. "Got anything old?" replies guitarist/vocalist Robyn Hitchcock, a tall, handsome and intense-looking fellow whose deranged gaze one only expects from the truly gifted. Hitchcock and the other Soft Boys — guitarist Kimberly Rew, bassist Matthew Seligman and drummer Morris Windsor — hardly have a kind word for any music under ten years old.

Unlike most of their contemporaries, England's Soft Boys are influenced not by the Dolls, Bowie or Roxy Music, but by the golden age of psychedelic pop — the years when rock went beyond beat-era simplicity, but before it lapsed into self-indulgence. In those few neat years, British and American music was filled with challenging sounds that were still identifiably pop. The Soft Boys aren't nostalgic or escapist but are merely trying to capture a wonderful aspect of music overlooked in the last decade or so.

The band came together about four years ago

has been inactive since 1970) was played up for *Can of Bees*' lyrical and musical oddities. By *Moonlight*, the band had established its own identity to the point where the Barrett influence isn't immediately evident (although Barrett's "Vegetable Man" is a B-side to their "Kingdom of Love" 45, and "Astronomy Domine" often turns up as a Soft Boys encore). "Inasmuch as Syd isn't anywhere," Hitchcock explains, "he can follow you around without taking too much baggage. He's always around the corner, but we just don't see him, so we have to put up with him." Clear?

If the trend-hungry UK music press ever decides it's time for a psychedelic revival, the Soft Boys will be the first to benefit. Hitchcock is not overly sanguine: "I don't think there will be a psychedelic revival. Reviving something means that it's not entirely fresh, but perhaps if it gets to a new bunch of people it will become fresh." Guitarist Rew picks up on Hitchcock's point: "There might be a revival or there might not, but it won't make any difference what we sing, what we play or what our attitude is."

Hitchcock sums up what the Soft Boys are doing and how they try to do it. "If there's any real point to make, it's just that pop music flowered then degenerated and it still hasn't picked up from the point it degenerated to. Psychedelia was great, but it was also destruction, the end of pop music; after that people gave up on tunes and it became endless jams. Rock became heavy and meandering, while pop became light and fluttery. There was this explosion in '77 but it hasn't yet set things to right. We work from the point of psychedelia — and we want to carry forth from that point and do it right, rather than imploding like Syd or degenerating into long jams or trashy pop music. That's what I'm trying to do. I know where we come from, so half the road is complete, even if I don't know exactly where the future lies." ∎

in Cambridge. Hitchcock, Rew and Windsor have always stuck together. Seligman joined earlier this year, after working with Knox (of the Vibrators), Alex Chilton and the Local Heroes; he says he turned down a high-paying job with the Bruce Woolley Band to become a Soft Boy.

The Soft Boys' first recording, an EP on Raw Records, came out in late 1977. They were among Radar Records' first signings the following year, but after releasing a single they scrapped a finished LP to start anew on an album to be released independently. *A Can of Bees*, complex and frighteningly psychedelic, appeared on their own Two Crabs label. Their latest album, *Underwater Moonlight* (on Armageddon Records), is the Soft Boys' Pop Record, showcasing the less bizarre and more tuneful side of the band. They still haven't gone beyond cult status in their homeland, however, and they claim over half their record sales have been in the U.S. as imports — which is partly why the band is in New York playing a series of dates before touring Britain.

The spirit of Syd Barrett — Pink Floyd's founding loony — hangs heavily over the Soft Boys. Hitchcock's vocal resemblance to Barrett (who

PRODUCED BY MARTIN RUSHENT
A NEW WAVE PRODUCER LOOKS BACK

TP 62, JUNE 1981

By Tim Sommer

New York's Electric Lady Studios is as security-conscious as a ritzy apartment building. To enter, you talk into a camera and somebody somewhere buzzes you in. The interior is like a McDonalds townhouse gone mad, with purple, green and blue walls and carpets on multi-levels. "Remember, Hendrix built it," a publicist notes while ushering me past long-haired people who claim to be Foreigner. "It's supposed to be psychedelic."

Producer Martin Rushent — blond, bearded, pleasant and very straight looking — sits in a little room with a hissing radiator. He's just put the finishing touches on a new Ian Gomm single and has a rare, brief breathing spell before going back to work that night. Along with Martin Hannett and Steve Lillywhite, Rushent is one of the few producers to emerge from the new wave (superficially an anti-"production" movement) with a reputation that often precedes the bands he works with. Over the last five years he's produced the Stranglers, Buzzcocks, Generation X, Visage, 999 and many others; as an engineer, his pre-'76 portfolio includes work with musicians as diverse as the Who, ELP, Petula Clark, Paul Anka and T. Rex.

"I'd been an engineer for years, and I was pretty bored with the whole thing," he says, explaining his involvement with the British new wave. "The thought of doing a rock band at night and then having to be back in the studio at nine in the morning for a TV jingle was not exactly my idea of fun. So, I thought I'd just pack it up and start producing, ha ha.

"For a year I starved, but I was hanging about at all the gigs, which a lot of studio people don't; they tend to lag someway behind the times. I was fortunate — or unfortunate, as the case may be — enough to have nothing to do, so I went to loads of concerts.

"I started seeing all these young bands that I thought were really exciting. I would be talking to friends who'd be doing an album by so-and-so, and I'd think, 'Blimey, how boring!' when there were all these great bands out there."

Rushent eventually found sympathetic companions in Andrew Lauder and Martin Davis, A&R man and managing director, respectively, at British United Artists Records. They made a couple of propitious signings — the Stranglers and Buzzcocks — and "the whole thing exploded."

THE STRANGLERS

I'd seen them a couple of times, and Andrew Lauder had seen them a couple of times, when a demo arrived at the office. We played it, looked at one another and said, "We've got to sign this band!" We knew no other record company in the world could stand this band, but we had to have them. We signed them in two weeks. It was easy; no one else cared.

Then we thought, who the hell is going to produce this? We went through a list of people, and it was always, "No, they won't do it, they won't understand what it's about." So, Andrew said to me, "Alright, you do it. Just record them exactly as they are: no frills, nothing special, just raw Stranglers."

Which is exactly what I did. We did "(Get a) Grip (On Yourself)" and that was a minor hit. Then we made the album, *Rattus Norvegicus*, and it just took off. I remember I had the flu, and I was lying in bed waiting for the week's charts; when I saw the album had gone in at number-four, my flu disappeared — immediately! I got up and banged on my next-door neighbor's door. I said,

"You won't believe this, but remember that tatty band I took you to see that you hated? Their new album's number-four in the charts."

At the end of "Nice 'n' Sleazy," there's a synthesizer solo that goes crazy. It was due to my plugging in the wrong socket; the whole system fed back. We played it back and I said, "Look, let's just ignore the synth solo. I know I fucked that up." [Stranglers keyboard player] Dave Greenfield heard it, and he said, "Great, that's unreal! I'll do it again and make it go on a bit longer." But I couldn't get the sound again. I tried for days; it was just one of those things that happened once and I could never do it again.

The development of Jean-Jacques Burnel's bass sound really took off when we did *Rattus*, because he had a couple of blown speakers and I had a dodgy mike. The combination sounded out of this world. He heard the playbacks and said, "That's my sound, that's what I've always wanted to get." Basically, it's just turning everything up full. It used to feed back like crazy, and recording it was a nightmare.

Everybody implies that the Stranglers peaked with *Black and White* and, just by coincidence, that happened to be the last album I did with them. I don't think they've peaked at all.

When *Rattus Norvegicus* came out, the Stranglers had already been together for three years. No one was watching them under a magnifying glass while they were developing that style. Now they've decided they're going to be something else, but this time a lot of people are watching their development and their mistakes. That's a real brave thing to do: to put your career, your reputation on the line because you believe you need something new. How many bands are prepared to risk that? In the last two years the Stranglers have gone through shit — financially, hassles with the law — and they're still together, still doing it.

The Stranglers are very strong individuals; and they fight like dogs and cats. The rows we used to have were unbelievable! Greenfield won't broach any shit about what he plays: "I'm playing this and that's that!" Hugh Cornwell is a great melody writer, and there's no way he can escape that.

THE BUZZCOCKS

The Buzzcocks turned up within a week after the Stranglers. Lauder gave me a tape and asked me what I thought. I said, "Wonderful, we've got to have them, too." There was a bit more competition there; when people found out we were interested in the Buzzcocks, everyone was interested in the Buzzcocks. But we got them because we were first at their door.

My first with them was "Orgasm Addict," a totally crazy record. Pete Shelley didn't know very much about recording at the time, so we sort of threw those things together up in Manchester. They were great, but now Shelley's very into recording technique. He'll come down to my house for weeks at a time and stay at the studio even if he's not on the session — just to hang out. Coming to a big London studio and seeing the possibilities really opened him up. He adopted a different approach to recording after that — double-tracking guitars, whatever gave him the sound he wanted.

They used to let me do a lot of backing vocals. I'm a frustrated singer, and I seem to wangle my way on to backing vocals on everybody's album that I ever produced. It's become a joke. [Buzzcocks guitarist Steve] Diggle and I used to do all the "oh-ohs," all those bits; any harmony line with Shelley is usually myself, because while Digs is good at "Oh-ohs," shouts and yells, harmony is a bit tricky for him.

The Buzzcocks felt trapped in the three-minute pop format. They were very good at it, but I think Shelley got a bit bored with it. He can rattle that stuff off while drinking his coffee after breakfast, he's that great a talent. But that's no challenge; Shelley wants to try different things, expand what the band is capable of doing. The new album will be quite a departure for the Buzzcocks. It'll be something different again; whether people will like it or not remains to be seen.

You can imagine what Shelley is going through. He's saying, "Our albums — our best work — is being ignored. No one will take it seriously, 'cause they're used to us churning out the old three-minute hits." There's a lot of good stuff on those albums, but people only wonder, well, what is the three-minute hit on this record?

GENERATION X

Generation X was recording an album with another producer, and it had been going on for months. Chrysalis [the band's record label] called me and asked if I could come in and have it done in fourteen days. I liked Generation X, and I realized that if they didn't get an album out pretty fast they were going to miss the boat — which they partially did. I went in and we did it in fourteen days (fifteen, actually). I enjoyed doing it. Derwood Andrews is a great guitar player; one of these days someone's going to realize how fucking great he is.

VISAGE, STEVE STRANGE AND MIDGE URE

I was working with Visage eighteen months ago and getting laughed out of London for buggering around with these poufy fashion guys. Steve Strange wears some amazing gear. I thought he was a star the moment he walked through the door, and I took to him straight away. Midge Ure persuaded me to do it. We were doing that eighteen months ago, and now, 1981, this is the thing. I saw Spandau Ballet's first concert nearly two years ago.

The English press slagged us because they didn't know what we were doing; they had no idea we were locked in a little shed in the middle of Berkshire making electronic music. All they knew was here were all these people with dodgy credibility at the time — Rich Kids [Ure's previous group with Glen Matlock] had been a disaster — who got together to make this record. No one took it seriously, and suddenly everybody's saying, "Great!" We did it because we thought it was a good idea and we'd have a lot of fun doing it.

Midge Ure is an amazing talent. Nearly all the different things he's done have been only marginally successful, but I think he's always been misunderstood. I get on really well with him, but he can be an aggressive little bastard, and that's hurt him. The people he's now with understand him and what he's about, and that's much better. He's in an environment where his talent is starting to show.

THE PRODUCER VS. THE ARTIST

New wave is not anti-production in my terms of reference. Glossing it all up, tarting music up so it becomes palatable, or salable, or sounds sweet, or sounds like the musicians can play — that's not what I call production. Production means getting involved with a band that is intrinsically good and capturing them at their best. If a band is truly great, they don't need any frills.

It's a challenge to me to resist the temptation to smother a group with multi-tracked guitars, choirs for backing vocals — the typical big producer trip. That's one of the reasons I stopped working with the Stranglers: They wanted to get into this incredibly produced area, and I felt they were making a mistake. If I wanted to do that I'd go back to TV jingles.

Producers have a reputation for being the people whom the record company tells, "Look, we've signed this band Glurk, and they're really good but they haven't got quite enough radio songs. They need this, they need that, go in there and mold them." I won't say I'm a producer in that sense. I look for bands I know are good that the record company has signed for the right motives — because they believe they're good.

A producer should draw the best out of a band rather than put icing on them — not try to hide their flaws but bring out their strong points so that no one notices the flaws.

You can do that by encouragement, giving them confidence, stretching them — it's a whole psychological trip. The actual recording, the sound of a record is the easy part. It's like learning to ride a bicycle: difficult at first, but once you can do it without falling off, you don't even have to think.

The part that takes effort is keeping people up, keeping people believing in themselves. The producer has to do that because the other members of the band can't. A band's interrelationships are like a family's: say the wrong thing and shock waves go through. But they respect an outsider, and respect is the first thing a producer has to get from a band. The producer becomes a yes or no man, with all the responsibility that entails. If he says something is good, and the band knows he's not trying to fool anybody, it gives them the confidence to press on. ■

Ira Robbins has stated Creem *magazine influenced the* Trouser Press *sensibility. I never doubted our true guru was Harvey Kurtzman, the creator of* MAD *magazine; hence TP's cover parody of 16 magazine, our end-of-decade/half-upside-down issue, etc. The following may or may not have much to do with music. But as avid readers of the British pop-music weeklies — yes, there were several way back then — we couldn't restrain ourselves. (SI)*

YOU TOO CAN SPEAK BRITISH!

TP 32, OCTOBER 1978

Research by Scott Isler

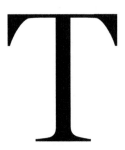

True or false: England and the U.S. share a common language. Wrong! as any reader of the British music weeklies can attest. The exotic words and phrases that abound can easily confuse the unprepared Yank.

To promote international understanding, *Trouser Press* has chosen a typical extract from one of the English music papers — a concert review, as it turns out — and submitted it to a distinguished panel of experts (names and degrees available on request) for linguistic analysis. The result is a milestone in the communications field and one small step for Anglo-American relations.

ACTUAL EXTRACT FROM REAL BRITISH MUSIC PAPER:

HAVING BLAGGED a ride to the venue, I tried flogging my tickets for a few quids outside. After sod all success I decided to slog the bovver and face the music. The support band, a poxy bunch of twee Geordie poofs, were still having a go. "Ramalamadolequeue rock," my mate noted, "naff wankers." "Shut yer gob," I proffered. I was knackered and well chuffed to take the piss out of her.

Which reminded me I was a mite pissed myself. Taking the lift, I queued up outside the bog with some cheeky liggers trying to pull birds. One poser in a drape had the heavy manners to gob on my badge, which was in bad nick (in fact I nicked it myself). I nutted the bleedin' prat with a full-colour bag I keep loaded with sand for just such emergencies. When the other berks started looning around I sussed the aggro and hauled arse back to my stall. I arrived as the duff spiv of a compere was introducing the headline wallies. After a few sodding piss takes I'd had enough of this bollocks. Someone had ponced my piece, so I joined the punters heading to the tube, thinking how much I'd enjoy slagging the twits.

MICK KEITH

INTERPRETATION BY PANEL OF EXPERTS: After managing to secure free transportation to the concert, I attempted to sell my tickets for a little money in front of the theater. My lack of luck compelled me to forsake the project and go in. Upon my arrival, the opening act, an unpleasant aggregation of homosexuals from Newcastle, was still on stage. My female companion observed that the band's music was unoriginal. I asked her to be quiet so I could concentrate on the music. In my fatigue, I enjoyed being rude to her.

At this point, feeling the effects of slight inebriation, I rode the elevator and joined a line of youthful rascals outside the bathroom; many of them were seeking to attract the attention of members of the opposite sex. One young man wearing a 1950s-style coat and affecting an attitude was impertinent enough to expectorate upon the button I was wearing which was already in a sorry state (I had stolen it from its former owner). I accosted the shameless ruffian and managed to strike a blow upon his skull with a weighted 45 picture sleeve. Now the rest of the lads started to behave in a socially unacceptable manner; I foresaw violence and returned to my seat.

I arrived as the obnoxious MC was introducing the top-billed group. Their playing was not to my taste, and I resolved to leave. My companion was not to be found, so I joined some youths on their way to the underground train and contemplated my aesthetic reaction to the music I had just heard.

(NB: We regret being unable to decipher the terms "arrived" and "joined." —Panel of experts)

THIS COMPARISON should serve to acquaint readers with the rudiments of British. As with any translation, however, the language's beauty can be conveyed only faintly in another tongue. Careful study of the two versions is suggested for those wishing to further their knowledge of this often-puzzling language (especially for those planning a visit). Try to incorporate as many terms as possible into your vocabulary; constant use alone will bring familiarity, and, of course, the British will appreciate your attempts, no matter how garbled. Remember: practice makes perfect! ∎

QUOTES OF THE DECADE

"Her boring bloody music is complete sub-hippie drivel dressed up in knickers for the sake of art."
—NICK LOWE, on Siouxsie (and the Banshees) (1981) TP 59

"We'd bump into each other in the studio and give each other dirty looks. He thinks he's too much of a star to talk to me, and if I talk to him I'm groveling. So we don't talk."
—JOE JACKSON, on Elvis Costello (1979) TP 38

THE NEW WAVE WASHES OUT

TP 22, OCTOBER 1977

By Ira Robbins

It may come as a bit of a shock, especially if you were just getting used to the idea, but Britain's new wave movement is over. Fini. Kaput. Although it has unalterably changed the course of rock music, the movement that was created in the British rock press has died partly through the sensationalist coverage given it in the regular journals of our day. Because of a variety of internal contradictions and external oppositions, this unique and wondrous era has ended.

Lest anyone jump to the incorrect conclusion that 287 bands have simultaneously bit the dust, it is not the music that has stopped, merely the driving creative force that brought bands such as the Pistols, Clash, Damned, Jam, Vibrators, Eater et al. into a position of national note: something they might never have achieved on their disconnected own. New wave will continue to be used as a banner, both to label diverging musics and to reject, exploit and defuse some; but articles now appearing purporting to be about the new wave are merely reporting the vestiges of a dinosaur that has not had the good sense to freeze. By the time the U.S. press and radio picks up on the British bands, there will be so little left to say about the movement that they will wonder why they are giving it coverage. There ain't nothing there anymore.

From here on in, the bands are on their own. No amount of brave talk or camaraderie will coalesce the same emotions that brought these groups into existence. Along with the independent record labels and the new wave fanzines, they will have to make their way on the basis of individual talent and/or creativity. It won't do any

changing the entire world of music overnight. Pioneers who opened the doors to a load of rockers who had been denied a chance put it on the line; the smart ones survived, the turkeys didn't. Since the '50s, there have been several revolutionary periods in rock: San Francisco in 1966–67, London and Liverpool in 1963–64, glitter-rock in 1972 and the accompanying art-school movement beginning that same year. While each of these major shifts have had long-lasting and far-reaching effects, the 1976–77 new wave has been the first instance where the social and cultural conditions have changed the music. In all the other cases, the music has been affected by forces within itself, new talents emerging and leading a new path. In the new wave, the change was based on the objective social conditions facing British kids: out of work, full of teenage frustration and fed up with the stiff-lipped British acceptance of their fate. When your culture abandons you, create a new one. And that's just what they did.

THE RESULT OF THIS grass roots movement has been the complete revitalization of the entire British music scene, and a major impact in other countries. A year ago, the British music papers were desperate for things to write about, so uneventful was the general atmosphere. Now, if a new Stones album comes out it may be a few issues before they can find space to mention it, so full of new wave news are they. Obviously, this is largely uncalled-for gossip about bands that have captured media/public (it doesn't matter which) attention and have become sensationalist fodder that sells papers. When someone pointed out recently that nothing was happening in the UK except for the new wave it was necessary to mention that the papers don't cover anything else, which doesn't rule out the chance that other, less eye-catching events are taking place. They merely aren't being covered.

Signs of this revitalization more trustworthy than press linage are the surge of new bands (some first-rate) and the popularity they have attained. Some of the records that have been created are classic, and they might never have

longer to write songs about boredom and anarchy; if you've got nothing unique to present, you're just an artifact, a relic who didn't hear that the bandwagon has run out of gas. Crapshit bands, ones who "made it" solely through the sufferance of the times (anonymity in the crowd), will fade and die as quickly as they appeared, leaving naught but a few disposable records to prove their moment of glory. So long; don't call us...

ON THE OTHER HAND, the truly meaningful talents that have shot into stardom courtesy of the press- fed new wave publicity have a few months to beat the clock and prove themselves to have some lasting merit — more than just their initial inspiration — to carry themselves for a few years. Like the Merseybeat movement, it wasn't until six months after the initial explosion that you could tell the bands who had it from those who just sounded like everybody else and couldn't progress off their lily pad.

As in the Merseybeat boom, there are several historical eras against which the new wave can be weighed. Twenty years ago, the entire birth of rock and roll from the embers of R&B, country and blues was the biggest and baddest of the lot, emerged had there not been the vacuum waiting to be filled. New bands are breaking rules that were in effect for the entire history of rock, bringing minimalism to music in a way that has been hinted at for years but was never successfully achieved. The influx of energy and inquiry makes the new wave the most-needed change in rock music this decade. Though many people have rejected it out of hand, they will not avoid its influence in later work done by more mainstream bands.

SO, WHAT'S WRONG? When the reports began to suggest early this year that the new wave was growing into something much more important than just an ersatz New York-type scene (i.e., lots of bands not making it), some basic problems became apparent. The development of a cohesive movement put a time limit on bands who had become too successful to continue to claim the political integrity of being just like their audience — kids on the dole with no future. While the ordinary rock fan was no better off than he [or she] had been (unless the identity of a new culture is a good substitute for a paying job), the bands had gained a job, a life and a future. Unlike the culty American bands of radical persuasion (the MC5 make a good f'rinstance), the British bands could not stay unsuccessful enough to remain honest to their fans. With all the press and public interest in the Pistols and their kind, groups were meeting with more sales and fame than many established first-tier bands (the week the Stranglers' album was number-four, Pink Floyd was number-five). Unassuming young punks were becoming media superstars, whether they cared to be or not. In the eyes of their original fans, no amount of fancy backtalk could prove that they weren't becoming just like the alienated groups against whom they were supposed to be rebelling.

In some cases, fame and fortune were the unconsidered result of an honestly pure artistic desire to state their feelings musically. Maybe. However, few bands have made a serious attempt to stem the tide. Even the Pistols, with their knack for getting thrown off labels, have earned as much in a year of near inactivity as a successful band does in a prosperous year. There's certainly no reason for them not to make money, but it's not a very revolutionary thing to do. After all, where do EMI's pounds come from? If you aren't totally blind to the fact that rock and roll is and always has been primarily a business that just happens to proffer a culture we all hold near and dear, then there is nothing at all wrong with new wave bands making money in the normal sell-records-sell-tickets fashion. As long as punters are willing to plunk down their money, the unavoidable chain of grey suits with their contracts and open palms will be there to collect their share. Them's the breaks. It doesn't change the music. Usually.

THE REAL HYPOCRISY ARISES when bands refuse to admit they are charter subscribers to the great R&R dream — the Big Time. Maybe they see it a bit differently than those who preceded them, but there aren't any new wave bands who have convincingly showed their opposition to the notion of fame and fortune — their distaste for the trappings, perhaps, but not the idea. Whether they say it or not, every punk band in England and America is just as fascinated by the Eric Carmen theory of Hit Record-dom as Peter Frampton is. I'm not knocking rock and roll success, but musical careers built on nihilism and anti-superstardom seem a bit wobbly when the groups begin to accept the star's life. Why walk when you can ride? Just because Joe Strummer of the Clash was arrested for spray-painting a slogan on a wall doesn't change the fact that he got off with a fine. A kid off the street probably wouldn't have. It's just one of those incontrovertible facts of life: when you become famous, your life changes.

There have been some telling remarks in the press recently. Johnny Rotten on the subject of unprovoked attacks on his person by reactionary thugs: "I don't want the star trip. All those silly twats trying to kick me off the street — they don't realize what they're doing. They're just turning me into another superstar." If it were only that simple.

Let's talk about co-option. Every movement has to be co-opted to be destroyed; I think Lenny Kaye said that. In the past few months, the new wave has been the subject of almost every possible form of exploitation: films, best-of albums, foreign tours, press junkets — the works. There's nothing left to be taken. For the bands, there's no turning back. Once you've done the major halls there are no club gigs for you, no future if you can't meet expenses. The new wave bands aren't gonna give their money away to charity; nihilism is not an altruistic affair.

IF THE TWO BASIC PRINCIPLES of the new wave are (a) total opposition to everything dull, boring and stagnant and (b) a refusal to take anything seriously, a few problems arise. Bands like the Damned have put a lot of effort into remaining ridiculous, but there's just so far it can go. When interviewed for the absurdist NBC-TV report on the new wave, Rat Scabies of the Damned proudly declared he'd like nothing better than to make a million dollars. If he intends to pursue that goal, the Damned will find themselves becoming serious before long. (In passing, while we're on the subject of silliness, a song titled "I'm Bored" appears on the first Bonzo Dog Band album, recorded in 1967. Viv Stanshall as proto-punk?)

Along with the induction of new wave bands into the rock hierarchy comes the inevitable onset of dry rot; no band can stay fresh forever. The idea of permanent change (essentially a political theory, but then many features of the new wave are Maoist) leads each new band that comes along to reject everything preceding. Now that the Pistols are stars, they get lumped in (from the newcomer's point of view) with all the star bands, such as the Stones.

The difference between 30,000 and 3,000,000 pounds a year seems inconsequential compared to 30 a week. (As long as the Stones have come up, remember that they were the original rebellious bad boys of rock, peeing on gas stations and such. It certainly didn't kill them to trade street-fighting for jet setting, but they were also able to change their public outlook.)

Like Keith with his drug problems, the Pistols and other new wave bands have no chance of being inducted into the good guy hall of fame. They are working hard at being rude and obnoxious, gaining legions by their outrage. That's nothing new, but the foolish English authorities are so paranoid that they are terrified of these paper punks and have taken unreal steps to ban live performances and hound the groups legally wherever they venture. This is the confusing factor: the new wave exists only as long as its enemies believe that it exists. A very shaky foundation.

FOR ALL ITS FATALITY, the new wave has served a few long-range functions. (I still can't believe the new wave fashion show in Macy's window.) Providing the opportunity for a veritable monsoon of young bands (some talented) to make their way from the clubs to the jukeboxes in a matter of months, not years, is the sort of situation that should always exist. Instead of farty old record execs signing three new bands a year, always choosing the ones that sound like whatever's currently popular (that of course being the reason for the worldwide magnanimity toward punk bands), both adventurous establishment record people and newly founded labels (designed to meet the needs of an industry expanding creatively much faster than normal outlets were prepared to comprehend) have made the break and taken some very long shots, some of which have turned into gold mines. Elvis Costello and Joe Strummer would've remained frustrated hackers, playing cheap gigs to ten people had open-mindedness not suddenly entered a business not known for its interest in talent. Where would the Stranglers be without the publicity of Hugh Cornwell wearing a (ooh-isn't-it-'orrible) T-shirt with one four-letter word printed on it to a concert one night. That sort of nonsense was gobbled up furiously by the sensationalist British press, making national villains out of a rock band. It's happened before, it'll happen again.

The other wonderful thing the new wave accomplished was the return of marketing techniques that actually add something. In this, the decade of the salesman, where a hit record is a scientific process only scarcely involved with music, the idea of putting a record out in blue plastic, or with a nice picture sleeve — just the idea of making singles an important item, not a trailer of coming attractions for an LP — is worth celebrating. Granted, singles are harder to store, but a lovingly produced single by a talented three-minute artist is worth lots more than a drecky album by a tasteless schnook whom the research department deems of star quality. Thank you Stiff, Chiswick and Island for leading the way and CBS, Polydor and Virgin for following. Special mention to EMI for never quite catching on.

GETTING BACK TO MY original point, new wave has ended. From here on in, everything that arises will be an imitation. There can be only one set of leaders per movement and this one's have already risen to the surface. Sorry, all the good jobs have been taken; come back and file an application when the next movement begins. Or begin it yourself. The style has been set, and now it's the duty of those who pioneered it to give it up. If they have the creativity and the good sense they will refuse to become the stagnant heads of a dying movement.

It's all been done; the new wave has run its course. From stinky little clubs where unknown bands all sounded alike, to the scramble for the free ride provided courtesy of the media over-blitz, the new wave has been transformed from a fresh revolution to a stale mockery. Before it all. gets totally sour — Johnny Rotten posters, etc. — the top groups should make the suicidal move and jack it in (wake up, you're only dreaming). Even the camaraderie that tied the young bands together has broken down to bitter disputes over bookings, contracts and egos.

As the groups have begun to feel their own power, they are learning how to wield it — at promoters, at record companies, at the press. It's just a matter of time before they begin staving off enthusiastic fans with burly gorillas in concert aisles. But then that's the way it's always been, hasn't it? ∎

RAVING FAVES

BEST POLITICAL ROCK SONGS

TP 56, NOVEMBER 1980

Rock's relationship with politics has been an on-again, off-again affair, subject to the whims of fashion. The response to this Raving Fave bore that out, with songs split between '60s protest rock and the heightened new-wave consciousness of the '70s. Indeed, as M. Sebasquian pointed out, punk was "another rebirth of protest music," and timeliness was certainly on its side (witness all the Clash nominations).

1. "Anarchy in the UK," Sex Pistols

2. "Won't Get Fooled Again," Who

3. "White Riot," Clash

4. "God Save the Queen," Sex Pistols

   "I-Feel-Like-I'm-Fixin'-to-Die Rag," Country Joe and the Fish

   "I'm So Bored With the USA," Clash

   "Power to the People," Plastic Ono Band

8. "Ball of Confusion," Temptations

   "Clampdown," Clash

   The Clash

   "Eve of Destruction," Barry McGuire

   "For What It's Worth," Buffalo Springfield

   "Ohio," Crosby, Stills, Nash & Young

   "Revolution," Beatles

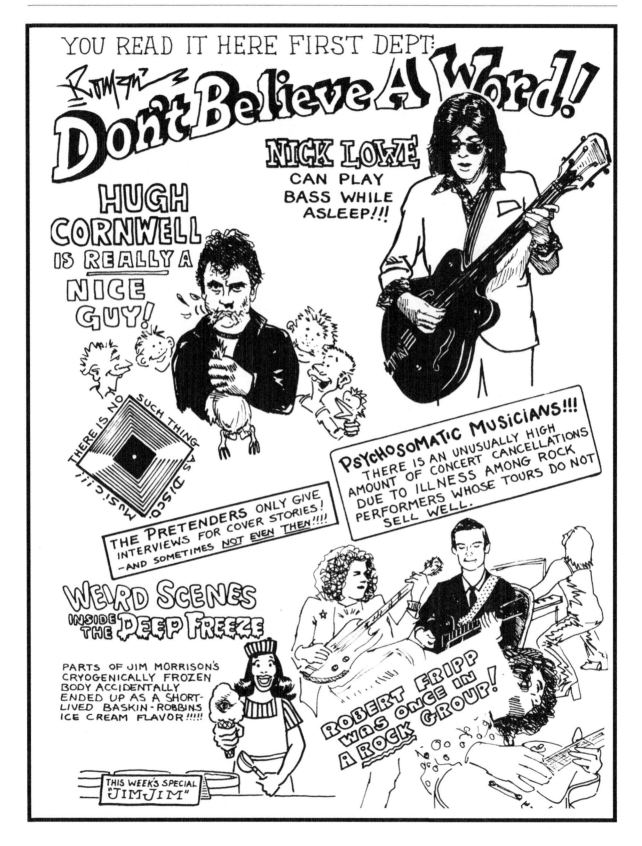

APRÈS PUNK

Armed with sophisticated videos and colorful images, a host of British pop acts who would not likely have gotten much notice otherwise were thrust into America's consciousness (especially among the younger set) by the advent of MTV in the early '80s. We thought of the colorful new bands as junior echoes of the glam era and felt inclined to cover them. But we were old (nearly 30!), a little bit seen-and-heard-it-all-before jaded and not completely sold on the superficiality and commercial commitment of the bands who supplanted the give-a-shit streetwise punks we so admired.

So, while we willingly put these acts in our pages and on our covers (with an increase in newsstand sales as a result), we didn't necessarily respect or revere them, and a hollowness, a "sure, but..." bit of nose-holding crept into the writing. Adam Ant was a likable enough character, and his singles were hard to resist, but none of us were enthusiastic in the same way we'd been about some of his late-'70s predecessors. Criticism is one thing — we had never been shy about shitting on bands we didn't like — but we did not wear skepticism so well, and that opened a chasm between us and our newfound audience.

There was more to the era than the nouveau pop acts and future stadium super-stars: new romantics, modern dancers, techno-poppers, punky funkateers, goths and assorted stripes of modern rock. Unfortunately, the left-of-the-dial American acts emerging from the Midwest, who would ultimately connect with us more strongly as music fans, arrived a bit too late in the story for us to properly address.

The characterization of Joy Division as heavy metal was an odd critical response to the sound of a few songs, but it was amplified by metal fans responding primarily to the band's lyrics and mood. Put that in the same box as the view that Television's guitar work merited comparisons to the Grateful Dead.

DEATH WILL KEEP US TOGETHER: JOY DIVISION AND NEW ORDER EXAMINED

TP 71, MARCH 1982

By Steven Grant

Joy Division disintegrated in the wake of singer Ian Curtis's suicide on May 18, 1980, leaving behind a confused legend we cannot even now unravel with great certainty. The legacy begins with the early punk-era band Warsaw and continues through the transformation of the remaining (one is tempted to say surviving) band members into New Order; it is wrapped in mystery and silence, intentional or otherwise. Add to this a surfeit of fanciful writing about Joy Division by the few journalists who got close to them, New Order's refusal to be interviewed, and the general unavailability of those who regularly dealt with the band (Tony Wilson, Peter Saville, Martin Hannett, et al.). Where is Philip Marlowe when we need him?

The first mention this writer can find of Joy Division is in *The NME Book of Modern Music*, a flippant tome c. 1978, that has this to say:

> ### Joy Division
> Bernard Albrecht (guitar), Stephen Morris (drums), Peter Hook (bass), Ian Curtis (voice)
>
> A young quartet formed as Warsaw in mid '77, a spiteful punk group with obvious pretentions. Released poor EP and appeared in Virgin's Last Night at the Electric Circus with sloppy, lethargic 'At a Later Date.' By mid '78 their motivation, direction, inspiration had sharpened considerably, and as modern metal makers, they rank on the line of Fall, Penetration and Banshees, whilst their philosophy remains hidden and perhaps disturbing.

Judging from this description, Joy Division is a band of minimal if interesting potential. Yet two years later, the same music paper pronounced Joy Division's "Love Will Tear Us Apart" the number-one single of 1980 and their *Closer* LP the number-one album. Now, almost another two years later, Joy Division — although long defunct — is making inroads into the American market, gaining exposure in such normally conservative papers as *Rolling Stone* and the *New York Times*.

To call Joy Division a huge success is something of an overstatement. The band's record sales have made no one rich. Their output — three albums, an EP, three singles, a flexidisc and a handful of appearances on compilation albums — is minimal; the official oeuvre is now outweighed by the volume of bootlegs that have appeared. The band's notoriety springs from very few elements: their sound, their songs' penchant for realistic depression and their breakthrough on an independent label (Factory Records) into a market controlled by conglomerates.

At first glance, Joy Division *was* a fairly unremarkable group. Even Ian Curtis's death — an event, two days before the band's first scheduled American tour, which triggered a new wave of popularity for them — fits neatly into a pattern that has become the stuff of rock myth. Yet the band's fame and influence hasn't crested. Why?

If ever there was a band that did nothing "right," it was Joy Division. Even their name sounds wrong, intimating a last, grey place of pleasure. (For those who came in late: the name "Joy Division" was supposedly first applied to the areas in Nazi prison camps where prostitutes were kept.) They flew in the face of conventional rock wisdom, mutating from punk to heavy metal, but didn't grasp for that huge audience. Instead, Joy Division made the next big jump, developing into a form of anti-metal music, being to heavy metal what anti-matter is to matter. In this mode they set themselves — accidentally or not — against the great rock dragon, romanticism.

Romanticism, as a tradition, originated in northern Europe in the 18th century. Colin Wilson writes about it in his *Mysteries*: "It was the age of heroes and of the imagination, in which men threw steel bridges across estuaries and railways across continents. The artistic schemes were grandiose: Beethoven's symphonies, Balzac's novels, Wagner's ring cycle; so were the engineering schemes: Brunel, the builder of the world's largest steamship, posed for a photograph against a chain whose links were larger than a man's head. Some historians have blamed Romanticism on the Industrial Revolution and the need to escape from 'dark, satanic mills.' This is to put the cart before the horse: it was Romanticism that caused the Industrial Revolution..."

The movement dies hard; rock's most cherished notions — we can change the world, love conquers all, there is always hope, etc. — come from romanticism. Yet romanticism ultimately climaxed in the formation of Nazi Germany, which gloried in naturalism, black magic and cultural superiority.

Romanticism reached its dead end in that great wrong place of the latter 20th century, the failing industrial North of England. It's no coincidence that this area gave birth to Joy Division in 1977, playing bills with the Buzzcocks and other Manchester bands. The Buzzcocks' Pete Shelley suggested the new band call themselves Stiff Kittens; they opted for the less punky, more serious-sounding Warsaw (from David Bowie's "Warszawa," a moody instrumental on *Low*) before settling on the ambiguous/ironic Joy Division. Early recordings (*An Ideal for Living* EP and "At a Later Date" on Virgin's *Electric Circus* sampler) were marred by shoddy sound, meandering music and Ian Curtis's nasty tendency to go for shock effects — a tendency he shook off as Joy Division became increasingly withdrawn from audiences and the dictates of the marketplace.

In these early works, the band's source material is apparent. "At a Later Date" shows a strong Stooges influence; the lyrics bear traces of Jim Morrison, likely filtered through Iggy Pop, a strong Morrison admirer. Curtis's singing and phrasing, both here and on later recordings, is far more American than British, setting him off from punk groups like the Sex Pistols who were prevalent in the Britain of 1977/78.

For all its relative crudity, *An Ideal for Living* has become an important relic in the growing Joy Division cult. Released on the band's own Enigma label (not to be confused with a later record company of the same name), it sported four lackluster songs and was released in both seven-inch and (later) higher quality 12-inch versions. Its interest derives not from the music but its packaging. A line on the back cover can serve as a roadmap for Joy Division's development: "This is not a concept it is an enigma."

TO A GREAT EXTENT, Joy Division was not a band but a fortuitous marriage of lesser parts into a greater whole. Evidence simply goes against the theory that they were an "experimental" band. The sonic components are quite normal. Curtis's voice, in particular, was logy and lacking in edge; bootlegs, as well as the live sides of the recent *Still* compilation, show a sloppiness which caused problems for the band when they toured in the wake of their highly polished studio releases.

Nonetheless, Joy Division — in tandem with their producer and unofficial fifth member, Martin (Zero) Hannett— made a quantum leap into the desperately original. Hannett was introduced to the band through Tony Wilson, the Granada TV producer who started Factory Records during the English independent label boom of 1978. Wilson became aware of Joy Division through their manager, Rob Gretton, a former club DJ. The label owner refined Joy Division's image, making a mystique out of their natural isolationism; the producer refined and developed the sound.

After several months of rehearsals and a few minor changes in the music — notably pulling drums up front where buzzsaw guitars had once been — the brave new Joy Division sprang forth on *A Factory Sample* (also featuring then-unknowns like Durutti Column and Cabaret Voltaire) with two Martin Zero-produced tunes, "Digital" and "Glass." The music was smooth, crisp and paced, as opposed to earlier frantic and fuzzy material — and it was matched by a new maturity and intensity in Curtis's vocals and lyrics. Though expressed primitively, all of Joy Division's themes can be found in "Digital." Sung in a tired, confused tone staving off panic, the verse erupts into a pleading, startling refrain. Curtis's voice cracks as he is stung suddenly by the horror of his situation. It was the end of a phase; Joy Division would never be as personal or straightforward again.

On "Glass," the band and Hannett added electronic noises to the mix, supplementing the guitar/drum attack with a whole new breed of sounds. Lyrical content, meanwhile, shifted to the elliptical; angst surfaces in the vocals but is perhaps too painful to put into words.

BUT "GLASS" WAS MERELY the promise; *Unknown Pleasures*, Joy Division's first album, was its fulfillment and remains the band's most fully realized work. In contrast to their messages of decay and acceptance (bemused, bewildered acceptance, not despair, was central to Joy Division's ethos), *Unknown Pleasures* is fired with the energy and excitement of the band set free in the studio for the first time. They had signed with Wilson's Factory label, despite overtures from Radar Records. The move was a shrewd one, exempting them from possible interference by executives and camp followers.

The tendency has been to separate Curtis from his bandmates, marking him as mastermind of Joy Division's depressive strategy. Wrong. The focus is on Curtis — his lyrics and vocals are the most immediately memorable part of Joy Division's sound — but *Unknown Pleasures* blends music, theme and expression for the first time. Even without lyrics, the chilling, despondent music leaves no doubt what Joy Division was on about. Hannett glazed any pop vestiges with a Teutonic sheen, fusing medium and message into a holistic brilliance.

Paul Rambali, a British journalist [and *Trouser Press* columnist] who was among the few to be granted an interview with Joy Division and who saw them infrequently until Curtis's death, describes the band's social structure:

"Three of the members were quite talkative, quite open. All of them were if you spoke to them casually. But if you put a tape recorder down, they'd refuse to talk. The bass player, Hooky (Peter Hook) got very intractable and argumentative, and refused to answer any direct questions, especially any probing the meaning of their music. He was not ill-natured, of course, and I ended up having a big argument with him about the meaning of interviews instead.

"I saw them at a TV studio in Manchester, where they were recording a song for a local program. They did a couple of run-throughs and weren't getting on particularly well with the director. The TV crew would say, 'Go through it again'; they would, and no one would say whether that was any good or not. Eventually the floor manager said, 'That's it, it's all over now.' They were unaware that that was the final take, and they went to the control room to see what was happening. The director had covered the group with video effects; he thought he was being really creative. Beaming with pride, he turned to the group and said, 'Well, what'd you think of that, then?' They were just silent; then Hooky said, 'I thought it was a load of fucking rubbish.' A few minutes after that, the whole group tromped out, and no more words were said. That's sort of what Hooky's like, and it's from him that their stonewalling thing came.

"The music had much to do with Martin Hannett. He defined Joy Division's sound to a large extent. He's obsessed with electronics; he'd buy all the latest equipment he could get his hands on. He'd arrive at the studio with these big boxes, hook them up and start recording.

"Once Hannett put Joy Division through phase shifters, equalized them, beefed them up in the right places and so forth, the music sounded very sophisticated technologically. Performing was a bit of a problem until they could duplicate the sound live. They were a great heavy metal band onstage and could really have cleaned up if they'd gone on. They looked completely wrong, though, because they didn't wear denim or long hair.

"What the music sounded like came to a great extent from Bernard Albrecht, the guitarist; Hooky, the bassist; and Martin Hannett. The atmosphere of the music and, of course, the lyrics came from Curtis. They all had a strong input; Joy Division was pretty much a combination of talents."

BY 1979, JOY DIVISION had driven themselves out of pop and into a land gutted by "art rock" bands of the early 1970s. *Unknown Pleasures'* ornately grim songs — punctuated by ambulance sirens and breaking glass — left Curtis crooning mournfully at his own echoing voice. The opening track, "Disorder," makes clear the band's aesthetic shift from earlier work. As a source of angst, "Digital"'s ephemeral shadows have been replaced by the world at large, speeding toward incomprehensible chaos. The theme is reiterated on "She's Lost Control" (also recorded by Grace Jones in a disco version that did much to establish Joy Division's credentials).

Curtis's characters are surrounded by madness. "Insight," perhaps *Unknown Pleasures'* most poignant song, outlines his world view, complete with a growing sense of isolation and a shutdown of all senses save those of clinical observation.

A FEW SINGLES WERE RELEASED, and two Joy Division songs appeared on Fast Records' *Earcom 2* compilation. The band had just completed a second album when Ian Curtis, reportedly despondent over a broken romance, hung himself at home in Macclesfield, England on May 18, 1980. He was 23. His death retroactively taints all of Joy Division's work, and — callous as it may be to say so — validates a mood that other bands (before and after Joy Division) have played for the sake of

dark fashion. Curtis, for one, acted on his convictions. Joy Division's last single and best expression of those convictions, "Love Will Tear Us Apart," stands as an exquisite suicide note.

The second album, *Closer* (we must now wonder, to what?), appeared two months after Curtis's death. It displays a dramatically different Joy Division from the one on *Unknown Pleasures*. The sound is emptier, more distant, with emphasis on a strangely out-of-kilter synthesizer. The whole album has a dislocated feel. Curtis is no longer the quiet observer, but an outraged participant in a world that has robbed him of joy and hope.

Curtis's death spurred a flurry of interest in the band, propelling their work into the charts and creating a demand for unreleased tracks. A recent flood of bootlegs, taped from concerts and lifted from Warsaw demo tapes, filled the gap and finally forced Factory to issue *Still*, a compilation of old Joy Division material and live performances. The release may be a shrewd move — death, in the music industry, creates goldmines (or at least cottage industries) — but *Still* is not sub-standard, and does no dishonor to Joy Division's reputation.

Death has always been the great romantic legend of rock music. The suffering artist, the youthful hero cut down in his prime — all of this has been applied to Curtis in the last two years, carelessly and with little concern for fact.

Curtis was no romantic hero; his songs held no romantic vision. They are editorials, observations of the human condition on this world in this time — specifically conditions in the northwest of England, where poverty, unemployment and despair mingle with past glories in a sorry mess — that grind any notion of romanticism underfoot. Curtis's cries were of loneliness in the dark; he was obviously an intelligent, sensitive man trying to make sense of a world he couldn't understand. The answers he arrived at, if that's what his lyrics are, are anything but comforting. His songs, the songs of Joy Division, point out that there is no romance in life. Curtis's unfortunate, ugly death points out that there is no romance in suicide, either.

Death tore Joy Division apart. The remaining members withdrew for air and reappeared a few months later as New Order. So far, they've released two singles and one album since reforming; the first single, "Ceremony" b/w "In a Lonely Place," comes out of the Joy Division repertoire; the rest of their output is grimly lackluster. Desperate as they might be to do so, it's unlikely New Order will ever shake off Joy Division's shadow.

AFTER CURTIS'S death, journalists romanticized him beyond recognition. He conveniently fit a predetermined mold — that of the romantic poet driven to suicide by an unfeeling world — and as such has entered the pantheon of rock martyrs. Joy Division has also been reinterpreted and made into something they were not.

Joy Division's music has been called dangerous, but this word is cheapened by overuse; it has been a long time since any kind of rock has been dangerous. Their music was confrontational; it looked life in the eye without flinching or retreating into fantasy. For Joy Division, reality, no matter how bleak or oppressive, is better than fantasy. That attitude can frighten and confuse some people.

Above all, Joy Division made intimate, personal music. Much of it deals with the inability to communicate feelings accurately, to break through barriers that isolate people from each other, which makes Joy Division the first existential band in rock history. Why, then, would a group seemingly so convinced of the impossibility of communication try so desperately to communicate — and how did they do it so well?

Perhaps their outlook was accurate, at least in regard to themselves. Whatever quality made Joy Division the special experience they were escapes words. The parts can be dissected and analyzed, but no resulting label or notion quite sums it up. All that can be said, finally, is that Joy Division transformed a moribund music into a vital if difficult experience. A shell of darkness surrounds Joy Division; once cracked, it yields up warm, afflicted souls, and listening to them just gets better and better.

Language may never quite represent Joy Division's appeal. Then again, if everything could be expressed by language, there would be no need for music. ∎

RAVING FAVES

ROCK SONG TOPICS

TP 59, FEBRUARY 1981

Bruce Simpson felt that "just about all subjects had been exhausted — all types of human emotions, bodily functions and favorite positions, machinery and animals as well as philosophical concepts (truths and falsehoods)." He went on to suggest a rock opera on the life of Nietzsche ("or perhaps Kierkegaard").

Others felt there were still crucial topics left to be explored in the context of rock songs, among them:

- old age
- Antarctica
- spinal taps
- sloppy sideburns
- toaster ovens
- Woody Allen
- eye tests ("in the tradition of 'S-A-T-U-R-D-A-Y Night,' 'D-I-V-O-R-C-E' and 'R-E-S-P-E-C-T'" —Tom Blumenfeld)
- 40-year-olds posing as punks
- White Castle hamburgers
- golf
- tight underwear
- polls in music magazines

Future songwriters, your work is cut out for you!

THE CURE

TP 67, NOVEMBER 1981

By Jim Green

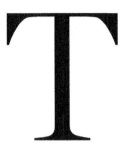

The Cure is the kind of rock band that encourages a blurring of distinctions between journalism and criticism. They simply must be considered subjectively; dealing with them otherwise would be unfair and unproductive. Take it on faith.

Or, rather, *Faith*, the band's third album, just released by A&M in tandem with the previous *Seventeen Seconds* as a two-record set called *Happily Ever After* — as misleading a title as the late Ian Curtis's band being called Joy Division. Much of the Cure's live set is deliberately, almost painfully slow. Onstage at the Ritz in New York, the band seemed to prolong the majestically lugubrious "Funeral Party" indefinitely; other numbers like "The Drowning Man" add new dimension to the word "miasma." Dance music for autistics?

There you go. In a hot, humid ballroom in the wee hours of a hard day's night, at the reserved table of the record company, whose people were either snoozing or had gone home, it was easy to make cracks about the music. Under more favorable circumstances, the Cure's moody mantras could be hypnotic instead of soporific. How about "melancholy ear candy"?

The Cure's music has been labeled and pigeonholed since the band started out. At A&M's offices the next day, they note that even their record company is having trouble describing them for a press bio.

"They did say, 'It's not your regular boogie,'" drummer Laurence (Lol) Tolhurst notes with a mixture of wryness and resignation. "You should have heard it before I started censoring it," counters guitarist/vocalist Robert Smith. "They said our sound couldn't be compared to anyone, and then further on say we're a 'cosmic Ventures' with overtones of psychedelia or something. Must be the West Coast office's version."

Smith's common name masks striking facial features. He resembles a less fantastic version of Marvel Comics' Sub-Mariner — without the pointy ears but with a shock of bristly black hair. He himself says he wouldn't bother trying to describe the band's music; the Cure's creative process is very much intuitive.

"We never theorize about what we do. There's no ulterior idea behind it. When we sit down and play something we know straight away if it's not right. When we started, and it was literally a toss-up that I picked guitar, I tried to avoid musical clichés. I never wanted to be a guitarist *per se* and tried to impress on the others [originally Tolhurst and bassist Michael Dempsey, now in the Associates] not to 'be' their instruments, The Drummer and The Bassist. That's so limited." The song, rather than musical role models, would dictate the course of action.

The Cure's debut album, *Three Imaginary Boys*, (released here by PVC in slightly altered form as *Boys Don't Cry*), consists of a dozen brief songs, most with gloomy/dire/stark scenarios, a spare instrumental sound and catchy riffs. "Fire in Cairo," "Grinding Halt" and two subsequent singles (included on the U.S. LP), "Boys Don't Cry" and "Jumping Someone Else's Train," suggested a growing affinity for pop hooks.

"But the Cure then has nothing to do with what we are now," Smith objects. "We were playing about 50 songs at the time, mostly in pubs and to people who didn't care if we fell over and died. I wrote most of them by myself without thinking they'd ever be heard by more than 30 people at a time. Chris Parry [head of Fiction, the Cure's English label] picked what he thought were the best of the 30 we recorded. They turned out to be some critics' ideas of 'classic pop,' but they obviously weren't, because they weren't popular. "Jumping Someone Else's Train" was the last song of that period — and, yes, the last we did with Dempsey. We could've gone on doing songs like that but it would've been like, er, a Vapors trail" — everyone groans at the pun — "and we had no intention of doing that."

Dempsey's departure spurred changes on many fronts. Besides current bassist Simon Gallup, Matthieu Hartley (since departed) was added on keyboards. The writing began to change, and with it the sound and aural shape of the Cure.

"Early on," Smith says, "the songs were credited to the group even if I had written them, so there wouldn't be any jealousy over my getting more money; I didn't want that to be a factor. Now the songs are group compositions. I couldn't just say 'Here, we're gonna do this song,' 'cause if everybody's unhappy with it they wouldn't play it. Though it's down to compromise, we all do tend to think along the same lines."

Tolhurst always had some lyrical input; now they're all involved, although Smith has last say on the words ("I have to sing them"). There's no set writing pattern.

Smith: "We played 'Charlotte Sometimes' [the latest Cure single] through for the first time when we went into the studio to record it. The first take was perfect — although none of us told the others what to play at all. The B-side, though, 'Splintered in Her Head,' was pieced together: the drums were put down, then we sat and thought about what to put on top. Simon tried bass parts until bass and drums meshed, then I tried some guitar over that. So, both sides were completely different processes. The only thing that runs through it all is that we are primarily concentrating on the atmosphere we want to create — and then, of course, Lol usually thinks of a title."

Seventeen Seconds had a richer texture than the first album. It was almost lush, even gentle in spots, not unlike ambient music — although its eight main tracks (not counting a brief instrumental introduction on each side) are definitely songs. The album almost made the British Top 30 and the single it spawned, "A Forest," nearly snuck into the Top 20.

"That's a joke," Smith says. "When we did 'Jumping Someone Else's Train,' Polydor, who distribute Fiction in England, said, 'This is it, a Top 10 single!' and it went nowhere. They also said they couldn't really hear 'A Forest' as a single, and it was a hit. Polydor doesn't understand us. One person likes us; the rest say, 'This is your year, boys' — and, after we leave, 'Who was that band?' The critics didn't understand us either, but we don't pay much attention."

Reviewers' potshots escalated when *Faith* came out. The term "self-indulgent" got thrown around, but as Smith says, "How do you define self-indulgent? Is ambient self-indulgent? Is Van Halen? My mother thinks Gregorian chants are."

"I have my own criticisms of the album. The production is really shit!" The band laughs, since they produced it with engineer Mike Hedges. More seriously, Smith continues, "We didn't allow ourselves enough time to develop the songs in the studio; then again, if we'd taken longer that would've been self-indulgent. The last album took under 20 days, this one a bit more — but even that was too much; we have self-imposed limits on how much time and money we should spend. It took so long because we kept getting thrown out of studios in favor of 'more important' people, and once we lost the mood, we never quite got back the atmosphere we wanted. Also, some of it could have been a little more cohesive.

"A lot of people are like us. Everybody I know has gone through the emotional trauma of *Seventeen Seconds*, which is learning you can't trust people as implicitly as you'd thought when you were younger. *Faith* is about having gone through that and trying to discover what you can have faith in, the loss of innocence and growing older, as in 'Primary,' and trying to sort out what your life's about." [*Sounds like jolly good entertainment. —Ed.*]

The band isn't aware of what an atypically raucous reception they received from the packed Ritz crowd. The closing jam, based on "Three" from *Seventeen Seconds*, is made up "as we go, to relieve the tensions of the day," Smith says. "Once it lasted 45 minutes!"

Irregular boogie men? In the last analysis, one can only say it's all very Cure-ious. Bad punning aside, the Cure wouldn't have it any other way. ■

Two issues after we reviewed Boy *("a startlingly good but flawed debut"), we ran this more enthusiastic one-page article, written by Tim Sommer, an NYU student whose encounter with the band the previous December (their first time in New York) had ended with Bono and the Edge performing four acoustic songs for him and a friend in their Gramercy Park Hotel room. Four decades later, Tim wrote about it in* Rock and Roll Globe. *"I distinctly recall thinking to myself, 'You better remember this really clearly, in case they become the biggest band in the world, because if that happens, in the future this will make for one hell of a story.' I really did think that." The long lag between interview and article was probably due to the delayed American release of the album.*

U2

TP 63, JULY 1981

By Tim Sommer

New music requires new classifications. Or is it no classification?

U2 is the sort of band that prompts the above riddle. The Irish group's sweeping and majestic music is "rock" in one sense, but simultaneously transcends all genres.

U2's uniqueness is probably due to the emotional depth charges they detonate live and on record. Their debut album, *Boy*, is a glorious roar of hope, drenched in emotion. The band has a wonderful ability to find the musical correlatives to the ideas stirring in their young hearts and minds.

U2 singer and main songwriter Bono Vox, 20, projects warmth and openness from the moment you meet him; when introduced, he grasps your arm with both hands, making you feel immediately at ease. He's quick to pick up a comment that *Boy*'s images and aural wash are startlingly vivid.

"What we were looking for in *Boy* was a sort of cinema sound, a Panavision — really textured and big, like a huge screen in a cinema. The lyrics are very picturesque; they don't tell a story as such, they're just various images in the album that link together to form one big picture. There are enough little groups around playing little sounds, very unimportant. We wanted a big sound. We're using a three-piece format — bass, guitar and drums — like the three primary colors. We're mixing them, trying to get the most out of them."

It works well. The Edge, U2's guitarist, lays down thick chords here, dreamy tonal support there, even a straightforward solo now and again just to bring it all back home. Bono's expressive tenor is always in control; Adam Clayton's bass, with Larry Mullen's drums, make a solid foundation. For all that, the music fits into a pop format, as full of hooks and memorable melodies as deeper moments that make you mull over — or just appreciate — what you're hearing.

U2 stands for hope — another singular trait. A lot of groups represent some form of nihilism, escapism, or despair; how many can honestly state the opposite case?

"It is a celebration," Bono says. "'Shadows and Tall Trees' on the album begins in a pensive mood, as the character — who is me — looks around him. He sees this pattern developing, the repetition of everyday life. It really gets to him, really irritates him, as he realizes 'Mrs. Brown's washing is always the same.' I was listening to housewives talking; in Dublin there's this expression — 'I *know*, I *know*,' they say to each other, 'I *know*' — but I realized that's very beautiful in many ways. It's often the everyday things that are beautiful.

"We chose the name U2 to be ambiguous, to stay away from categorization. People who work in print tend to tidy things up a bit — put a stack of bands in that way, a stack of bands in here. People don't fit into boxes. We all smell different, we all eat different, we all *are* different. There's a huge audience out there of individuals." ∎

Win Sony Video 45s™—details inside!

Scene reports from:
● NEW YORK
● CHICAGO
● NASHVILLE
● VANCOUVER

Trouser Press

JULY 1983
TP 87
$1.75
Canada $2.00

U2's heart beat

WALL OF VOODOO
Rock from the twilight zone
STRANGLERS
Autodiscography
ULTRAVOX
State of the art

Bono, the Edge, Adam Clayton of U2

HOT CHOCOLATE   D.O.A.
LENE LOVICH   TIN TIN
DREAM SYNDICATE   INXS

*A*n innocent design decision to make a horizontal Ebet Roberts photo work on a stubbornly vertical cover led us into a huge row with the band's label over the elision of drummer Larry Mullen. Sorry, gentlemen.

U2: A WAY OF LIFE

TP 87, JULY 1983

By Scott Isler

"Tell me, what do you like about U2?"

The question comes from Paul Hewson, better known as Bono, U2's singer. It's aimed at the *Trouser Press* writer. Who's interviewing whom here?

Hewson, 23, isn't being presumptuous, just disarming. It's the day before U2 sets off on a two-month, 42-date tour of the U.S. that should certify the band's status as conquering heroes of 1983. *War*, U2's third album, has crashed into the upper reaches of American record charts. With FM radio plugging the "New Year's Day" single, very few people seem not to like U2. Hewson doesn't want ego-stroking praise. He's genuinely curious how his suddenly popular band is being perceived Stateside. Why? Because U2 cares.

THE MANHATTAN HOTEL ROOM shared by Hewson and drummer Larry Mullen has a comfortably disordered appearance. A big acoustic guitar case (Mullen's; he's started writing songs) lies on the floor. The coffee table in front of the couch bears magazines, a basket of fruit and an open box of chocolates with one piece in it. The band arrived in New York the previous day; before flying to North Carolina that evening, where the tour will begin, they want to see *Tootsie*. Hewson also wants to check out the city's hipper dance clubs — surprising, in light of U2's own rather "traditional" rock music.

"It's not how you play it, it's why you're playing it," the singer comments on the band's disregard of musical fashion. "Instruments are just bits of wood and metal nailed together, plastic skins stretched over boxes. It's what you do with them that's important."

U2 has taken its wood, metal and plastic and used the conventions of rock as a basis for evocative combinations of words and music. In June, Hewson will be declaiming his introspective (if exuberant) lyrics from the Los Angeles Sports Arena; the band is also considering playing New York's 20,000-seat Madison Square Garden. Not bad for a one-time punk outfit from Dublin. But what happened to the anti-big biz ethic that nourished U2 in the first place?

"If we stay in small clubs," Hewson counters, "we'll develop small minds, and then we'll start making small music." U2 likes to think big.

HEWSON IS DRESSED all in black, but casual: black shoes, black pants, black peasant shirt. His spiky hair is long in the back; some dyed-blond tufts in the front are the only touch of affecta-tion in his appearance. Broad of face and stocky of build, he talks slowly and intently, hesitating between phrases. Overall, he gives an impression of unforced sincerity.

U2's albums identify him only as Bono (pro-nounced "bonno"), a childhood nickname short for Bono Vox, shorter still for Bono Vox of O'Con-nell Street. His name, as well as guitarist the Edge's, is a legacy of growing up with friends who invent-ed their own town, Lypton Village, and peopled it with arbitrarily renamed acquaintances.

"People think, 'They're into pseudonyms, they must be really pseudy-type people,'" Hewson says. "'They want to hide their real names.' I can think of a lot better pseudonyms than Bono! Why couldn't I have thought of something like Sting?" Actually, Hewson didn't think of Bono; he was given it by an especially creative Lyptonian. As a "return serve," Hewson dubbed *him* Guggi, and that name stuck as well. Guggi now sings in another Dublin ex-port, the Virgin Prunes.

More likely, U2's members abjured surnames out of folksiness. Nonetheless, Hewson is getting tired of misrepresentation. "Publications keep calling me Bono Vox," he sighs. "I'm not Mr. Vox." U2's early history is intertwined with that of the Virgin Prunes. Before both groups stabilized, their personnels were interchangeable. Dik of the Prunes is older brother to U2's the Edge — David Evans, to his parents.

(As a mini-revelation, *War* marks the first time Larry Mullen's full name has seen print on a U2 album cover. "He's become a man," Hewson teases the youthful drummer, who turned 21 early this year. "He now knows how to drink a pint of Guin-ness.")

The magnet for all these musicians — and would-be musicians — was a notice posted in school by Mullen, who was looking to start a band. ("If I see that in print again, I could do a nasty," Hewson warns.) It was 1976, and Mullen was 14. The drummer now resembles Billy Idol's kid brother in a blue denim vest over a T-shirt with rolled-up sleeves, blue jeans and sneakers. His hair is '50s-rebel length and newly dyed blond. He wears a solitary earring.

"I had two days of glory when I was tellin' peo-ple what to do," Mullen says. "Then Bono came in and that was the end. He took it from there."

IT'S NOT HARD TO imagine the outgoing Hew-son taking charge. Back then, though, there wasn't much to take charge of, as no one was very profi-cient on his instrument. But the four — Hewson, Evans, Mullen and bassist Adam Clayton — be-came friends, which seems as important to them now as anything else. They took the deliberately ambiguous name U2 to avoid categorization in those heady punk days.

About a year after coagulating, in 1977, Clay-ton convinced manager Paul McGuinness to at-tend a gig. "He came down to talk us out of it," Hewson remembers, "how we shouldn't do this, it's really a dead end." McGuinness came, saw and was conquered. The band rechristened him Magoo. "His first assignment was to get us served in the pub next door, 'cause we were too young," Hewson chuckles.

McGuinness formally took on U2 in 1978. The band was constantly improving and building a local following. After winning a lucrative talent contest, U2 was offered a record contract by the Irish arm of CBS. They issued a three-song single on that label but refused to commit themselves.

In spring 1980, U2 signed to Island Records worldwide. "People there really believe in the group," Hewson says. "They never wanted us to be a pop group. We wanted '11 O'Clock Tick Tock' to be our first single. It was four-and-a-half minutes long and was never going to get played on radio. They stood by us."

U2's first U.S. release was *Boy* in early 1981. The twin themes of adolescence and growth run through this debut LP, matched by swirling, misty music. Producer Steve Lillywhite's echoic approach gave U2 the phosphorescent quality of swampfire; Hewson's passionate stream-of-consciousness vo-cals combined with the basic guitar-bass-drums lineup to create an album that's both accessible and enthralling. For a new band receiving little airplay, U2 sold respectably well.

The group came over to tour and fulfilled expectations with a dynamic stage show. Unfortunately, the climax of the trip occurred in Portland, Oregon, when two women walked into U2's dressing room and walked out with Hewson's briefcase, containing his notes for the following album's songs.

"I'd like to meet them," he says wistfully of his robbers — "those big blue eyes." He pauses. "It's the $300 I want back! Keep the lyrics!"

HEWSON MAY joke about it now, but at the time the loss of his lyrics was no laughing matter. In between extensive tours of the U.S. and UK — U2 played over 200 shows in 1981 — the band had booked studio time to record its second album. In the past, the group-credited compositions evolved out of soundcheck jams, with lyrics often improvised onstage. Now Hewson was forced to push his creativity to the limit.

That summer, with the backing tracks already done, the singer went into U2's recording haunt, Windmill Lane Studios in Dublin, and literally expelled lyrics through massive amounts of free association. Afterward, a harried Lillywhite helped piece together snippets of Hewson's extemporizing. The technique would have pleased James Joyce.

"It's best to do it under stress," Hewson avers with hindsight. "Maybe I have a few lines in my mind, or words or images. I play around with them, fill up a [vocal] track, move on, fill up another track. Then I go back with Lillywhite, and maybe Larry or Adam, and see a train of thought.

"I try to pull out of myself things I wouldn't be able to do with pen and paper. At the front of your brain is a lot of rubbish: You write about things you think you're concerned about, but that may not be what you're concerned about at all."

The album was entitled *October* for its month of release and the autumnal nature of its songs. To American ears it lacked the impact of *Boy* and didn't even dent the Top 100. But it entered the British charts at number-11, serving notice that U2 was no one-shot wonder.

Hewson admits *October* "was quite an introspective record" and not "as immediate" as *Boy*. More importantly, its subject matter shoved U2 out of the Christian closet.

Hewson had started to talk about his deeply held but slightly unorthodox religious beliefs at interviews. While professing contempt for organized faith — understandably, having seen it divide his native land — he could still take on an evangelical fervor.

"Christ is like a sword that divides the world," he told one reporter. "It's about time we get into line and let people know where we stand." It wasn't exactly sex 'n' drugs 'n' rock 'n' roll, but then U2 has never worried much about appearances.

TO BOLSTER *OCTOBER* in the U.S., U2 toured here a second time. Swallowing its Irish pride, the group even accepted opening-act status for several shows with the J. Geils Band. Hewson, who says U2 doesn't "believe in playing a venue unless we sell it out," flatly denies the exposure helped U2's subsequent commercial breakthrough.

The band recrossed the Atlantic and played some European dates. U2 finally retreated to Ireland by the end of summer 1982 to recuperate and plan a third album — the first since their debut they *could* plan.

As early as 1981, Hewson was hinting that Ireland's civil strife "was starting to affect me." Now he admits the concerns behind *War*, U2's current LP, were originally going to surface on *October*. His purloined lyrics were different from those on *War*, "but they had that same [feeling of] conflict."

War, released in early 1983, topped British record charts its first week out. Over here, the record's gradual acceleration into the Top 10 has been less dramatic but more impressive, given chronic American indifference to new and/or imported popular music.

Lillywhite, who normally tries to vary his clientele, once again produced a U2 album. The band had been thinking of changing producers; having decided to strip down their sound on the new record, however, they realized Lillywhite was the most empathic choice to carry out their intentions.

"I rang up Steve," Hewson says, "and in a flash he said, 'I'll be over.' He said we're his favorite group. It's a very close thing."

War opens with the claustrophobic attack of "Sunday Bloody Sunday," whose violent imagery tackles the Northern Ireland situation head on. But the mention of Jesus at the song's end implies it isn't just about politics.

"In the Republic of Ireland," Hewson says gravely, "if you make a statement against a man of violence, you are in danger of coming into a certain amount of violence — a brick through a window. Some of the lines in that song were very strong in castigating the IRA. At the time I felt very angry. But that had to be tempered, 'cause I realized I was dealing with a blinkered situation, where people really believe in what they're doing; they're not just bad men. I'm prepared to say it's wrong, but I wanted to make it more than a song about the IRA. That's why I contrast it with Easter Sunday, the ultimate Bloody Sunday."

He acknowledges the lyrics were "tempered by other members of the band. They redeemed a very volatile situation." Still, "we have the right to speak out."

WAR SPEAKS OUT ON other topics as well: Poland ("New Year's Day"), atomic Armageddon ("Seconds" — "black humor on the bomb"), the senselessness of all armed combat ("The Refugee"). As on "Sunday Bloody Sunday," the specific is a jumping-off point for more generalized observations.

"I'm trying to get across the theme of surrender," Hewson says, "the white flag that applies to every area of your life — whether it's the factory, the campus or just being on the street. I think the revolution begins at home, in the heart."

Whew. Does Hewson think everyone slapping down their money for *War* is getting the message?

"I'd like to say they are, but I couldn't. I'm sure there are many levels on which people come into our music. You may find 16-year-olds into the phenomenon of the Edge. I don't look down on that; I hope the music draws people in further."

On that point, the packaging sure is right. U2 has consistently shunned synthesizers and other trendy electronic hardware in favor of the good old power trio — the "primary colors" Hewson invariably mentions to the press. He has nothing against synth bands as such, but just likes some meat with his potatoes.

"It is a breakthrough hearing Human League on radio — they play synthesizers, they're non-musicians and they come from Sheffield — but the content of the songs is the same as ABBA."

U2, on the other hand, is concentrating on message more than form?

"Well, 'message' always gives an image of a prophet [*pointing*]: 'This way!' It's not like that. We only use it in a very personal way."

The singer, who calls himself an "aggressive pacifist," can be similarly convoluted explaining his music's conflicting components.

"There are few instruments that get across aggression as well as a distorted guitar; it's physically brutalizing. The power of a rock and roll concert is that it stimulates you emotionally, as you follow the singer, and physically, as you dance and are hit by the music. It also has a cleansing effect; it's a great release. The brutalizing effect of guitar has been used in a very negative direction at times. But our aggression is not, uh — masturbation. It's much warmer, much more communicative than that."

THE MASTER OF U2's warmly brutalizing guitar, 21-year-old Edge (Evans), is sharing a hotel room with bassist Clayton, 23. With his receding hairline and couple of days' stubble, wearing blue jeans, black T-shirt and checked wool jacket, the thin, soft-spoken Evans could pass for almost anything except a high-powered rock guitarist. A steely gaze and lupine face help explain his nickname.

Clayton, by contrast, sports a tie-dyed tank top, bracelets, a necklace and studded belt through his black Levi's. His blond hair trimmed down from its former curly thatch, he looks like a serious hedonist.

According to Hewson, Clayton was bounced out of several schools before ending up at Mt. Temple Comprehensive with the other budding musicians: "People usually have no problem at our school, but he did! He was thrown out and became a full-time hustler for the group."

"I'd never been particularly interested in school," Clayton admits in cultured tones. "Then playing an instrument occurred to me."

Superficially, at least, Clayton is U2's odd man out. "Adam was more and more into the rock and roll circus," Hewson says, while the rest of U2 was "getting more and more estranged from all that." Besides his distinctive (for U2) dressing up, he is the sole non-believer among his spiritually devout bandmates. Yet all concerned agree the group has no personality problems.

During the *War* sessions, Hewson says, Clayton "was becoming a caricature of himself, with a bottle of brandy. But there was never tension. There's always great love and respect for him, and vice versa."

"I don't think there are any particularly sensitive or vulnerable relationships within the band at all," Evans says. "We're pretty open; we're not afraid to talk to one another."

Something else all U2's members agree on is the band's continuing growth over the years. "We now know a lot more about what we do and how we do it," Clayton says. "In the past, we'd have a rough idea how a song was going to turn out, but we'd never really know how good it could be. Nowadays, we're in control a lot more."

"I don't think U2 will ever get to the stage where there's a formula," Evans adds. "Our way of writing is always so much a part of experimenting, and a feeling at the time. It's not a conscious thing." Indeed, Hewson may change lyrics or add them to a song (like "Twilight," on *Boy*) the band has been playing as an instrumental for a year or more.

"Essentially, there are no rules to what we do," the guitarist says. "That's what people can't understand."

Where do they go from here? U2's next music will be a score for the Royal Dublin Ballet, to be presented this summer. That work may involve outside musicians on traditional instruments. Evans, who started out on acoustic guitar, hints at picking it up again. (He's also just recorded with Jah Wobble, Holger Czukay and Jaki Liebezeit.)

Hewson also implies U2's next album will mark a break with its past. "Everyone feels a weight off their shoulders," he says. "We feel like we're in a new group now. I can't sleep at night with thoughts about the next record."

What a come-on. How about some details? "We're not allowed to say," he laughs.

U2 ADMITTEDLY has not revolutionized music through stylistic innovation. What they have done, though, is perhaps more daring: injected commitment into an escapist pop scene.

"We open ourselves up to people to such an extent it gets embarrassing," Evans says. "We sacrifice a certain amount of cool. There's so much theater involved in this business, and to a certain extent we've opted out of that. A performance must be larger than life, but to be worthwhile you must have an element of humanity. It has to be more than an intellectual pursuit."

Asked what effect he wants to have on audiences, Hewson replies, "Uplifting. That's the effect the music has on me. I hope that's the effect a U2 concert has: 'Let's all go get uplifted at a U2 show!'"

At least he's kept his sense of humor along with his ideals. At the same time, Hewson presents himself as a worldly character — a depiction that, to his credit, he doesn't bring off very well.

"Because we used a child's face on the cover, and *Boy* was about innocence, people thought, oh, they must be four good Catholic boys from Ireland, wide-eyed to the world. I've probably been through more than a lot of people," he laughs.

"We were never innocent. We still have a lot to learn, and we've always felt if we didn't know something we should find somebody who did. But it would be complimenting us to portray us in that way. We're actually really nasty people." He laughs again.

Somehow, that doesn't jibe with Hewson's belief in the power of music to change, just as he feels '60s music united a culture to stop the Vietnam war. "It would be wrong for me to say, yes, we can change the world with a song. But every time I try writing, that's where I'm at!" Another self-deprecating laugh.

"I'm not stupid. I'm aware of the futility of rock and roll music, but I'm also aware of its power. We're only coming to terms with our trade. We've yet to become craftsmen. Well, maybe we should never become craftsmen. It's great fun being in this band." ■

AT HOME
— IN THE STUDIO —
WITH
STEVE LILLYWHITE

TP 72, APRIL 1982

By Karen Schlosberg

He's been associated with early British punk (Ultravox!) and sophisticated art rock (Peter Gabriel), all shades of new wave from Siouxsie and the Banshees to the Psychedelic Furs, XTC and the Brains, from U2 to Joan Armatrading. The man who's had his finger on some very important buttons in almost every new rock style is producer Steve Lillywhite.

The phrase "boy wonder" could have been coined specifically for Lillywhite. Twenty-six years old but looking 18, he's fair-haired, open-faced and modest about being a prime mover of punk and post-punk rock.

"I get a few letters from young kids," Lillywhite says from the unassuming London office of his manager. "I got a funny letter once from a 16-year-old who said, 'I've been thinking of becoming a record producer for *quite* a few years now.'"

That kid is probably the same age now as Lillywhite was when he was hired as tape operator in Phonogram's Marble Arch studio — a classic case of being in the right place at the right time.

"I just happened to know someone at a studio," Lillywhite recalls. "I went up to have a look 'round, and just the same day someone happened to be sacked. I bluffed my way into it by pretending I had all of the right qualifications."

From a town just outside London called Egham, Lillywhite is the oldest of three children in a musical family: his parents both play instruments and his younger brother, Adrian, is the drummer in the Members, whom Steve has produced. He "fiddled about" with piano, guitar and bass, and played in school bands, but Lillywhite found that he didn't have time to continue his own playing as his job at Phonogram progressed.

His "lucky break" at 17 started Lillywhite off on a career. In four and a half years at Phonogram, climbing up the ladder from "tea boy" to house engineer, he worked on everything from Status Quo to Welsh singer-comedian Harry Secombe.

"It was a complete cross-section, which was great for me. One morning you'd be working with a 40-piece orchestra with strings; then that same afternoon you'd have a rock band with four blaring guitars. You got to know a lot about your job because it wasn't just one style of music.

"But," he continues, "as it was a studio that was affiliated with a record company, it was very much like a little bubble. The head engineer had been there 21 years. There was not that much of a chance of anyone being sacked."

Lillywhite also had the opportunity to use the studio on weekends for outside projects (providing it was not occupied). Demos he did with a band called Ultravox! led to them being signed to Island Records.

"I hadn't produced anything then. The band wanted me to work with them, but Island said, look, you've got to have somebody come in as well. That's how Brian Eno was involved. That was my first production credit, a three-way production; Ultravox!, Eno and myself. The album got absolutely slated; 'Ultrahype' was one of the headlines."

Critical reaction notwithstanding, Lillywhite was off and running. "I got offered this quite abstract job by Island. It wasn't as engineer, it wasn't as producer and it wasn't A&R, but bits of all those things. To this day I still don't know what I was supposed to be called," Lillywhite smiles. "God, it was terrible! I didn't know anybody except for the person who had hired me. When I arrived on Monday morning, I was told the person who'd hired me had left the Friday before! I really started off on the wrong foot."

Lillywhite soon settled in. In his two years with Island, he would produce Eddie and the Hot Rods, reggae band Steel Pulse and the second Ultravox! album. Chris Blackwell, Island's president, offered him a producer's contract through Island Artists (the label's management arm) that would give him a set amount a year as an advance against royalties, plus the chance to work for others. Lillywhite accepted.

"This was just as punk was starting," he says. "Punk was the first thing that really made my ears prick up. London in '77 was fantastic. I was going out to all these punk clubs and meeting the bands. I started working for these people, who started getting hit records — but none of them were for Island. I suddenly realized, well, they're not really looking after my career. So, Chris Blackwell and I terminated the contract; I decided to branch out on my own. The first time I've worked for Island since then has been with U2."

Lillywhite hasn't gone hungry or had to compromise his principles. He only works on what he enjoys, and he tries to vary his style as much as possible.

"Lots of producers become known for a certain type of thing, and then if that becomes unfashionable, they go down with it. I like to keep fresh with everything I do. It's for the artist's sake as well, you know. If they work with different producers, they can get different influences. A producer is a floating member of the band." Lillywhite pauses, then resumes, playing devil's advocate. "But, you can also argue, would the Beatles have done what they did if they didn't have George Martin?"

ONE BAND Lillywhite has most enjoyed working with is U2. His full yet crisp, clean sound on the band's debut album, *Boy*, was almost an instrument in its own right.

U2 bassist Adam Clayton has conceded Lillywhite is a virtual fifth member of the band: "I'm sure if he wasn't producing us he'd probably be a member of the band anyway."

"Everyone was in such a good frame of mind," Lillywhite remembers of the session for "I Will Follow." "Ideas would just flow. I had a bicycle turned upside down; Bono and I would spin the wheels and hit the spokes with a knife. There were also bottles smashing all over the place. We were having a great time — just like little kids."

Lillywhite says most bands now have their arrangements sorted out before entering the studio, and he only offers suggestions from time to time.

"But there's the other way of doing it, which is to write something in the studio, be creative there. I always try to keep one or two songs on a record completely unwritten, and just work on them from scratch."

In that respect Lillywhite got more than he bargained for while producing U2's second album, *October*. Singer/lyricist Bono lost his notebook full of lyric jottings while on tour; Lillywhite calls the compensatory efforts in the studio "not so much time-consuming as just, uh, quite a harrowing experience. It didn't really flow as well as the first album because they hadn't had that much time to write it. When we went into the studio there was only one song ['I Fall Down'] that was completely finished. The rest were snatches of ideas, not really many melodies or lyrics. Considering that, it turned out very well."

JOAN ARMATRADING was one of three artists Lillywhite had most wanted to produce. (The other two were Bruce Springsteen and Talking Heads.) He approached A&M, Armatrading's label, and turned out to be in the right place at the right time once again. Armatrading had just scrapped an album due to problems in the studio. In stepped Lillywhite.

"I met Joan, and she played me the shelved album — once. I've never heard it again," he laughs. "She won't let *anybody* hear it. We used a bit more than half of those songs on *Walk Under Ladders*.

"She's fantastic. She's extremely shy when you first meet her, but she blossomed as the album went on.

"She let me choose the musicians. I really wanted the Edge from U2 to do some guitar — that would've been incredible! — but then she put her foot down. Which is a pity, because he is my favorite guitar player. Finding the right guitar player was one problem on the album. We used four guys total, I think."

THE PSYCHEDELIC FURS are a Lillywhite-produced band that seems to have successfully avoided what he calls the "stumbling block" of a second album.

"They've got something. I can't put my finger on why I like them, because really you shouldn't like the Psychedelic Furs; it's just that the sum is definitely greater than all the parts. It's sort of a mishmash of sound, although they're changing now. They improved a lot on the second album [*Talk Talk Talk*]. The first one had some really good things on it — 'Sister Europe' is probably better than anything on the second album — but the second album's consistently better.

"They're great to work with. Richard [Butler] is definitely improving as a singer. On the first album he wouldn't do anything more than once, and I wasn't allowed to put any effects on his vocals. I think it's just insecurity on his part. It was sometimes quite difficult to get him into the studio for a vocal."

Part of a producer's job, of course, is not only to get the best sounds in the studio, but to create the best moods for getting those sounds.

"It's a bit like being a psychiatrist. You find out what each member of the band is worried about, then spend a little more time with people you think might have problems.

"When I'm in a studio I come to life. It's the only place I really feel at home. It's really good fun, and fun is basically what it's all about. If you enjoy yourself, and if everybody's enjoying themselves, you get the best out of the artist."

Lately Lillywhite has been keeping active with the Thompson Twins ("part African music with a touch psychedelic").

"I might be trying something with the Pretenders," he hints, but "not until March or April — just a couple of tracks to see how it goes."

Long-range plans — remember he's only 26, so he's still got a few years left — might include a custom label and his own studio. Lillywhite doesn't sound like a producer who relishes time off.

"I spend all my time at work. I'm the most boring person in the world." He laughs again. "Thank goodness people want to hear about what I do. If they didn't, I'd have nothing to talk about." ∎

THE ELUSIVE JOAN ARMATRADING

TP 51, JUNE 1980

By Marianne Meyer

The 32 floors that separate A&M Records' Manhattan offices from Madison Avenue street level are going by very slowly. Having picked up publicity materials for an upcoming interview with Joan Armatrading, I am surprised to find the artist herself sharing the downward elevator ride. My attempts at light conversation are not going over well. We have both been caught off-guard, outside a safely "professional" context, and Armatrading seems no less shy or ill-at-ease than I am at having to make superficial comments about the city and the weather. There is also a coolness in her demeanor and a lack of enthusiasm for the interview mentioned that makes the sight of the ground floor lobby that much more welcome.

Four days later, we meet in the Mayfair Hotel lounge to speak in earnest. Although this went better than the elevator ride, my first impressions are not totally untrue. The Black singer-songwriter's press clips are rife with reports of her desire for privacy and reluctance to divulge personal detail under friendly cross-examination. (One frustrated writer even calls her Joan Armorplating.) That reputation is enough to make the proceedings somewhat tense at the start. Dressed unassumingly in a dark blue sweatshirt and pants and sneakers, Armatrading answers questions in a slow, deliberate manner; the cool efficiency is frequently punctuated with a short, clean laugh.

She is recording in New York for the first time, working with producer Richard Gottehrer at the Record Plant. "Derek Green, managing director of A&M in England, suggested [that Gottehrer and I] might get together. I fancied a change in studio, and since Richard was here and he knew totally different musicians than the ones I was used to, it just seemed a good idea to do it here."

The interview barely begun, we are interrupted by the incessant drilling of a pair of telephone men. I have to wait until we relocate to an unused dining room to ask what Gottehrer's involvement means to Armatrading's longstanding collaboration with Glyn Johns. He was responsible for producing the last three of her five albums, including the 1976 breakthrough *Joan Armatrading*, which went gold in England and was, according to Johns, the best work he'd ever been associated with — not faint praise from a man who's worked with the Eagles and the Rolling Stones.

"We worked together up to a point," Armatrading explains, "but it was just a matter of my wanting to try something different. Glyn is an engineer as well and he has his sound. When I worked with him, I was into what I was doing then, but by the third album I was sort of getting out of that." Can she be more specific? "Just the way I wrote, the structure of the songs. I was getting into a very jazzy thing, onstage it would be even more jazzy than on the record. Now I'm into a more rocky thing, simpler chord structures and, just to get that across, I felt I needed to change producers."

CHANGE IS A RECURRING process in Armatrading's musical methodology. A renowned perfectionist, she prefers to use new session players on almost every album and to reshuffle her lineup again when she goes on the road. She says the subtle injections of new styles keeps the music fresh. The real surprise may be that she was with Johns as long as she was.

Unlike many singer-songwriters, Armatrading avoids self-absorption or cosmic commentary in her work. Her lyrics have an intimate narrative quality (which she insists is not autobiographical) balanced with innate intelligence and a strong (albeit sometimes vulnerable) sense of self-worth. Her astoundingly versatile voice explores every crevice of tone and scale suggested by the lyrics and is the focal point around which the music revolves. The songs, rooted in her folky acoustic guitar playing, incorporate undercurrents of blues, soul, rock and jazz. The sum of these parts is vaguely reminiscent of Joni Mitchell or Phoebe Snow, but with a sharper edge and eclecticism that is wholly unique.

Armatrading's first two albums were cluttered and a bit grandiose, betraying the elegant simplicity and taste of her songs. Johns' largely acoustic-based production, with its jazz-tinged passages, was the first to focus her lyrical passion and crystallize her musical style. *Joan Armatrading* became one of 1976's best-selling albums in England, spawned two hit singles (one, "Love and Affection," was a minor hit here) and was named album of the year by the British weekly *Sounds*.

Hitting full stride as writer and singer, Armatrading's 1977 release, *Show Some Emotion*, was another European hit, but when *To the Limit* came out the next year, some felt her work with Johns was growing stale. One writer cited her static musical settings and blamed Johns for apathetic production, terming the LP "Joan's Armageddon." (Such are the problems of having a punnable name.)

While these critical rumblings did little to hurt Armatrading's headliner status in England and Europe, they certainly didn't help in the U.S., where she maintains a fierce if cultish following stabilized in the large-club/small-hall range. Her first tour of the States was less than triumphant (supporting such acts as the Ozark Mountain Daredevils) but she looks back with the good-natured understanding of one who knows about paying dues. "They weren't difficult times. I was just new, and I imagine everybody goes through that." She tells of one particular gig in Chicago in which the headliner canceled, and she was left playing to an audience of ten people. "But it's not as if it's staying to those ten people; all the time it's growing and growing." She professes to be quite happy with the size of her American audience.

Uncomfortable on stage at first, and a bit skeptical of her frequently fanatical listeners, Armatrading says she is much more at home now in the spotlight. "I really enjoy it now. The audience puts you in a good mood to try to do it better. It's really nice when they come to the gigs, and they're all singing along and shouting out what they want to hear."

IT'S A LONG ROUTE backwards from that stage to the West Indies, where Joan Armatrading was born 30 years ago. To hear her biography, one would think the journey was simply a series of fortunate accidents. Her father was a fireman and carpenter who played bass in a band at night; far from encouraging his children musically, he used to hide his guitar. Armatrading admits that the air of secrecy made music that much more attractive to her.

While she was still a child, the family moved to Birmingham, England. Although an exotic influence in her rhythms would seem to be a product of those early years in the Indies, Armatrading dismisses the idea with a slightly incredulous, "I was seven!"

The music she was conscious of was Otis Redding, Jim Reeves and Aretha Franklin — records owned by her brothers — but even these did not particularly impress her.

"The first person who made me listen to a record properly," she has often been quoted, "was Van Morrison." Her enthusiasm for his work is obvious. "I go to all [his] shows and I'm the last one out." Curiously enough, she had steadfastly refused offers to sing backup on his records. "I like him too much, and I don't want anything to spoil it. I've heard so many weird stories about him."

Settled in England, her mother bought a piano "as a piece of furniture." Armatrading was assigned the task of cleaning it. That led to playing it and, around the age of 14, the girl who had thought of becoming a lawyer started to write. When an elder brother heard her songs, he convinced her to play at the local school; by 16, she was playing cover material in local clubs.

Not long after, she accompanied a friend to an audition for the London company of *Hair*, just as a lark. The friend didn't get a part, but Armatrading did — and toured the provinces for 18 months. Afterwards, she went on the dole and spent a year writing songs in almost hermetic solitude. She read the poems of a woman named Pam Nestor, suggested some music of her own to augment them and, "Before you know it, we were writing songs. That's how it started."

A British record label, Cube, liked the songs and Armatrading's voice and offered her a recording contract. The first album, *Whatever's for Us*, was produced by Elton John associate Gus Dudgeon and released in 1972. Up to that point Armatrading had always considered herself primarily a songwriter ("In my head, that's how I started off") and she wasn't sure she enjoyed being in front of a microphone.

"I had to get used to that," she says thoughtfully over a glass of orange juice. "I enjoyed writing, but I never thought in terms of, 'This is what's going to make me money' or 'This is going to make me famous.' I was still trying to figure out what job to get, not to fall back on — just what job I was going to do to run my car and stuff like that. I didn't consider music my job."

When did she? "If you want to say when did I decide that music was my career, it was definitely after I made the second album [*Back to the Night*, released in 1975]." Between the two records was the all-too-typical case of a new talent's problems with record company legalities. Some observers felt that Cube pushed Pam Nestor into the background on the first LP, causing tensions that sundered the women's relationship and led Armatrading to seek release from her contract. The artist herself says, "Pam was just involved in publishing and that was a different thing. I always wrote songs on my own anyway, so it wasn't as if I had to find somebody to work with." (Nestor has since recorded a few songs on her own in England.)

Armatrading does have harsh words for Cube, though. "They were just a terrible record company," she recalls. "It took me 18 months to get away from them. It wasn't easy. I didn't just say 'bye' and that was it." But for the most part she stayed out of the battle.

"I certainly kept writing, anyway. But because I didn't think, 'This is what I have to do, I have to be famous,' it didn't get me in a state. A couple of times it would get me down because the legal thing was a bit frustrating — not because it was stopping my career, it was just a boring thing to be involved with. My manager, Mike Stone, who's still my manager, was really good, so it was his job to sort all that out. When you've got a good manager a lot of worries are taken off. All I did was sit and wait for him to finish and then begin again."

She traded Cube for A&M (who had released the first LP on these shores), and Dudgeon for Pete Cage to produce her second album. Then came her first concert appearances, the steady growth of her audience and, ultimately, the success of her first recordings with Glyn Johns.

WHICH BRINGS US BACK to Joan Armatrading today. Naturally, A&M would like to see her achieve the status in America that she has elsewhere in the world, but the label has proven its willingness to stand by her for as long as it takes. I wonder if, earlier in her career, she might have been given a make-it-or-go ultimatum. "A&M is not that sort of label," she contends. "Not just for me, but for all their artists. They tend to think in terms of growth. They don't like to just sign people for a year, hope for the best and then drop them. They tend to build their artists." She mentions Fairport Convention (perhaps because guitarist Jerry Donahue was in her touring band for a few years) as an example of a group that recorded seven or eight albums without having to live up to the gold standard.

The only charge that might be leveled against A&M is that the company's promo department is sometimes too clever for its own good. Last year, Armatrading recorded four songs which were released on a one-sided 12-inch called *How Cruel*. After a steady diet of gimmicky releases to promote other A&M artists, many fans thought Armatrading's EP was yet another tricky promo item unavailable for commercial sale. Meanwhile, misinformed DJs were touting the songs as a sampler from her forthcoming album, due sometime in May. Neither fan nor DJ assump-

tion is true. The EP is an independent collection of material for regular sale. Armatrading is a bit perplexed by all the confusion. "I thought people knew what an EP was," she asserts with a trace of annoyance.

How Cruel's appearance also undermined plans for the U.S. release of a live album circulated in every other country. Armatrading fans will have to seek out the Canadian import, because it will not be showing up in domestic racks. As for the rumor that Armatrading was dissatisfied with the live tapes and fought their release, she contends it was just a matter of not wanting an album and EP to compete. "It sounds alright," she says of the concert LP, "but it's not my all-time favorite live album; Van Morrison's is. It sounded good at the time, but somewhere along the line it lost something."

AS A YOUNG BLACK WOMAN growing up in England, Armatrading takes on charged political symbolism. "All that means is I'm a young Black woman growing up in England," she exclaims with a slightly irritated laugh. She doesn't feel her position as one of England's few major Black female performers gives her the right to comment on things?

She softens. "If you're gonna do something, you should be able to follow it through a bit." She mentions the Rock Against Racism movement as one in which the musicians didn't follow through. "I don't know, because I didn't get involved in it, but from what I read and what I saw of different bands and how they behaved, I just felt they did it for the publicity. They got onto the bandwagon because whoever did that at the time got in the papers, and it was misleading a lot of kids who tried to follow them. It's a serious sort of business, and I don't feel qualified to try to tell anybody what to do in that sense."

She pauses for a moment, then returns to the subject. "The other thing, I think, is that it gets in the way of what you're really trying to do. If you're trying to say, 'Vote for me,' then do that. If you're trying to say, 'Listen to my music,' then do that, because the two sometimes get so mixed up that you're gonna lose out on one." She expresses no doubt about the sincerity of Tom Robinson's "gay thing," but wonders if he might not have hurt himself in becoming such a politicized performer. "His music became something totally different. He's still trying to be a singer, and he's trying to get more people interested in his music, which I think could be hard now."

Relieved that the interview has proceeded with no incident to affirm Armatrading's reputation as a "difficult" subject, I ask her why she feels she has been pegged as such. "It depends on the interviewer," she states simply. "Sometimes you get funny questions, or an awkward person you just don't want to talk to."

And yet, a few minutes later, we are in just that kind of situation that gives rise to a sense of tension between reporter and subject. In response to an offhand question about her new album, Armatrading says it will be a rocker, as Richard Gottehrer's name would lead one to believe. She begins to speak of the session men who will be playing on it.

"If you're going to mention anybody," she suggests, "I'd mention Anton Fig." She points to a small pad on which I am keeping minimal notes. "Write that down, he's incredible." Her manner has such a quiet authority that I instinctively obey. While Armatrading goes on about the South African drummer, the publicist with us mentions [English guitarist] Chris Spedding, who is also helping out with the album. "I'd rather you just mention Anton," Armatrading interjects casually, and I promise to highlight her remarks about him. No, she insists firmly, don't mention Spedding at all, just Anton.

That, perhaps, is the essence of Armatrading's tenuous relationship with the press. It is not so much arrogance as an unyielding desire to reveal only that which she considers relevant.

Whatever ill feeling Armatrading may occasionally create in presenting her personal image, her musical one stands solid as a woman of great talent. As I pack up to leave, she points to my portfolio case and bemoans her unfortunate loss, in a New York cab, of a similar case filled with notebooks of unrecorded songs. I hope she's gotten it back. ■

OUTSIDE THE BANDS DON'T TOE THE LINE: GANG OF FOUR MAKE MUSIC THEIR WAY

TP 59, FEBRUARY 1981

By Jon Young

Would you like your rock with politics or without? Today pop music offers a wide variety of choices: from the violent invective of stereotypic punk bands to the complacency of boogie-'til-you-puke clods and stupefying sensitive folkies. But it's been a long time since rock evidenced any consistent awareness of the real world. Much '70s music seemed insular or self-serving — at least until 1977, when the Sex Pistols, Clash and others revived the illusion (if not the reality) of rock as a social influence.

Those with long memories can recall a different state of affairs. Elvis Presley shook up the world with a vengeance, angering and frightening an unprepared Establishment. The King would have looked pretty silly gyrating to lyrics critical of Eisenhower's social programs, but his rambunctious, open sexuality and mobilization of the kids into a (here it comes) youth culture had a deep and permanent political effect. Likewise, the Beatles whipped their audiences into a frenzy that had broad implications by virtue of its very intensity, although again the content was vague. By the mid-'60s folkies like Bob Dylan had picked up electric guitars, bands like the Byrds presented neutered protest songs, and even the Supremes took a stab at relevance.

The ascendance of Jimi Hendrix, the Doors and others repeated the process somewhat, with even heavier sexual content than Presley and (what the world saw as) drug proselytizing. Unfortunately, that era also ushered in a new emphasis on theatrics, so that bands often played down to their listeners rather than for them; the result was grand spectacles of spiritually cool showmen like Yes and Queen. Hendrix and Cream gave the instrumentalist unprecedented prominence; heavy metal and synth-rock were the outcome. Potentially subversive forces eventually became conservative. The high drama of Led Zeppelin and its progeny lent itself more to militarism than socialism.

You could make a case that a few have never stopped commenting on the world around them. Ray Davies continued to spout his hazy Muswell Hill politics, and the Stones, though probably more interested in cheap thrills than explanation, at least checked the social pulse occasionally. But the majority of mainstream bands came to represent a status quo hostile to change, sustained against other waves by devoted fans — just as partisans of Tony Bennett and Frankie Laine resented the intrusion of Elvis Presley in the '50s.

Another camp felt offended by the Hollywood-like ostentation of contemporary rock's star system. These egalitarians felt the performers' distance from audiences was contrary to rock's populist spirit (whether illusion or fact). The punk explosion spoke directly to those reservations. Suddenly rock was people's music again; even the stars were to remain part of the audience, somehow. The Pistols' shock treatment, with its heavy moralistic streak, sought to banish complacency; Tom Robinson did his best to revive protest music, with little support.

Show business conventions can't be killed off with a few shocking singles and outrageous pronouncements, of course. Consequently, some artists feel compelled to protest repeatedly that they're not part of the same old routine; others exhibit defensiveness because they are. Interest-ingly, many British bands who've visited the States lately have expressed disappointment and even bitterness at the way the Clash turned out. The general feeling seems to be: "They led us to believe they'd be something different, but all they really stand for is the traditional arrogance and greed."

BRITAIN'S GANG OF FOUR, with their stern pronouncements about the state of the world, have ventured bravely onto the music scene as charges of sellout and dishonesty fly every which way. *Entertainment!*, their debut LP, is primarily a treatise on the exploitation of the have-nots by the haves. The Gang of Four is not subtle; the following message (among others) is on their LP cover: "Those who will decide what everyone will do grow rich because the decisions are made in their interest. They are pleased at how well they rule others. The others smile too, thinking that their rulers know best."

The Gang's songs probe for the rotten core. "Ether" talks about "dirt behind the daydream." "Contract" considers the way a couple uses each other sexually. "Not Great Men" addresses the class system. The Gang of Four plays serious music.

But they play party music, too. As a band they are startling and original, using a formula that's so simple it's brilliant. Jon King sings in a vigorous chant-shout, never quite forgetting the melody. Andy Gill rakes the guitar, producing challenging chords and bristling feedback. Though both are fine, the musical emphasis is often on the amazing rhythm section of bassist Dave Allen and drummer Hugo Burnham. Together, they provide a supple, steady beat that's irresistible and more flexible than much conventional funk. The combination of King and Gill's prickly top with Allen and Burnham's rubbery bottom creates a bracing experience akin to a pleasurable electric shock.

The Gang of Four can't get much airplay on stodgy American radio, but their obvious musical excellence has garnered them a respectable audience; they already sell out clubs and small halls. When finally tracked down for an interview — not an easy task, with their hectic schedule — they're waiting for a soundcheck in a Manhattan hall, preparing for the last date of a short but grueling third tour of the States. Gill and Allen, who've been drafted to speak, look bleary-eyed and half-dead from the cumulative effects of long car trips and post-gig interviews at four a.m. Word is that they'll talk to anyone, anytime.

Are they burned out?

"Yeah, fuckin' hell," Allen mutters. "This was supposed to be a 10-day tour to try out some new material and help the release of the EP. But it's turned into nearly four weeks and 18 dates — not quite what we wanted."

How did that happen?

"Dunno. That's the way it goes. You can't just tell promoters when you want to come. It's when they want you."

Rubbing his red eyes, Gill grunts something about the hair of the dog. Allen adds, "I'd like to have a few drinks before I go on," and trails off, mumbling in Scottish.

Part of the problem with braving America on a low budget, Allen explains, is that the stretches between cities are a lot bigger than in England. "If you did a well-ordered 40-date tour of England you'd only travel 50 miles a day. But on the 18 dates we've been doing, we've been driving up to 400 miles a day and playing that night."

He adds that they see no alternative to going through the wringer. "It is difficult to talk about it, because what can you do? How can you change it? It wouldn't be very effective at all just putting out records. We were almost on *Saturday Night Live*; that would have done the work of three months of gigs."

Contrary to assumptions, the Gang harbors no hangups about selling their music. "You want to sell a certain amount of records," Gill states. "It would be silly to say we don't," Allen adds. "Otherwise, we wouldn't be touring at all." Allen feels that Warners may have been a little nervous about signing them because of their art-student overtones. He doesn't feel the company was worried about their politics, which could easily be construed as anti-capitalist. "It didn't even cross their collective minds."

Drummer Hugo Burnham, who has just joined the discussion, has other ideas: "I think there was probably a certain amount of wanting to sign a radical English band. We are known as a political band to the American market. CBS has the Clash, and I think possibly one of the assumptions was that we're a band in that mold."

Allen: "I would disagree on that, because the Clash obviously mold their songs to the States."

Burnham: "But that's irrelevant. It's an image. They were signed as young radical English punks, angry young punks."

Allen: "What I'm saying, though, is that I doubt whether Warners would ever have expected us to change our music."

Gill: "They just wanted their equivalent of a heavy white band, not a pop band or a rock band."

Yet Gill professes optimism that American audiences will be receptive to the band's message. "I feel Americans can probably handle the idea of serious lyrics less problematically than their British counterparts, because there's a terrible fear of being pretentious in England."

"There's a fear of people being educated, of displaying any sort of intellect in the sphere of rock and roll," Allen says. "There's an obsession with this dull brain working-class attitude or image."

But do American audiences actually listen to what Gang of Four has to say? If you've seen one of their shows you might find it difficult to answer yes. Plenty of people at the band's gigs obviously know the tunes by heart, and when that magnificent rhythm of section kicks into gear the fans are off and dancing — digging the groove and oblivious to all else.

Allen disagrees: "I don't think they could avoid listening. If you read a review of tonight's gig next week it'll probably give you quite an insight into the band. It'll go beyond, 'They strutted around and posed,' which is what you get with most bands. It'll go into the lyrics."

"'Great guitar' or 'great rhythm section' means fuck-all anymore," Burnham says. "Because it's so different, they'll try to qualify it, describe it."

"A whole new set of criteria have appeared in the press — I'm not saying it's just us," Gill says. "The way bands are talked about has changed quite a lot."

They claim to be satisfied with the public stance they've hammered out for the band but confess to worrying still about avoiding clichés. Burnham explains the problem is not so much changing the way the band is now, as "maintaining the standards we have in six months or a year's time. People say, 'Has success changed you' as soon as you've got a few bob in your pocket. People expect you to go and do what the Clash did, which was totally become the boys in the band, jumpin' up and down, regurgitating the old myths of rock and roll, with a strong gang image."

Weren't the Clash always that way? Gill thinks not. "What they first came out with was original, different, startling sort of music."

"It was," Burnham maintains, "very anarchic. It was: 'We're making a lot of noise and we're very angry. We're not sure why we're very angry or what we're going to made a lot of noise about, but we're doing it, and this is the way we're doing it.' And it changed — developed, if you like."

"It's the same with many groups," Gill adds.

"Unfortunately," Burnham says, "that's the example that's easiest to draw upon. It always seems to come up. Continuous comparisons are made between us and the Clash in America." Insultingly so, judging from the tone of his voice.

Well ... ahem ... is the Gang of Four a political band? By now Allen and Gill have drifted off to the soundcheck, leaving Burnham to field the queries.

"Yes. It's down very much to what people understand by the word 'political.' A lot of people think 'political' is solely on the level of governmental-type politics. We are political in that the things that we talk, discuss, argue and sing (or whatever) about are the politics of your daily life: the individual attitudes you've been taught or trained, wrong or right. Everything you do, ostensibly, is a political act, even if it's saying, 'You shouldn't mix rock and politics, 'cause I hate politics.' That is a political act.

"None of us belongs to a political party. Our politics are socialist to differing degrees." He adds that while there are Marxist aspects to the band's attitudes, he doesn't feel he understands enough of the philosophy to call himself a Marxist.

Asked to detail more of the Gang of Four party line, he mutters, "I'd better be careful," and pauses to think. "Generally speaking, we try to encourage wider thought, appreciation of different attitudes — not just accepting the status quo of attitudes towards other people, be it your wife, your kids or the Russians."

On a slightly lighter note, Burnham says the band signed with EMI in England because the company "gave us the contract we want, which gives us freedom, control and autonomy." EMI, he adds, "has the wherewithal and finance to market a record properly. We want to sell records, which is why we make records — not just so I can give one to my mum or my friends."

And what of those who charged sellout? "Fuckin' naïve wankers! It's very naïve to say, 'How can you be socialist and sign with that?' People should be putting their own houses in order before they criticize things they don't understand. I have no qualms about being with either Warners or EMI. That is no reflection on how happy I am with either of them."

WILL THEY BECOME POPULAR? Will success pervert them? Will they become too doctrinaire to function? The band still subsists largely on its original repertoire, and their equal partnership seems to ensure that fresh songs will be produced slowly. (Their musicianship is impeccable, fortunately.) They believe people really do listen to what they say, and, crucially, they're willing to work themselves silly to make their points. The Gang of Four may agonize over the moral implications, but they're realistic about the business they're in.

Can a mortal rock band walk the path of righteousness and stay sane? If the Gang of Four can't do it, nobody can. ■

QUOTES OF THE DECADE

"We didn't look at music as an art form but as a job we're best suited for, for which we can get paid wages."

—TERRY HALL OF THE SPECIALS AND FUN BOY 3
(1982) TP 74

This piece accurately reflects my experience with Adam that day. He came across as articulate, driven and joyless. Other band members were in the limo on the ride to the gig, but they were mostly silent as Adam engaged in his endless spiel, occasionally detouring to make a snarky remark to one or another of them that they probably weren't allowed to respond to. I remember an inside joke about bassist Gary Tibbs (present at the time) and his previous involvement with Roxy Music, which felt like mean-boy teasing afterward.

A close after-show look at the sweaty Adam in full, crude makeup added a tawdry vibe. (JY)

SINGING IN THE RAIN:
ADAM ANT TAKES THE U.S. BY STORM

TP 69, JANUARY 1982

By Jon Young

You may not like us now, but you will
—"DON'T BE SQUARE (BE THERE)"

A threat? A promise? An idle boast? Over the last year, Antmusic has established a foothold on these shores, and the small but hardy legions of American Antpeople may eventually become a swarm.

Friend and foe alike must prepare for the possibility that Adam and the Ants will achieve massive popularity here. They have already done it in England and a score or so of other countries all over the globe. "For me that just goes to prove the belief I have that there's a need for show business and color everywhere in the world," remarks 27-year-old Adam Ant (Stuart Goddard).

Whether the specter of Antmusic is to be regarded as cause for celebration or despair depends on your preferences in pop and your prejudices regarding the nature of mass culture. Adam and his fellow Ants — Marco Pirroni (guitar), Terry Lee Miall (drums), Chris Hughes (a.k.a. Merrick: drums, producer) and Gary Tibbs (bass) — play bubblegum music, more or less. *Kings of the Wild Frontier* and the new *Prince Charming* are loaded with snappy beats, ingeniously simple melodies and Adam's exhibitionist singing. For visual impact, the gang dons showy costumes: pirate garb, native American paint and feathers, highwayman capes and just about anything else suitable for a masquerade party — sometimes all at once. The implication is that you're not to take this too seriously; just have fun and feel free to dress up yourself. Adam and the Ants recall the flash of glitter rock with a reaching out to the audience that hints at the idealism of punk.

Boasting five consecutive smash singles in the UK, Adam is now having a go at America. *Kings* has reportedly "shifted" over 300,000 units, quite respectable for a debut. The Ants already headline middle-level venues here, and many of their enthusiastic fans dress up and make up just like the group, sometimes even better. Shades of Kiss!

Adam Ant regards the plump U.S. market with the coolness of a sharp businessman, not the passion of his persona. "We have to go through a process of proving ourselves by our work," he muses, "and it will be a very gradual process. I think we'll build in the U.S. 'cause I'm willing to work hard; I'm willing to wait. I'm in no hurry."

REO Speedwagon couldn't have said it better.

THE ANTS ARE IN NEW YORK CITY for less than a week. After a handful of shows they'll move to the West Coast for a few more, then to Australia, where they're stars, and Japan, where they hope for the kind of reception Kiss and Cheap Trick got. This Friday afternoon, band and crew gather in the lobby of their Manhattan hotel before motoring to the evening's venue, a Long Island concert hall. Being the star, Adam is naturally the last to appear. His blue Adidas jogging suit serves as a disguise of sorts — what does Adam wear on the street anyway? — but the braids in his hair belie the half-hearted stab at normalcy. A few nervous kids stop Adam for autographs at the main entrance and then the caravan hits the road.

Though not yet a big star here, Adam Ant runs on a tight schedule: he's a hit with the media. In *TP*'s case, that means he'll conduct the interview as the limo makes its way out to Long Island. The prospect of competing with noisy rush hour traffic, coupled with Adam's fatigued and vacant expression, does not bode well.

Never fear; this guy is a professional. Once we're rolling and the conversation begins, Adam Ant comes to life like a switched-on TV. He speaks quickly, courteously and articulately, not always in response to the question, but he certainly has his lines memorized cold.

Adam is well aware that other UK sensations have met an indifferent response in the States.

"I'm very intrigued by what's happened to people that were in the position I'm in right now," he says. "For instance, T. Rex came over with massive success in England and just did nothing. That happened even to bands respected in England, like Roxy Music."

A self-styled student of the "history books of pop music," Adam has an idea why his predecessors failed. "I think it's because they didn't make the idea simple enough for the commercial marketplace. A good designer makes it simple; a bad designer confuses it. Simplicity is an art.

"In England, you can achieve overnight success. The beginning of my success was going on *Top of the Pops* on TV. Overnight 250,000 people decided they wanted to buy our record, which suddenly made us important from a commercial point of view, and the media followed it through." A quick score is far less likely in the vast U.S.; with its thousands of radio playlists, the States must be conquered a piece at a time.

As he does so often, Adam muses on the importance of media attention. "People forget that even Bob Dylan was as much a product of press coverage as anything else, which doesn't negate the guy's status as a genius. Everybody in the past 20 years of pop music has been given to the public through the media. If you deny that you're very foolish. I think a lot of my colleagues in other bands won't admit that. They seem to expect audiences to believe they have some kind of divine inspiration.

"I know I'm not a genius because I have to work too damn hard. I think the only originality I have is the way I put ideas that have taken place in history together. Lenny Bruce is the first one I heard admit that; I'm just following it up. He's a big inspiration for me." (Indeed, Adam praises Bruce throughout the interview and quotes from the comedian's routines afterwards.)

"Any status I achieve will be the result of hard work and nothing else, so I have to be very methodical. I know my limitations. I don't ever fool myself into thinking I can sit back and let it all happen. I don't trust that."

As for who *is* a genius — that is, "someone who

thinks completely differently" — he cites Bruce, Muhammad Ali, Mel Brooks, Michael Jackson, Stevie Wonder — and his own ex-manager, Malcolm McLaren.

Adam talks at length about his (mostly American) heroes, switching effortlessly from the role of star to fan. "I met Robert De Niro the other day," he recalls, "and I was as speechless as some kid who likes Adam and the Ants and meets me." He also shows he's not just one of rock's cultural illiterates by remarking that he likes Perry Como and Frank Sinatra. "I'd be honored to meet them. Some people think I'd be far more honored to meet somebody a little more hip, Johnny Rotten or somebody like that, which I wouldn't be."

Adam exhibits excusable pride at his acceptance by the old guard. He recalls that Bob Dylan expressed interest in Antmusic on his last visit to London. He relates how Paul McCartney's kids asked *him* for an autograph and various Led Zeppelin offspring brought their parents to an Antgig. "If you cut all the crap out," Adam concludes, "there always should be respect between musicians. It's basically only record company and press antagonism that says everybody's gotta be better than everybody else."

LISTEN TO ADAM ANT long enough, however, and his hostile attitudes emerge. The British music press, dreaded and hated by so many rock and rollers, receives special venom. "When you start out, you need as much coverage as you can get," he says, blood pressure slowly rising. "They [the music press] are in a position to take a group that looks exciting, build them up and claim the credit — and when the group makes it, they hammer 'em. But I decided they were gonna have no part in it; our success was the result of going on TV and doing interviews with the national press [daily newspapers]."

He continues with angry satisfaction. "They've called me the flavor of the month for the last 18 months, but I don't care. [*Sure! —Ed.*] I don't write songs for them; I write songs for the kids and myself. The press don't buy 'em anyway; they just lig 'em off the record companies." Elsewhere, Adam slips and concedes that nasty re-

views can be "very hurtful."

"The reviews of our single ['Prince Charming'] in Britain were great. They didn't have the guts to come out and say, 'I hate it,' because they might want to do an interview with me. Quite rightly. I can sell papers for them. They know that."

Despite his obvious sensitivity, Adam also expresses confidence. He says the papers "can call me all the names under the sun and it doesn't make any difference. If they say anything false, I'm gonna sue 'em. I've got very, very good lawyers and I use them a lot. I'll win most of the time as well. Maybe it's some kind of crusade for artists, if you like, 'cause I think they [the press] are assholes." Adam and Carol Burnett would probably hit it off.

Among the successful Antsuits to date are an injunction to prevent British Decca Records from releasing old demos and a damage action against a major daily for publishing without permission a years-old caricature Adam drew of Margaret Thatcher. "Early in my career I got taken for a ride," Adam remarks by way of explaining his fondness for lawsuits. "I'm not impressed by what people say. I only go by what they do."

As for critics, he feels they "should be able to make an opinion of any artist's work without involving personalities. If a guy doesn't like you, that's his prerogative, but he should say why, 'cause then he's being constructive, and maybe that'll help the artist to be better."

IF ADAM SEEMS unduly sour for someone so popular, consider this: Until the Ants conquered England in the latter part of 1980, he suffered years of failure and neglect. From 1976 on, he was active in a London music scene that produced the Sex Pistols, Clash, Siouxsie and the Banshees and numerous others, but it always seemed to be Adam Ant who got the shortest shrift and the least encouragement. The Ants' recorded debut, two tracks on 1978's *Jubilee* soundtrack LP, was truly embarrassing. Even an official Antbiography written in 1980 acknowledges that, in 1978, "The Ants were very unfashionable and used to get slagged off by the rock press with monotonous regularity … The Ants continued to languish in relative obscurity."

Dirk Wears White Sox, recorded in August 1979 and released a few months later, did little to help. A grim, lyric-heavy disc, it explores alienation ("Digital Tenderness"), John Kennedy's assassination ("Catholic Day"), sexual excess ("Cleopatra") and the like, crippled by weak music and listless musicianship.

Adam looks back on the LP as an "apprenticeship" and adds, "I was going through a very esoteric, deep, self-searching period. There were certain things that were hurting me emotionally that I just ripped out of myself. I hadn't really discovered what I wanted to say clearly; I was very confused. It's a very heavy album for me. I can't listen to it." In other words, *Dirk* was little more than a cult record.

"When I'd done that album, I realized that wasn't enough," he reflects. "I did want everybody to buy an album I'd made, so I faced up to it and got on with it."

The catalyst in Adam's transformation from [zero] to hero was Malcolm McLaren, infamous ex-manager of the Sex Pistols and the man behind Bow Wow Wow. Adam calls McLaren a genius, but then he'd probably call the devil a genius, too. McLaren assumed management of the Ants in late 1979; by January 1980 he'd "stolen" Adam's original band for his own project, Bow Wow Wow, and the head Ant was forced to start all over from scratch.

Two years later, Adam looks back on the relationship with a feeling of vindication. "I think McLaren has a big effect on everybody that meets him, 'cause he's a very clever man. I paid him about $500 a week to work for me for two months; he was well-paid for what he did. He came up with a few ideas, but there's always good ideas about; it's much harder to make an idea into reality. He can't make his ideas reality because otherwise Bow Wow Wow would be selling the records we're selling. That isn't bitterness, that's a statement — a hardcore business statement.

"He's a great one for telling you you're making it difficult for yourself, but he can't seem to do things for himself. The Sex Pistols were an accident, really, and he knows that. He didn't make any money out of it, Virgin Records did. So, for somebody who tries to tell the world he's in it for the money, he's not a very good businessman." Excuse Adam Ant for gloating a little.

FOR LIGHT AND LIVELY FUN, it's hard to beat *Kings of the Wild Frontier*. Featuring the fab hits "Dog Eat Dog" and "Antmusic," the first LP from the current Ants cajoles rather than assaults; though Adam offers substance along with the high spirits — his grasping at innocence is bittersweet — a good time comes first. He views the difference between *Dirk* and *Kings* as comparable to "the Velvet Underground and *Transformer* by Lou Reed. Or listen to Jonathan Richman on the first Modern Lovers album and then listen to *Rock 'n' Roll With the Modern Lovers*. They're completely different varieties."

Adam makes no bones about his craft. "I'm involved in escapist entertainment. That's good when you have a worldwide depression, you're going through a terrible austerity period and there's not much money about. I think it parallels what happened in Hollywood during the Great Depression. Busby Berkeley was escapist. People went to the cinema to hope. It made them feel good, and I think that's what Adam and the Ants do. About the only service one can offer onstage is to provide an escape from reality for kids. If you don't, you're not doing anything: that's not show business."

Typically, he draws another parallel with film. "When I go see *Raiders of the Lost Ark* or *Star Wars*, I'm not thinking about business I've gotta do; I'm thinking about what's on the screen. The scripts are very good scripts, they may seem banal, but they're very good. If you go into it, you realize there's more to it. It's really quite serious. It's like being a comedian. People think it's dead easy to make people laugh. It isn't. It's very hard.

"Same with Adam and the Ants. Some of our lyrics have got quite serious social ideals behind them, but they're personal ones and they're only opinions. I don't intend to preach."

Lest anyone think he undervalues his work, Adam adds, "I'm serious about what I do. If I wasn't, I couldn't have a conversation about it. I'm very self-analytical because I think it's important to know what you're saying. That's why I classified the music as Antmusic, which is a very pretentious, very arrogant thing to do — but not in a negative way. We're arrogant out of necessity. If you don't classify yourself, you're classified in a derogatory way by other people. They'd call it mindless tribalism and it would catch on, just like punk did.

"I think the slogan 'Antmusic for Sex People' means nothing, but it could mean everything. I think the group is interested in making music, dressing sexy, looking pretty and young and not listening when we're told there's no fun."

In brief, Adam Ant is anathema to those who demand meaning in their music. "I think far too many people are looking for messages and directions from artists when they should listen a bit more to the music, look at what they're wearing and enjoy it."

THE NEW *PRINCE CHARMING* LP should solidify Adam and the Ants' position back home and establish the band further here. In effect a second album, it suffers a bit from the sophomore jinx but offers enough thrills to satisfy Antpeople. More objective observers will note the title track's soliloquy contains the line "Ridicule is nothing to be scared of." The artist's chip-on-the-shoulder attitude sometimes intrudes on the entertainment.

In his metamorphosis from punk rock also-ran to king of the UK charts, Adam Ant resembles the loser in the Charles Atlas ads who develops muscles and goes back to the beach to punish his tormentors. Adam has proven something to those who once brushed him off, just as the former weakling gets back at the guys who kicked sand in his face. You have to wonder, though, when Adam Ant will start to enjoy himself. ∎

QUOTES OF THE DECADE

"It's all very well being clever and playing in ridiculous time signatures, but it doesn't make for a good pop song. "
—NICK RHODES of DURAN DURAN (1983) TP 90

RAVING FAVES

MOST IMAGINATIVE PACKAGING OF AN LP

TP 69, JANUARY 1982

A lot of readers seemed to think "packaging" was synonymous with "cover art." We wanted concepts, not misconceptions — the whole banana (which is what some Favers gave us by nominating the first, peelable Velvet Underground album).

Robert Johnson, for one, was "shocked at how little imagination is used to package a record," although "most of the bands that have amusing ideas in this area spend so much time on the damn packaging that they almost forget to make a record."

One of Johnson's choices, Public Image Ltd.'s *Metal Box* ("provokes as much thought or arguments as the records that come in it"), was shared by enough people to propel it into a first-place tie with that classic of flashy marketing and bad design, the Rolling Stones' zip-up *Sticky Fingers*. (Unlike the PiL box, which protects the records, the Stones' zipper was notorious for scratching them.) The Who's *Live at Leeds* is fondly remembered for containing (in Michael Dawson's words) "more giveaway junk than any other album." Next up are Alice Cooper's old desk and panties ("a perfect fit"—Fruff) with *School's Out*; and the *Metal Box* of its time, Small Faces' (cardboard) tobacco tin, about which Barnes Newberry wails, "I never could figure out how to open the UK version!"

1. Public Image Ltd. *Metal Box*
2. Rolling Stones *Sticky Fingers*
3. Who *Live at Leeds*
4. Alice Cooper *School's Out*
   Small Faces *Ogdens' Nut Gone Flake*

More Spin Art:
Beatles *Sgt. Pepper*
Return of the Durutti Column
Jethro Tull *Thick as a Brick*
Orchestral Manoeuvres in the Dark
   first UK LP (die-cut hole cover)
Velvet Underground and Nico

We had a checkered relationship with the future Rock and Roll Hall of Famer. When the Runaways played CBGB in August 1976, their forced jailbait salaciousness and traditional guitar rock put them out of step with the more innovative bands we were used to seeing on that stage. So, when Jett later launched her solo career with an album of (mostly) covers performed with an equal lack of contemporary style, we published a harshly negative review that prompted indignant-going-on-angry letters from Joan and her manager. Perhaps as a way to make amends, we ran a short, uncritical profile in TP 56, giving her the last word about the record we'd panned. "The album was fun for me to do. I wasn't trying to prove nothin'. It was a transitional album from the Runaways to a solo thing, to keep my name out there until I had a new band.'"

Eighteen months later, by which time Jett had proved her commercial potential with a chart-topping single, we bowed to our own sense of commercial potential and put her on the cover. We even did a flexidisc with her later on.

JOAN JETT: SELLING RECORDS IS THE BEST REVENGE

TP 74, JUNE 1982

By Jim Green

"I love rock and roll" has to be one of the corniest, old-hat, lowest-common-denominator clichés of all time, right? The phrase conjures images of bare-chested blue-jeaned males (species *beerbelli beerswiggerus*) at open-air concerts bellowing "Boogie!" in hopes of another 20-minute guitar solo.

Some might say that Joan Jett's smash recording of "I Love Rock 'n Roll" is puerile airwave fodder. The typical *Trouser Press* reader, sipping Perrier while Throbbing Gristle or the Fire Engines hack away on the headphones, would probably note that the song, while not without charm, lacks specificity and is a sort of received innocence.

Well, it is, and it isn't. First of all, it says "rock and roll," not "rock," that fatuously open-ended category that includes such sludge as Styx (*and all those other popular groups—Ed.*). "Rock and roll" has maintained its artistic integrity; "rock," its once-progressive descendant since revealed to be artificially flavored and colored, is a term now used for elevator music or combos at weddings ("Play a rock, fellas").

From the cultural angle, Chuck Berry played "Rock & Roll Music," the Velvet Underground affirmed that "Rock & Roll" was definitely "all riiight" and Gary Glitter kicked off a string of

11 British Top 10 hits with "Rock & Roll (Parts 1 & 2)," half of which crystallized the essence of the music with no more lyrics than "Hey!" and the title. These songs are simple, even trashy, and meaningfully basic yet basically meaningful. You can chase your tail trying to define the spirit of rock and roll but the above trio explain it without even trying. If you have to ask, you'll never know.

Now the Stones may like rock and roll, but Joan Jett loves it. Indeed, who else could have the best-selling album and single in the country stating, "I love rock and roll" and mean it? But Joan Jett is for real. How much she means what she sings — lives it — can be approximated only by unfolding her story. Joan Jett couldn't have sold out, 'cause she couldn't even buy her way in.

JOAN JETT wasn't kidding when she sang about having a "Bad Reputation" on her solo debut LP. Manager-producer Kenny Laguna notes that when he first encountered Jett, "She was the wildest kid I ever met in my life, especially for a girl."

Sitting in her publicist's office, demurely sipping a diet cola, the 23-year-old Jett (she was always Joan) discusses her indiscreet past. Born in Philadelphia, she moved around the East with her family before coming to Los Angeles (from Baltimore) at age 14; a few years later her parents separated.

Jett's new hometown had plenty of nightlife, but not for female teenagers. A kid walking around West Hollywood in the wee hours was a likely target for police hassling. Jett later wrote "Victim of Circumstance" from experience: "The cops were waiting when the sun came up ... The cops knew who I was, where I lived."

By 1976, Jett was rhythm guitarist in the Runaways, the teenaged, all-female band that erupted like a ripe pimple on the face of L.A.'s forever-acne youth scene. Jett is tired of recounting the Runaways' complicated story, but feels the group was historically important: "We were breaking barriers, in a sense — opening doors for others, taking all the shit so other people could get in." Surprisingly, she sounds uncomfortable giving herself that credit. To her, the Runaways were

something she was determined to do — and did.

At the time, though, the Runaways came across as the latest hype from Kim Fowley, a multi-talented character whose greatest ability is a knack for blurring the extent (in his favor, of course) of his involvement with every artist with whom he's worked. No doubt Fowley was crucial in getting the Runaways off the ground, but his self-aggrandizement made the band appear to have sprung full-blown from his brow.

"Kim was the middleman," Jett recounts. Two days after meeting this guitar-playing girl who wanted to form an all-female band, Fowley introduced Jett to drummer Sandy West, who wanted the same thing. "We lived an hour and a half away from each other. We exchanged phone numbers, I went over to her house, we jammed — me on my Sears guitar. We called up Kim, said, 'Listen to this,' and played some basic Chuck Berry nonsense into the phone. He said, 'Sounds great, let's form a band.'

"There weren't lots of girls who played instruments in those days. Who was there? Fanny? I mean, who played sweaty rock and roll?"

Good question. Goldie (Genya Ravan) and the Gingerbreads were an all-female group that played a few chic parties and scored a British Top 30 hit — but that had been 10 years earlier. Fanny was a light pop-rock outfit noted more for its producers (Richard Perry, Todd Rundgren) than its own prowess. Birtha, a Fanny knock-off, was destined for instant bargain-bindom. Suzi Quatro was a gutsy role model but had all male bandmates. "It was a prime opportunity, but it seemed like we happened too soon. It was amazing the way people who'd never even heard the group would say we sucked!" Jett spits out disgustedly. "I'd say, 'What songs of theirs have you heard?' 'I haven't heard any of their songs, I just heard they suck.' That's how intense it got. It made me wanna puke."

This was before punk reared its delightfully ugly little head. But while the Runaways had the same nose-thumbing spirit as the new-wavers-to-be, they aspired to play mainstream-oriented music, however hard-edged their approach. And mainstream American rock, as we all know, is played by seasoned pros, not green upstarts — and certainly not girls.

Joan Jett always personified the Runaways. She was the band's most prolific songwriter and, although neither lead guitarist nor lead singer, was most often singled out as the fave Runaway. When singer Cherie Currie left for a solo career, Jett took over as lead vocalist.

In 1979, the Runaways were out of money, out of a recording contract and, Jett says, "out of spirit. The press had always given us a hard time — that was constant. A couple of the girls wanted to go in a more heavy-metal direction while I wanted to stay more mainstream rock and roll. One day we had a meeting and I said, 'I quit.'" (It was an amicable split; Jett is still on good terms with her ex-bandmates.)

KENNY LAGUNA and his partner Ritchie Cordell met Joan Jett when they worked with her on the soundtrack to a film called *We're All Crazy Now* in August, 1979.

"She was a rock and roll lunatic," Laguna remembers. "She was giving me this strong vibe that here was something special. At that time, though, she wasn't looking so good. She'd been through the Runaways, and she'd abused herself. It scared me because here's this little girl who reminded me of a lot of people I knew when I was that age, that I watched deteriorate because they were ignored and frustrated by the business."

Laguna had experienced the depredations of the music business firsthand. In the late '60s, he was one of the studio musicians who churned out bubblegum music, playing on the Ohio Express's "Yummy Yummy Yummy" and "Chewy Chewy" and the Archies' "Bang Shang a Lang." He also worked with Tommy James & the Shondells, singing backup on "Mony Mony."

"I don't say I was as significant as Joan Jett, but I was playing on hit records, making $2,000 a week and all I was thinking was, 'Where can I get the next 25 ups so I can keep doing this?' I wish I'd had someone to take care of me at some point in my career. We didn't know all this business was going on above us, and that when this thing would end it would end suddenly. The awful part

was watching a few friends die. I felt so bad for this girl [Jett]. I didn't want to see it happen to her, and I, like, adopted her. She had one pair of pants!"

We're All Crazy Now, a film which was never released, was supposed to star the Runaways. Laguna had no idea what he was getting into when he and Cordell (who produced and wrote for Tommy James) were asked to help Jett compose the soundtrack. "I'd heard of the Runaways," Laguna says, "'cause there was talk of my producing them, but I'd opted for Greg Kihn instead. The name Joan Jett didn't mean anything to me, but my old lady" — wife Meryl, who now co-manages Jett — "said Joan was really significant and told me to go ahead." The film, referred to by Laguna as "that horror," turned out to be a "no-class move — but then, Joan's been involved with a lot of no-class moves in the past."

Laguna's "adoption" of Jett was more than an act of pity. "She gave me the same tingle I got when I worked with Darlene Love. It was long after Phil Spector had made her legendary, [but] Darlene still did something that was magical — she made a song sound more intense than it was written." In her own way, says Laguna, Jett did the same thing.

As they worked together on the film soundtrack Laguna became convinced he should do an album with Jett. She had already dabbled in post-Runaways recording with some classy help.

"I was in L.A., wondering what I was gonna do with my life," Jett recalls. "The Sex Pistols, one of my favorite bands, had broken up by then, too, so I gave [drummer Paul Cook and guitarist Steve Jones] a call and said, 'You wanna cut a couple of sides with me and produce?' They said, 'Yeah.'" Three tracks, cut in London, were issued on an EP in Europe, but Jett wasn't pleased with the way it was being promoted and had it quashed.

Laguna and Cordell agreed to bankroll an album. ("I was just helping her out," the former says modestly.) Laguna used his Who connections to book recording time in the Who's Ramport Studios during the winter of 1979/80, and an industry friend arranged a European label deal.

A good start, right? Well, this is just when it began to get tough.

"I DIDN'T WANT to be her manager in the worst way," Laguna now groans in simulated pain. "I had a policy of never holding someone's life in my hands." Unfortunately for Laguna's resolve, there'd been a communications breakdown between Jett and her previous manager, ending that hook-up, and a replacement manager fell through as well.

"I didn't want to see her lose herself, so I figured I'd just try to help her survive until she could get other management. That I was stuck being responsible for her career would keep me up all night. In Holland once, I went to the hospital for two days with a migraine headache. I kept telling people, 'I'm not her manager, I'm her producer.' I was embarrassed, like managing was some kind of disgrace. I thought if she could get up to the level of $2,000 per gig, they could make a living out of it."

That's right, "they": Joan Jett and the Blackhearts. She'd auditioned musicians in New York and come up with guitarist Eric Amble (later replaced by Ricky Byrd), drummer Lee Crystal (who's played with Johnny Thunders, Syl Sylvain and a New York band called the Boyfriends) and young bassist Gary Ryan.

Money worries were at the root of Laguna's migraines. "I was ready to jump off a building. Everybody wanted money, you can't do anything without money, and nobody wanted to pay us. On the road, the band rented a motor home, which they all slept in, except for Joanie — unless they drove all night between gigs to save on her hotel room. They were living — including Joan — on $10 a day. That was it."

Laguna received help, gratis, from his own manager, Steve Leber. Ian Copeland's Frontier Booking International helped out with gigs. The free advice temporarily dunked Laguna into boiling water when Leber suggested that having Jett's album, *Bad Reputation*, out domestically could up the nightly take a couple of C-notes. An initial pressing of 5,000 copies on their own Blackheart label sold out in a week. That was okay. At such a low level of distribution, Laguna could get away with shipping to stores COD. (He had to, since the money to manufacture the records was borrowed in the first place.) As sales neared the 20,000 mark, though, "Everybody wanted to do it like a real business, where you wait three months to get paid," Laguna says. "I was selling so many records that I couldn't afford to print them up!"

It then occurred to Laguna to get Jett a label deal for the U.S. "Surely Joan Jett will be picked up by a label now, am I right? No. I have Bill Curbishley, who manages the fuckin' Who, and Steve Leber [whose management firm, Leber-Krebs, has handled heavyweights like AC/DC, Aerosmith and Ted Nugent] calling in favors to get Joan Jett signed, and they still won't sign her." Even clout wasn't working for Joan Jett.

"We had guys saying, 'If it's Joan Jett, we don't even want to listen'; letters from famous A&R men about how her voice isn't up to the standards of their label. Everybody passed on her, most of them three or four times. I even offered it to one of the big companies for free: 'Look, manufacture the fuckin' record, collect, then pay me at the end of the month.' They passed. They thought she didn't have enough class for their label."

Today those same industry people claim they never heard Jett do the song that made her a star. "Bullshit," Laguna snorts. "'I Love Rock 'n Roll' was on the tape I'd been showing people all along, even three years ago. They all heard it, and they didn't want it."

Jett had recorded the ditty (originally done by the Arrows, a trans-Atlantic group, in the mid-'70s) with Paul Cook and Steve Jones. Unlike her other tracks with the former Sex Pistols, it went unreleased mainly due to a slight fluff on Cook's part.

Enter Neil Bogart — or rather, re-enter Neil Bogart. The mogul behind Buddah Records, where most bubblegum rock stuck, needed no introduction to Laguna. Now he was head of Boardwalk Records, and he was interested in Joan Jett.

"Neil was hipped to the record by the attorneys," Laguna says — in the music business, lawyers are increasingly assuming the role of A&R liaisons. "He came down to see Joanie and signed her." You can exhale now.

JOAN JETT HAD NOT YET begun to fight. She was signed, but how could her album be sold?

Concerts were a start. Jett was gigging frequently, and Laguna reckoned her live rep had already sold her album with a great degree of efficacy. Live shows were also a hook for radio people, like Dan Neer at New York's WNEW-FM, a key station in what came to be called "the Blackheart network."

John DeBella of Long Island's WLIR-FM was turned on to *Bad Reputation* by the station's music director, Ray White. DeBella was skeptical of Jett's punkette cover pose but, by his own account, fell in love with the record. His on-the-air persona dictated making wisecracks about her appearance, however. One day Jett called him up during his show, saying she'd heard he was bad-rapping her music.

Not true, but DeBella seized the opportunity to put Jett's call over the airwaves. After some verbal sparring, Jett invited herself up to the station to pull down DeBella's pants while he was on the air. And she did. This made hay for Jett on Long Island. A local club last summer turned away business ("Traffic was backed up for miles," DeBella claims), and fire marshals barely let her do a short set. To make up for it Jett played a free open-air concert sponsored and broadcast by WLIR. "It was scary," DeBella says, "a half-mile strip packed so tight there was nowhere to move. The estimate was a crowd of 27,000" — but he terms that conservative.

Not everything was rosy just yet. Radio stations that looked on Joan Jett with favor were definitely in the minority. Independent promo man [and former ad salesman for *Trouser Press*] Joel Webber was "working" *Bad Reputation* and meeting stiff resistance: "The consultants, firms and individuals that tell stations who hire 'em which records to pick and which to avoid were openly hostile to Joan Jett's image. The catch phrase was, 'If we have Pat Benatar, why should we have Joan Jett?'"

JETT'S SECOND ALBUM promised to be much more consistent than her solo debut. "We'd been doing the songs live on stage first," she says, making for a high polish.

A Jett/Laguna writing partnership also was blooming. "We brainstorm," she says. "I'm always writing, but sometimes I'll come up with a good chorus but no words, or I'll have words and he'll have a musical idea." "(I Think I'm Gonna) Run Away" is the only number on *I Love Rock 'n Roll* written in the studio; it took about 15 minutes to complete but is one of the album's standouts. "You're Too Possessive" is a Runaways tune to which that band didn't do justice.

Then there are the non-originals. Jett ran across "Nag" by the Halos in Laguna's record collection. "Crimson and Clover" was the first single Jett ever bought. And, oh yes, that song. Jake Hooker and Alan Merrill, two Americans, went to England to make their fortune. They formed the Arrows, signed with Mickie Most's glitter-laden RAK Records and, in 1974, rode a toned-down pseudo-Sweet song ("A Touch Too Much") into the British Top 10. "I Love Rock 'n' Roll" was the B-side of the Arrows' only other chart record, which had considerably less success. (For the curious, Hooker married and now manages Lorna Luft, soon to star in *Grease II*; he also manages Rick Derringer. Merrill now plays in Derringer's band.)

Jett had seen the Arrows perform "I Love Rock 'n' Roll" once on British TV, but the song stuck with her long enough to try it with the Runaways, then with Cook and Jones. Third time lucky?

Not without a lot of work. Laguna established a working relationship with Neil Bogart's liaison in New York, Irv Biegel, and consulted with friends and advisors about the best marketing strategy for the second album. He wrangled with Leber over which were the best ideas. He then went to Biegel, wrangled some more, and finally to Bogart, emerging with a master plan — not so much Machiavellian manipulation as plain hard work.

Radio hostility was still there in great measure, but something happened. Now more than hardcore Jett supporters were giving "I Love Rock 'n Roll" a shot, and listener call-in response was phenomenal. Live gigs continued to build a following, but suddenly the single was being snapped up at an incredible rate, selling a million copies in just over four weeks. Radio stations, daring to disagree with their consultants, began playing the record. Less than two months after its release, "I Love Rock 'n Roll" was the number-one single on all three major trade charts.

Nobody expected Joan Jett to "break" this big and this fast — including Jett herself. She and Laguna have yet to reap the monetary rewards success is supposed to bring, only now are they beginning to enjoy a comfortable cash flow.

Both are still moving at an outrageous pace. Laguna could barely tear the phone from his ear long enough to say hello the day I interviewed Jett — he had a glazed look in his eyes and had forgotten what day of the week it was (although he somehow found time to dive into the studio to produce Bow Wow Wow). After 30 straight concert dates, amid radio and press demands for her time, Jett grew so restless after two days off the road that she called a band rehearsal.

"I'd like [Joan and the Blackhearts] to end up like Waylon Jennings," Laguna envisages, "someone who's got a tour bus and goes and plays for his adoring fans every night. That's all Joanie really wants. As far as the megabucks and mega-platinum sales go, she'd be really happy, but if this could be a touring band that'd be enough for us. In my eyes she's already a legend anyway."

Funny, Jett didn't seem too legendary when we drifted off into a discussion on baseball, of which she's a super buff. She roots for the Baltimore Orioles but could almost have been describing her own situation: "We've got the best manager in baseball, added power... I'm a firm believer in fate and faith. Do I look worried?" ∎

QUOTES OF THE DECADE

"I may throw my crotch about a bit but I can still be innocent inside. "

—ADAM ANT (1982) TP 80

The late Harry Robinson was a lovely man and a fine writer. His articles for us used his middle name rather than his surname: he had some concern that his day-job employers would not appreciate his detours into the world of rock writing. He was generally game for whatever we sent his way: he also penned profiles of the Pretenders, Buzzcocks, Specials, The Teardrop Explodes, Bad Manners, Echo and the Bunnymen and Rocket 88.

FROM HERE TO *DARE*: THE HUMAN LEAGUE

TP 76, AUGUST 1982

By Harry George (Robinson)

Every mega-success tends to rewrite the ground rules slightly, but the Human League's route to UK domination and a healthy position on the U.S. charts makes for a bewildering catalogue. Formed in 1977, by 1980 their record sales had repeatedly failed to match their press; in October of that year they split down the middle, losing the duo responsible for ninety-percent of their musical input.

Possibly the only thing standing between the Human League and extinction was that old showbiz standby, Contractual Obligation. Just as Jimmy Page had to muster some New Yardbirds (you may know them as Led Zeppelin) to tour Scandinavia in 1968, so Europe expected a Human League tour in November 1980. Page found his recruits by reputation and recommendation; Human League singer Phil Oakey's methods were less systematic. In the Crazy Daizy disco in his hometown of Sheffield, he spotted two girls "dancing differently to anyone in the building." Could they sing, he asked? Undeterred by a negative reply, he persuaded Susanne Sulley (17) and Joanne Catherall (18) to shelve their studies for the duration of the tour. By Christmas 1981, the former was trading verses with Oakey on Britain's number-one single, "Don't You Want Me."

Sheffield, one of northern England's more attractive industrial towns, saw the formation of a band called the Future in 1977. Based around computer operators/synthesizer players Ian Marsh and Martyn Ware, it also featured one Adi Newton, later to form Clock DVA. Upon Newton's departure, the Future acquired former hospital porter Oakey and became the Human League. About four gigs later, they were augmented by Adrian Wright, previously employed on an ice cream van and now charged with showing slides as a backdrop to the set. Despite a commendable aim of bringing warmth and humanity to electronic music, they regularly inspired spontaneous bombardment from audiences.

The Human League was doing something right, though. In 1978, they were signed by Edinburgh entrepreneur Bob Last (who also spotted Gang of Four) and released "Being Boiled" b/w "Circus of Death" on his Fast Product label. These songs set the tone for much of Human League's future output, harnessing slightly predictable melodies to diverting (if somewhat inconsequential) lyrics.

On this latter point, it is worth noting a remark of Last's printed in *Melody Maker* (June 1980): "As far as I'm concerned, the only world I live in is the one presented to me by the various bits of media that I see." Similarly, Ian Craig Marsh (as he became) states in a post-League publicity handout that he never reads books, only *Newsweek* and *Time*. Human League and Marsh/Ware's subsequent vehicle, Heaven 17, both present a cartoon-like view of the world in their lyrics, which can be artless to the point of banality. The "trash culture" element makes an early appearance on

"Circus of Death," with its opening monologue about Steve McGarrett of *Hawaii Five-O* fame. And Wright's slides of bubblegum cards, comics, etc. went down well with the flourishing anti-intellectual faction of the British music press.

BY MARCH 1979, David Bowie had seen Human League perform and *New Musical Express* writer Paul Morley announced he had placed several bets on the band's scoring a hit single that summer. An opening slot on a Siouxsie and the Banshees tour gave the band its first crack at a wider audience. Morley lost his money, but the League continued to advance, signing with Virgin Records in April, supporting Iggy Pop in Europe and appearing at the Leeds *Futurama '79* festival with Joy Division, The Teardrop Explodes and the Hawklords.

Until then exclusively a synthesizer lineup, the Human League's first Virgin release was under the pseudonym of the Men and featured a bass player and drummer. It's intriguing to ponder whether, if "I Don't Depend on You" had been a hit, they would have added orthodox instruments again. Was their belief in electronic self-sufficiency beginning to falter? More likely they just wanted to avoid the predictable, as when they cancelled a string of gigs for "reprogramming" that October.

An opportunity then arose to tour England with Talking Heads. Virgin was naturally keen, but the band proposed instead to supply a specially made film of themselves: "The Human League, intrigued to experience their own performance, have designed a remotely controlled touring entertainment. Therefore, 30 Human League minutes will be available on the Talking Heads tour. The League themselves may join the audience on some evenings to savor the occasion."

"It was an inspirational compromise which we thought Talking Heads would go for," Martyn Ware told *Melody Maker* later. No such luck. The tour promoter and agent, reportedly at the Heads' instigation, turned thumbs down "due to the format of the League's show" — despite Bob Last's offer to indemnify the presenters against complaints, and after considerable advertising to forewarn the public.

THIS WAS NOT a good period for the Human League. *The Dignity of Labour* EP was an almost willful expression of serious intent before the nursery rhyme-like "Empire State Human" inauspiciously launched an assault on the singles chart. Even admirers began to feel the band had missed the boat, and *Reproduction*, the first League album, was released to lukewarm reviews. In its end-of-year roundup, the *NME* commented that "the electronic pop boom never really materialized" (although Gary Numan had two number-one singles). By next May, Ware was musing, "It's no use being ahead of your time, is it really?"

THE HUMAN LEAGUE had shrewdly invested its money in equipment and its own Monumental Pictures studio in Sheffield, allowing the band to record fairly cheaply.

"I got dressed up in this suit and went round telling estate agents we were an audio-visual company ... which we are, in a sense," Marsh told *Record Mirror*. (The habiliments were seen more often when Marsh and Ware started British Electric Foundation after the split.)

But studios aren't everything. Despite production assistance from John Leckie and Richard Manwaring on *Reproduction* and 1980's *Travelogue*, respectively, both albums are muffled representations of the group and lack a successful aural substitute for Adrian Wright's contribution to the live show. It must have been small consolation for the band to hear the Undertones sing about them in "My Perfect Cousin."

Having played one gig in the last year, the Human League preceded *Travelogue* with *Holiday '80*, a double-45 package that paid tribute to two prime sources of inspiration with versions of Gary Glitter's "Rock and Roll" and the Bowie/Pop composition "Nightclubbing." Significantly (in view of future events), Wright began to appear onstage and generally make a wider contribution. As the months wore on, however, the smart money must have been on Virgin to drop the Human League.

Then came the Big Split. For the above-mentioned European tour, Oakey and Wright beefed up the group vocally with Sulley and Catherall, musically with Ian Burden and former Rezillos guitarist and songwriter and (doubtless the clincher) comics addict Jo Callis on synthesizers. Somehow this makeshift coalition — Burden had never played synthesizer before — clicked. Among the numbers featured in Europe was Judas Priest's (!) "Take on the World," its sentiments no more portentous than those found in several Human League originals.

Success on record, though, still lay in the future. The first single with the new lineup, "Boys and Girls," made the Top 50, but the band was in transition between glam and the old scruffy student look. With miracle ingredient Martin Rushent as producer, though, the new League came into focus. A vast increase in aural and visual polish culminated in the band's mannequin-like appearance on the cover of the *Dare* album, released in England in October 1981.

The League's collaboration with Rushent had begun in May with "The Sound of the Crowd," the first of *Dare*'s four successive British hit singles. The climax came with "Don't You Want Me," a more emotional number than usual. The ugly ducklings were swans at last. What had caused the transformation?

Martyn Ware had no doubts. "If Rushent split with the band he could impart their sound to any band on Earth," he told *The Face* earlier this year. "He programs everything on his gear and gets minute credit for that. The League put him in the background, even though in many ways he's more a member of the band than Burden, Callis and the girls."

I MET RUSHENT at his Genetic Studios on the eve of his departure for Nassau on a working holiday. Abandoning discretion, I fed him the above quote and stood well back.

"That's the statement of a jerk. Anybody that could say that without having been at the sessions ... to come out with such a sweeping statement is just idiotic. The League and the people at Genetic are a team; the whole is much greater than the parts. To even suggest that I could function with minimal contribution from the League is stupid and naïve.

"As to me being more a member of the band than Burden or Callis, that's equally nonsense. Callis wrote half of 'Don't You Want Me,' including a lot of its catchy lines. That's not to say I don't come up with ideas and contribute to the arrangements, but a lot of the ideas are already formed when they walk through the door. Some songs come together in the studio. 'Don't You Want Me' was virtually conceived in the studio, apart from a couple of brass lines they'd written. It varies from track to track."

Was the Human League confused as to their direction when they began working with Rushent?

"No, not at all," the producer replies. "Phil Oakey had quite a solid master plan. He's always wanted to be a pop star and sell lots and lots of what he regards to be good quality records. I happen to agree with his criteria, but I know there are those who don't. Once Oakey was able to pursue his own ideas in terms of production and of putting the League together, then it started to work. He walked through my door with all that in his head.

"There seems to be an idea in certain quarters that I manufactured them, and it's time it was laid to rest. I'll accept the fact that my contribution was important, but it was only part of seven people contributing to the League."

Does Adrian Wright contribute much in the studio?

"Yeah, a lot. Adrian's contribution in a musical sense is slightly less than the others', although he's co-written two or three songs on the album [five, actually]; the whole lyric to 'Darkness' I think was his. But his personality and the things he has to say are crucial in terms of maintaining that organic balance that makes the whole thing work.

"The great thing about doing that album was that we all had a lot of faith in one another. When it was Callis's department, Callis had the floor. When it comes to mixing, I've got the floor, and I call the shots. It works really well. Nobody tried to tell Oakey how to sing the songs.

"Their direction was defined, but they didn't quite know how to get it recorded properly. I don't think the League has ever been short of good songs; they just never seemed to be able to record the bloody things properly."

RUSHENT INTRODUCED the Human League to the Linn drum computer, which enables the user to program beats recorded off an actual kit in any desired order and, if necessary, inserting an intricate pattern slowly for speeding up later.

"I got one of the first ones. On 'Sound of the Crowd,' we hadn't [yet] got a Linn drum, and were using some synthetic Simmons drums. They didn't want a drummer, but we couldn't get a really good recorded drum sound. There wasn't a machine available that gave you the real thud on the bass drum and crack on the snare.

"Then I got one of these, and I said to them, 'I've found the solution to our percussion problem. It's got all the poke that real drums have, but it's a machine.' They took one look at it and said, 'This is what we've been waiting for.'

"On their demos they'd have a basic idea for a drum part with no drum fills or anything. Then we'd overdub the track and they used to leave it to my discretion to put in drum fills and accents where I thought appropriate. We'd alter them if they didn't like part of it. They let me have the most programming freedom with the drums 'cause none of them are drummers. I used to be a drummer and I still play a bit."

Rushent also programmed the Roland Microcomposer, which he praises to the skies.

"It's a very complicated sequencer. You program a series of notes into it and instead of using a keyboard to play a synthesizer, this sends out the signals instead. It can be locked in time to the tape, so it can overdub. If the bands wants a brass line, I'll just write it down, program it and then we can play with it for a couple of hours without anyone wearing out their hands. It never makes an error, never goes to sleep, never gets drunk. You can make up highly articulated lines. There's a French horn-sounding line at the beginning of 'Things That Dreams Are Made Of' that you feel is played with all the emotive quality you would put in if you were playing a horn."

For all his electronic enthusiasm, Rushent

denies the Human League sold him on synthesizers. Rather, he says there was more of an aesthetic give-and-take.

"I wanted to make a pop electronic album. Not a DAF or a Kraftwerk, but something that was accessible to everybody. The Human League just walked through the door at the right time.

"We were starting the rest of the album when 'Love Action' charted. We sat down and said, 'Right, we've really got to make every track a single, 'cause it seems like we've got something here.' So that's what we did."

THE HUMAN LEAGUE HAS understandably been busy since the release of *Dare*, touring heavily in Britain (where "Don't You Want Me" has gone platinum), Europe and, most recently, the U.S. Rushent can't wait to get started on the next album.

"I've heard two or three of the new songs, and they're just as good, probably better. All the personalities are basically the same, so the vibe will be the same hopefully. When we were making *Dare* no one was expecting anything, so we were tucked away in here having a good time. This time everyone's waiting to see what we're gonna do, so there is gonna be a pressure that wasn't there last time. We've got some new machines and some new ideas. I think it should be all right."

So far, the only revolutionary aspect of the current Human League's music is its means of creation. The pressure of success may be a positive influence if it spurs them into attempting more ambitious song structures, with "Don't You Want Me" as a starting point. But the Human League story offers powerful encouragement to anyone who believes in their ideas and can sustain the will to carry them through. ■

QUOTES OF THE DECADE

"If they played our records on the radio and MTV as much as Duran Duran, I think they'd sell like hotcakes."

—BILLY ZOOM of X (1984) TP 94

MALCOLM McLAREN: FROM THE EYE OF THE STORM

TP 85, MAY 1983

By Scott Isler

Record companies have learned to fear the name Malcolm McLaren. First gaining prominence as manager of the Sex Pistols, McLaren seemed a Machiavellian pied piper: leading his notorious charges (and the whole mid-'70s punk movement behind them) from label to label, he was the purveyor of outrage for Queen Elizabeth's Jubilee Year.

McLaren had dabbled in the rock business before. In 1975 he oversaw the demise of the New York Dolls. That band, forerunners of the Pistols in the shock-rock sweepstakes, had peaked musically (*sic*) and commercially (*sic*). Under McLaren, they went out in style, garbed in red vinyl and performing against a Communist Chinese flag backdrop.

Style has always been a McLaren specialty. The 37-year-old native Londoner went to art schools and painted for ten years as a student. Around 1970, he opened a clothes shop with partner Vivienne Westwood: Let It Rock sold 1950s teddy-boy gear, and introduced McLaren to the Dolls when they wandered in one day. The store changes its name (Sex, Seditionaries, Worlds End) as regularly as its fashions.

In the late '70s, the Sex Pistols collapsed amid a shambling backroads U.S. tour, a shelved film project (*The Great Rock 'n' Roll Swindle*), internal dissent and bassist Sid Vicious's last heroin over-dose. McLaren's corporation went into receiver-ship following a lawsuit brought by Pistols singer Johnny Rotten (John Lydon); the entrepreneur fled to Paris for a year.

He reemerged with Bow Wow Wow, Adam Ant's former band fronted by a 14-year-old girl rattling off a paean to home taping. The ensuing uproar proved McLaren's instincts were still in-tact. Now, instead of stealing the spotlight from his protégés, McLaren has stepped in front of the microphone himself with "Buffalo Gals" — a square-dance lyric plopped down in an inner-city streetwise musical setting — and an accompany-ing album of ethnic musics drawn from travel in Africa, Cuba and the Appalachians.

This interview took place in the New York of-fices of Island Records, McLaren's U.S. label. He had just come from a meeting with Bob Pittman, Warner Amex's senior vice president of program-ming for MTV. The cable music channel had refused to show the video of "Buffalo Gals," de-picting breakdancers and other aspects of urban Black culture.

For someone who co-owns an ultra-trendy boutique, McLaren dresses as casually as possi-ble short of sloppiness: a V-neck sweater over a pink T-shirt, brown cords and lace-up boots. His strawberry-blond curls are hidden under a floppy felt hat which he says he made himself.

Despite the contentious nature of his remarks, an open countenance and high-pitched voice lend McLaren an elfin quality. He laughs often at the absurd state of the world as he sees it; his dynamic range fluctuates between soft-spoken and forth-right, varying with emotional temperature.

Still very much the '60s activist, McLaren has a good deal of the crusader in his make-up. Un-like humorless "political" types, though, he seems unwilling to achieve his ends regardless of the means. This may be why, no matter that they in-evitably get burned, record companies can't stay away from McLaren's combustible concepts.

"Let's get rid of these innocuous bands that use 'fun' in such a horrible way," he says. "They've made that word ever so grey. Fun can be subver-sive too, you know."

HOW DID YOUR MEETING with Bob Pittman go this morning?

He really is acting out the role of the politician. He never says yes or no to anything, but when the door slams it's definitely no. Rock and roll's basi-cally a very conservative industry.

There's rock and roll, and then there's the rock and roll industry.

Well, you'd go a long way to find rock and roll. I would say it's very close to the industry.

Does it look like MTV will show your video?

Very doubtful.

What was their objection?

Too Black. You've never had a tradition of lik-ing Black people in this country.

Unlike your country.

It's too Black and too threatening — too much to do with street culture and things they don't want to be promoting. They want to promote things that come out of the industry — like sausages that come out of a machine — the Blancmanges and all this other rubbish [*gesturing around office*]. It's a funny thing, rock and roll. It's become part of the politics of this country. It's probably as responsible for Ronald Reagan as anything else is.

Do you care if MTV plays the video?

I care because people who set about creating information and music always care that it's trans-ported to as many people as possible. Isn't that the intent? I do care, but I'm not surprised. I'm not surprised by anything in this industry.

What was the source of "Buffalo Gals"?

The source of that song was probably the only thing white people in this country have in prox-imity to what I suspect the origins of rock and roll are all about: something very pagan, some-thing that harks back to the love rituals of forgot-ten days, when dance was very serious and sacred, when people really understood the magic of their bodies. That's what square dancing really is all about, isn't it?

More like an African approach to music?

Oh no, not at all. What do you think "duck for the oyster" means? Or "dig for the clam, dig, dig, dig"? "Knock a hole in the old tin can"? Think about it. It's just as primitive as "Tutti Frutti."

How did you get the idea to combine an Appa-

lachian lyric with an Afro-American rhythm track?

I decided that whitey ought to put something back into the culture he'd been plundering for many years. I just thought it was a nice gesture finding something as dramatic as a square dance in this country, in a part where probably there's no electricity, and the people there don't realize the country's called "the United States of America" — and to take that to the ghettos of this godforsaken place and realize there isn't really a hell of a lot of difference between the caller and the rapper. That parallel really brings together the pagan ideals of both countries. "Buffalo Gals" is a song that's been in your heritage for over a hundred years. I guess it was your rock and roll 150 years ago.

HOW DID YOU MEET the World's Famous Supreme Team?

They were 42nd Street hustlers in New York, playing red card. They'd steal as much money as they could, particularly off white men. Then they'd hurry down to ethnic radio station WHBI, where they could slap a certain amount of dollars on the table for a time slot, enabling them to get a moment of fame. I guess a DJ is closer to aspire to than Stevie Wonder.

I heard their show at two o'clock in the morning and thought it was full of tremendous humor, not unlike the Marx Brothers — the same anarchic flavor. It was all about getting off with every girl who phoned up on the air, whilst they "scratched" records underneath. Made that scratch sound very sexual, not unlike medicine men in Africa who concoct similar things. I thought it was terrific, and a marvelous discovery — like the thrill when you first heard Elvis Presley sing.

Did they contribute to the rest of the album!

No, but they anchored it all for me. They gave it a kind of logic: the basis of allowing me to mix songs from Zululand and the mountains of Lima and the Dominican Republic and Cuban priests and Appalachian hillbillies all together under one roof. The dances and styles, and maybe the rhythms, are different, but they all have essentially the same purpose. They're all part of the dispossessed cultures of this world, and probably ally themselves better to the term "rock and roll" than

most other things we know of. A radio show was a marvelous way of introducing all those ideas, so I used that as a "carrier."

HOW SHOULD "Buffalo Gals" affect people?

They should receive information, instruction, about dances that shouldn't be considered other than in a pagan way. They should start to belong to and spread this culture to get rid of the pop packaging that exists in an industry that's been trying to feed you so much pap and bland information. It's criminal, really; those in charge are cultural criminals. We sit in a place not unlike what I've just talked about, and I would like to destroy that. I'd be the first guy with a grenade.

You're not pagan yourself.

No, but I dream of being one.

So, this is all fantasy?

It's not fantasy at all. Deep inside my heart I'm just like you, preconditioned at an early age: reds [Communists] under the bed and all the propaganda your country's been corking for a long time. Just like that poor kid in *E.T.*, 'cept he could relate to E.T. That's what made you all pour your hearts out.

You can escape your preconditioning?

Yes, just like he did. You get involved with the sentiments of that young boy: I really am just like E.T. and wish to be!

How do you know what's in your head isn't just your own fantasy?

Don't keep talking about fantasy. It's reality! It's what you actually see in front of you. It's there, you can touch it. I go to the Appalachian mountains; it's not fantasy, those people exist! They exist without electricity and without toilets. They hunt rabbits and play music. They've resolved a lifestyle and they've never seen a $100 bill. Tradition doesn't die, only business dies.

How much time did you spend in that area?

About ten days, on the border of east Tennessee and Virginia.

How did you decide on that area?

The English are marvelous anthropologists. We do our research right well. A guy I knew from the BBC pointed me in that direction. He said, "Get off at Kingsport and drive this way."

WHY DID YOU TURN from a manager to a recording artist?

When people ask me that, I really can't answer clearly other than to say I got fed up with being piggy in the middle — the guy that has to secure himself between the band, or "product," and the record company. I've always been known as a tremendous troublemaker; after being locked in the middle for a while, I realized Bow Wow Wow would rather be closer to the record company than I would, and the record company would rather be closer to the band than I would. I just thought, well, why doesn't the band join up and let me make my fabulous exit? So, that's what happened.

I'm afraid I find more often than not there isn't a lot of difference between the record company and the band at the end of the day. I was really the odd one out. I was often the fifth silent member who was the *agent provocateur.*

Bands feel too insecure today. They're very concerned with holding on to the industry that's been created, and to get as much money as they can in the shortest space of time. Rightly so, in a way: jobs are difficult to come by, particularly in England. It's one career that seems exportable enough for people to take it very seriously.

Do you feel you'd ever want to go back to managing a group?

Oh god, no. It was a bit like having a noose 'round your neck, or a monkey on your back. I was strangled beyond belief when I had to worry about mothers, and having to explain why you have to do this and that, and whether somebody can write a song and ending up having to write it all yourself, then describe it to them, then try to explain it to the record company. God, man, it's a fucking nightmare!

The funny thing now is, being an artist and not having a manager, I never realized how hard you have to work! One gratifying thing is that exploiting yourself is much better than exploiting others. When a painter paints figures, they can't talk back. Exploiting yourself, you've got only yourself to blame but nobody to answer to.

On the other hand, you have so much explaining to do. Music ought to be self-explanatory! I didn't realize you have to put chapter and verse before anybody pretends to be interested!

DO YOU BELIEVE WHITES can make a valid contribution to a Black art form?

Without a doubt. It's already happening in England. That's what "Buffalo Gals" was all about. Making it work in the context of England and Europe, and exposing people to such technique is marvelous! It makes people realize the dance floor of a discothèque and radio itself can be an awful lot more exciting.

But at what point does it become exploitation of Black culture?

It's never exploitation. Rock and roll's free for everyone. It's spreading the word, isn't it? Anything that has subversion as its objective should be copied by millions, in my opinion.

Why do Blacks never seem to borrow from white musical traditions?

Probably because they're not as interesting! Or as pagan. That's why I introduced the square dance. That's all you've fucking got!

All we've got. You don't consider yourself a cultural voyeur?

No, I'm a troublemaker, a mischief guy — like the god Pan. I set up things and get explosions going, get everybody caught up in it, rant and rave. Hopefully, out of that chaos we might produce something that's got a sense of purpose.

HAVE YOU ALWAYS BEEN attracted to music?

Never. I've always found musicians very coarse people, often quite uninspired and unintelligent. But I must say the vulgarity of the medium appealed to me. I've always believed in impolite people. I think there was something very strong in my background to which rock and roll had a very powerful relevance. I like the practical use of music. I don't like music for music's sake.

So, you weren't impressed with rock and roll in the '50s?

I *was!* Quite impressed. I listened avidly to radio during my boyhood. I even saw Eddie Cochran onstage.

Have you heard anything recently that you like?

I don't listen! I have no interest at all. I'd much rather look at a picture or read a book. I might listen to certain things that are peculiar to my endeavor to understand the world around me, be it square dance or those guys in the south Bronx you see on street corners electric boogalooing. I can see an affinity between them and Zulu warriors living on the time bomb in South Africa waiting for their chance to strike.

I love it all when it's pagan. I think there's more truth in it then. That's what rock and roll always was: very pagan, very primitive, very jungle, very ethnic. Africa has the oldest civilization in the world, and probably the most sophisticated. Therefore, its music, with respect to the barbarism we've created in society, is probably the most subversive and revolutionary.

I think rock and roll always was that. When it ceased to be that it had no significance! It was just fodder for the industry to sell, like another pair of gloves in a different color. It's a complete fallacy that the industry was ever needed to secure rock and roll's place in the world. God, it existed here long before Jesus Christ.

It just hadn't been marketed properly.

That's all. It was an accident, wasn't it?

DO YOU THINK IF the New York Dolls hadn't walked into Let It Rock your career would have taken the turns it did?

I would never have known they existed! I didn't listen to any of that music. I didn't even care about what they played. I cared more about their personalities. I came to America and was quite shocked when they tried desperately hard to play me their record. I said, no, I don't need to hear your music; it's all right, you're good guys! They played it anyway and I was appalled — what a load of rubbish! Funny thing was, Johnny Thunders agreed with me. Thereafter I took up the gauntlet and worked with them at the tail end of their career.

You've been talking about a Sex Pistols reunion?

I said that 'cause I got so bored giving the same interviews about "Buffalo Gals" that I decided to change the subject once, on television. Everybody went mad! It got reported in the papers, and maybe John Rotten, who looks somewhat like a pear these days, will wake up to the fact that he was far more relevant, poignant and truthful then than he

is today. If he could shake off all the bitterness and paranoia that exists around him, perhaps he could do himself a lot of good by reliving those days just to resolve that in his head.

I made that statement quite flippantly at the time; seeing it have those effects demonstrates the need for such a group again. Rotten was a marvelous poet. With me inspiring him here and there, he was able to eloquently portray the feelings of a generation. The Pistols didn't sell that many records but gave a tremendous amount of inspiration to everybody.

How do you feel about hardcore punk bands?

They've become modern-day hillbillies, haven't they? It's funny: You declare an idea. It's not often that everybody understands the essence of the idea. Those are the repercussions. I guess those groups are the debris of the fact, after the holocaust. What about reconstruction? That's why I've recorded "Buffalo Gals"!

WHY DO YOU think Adam Ant is more popular than Bow Wow Wow?

Because he's far more tenacious and understood the ideas. He was a terribly good student. I worked with him for four weeks. Each day he came with a notebook; I felt like I was his teacher. He would sit there with his group and write down everything I said. Then he'd go off to the toilet and read it again and again. He held me in great esteem. I thought, this boy grabs these ideas and is going to do it.

Annabella was still too worried about her mother and whether she wanted to be an airline stewardess or not. When you're thinking like that, there's no way you're going to make it. You have to act out of desperation.

Why didn't you stick with Adam?

I didn't stick with any of them. It was only a mercenary job I undertook for four weeks because Adam's girlfriend worked in my store.

Adam and the band separated because I'd made them all equal and the natives got restless. I'd never realized the politics of the group. He'd obviously been very dictatorial in the past; now I was the dictator and they were all my minions.

Adam had a terrible time writing lyrics, or

even fitting them with the rhythm. So, they were looking at him, thinking he's not doing his job very well, and suddenly they were able to comment. Adam's ego was burst, and I saw it would be better for him to depart because maybe he could take it down a more traditional rock and roll route. The band, particularly the drummer and bass player, seemed more astute musically.

I had the intention of going back to Paris to work on a film. I was also hired by a TV company to write a script called *An Insider's Guide to the World of the Music Industry*. They thought I was the right man for the job. I wrote a script based around a rather elegant Negro with a cassette player on his shoulder, home taping. He seemed the most fashionable man in London at that time.

I also wrote a theme tune called "C30 C60 C90 Go" using a Burundi beat I'd picked up in Paris. The chairman of the TV company thought the script was too over-the-top — they didn't want to lose all their record company advertising, I suppose — and decided they couldn't put on such a program. But I was so infatuated with the song that I had to record it myself.

I went into the studio with Adam's musicians, but I needed a singer. Adam was off finding other musicians, trying to develop his own group with my ideas. There was no point getting involved with that; I wanted someone a bit more exotic anyway. I also liked the idea of someone very young, with a sweet, angelic voice — perhaps a female equivalent of Frankie Lymon.

The band and I looked everywhere. I got so fed up I thought perhaps they couldn't record the song. I was going to go back to Paris. Then I walked into a dry cleaner's with a friend, talking about this idea, and he said, there's this girl here who's Burmese, about 13, always singing Stevie Wonder songs. So, I went in and noticed. She wasn't singing any Stevie Wonder songs whilst I was there, but she seemed cute. I talked to her about an audition — very straightforward. I suppose she looked at me as if I were trying to pick her up, a bit of a pervert or monster. Nevertheless, with this friend of mine she understood I was a little more legit than that and decided to take a shot.

Annabella had a very good voice. But more than the voice, which wasn't so unique, she had a marvelous sense of rhythm. Also, she had very good intonation; I needed someone who could speak clearly, since the words were fast and clipped. I thought, she's got to sing this song. Then I had to give the band a name, sign them to a record company to get the record out — and I was lumbered with the old-fashioned task of managing a band again.

I got terribly caught up with it, what with not getting success. I suppose my ego persuaded me to continue with a "cassette pet" package developing the idea further, and to continue writing lyrics.

WHEN DID YOU START phasing out your involvement with Bow Wow Wow?

Directly after I wrote "Go Wild in the Country" and photographed the recreation of that Manet painting, "Déjeuner sur l'Herbe." Those two things were to go hand in hand. But, of course, the mother and the corporation were all up in arms. It's amazing how a painting that was done 120 years ago can still cause such trouble.

I just got very bored. I used to end up sitting in Foyle's bookshop on Charing Cross Road rather than go to marketing meetings; it was more instructive. I don't find the people intelligent enough, I'm afraid, and I don't think the job did anything for me. You can put a lot in, but if you don't get anything out, after a while you get very frustrated.

One of the horrible experiences of my life is explaining things to people and realizing I'm just wasting my time. I wasn't counting for anything. I was acting as a mercenary, and I've never acted as a mercenary in my life. [*Earlier: "It was only a mercenary job I undertook…"*]

A mercenary for whom?

For the band, who wished desperately for success. (Meaning, I suppose, commercial success, and money.) Likewise, the record company. I was the poor fuck who wasn't thinking about that at all! They didn't need someone like me. After about 18 months I thought, I can't do it anymore, I must leave, and I did. It was silly, me getting Annabella to sing songs I'd written about the work ethic or advocating home taping, because none of these people were interested in that. I was just using them. It was nice to exploit them for that — I'm quite proud of the fact.

One thing I learned, though, was that ideas are one thing, but people listen to people, not ideas. There's a terrible conflict if the person singing your ideas is a different person than the ideas. Sooner or later, it's going to be discovered. That's what was happening.

I felt a bit silly and, frankly, I got despondent. I felt, you want to be a successful band, get over to the United States and play all this "I Want Candy" stuff, you better do it. You don't need me for that. Bo Diddley's been doing it for years, just copy him!

Bow Wow Wow was a lot more mellow than the Sex Pistols. They conjured up a different feeling — of escape, getting out. It didn't penetrate because the people themselves were too much like cartoons, they weren't real enough — all of them, not just Annabella.

Weren't the Pistols also cartoon characters?

People would suggest that because it looked so obvious, but they were very believable, the more you thought about them. They were English ragamuffins, absolutely true to culture. They were your working-class hoodlums in the best sense of that word. That's why they reigned for so long, and still do. Punk rock will never die 'cause it didn't have as its essence the idea of selling anybody anything. It was a spirit; you can't kill that.

There's no doubt in my mind the Sex Pistols were England's greatest contribution to rock and roll, well over and above the Rolling Stones or the Beatles. Twenty years from now they will be remembered far more than the Beatles. We have posters on English buses with portraits of Ringo Starr and the slogan, "Did you know this man was in the Beatles?" I don't think they'll say that that of Sid Vicious!

How do your parents feel about your career?

My parents hate me. I'm the black sheep. I come from a very nouveau riche Jewish family. I wasn't really brought up by my parents, I was brought up by grandparents, my grandmother in particular.

So, they were too permissive.

She was one of those Victorian Jewish liber-

als, who loved the stage but was unable to act because a woman was considered a whore if she did in those days. So, she had a fondness for anything to do with breaking down the establishment that she failed to do at the time. She taught me to question everybody, especially the establishment. She never thought she could rely on anything they said, ever. "Boys will be boys" was her statement after any catastrophe.

I'm self-taught, basically, because I was a tearaway at school. I didn't learn anything. Although my grandmother was an elocution teacher — I was forced to read *Jane Eyre* at the age of six with a dictionary beside my lap. After that I stopped reading for about ten years! The visual world seemed more basic and common, more seductive

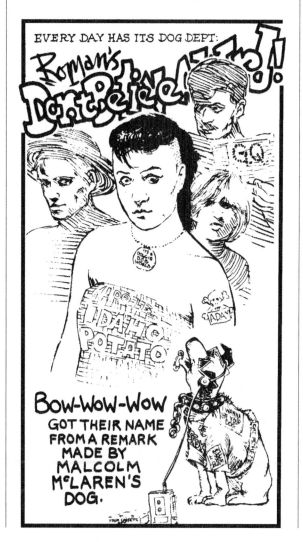

to me. I learned an awful lot from looking at pictures and looking at the world around me.

Do you see anyone else doing what you do?

No. That's a great tragedy, isn't it? People are scared too much of their jobs. They probably didn't have the same childhood I did. I've never been scared of such things. I think that's because I've never had anything to protect. I didn't have parents to hold me back. I only had a grandmother who told me to get out!

Does your store provide a modicum of security?

No, it's always a desperate task to keep it going and constantly breed new ideas. It's a tiresome occupation but a lovely one. I don't know a better thrill than putting on a fashion show. I can use music, and make that parade, and it all happens in 35 minutes and isn't repeated for three months. When you're with rock and roll bands, you see the same show night after night.

Fashion seems so opposed to what you're doing in other areas. It's superficial.

People say that, but it isn't. Jean-Paul Sartre said appearances are evil, but appearances are everything. When you live in a tradition of the ideals of a gentleman, to get out of that class structure a boy may have to wear a dress — à la Boy George. It's the only alternative.

Fashion encapsulates the thoughts and processes of your culture, and usually comes first because it's most important and most direct. Seeing is believing; hearing is sometimes suspect. Music is a secondary medium.

Do you think of your future?

I'm evolutionary, like everyone. Your tide comes in; you see a boat and get in it if you are an adventurer or stay panicking on the beach if you're not. It might sail out and you'll never see it again, so I usually jump in — for better or worse. You sometimes learn from your mistakes, but you don't learn a whole lot. You learn more from your success. Your mistakes you tend to disregard.

How do you relax?

I read a lot. And I have a lot of sex.

Do you have many friends?

No one has lots of friends in London unless they've got lots of money. I never have. It's never been my profession. I'm rich in ideas. ∎

FEAR AND LOATHING ON THE WEST COAST: PUBLIC IMAGE LTD.'S NEW CAREER IN THE SAME OLD TOWNS

TP 51, JUNE 1980

By Scott Isler

Don McLean had it all wrong. The music didn't die when Buddy Holly plummeted, but on January 14, 1978. That night in San Francisco, the Sex Pistols dismantled their only American tour (all of seven dates), their career as a functioning unit and, according to John Lydon (Johnny Rotten back then), the entire rickety structure of rock music as well.

But rock and roll never forgets — unfortunately. Two years and two months later, Lydon is back in the little city by the Bay, and to the local yobbos it's like the Pistols never left. The occasion is a press conference heralding the domestic release of Public Image Ltd.'s *Second Edition* LP. Lydon's post-Pistols band (referred to more handily as PiL) has existed for over a year and a half; scheduling foul-ups, however, prevented their self-titled debut album from coming out here. Now, with a sense of cooperation unthinkable a few years ago, singer Lydon and guitarist Keith Levene have flown over for interviews and publicity. Could they possibly want to (choke) *sell their record*?

The City is a disco with mirrored walls, columns and revolving balls suspended from the ceiling. Twenty years ago, this sleazy North Beach area of San Francisco was mecca for beatniks; there don't seem to be any milling around before PiL's conference gets under way, but beards and long hair in casual attire are uncomfortable reminders that this town also gave birth to the hippies, which the Sex Pistols (and/or abrasive mouthpiece Rotten/Lydon) so detested. There are studiedly new wave types, too, from black-garbed punks in various flavors of hair to the latest porkpie chic. The cross-cultural chaos is impressive, but all will seem irrelevant when the anti-stars arrive.

Lydon and Levene show up looking positively etiolated. Lydon, 24, who selects his wardrobe from second-hand shops ("I never wear jeans"), is decked out in a bulky, dark checked jacket, rumpled shirt and loosely knotted tie. The jacket and baggy pants almost make him look stocky, accentuating his stumpy proportions. (He is definitely not a hunchback, though, as once rumored.) His red hair is greased back casually; the beady stare — only a sliver of dark blue iris extends beyond large pupils — could melt glass. By contrast, Levene, 22, looks almost dapper, although similarly attired. Just as intent as Lydon, the blond, tousled guitarist lacks his partner's manic charisma but makes up for it in more conventional good looks. Both clutch Heinekens (Lydon is rarely without one for the next eight hours) and seem a bit unsure (behind glacial façades) about the whole set-up.

Their fears are borne out after they ascend the podium. An intelligent rock press conference is an impossibility in the best of circumstances, and Lydon's former notoriety has brought out thrill-seekers. A much-needed moderator is unable to attend, members of a local band bait the subjects mercilessly and a video crew blinds them with third-degree lights. Under the circumstances, Lydon and Levene are models of restraint — or maybe it's resignation. Lydon's weary monotone (he does almost all the talking) is so low the microphone can barely pick up his dry, acerbic comments. "This is definitely not my doing," he says by way of introduction, swigging the Heineken. A portion of the audience — the sympathetic ones — cackle uproariously at his every statement. They've come to see Johnny Rotten, and Lydon doesn't want to know.

"The Pistols finished rock and roll. That was the last rock and roll band. It's all over now ... Rock and roll is shit. It's dismal. Granddad danced to it. I'm not interested in it ... I think music has reached an all-time low — except the Raincoats."

And, he forgot to add, Public Image Ltd. Lydon and Levene obviously consider their band of vital importance, which is the only reason they're putting up with this circus. "This is a joke, I think, personally," Lydon injects at one point, "but we'll go on with it." Soon after, while anonymous catcallers repeatedly ask if he's a punk and where he bought his green glitter socks, he adds, "I feel like a fool."

"It is essential that everyone is aware that this band exists," Lydon enunciates slowly. "There's no competition ... No one is forced to buy our records. We just want people to know they exist." PiL is "not rock and roll, not disco; it defies any category. It's PiL ... We do it; you either like it or you don't. It's simple. There's no intellectual ideology behind it ... Call us what you like. It doesn't matter; I've been called lots of things ... I'm a pretty good target for people's particular bickerings and hate and their ridiculous egos. I'm used to it."

After what seems like infinity, the conference ends. The crowd strips *Second Edition* cover slicks from the walls for souvenirs, and Lydon and Levene repair to a nearby hotel for one *mano a mano* interview. They've already done lots of these in New York and Los Angeles; the San Francisco sideshow was to avoid more. When their interviewer leaves after an hour and a half, Levene comments, "He acted intently interested." "He didn't act intently interested, he acted intently *dull*," Lydon shoots back.

"DULL" AND "BORING" ARE Lydon's favorite expressions of contempt. Not that he leads a swashbuckler's life himself; Lydon says he divides his time between recording, playing with video equipment (the latest PiL toy), writing songs, practicing piano and synthesizer and watching television. "I can't be bothered to socialize. I'm not a social person."

Yet PiL in many ways is an exciting enough

project. The "Ltd." is not just for effect. "It's a company," Lydon explains. "We're all shareholders. Everything we do we work out together. [Besides Lydon and Levene, PiL currently includes bassist Wobble (John Wardle), and Jeanette Lee and Dave Crowe for "visual assistance."] We don't see ourselves as a group — no way at all. We see ourselves as a company. Music is only one of the things we have in mind." Another is the construction of a video studio.

The Clash sings about complete control, but PiL actually seems to have achieved it. The band produces itself and has no manager, much to the chagrin of Warner Bros. (who released *Second Edition* through its subsidiary Island label).

"They just don't understand," Lydon complains. "They want us to get a manager. They seriously doubt whether they can deal with us as people unless we have some business cunt. They like to have very little personal contact with the bands themselves. Very cruel and savage decisions can be effected with the greatest of ease that way, rather than have me screaming."

He is already annoyed about the American label's pressing only 50,000 copies of *Second Edition*. "I don't understand their reluctance on us at all. I'm sick and tired of listening to these businesspeople going on about how they need something 'new' and 'exciting.' Well, we're new — and we're not dull. So, what's happening, baby?"

As part of their assumed responsibilities, Lydon and Levene have used this American jaunt to set up PiL's debut US tour. En route to the San Francisco airport for the return hop to Los Angeles (their temporary base), they negotiate terms with a local promoter. Levene now takes over, going over every detail from ticket prices ("Ten dollars is too much ... you'll only attract our ardent fans") to the venue's capacity (PiL is anti-seating) with hawklike vigilance. Expenses are pared to the bone: the band doesn't want fresh-roses-in-the-dressing-room star treatment; they'll even supply their own lighting (a few white spots). ("Everything we earn goes immediately into building the studio and video equipment," Lydon says later.) While Levene is on the offensive, Lydon questions the promoter's every statement, frequently

contradicting him. Later the two will joke about the Californian's height.

Lydon and Levene's long-standing friendship is the kind that doesn't require verbal communication. On the evening flight back to L.A. they huddle together conspiratorially, their blanched faces almost luminescent in the surrounding darkness. Wobble is another member of this select club. "He'll steal your socks and underwear; he's a good mate," Lydon admits in a rare moment of praise. It's not his style to speak well of anyone — sometimes not even excluding himself. Lydon's impenetrable armor consists of simply denying everything and refusing all commitment; cornering quicksilver is an easier task. Only the death of his mother last year is said to have brought a conventional response. He amuses himself by singing "Don't cry for me, Argentina" in a mock-operatic American accent; compliment him on his dialect and he replies, "I think it's poxy." One can't imagine him asleep, and indeed he says he hasn't been the last few days. He apparently lives on a diet of beer and cigarettes (although he doesn't drink so much as open a bottle, let it go flat after a couple of sips and open another one).

Back in the Continental Hyatt on Sunset Boulevard, Lydon reflexively turns on the TV ("I was brought up surrounded by noise"), peruses a fan note and collapses on the sofa. One learns not to push him into conversation; confronted with silence, he'll take the initiative. His speech assumes numerous dramatic inflections, and he'll occasionally flash a grin (exuding playful malice) for emphasis. Nearby tables are covered with Japanese toys — robots, model cars — he is bringing back to England. He says he is "blind, paralytic drunk," has a headache and is nauseous from the airplane flights. Calmly, in the deliberate drawl that set off still-reverberating waves four years ago, he runs down the benefits of jet-age travel. "Me guts keep grumbling; I can't fart, and I can't burp. I can't bear food. I can't sleep because of central fucking heating and air conditioning. All of my skin is flaking off. I wash my face and come out in a red rash. I'm falling to bits! It doesn't seem to bother anyone else, just me. I've got more problems than the rest put together."

For all his kvetching and nay-saying, Lydon is in deadly earnest about PiL (which he never calls "pill"; he also pronounces his own name LIE-din). He can't conceive of doing anything else: "There is no alternative right now. Anyone who has an idea, it's used. We enjoy it and [*tongue in cheek?*] it's very relevant to society today as we know it."

IT'S HARD TO THINK of another (so-called) rock band that's provoked as much extreme reaction as Public Image Ltd. People tend either to fall head over heels for them or dismiss them as unmitigated poseurs. The band's musical orbit has steadily removed them from anything normally thought of as commercial pop music.

The Sex Pistols (with Johnny Rotten) were still a fresh memory when the "Public Image" 45 debuted; it was conventional enough for Lydon to claim that the Pretenders ("whom Keith has been giving a few lessons to") swiped its guitar lick. Their first album, though, struck many as a prolonged exercise in self-indulgence, from Lydon's caterwauling on the first cut ("I wish I could die" — a pretty good set-up line) to the intentionally obnoxious falsetto chanting ("We only I wanted to be loved") on the last. The album cover and inner sleeve are parodies of different magazine covers; Lydon incredulously (and contemptuously) notes that some reviewers didn't even get the point.

"I just thought it was a real fun piss-take: the 'public image.' I mean, we looked as ridiculous as you could possibly hope. There's no fun left," he complains. "People are just prepared to condemn without seeing."

One of the album's numbers, "Religion," appeared to be an excoriating attack on organized worship. On an album whose vocals are buried under bass, guitar and echo, "Religion" is remarkable for being preceded by an unaccompanied recital of the lyrics … In view of Lydon's Catholic-school upbringing, one might conclude that he was holding a grudge. "It wasn't serious," he states gravely. "It was totally over the top — for the sheer fun of it." Earlier in the evening he had expressed annoyed disbelief over Los Angeles radio stations' late-night religious broadcasting.

About a year elapsed before Public Image Ltd. released another album. (In the meantime, they issued one 45, "Death Disco," which, Lydon notes amusingly, made number-eight in a British list of the year's best disco singles.) They were not particularly visible. "We don't like gigging — not continuously," Lydon says, and estimates the band has only played live 15 to 20 times prior to their nine-city U.S. tour. Their most recent pre-America date — in Paris, where they've performed three times before — was "brilliant; we never even rehearsed for it."

The band had been recording bits and pieces here and there, according to "how much studio time we could get for half price" (Lydon estimates about 20 studios, scattered throughout England, were used). The results comprised *Metal Box*, three 12-inch 45s wedged firmly inside what looks like a film can embossed with the PiL logo. Virgin, PiL's British label after the Sex Pistols defaulted, was resistant to the custom packaging. "They made us pay for it. They thought, we were, like, pissing about." There was "no intellectual reason" behind the design; "it just looked good." (At the press conference, Lydon hinted it was to make it hard getting the records in and out.) His voice rises in undisguised anger when discussing *Metal Box*'s stiff price tag (about $25) in this country: "I'm getting sick of being blamed for imports. That's fuck-all to do with us." He says the package sells for the price of a regular LP (about $11) in England; actually, it goes for more like $20.

Once *Metal Box* sold out its limited supply, PiL's 60-minute opus was transferred to a two-LP set titled *Second Edition*; this is the album Warners has issued in America, after refusing to produce a *Metal Box* of their own. There's a minor change in song sequencing, but for once Lydon is resigned.

"That's the only way we could get the fucker out here. The quality's still quite superb [on LP] but on the 12-inch 45s it's absolutely excellent. That's where all the effort that we put into it shows. There's so much scope on a 12-incher: you can go to an all-time low on bass, and incredibly high. I loved that. I'm definitely into hi-fi."

One advantage *Second Edition* has over *Met-*

al Box is the printed lyrics on the back cover. A lyric sheet was left out of *Metal Box* when Virgin informed the band it would drive up the price another $2.00. Although indecipherable on record, Lydon considers his stream-of-consciousness phrases more than sound effects.

"I wouldn't waste my time writin' 'em down if it wasn't important. Each song deals with a separate story. They all deal with people. I'm not one to moan about fucking wildlife, or fucking buildings or airplanes — or anything abstract."

"Suit," for example, is about social climbers, "people of low origins trying to be posh." Lydon had specific individuals in mind, "as in everything I do." "Poptones" had its origin in a newspaper account of a rape; mass media often inspire him. "I'll read a newspaper article, tap my foot to it and get a tune. Those songs definitely create illusions, patterns ... nightmares."

LYDON ADMITS PiL was "going in all ways at once" on their first album, a charge that cannot be leveled at *Second Edition*. Its monomania no doubt encourages violent reactions. Wobble's overwhelming bass derives from reggae (Lydon, a reggae fan, won't acknowledge any musical influences), but Levene's ethereal guitar and Lydon's variety of vocal timbres ("I'm adapting brilliantly to each situation," he smirks, trilling the last syllable) unite in a disturbing challenge to all preconceptions of "pop" music.

"We don't make music — it's noise, sound. We avoid the term 'music' because of all those assholes who like to call themselves musicians or artists. It's just so phony. We don't give a shit about inner attitude, just as long as it sounds good. We're not some intellectual bunch of freaks. I think we're a very, very valid act. For once in a lifetime a band actually has its own way, its own terms — that would really make extreme music. We just want to make sure you have a choice. I mean, we can only be hated on a large scale. I'd much rather be hated by millions than thousands. That's why I'm here: I want people to know that we exist and let them make the decision for themselves."

Lydon knows what he likes, though, and isn't afraid to say so. "Maybe it's very egocentric of me but I do think it's a fucking good album. We spent a lot of time — we always do — on our stuff. I think our ideas are better than anything available — most definitely. It's a jolly good record. It's danceable. It has strength. It exists on many levels. It's a serious effort by so-called incompetent assholes actually proving any cunt can use a studio and *get what they want*.

"We revel in our own fucking genius. Why the hell not? Self-indulgence is what we're full of and we're proud of it. 'Self-indulgent' means totally involved with what you're doing. We consider no one's viewpoint until we're finished. I'm quite aware of the fact that we can make good records and bad records. There's no guarantee; just give us a chance. I think we deserve a listen."

One would think from the above that Lydon might have appreciated the *New York Times*' rave review of *Metal Box*; Robert Palmer wrote that the album "sounds suspiciously like a genuine masterpiece." But PiL is equally suspicious of enthusiastic outsiders.

"I suppose it would be boring if people just permanently thought, 'Oh man, everything you do is so great.' I find that more irritating [than being put down], frankly, 'cause that's patronization. I find it vile. We're not brilliant; we make mistakes, just like everyone else."

For example?

"I'm not telling you. I'm not here to condemn myself.

"I don't like that 'masterpiece' shit; that's a real put-off. The normal person just reading that thinks, 'Fuck you, cunts.' It's bad news when people do that, going over the top. It's only music; so? Music isn't the be-all and end-all of the universe."

What is?

"Nothing. Well, actually, politics is."

In contrast to Lydon and Levene's deadly serious demeanor, PiL maintains a loose approach to music-(sorry, sound-)making. Lydon says a lot of PiL's songs are made up on the spot, "literally live recordings." "Albatross," *Metal Box/Second Edition*'s longest cut, was done in one take. "I had about four ideas running around me brain. I knew I could do it and I just went off and did it. Had some good fun — was jolly pleased. We almost threw that away."

The same casual attitude is evident in the band's internal organization. There are four drummers on *Second Edition*; Wobble ("We call him that to get him really annoyed") is currently cutting a solo album. (Lydon claims that by using tape loops it will take longer to listen to than it did to record.) Levene, however, is meticulous about his share in the group.

"Guitar playing is sometimes an effort — a real effort, when I don't bother to walk out. Sometimes it flows, when I'm on form, and that's good 'cause I'm only on form when I'm inventing by the second. It's hard to do; I've always got synthesizers to turn to."

A standing joke in the band concerns Levene's classical music training, mentioned by Palmer and others.

Lydon: "Bullshit. That was just to annoy someone; it works a treat." He turns to the guitarist. "Remember all that 'classically trained' crap?"

"Yeah. Three people said to me, 'I can see how well you fit in since you had 17 years of classical piano.' They're all taken in. Big lie."

"The only way these crummy English journalists would consider him a guitar player was by waffling shit to them. And they swallowed it."

(One impressive — and factual — credential in Levene's past is his founding membership in the Clash, although he didn't stick it out long enough to record with them. Typically, Lydon finds them detestable; at the press conference he called Joe Strummer his favorite comedian.)

Lydon, as well as Levene, "messes about" with synthesizers, particularly string synth (*vide* "Chant" on *Second Edition*). "That's my *favorite* instrument," he almost gushes. "I just love murdering it; you get such glorious, tortured violins."

He's not obsessed with technology, though. "Machines aren't props, they're there for you to use. Use them properly; don't fucking use them as gimmicks or fronts to your lack of personality."

Humanistic, no? Yet Lydon's views on interpersonal relations remain fiercely scabrous.

"I've grown very far away from human beings. I like being detached; I don't even like shaking hands. I don't like sweat. I think everyone is ugly. Faces disgust me and feet really make me reek. I think the human body's about one of the most ugly things ever created. It's abysmal. Everyone has lumps and distorted bits and pieces." He laughs mirthlessly. So, what does John Lydon find attractive?

"Machines. Lots of buttons on record players. Knobs and gadgets, electrical equipment of any kind. They're man-made creations; that's what's so good. They're here to make life better. The flaws come in when people let machines dictate. A vacuum cleaner's a machine; my god, I'm not gonna let that run my life, should I? People shouldn't be frightened by things like that." For the first time this grueling day he seems relaxed; maybe it's just fatigue. He leans his head on the sofa arm, flicks cigarette ashes on the carpet and belches.

"Do you know," Lydon confides, "when I was in the Pistols, Malcolm [McLaren] and the rest of the boys thought it was a *bad idea* me mixin' with Sid [Vicious], Wobble and Keith. Definitely leading me astray with those people." Lydon usually refuses to discuss his past, but he seems in a (relatively) expansive mood. He says he didn't find the death of his close friend Vicious upsetting.

"Between Malcolm and Sid's old dear [mum], they fucking just about killed him. He didn't know what the fuck was going on. Malcolm was getting him to sign contracts left, right and center. During all that business, in and out of jail, they were getting him to record songs — while Sid's mum and Malcolm shared the money half and half. Sidney, even if he'd remained alive, would never get a penny of it. It's just sick, what was happening — really fucking sick. Then they went and got him the worst lawyer in the world; he doesn't win anything, he just makes a big showcase out of it. Well, that was definitely not for Sid's benefit. I set about trying to get Sid another lawyer and had no way of contacting him except through Sid's mum, who wouldn't speak to me. They definitely had him sewn up. I don't like what happened then. Someone's got to pay their dues for that." He sounds ominous. "I don't think Sid's life was made very easy by those bastards. Not that he was a very wonderful person, anyway."

WELL, ENOUGH NOSTALGIC strolling down Memory Lane. Lydon (and PiL) is here and now and expects everyone to be similarly progressive.

"I'm quite disgusted the past is still here. That's boring: now I'm doing something else. Why can't I be appreciated for just that? It took the Pistols four years, and then they had to break up before people knew of their presence. The only reason we ended up in America is we wanted to see the country. We were tourists. In Frisco there was like this hate — seething hate. Now in San Francisco the Pistols are god's gift to the universe." He laughs again. "The Ayatollah could be a folk hero here soon. It's the way America runs. They need to absorb everything into their system.

"I'd like to make it very clear that we want no assholes turning up [at PiL gigs] expecting rock and roll or third-rate punk riffs, 'cause they won't get it. We don't want people who are only interested in what we were; we also don't want trendies. We don't care a tub of shit what we look like or are part of or any of that. Life is fun and people should stop squabbling over silliness," he sneers.

"After all that fucking shit today it makes you fucking wonder whether it's really worth the bother. Of course, it is. That fiasco in San Francisco — if that's how press conferences are run, they're really inefficient. We're here to get publicity, which is important. I'll never go through that ever again. I should have known better. It appears to me that I have to tolerate more bullshit than just about anyone in this entire business. I don't understand it."

LIKE A BECKETTIAN HERO, Lydon seems to exist apart from the world, yet must remain in contact with it. He can't go on. He'll go on.

"I don't want to be no superstar. We just want to make enough money to continue doing what we're doing. We do nothing but improve. We've been slagged off because we firstly make [music] for ourselves. We do not sit down and think, 'What will people like?' That would be very wrong, and I don't like bands that do that. We do what we enjoy. I think we guarantee we come up with the goods."

Or, as Lydon stated at the press conference, "I just do what I want. As long as I can get away with it, I'm smiling." ∎

PUBLIC IMAGE LTD. LIVE

TP 64, AUGUST 1981

By Scott Isler [uncredited]

It was a weekend the staff of New York's Ritz club would probably like to forget. The trouble started May 13, when Bow Wow Wow — the British group masterminded by former Sex Pistols manager Malcolm McLaren and fronted by 15-year-old Annabella Lu Win — abruptly cancelled a five-city U.S. tour. The band was to have made its American debut at the Ritz two days later.

Bow Wow Wow's blow-wo-wo-out didn't surprise cynical McLaren-watchers who doubt the band ever intended to come over in the first place. While handling the Pistols, McLaren used to set up European tours then cancel them and notify the press that his group had been banned. More recently, Bow Wow Wow has acquired a spotty track record in regard to English appearances (due to a dispute with English label EMI over who would pay for Lu Win's on-the-road tutor).

Ian Copeland, who set up the U.S. tour through his Frontier Booking International agency, had to laugh. "I fell on the floor. I thought, 'That sucker, he's done it again!' It's like a one-trick special." This time, though, there was a valid reason. Bow Wow Wow had been in the recording studio prior to the scheduled U.S. tour — and joining them was Lu Win's domineering mother, a feisty dame by all accounts. As a result of a shouting match, the younger Lu Win lost her voice; McLaren's press release cited "nervous and physical exhaustion." (Maybe Malc should replace Annabella with her mother, who sounds like she has better pipes.)

The Ritz was thus left staring at a looming weekend with no group to pack 'em in. Then someone at the club remembered that Public Image Ltd. was in town. Guitarist/synthesizer player Keith

Levene had been holding interviews all week, and, with recently arrived singer John Lydon — in ancient times Johnny Rotten of the Sex Pistols — and aide-de-camp Jeanette Lee, planned to settle in the Big Apple. Evidently impressed with the club's huge video screen and facilities, the "band" agreed to present a video-oriented show as a last-minute replacement for McLaren's latest protégés. (Perhaps Lydon, never an admirer of his former manager, derived some satisfaction from the turn of events.) It was too late for print advertising, but word spread fast and, came Friday night, the Ritz was jammed.

It's hard to figure out exactly what the crowd was expecting. A reprise of Public Image Ltd.'s New York shows from a year earlier? A trace of Sex Pistols glory? What they got, in any case (after a tediously grating Levene "interview" on videotape, brimming with high-school wit), was Lydon, Levene and pick-up drummer Sam Ulano playing behind the Ritz's screen. Bright lights backstage rear-projected Lydon's capering shadow, while video cameras relayed PiL's image in front.

Unfortunately, the concept was flawed in execution: backstage lights made the video projection nearly invisible. As the boisterous crowd made its displeasure known, Lydon switched his abusiveness into overdrive. "So glad you're enjoying the show," he egged on an increasingly ugly (and now bottle-hurling) throng. "I'm safe... 'Boo hiss, they're cheatin' us, we want rock and roll,'" etc. etc. Lydon also threw in a chorus of "New York, New York" — and knew the words!

The group did essay a couple of numbers from their new *Flowers of Romance* LP, in between extended synthesizer noises. Levene added a couple of stanzas of the well-known chant, "silly fucking audience," before deciding he'd had enough of the preliminaries and emerged in front of the screen to cool down the crowd.

He didn't have a chance to try his crowd control technique. A Ritz security guard quickly removed him from harm's way, whereupon the show was declared over after 20 minutes. The crowd, yanking on the plastic tarp under the band's set-up, damaged Levene's synthesizer and ripped the Ritz's $10,000 screen. Public Image

Ltd. did not perform the following night.

On Tuesday, May 19, Warner Bros. Records, PiL's American label, hosted a hastily arranged press conference at which the band (or company, as they like to think of themselves) could explain themselves. Arriving an hour late, thin-skinned genius Levene (whose idea the conference was in the first place) declared, "I've got nothing to say. I think I'll just... film it." (The guitarist seems to like bearing decorative video equipment.)

"This looks like fun," said Lydon — divine in a pseudo-leopard-skin baseball cap, matching doublet over a billowing, untucked Yankees pinstripe shirt that could have doubled for a maternity dress and baggy pinstripe pants. He immediately disappeared into an adjoining room.

The assembled journalists were shown a video of the Ritz gig — the same one that viewing conditions at the club made impossible to see — after which Levene showed his mettle and provided generally hostile responses to questions. Although he stated the decision to cancel the second night's show was mutual between PiL and the Ritz, Levene rationalized that "We did two shows in one; it was that intense. Didn't need to do another show."

Levene claimed "We didn't plan anything," but then admitted they intended to raise the divisive screen; "We never got to the end of it." He snappishly maintained PiL's innocence of crowd-baiting. "We were not provoking a negative response ... We're too loving, that's what it is. The whole thing was positive until the audience moved in." No one suggested PiL play dates without an audience in the future.

"Listen, they're gonna get more out of that [show] than they got out of the last fucking 15 years of what they've been watching," Levene summed up modestly. Making a virtue of necessity, he noted the group had bought the damaged screen from the Ritz for their own use. Actually, the club withheld the screen's cost from PiL's fee, which Levene refused to divulge. "Nobody left disappointed," said Lydon, coaxed out of hiding by Levene's pleas. "They participate one way or another."

Sam Ulano could not be reached for comment. ∎

Steven Grant, a droll and erudite Wisconsin film journalist with prematurely grey hair, found his way to us after moving to New York in the late '70s. Trouser Press took full advantage of his talent and willingness to write about forward-looking rock music and, over the next five or six years, ran articles and interviews by him about Eno, Joy Division, Ultravox, Gary Numan, Killing Joke and Magazine. He was also responsible for the TP 66 cover story about the rise of sleaze in rock.

He went on to become a legendary figure in comics, creator of The Punisher *and* Whisper *and writer of countless other books. His* 2 Guns *was made into a 2013 Denzel Washington film.*

WHAT IS REALITY?
EURYTHMICS DREAM THEIR WAY TO SUCCESS

TP 90, OCTOBER 1983

By Steven Grant

Sweet dreams are made of this: A Motown-stricken damsel from the Scottish coast ... a gadabout British minstrel ... a band ... a song ... a hit...

"We don't want to be a part of it," Annie Lennox says of the New Music Seminar din outside Eurythmics' New York hotel suite.

This is a contradiction: Eurythmics *are* part of it, if only by virtue of being RCA's guests/product at the conference. And they have, it seems, played the biz with cool cunning: Their second

LP (functionally their debut), *Sweet Dreams (Are Made of This)*, has gone Top 30, while the single of the same name hovers in the Top 10. Accidents will happen, but this isn't one of them.

Eurythmics are an exercise in harmonious but unresolved contradictions; there's an unnerving edge to even their most benign material. "Sweet Dreams," an electronic lullaby, consists of repeated stanzas punctuated by Dave Stewart's searing synthesizer. Lennox's siren voice, maybe the best in English pop today, sweeps and surges from summer breeze to tempest. The song is simultaneously urban and pastoral, comforting and menacing, familiar and strange.

EURYTHMICS TIME CAPSULE

Annie Lennox from Scotland listens and dances to Tamla/Motown as teen ... attends Royal Academy of Music for classical training, drops out ... moves into London flat, listens to Stevie Wonder and Joni Mitchell ... decides to sing and write songs...looks for band situation...

Dave Stewart grows up in Sunderland in the northeast of England ... plays guitar in various styles ... escapes from home ... gypsies ... becomes the protégé of Amazing Blondel, opening shows for them ... begins to work with Peet Coombes ... Annie meets Dave ... songwriting team forms immediately ... Coombes, Lennox and Stewart form the Tourists ... travel the world and the seven seas ... three albums ... score novelty hit with less-than-inspired remake of "I Only Want to Be With You"... Coombes takes more control...

1980 ... Lennox/Stewart leave to form Eurythmics ... sessions with German producer Conny Plank ... sign with unnamed independent label ... label bought out by RCA ... UK RCA issues *In the Garden* (with Clem Burke of Blondie, Robert Görl of Deutsch Amerikanische Freundschaft, Holger Czukay and Jaki Liebezeit of Can) ... US RCA refuses LP....

Lennox: "After we made that album, we said, 'Okay, we've made this first statement.' Those were our first experiments with just the two of us as songwriters and instrumentalists. Now we want to do something where we can define what we—"

Stewart: "That's when we made a manifesto,

really. Our own manifesto."

On paper, this sounds disingenuous; the term "manifesto" smacks of political intrigue. There is nothing pretentious in Eurythmics' use of the word, however: it is their shield from commercialism, their roadmap to personality. Yes, political.

EURYTHMICS MANIFESTO

1) *We have no commitments to anyone but ourselves.*

Stewart: "There are a lot of synthesizer bands that are reenacting a cold statement and delivery — not really much passion in it. Which is a fair statement; too much of life is all automatic, put your ticket in the machine. We aren't really like that as people, we're more earthy, more passionate. And we've experienced a lot. We've been through the thing of being in a band that became famous. We've been through making an album with the most experimental producer. Now we buy our own equipment and it's totally down to us. No commitments to a record label. What would we like to do? Let's not go off on the track of what people expect us to do.

"In the Tourists, Annie had never been given the songs to sing the way she wanted to sing. It was always third harmony. But what she really loved was Tamla/Motown material."

Lennox: "I identify my vocal style very much with black soul music. Not with blues, but with '60s soul. It really struck a chord in me, and I can't get away from that.

"The next strongest identification was folk music from Scotland, but I don't want to be a folk singer. I see myself as a white European, but I'd like to restate the black values of the '60s. Black music in the '70s and '80s has become impotent, clichéd, repetitive. Diana Ross, whom I had so admired, and still do in many ways, makes an appeal to a general MOR white market."

Stewart: "We had just come out of the punk thing, which was very aggressive. We wanted to put that element into it, so it wouldn't be soppy soul scene, it would be very edgy. We wanted to give the soul back to music but coming from a funny place.

"We also love the power of bass synthesizers, not the ones that do frilly bits of music. We use very powerful bass lines on the album. We left in the automation of a drum machine because it's so irresistible; you can't stop it, it's incessant. That mixture with Annie's singing we felt would give the music an edge."

Lennox: "There's friction between very dark, abrasive elements and very sweet, harmonious, melodic textures. I find that very exciting. It's representative of life. That sounds *too* profound."

Stewart: "This clash is our subject, what we're living in. The most extreme example is in Bangkok, where they have this leftover American junk mixed up with their little worship temples. At an altar you might see a Campbell's soup can bent into a sacred shape."

Lennox: "As musicians, what you must do is be representative of yourself. As a European, that's a very hard thing to do. We're very much a mishmash of things. I come from the northeast of Scotland, but I identified most strongly with Motown. It has taken me a long time to realize that this was representative of me. Punk music represented me to some extent, but when the people into punk were 18, I was 23. It wasn't quite my generation. When I was 18, the hippie movement was already having its swan song.

"I now feel that I am coming into my time. I am coming to a clarity of vision. I see what I am representing. Yes, it is a mishmash, it is a mixture, it cannot be this movement or that."

2) *Eurythmics are a project, not a band, that involves different people at different times.*

An English TV show. Eurythmics, promoting their album, appear with grand piano and gospel choir. They perform "The Walk" and "This City Never Sleeps." "It was so obvious," Stewart says, "that it almost sounded like a famous gospel song."

The filtering process: new becomes old, familiar becomes unpredictable. Jump cut to: Lennox and Stewart singing the same songs a cappella. A jarring moment.

Lennox: "Synthesized sounds alone couldn't possibly represent us. Dave used to be totally into minstrel music. I think cultural elitism about liking this or that kind of music is almost fascistic."

3) *The traditional commercial route dilutes the core of the music. Protect yourself.*

Lennox: "Eurythmics razed everything to the ground. We started from scratch, got every penny together that we possibly could, and went to a bank manager for a loan. We invested that money in a studio: an 8-track machine and an empty warehouse."

Stewart: "We purposely set about creating a place where we would have nothing whatsoever to do with the music industry. We were like kids playing with a new toy. We have stacks of tapes from playing with the 8-track. It had nothing to do with music, really."

Lennox: "RCA was running hot and cold about the deal. When they heard the material we produced and felt they could do something with it, they ran incredibly hot. That was a nice coincidence. Now that we have a good deal of commercial success, we have to go back to the drawing board. I don't want to do remakes of things because they were successful. Artists must — I don't want to get too pretentious here — redefine what they are doing constantly."

IT IS EASY TO QUESTION Lennox and Stewart's seriousness. They espouse all the bugaboos of pop music: art, self-control, self-expression. One's immediate response is to wince at these self-pronounced artistes brought low.

What, specifically, is new about Eurythmics? The white soul craze that hit northern England a few years back parallels Lennox's fixation with the source material. The manifesto/isolationism/project-not-band stance was prefigured by Public Image Ltd. Then there are the thoroughly disconcerting elements: the songs' almost perfect pop construction, the mélange of source material, the careful consideration of image.

With her business suits and cropped flaming red hair, Annie Lennox could be the female counterpart of Boy George — except that she escapes androgyny. Her appearance is initially shocking but not bewildering (Boy George is just the opposite), unexpected but not exactly out of place. She sidesteps both male and female images instead of absorbing them, but her stance prevents a blurring of roles: there are no lesbian overtones, no feminist statement. She is less image than anti-fashion.

EURYTHMICS, THEN, are appealing because they dodge a communicable aesthetic. And their music is less immediately striking than their image. *In the Garden* was calm and pastoral, with vast distances between the sounds and a romantic lyrical quality. *Sweet Dreams (Are Made of This)* moves the duo into more commercial areas; cosmopolitan urgency pervades the songs. Lennox's voice, with its pure tone characteristic of English folk music, sometimes seems a pretender to rock.

Abrupt changes in technique and style, a mad rush up the charts both here and in the UK, artistic posture and image manipulation — these have the sting of calculated promotion to them. And somewhere a dog thinks it's dinnertime.

Let's say the image is calculated. (It is.)

Lennox: "I don't want to wear a frilly dress, because I feel vulnerable. To wear something more neutral — like a man's suit — I can go along with that. The suit is a functional thing, and it also makes you stop and think, 'What sort of person wears a man's suit?'"

Stewart bought his suit at an esteemed London tailor known as "*the* Mister Average place. No style to the clothes whatsoever. Right in the middle."

LET'S SAY EURYTHMICS' shift between their two albums — the acquiescence to more popular forms — was machinated. (Half right.)

Let's say the Eurythmics plant themselves squarely in the avant-garde cerebral dance tradition of electropop music. (Almost accurate.)

If that were true, it still wouldn't matter. Eurythmics do all of these things right. They have intelligence rather than art-school cleverness, critical faculties rather than cynicism — and an honest love of music for music's sake. Their songs offer one contradiction after another: past and future, black American artifact and white European experience, erotic flamboyance and sexual neutrality, the experimental and the familiar.

Lennox likes pop music "that has some abrasion in it. The trick is to get as much through as possible without them realizing it. We don't have anything that subversive in our music, but we have our moments. The next lot of material, which we've all got ideas for, will be a development in that sense."

(Lennox/Stewart's fave pop songs: the Kinks' "Waterloo Sunset," the Pretenders' "Stop Your Sobbing," David Bowie/Iggy Pop's "China Girl.")

Eurythmics' highly stylized music remains highly accessible, vivacious, perspicacious. Beneath the smooth electronics and Lennox's sweet, lulling vocals lie depths of experience and a feel for paradox. It's subtly dangerous music. This is not *just* another pop group.

THE JOURNALISTS and photographers, the promo people, the would-be rock writers and would-be rock musicians have all packed up. The free bars are closed and the bottles empty. The New Music Seminar calls it a day — and Eurythmics couldn't be happier about it.

Annie Lennox has largely remained locked up in her room, nursing a potentially failing throat. Dave Stewart, though, has spent some time mingling, to see what the ado is about.

"I just had a great conversation," he says. "This guy was from Austin, Texas. Within 10 minutes I found we were on the same exact wavelength. His favorite record of all time is the same as mine: Beaver and Krause's *All Good Men*. Every track on that album is completely different. His favorite groups included Abba, Chris and Cosey from Throbbing Gristle ... all these different types of groups.

"It's the same way I feel. I don't see why you should be stuck with just one ... the sort of thing this New Music Seminar is about."

"I think it's a kind of fear," Lennox says. "This endorsement of something somehow exclusive is also typical of the music industry. Inverted snobbery.

"New music? That's a very handy label. And everyone knows it's bullshit. Music is new all the time. There's no old music or new music. It's just *music!*"

Who am I to disagree? ∎

THEY'RE ALL DANCING TO EDDY GRANT'S TUNE

TP 91, NOVEMBER 1993

By Jim Green

Eddy Grant is a man of many parts and curious contrasts.

His first American hit, "Electric Avenue" (from his current *Killer on the Rampage* album), combines soul, rock and funk in just the right proportions for these musically cross-fertilized times. The genre-bending recalls Eddie Van Halen's collaboration with Michael Jackson on "Beat It" — but, for some, Jackson's slick façade rings a touch less true than Grant's more down-to-earth approach. Also, Grant does it all himself: writing, production and performance.

At New York's Ritz, Grant bounds onstage clad in coordinated black leather trousers and vest and black T-shirt. He swings his (unreligiously) neat dreadlocks and flashes a toothy grin as he dons his guitar. The tight little band behind him vamps on the ominous reggae chords of "Living on the Frontline," then suddenly switches gears to the buoyant bounce of a song the crowd can't be expected to know, "Can't Get Enough of Your Love." (Grant's 1980 *Can't Get Enough* LP was never released here.)

But the crowd is with him from the first note. Grant presides over his two-hour set with a mix-

ture of grateful humility and confidence verging on bravado — as if to say, "It's great to be here, thank you!" (which he does, in several variations), followed by "And don't I deserve it?" *That* he doesn't need to say at all.

This promising new face with potential to burn is a 16-year veteran of the music biz wars. His music has sold in great quantities around the world — both under his own name and in versions by other artists — virtually everywhere but (until recently) Britain and North America. Grant's status as a Third World star is striking only in light of his having started in the Equals, a [British] band whose millstone was getting tagged as too black for white audiences but far too white-rock for the black market.

Now, however, it doesn't matter. Eddy Grant has arrived. *Killer on the Rampage* made the Top 10; ironically, "Electric Avenue" was denied the honor of heading the pop singles list by (of all people) the Police's "Every Breath You Take." But the deed's been done, America has been broken. "Electric Avenue" is a certified million-seller, and the album seems destined to share the honor — especially with the second single, "I Don't Wanna Dance," bulleting up the charts.

Grant is not worried. Life is sweet when you're in the driver's seat; in his Hotel Pierre suite on his tour's Manhattan stopover, Grant seems eminently comfortable. He no longer has to oversee every stage of his records' manufacture and distribution. For touring purposes, he shares musical control with members of his road band, but Grant still holds the reins of his career.

Lounging barefoot in an olive-drab jumpsuit, Grant indicates the pattern was set at an early age. He was inspired by his father Patrick, one of Guyana's top trumpet players.

"I'd wanted to play trumpet since I was six years old, but I didn't have the facility, and my father kept me away from it. Every time I tried to take his trumpet out from under the bed, he'd throw a cuff at me."

In December 1960, the senior Grant, hoping for a more lucrative return on his professional rep, resettled his family in north London. Twelve-year-old Eddy immediately gathered his gumption and asked for his own horn. He got it and was soon playing in his school's symphony orchestra. Later he turned to traditional jazz.

It wasn't long before rock and roll, soul and blues beckoned to Grant. Again, he went to his dad and requested an instrument: an electric guitar.

"My father thought it was going to be another fad. He said, 'I don't want you to play no guitar. Anyway, the guys who play guitar are all yobs, they *smoke* and do all kinds of terrible things' — you know, that kind of talk.

"I said, 'Naah, I wouldn't be like that'" — he still avoids demon nicotine, at least — "'I just wanna play.' So, in the end he struck a compromise."

If young Eddy built himself an electric guitar, his father would buy him an amplifier. The offspring went off and did it; his dad not only bought him the amp, but — being versed in the fretboard himself — showed his son some chords as well. "Bit by bit, I met people who reckoned that I was quite good," Grant says, although he admits it was a generous assessment. All the same, he was invited to jam with a group in London's nearby Highgate area. Grant was skeptical it would amount to anything but went anyway. "I'd just finished my exams" — it was 1966 — "and there was nothing much to do."

HE MET A young white drummer named John Hall, with whom Grant started the Equals. "We put word about, and in a couple of weeks or so the Gordon brothers, Derv and Lincoln [from a relocated Jamaican family], came into the picture, and eventually Pat Lloyd [another white Londoner] as well. None of them could play. I could just about play, but the others didn't know a chord amongst them."

That was soon remedied by lots of hard work. "We played right across the board. We did some blues gigs too, concerts and smaller gigs with, like, Fleetwood Mac — in those days, a blues group — and John Mayall. We —or I — was really involved with those kinds of eclectic musics. But we were basically a pop band; that was our arena." As such the Equals signed to President Records in 1967.

"Our first record was 'I Won't Be There,' a hit in Germany and nowhere else. We did become very big and successful in Germany that year. Our debut there onstage was on the same bill as Cream, at Bremen Stadthalle. We were playing with real heavyweights, but it didn't make any difference to us. Playing to 20,000 people was the same as playing to 150 people at the All Star Club in Liverpool Street. The difference was between Cream and us, in that we knew when the time came how to handle such an audience, by having worked with all these great guys.

"Cream had all this adulation heaped on them, but they didn't have the experience of how to work an audience, so they came out much the worse for it. People were watching us and saying, 'Oooh, these young guys, cor, they're freaking everybody out' — doing somersaults and all kinds of incredible things onstage.

"We later opened for Spencer Davis, Jeff Beck, Procol Harum and, in most cases, we blew those people off the stage. We were a young band, but with lots of energy and lots of experience. While most of these pop bands, like the Yardbirds or whoever, were learning their art musically but not learning any stagecraft, we had the best of stagecraft from all these soul guys —

and we had the musical thing coming along from the pop side."

Lead singer Derv Gordon was a pretty fair frontman, according to Grant, but even better was his brother Lincoln on second vocal and sometimes rhythm guitar along with Pat Lloyd. "Lincoln would imitate, like, James Brown on one number and win everybody over." (Wait a minute — who played bass? "We never had a bass onstage, just the rhythm guitars and myself playing solo. We used one on recordings a lot of the time, but never onstage.")

"I Get So Excited" almost made the British Top 40 in early 1968. A few months later, "Baby Come Back" fought its way up to number-one. The Equals, Grant claims, "broke attendance records wherever they played." The group stood on the verge of getting it on (as George Clinton might say) in a big way. But what happened?

Over the next two and a half years, the Equals placed only two more Top 10 UK hits, "Viva Bobby Joe" and "Black Skin Blue Eyed Boys." In the U.S., the group's first LP, *Unequalled*, came out on the tiny Laurie label and sank without a trace. Grant estimates that "Baby Come Back," picked up here by RCA, sold perhaps a half-million copies Stateside, "but it was over the course of maybe six months, happening in different places at different times," so the single charted only in the low thirties. RCA also assembled a *Baby Come Back* LP from various UK tracks, a move not appreciated by Grant; it became a bargain-bin special in no time flat.

"The Equals got all the success they deserved in Europe and Africa and South America. Overall, just about every one of the singles sold a million copies. But in America and England, our career wasn't very well orchestrated. President was a very small label; [our chart placings were] very much music-business politics; we had no real manager; we never came over to tour in America, which would've made a great difference."

FOR A MAN SO outspoken on record, Grant seems loath to accuse the record industry of racism. A somewhat leading question only elicits the response that the Equals' straddling of Stones/

Who rock and roll, Memphis soul and Britpop bred confusion, particularly in the U.S., as to how they should be promoted.

"If the Equals had been treated right, we would have been enormous. If we had toured here, if we had broken here, a band like Sly & the Family Stone would never have existed."

But history isn't made of "ifs." After a handful of singles and albums, the Equals were ready to move on, musically and contractually. In search of a more striking sound, Grant wrote "Black Skin Blue Eyed Boys," which he considers a milestone of the band's career.

The Equals made that the last record they would record for President — they *thought*.

"We went to CBS and made one album, *Stand Up and Be Counted*, a departure from the Equals sound. I realized a lot of people were trying to get on that bandwagon — groups like Slade, who were coming up and getting hits — and I thought it was time we moved away from it."

Unfortunately, President filed suit, claiming the Equals had no right leaving them just yet. *Stand Up* was tied up in litigation. The band was disgusted and lost direction, other than moving back to the President stable.

"There was no output from the band until, as part of the settlement, they had to do another record for President. The label boss wanted it to be real old-fashioned rock and roll stuff, some just in that style and some actual covers. We did two albums' worth of material; eventually one came out [in 1974] called *Equals Rock Around the Clock*. Interesting, because I really messed around the arrangements of these standards that *everybody* had done, trying to do them differently."

Grant's reference to the Equals as "they" is significant. "By now I was no longer a member of the band; I'd left in '72. But when they did an album for Phonogram in '76, called *Born Ya!* [patois for "born here"], I produced because I didn't have my solo career on a firm footing yet.

"I was really doing what I'd been doing all along: writing, producing the band and playing, too. There was the desire on the part of certain people to keep me in the band, because it was worth more with me in it. It was also a ques-

tion of friendship; Pat Lloyd kept urging me to work with them, and he's still my best friend out of that situation. A series of guitarists replaced me, but whoever came in seemed to feel it wasn't their place. In the end I wound up playing with them as well as producing and writing for them."

Grant was beginning to take a broader view of his career. In 1974, he built a studio in an old carriage house in northern London. He had decided to begin as a behind-the-scenes man rather than an artist in his own right. His work on the Equals' Phonogram album was part of a production deal he'd signed with the label; he also produced stalwart British reggae band the Pioneers (best known for "Long Shot Kick the Bucket" and "Let Your Yeah Be Yeah") and the more experimental reggae amalgam of 90° Inclusive.

"The Pioneers were established reggae, but I wasn't making reggae with them. If you ever listen to *Feel the Rhythm*, you'll be amazed: Suddenly you find a guy with a great voice in a completely new light. 90° Inclusive was a young band with whom I was experimenting in different forms. With the Equals, I wrote the songs, the interpretation of the music was always mine, I produced the records. *Born Ya!* is a transition between what the Equals had been and what I am now."

This, then, was the ideal way for Grant to operate, since he felt record companies wouldn't give him a free hand by himself. The Equals had "a name that would sell records *somewhere*, at least. So, if I wanted to experiment a little and drop this funny kind of music in, they could accept that."

Not for long. All three bands' albums came out in 1976 and were instant stiffs. "They said, 'We're not selling any of "your" artists — mind you, they weren't *marketing* 'my' artists. They simply expected me to come in and sell millions of records *for* them." Phonogram wanted Eddy Grant as an artist, not a producer. "If I had been under contract as a member of the Equals at that time, my career as it is now would never have existed. But I wasn't. When Phonogram found this out, they tried all kinds of deals to keep me — to buy up my studio, to fund me, to give me a label and so on. I knew it would come down to that, but I didn't want that, 'cause they hadn't made an effort to sell my music.

"Then they said, 'What do you want to sign with us as an artist?' I said, 'A million pounds. I don't care how you actually give it to me, I just want to be able to tell the press I've signed a deal for a million pounds.'

"They laughed. They rolled on the floor. They said, 'You've got to be joking. You'll never make a million pounds in this business.' So, I told them to kiss my ass. I had nothing to lose, really.

"I'd already started my own label, Ice, in the Caribbean in 1974. Phonogram didn't know about it; it was none of their business. I picked the Caribbean because of the access to the radio, to get the music I wanted to do heard there and let other markets pick up on it.

"I reasoned that I couldn't go to America. It's so big; how could little me come to America with a couple of thousand pounds and try to impress these people? But the heads of all the record companies go on holidays, and most of them go to the West Indies, where I knew I could create some airplay for my music. If it's good, I thought, they'll want it, and then I'll say, 'Right, you lot, let's talk a deal.'" It didn't quite work out that way. However, that's how Grant hooked up with Tony Calder, who's been his manager ever since.

BY MID-1977, Grant had set up Ice in England, modeling the label after what he learned at Phonogram. "Jesus, it wasn't so easy," he laughs at his own naïveté. "But once you've made the decision you're committed, you just have to carry on." Grant knew the global nature of the record business (and of his music's appeal) from his Equals days. He directed his output not only at Britain and the Caribbean, but at Africa, too. His first Ice single was "Hello, Africa"; *Message Man*, an LP which included it, followed. "Neighbour Neighbour," another single from the album, was also successful outside Europe and North America.

"We were an *independent* independent label," Grant chuckles, "although towards the end of [the album's] run we did a distribution deal with Pye." (Several *Message Man* songs are on Grant's 1979 *Live at Notting Hill* album.)

Then came *Walking on Sunshine*, a key album in a number of ways.

"It was selling fantastically throughout Africa," Grant says. "By now I had bought a pressing plant, and we were manufacturing vast quantities of this record and exporting them. Around that time, I also recorded a couple of albums in Yoruba, for sale only in Africa. I did an 18-minute version in Yoruba of a track from *Walking on Sunshine*: 'Say I Love You' must be the biggest-selling record in Nigeria ever, bigger than Sunny Adé, Fela, Ebenezer Obey, you name them. Big. It was so ridiculous that I had to press records in London and Nigeria.

"Then Nigeria banned all imports, so I was pressing in Nigeria and commuting back and forth! But meanwhile we were stuck with 10,000 copies of *Walking on Sunshine* in England, and nowhere to sell them. Tony was trying desperately to make a deal, but it just wasn't happening. We started giving them away — to discothèques, boutiques, anyone who'd have them. Eventually it started getting popular in a town called Slough, especially the first side, which consisted of five-and-a-half minutes of 'Sunshine' and thirteen minutes of 'Living on the Front Line.' They loved the whole side. But being told you're going down really great in Slough is roughly like being informed you're number-one in Poughkeepsie.

"People were telling me I should press up disco singles of the tracks. I thought, 'Aah, leave it alone.' But it got to epidemic proportions; we had no more copies, and kids were offering all kinds of money just to get the two songs.

"I thought, I think we've got a hit, if we can get distribution. Not long after I got a call from Chris Hill, who worked with Nigel Grainge, the guy who'd signed me to Phonogram and now had his own label called Ensign. He said, 'Look, you've got a hit on your hands. Let us help you get it into the charts.'"

After some coaxing, Grant agreed to let the record — just a single version of "Front Line," edited into two parts — go out as an Ice/Ensign 45, a one-off deal. It was a substantial success in Britain and on the Continent. Virgin Records head Richard Branson noticed and enticed Grant to license Ice distribution to Virgin — a complete flop. Epic picked up the record for the U.S. and fared little better.

In 1980, *Love in Exile* came out independently in Britain. Epic retitled it *My Turn to Love You*, but it's as if the record never existed here.

"It wasn't until the single 'Do You Feel My Love' from the *Can't Get Enough* album in 1980 that I got back with Nigel on another one-record situation. We got lucky again. The same with the single of 'Can't Get Enough of Your Love' and once again with 'I Love You Yes I Love You,' also from that album.

At that point Grant decided to assert his own corporate identity. He wanted Ice to be his label, not a logo on someone else's. Grainge agreed.

In 1981, Grant was busy moving to Barbados and setting up a studio and branch of Ice there. By the end of 1982, *Killer on the Rampage* was a fait accompli, and the stage set for his 1983 coup.

In the meantime, Grant found many of his songs succeeding in markets where he himself was unknown.

"'Hello, Africa' and 'Neighbour Neighbour' entered the U.S. soul charts on an album by a group called Kalyan. People didn't know I wrote it, but they were listening to the Clash do 'Police on My Back' [which first appeared here on RCA's *Equals* LP back in 1968!] on the *Sandinista!* album. Bonnie Raitt just did 'Baby Come Back' on her new album. Rockers Revenge had a local hit in New York with their version of 'Walking on Sunshine.' In 1982, I had a number-one hit in Australia with 'Say I Love You' sung by a white female singer called Renee Geyer; not even the ever-wise press knew it was my song. In Venezuela, Willie Colón's version of that song — he called it 'Amor Verdadero' and didn't give me any credit — was an enormous hit, which I only heard about when a friend went down there and heard it."

Such eclectic appeal recalled the Equals' problems with categorization. "It seemed to carry over into my solo career. I thought, 'Oh Jesus, don't tell me I'm gonna be doomed to "If only we could find somewhere to put you!"' Why don't you just play me across all the categories?" That's more or less what finally happened, and it had to be that way. "I don't make music specifically to sell it. I just do it because I like it, and if it sells too, that's nice. Otherwise, I would never have made a record like 'Front Line' — it's just not a commercial proposition to make a 13-minute record like that."

A virtual one-man band in the studio, Grant necessarily has to rely on others to bring his music to life onstage.

"I work alone in the studio because then I have total concentration. I don't need a man mixing my paints or holding the easel up for me, so to speak.

"My live musicians, then, do not have an easy job. They have to transcend all the musical barriers, to articulate in and around all of them, comfortably. These guys have been with me a long time, since before the Notting Hill live recording. They're Marcus James (bass), Tony Scantlebury (drums), Tony (Zap) Edmunds (keyboards), Valentine Pascal (guitar), Sonny Akpan (percussion) and Rose Hibbert, Pamela Robertin and Doreen Henry (backing vocals). And me!"

One last question: Why does Grant think he's succeeding now?

"You know, when it is your time, it is like when it is your time to die: It just is. No explanation, no set of circumstances you can put together to create the situation. It's like playing squash: You do an impossible shot behind your back and the other guy's got no chance. Normally it wouldn't work; you'd miss it, or if you did hit it the guy'd slam it down your throat. I took my shot and it worked; it's just my turn.

"I don't examine it, because once I start examining it, I start making mass-production music, and that would make me unhappy. I don't wanna be unhappy making music, so I just carry on. If tomorrow I wanna make a track that's ten minutes long, I will feel totally free to, because I'll be doing it for the right motive, not because it's commercially expedient."

Pride combined with enjoyment — that's what's at stake for Eddy Grant. Otherwise, as he might say, there'd be no reason for Portrait, his U.S. record company, to feel confident "I Don't Wanna Dance" will have a shot as a follow-up single. It's completely unlike "Electric Avenue" in every way — except that it's by Eddy Grant and it's good. It's also Eddy Grant's time. ■

COLUMNISM

Magazine publishing, on our small scale, could easily switch from "How can we fit all this great stuff into one issue" to "What are we going to fill all these pages with?" So, it was prudent and practical to establish regular elements that we could count on month to month. Our mainstay columns for nearly the entire existence of the magazine were *Hit and Run*, Jon Young's collection of one-paragraph album reviews, and *Green Circles*, Jim Green's singles reviews. We also had *America Underground* (domestic indie releases and local scene reports), *Media Eye* (books, films, magazines, etc.), Mick Farren's *Surface Noise*, Ira Robbins' *Lip Service*, Paul Rambali's *English Ramblings*, occasional coverage by various writers of European music in *Across the Channel* (later renamed *Outer Limits*) and a half-dozen amusing *Rock Therapy* columns by Joe Sasfy.

*O*ur high school pal Scott Kempner (a.k.a. Top Ten) was, like Dave and Ira, a diehard and knowledgeable rock and roller, Who freak, New York Yankee diehard and Richard Meltzer acolyte. We formed a band together that did a couple of jams in a living room and then got written about in Fusion *magazine by Meltzer. But that was just a teenaged lark. We were totally knocked out when he became a certified professional musician with the Dictators and remained enthusiastic when he went on to form the Del-Lords with Eric Ambel and the Little Kings with Dion.*

Although he continued to prove himself to be an engaging writer of both songs and prose, this was the only thing Scott ever wrote for us.

Scott spent the last years of his life in a Connecticut nursing home, being cared for as he suffered through early onset dementia. He died, at the age of 69, in November 2023.

MEDIA EYE

TP 14, JUNE/JULY 1976

By Top Ten (Dictators guitarist)

This is the very first article that I've ever written. Ira's been asking me for an article for a long time and I've been promising him one for almost as long. Writing it was tough enough, but to complicate the assignment, the subject is a real good friend of mine. To complicate things further, I regard my subject as the tops in my new field of endeavor. Before I go any further, I would like to say that, although we are real good friends, I was an avid, if not fanatical, fan first and friend second. All of which brings us to the legendary Richard Meltzer.

For me, meeting Richard Meltzer was a thrill comparable to shaking hands with Roger Daltrey (lead singer of the Tommys, a top rock combo) the night of the famous Fillmore fire. The historic meeting took place in Ungano's, a now-defunct rock club in Manhattan. It was a hot August night in 1970 and about fifteen of us were there to see the Stooges. Having arrived four hours early (intentionally, of course), we were waiting not-so-patiently for the show to begin when I spotted a familiar face by the bar (of course). I recognized him by his baseball cap. After all, was it not the very same cap that he was wearing on page 9 of the second incarnation of *Crawdaddy* (Vol. IV, No. 12)? That photo accompanied his article describing *Flamingo* by the Flamin' Groovies as the greatest LP ever. Being madly in love with both the group and the album, I decided that I had a damn good opening line to whip on this amazing human bean and personal idol. I collected my nerve (I only use drugs, never abuse them) and went up to him and asked, "Do you really think that *Flamingo* is the greatest of them all?" Not used to being recognized by young citizens, he was both impressed and surprised, but managed to expertly retort, "No! Never did." Snappy answer, huh? Much impressed by his coolness, I watched the Stooges' set, which was just beginning. After the rather incredible show, I again approached the world-renown scribe and asked if he was going to write about the show. He said, "No, I'm going to write about you." We then exchanged addresses, and a long, historic friendship was under way. About three months later, a high school pal brought me an article he had found while reviewing the literary content of one of his dad's *Screw* magazines. It was an article on the Stooges' show and, sure enough, the fifth and sixth words of the article were my very own two names.

To backtrack, my discovery of Richard Meltzer occurred when I was in junior high. Since September of my ninth year (when I bought *Meet the Beatles*), every cent that I've ever had has gone to rock and roll. When it wasn't records, I was buying rock and roll magazines. One day, as I was drooling over some new releases in a local record store, I noticed a magazine that I had never seen before. It was *Crawdaddy* #9, and I bought it immediately. On the bus ride home, I became entranced by an article entitled, "The Stones, the Beatles and Spyder Turner's Raunch Epistemology." Although I could only understand about one-fifth of it, something about it kept drawing me back. For the next week, it baffled all of my seventh-grade cronies and anybody else that I showed it to. Finally, after the tenth reading, and with the help of a large dictionary, it made a lot more sense than anything else I had ever read (on rock). It was more than just one a-hole's review of another a-hole's record. It wasn't stuffy and boring. Instead, it was entertaining, perceptive and every bit as danceable as half of my record collection. Here was a genius! The writer was, of course, Richard Meltzer.

(It's also worth remembering that the whole magazine knocked me out as well. There was one other writer in particular whose style was close to Meltzer's; Sandy Pearlman, who is now the manager of my band as well as the manager and main lyricist of the Blue Öyster Cult.)

Richard Meltzer is a man of many talents. To list only a few, he is: (1) an author of two books (as well as others awaiting publication), (2) the king of all rock critics, (3) former lead singer (very early BÖC), (4) grandfather of the Dictators, (5) genius, (6) piss artist, (7) lyricist extraordinaire, (8) visionary and philosopher, (9) sports writer, (10) funnyman, (11) pal to the stars (Iggy, Balin, K. Fowley, Groovies, Alex Harvey and more), (12) great drinker, (13) boyfriend of 10 years to the adorable and equally wonderful Roni Hoffman (you all remember her), (14) great pal and the most inherently cool guy I know, (15) and, last but not least, the first guy to put Ira's, David's, Hank Frank's and my own name in print.

This being a rock magazine, it appears proper to concentrate on the rock aspects of Meltzer's career. First, R. Meltzer as rock critic. There are three kinds of rock critics: The dull parasites who, unfortunately, make up about 80 percent of all rock critics. These are the ones who have nothing to say but can't seem to find enough space to say it in. They merely make condescending remarks about an art that needs them as much as Ed Cassidy needs a barber. Then there are those whose love and enthusiasm for rock is so genuine that their writing is exciting as well as justified. This magazine is a perfect example. Finally, there are the true artists whose work stands on its own. It

is in this category that our hero's moniker stands out above all others. Just check out any of the old *Crawdaddy* articles, either of his two books or any of his columns for *Fusion* or *Creem*. Start with the assumption that he is COOL and then settle down to the most unique and entertaining stuff that you could ever find on the subject of rock. Read them a few times (just like you would approach a new record) and see for yourself. (Some of the *Fusion* articles were written under pseudonyms like Borneo Jimmy and Lar Tusb.) To describe them and do them any sort of justice would be impossible, but some of the more amazing ones are "What a Goddam Great Second Cream Album," "Spyder Turner etc." and any of the "Outer Pumice" columns for *Crawdaddy*.

Then there are the two books, *The Aesthetics of Rock* and *Gulcher*. *The Aesthetics of Rock* was originally written as a master's thesis entitled "Tomorrow's Not Today: A Sequel." True to form, Meltzer handed his prof the paper inside the jacket of *Beatles VI*. The teacher, who failed to see the point or the humor, failed Meltzer. An excerpt from the paper appeared in *Crawdaddy*, accompanied by enthusiastic praise from Paul Williams (the editor, not the cretin that you see on *Hollywood Squares*). Also accompanying the excerpt was the announcement of the forthcoming book. When the book finally appeared three or four years later, it was hailed as genius by sources as diverse as the *New York Times* and me. It was the most unusual rock book ever to surface on G-d's green earth. The style was roughly like Socrates shooting up and being transferred to nowadays and being a VERY COOL GUY WHO LUVVED ROCK'N ROLL. Instead, we have the only philosophy book that you can Twist to. At this point, I feel obliged to brag that I am the proud owner of the original manuscript (that's right, the master's thesis) and you, boys and girls, are not.

A few years later, a second book appeared, entitled *Gulcher* (gulcher ... gulture ... culture, get it?). Like the first book, one can start at any point and read in any direction. *Gulcher* is subtitled *Post-Rock Cultural Pluralism in America (1649-1980)* and is the official document of the under-the-counter culture. Recognizing that rock itself is no longer the true focal point of the culture, Meltzer covers everything from wrestling and booze to television and bottlecaps (of which he has the world's largest collection). The styles of both books are in complete contrast. Where *T.A.O. Rock* had more ten-letter words than you ever knew existed, *Gulcher* is deceptively simple. Both books are definitive Richard Meltzer and YOU SHOULD BUY THEM IMMEDIATELY!!

It is Meltzer's attitude that carries everything he writes. Whether it's rock or sports or even his infamous dead animals in jello, it all becomes rock and roll under his expert touch. This has less to do with mastery of his own craft than with the fact that Richard Meltzer lives, eats and breathes rock and roll every day of his life. After all, what is rock and roll if not an attitude and a way of life? Richard Meltzer is this attitude more than anybody else that you or I have ever met.

Why then has fame and big bucks eluded a genius of Meltzer's caliber? The answer is all too simple. When Meltzer's style was complex and "serious." people were turned off by the big words and elusive style. Not everybody was. There were certainly many others like myself who kept coming back to his stuff and felt like we had made a great artistic discovery. Then when Meltzer's style changed to what it is now, people were turned off by the seeming simplicity of it. Again, there were fanatical fans, but they remained a cult.

Hopefully the future will bring the long-overdue success that Meltzer deserves. For one thing, the Dictators are dedicated to his success. His lyrics will appear on the forthcoming Dictators' second album on at least one masterpiece entitled "Tender Was the Night." Other possibilities are "Gimme Puppy" and "I Live With the Roaches." I also believe that Meltzer will derive great personal satisfaction from the inevitable success of Handsome Dick Manitoba. Manitoba is the living embodiment of cool as defined by Meltzer. They are great friends, and together can level mountains.

Richard Meltzer has now left Noo Yawk in quest of the pot of gold under the warm California sun. He has far too much integrity to change a style that anyone who is really cool knows is the cat's pajamas. We all pray for his success and are confident that he will return home a star. Next time you run into some critic, ask him or her about Richard Meltzer. If they don't acknowledge their debt to him, they're just lying. Meltzer was, is and always will be the King. ∎

Having Mick Farren as a columnist (1980–84) was an amazing thrill for us: he was a genuine voice of the British counterculture, a veteran of London's underground press, leader of rock's (Social) Deviants, someone whose music writing we'd read and admired in the weeklies and a larger-than-life character in a black leather jacket who'd fortuitously taken up residence in New York. We were honored to be a monthly host for his thoughtful emanations. This was not, in fact, his last column, but it is fully representative of the voice he brought to our pages.

Mick eventually left New York for Los Angeles and then back to Blighty, where he died in 2013 after collapsing onstage during a Deviants gig.

SURFACE NOISE

TP 85, MAY 1983

By Mick Farren

At times the profession of rock critic seems marginally lower than that of pimp. On a scale of social usefulness, you're scrambling to make zero. A feeling of depression comes and goes often enough to start a reasonable person wondering if this is any way for a grown-up to make a living.

Every art form has critics. Some are respected, even recognized as artists in their own right. Most receive some attention for their opinions. It's nice to believe that's the way it is in rock. Oh yeah? Let me quote from the Plasmatics' "A Pig Is a Pig": "This song is dedicated / To a special kind of person … The cowardly journalist / Who hides behind his typewriter / Exploiting people who can't fight back."

When Wendy O. Williams and Rod Swenson can talk thus, something must be rotten in the profession. Could it be we've sunk so far into the scumbag league that we're beyond all salvation? In attempting to play a productive role in popular music, have we alienated its primary producers? Do the majority of recording artists secretly share the Plasmatics' sentiments?

The truth of the matter is that vast areas of the music industry would much rather that rock writing had never progressed beyond noting rock stars' favorite food and color and printing his or her picture nice and big.

On one hand, the writer is beset by petulant, would-be stars who become venomously hostile if you point out that they are anything less than the left hand of god and may even try to punch you out if you meet in the same bar. They are often accompanied by a press agent who not only despises you and all you stand for, but also believes you are so hopelessly corrupt that you will sell out for a free lunch and a few lousy albums or stand your integrity on its head for a free trip to Cleveland.

On the other hand, certain readers take it as a personal insult if you mention the smallest flaw in the work of their favorite artiste. They also may punch you out if they find you in the same bar. This itself can be adequate reason, regardless of ego, never to let the readers find out what you look like.

Part of the problem is that few people apart from critics themselves realize they serve a purpose. The classic role of the critic has always been to stand slightly apart from art and act as a stimulant — a combination stick and carrot, if you like, pushing for the highest possible standards. This applies to everything from restaurants to bullfights. (Yes, Spain and Mexico host a flourishing breed of bullfight writers.)

Unfortunately, all too often neither musicians nor the industry see it this way. For too long they have embraced the idea that rock journalism is simply a gratuitous aid to selling records, a kind of free advertising. If a writer's response to a show is less than positive, nobody reevaluates or tries to figure out why the critic didn't like what they

did. They simply assume the review is a product of a twisted, vindictive mind.

The phrase is "getting some press." A great rock tradition is that "press" is a stepping stone to stardom and the unlimited sex, drugs and money at the end of the rock rainbow. Even friends hit on you: not "Hey Micky, I'd really appreciate your critical evaluation of my record" — hell no — just "I want some press."

It starts to sound uncomfortably like "gimme some head." A writer who doesn't put out is clearly and viciously standing in the way of the unrestrained luxury that's the birthright of every rock and roller. Kill the writer! Or at least banish him from the free list. (Lou Reed, unhappy with his treatment at the ballpoint of *New Musical Express*'s Nick Kent, once decreed that not only would Kent never again receive press tickets to one of his shows, but he was to be prevented from even *purchasing* tickets to a Lou Reed concert. Reed, later famous for verbally abusing writers like Robert Christgau and John Rockwell on a live album, was less than happy when shown the impossibility of this conceit.)

There was a time when rock writers attempted to become sub-stars in their own right. Dave Marsh, Charles Shaar Murray, Nick Kent and Lester Bangs all felt they deserved better than simply being appendages of the music industry.

I could never quite come to grips with this critic-as-star business. I'd already had a somewhat farcical career as a singer. I'd cut records. To attempt luminescence in a kindred trade might lead to identity confusion, but record companies were then handing out booze, bowling jackets and airplane tickets like they were going out of fashion, so what the hell.

When other writers started making records (Kent, Murray, Bangs, Vivien Goldman) the identity confusion was complete. Some, like the Pretenders' Chrissie Hynde, even had hits. Boomtown Rat Bob Geldof, now a noted press hater, was once the *NME* stringer in Dublin.

As rock diminished, rock writing, to a degree, diminished with it. It was saved in part by a flood of rock books. For a while it seemed more people wanted to read about music than hear it. This proved to be largely a publisher's illusion.

The real situation was that half the practicing journalists were cultivating a massive enthusiasm for the obscure. The rest — primarily the young and the English, in the wake of Tony Parsons and Julie Burchill — adopted a judgmental, almost Stalinist approach: grading, rewarding and chastising according to age, income and degree of deviation from current (and momentary) concepts of "correct" thinking.

It all became a bit much. I'm not saying I'm giving up writing about popular music; I figure I still have some comments that might be relevant. What I am going to do is hang up this column for a while. The ideas are not coming as fast as they once did. The surface is worn and the noise is becoming repetitive. I think this particular vein of rock metaphysics is about worked out and it's time to prospect elsewhere. It's time to recharge. 'Bye for now. ∎

Jim Green, a native New Yorker recently returned home from college in Berkeley, California, reached out to us in the magazine's early days and became one of the new friends who pitched in in various ways, joining assorted college pals of ours who we had already pulled in to help. Although he initially served as the magazine's distribution manager (that meant carting issues to the handful of Manhattan stores and newsstands that had agreed to take them on consignment), in issue 10, Jim began writing a singles review column, cleverly titled Green Circles *to invoke not only his name and the shape of 45s but a classic Small Faces song. He kept that up for the remainder of the magazine's existence, reviewing some 1,300 singles in all. Fortunately, there were many, many great ones, a lot of them imports, released during that stretch. Pithy, honest, funny and knowledgeable — * Green Circles *was a prized TP mainstay.*

The idea of getting musicians in to rate records (a feature usually dubbed Blind Date *in the UK) certainly wasn't original with us, and we only did it a handful of times. Here are two of those.*

GREEN CIRCLES
(WITH THE RAMONES)

TP 27, APRIL 1978

By Jim Green

It was a freezing January day in downtown Manhattan, hardly a stone's throw from City Hall, the World Trade Center and Wall Street. I emerged from the subway only to be nearly blown halfway down Chambers Street by an icy blast of wind rushing from the Hudson River. I hastily entered the building where Ramones manager Danny Fields has his apartment/office, and where I'm about to spin records with Joey and Dee Dee Ramone.

Joey was late, so Dee Dee and I shot the breeze about underground comics and such, eventually meandering onto more germane topics, touching on the Ramones' recent British tour.

"We couldn't even go out of the hotel," said Dee Dee, apparently amused and still surprised that the fans' reaction was so intensely favorable.

"We sold out everywhere. They pogo and go crazy. I dunno how they stand bein' in the audience. In the States we get a real good response in California and Texas. New York, it's always been more reserved."

I mentioned that I couldn't speak for the whole Palladium the previous Saturday when the Ramones topped the bill, but roughly half of the loge was so frenzied that its very foundation seemed to be moving. "We played the Apollo in Scotland, and the balcony looked like it was gonna go. You could see it moving. They said that once they had a Status Quo concert there and then the next night they had a Slade concert, and the balcony caved in. Everybody compares us to Status Quo over there." I admitted that musically there was some general basis for comparison.

"They say that's the audience we get. Status Quo's the biggest group there. They'll sell out the Apollo three nights. We were told it was great that we did it for one. The new wave doesn't draw that well over there, they play, the Clash or someone like that, before a thousand people a night.

"We've seen the Clash twice. They're real good. The problem with the Pistols is they don't know what to do onstage, so they huddle together, freaking out. The Clash have been working live a long time. They have a confidence, you can tell. They have a chemistry that works. I love their album, I play that all the time. They wanted to put 'em on an American tour with us, but I think us and the Runaways are a better package. We wanna be sure we can fill up the places. I don't know if America's ready for them yet. They're real nice guys, though, Joe Strummer's real nice. All those guys are. We really get along well with the Sex Pistols, too."

Around this time Joey arrived, wearing woolen leg warmers but only over his knees (Joey has huge holes in his jeans, uncovering his kneecaps). "Fashionable," said Dee Dee. Joey mumbled a bit, his way of saying hello. Both he and Dee Dee were tired out from having played the night before (and from contemplating the gig the next night, to which they would be driving for seven hours over icy roads). While Dee Dee was amiable, if a bit languid, Joey was reticent at first; he's by nature diffident, anxious for acceptance but too unsure to seek it.

We got into the swing of things with "Orgasm Addict" by the Buzzcocks (UA UP 36316).

Joey: "All right, nothing special. It's the Buzzcocks? I like them. 'Boredom.' I liked *Spiral Scratch*. This just sounds like another English record."

"Sounds too cluttered, too many lyrics," chipped in Dee Dee.

Joey: "Voice sounds a bit like early Bowie. Nothing special, though [Laughs] I'll give it 'Z'."

Dee Dee was puzzled. "I think the Buzzcocks are good, though. They have better songs than this. We've seen 'em. I don't understand why they used this."

I put on "Mannequin" by Wire (Harvest HAR 5144), which had a striking picture sleeve. The latter half of the song consists vocally of repeated "tell me's," "oo's" and "la-la-la's."

Again, Joey put his oar in first. "I like it."

Dee Dee: "I think they shouldn't'a had any other lyrics except 'tell me.' They should'a called

it that. Would have been incredible. I liked the break. The bass player sounds good. It [*Pink Flag*] should be a good album."

Next up was "Wild Youth" by Generation X (Chrysalis CHS 2189). "Sounds a lot like Slade," remarked Dee Dee admiringly. Joey agreed. "A little long though," said Dee Dee. "How long is it? About three minutes? They should have cut out a half minute. I think it could make the charts. They're really going all out pop, that band, their image. That's supposed to be the next big thing this year in England, going back to pop instead of punk."

I decided to throw them a curve and trot out some genuine pop. The next track I played was the Dead End Kids (Roller soundalikes) doing "All My Love Always" (CBS 5826).

Dee Dee was enthusiastic: "Sounds like a hit! I like it, but" — looking over at Joey, — "Joey doesn't like it..." Joey thought it was much too wimpy. We discussed the Rollers' influence on Ramones music, and Dee Dee admitted he was a fan ("...and they really *can* play live!"). Joey said he liked some of it a lot, but that the Dead End Kids just weren't up to the better Rollers stuff. In the meantime, I put on a gen-u-wine new wave hit, the Banned's remake of "Little Girl."

They recognized it at once, having been in England while it was in the charts. And they didn't think much of it either. Dee Dee: "Really stiff. They sound like metronomes." Said Joey, "I don't like the way the guitar sounds." Limp, eh? "Yeah. Doesn't flow, man. The Dead Boys did it, then *these* guys..." he added, decrying the vapid trendiness of bands who, in resurrecting old songs, "butcher" them. Not at all like the Ramones and "Do You Wanna Dance," as I was about to say, when Danny Fields announced that coffee was ready, and we scrambled into the kitchen.

"I couldn't live without it," said Dee Dee, "but in England they serve this stuff that's not real coffee, and it's awful." Postum? Chicory? "I don't know, but it's not coffee. But they drink tea a lot. All the roadies, they have vats of tea."

Then it was back to the listening room, and I put on "Just Another Teenage Anthem" by the New Hearts (CBS 5800). Joey thought the title was all too accurate. "It's amusing, but that's about it. Maybe if I was isolated for about three weeks..." He thought that a lot of the new wave stuff was getting better, but most of it seemed just to be reaching mediocre competence. The remark was all the more telling after we ran through three singles in quick succession without finding much to get excited about. "Lipstick" by Advertising (EMI 2710), which I thought resembled primitive Roxy, was judged by Joey to be boring and too calculated. Upon hearing Celia and the Fabulous Mutations run through "You Better Believe Me" (United Artists UP 36318), Dee exclaimed, "All these singles sound alike!" "Lovers of Today" by the Only Ones (Vengeance VEN 001), who have among them ex-Spooky Tooth drummer Mike Kellie and who were just signed to CBS in England, brought no response from the pair except Joey's "I wish I could say I like it" (he seemed a bit embarrassed that I was pulling turkey after turkey out of my bag of singles).

I countered with "Living on Dreams" by the Depressions (Barn 2014 112), a cut [critic] John Rockwell might describe as neo-folk-punk-pop-rock. This fizzled too: "They coulda had more substance behind it. Sounds like they sold out before they started," said Dee Dee. Joey said it reminded him of filler on mid-'60s albums.

Only slightly daunted, I turned the record over and played the flip, "Family Planning," which I thought was not bad. Eureka! "Best record you've played us. Going in the right direction," declared Dee Dee. Joey agreed; it was a bit more forceful, more muscular than the A-side. "Great sleeve," he noted (head shots of four guys with grimly ugly mugs and spiky white hair on a black background). Nevertheless, the band's dour name got Joey talking about a particular gripe he had with the English scene.

"In England, it's like a fad to be depressed and miserable, y'know." He could understand the anger of the scene's first groups, like the Clash and the Pistols, "but now it's pretentious, you walk around and everything out of their mouths is like that. It's just the thing to do. But the kids aren't like that. I don't think they give a shit about that, they just wanna have a good time. Everybody's a fuckin' poser now, man. Like, the Clash are great, but a lotta groups, they can't play, the songs stink and all they talk about is how bad things are."

Said Dee Dee, "When you get a bunch of new wave singles, you have to really sort through them." On the British tour before this last one, "We went out and bought about 30 singles, like everything that was out at the time. Out of 30 records there was maybe three that were really good."

WHY ARE THE Ramones are so popular? Joey was getting into talking now. "The music's good, the songs are exciting, it's our humor, the way we look, our show. It's us, man, nothing we put on. It's completely different.

"There's a second or third generation [of new wave bands] in England and maybe a third or fourth here in New York, and the groups coming out now are just — like, Suicide are great, I think the Cramps are good, and that's all I've heard of the later generations in New York that I like. The Sic F*cks are kinda good. It's amazing that they started out just as a joke, and now they could get signed tomorrow. They're just above everything now, they take it as a joke. That's good.

"Things are looking up, though. There are some great records. 'Watching the Detectives' is a great song, and it's nicer to hear than all this progressive crap, with long guitar solos. It's affecting the bigger groups, too. Things are becoming more rock-oriented, songs are getting shorter. Nazareth's got this song, 'No Mercy,' y'know, the Kinks got 'Father Christmas.'"

The Ramones are far more astute than their detractors — and even many of their fans — give them credit for. Even before Dee Dee offered his lone criticism of the Generation X single, I realized that many bands would profit by employing some of the economy by which the Ramones are habitually characterized. Loud, short and simple rock isn't all there is to it, of course, as anyone who's listened to, say, the Users will testify. In any kind of music there are a few greats, a slightly larger portion of goods, barrels full of "all rights" and barge-loads of bilge. No matter how much you like the genre.

After all, there's only one band of Ramones. ∎

GREEN CIRCLES
(WITH BILLY IDOL)

TP 64, AUGUST 1981

By Jim Green

Ain't no percentage in trying to second-guess a guest reviewer. This time around we've got Billy Idol, newly parted from Gen X and residing in New York. The former teenypunk wet dream looks wildly incongruous in the conference room of Aucoin Management: a sprinkling of men and women go about their business; an electronic Kiss pinball machine bink-bonks in the distance; a set of Kiss marionettes stand next to a video playback unit; and in walks the spike-haired Idol, a mass of stylishly punky shreds and vents in T-shirt, leather trousers and vest/jacket.

Aucoin is betting that Idol will be the right mix of teen appeal and rock credibility for '80s America. Idol mentions, however, that his taste in music is not necessarily that displayed on his former group's three LPs — and his reactions to the records I bring along bear that out.

He also protests, "This is an unnatural way to listen to records. Music is a personal, private thing; a lot of times a record that sounds unremarkable the first time will gradually pull your ears in — but not in the middle of a whole lot of others."

We hit a responsive chord straight away, in the form of "W.O.R.K. (N.O. Nah No No My Daddy Don't)" by Bow Wow Wow (UK EMI 5153), the latest protégés of Great Rock 'n' Roll Swindler Malcolm McLaren.

"It's great! It's not like a conventional song, although it's easy to jump to. Sure, it has that sort of 'rap record' feel and the disco bits, but in the end it's not a conventional record."

Bizarre as it may seem, "W.O.R.K." was produced cleanly by Alan Tarney, a songwriter/producer associated with Cliff Richard. "While it's not as rough as their first record, 'C-30, C-60, C-90 Go,' they'll have that rough guitar sound with any producer, and the song does come through. One of their best." Idol also applauds the Spanish version of "C-30" on the flip.

He is less enthusiastic about a tune I quite like, the Plimsouls' "Now" (Planet P-47923, with an instrumental version of an old Nerves number, "When You Find Out," on the back). "Was it a tribute to John Lennon?" I have to admit it's flawed by a clinical sound, which even the Plimsouls had remarked on.

"I don't really like this kind of American-sounding record anyway. It's very professional — or *sounds* it. Even though Bow Wow Wow were produced by Cliff Richard's producer and may be professionals, in a way, even more than the Plimsouls, they sounded less professional, and had a feeling that this doesn't."

Even after scrutinizing the lyrics on the sleeve of "Plan B" by Dexys Midnight Runners (Parlophone R6046), Idol still can't figure them out. He doesn't relate particularly well to the "young soul rebels" stance.

"Quite nice, I suppose, if you like tight little band sounds — a bit like Elvis Costello on the chorus — but to me it's like great old soul music done by lesser people. It's so painful to talk about these kind of groups. I mean, I suppose it's not a total drag backward in time, done as it is today by white people in England in totally different circumstances, but I don't care for it." He declined to listen to Dexys' remake of the BarKays' "Soul Finger" on the flip side. (Dexy mainman Kevin Rowland claims the record was put out by EMI over his objections, for whatever that's worth.)

The Bureau consists largely of original Dexys personnel. Since Rowland refuses to speak to the press, the Bureau has dominated UK accounts of the two groups' post-split activities. "Only for Sheep" b/w "The First One" (UK WEA K18478), less faithful to '60s soul sources than Dexys, is so irritating (vocally and instrumentally) we can't last through either side. Asked what he didn't like about the record, Idol replies, "It."

[Next up…] "I thought the Stray Cats wouldn't have as good a record as 'Runaway Boys.' Everybody kept telling me I was wrong, and when it came out, I said, 'Mmm, well done, lads.' But 'Stray

Cat Strut' [UK Stray Cat/Arista SCAT3] is pretty average, as was 'Rock This Town.' Good drum sound and so on; I like the bluesy feel as a change of pace, and it must be nice when they play it live.

"They're an exciting live band, a 10-star presentation, but I'm not really moved by this new rockabilly thing — although I love the old Sun records. The Polecats doing 'John, I'm Only Dancing' was all right 'cause it wasn't playing into the rockabilly thing directly; it was sort of breaking the rules. But as far as 'Stray Cat Strut' — fuck's sake, Billy, give 'em a break. I do like that it's not overproduced, and that they tried to keep it at least a little rough. And they sound like they do mean it, which is more than I can say for most of this sort of thing."

The flip is a live take of "Drink That Bottle Down," but we agree the only single worth pulling from their album was the first.

Bauhaus "Kick in the Eye" (b/w "Satori"; UK Beggars Banquet BEG54) didn't reverse the negative trend. "I do like that *kind* of thing, that smacking drum sound, but every day someone'll put on a record and I'll sit there grumbling that it sounds like somebody else. 'Fuck me, that's the *Low* drum sound, the David Bowie bit, the harmonizer on the vocals.' And I don't even know *nothing* — I've only been in the studio about three times and I didn't know what they were on about then — but I can tell that it's a fucking copy. 'Yes, add the little disco bit to pull them in.' Maybe that's unfair, but at least Bow Wow Wow is different. 'W.O.R.K.' is noise, but a great noise. This is shit noise.

"At the same time, I'd rather play this crap than Led Zeppelin or REO Speedwagon. I wanna see the floor wiped with groups like that. The frightening thing about making records today is that you've really got to make sure what you're doing is for *real*; it isn't just copying all the little bits and hoping they're gonna sound different. 'Kick in the Eye' sounds like four or five different things glued together."

Fortunately, Robert Fripp came to the rescue. "Dislocated," from the *League of Gentlemen* LP, backed with "1984 (January 13th-May 16th)," from the Frippertronics LP *Let the Power Fall* (UK Editions EG EGEDS2), presents two contrasting

views of the master at work. Idol gives the danceable first side points just for being a non-nostalgic instrumental, even though it's too long, and remarks on the other side's striking guitar work.

"He's got a great sound, doesn't he? Of course, it's always better when a great guitarist is inserted into an outside context, contained by something. With Bowie or Blondie, Fripp comes in and goes crazy, like he's just come from outer space, and gives a whole new idea of what the track's about. These two sides are kind of like dub reggae, the good bits being worth sticking it out. It's a different way of playing guitar, and that's the important thing. Fripp's always looking for something new."

It's back to the world of lesser mortals, however, when confronted with the Beat's disappointing new single, "All Out to Get You" b/w "Drowning" (UK Go-Feet FEET6). The topside doesn't happen; Idol is impressed by the flip's sliding, dipping bass line, and is disappointed that's all he can enthuse about, as the Beat is a personal fave.

"They sing about things most people can relate to, have clever riffs, catchy tunes — like the Police, they succeed on good dynamics. But there's nothing much here; it's really poor in terms of their previous records. They've been working really hard, haven't they? Could be they're stretching themselves too far."

"I don't like Echo and the Bunnymen," Idol says apropos of their live 12-inch EP, *Shine So Hard* (UK Korova ECHO1). "They might be great blokes, but this '60s sound doesn't move me at all. It doesn't sound like they're enjoying themselves playing it." For the record, it leaves me flat, too.

To close the proceedings, we checked out the 12-inch EP (99 Records 99-04) by New York's own ESG, a band Idol rated as the Apple's best after seeing them live. "You're No Good" (not the oldie), "Moody" and "UFO" are studio tracks produced by Martin Hannett; "Earn It," "ESG" and "Hey" were recorded live at Hurrah.

Idol bubbles with excitement. "It's absolutely fantastic! They're up there with Public Image, the Cramps and Suicide. Just some percussion, bass, one-string guitar and vocals. It's like Motown dub!"

He just *has* to tape it so he can take it home, and I leave him still raving about it. ∎

From that same issue, Tim Sommer — who arrived in our Times Square office in 1978 as a timid 16-year-old intern and grew up to be a highly regarded music writer, radio star (Noise! the Show on WNYU-FM), MTV host, recording artist (Hugo Largo, HiFi Sky), producer, A&R man (yes, he signed Hootie and the Blowfish) and author — shared his America Underground *column with Jello Biafra of the Dead Kennedys.*

AU *began as a spinoff from* Green Circles *— a way to ensure that independently released singles were not given short shrift — in issue 18, doubling Jim Green's workload. After a while, the column began incorporating scene reports from various locales around the country; we eventually expanded that into a monthly trio of dispatches that allowed local writers to tell the rest of us what was happening in their towns.*

At some point, at a time when mail order was the primary distribution channel for home-brew records, we recognized the challenge of getting the word out on a shoestring budget and began offering independent artists a discounted advertising rate. We called the program Band Aids.

> We know how hard it is to be a new band in this business, and we offer special advertising rates to unsigned bands who have gone to the trouble of putting out a record on their own label. This rate applies only to advertising mail order records of that nature, and the only sizes available are:
>
> 1/6 page - 2 3/8" wide by 5" $50
> 1/3 page - 4 7/8" square $75
> 1/2 page - 7 1/2" by 4 7/8" $100
>
> Ads must be camera-ready. Photo-screening (when required) costs $8.00 as do reverses, reductions, and tints. Deadline is the first of the month, two months before cover date. Payment and two copies of your record must accompany your artwork; if there are any additional art charges incurred, you will be billed.
>
> Please make an effort to do a nice-looking ad. If it looks like shit, we probably won't run it — we'll just send it back to you. We work too hard making TP look nice to have it messed up by a hasty, scribbled ad. Thank you.

Tim took over in 1980 and wrote it for a year and a half. Jim reclaimed the role in issue 68 and then handed it over to Robert Payes, who stayed on the case until the middle of 1983, when future New York Times *staffer John Leland arrived.*

AMERICA UNDERGROUND
(WITH JELLO BIAFRA)

TP 64, AUGUST 1981

By Tim Sommer

The Dead Kennedys are the first band in a long time to arise from the American underground and impress the "real" world (particularly in Britain). We thought it might be interesting to have the Dead Kennedys' lead singer and focal point, punk lunatic/legend Jello Biafra, revisit his vinyl alma mater and sit in as guest reviewer for this month's *America Underground.*

He turned out to be an excellent choice for the job. Biafra knows a lot about the underground band scene, and not just from personal experience. He's truly a fan, a record and fact hoarder with a passionate interest in alternate rock. The number of underground bands Biafra can talk about knowledgeably is amazing.

My own comments are in italics. All the rest is Biafra. (TS)

The Teen Idles: *Minor Disturbance* **EP (Dischord No. 1).** [*Fast, no-nonsense hardcore punk — eight songs' worth — from Washington, DC.*] A very important band. The Teen Idles played in Los Angeles and San Francisco last summer, and they took the West Coast mentality back to DC with them. Then they split up into three other bands: Minor Threat, Youth Brigade and SOA. There are about six or seven real young punk bands in DC now. They're real wild, but they don't go out to hurt people; if they're dancing all over the stage and knock over a drum mike, they'll bend down to pick it up, *then* they'll dive headfirst into the audience. The singer in this band works in an ice cream parlor where the Kennedy children hang out.

The Washington, DC scene is my favorite on the East Coast. The bands aren't under the constant glare of the media, so they just develop on their own and play for fun — which is pretty damn important, especially after you've seen people who put too much planning into things. People can cry "dated" all they want about records like this, but the energy speaks for itself. Punk will never die until something more dangerous replaces it. The closest anything has come to that has been Flipper.

Flipper: "Ha Ha Ha Ha Ha Ha Ha Ha Ho Ho Ho Ho Ho Hee Hee Hee Hee Hee Hee Hee" b/w "Love Canal" (Subterranean LT1). [*Like Crass with a sense of humor. Wall of noise, absurd lyrics — one of TS's faves of the year so far.*] This is the Flipper mentality in a nutshell. They've done away with such rigid musical bullshit as tuning their instruments properly or playing with proper techniques. Try learning the chords to either of these songs and you'll have lots of problems. Wait till "Boom Boom Boom" comes out; you need a Bacardi bottle to play that one right. What they do to annoy the punks is play excruciatingly slow. I figure this is closer to new psychedelia than Echo and the Bunnymen could ever hope to be, 'cause there's danger involved here. Flipper, like some other people (including us), does not play to entertain, but to attack. And Flipper does this better than anyone I know.

SF Underground 2 **(Lewd, Undead, Society Dog, Spikes) (Subterranean SUB10B); No Alternative:** *Backtracks* **EP (Subterranean SUB9).** [SF Underground 2 *spotty but worthwhile; No Alternative roarin', rockin' stuff.*] Subterranean is probably the West Coast label with its ear closer to the ground than anyone else. *SF Underground 2* is better recorded than the first one, but only time will tell whether these bands will have the impact of the bands on *SF Underground 1* (Flipper, No Alternative, VKTMS, Tools).

The best cut on here, I think, is Society Dog's "Title Role." Their singer, Jonathan Christ, is a real intelligent guy and the rest of the band is slowly but surely catching up to him. "Hitler's Brain" got the (San Francisco) Undead in a bit of hot water; the song was meant to be sarcastic but came off to some people as being pro-Klan, pro-Nazi.

The Lewd put out an EP in Seattle a while back before moving to San Francisco. Their "Mobile Home" is real good. It's the sort of subject matter everyone kicks themselves for not thinking of first; nobody's really gone after trailer-court life in America before.

No Alternative has a lot of good songs and should have recorded more by now. This EP is different from their live stuff; there are a lot of overdubs. The band is basically the creation of Johnny Genocide, who will go far one day. I think he's only 18 or 19, though he's been around; he was in the Offs for quite a while.

Half Japanese: "Spy" (UK Armageddon A5009). (*A plodding riff with all manner of things going on over it.*] We played with Half Japanese in Washington, DC. They were amazing; I was afraid they might be a total art-student disaster, but only Flipper can top them in the "wall of abrasive noise onstage" department. I think this is their first record as a six-piece. David and Jad Fair play untuned guitar — David's is fretless, as well — and they have another guy playing tuned guitar with regular chords, a horn section and a very abstract drummer. One saxophone plays Psychedelic Furs-like runs, while the other one does Beefheart-type cacophony. They didn't do anything as slow as "Spy" live. Armageddon is a great label. I'd dearly like to meet [label head] Richard Bishop; he's obviously interested in American stuff.

Kevin Dunn and the Regiment of Women: "Oktyabrina" (Armageddon AS014). [*Synthesizer pop.*] He's in the Fans. Kevin Dunn on his own is really bizarre. The Fans are real pop, which isn't quite my cup of tea; I like Dunn's solo stuff better. This may be a different recording, but this is the B-side of "Nadine," his first single, and disappointing in comparison. "Nadine" is so weird.

The Feederz: "Jesus" + "Stop You're Killing Me" b/w "Avon Lady" + "Terrorist" (Anxiety 666A). A cross between Wire and Teenage Jesus. "Jesus" is one of the most direct anti-church tunes I've ever heard; I think [lead singer] Frank

Discussion got sent to church a little too often when he was little. At their first gig in Phoenix, Frank came out with a live rat in his mouth. He threw it into the crowd, it landed on a girl and bit her. They weren't allowed to play Phoenix for six months after that. So, the second time around he came out with live crickets glued to his shaved head and shampooed people with them — and didn't play Phoenix again for quite a while.

This recording isn't quite what it could be; the Feederz are a lot more powerful live. They consider themselves musical terrorists, and Frank is one of the most twisted people I've ever known. Needless to say, the members of his band are not very well liked by the police in their hometown.

Teddy and the Frat Girls: "I Wanna Be a Man" (Hospital). Ah! Shades of Flipper, always a healthy sign. Pretty good lyrics, too — very anti-male. "If I was a man, I could fuck anytime, and be as hard as a rock, spend my life worrying about the size of my cock." Eat your heart out, Raincoats. I like this group because they are so absolutely *cruel* to people.

The Wipers: "Alien Boy" (Park Avenue PA10 EP). They're real inventive. They have good punk songs, but they can mix them with ballads and make that work, which I've never heard anyone else do. This is their morbid psychedelic side; it's an extended version of a track on their album. The other side's three songs are non-LP. Greg Sage, their guitar player, produces and records a lot of Portland bands himself, putting them out on his own Trap Records label. He and the bass player once backed a professional wrestler on an album.

Art: *Only Record in the World* EP (The Only Label in the World EP1). An absolute classic — the most accurate record about New York in who-knows-how-many years. Instead of love songs or blues about living in the city or how wonderful it is to slowly amputate your career due to smack, this is an insight into people who consider themselves insightful and work so hard to make other people think they are as well. I'm so glad New York has a band like this that's willing to put them in their place. I just love bands that go out of their way to annoy people. ∎

Touring: end of November, and in December

Single: Academy Fight Song/Max Ernst

Information: Ace of Hearts Records
P.O. Box 579
Kenmore Station
Boston MA. 02215

From 1980: one of the hand-made Band Aid ads we ran from artists destined to become a lot better known.

BAND AIDS

Presented for their historic value, this selection of ads that ran in *Trouser Press* back in the day (so don't try and order anything!) demonstrates the range of design approaches: handwriting and scissor-cut photos, typewriter lines pasted on pictures, drawings, Letraset layouts and actual typesetting.

The explosion of d.i.y. record releases was the herald of an alternative music industry that helped many of these artists build actual careers.

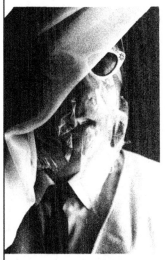

SURVEY SEZ

> **“** *I asked a ouija board once if I'd ever be in a rock band. It said no and I was crushed.* **”**
>
> **—FRED SCHNEIDER**
> of the B-52'S

At the end of the 1970s, and for our fifth and tenth birthdays, we reached out to every publicist we knew and asked them to put a question to their artists for the purpose of an article we had dreamed up. Whatever we may have thought about this then, it is mind-boggling now to see how many (not to mention who) bothered to respond. And all in the pre-Internet era, when this sort of thing had to be done over the phone.

WHAT WERE YOU DOING IN MARCH OF 1974 AND/OR WHAT HAVE YOU BEEN DOING SINCE?

TP 37, APRIL 1979

We here at *Trouser Press* are painfully aware of what we've been doing for the past five years, and those of us who were there for the magazine's inception can remember exactly where we were and what we were doing in March 1974. However, we thought it would be interesting to find out what other folks in and around the rock and roll world have been up to. So, we put the following question to everyone we could think of and waited for the results to stream in.

Jerry Casale, musician (Devo): Personally, I was teaching art spuds at Akron University. The group, at the time, was planting tubers and sorting out the gene pool. Since ... we've devolved.

Lou Reed, musician: I was doing 85 in a 55-mile-per-hour zone ... I still am.

Tom Scholz, musician (Boston): I was working at Polaroid and playing in a band called Mother's Milk along with Brad Delp and Barry Goudreau...

Savage Pencil, rock cartoonist: I was waiting for the next Frank Zappa album to come out. Now all I'm doing is waiting for the next Residents album to come out.

Peter Hammill, musician (ex-Van der Graaf Generator): I was living in Sussex, England writing and thinking. I'm still doing it, more or less, with quite a lot in-between.

John Rockwell, pop music journalist (*New York Times*): Sorry, but I'm just not feeling clever. I like your magazine, but nothing much has changed for me in the last five years.

Richard Gottehrer, record producer: I was with Sire Records. I remember going to a Deep Purple / Savoy Brown / Tucky Buzzard concert at Madison Square Garden. Someone selling a mimeoed *TP* stopped me as I was going in. I remember how silly I thought the name was. Since then, I left Sire, took time off and — two years ago — got back into activity. Now I produce and manage Robert Gordon and have recently produced Blondie, Dirty Angels, Richard Hell, Stumblebunny, the Feelgoods and the Yachts.

Toby Goldstein, freelance journalist and publicist: I was a press agent with Ren Grevatt Assoc., where I tried to convince people that some of the clients, like Steve Martin, Linda Ronstadt and Steve Miller, weren't has-beens. Since, I gave up flacking for writing, went to grad school, was musically revitalized by seeing the Sex Pistols and Clash in 1976, and now work as a freelance journalist, hopefully without acting like a camp follower, gossip monger or pompous asshole...

Pat Travers, musician (Pat Travers Band): I was playing in a club band called Red Hot, based in Ottawa, Canada and that month was probably somewhere between Thunder Bay, Ontario and Remusky, Quebec. Since then, I left that band, went to play with Ronnie Hawkins from Sept.–April 1976, moved to London, started this band and brought it over here, toured a lot and tried to sell some records.

David Byrne, musician (Talking Heads): I was working at the Yankee Clipper in Providence, RI, I was working the aft[ernoon] shift. They put me on the morning shift, then I got fired. I couldn't handle working in the morning — I couldn't take the pressure, I couldn't fry those eggs that fast. Moved to NY in May 1974, I joined a band and learned how to make records.

Janine Safer, publicist, A.R.S.E. Management: I was ridiculously idealistic; in the ensuing time I've become ideally ridiculous.

Robert Gordon, singer: I was fantasizing about someday signing with RCA. Since then, I signed with RCA.

Nick Lowe, musician, producer: I was hanging out. Since then, I've been having fun.

Spencer Davis, producer, former bandleader (Spencer Davis Group): I was playing with a group called the Larks up in the Pacific NW. Doug Weston of the Troubadour was responsible for getting us together; he needed a band for a few dates. We

were an acoustic band with Peter Jamieson, Tom from Locomotiv GT, Tret Fure and Andy Way. We recorded some of the performances, but I've yet to do anything with the tapes. Since then, I translated legal and aerospace documents in 1975, went to Island Records as head of Artist Development, where I was reunited with Steve Winwood. Just recently, I moved to Janus Records, where I've just produced an LP by Paul Korda, using some of the musicians who had previously played in my bands.

Dave Marsh, rock writer: I had just moved to Boston to edit the *Real Paper*. Then I went to *Newsday* and then *Rolling Stone*, where I am currently situated, among other things.

Bun E. Carlos, musician (Cheap Trick): I was a happy man then, but that was a long time ago.

Peter Gabriel, singer, bandleader: I was writing *The Lamb Lies Down...*, moving out of London and waiting for Anna, our first child. The rest has been well chronicled.

Dr. Joseph Sasfy, creator of Rock Therapy: I was in Central Pennsylvania, studying to be a social scientist, drinking Rolling Rock beer, wondering how the Dodgers blew the World Series to the A's and listening to Buddy Holly records. Now I'm suffocating in D.C., practicing social science, drinking Stroh's beer, wondering how the Dodgers blew the World Series to the Yankees and listening to Buddy Holly records.

David Fricke, rock writer: I was wondering what I'd be doing five years from now. Now, I'm doing it.

Lenny Kaye, musician (Patti Smith Group), rock writer: I was attempting to get the Sidewinders signed to Casablanca Records via Aucoin Management, working at Village Oldies, writing a Sweet vs. Mud story for *Rock Scene* and preparing for a Reno Sweeney's date with Patti Smith and our newly discovered piano player Richard DMV Sohl. Since then, my career has become public record (on blue vinyl, of course).

Tom Robinson, musician (Tom Robinson Band): I'd been in London for one year and had just been signed with Konk Records by Ray Davies. I had stars in my eyes and holes in my shoes. Since then, I've worked my way up to a good pair of black boots. Congratulations to *TP* on the first five and here's to straight creases for the next five.

Robert Fripp, musician, producer: During March 1974, Fripp lost faith in King Crimson as an appropriate education, retiring between Sept. 1974 and Aug. 1977 to train as a small, mobile and intelligent unit. During the first year he prepared for a course at the I.A.C.E. in Sherborne, Gloucestershire; during the second he attended the course; the third he spent assimilating the course. During this period, King Crimson's *Red* [1974] and *Young Person's Guide to...* [1976] were released, also *Evening Star* [1976] with Brian Eno. With Eno he mini-toured Europe in May 1975. Fripp appeared scantily on *Peter Gabriel 1* [1977] and pseudonymously toured with Gabriel [Spring, 1977]. Returning to active duty in August 1977, he has recorded on Bowie's *"Heroes,"* Blondie's *Parallel Lines*, Walter Steding's *Hangdog*; produced Daryl Hall's solo non-album, *Peter Gabriel 2*, *The Roches* [for March release] and is finalizing his first solo album, *Exposure*, for March release.

Paul Weller, musician: Five years ago, I was playing my guitar and going to school — I wasn't into the contemporary music scene. I played then, as now, what I wanted to play — I jammed with different people. I've always taken my work very seriously. It's about time we (the Jam) were taken seriously — we're not here for anyone's amusement. I basically ignore the music press, except for *NME* and *Sounds*, and some of the British fanzines. The other ones all copy what the others say. With the press, your popularity seemingly goes in cycles, but with us, no matter what the press has said, our fans were always there. The American press feels as though it has the British music scene all sewn up — but they don't know anything about it.

Jonathan Richman, musician: March 1, 1974, the Modern Lovers played their last gig with Ernie [Brooks] and Jerry [Harrison] in the band (David [Robinson] had already left) at a big warehouse party in Jamaica Plain, near Boston. I went off to experiment. After five years of experimenting, I decided to go back and sing alone, just like before. People ask me why ... well, because it's more naked this way.

Mark "Moogy" Klingman, musician: I was touring as a member of Todd Rundgren's Utopia.

Since then, I have seen many of my hopes and dreams realized. Producing Bette Midler and Bob Dylan being one of them. Seeing my second solo album finally released here as well as in Europe being another.

And, finally, the formation of Moogtown Productions — a recording studio, publishing, production and management company housed under one roof with a staff of artists, writers, producers and engineers working together under my guidance. I see only steady growth in the years ahead both for Moogtown Productions and my fave rock mag, *Trouser Press*.

Paul Atkinson, A&R man, former musician (Zombies): I was working for CBS in England as International A&R Director. We'd just signed ABBA after they'd won the Eurovision Song Contest, and they were becoming really big for us. I moved to the U.S. in 1976, first as Director of A&R for CBS International, and then transferring to the U.S. division in late 1977.

Wreckless Eric, musician, bandleader: I was working at a way to change the world a bit. Now, I'm putting the scheme into operation.

Chuck Pulin, rock photographer: That month I shot Genesis, Barry White, 10cc, Deep Purple, Frampton, Stevie Wonder and other assorted turkeys. Since then, I've been doing the same — taking pictures of rock people.

Captain Sensible, musician (Damned): Five years ago — a monologue: Brigstock Arms public house, the Great Croydon Talent Contest. Now about my thoughts for the day, namely ecology as it is a subject close to my heart (I'm sure I left my notes in my breast pocket) — aside stage left — I feel a right tit. No, seriously, I don't wanna preach about ecology, but this city is beginning to smell of pig's dung, and I don't even like pork. No, honestly, life just ain't worth living anymore, funnily enough the reason I took up playing the guitar is because of pollution in a way. I discovered that Tunes help you breathe more easily.

Ted Carroll, owner, Chiswick Records: I was co-managing Thin Lizzy with Chris Morrison. Gary Moore had just walked out of the band, and we didn't have a record deal and Chris and myself were having 19 nervous breakdowns as we: tried to put the band back together, tried to get a record deal together and tried to hold back the creditors. However, things always work out. Scott and Brian joined Thin Lizzy, we got a record deal together with Nigel Grainge at Phonogram and paid the bills. Since then, I have been running Rock On, a record collectors shop in North London, with the help of fab Barry, and also learning how to run a record company with my partners Trevor and Roger. I'm looking forward to retiring in 1984.

Andy Ellison, singer (Radio Stars): Needed prolonged session with hypno-therapist to take me back this far. Spent two months non-stop on acid, ended up in the south of France and subsequently got deported over unpaid hospital fees. July formed Jet and toured with Hunter-Ronson and tried to keep Davey O'List awake, Bonfire day was nice.

Ebet Roberts, rock photographer: I was painting, doing photo collages and working at the Guggenheim Museum. Since then, I did waitressing and manipulative photography and became a rock photographer two years ago.

Meat Loaf, singer: I was returning from London where I'd just finished filming *The Rocky Horror Picture Show* and had lost 25 pounds due to sexual excess...

Rodney Bingenheimer, disc jockey (KROQ-FM, Los Angeles): My rock and roll night club, Rodney Bingenheimer's English Disco, was just closing. Disco music was coming in, and I wanted to get into radio and bring what I was playing into people's living rooms. Since then, I've had my show — 8 p.m. to midnight, Sundays, on KROQ.

Bill Nelson, musician (Be-Bop Deluxe/Red Noise): The mists are clearing... I see a thin young man wearing heavy black eye shadow playing a white imitation Les Paul guitar in small pubs and clubs and the occasional college theatre. He is surrounded by three other young men also wearing funny make-up. Is it a bird, is it a plane, is it Kiss? No, it is Be-Bop Deluxe Mark 1 about to give up their day jobs and become full-time musicians prior to recording an album called *Axe Victim*. He wonders if he'll ever get to play in America but doubts it. A few months later, a friend hands him a copy of an obscure American magazine in which *Axe Victim* is being given an inordinate amount of praise. He scans the page to see what paragon of good taste is responsible for such an article... "Ira Robbins" it says. So, Americans are not all old hippies and cowboys after all. Perhaps there is still a chance for Be-Bop Deluxe to play the States and, in fact, they eventually do and yes, apart from a select few, Americans are still old hippies and Be-Bop Deluxe soon become largely misunderstood.

And today? I see a slightly less thin, slightly older young man playing a non-imitation Japanese guitar about to stick his imitation rock star's neck into the public gallows once more. This time the band is called Red Noise and cares not at all about pleasing guitar freaks, MOR freaks or senile old hippies. However, we do care about playing hard, fast, witty, metallic, fun music for people who have woken up to the mood of the times. Maybe if enough of you catch on, *Trouser Press* won't be the only magazine in the States aware of the fact that we're living on the threshold of 1980. All the best for the Future.

Gary Kenton, publicist, Warner Bros. Records: I was working and living with Susan Blond. Now I'm working and married to Susan Blond.

Susan Blond, publicist, Epic Records: I was working and living with Gary Kenton. Now I'm working and married to Gary Kenton.

Nancy Lewis, general Manager, Charisma Records, U.S.: I was working for Buddah Records and had just gone to London to formalize a management agreement with Monty Python. They were playing the Drury Lane Theatre at that time. I worked for Buddah until 18 months ago, when I came to Charisma, where I am today.

Tom Petty, musician, bandleader: I was saving money to buy a multitrack recorder to record over 1,000 dogs barking at once. Since then, I have recorded 568, and I am on the road to a dream come true.

Robin Zander, singer (Cheap Trick): I was wandering around the UK looking for work and lucked into meeting. Rick, Tom and Bun E. Everything just seemed to fall into place. Now I'm working, having fun, meeting girls and playing the kind of music that I love. What more could a poor boy ask for?

Willy DeVille, singer, bandleader: I was bumming around the country. I made my way to San Francisco, where I teamed up with Ruben Siguenza, but we couldn't even find a gig in a club there. About three years ago, I noticed in the NY papers that a lot of bands I'd never heard of were playing in clubs, so I moved back to NY, got a band together, and started playing CBGBs and Max's. We got onto the *Live at CBGBs* album, then Ben Edmonds, who was doing A&R for Capitol, saw us and signed us. We're about to do our third LP in Paris — I'm glad *TP* is finally doing American groups, there's a lot of good music here.

Tom Petersson, musician (Cheap Trick): About five years ago I saw the NY Dolls on New Year's Eve in Detroit and had to be carried from the stage after smashing half their lights with my empty tequila bottle ... sorry, Johnny.

Jon Tiven, musician (Yankees), rock writer: I was fronting a band occasionally called the Yankees, jamming with Big Star at Max's, feeling my journalistic oats and sporadically attending journalism classes at Sarah Lawrence College. Since then, I recorded a single for Andrew Oldham's non-existent record label and 200 song demos, flacked for Chess Records, produced Alex Chilton, joined a band with Chris Bell, Van Duren, and Jody Stephens, formed Prix with Tommy Hoehn, joined Ork as a staff producer, founded Big Sound Records, produced Van Duren and the Werewolves, and reformed the Yankees.

Ian North, musician (Neo): I was in Milk 'n' Cookies playing Italian restaurants in Rosedale and some college in Brooklyn. Then John Hewlett came out of nowhere and the next thing you know we were in England making an album. Next thing you know we were back, in total shock, in Long Island, where we started. The Cookies broke up in 1976, just before the LP came out, two years after it was recorded. I went back to England and put together a band with Martin Gordon that metamorphosed into Neo in May 1977. We signed with Jet in Jan. '78 and recorded an LP, out in February.

Chris Stamey, musician (the dB's): I was a freshman at UNC-Chapel Hill; a computer science major with a minor in physics; playing cello and listening to Pink Floyd and Genesis; had

joined a group called the Pandemonium Symposium, but it was just a hobby; in love with my best friend's girl. I've done nothing worthwhile since, except spend a lot of money.

Rick Nielsen, musician (Cheap Trick): I was thinking about joining the Foreign Legion. Although my mind was quite sane and only a handful of friends — the number is still small — thought I'd ever amount of anything more than President of the U.S. Well, that would never be good enough for me, I'd rather be the musical good-will ambassador to the rest of the world I am today — a travelling minstrel of the '70s, '80s, '90s, etc., spreading music and pillaging nations. But ho, it wasn't easy. As luck would have it, five years ago I read my first *TP* and now my dreams are coming true. Thank you, guys, you're the inspiration that I needed — then and now.

Elvis Costello, recording artiste: [unprintable.]

TROUSER PRESS APPRAISES THOSE SAME FIVE YEARS

TP 37, APRIL 1979

Wow, what churlish grumblers we were!

1974: What a non-event this year turned out to be! We entered it with an energy crisis that threatened to cut down the number of records released and the quality of vinyl used and closed it out with plenty of low-quality records. In the United States, the John Denver-Olivia Newton-John-Helen Reddy-Jim Croce kind of country was reigning supreme. In England, festivals and concerts were announced and almost always immediately cancelled, towns began to regulate decibel levels and the new Britrock was steering its way toward its own collapse. It was the year of the superstar, with everyone leaving the groups that took them to fame and striking out on solo careers. It was the beginning of the great revival age, and it saw the return of Bob Dylan, Neil Sedaka, Paul Anka and Adam Faith. It was the start of Casablanca Records and Clive Davis's Arista.

But it seemed much more exciting than it actually was. The first half of 1974 was a time of great promise for rock and roll; the second slumped into ennui. By August, things had fallen into eclectic disarray. By December, the forces of syrup had taken the field, even as disco was just beginning to raise its head. As we slouched toward 1975, it was apparent that the worst was yet to come. (Steven Grant)

1975: And that's the way it was ... boring. 1975 was a limbo year, if not the dullest in recent memory, undeniably right up there. The zombie movement of '70s rock was consolidating strength; *Frampton Comes Alive* would soon be the dominant force of western civilization. "Artists" like McCartney and the Eagles were setting the stage for the overfed, multi-platinum acts of today. "Feelings" by Morris Albert was on the charts for 32 weeks.

On the debatably brighter side: Elton John had a number of agreeably commercial hits, including "Philadelphia Freedom." Bruce Springsteen emerged as a major star. Fleetwood Mac began to emerge. Ace registered the only-ever U.S. pub-rock success with "How Long." Bowie achieved his first and only American number-one with "Fame." Kiss got bigger and bigger. John Lennon released *Rock'n'Roll* and subsequently disappeared. Other good guys had hits: Sweet ("Ballroom Blitz"), 10cc ("I'm Not in Love") and Dwight Twilley ("I'm on Fire").

Overseas, the discontent with mediocrity was becoming obvious. The *Naughty Rhythms* package introduced Dr. Feelgood to England at large; by the end of the year, they were headlining their own tour. And you know where that eventually led. (Jon Young)

1976 will be remembered as the pivotal year in '70s rock, the year in which the first attempts were made to counter the growing distance between audience and superstar performer. On the surface it was business as usual — with the old-old superstars (Stones, Zeppelin, Aerosmith, Dylan, Wings) being joined at the top of the charts by new-old superstars (Peter Frampton, Fleetwood Mac). But away from the high-powered, big-spending record biz world of accountants and swimming pools, the seeds of an alternative were being sown.

In Berkeley, Matthew Kaufman's Beserkley label set an irreverent example of what could be done. Stiff Records, run for a laugh by two former pub rock scenemakers, Dave Robinson and Jake Riviera, took a chance and released a single by ex-hippie-turned-pop-genius Nick Lowe; though Chiswick Records, run by record store proprietor Ted Carroll, had beat them to the punch by releasing their first record, by the Count Bishops, earlier in the year. Small labels took more chances and had more people in the biz committed to the rock lifestyle, and this new awareness led straight to "punk," the notorious updating of the rawest rock and roll styles. In Britain, that meant the Sex Pistols and, shortly after, the Damned, the Clash, the Vibrators and the Stranglers. The famous incident on Bill Grundy's *Today* show in December made sure that even those who disapproved, or just couldn't have cared less about pop music, knew that something weird was afoot as we entered 1977. Whether or not anyone outside of the handful who had started it would accept it remained to be seen, but a schism could be seen developing in British and American tastes, the effects of which are still with us. (Dave Schulps)

1977: Non-stop excitement. Amid the obviously notable records released were scads more of less-lasting impact. The joy of looking forward to each new 45 and LP by a seemingly unending stream of new bands will not be soon forgotten. As a breath of fresh air, the year neatly put aside all memories of boring superstar bands, although the possibilities of mega-selling albums had only begun to become evident.

In terms of the magazine, *Trouser Press* followed events with an enthusiastic, yet objectively critical eye. While some readers might have objected to our coverage of new wave bands, the fact remains that nothing in 1977 was as significant or active, and we tried to act as an observer and reporter, using our abilities to sample records and gather news for the benefit of those readers who were also thrilled with the reemergence of rock and roll. Looking back, we did a pretty good job.

Towards the end of the year, it became pretty apparent that the level of activity had peaked, and that some finality was approaching. Little did we know that it would all fall apart in January, with the dramatic dissolution of the Pistols in America. From there on, the end was merely a formality. We warned you... (Ira Robbins)

1978 was a wild and woolly year in the record business, but it's hard to tell whether the music suffered irreparable damage, either consequently or incidentally. Unusual packaging ploys, largely inspired by the new wave and alternative labels' sense of having fun by being different, attained a popularity that could only have brought grins to the faces of entrepreneurs large and small. Yet some observers could not help noting that all too often the music was not the main selling point of 12-inch singles, colored vinyl and picture discs.

Nonetheless, consumers sat still for price raises; LPs continued to rack up multiple platinum (a million units) sales; singles approached platinum status more consistently; and even small independent labels turned over thousands of records made on minuscule budgets. And disco reigned supreme, as *Saturday Night Fever* became the best-selling LP of the year.

In spite of many new wave and related acts touring the States, including several from England, the new wave failed to break in America. Even the Warner Bros. colossus failed to break the Sex Pistols and Devo — although they nearly (but not quite) succeeded with Sire's Talking Heads, as did CBS with Elvis Costello. Patti Smith did get a genuine hit with "Because the Night," but it was co-written by mainstreamer Bruce Springsteen and, had she cut it under a different name, would never have been labeled new wave. And except for Blondie's "Denis" and the Boomtown Rats' "Rat Trap," in England, new wave 45s and LPs made dramatic leaps into the charts only to recede quickly. (Jim Green)

1970s SURVEY

TP 46, JANUARY 1980

A. What were your favorite records of the '70s?

B. What were the most significant musical events (concerts, deaths, etc.) of the decade?

C. Personal high and low points?

D. What have the '70s done for you?

E. Miscellaneous '70s faves and dislikes

Drummer Bill Bruford

A. LPs: *Walls and Bridges* (John Lennon); *Drums and Wires* (XTC); *One World* (John Martyn); *Bitches Brew* (Miles Davis)

B. The Arabs jacking up the price of oil; Miles Davis going electric. (P.S. A death is not a musical event.)

C. Low point: Half-hearted attempt while unemployed to infiltrate the miserable London "commercial" studio scene of jingles, TV themes, etc. After three weeks, attempt ended in merciful failure.

High points: Sitting in a hotel room in San Francisco with the other members of King Crimson watching our pre-recorded performance on *Midnight Special*. "Larks Tongues in Aspic" live to twenty million Americans. Also recording latest LP with Ron Malo.

D. Have moved from timid and slightly idiosyncratic drummer at the back of a group to leader/conductor/composer in my own band, in the process gaining a much broader knowledge of music and a clearer sense of what to do with the stuff.

Blondie drummer Clem Burke

B. David Bowie at Carnegie Hall (1972), first Ramones album, glitter rock, punk rock, *Stardust* movie, "Anarchy in the UK," New York Dolls, independent record labels.

C. Personal high points: "Denis" going to number-one in England, appearing on *Top of the Pops*, recording "X Offender," meeting Paul McCartney, making the covers of *Rolling Stone* and *Trouser Press*. Personal low points: working in the post office, Keith Moon's death.

Predictions for pop music in the '80s: return to good AM radio, more rock and roll movies, what is hip now becoming unhip via media overkill, electronic and disco music being assimilated into the pop mainstream, Joey Ramone solo album, Debbie Harry solo album.

D. I've become rich and famous — also more cynical, egotistic, perverted and disenchanted with music biz bullshit but ultimately better off.

E. likes: Perrier water, videocassette machines, high tech, holograms, Johnson's on King's Road, cable TV, Concorde, CBGB's, short hair.

dislikes: Fiorucci, nuclear power, designer jeans, Barry Manilow, long hair.

Robert Fripp

A. *Blue* (Joni Mitchell); *No Pussyfooting* (Fripp and Eno); *Another Green World* (Eno); *"Heroes"* (David Bowie); *Parallel Lines* (Blondie); *Fear of Music* (Talking Heads)

B. As a young guitarist lacking in music [*skills?*] I worked to reach a point at which better musicians would let me play with them. In this respect I have been particularly fortunate to have worked with many of my favorite performers. The punk and new wave movement which unsettled the complacency of the music industry and its established performers. In a sense it was contemporary Dadaism although it is currently facing all the particular challenges of maintaining this spirit in front of marketing and marketplace success. The proliferation of small groups, record labels, garage recording and clubs which the movement brought with it offer a malleable form of organization which might prevent the solidification which is almost inevitable if the music works through conventional channels. One will recognize this by a collapse into style.

C. My personal high was a remarkable experience in July, 1974 which granted me a glimpse of what a human being can really be and the freedom which is naturally part of that. The low point was simultaneously seeing the price that had to be paid for this and recognising my own level of development. All subsequent events in my life have been governed by this experience and the insights that went with it. The recent *Frippertronics Tour* was a continuing high by giving me so many practical opportunities to work with these insights and the ideas I received at Sherborne House and validating them in the blast of the marketplace.

D. Rather than seek information to argue in support of what I instinctively feel to be right I act on my instincts and let the results be my validation.

E. Dislikes: The collapse into style and the vaporation of intent in the so-called English progressive/art rock music. Even more do I dislike the uncritical support of it. "Art rock" took the wrong turn and became more intrigued by pseudo-gothic visitors than giving a genuine impression of multidimensionality which at best it implied. Likes: Overcoming the mystique that only musicians can make music.

Gregg Geller, Columbia Records A&R

A. 45s: "Burning Love" (Elvis Presley), "Take Me to the River" (Syl Johnson), "So It Goes"/"Heart of the City" (Nick Lowe)

LPs: *Ziggy Stardust* (David Bowie), *Late for the Sky* (Jackson Browne), *My Aim Is True* (Elvis Costello), Charly Sun reissues

B. Death of Elvis Presley; advent of Elvis Costello.

C. Low point: Living in Los Angeles. High point: Living to tell about it.

D. Lost weight, lost hair, shaved beard, got glasses, grew older and hopefully wiser.

E. Faves: Baseball; rockabilly (forever). Dislikes: Disco, disco, disco, disco, disco.

Alex Harvey, Scottish rock and roller

A. 45s: "Anarchy in the UK" (Sex Pistols), "Jocko Homo" (Devo), "In the Navy" (Village People)

LPs: All Pere Ubu; all Residents; all Jimmy Rodgers, the Singing Cowboy

B. The punk movement and Watergate!

C. High point: Forming the Sensational Alex Harvey Band. Low: Disbanding SAHB. High: Considering entering my dogs in dog food commercial competition; finding book about "tomahawk" in museum of American Indian on Broadway.

D. They've made me 10 years older!

E. My favorite thing about the '70s is that youth springs eternally, and that's always good. Dislike the fact that the most attractive thing for young people to be today is to be a terrorist — to males this is especially attractive.

Marilyn Laverty, Columbia Records publicity

C. Meeting the Clash (high) and Bowie (high) and Bruce Springsteen (high); getting kicked out of Cornell's music program (low); my first article printed in *TP* (high); getting paid for my first *TP* article (low!).

Genya Ravan, artist producer

A. Ones that never made it and Television and CBGB Live. (It brought me back. I felt a heartbeat.)

B. Death of a roach I trained—he had good commercial ears. I moved him from Rivington and Pitt St. to the upper West Side. He's still on his back, but I had him stuffed.

C. High on coke; low on Quaaludes.

E. I hate the dead end of the music business. I love the live end of music. (A long-lost feeling.)

Lisa Robinson, Syndicated columnist, *Hit Parader* editor

A. LPs: *New York Dolls, Horses* (Patti Smith); *Some Girls* (Rolling Stones); *David Johansen*; first Clash album; *Paris 1919* (John Cale); *Never Mind the Bollocks* (Sex Pistols); *The Great Rock'n'Roll Swindle* (Sex Pistols); first Stooges album; *Funhouse* (Stooges); *Imagine* (John Lennon); *June 1, 1974* (Nico, Cale, Eno and Ayers); first Ramones album; *Marquee Moon* (Television); *Tom Verlaine*

B. *Anarchy in the UK* tour/1976; Television sets at CBGB's/1974; Patti Smith/Lenny Kaye poetry reading at St. Mark's/1971.

C. High: all Patti Smith performances, especially early days; seeing the Clash and Sex Pistols/Manchester, England, 1976; touring with Rolling Stones/1975; the early days of *Rock Scene* magazine.

Low: The death of Lillian Roxon in 1973.

D. Reaffirmed my original tastes. I still like the same noisy, "inaccessible," "uncommercial" rock and roll I always did. Other than that, much of my "work" in the field has become routine. Too bad.

Dislikes: *Rolling Stone* magazine; REO Speedwagon; Kansas; Boston; Foreigner; Firefall; Eagles; Fleetwood Mac; Yes; ELO; ELP; Styx; Supertramp; most FM radio except WPIX/NY and WMMS/Cleveland. (There may be other good ones, but those are the only ones I really know.)

Andy Scott, Sweet

A. 45s: "Layla" (Derek & the Dominos); "Let's Go" (Cars); "Feels Like the First Time" (Foreigner)

LPS: *Can't Buy a Thrill* (Steely Dan); *Kids Are Alright* soundtrack (the Who); *Made in Japan* (Deep Purple)

B. Keith Moon's death; punk came and went; Deep Purple split; but new wave stuck!

C. I'm high when I work! And low when I don't.

E. Disco sucks; I rediscovered Frank Zappa; I'm enjoying playing so much I can't wait for the '80s.

Gloria Stavers, National Rock Treasure (former editor of *16 Magazine*)

A. *New Boots and Panties!* (Ian Dury); Vivaldi's "Four Seasons" (New Koto Ensemble of Tokyo); *Alive on Arrival* (Steve Forbert); *Einstein on the Beach* (Philip Glass); *Slow Train Coming* (Bob Dylan)

C. High: Finally leaving *16* magazine after 17 years of fun-fun-fun that finally began to pale.

Lows: Seeing how lazy and nonproductive we've become — hence, inflation (gobble gobble). Also disco-zzzz...zzzz...

D. Made me delight in and love life, friends, nature, intelligence, etc. More: Life's a groove! I've become less compulsive, more loving (truly) and generally gotten happier!

1983–1984: A SURVEY

TP 92/93, DECEMBER 1983/JANUARY 1984

The end of any year is a time for taking stock of the past and looking ahead to the future. As we hover on the edge of 1984, however, the moment seems especially propitious for pop music— least of all for the date's Orwellian significance. Record sales, radio airplay and this summer's New Music Seminar in New York were conclusive: The current descendants of the original new wave explosion have entered the pop mainstream.

So far, so good; where next? *TP* contacted various musicians for their views on the scene, present and future. Their answers speak for themselves — but it's interesting to note that more than one hints of an imminent synthesizer backlash and the increasing influence of video.

Adam Clayton, U2

1983: People are reevaluating what they're going to be doing, where they're going — trying to get more of a firm direction. It's been very much a year of reassessment. A lot of bands are coming and going, particularly bands that have done three or four albums and have gone as far as they can go in that format: Paul Weller and the Jam, the English Beat, the Clash. U2 certainly intends to make a change from what we've done so far.

1984: I think music will become a lot more vital, maybe a bit rougher, not as smooth and produced as it has been. It may go in a more political way overall. The synthesizer bands are already having problems: They can't really tour, and they're very reliant on that floating market that buys hit records. They have no more longevity than their next song. A lot of those bands may well disappear. The vanguard of the new direction is certainly the Alarm and Big Country.

Jerry Casale, Devo

1983: This was the best year since 1978. With the success of bands like U2, Eurythmics and Heaven 17 (in Europe), a degree of style and intelligence has been allowed out once more from the narrow-casting chokehold of the music biz. Good things have been rewarded.

1984: There seems to be a widening chasm between the forces of goon regression and the forces of true mutancy. Nineteen eighty-four promises to be the year they come together in some big crunch. It's a mythical year everybody's been looking forward to, and it's sure to affect everyone on an unconscious level. Devo will be right there with our customary ambivalence and exuberant cynicism. We know, of course, that with every move we make and every step we take, the police are watching us!

Adam Ant

1983: Music got a little bit safe and precious last year. I think it could become a lot sexier with more humor. Live shows could become far more colorful and theatrical than they have in the past. In fact, due to the video revolution, we may see some of the style of the videos reproduced live. Video has fulfilled more than anyone ever dreamed.

1984: I would like to see more artists getting involved in controlling their own video imagery. It's important to realize that videos are the product of the artist's imagination and should reflect the lyrics the artist has written. Videos have to be worked through in the same manner that one writes a song. It is a craft to be learned by the artist and not just handed over to outside producers. Otherwise, it may be turned into cosmetic with no musical guts.

In the coming year audiences should be given a lot more credit. Live performances are very important, and kids should demand a higher level of entertainment than ever seen before.

Iggy Pop

1983: You could call 1983 the Year of the Sobering Experience. A lot of the mystery and maybe mysticism that was once attendant upon music has gone out of it, which is good: As new wave becomes a dominant musical force you can actually hear on radio, musicians are beginning to realize this can be a lifetime role. Bands are getting more serious and a little more normal about their lifestyle.

I'm finding the people in the audience at my shows are living a life not terribly different from mine! Before you could have an Elvis living in the Hollywood Hills with starlets around the house, and his fans would be hillbillies. Now half the people in the audience have bands of their own! There's an integration between performer and audience — something I tried to push a long time ago.

1984: Because of MTV and a lot of other channels, people are going to start writing music much more with video and a story in mind. A long, arduous tour will no longer be something you have to do to get yourself seen everywhere. That's good for the audience, because a lot of people used to get ruined from touring too much. You can give more thought to what you do in a video than trying to deal with the frustrations of a small club with a bad sound system 10,000 miles from home.

Henry Rollins, Black Flag

1983: I'm kind of a rare bird in that I don't keep a finger on the pulsebeat of rock movements. Radio is awful. Hardcore is not very hard. I don't see anything that vital except a handful of bands: Minor Threat, Minutemen, Hüsker Dü, Meat Puppets, Big Boys, St. Vitus. Mostly I listen to older records; my favorite band is the Stooges. I start with the Stooges and Velvet Underground, and then I look at bands.

1984: Black Flag's going to tour a lot and put out a lot of records. We are a live touring band, and this sitting-at-home shit is not happening.

Fred Schneider, B-52's

1983: More avenues are open for non-MOR groups. New British music, good and bad, and MTV have opened up radio. People are finally getting to see the groups they wanted to see and hear.

1984: I guess it will continue the way it has been for the past year or so: more British music coming in, more American groups getting better exposure. Groups who might not get radio play will take advantage of video, getting the expo-

sure they need and deserve — or don't deserve. My family watches MTV; they let me know what's going on.

Joey Ramone

1983: I'm disgusted with elevator music, all this English synthetic Motown. I'd like to see music get exciting again. Rock and roll is exciting music, but this is schlock: A Flock of Seagulls, the Fixx, all this crap. Everything now is just so artificial and superficial. There's no feeling, no guts or soul. I'm not saying everybody's doing this, but it seems most people are jumping on the bandwagon; it's the easiest thing to do. It infuriates me when bullshit like Wham! is the hottest thing in England.

If you grew up on rock and roll, you know what's good. I like music that's real, with some emotion. I've had enough of all this shit, and I think kids have, too.

Gordon Gano, Violent Femmes

1983: I'm fairly ignorant of the music scene, even though I'm part of it. We don't make it our business to stay up on what's happening. But it's certainly been a good year for the Femmes!

1984: If we were to play it relatively safe our popularity would grow. But what we're planning for the second album will throw some people for a loop. We want to continue to make the best music we can, and we hope people will continue to be open-minded and get into it. I think it will be a good year.

Peter Buck and Michael Stipe, R.E.M.

1983: There was a bit more willingness on the part of the media to spotlight independent labels and uncompromising music.

1984: The record industry is going to die like the dinosaur which it so much resembles.

Suggs, Madness

1983: I really hate the phrase "new music." That's one of the worst trends in America, segregating music.

It's a funny period. Everything's been done, and anything that anybody's doing has been recycled. Maybe that's how it's always been, but it seems like there's nowhere to go. People are burying themselves in synthesizers, finding nothing at the bottom and flinging themselves around trying to find new things.

Madness. That was my favorite trend this year.

1984: A good sign is that the young seem more involved in popular music than they were a few years ago. Punk is the best thing that's happened.

Stiv Bator, Lords of the New Church

1984: I see a return to glam-punk coming in, along the tradition of the Alice Cooper "nightmare" look as opposed to the feminine/drag queen look. There'll be a weird undercurrent of punkadelia thrown in, too.

Ray Manzarek

1983: The new music scene is extremely exciting. I'm finding people are committed to the importance of music once again. It reminds me of what was going on in the mid to late '60s, when music was important. Music should be entertaining, but it shouldn't be just entertainment. Certainly, X is in the forefront; that's why I'm working with them. Some people coming out of England and Australia are starting to do very meaningful things. There's a lot of bullshit going on, too.

1984: George Orwell said 1984 is the year of Big Brother, but it's not going to go that way. Instead, individual human beings are going to find out that music is one of the most important things in their lives. Music matters, and the words singers are singing matter. I see some important things going on in 1984 that will be generated by the young people of America and the whole planet, committed to the intoxicating rhythms of rock and roll. Either that, or the shit hits the fan.

Paul Weller, Style Council

1983: Very cloudy and overcast. Lots of drizzle.

1984: More grey clouds, but outbursts later, followed by extreme sunshine.

Andy Gill, Gang of Four

1983: I don't think there's been an enormous change in the last 12 months; the change happened more like two years ago. The synthesizer

thing is still sticking around. The American Top 20 has been dominated by English groups the last couple of years, with well-crafted pop songs. As in the classic pop song tradition, those songs are about nothing. I like a little bit of interest.

1984: Changes will be occurring soon. People are going to get tired of being fed this pap all the time and will look for something with substance to it — which will be good for Gang of Four. What we feel we're doing makes sense when it's nestling shoulder to shoulder with Barry Manilow and REO Speedwagon. That's the context in which Gang of Four should be heard. Perhaps we've not achieved that because we've been so difficult in media terms. We felt we could get away with more radical moves than people are prepared to accept.

Lenny Kaye, Patti Smith Group

1983 gave us the technology for the music we're going to be listening to, and the ways we're going to listen to it, over the next ten years. It completely split apart old musical categories and created new ones. You can hear that in radio, if nowhere else. It was a year, for instance, when disco music, once the most conservative of forms, became the most radical — and rock and roll, vice versa.

It's form over content at this point. In England, form has taken total precedence over everything; whatever content you get out of the music is incidental.

1984: Perhaps people will learn to harness technologies and style. Now that we have a bunch of new styles to work with, I'm curious to see whether we can get into what these styles can teach us about how we live and breathe. African music — a novelty, from a white viewpoint — will have a lot more relevance than just "this week's foreign music." The most relevant album to all this — so relevant it's almost a theoretical work — is Malcolm McLaren's *Duck Rock*.

Obviously, new wave — which began in the mid-'70s — has run its course. You can see it in the music and sense of possibility that looms right over the horizon. I'm kind of anxious for the next year to begin, because I think that's when things are really going to start rolling, and the true personality of the '80s will make itself manifest.

We celebrated reaching the ten-year publishing milestone in our last issue (we knew it was our last issue, but nobody else did). This cull of pungent one-liners from our back pages conveys as much about what the magazine accomplished as anything. Dada for now, as we (and the Bonzos) used to say.

QUOTES OF THE (*TROUSER PRESS*) DECADE

TP 96, APRIL 1984

SELF-ANALYSIS

I'd rather make music than write about it.
—Future *TROUSER PRESS* editor SCOTT ISLER (1974)

I'm really great at listening: I'd rather do that than anything else.
—MARSHALL CRENSHAW (1983)

It's not like I have pretensions to high art.
—JOHN HIATT (1980)

I know I'm not a genius because I have to work too hard.
—ADAM ANT (1982)

My artistic integrity is 100% uncompromised.
—TODD RUNDGREN (1979)

I think Phil [Collins] is technically a better singer than I am.
—PETER GABRIEL (1980)

Drummers shouldn't sing — except Levon Helm.
—DAVE EDMUNDS (1981)

I wouldn't call myself a singer...Sam Cooke's a singer.
—JOE STRUMMER (1981)

It's hard to sing a song that makes you puke. You can't do both at the same time.
—GRACE SLICK (1981)

I'm not a thief. I've never taken anything from anyone. I don't have to. I have too much respect for myself to take anything from anybody.
—CAPTAIN BEEFHEART (1983)

I wasn't an outcast, I cast myself out.
—IAN DURY (1978)

PUNKARAMA

Punk will never die until something more dangerous replaces it.
—JELLO BIAFRA (1981)

I don't like walking the streets and seeing 30,000 imitations of me.
—JOHNNY ROTTEN (1977)

Just because we use the word "spit" in a song doesn't mean we're trying to be like the Sex Pistols.
—EXENE (1980)

In ten years, I hope there will be plenty of young bands around who'll tell me I'm boring and continue the tradition of rock and roll.
—BOB GELDOF (1977)

At this particular point, if it wasn't for punk, which is taking it right back to the roots of shit-kicking rock and roll — back to "fuck you" music, sheer adrenaline — [rock and roll] would be in a sad state of affairs.
—JIMMY PAGE (1977)

The fuck-you finger must be the new peace salute of the '80s.
—ALAN VEGA of SUICIDE (1982)

I was duped by the punk thing. I thought this was gonna save the world.
—ANDY PARTRIDGE of XTC (1981)

THE NITTY GRITTY

I've always found musicians very coarse people, often quite uninspired and unintelligent.
—MALCOLM MCLAREN (1983)

In our music we're looking for the big enema, the big catharsis.
—GERALD CASALE of DEVO (1978)

We're an up band. We're not a fucking downer.
—ANNABELLA of BOW WOW WOW (1982)

We don't have no big-ass fucking lawyer who goes down and gives a blowjob to some asshole at CBS. **—CYRIL JORDAN, explaining why the FLAMIN' GROOVIES haven't succeeded in the U.S. (1978)**

Tits and asses are gifts god gave us and it's to my best interest to use them.

—DALE BOZZIO of MISSING PERSONS (1983)

I think the human body's about one of the most ugly things ever created. Everyone has lumps and distorted bits and pieces.

—JOHN LYDON (1980)

AMERICAN RUES

I don't think America would know a good rock and roll band unless they were advertised on TV. **—DAVE HIGGS of EDDIE & THE HOT RODS (1978)**

A quick spree 'round the States taking in all the sights and buying all the crap you can lay your hands on — that's what we call fun. So long as we don't have to live there.

—JOE STRUMMER of THE CLASH (1980)

I wish [Americans] would bring up their kids with a little more discipline, stop giving them hamburgers and shit like that.

—RITCHIE BLACKMORE of RAINBOW (1978)

We'd love to come to America, but we won't until Virgin releases our albums here... They don't think we'll go over. I think we could conquer America.

—MARTYN WARE of THE HUMAN LEAGUE (1980)

REMEMBER MY NAME

We had a number-one single and were still getting $40 a week.

—STEVE MARRIOTT, on THE SMALL FACES (1981)

I'm not making a comeback. I'm making a living. **—RICHARD HELL (1982)**

One disadvantage to having our own company is that if the next record doesn't sell, we may have to drop ourselves.

—SGT. BLOTTO of BLOTTO (1982)

We're definitely not an underground group anymore. The only place left for us to go where people think we're crazy is to hang out with Chuck Mangione.

—CLEM BURKE of BLONDIE (1981)

I want our records to be hits. I want my kids to go to college.

—MARTHA DAVIS of THE MOTELS (1980)

People change when they get a hit. Your back straightens. Your acne goes. I know, because it happened to me.

—PETER NOONE of HERMAN'S HERMITS (1980)

I pull a lot more chicks now since they've seen my name in the papers. **—NICK LOWE (1977)**

Cute English boys will always be more popular than talented American bands. **—EXENE (1984)**

I think you can be successful and still keep a certain amount of self-respect.

—PAUL WELLER of THE JAM (1979)

We haven't made too many of the obvious mistakes. Nobody has killed themselves off with dope, nobody has done anything wildly dishonest, nobody has killed anybody. We never put out what I feel was a dishonest record, we've never deliberately gone out to exploit large numbers of people.

—PETE TOWNSHEND of THE WHO (1978)

This is glamorous, yeah: You drag your butt all over the world. It's a regular job.

—RICK NIELSEN of CHEAP TRICK (1980)

The only thing I could see doing is the opposite of touring, where I stay in one place and the audience tours to see me. **—BRIAN ENO (1978)**

HI-Q'S

Is it true you're an idiot?

—LOU REED, to a Cleveland disc jockey (1976)

We've got a pretty wide demographic.

—MARTYN WARE of BRITISH ELECTRIC FOUNDATION (1983)

I never claimed to be original.
—GARY NUMAN (1981)

We're just a bunch of fucking lamebrains.
—FRANCIS ROSSI of STATUS QUO (1975)

Stupidity is like hydrogen; it's everywhere, it's the basic building block of the universe.
—FRANK ZAPPA (1980)

We've been told we can be successful here if we want to. But we'll decide that after we've worked out whether America deserves us or not. —TERRY HALL of FUN BOY THREE (1983)

THE PHILOSOPHY OF ROCK

The characteristic organization of the new world is small, independent, mobile and intelligent.
—ROBERT FRIPP (1975)

I'm ready for the new soul era.
—FRED SCHNEIDER of THE B-52'S (1980)

Creativity is on the streets. Pop is reactionary.
—RIC OCASEK of THE CARS (1983)

De-evolution is basically an extended joke ... a mythology for people to believe in.
—GERALD CASALE of DEVO (1982)

Among the first companies we approached with our demos was Stiff... [Jake Riviera] dismissed us as "fuckin' queer music."
—TOM ROBINSON (1978)

We wouldn't have girlfriends if we weren't in the Ramones.
—JOHNNY RAMONE (1978)

We did one straight, raunchy rock and roll album, and one is enough.
—JOHN LYDON on THE SEX PISTOLS (1979)

Our songs are about personal politics, not a nation's politics. We've all got our own views, but I don't see why Jerry-in-the-street needs to know how I feel politically.
—NICK RHODES of DURAN DURAN (1983)

We wouldn't endorse a car. We've also been asked to do political things, and we won't do them. You have to remember what you're really doing this for. —RIC OCASEK of THE CARS (1980)

CAREER CHOICES

I don't intend to wind up parking cars somewhere.
—KEITH MOON of THE WHO (1976)

I'm extremely uncommitted to music. It's like a hobby to me.
—NICK LOWE (1982)

I don't like being stared at when I'm playing.
—ROBERT FRIPP (1978)

I don't want to keep regurgitating the same rituals.
—STING (1982)

I've been developing my career as a moviegoer.
—TOM VERLAINE (1982)

If I had my way, I'd be touring five or six months a year all over the world. I'd go out onstage and play "Substitute" all night — I don't give a damn as long as I'm playing.
—JOHN ENTWISTLE of THE WHO (1978)

When we started, I looked at the bands in England and said, "I can't relate to this," but the New York bands were a different story.
—BONO of U2 (1982)

We're not fascists, and that's all that matters.
—BERNARD SUMNER, defending the names JOY DIVISION and NEW ORDER (1983)

It wasn't the easiest thing I've ever done, that's for sure.
—SANDY PEARLMAN on producing *Give 'Em Enough Rope* for THE CLASH

CULTURE SHOCKS

I'd rather see Liza Minnelli than any rock performer.
—ADAM ANT (1982)

I'd rather not become totally dependent on the technology I use.
—THOMAS DOLBY (1982)

It just wasn't enough for me to be a guitar player for the Rolling Stones.
—MICK TAYLOR (1979)

SERIOUSLY, NOW

You shouldn't be in a band if you don't want to influence people. Or you should just play instrumentals.

—DAVE WAKELING of THE BEAT (1982)

We did a gig in front of six people in Poughkeepsie and they loved us.

—ANDY SUMMERS of THE POLICE (1979)

Around '76, Joe Strummer told me that people have got to start writing about more important issues. That made an impression.

—PAUL WELLER of THE JAM (1981)

If you wrote about death completely convincingly you'd kill all your readers.

—Writer WILLIAM S. BURROUGHS (1982)

I never leave the songs behind. I might leave the arrangements and the mood behind, but the songs, I never leave them behind.

—BOB DYLAN (1979)

Nothing I do is fashionable at the time I do it.

—TODD RUNDGREN (1978)

I wouldn't want to think people doted on us, hung on every word, or wanted to look like us.

—ROBERT SMITH of THE CURE (1980)

FAMOUS FIRST WORDS

You *Trouser Pressers* are always up to something…—JAKE RIVIERA, ELVIS COSTELLO's manager (1978)

The first time I ever got any press was in *Trouser Press*.   —ALF MOYET of YAZ(OO) (1983)

The Australians are coming.

—Writers JIM GREEN and DAVE SCHULPS (1976)

AC/DC will surely find a place in the hearts, minds and bodies of the kind of 12-year-old girls who look three times their age.

—Writer KAREN ROSE (1976)

Much love and respect to your fine paper…

—PETE TOWNSHEND (1974)

A lot of people tell us that these are the best years even though we are struggling.

—MARGOT OLAVARRIA of THE GO-GO'S (1980)

It was doomed to fail: four blokes, not even out of their teens, shoved together, living in squalor.   —STEVE WINWOOD, on TRAFFIC (1981)

The Human League does little to encourage belief that the dropping price of synthesizers will usher in a new age of popular music.

—Writer STEVEN GRANT (1980)

I always thought *Trouser Press* was an English paper.   —ADRIAN BELEW (1982)

MEOW!

[Jerry Harrison] *is* Talking Heads: he's responsible for that sound. [He] was playing the things people have assumed Brian Eno or David Byrne were doing.

—TINA WEYMOUTH of TALKING HEADS (1982)

I'm not really bothered by what people think. As long as they don't say it to my face, who cares?   —PETER HOOK of NEW ORDER (1983)

Rolling Stone said I was trying to destroy pop music; they're out of their minds.

—CHRIS STEIN of BLONDIE (1982)

The Stones? I considered them idiots. I respect them but I don't like them.

—RITCHIE BLACKMORE (1978)

I like Jonathan Richman. I think he's got a great sense of humor … if he's kidding, that is.

—JOHNNY ROTTEN (1977)

Most people don't notice he's not there.

—PHIL COLLINS, on PETER GABRIEL's departure from GENESIS (1976)

Nobody compares us to the Velvet Underground and that's probably the one group we all love.   —MICHAEL STIPE of R.E.M. (1983)

My old man still shouts at me for not doing the dishes before I go to bed.   —BONO (1982)

I listen to the first album now and I just cringe, it all sounds so primitive.

—PAUL WELLER of THE JAM (1979)

Time has just flown since Rockpile broke up. You've no idea how happy I am to be, not just out of the band, but out of the whole thing.

—DAVE EDMUNDS (1982)

I can think of a lot better pseudonyms than Bono! Why couldn't I have thought of something like "Sting"?   —PAUL HEWSON of U2 (1983)

Not to say anything bad about Eno, but whenever we'd do something great while working with him he'd say, "No, that sounds too good."

—TINA WEYMOUTH of TALKING HEADS (1982)

AND SO FORTH

I think the worst thing in pop music is how people overstay their welcome. I hope we don't go on for more than two or three years.

—DAVE WAKELING of THE BEAT (1981)

I'm sick and tired of waiting around for people gradually to discover us. I don't want it happening in nine years' time, when maybe all our best songs are gone and we're just churning out rubbish.   —GLENN TILBROOK of SQUEEZE (1981)

If the Clash stay together for five years they'll probably be the new Rolling Stones.

—IAN HUNTER (1979)

George Martin would have been a terrific producer ... if he'd only known the right time to go to the toilet.

—Manager/producer ANDREW LOOG OLDHAM (1978)

Phil's a little temperamental...

—JOEY RAMONE, on SPECTOR (1979)

We were trying to do a Phil Spector thing with as few instruments as possible.   —JOHN CALE on the first VELVET UNDERGROUND album (1983)

There's nothing more pitiful than someone who's lost touch with what's going on.

—NICK LOWE (1978)

Pain is my girlfriend. I feel pain every day of my life.   —HENRY ROLLINS of BLACK FLAG (1983)

We're gonna learn our fourth chord next week. Three chords in thirteen years isn't bad. What takes the time is learning to go from the other chord to the new one.

—FRANCIS ROSSI of STATUS QUO (1975)

I'm an extraordinarily bitter person.

—ELVIS COSTELLO (1977)

It's very difficult to rise above the level of your own best clichés.   —BILL NELSON (1981)

I've always been optimistic about life. I've not always been optimistic about my role in it.

—PETE TOWNSHEND (1978)

We paved the road for bands like Duran Duran. We might even have helped Culture Club get accepted more quickly, at least in the area of strange hairdos.

—MIKE SCORE of A FLOCK OF SEAGULLS (1983)

A Flock of Seagulls are just Genesis with moronic haircuts, aren't they?

—TERRY HALL of FUN BOY THREE (1983)

I feel degraded to compete with a lot of the music that goes up the singles charts.

—JOHN ENTWISTLE of THE WHO (1978)

We don't want to sound discomforting or unsettling or make people feel uneasy.

—DAVID BYRNE of TALKING HEADS (1976)

I think kids are bored enough that if they got a chance to hear my music, they'd like it.

—CAPTAIN BEEFHEART (1981)

If all the things that happened to me when I was little had happened when I was a lot older, I'd probably be dead by now.

—LENE LOVICH (1983)

I can't stand being in a room full of people who have taken drugs.   —BRIAN ENO (1981)

If the records weren't free we'd be rating cheeseburgers.   —TROUSER PRESS (1978)

LAST CALL

> "
> *When your
> culture abandons you,
> create a new one.*
> "
>
> —IRA ROBBINS

T rouser Press *ceased publication after a tenth anniversary issue in April 1984. There was no article about him inside, but our cover star, Joey Ramone, was a good sport — even when the carefully crafted headline card was ignited by the candles on the cake and had to be replaced by a hastily scrawled version. (Honest, we didn't know that* Creem *had done virtually the same cover with Frank Zappa a decade earlier.)*

Looking back over our experience (but not letting on that we were headed for an exit), we shared some of our history in this mildly rueful (and deeply sarcastic) article, dressed up as an instructive warning to anyone inclined to do what we had done.

HOW TO PUBLISH A ROCK MAGAZINE

TP 96, APRIL 1984

By Scott Isler

S o, you want to put out a rock magazine? Great!

But wait! Before you become too involved to answer the phone, you might want to peruse the following pages. After ten years in this here rock rag biz, we at *Trouser Press* think we've learned something about How to Do It. To celebrate this anniversary, we considered running a thoroughly intimidating article detailing the unique mixture of genius, intelligence, creativity and sheer nerve that makes *Trouser Press* what it is.

However, we're too modest to brag. Instead, we're offering a public service: advice to aspiring rock publishing magnates. In a truly selfless move, we're sharing the fruit of ten years' labor. We've dug into *Trouser Press'* voluminous archives for case histories — many never before revealed — typical of what you can expect with your own publication. Read, and prosper! (If only someone had told us...)

HOW TO BEGIN

Scared? Don't be. Anybody can put out a rock magazine — and they do! Of course, it helps if you have an angle. Back when *TP* got rolling, British musicians were [rarely] featured on the cover of *Rolling Stone* (est. 1939), let alone *Time* or *Newsweek*. Now, with so many music 'zines out there, you've got to be pretty clever. How about a magazine dealing only with MTV veejays? Or giving plot outlines of all the videos shown on MTV? Your ingenuity is the limit. Just make sure the concept has something to do with MTV.

THE FACTS OF (PUBLISHING) LIFE

There are a variety of ways to produce a magazine. Lettering and drawing each issue by hand is the slowest, and not recommended by *Trouser Press*. You may want to start out — as we did — with a mimeograph machine, supplemented by offset printing for pages with photographs.

If you hang in there long enough, you'll probably move up printing's evolutionary scale. When you stop cranking 'em out yourself and give the job to a printing press, you'll be major league.

Printers are as human as anyone, sometimes too much so. *Trouser Press* switched to a new one for the magazine's first full-color cover (TP 20, 1977). The day blueprints were to arrive for final checking, we learned that the printer — located in New Jersey's Bible Belt — had discovered a four-letter word in the issue and refused to have anything to do with our slimy kind. We went begging back to our previous printer, who gleefully charged us double for the rush job. So, know your printer or watch your f*#in' language. (Or how about a magazine on born-again Christian rockers?)

GIVING THE PEOPLE WHAT THEY WANT

You may have difficulty at first getting interviews with big stars who never heard of your diddly-squat little magazine. Don't despair; take what you can get. *Trouser Press*' first exclusive interview (TOTP 5) was with Moogy Klingman. He's not the type to get mobbed on the street but, at the time, we hung on his every sentence. Keep pestering people at record companies, and soon they'll know who you are (and learn not to take your calls).

Fortunately, rock magazines can get away with other types of writing than interviews — record reviews, for instance. Everyone's got opinions; what makes yours more valuable than the others is that you're going to the trouble of forcing it on strangers.

Don't be afraid to make fun of a recording artist's sexual preference or body weight because you didn't understand his or her hit single. Remember, it's your responsibility to educate the public! You will sound even more authoritative if you quote song titles correctly.

WRITERS LOST IN SPACE

In the beginning — whether from force of circumstance or bloated ego — you might be writing most of your magazine yourself. Eventually, though, you'll develop a squad of writers. Some you may seek out; others will seek you out, drawn by the common bond of love of music matched only by love of free records.

Once you give assignments to writers, you'll discover a curious phenomenon: They inhabit a time zone of their own, regardless of geographic location. What you think of as "next week" doesn't reach their district until a great while later. Magazine editors learn to compensate for this time warp by assigning early and/or giving spurious deadline dates. In extreme cases, phoning a tardy contributor every 15 minutes also helps.

Other facts have to be considered, too, in dealing with outside writers — notoriously the mail — and you're sure to be delighted by unpredictable variations. Back in the heady summer of '77, we eagerly expected a Sex Pistols feature from a London writer.

A couple of weeks went by, and still we expected it. At the last possible moment, we learned the precious manuscript had been pouched via jet to a New York record company, from where it would be hand-delivered to us. On a Friday — the deadest of deadlines — the article landed, and a messenger was dispatched to our office. The messenger never showed up. Some frantic phone calls revealed our messenger to be a practicing Muslim who hurried home before sundown, taking our article with him. No, he had no phone. We sent him a telegram. The article showed up the following Tuesday, by which time the *TP* office resembled post-Kool Aid Jonestown. Needless to say, it got into the issue.

OKAY, ENOUGH OF THE BASICS. You'll find out soon enough what a nerve-wracking, wearying, soul-destroying experience rock magazine publishing can be.

"Are there no rewards?" you ask. "No wealth? Sex? No sealing my nose with cocaine?"

Fool! The rarefied pleasures of this business cannot be calibrated on such an earthly scale. Among the finer delights in store for you are:

FIGHTS WITH THE STARS

No matter how careful you think you are, you are bound to offend somebody sooner or later. Celebrities — especially rock celebrities — don't think like us normal people. Left Banke/Stories maestro Michael Brown abruptly ended an interview when *TP* publisher Ira Robbins innocently asked him what his protégés, the Beckies, would be wearing onstage when they toured.

Two years after we met, Flamin' Groovie Cyril Jordan — apparently miffed by an unfavorable record review — lambasted this writer and Robbins, who wasn't there, in the pages of *New York Rocker*. The attack provoked an even more virulent letter from Robbins, printed in the following *Rocker*. Jordan finally called to apologize, and we all made nice again. But the incident demonstrates the unseemly rancor some musicians hold for being one-sidedly attacked in print. Well, nobody's perfect. (And beware of stars who demand photo approval.)

FIGHTS WITH THE STARS' REPRESENTATIVES

As a magazine baron, you will be in touch less with superstar musicians — who have more important. things to do, like taking drugs — than with those who represent them, i.e., managers and press officers. Unfortunately, these people, naturally desirous of pleasing their clients, can be even worse to deal with than the stars themselves.

To illustrate a pathbreaking article on Kiss in 1978, we ran a sequence of photographs [by Mitch Kearney] showing the newly merchandized Kiss dolls in a group grope with Barbie dolls. The band thought the photos were hilarious. The president of their public relations firm sent a letter expressing "total disappointment": "We surely believed that *Trouser Press* worked on a high caliber level and would not resort to such a disgusting display." In the accompanying article, Gene Simmons showed his high caliber by stating, "Even a non-fan's got to say, 'God, I hate those guys, but they sure have big dicks!'"

When he founded Stiff Records, Jake Riviera used to send us the friendliest letters. Then he left Stiff to devote himself to managing Elvis Costello; despite being the first U.S. magazine to splash El on its cover (in late 1977), we've never gotten near him again. Now that Costello practically grants interviews to toy train collectors' journals and still snubs us, we have to wonder: could it have been that *TP* cover in 1979 — the one with the Costello puppet on it and the legend, "Who pulls the strings?" (Our think piece didn't say.) Nah!

FIGHTS WITH READERS

The glory of this free country is that you can print anything you want as long as you're prepared to take a pounding for it — verbally, at least. You'll find your readership will rarely write in to congratulate you for critical taste or journalistic excellence. They will sniff blood, though, at the merest hint of disrespect toward their musical heroes or ideals.

Ira Robbins took a lot of flak for his prescient "new wave is dead" editorial back in 1977. But the all-time winner in the *TP* hate-mail sweepstakes is this writer, thanks to a pan of the Ramones'

Pleasant Dreams. One anonymous fan evidently fed the offending page into a paper-shredder, then diced it into a fine powder, poured it into an envelope and returned it to us. Impressive.

FIGHTS WITH PERFECT STRANGERS

Accustomed as we are to constant psychic warfare, we can still be caught off-guard sometimes. The upper echelon of *Trouser Press* management, for example, has learned to dread the monthly arrival of *Don't Believe a Word!*, the cartoon by Roman Szolkowski. Szolkowski, "the Polish madman," speaks no recognized language. His column is delivered to our office by a small mute hunchback, who has been seen disappearing down manholes afterwards. The best we can do is pray that the artist's outrages, committed in the name of humor, be not too libelous. One month last year, we were pleased that *Don't Believe a Word!* contained nothing more offensive than a drawing of the Clash in designer battle fatigues. (For that, we received a negligible number of death threats from Clash fans.) The other illustration depicted Alvin the Chipmunk for a joke about the Chipmunks suing the Bee Gees for plagiarism.

A few months later, we got a letter from a lawyer representing the Chipmunks. Mr. Alvin was not pleased with the unauthorized use of his likeness, nor with any false rumors about the Chipmunks' legal activities. Mr. Alvin kindly requested we honor his trademark, or he and his pals would take legal action against us.

In this business, you never know who your friends are.

WE HOPE THE ABOVE has given you an idea of the joys of rock magazine publishing. Some rock writers — frustrated musicians, no doubt — hobnob with their subject matter just to soak up the fame by association. We, too, have had our memorable encounters — the Jam visiting our humble establishment and stealing all the wall posters — but, after ten years, one starts thinking about posterity. Many have proven that rock writing can also be great literature. May your publication attain the aesthetic heights scaled by *Trouser Press*. Like, y'know? ∎

CREDITS

The issue covers featured inside the book are marked, along with the page numbers on which they appear.

❖ **TOTP 1** (March 1974) The Who (press photo) **Page 9**

TOTP 2 (May 1974) Mott the Hoople (M.C. Escher)

❖ **TOTP 3** (June 1974) The Who (cartoon by Marc Nadel) **Cover**

❖ **TOTP 4** (July/August 1974) Jeff Beck (photo by David Kearns) **Page 45**

TOTP 5 (October/November 1974) Roger Ruskin Spear (photos by Ira Robbins)

❖ **TOTP 6** (December 1974/January 1975) Robert Fripp (photo by Ron Gott) **Page 181**

TOTP 7 (February/March 1975) The Animals (photographer unknown)

❖ **TOTP 8** (April/May 1975) Marc Bolan (photo by Linda Danna) **Page 140**

TOTP 9 (June/August 1975) Stones on Film (photographer unknown)

TOTP 10 (September/October 1975) Jeff Beck (photo by Ron Gott)

TOTP 11 (November/December 1975) Alex Harvey (photo by Ira Robbins)

TOTP 12 (February/March 1976) Roxy Music (photos by Linda Danna and Ron Gott)

TOTP 13 (April/May 1976) The Kinks (photo by Linda Danna)

❖ **TP 14** (June/July 1976) Keith Moon (photos by Chuck Pulin) **Cover**

❖ **TP 15** (August/September 1976) Dr. Feelgood (cartoon by Roman Szolkowski) **Page 218**

TP 16 (October/November 1976) Queen (photo by Linda Danna)

TP 17 (December 1976/January 1977) ELO (photo by Charles Charas)

TP 18 (February/March 1977) David Bowie (photo by Chuck Pulin)

TP 19 (April/May 1977) Thin Lizzy (photo by Janet Macoska)

❖ **TP 20** (June/July 1977) Peter Gabriel (photo by Ron Gott) **Page 174**

❖ **TP 21** (September 1977) Jimmy Page (photo by Neal Preston) **Cover, Page 51**

❖ **TP 22** (October 1977) Johnny Rotten (illustration by Rob Burger) **Cover, Page 332**

❖ **TP 23** (November 1977) Bryan Ferry (photo by Janet Macoska) **Page 160**

❖ **TP 24** (December 1977) Elvis Costello (photographer unknown) **Cover, Page 308**

TP 25 (January 1978) Steve Winwood (photo by Dick Polak)

TP 26 (February 1978) Paul McCartney (photo by Richard. E. Aaron)

❖ **TP 27** (April 1978) Pete Townshend (photo by Mike Putland/Retna) **Page 75**

❖ **TP 28** (May 1978) Pink Floyd (illustration by Rob Burger) **Cover, Page 33**

❖ **TP 29** (June 1978) Rolling Stones (photo from Rex Features Syndicate) **Cover, Page 22**

❖ **TP 30** (July 1978) Todd Rundgren (photo by Richard. E. Aaron) **Page 96**

TP 31 (August 1978) Cheap Trick (photo by Linda Danna Robbins)

❖ **TP 32** (September 1978) Ray Davies (photo by Richard E. Aaron) **Cover, Page 105**

❖ **TP 33** October 1978 *16* magazine parody (illustration by Amy Horowitz, photos by Ebet Roberts and Linda D. Robbins) **Cover**

❖ **TP 34** (December 1978) 100 Top Rock Guitarists of All Time (photo by Mitch Kearney) **Cover, Page 130**

TP 35 (January 1979) Devo
(photo by Ebet Roberts)

❖ **TP 36** (February 1979) Lou Reed
(photo by Mitch Kearney) **Cover, Page 210**

TP 37 (April 1979) Fifth Anniversary Issue:
The Who (color photo by Kevin Stein;
design assistance by Mike Masucci)

TP 38 (May 1979) John Lennon
(photo by Bob Gruen)

TP 39 (June 1979) Elvis Costello
(photo courtesy of *Record Mirror*)

TP 40 (July 1979) New Barbarians
(illustration by Brad Hamann)

TP 41 (August 1979) The Cars
(photo by Ebet Roberts)

❖ **TP 42** (September 1979) Blondie
(photo by Roberta Bayley) **Page 243**

TP 43 (October 1979) David Bowie
(illustration by Brad Hamann)

TP 44 (November 1979) Talking Heads
(photo by Ebet Roberts)

TP 45 (December 1979) Police
(photo by Ebet Roberts)

TP 46 (January 1980) Turn of the decade *Mad*
magazine parody (photo by Mitch Kearney,
illustration by John Ebersberger)

❖ **TP 47** (February 1980) Frank Zappa
(photo by Mitch Kearney) **Cover, Page 126**

❖ **TP 48** (March 1980) The Clash
(photo by James Lee Soffer) **Cover, Page 296**

TP 49 (April 1980) Neil Young
(photo by Chip Rock/Lynn Goldsmith Inc.)

❖ **TP 50** (May 1980) The Ramones
(photos by Mitch Kearney) **Cover**

TP 51 (June 1980) The Beatles
(photo by R.D.R. Productions)

TP 52 (July 1980) Pete Townshend
(photo by Terry O'Neal)

TP 53 (August 1980) The Kinks (photos by
Ebet Roberts and Nick Sangiamo)

TP 54 (September 1980) The Rolling Stones
(photo by Ebet Roberts)

TP 55 (October 1980) Springsteen in the
studio
(photo by Mitch Kearney)

TP 56 (November 1980) The Cars
(photo by Ebet Roberts)

❖ **TP 57** (December 1980) Cheap Trick
(photo by David Tan) **Cover, Page 118**

TP 58 (January 1981) Gary Numan
(photo by Mitch Kearney)

TP 59 (February 1981) Rockpile
(photo by Mitch Kearney)

TP 60 (April 1981) The Clash
(illustration by Amy Horowitz [Hill])

TP 61 (May 1981) Elvis Costello
(photo courtesy Columbia Records;
inset by Bob Leafe)

TP 62 (June 1981) Blondie
(illustrations by Brad Hamann and
Alba Acevedo)

TP 63 (July 1981) Sex Pistols in the Cinema
(illustration by Amy Horowitz [Hill])

TP 64 (August 1981) Tom Petty
(photo by Ebet Roberts)

TP 65 (September 1981) The Doors
(photo courtesy Danny Sugerman)

TP 66 (October 1981) Sex & Sleaze in Rock
(photos by Bob Leafe and Lou Kish,
design by Judy Steccone)

TP 67 (November 1981) The Pretenders
(photo by Ebet Roberts)

TP 68 (December 1981) Bill Wyman
(photo by Harrison Funk)

❖ **TP 69** (January 1982) Adam Ant
(photo by Mitch Kearney) **Cover, Page 361**

❖ **TP 70** (February 1982) Devo Meets Burroughs
(photo by Mitch Kearney) **Cover, Page 258**

TP 71 (March 1982) Genesis
(photo by Ebet Roberts)

❖ TP 72 (April 1982) Talking Heads
(photo by Godlis)

TP 73 (May 1982) The Police (photos by Bob
Leafe, Laura Levine and Ebet Roberts)

❖ TP 74 (June 1982) Joan Jett
(photo by by Ron Akiyama) **Cover, Page 366**

❖ TP 75 (July 1982) Nick Lowe
(photo by BC Kagan) **Page 320**

TP 76 (August 1982) Squeeze
(photo by BC Kagan)

❖ TP 77 (September 1982) Blondie
(photo by Brian Aris) **Cover**

TP 78 (October 1982) The Who
(illustration by Roman Szolkowski)

❖ TP 79 (November 1982) The Go-Go's
(photo by BC Kagan) **Page 269**

TP 80 (December 1982) Adam Ant et al
(photos by Ann Summa, CBS Records UK)

TP 81 (January 1983) Peter Gabriel
(photo by Mitch Kearney)

TP 82 (February 1983) The Cars
(photo by BC Kagan)

TP 83 (March 1983) Jefferson Airplane/
Starship (photos by Herb Greene)

TP 84 (April 1983) The Clash
(photo by Ebet Roberts)

TP 85 (May 1983) The Pretenders
(photo and tinting by Ebet Roberts)

TP 86 (June 1983) Boy George
(photo by Laura Levine)

❖ TP 87 (July 1983) U2
(photo by Ebet Roberts) **Cover, Page 346**

TP 88 (August 1983) Tabloid parody
(photos by Ebet Roberts, Craig Dietz and
Polydor Records)

TP 89 (September 1983) A Flock of Seagulls
(photo by Ebet Roberts)

❖ TP 90 (October 1983) Duran Duran
(photo by Brian Aris) **Cover**

❖ TP 91 (November 1983) Eddy Grant
(photo by Ebet Roberts) **Cover, Page 394**

TP 92/93 (December 1983/January 1984)
Madness (photographer unknown)

❖ TP 94 (February 1984) Stray Cats
(photographer unknown) **Cover**

TP 95 (March 1984) Big Country
(main photo by Chalkie Davies, inset by
Allan Ballard)

❖ TP 96 (April 1984) Tenth Anniversary
Issue: Joey Ramone (photo by Godlis)
Cover, Page 433

Printed in Great Britain
by Amazon